ECONOMETRIC MODELS OF CYCLICAL BEHAVIOR

Volume I

NATIONAL BUREAU OF ECONOMIC RESEARCH
CONFERENCE ON RESEARCH IN INCOME AND WEALTH

ECONOMETRIC MODELS OF CYCLICAL BEHAVIOR

EDITED BY **BERT G. HICKMAN**
STANFORD UNIVERSITY

Studies in Income and Wealth • NUMBER THIRTY-SIX
by the Conference on Research in Income and Wealth,

Volume I

Cosponsored by the National Bureau of Economic Research and the Social Science Research Council Committee on Economic Stability.

Distrb.
DISTRIBUTED BY **COLUMBIA UNIVERSITY PRESS**
NEW YORK AND LONDON   1972

Printed in the United States of America

RELATION OF THE NATIONAL BUREAU DIRECTORS TO
PUBLICATIONS REPORTING CONFERENCE PROCEEDINGS

Since the present volume is a record of conference proceedings,
it has been exempted from the rules governing submission of
manuscripts to, and critical review by, the Board of Directors
of the National Bureau.

(Resolution adopted July 6, 1948,
as revised November 21, 1949,
and April 20, 1968)

PREFATORY NOTE

THIS volume of *Studies in Income and Wealth* contains the papers presented at the Conference on Econometric Models of Cyclical Behavior held at Harvard University on November 14 and 15, 1969, under the joint sponsorship of the SSRC Committee on Economic Stability and the NBER Conference on Research in Income and Wealth. We are indebted to the National Science Foundation for its support. The Program Committee consisted of Bert G. Hickman, Chairman, Zvi Griliches, Lawrence R. Klein, and Geoffrey H. Moore. This group also served as the Editorial Committee, with Bert Hickman as Conference editor. Our thanks are due to Ruth Ridler who prepared the proceedings for press and to H. Irving Forman for his fine charting.

CONTENTS

PART II. OTHER DYNAMIC STUDIES

PART III. EVALUATION OF FORECASTS

ECONOMETRIC MODELS OF CYCLICAL BEHAVIOR

Volume I

INTRODUCTION AND SUMMARY
BERT G. HICKMAN · Stanford University

IN ONE sense the title of this Conference is a misnomer. With a single exception, the authors included herein did not set out deliberately to construct econometric models which are mathematical versions, or translations, of particular business-cycle theories. Rather, their purpose was to specify and quantify empirically valid behavioral hypotheses about the decisions and actions of various economic agents, and to integrate the estimated relationships into a complete system capable of determining the values of all the current endogenous variables for known, or assumed, values of the predetermined variables. Once built, the dynamic properties of the resulting models are a proper subject for investigation, but the models were not intended to test any specific theory of the cycle and, indeed, were constructed primarily for short-term forecasting and policy analysis.

In another sense, however, the tests of dynamic properties reported at the Conference are natural extensions of the mathematical literature on business fluctuations. Thus, it is well known that self-contained systems of linear difference equations, such as those specified in multiplier-accelerator and similar analytical models, may or may not have cyclical (complex) roots, depending on the numerical values assumed for the parameters. Moreover, such systems may, or may not, exhibit maintained cycles in the absence of stochastic shocks. Since modern econometric models are both large and nonlinear, it is usually necessary to resort to simulation techniques rather than direct mathematical analysis of the equation systems, but the aim of the simulation exercises is to answer the same questions about dynamic properties as may be asked of the simplest multiplier-accelerator model.

The four papers on business-cycle simulations in Part I were planned as a unit. The prototype for this set of complementary papers was the seminal 1959 *Econometrica* article: "The Dynamic Properties of the Klein-Goldberger Model," by Irma and Frank Adelman.

1

Just as in the Adelman study, the dynamic properties of the contemporary generation of macroeconometric models are studied in both a deterministic and stochastic context by the use of simulation techniques. The scale of the present effort is much greater, however, because more and bigger models are studied, the stochastic assumptions are more highly elaborated, and the simulation results are subjected to a larger battery of tests. The entire enterprise was feasible only because of the cooperative endeavors of the several model-building groups and the NBER team of cycle analysts.

In the first three papers of Part I, the OBE, Wharton, and Brookings model-builders describe and analyze stochastic and nonstochastic simulations prepared according to a common plan. The original program had called, also, for simulations to be done by the FMP (FRB-MIT-Penn) and the NBER (Chow-Moore) Models, and for all five sets of simulations to be turned over to researchers at the NBER for an independent analysis of their cyclical characteristics. It was recognized from the outset, however, that the last two models might still be in the developmental stage when the deadline for submission of the simulations for NBER cycle analysis was reached. As it turned out, the FMP group completed some of the simulations in time for the NBER analysis but were unable to complete the entire set, or to prepare a paper for the Conference, whereas Gregory Chow and Geoffrey Moore finished their model in time to describe it in a paper included in Part II, but not early enough to do the simulations. Finally, the Brookings group completed all simulations and submitted a paper discussing them, but again not in time for inclusion in the NBER analysis by Victor Zarnowitz, Charlotte Boschan, and Geoffrey Moore. The final outcome is that the NBER analysis deals only with the OBE, Wharton, and FMP Models and is incomplete in its coverage of the latter. Even so, it is a comprehensive and stimulating analysis, and the NBER plans to continue applying the methods developed in the paper in its future work on model-testing and evaluation.

Apart from the charge to supply simulations on a common scheme to the NBER, the model-builders were left free to structure their own analyses as they wished. Thus, the papers on the OBE, Wharton, and Brookings Models include materials that augment and complement the independent analysis of the NBER group. These papers can, and should, be read as self-contained and highly informative pieces on the structures and cyclical properties of the several models, as they existed circa 1967–69. For the purposes of this Introduction, however, it will be more enlightening to discuss certain common features of the simulation studies than to attempt an independent commentary on each paper.

The first point to emphasize is that the models are dynamically stable when treated as deterministic systems. This feature emerges clearly from the control solutions used for the long-run postsample simulations of the OBE, Wharton, and Brookings Models. For the most part, the exogenous variables were projected to follow smooth trends over the twenty-five-year interval utilized in these simulations. (The purpose was to provide a control solution for comparison with the stochastic simulations, of course—not to make an unconditional forecast of U.S. economic performance in the next quarter century.) Given the initial conditions at the beginning of the simulation period and the time pattern of the exogenous variables, the models were solved for the endogenous variables, which were found, in general, to follow trendlike paths rather than fluctuations. It may be objected that this result would follow even for an unstable model structure if the initial conditions happened to be consistent with the equilibrium solution. This would occur only by accident, however. In the case of the Wharton and Brookings Models, moreover, temporary perturbations are introduced in some of the exogenous and policy variables early in the simulation period to reflect an assumed Vietnam settlement during 1970–71. The economic response to this disturbance is perceptible but highly damped in both models. This is partly because effective compensatory policies are assumed, but it also reflects the stable dynamic structures of the models.

Further evidence on the point is found in the deterministic long-run simulations for the sample period. These are complete model-solutions, using the actual values of lagged endogenous variables at the beginning of the sample period as initial conditions, and setting the exogenous variables at their actual values throughout the period. It should be noted that these ex post simulations are rather stringent tests of the model structures, despite the use of observed values for the exogenous variables, and of parameters estimated from the same data that is being predicted, since errors can cumulate both across equations and, through the influence of the lagged endogenous variables, over time. Thus, "even if the model were perfectly specified, the neglect of stochastic elements would in itself give rise to errors which, due to the presence of lagged terms, would be carried forward," as George Green, Maurice Liebenberg, and Albert Hirsch note in the OBE paper.

In the course of summarizing their examination of the continuous sample-period simulations, Zarnowitz, Boschan, and Moore observe:

> Each of the models shows the economy . . . as declining during the first recession period covered (1948–49 for Wharton, 1953–54 for OBE, and 1957–58 for FMP). . . . The three models also have GNP^{58} contracting, or at least flattening out during the contractions in 1953–54, 1957–58, and 1960–61, respectively. The Wharton Model does not produce a fall in GNP^{58} during the recession of 1957–58, and neither the Wharton nor the OBE Model produces one in the 1960–61 recession. . . . The important conclusion is that there appears to be a progressive dampening of the fluctuations the further away a model's simulation proceeds from its initial-conditions period.

This same generalization might be made about the Brookings Model sample-period simulation for 1957–65, as reported by Gary Fromm, Lawrence Klein, and George Schink, in which "real GNP does follow the 1957–58 period, but fails to decline in 1960–61."

On one interpretation, the tendency toward progressive dampening could be attributed to damped cyclical roots. This may indeed be partly valid, but it cannot be the sole explanation. The cyclical roots are quite weak, to judge from the nonstochastic postsample simulations already discussed. The better cyclical performance of the models during the sample period must in large measure reflect the different treatment of exogenous variables. These variables are entered at their actual values in the sample-period simulations, where their movements represent an external source of disturbance to the model systems. The Wharton Model actually does better in reproducing the contraction of 1953–54 than that of 1948–49, despite the fact that the initial conditions had been left far behind by 1953. This superior performance during 1953–54 doubtless occurs because a sharp reduction in military spending was a prominent feature of that contraction, and such spending is exogenous in the Wharton Model, as in the others. Similarly, the OBE Model benefits from the exogenous fluctuation of government spending in 1953–54, so that its better performance in that recession than in those of 1957–58 or 1960–61 may be due as much, or more, to exogenous factors as to the proximity of the initial conditions.

Whether or not the models should be interpreted as endogenously generating progressively damped cycles in the deterministic sample-period simulations, there appears to be little doubt that they are highly stable as specified. If it is provisionally assumed that the models are correctly specified, cycles could nonetheless result from a damped cyclical response-mechanism which was kept going by erratic shocks, as in the Wicksell–Slutsky–Frisch theory. This hypothesis was extensively tested in the stochastic simulations prepared for the Conference by the OBE, Wharton, and Brookings groups. The general procedure was to generate random shocks to be applied to the endogenous behavioral variables in the long-run postsample simulations. The shocks were generated by a method developed by Michael McCarthy, and are explained in the Appendix to the paper on the Wharton Model by Michael Evans, Lawrence Klein, and Mitsuo Saito. The method allows for intercorrelation of the errors in different equations and, in some applications, for serial correlation in the errors of individual equations. In these respects, it is more realistic than the one employed earlier by the Adelmans, in which it was assumed that the disturbances in individual equations of the Klein-Goldberger Model were independent across equations and over time. On the other hand, their procedure achieved greater realism in other respects by scaling shocks to maintain the same ratio of the standard deviation of residuals to the value of the dependent variable as observed in the sample period, and by experimenting, also, with random shocks to the exogenous variables.

Fifty stochastic simulations were made for the OBE and Brookings Models and one hundred for the Wharton Model. In all runs for a given model, the exogenous variables and initial conditions were the same as in the nonstochastic control solution. Serially correlated disturbances were assumed for all fifty Brookings simulations, and for half of the runs for the OBE and Wharton Models. In all experiments, the shocks were chosen so as to reproduce the statistical properties of the sample-period residuals of the various models.

The stochastic simulations were analyzed in two different ways at the Conference. First, each model-building group studied its set of simulations by spectral methods to ascertain whether crucial endogenous variables displayed cyclical periodicities. Second, the simulations from the OBE and Wharton Models were subjected to NBER cycle analysis by Zarnowitz, Boschan, and Moore.

The principal conclusions reached by Green, Liebenberg, and Hirsch from their analysis of the stochastic simulations with the OBE Model are as follows: the real GNP series from the fifty different runs rarely showed absolute downturns, presumably because of the strong growth trends assumed in the exogenous variables. When expressed as deviations from control-solution values, however — i.e., approximately, as deviations from trend — the shocked GNP series show definite cycles. The "cycles" from the runs using serially uncorrelated shocks are unrealistically ragged, as compared with observed business cycles, however; and the average power-spectrum for these runs fails to reveal significant peaks at business-cycle periodicities. The runs with serially correlated shocks are considerably smoother, and a spectral analysis based on a preferred method of trend-removal reveals peaks at periodicities consistently falling in the range of two- to five-year cycles.

The findings are much the same for the Wharton Model as reported by Evans, Klein, and Saito. That is to say, serially independent shocks do not lead to average spectral-density functions with distinct peaks, whereas the application of serially correlated disturbances does produce a high concentration of spectral peaks for real GNP in the range 26.7 to 10 quarters, with a mode at 16 quarters — or the average duration of business cycles in the NBER chronology.

The NBER analysis of the stochastic simulations confirms the general findings of the OBE and Wharton groups, and adds a great deal of information on the cyclical attributes of the simulated series. Thus, in an analysis of the average durations of rises and declines in all of the simulation runs for current- and constant-dollar GNP, Zarnowitz, Boschan, and Moore conclude that many fluctuations do occur (especially for the runs with serially uncorrelated shocks), but they are in large part too short to qualify as cyclical movements. When the stochastic simulations are expressed as deviations from the control solutions, however, they reveal characteristics which are closer to the cycles of experience. Again, as in the earlier papers, it is found that the simulations based on autocorrelated shocks are substantially smoother than those with serially uncorrelated shocks, and are generally of more plausible appearance.

The NBER group did not attempt to identify business-cycle peaks and troughs in the detrended GNP simulations, although they did compute measures of the average duration, and amplitude of rises and declines, where declines as short as one quarter were included. Of considerably greater interest in the present context is the more exhaustive analysis they undertook, employing a random sample of three runs each from the OBE and Wharton Models. The plans for the Conference called for simulation results for a specified list of endogenous variables, so that each stochastic simulation for the Wharton Model included output for 17 variables, and 22 variables were available in the OBE simulations. For each of the six simulation sets examined, the NBER group dated the specific cycle-peaks and troughs in all of the detrended series, and computed a diffusion index of the percentage of the series undergoing expansion in each successive quarter. The diffusion indexes were expressed in cumulative form to derive a relatively smooth index, whose peaks and troughs would be centered on periods of greatest concentration of peaks and troughs in the component series. The cumulated diffusion indexes for both models show distinct cyclical fluctuations, whose average durations are similar to those of the cycles in trend-adjusted GNP during 1948–68. This finding provides interesting independent confirmation of the existence of cyclical periodicities in the detrended stochastic simulations, as established by the spectral analyses of the OBE and Wharton groups.

Does all this evidence amount to confirmation of the hypothesis that cyclical fluctuations are caused by stochastic disturbances impinging on a dynamically stable response-mechanism? Certainly, the evidence is consistent with at least one version of that hypothesis, but some major qualifications are in order. First, on the evidence of this Conference, it is necessary to reject the classical version of the hypothesis. Second, inadequate attention was paid at the Conference to the effects of shocks or fluctuations in exogenous variables. Third, it can be argued that the apparent success of the stochastic simulations is due to mis-specification of the model structures. Finally, if the models are indeed seriously mis-specified, the hypothesis of a deterministic cyclical-mechanism cannot be rejected on their account.

It is convenient to discuss the first two qualifications in the context of the elegant analysis of the dynamic properties of the Wharton Model by E. Philip Howrey. This paper, included in Part II, is a completely independent attack on the same problems that were studied in the stochastic simulations of Part I. Howrey uses an analytical technique based on the spectral representation of a stochastic process to determine whether a condensed, linearized version of the Wharton Model exhibits cyclical properties. The method has some drawbacks—especially the need to linearize the model, with unknown effects on its properties for large departures from the neighborhood of linearization—but it permits a rigorous statement and analysis of the alternative hypotheses on the nature of cyclical fluctuations.

In Howrey's notation, the linear econometric model can be written in the form

$$(1) \qquad B(L)y(t) = C(L)x(t) + u(t)$$

where $y(t)$ and $x(t)$ are vectors, respectively, of endogenous and exogenous variables at time t; $B(L)$ and $C(L)$ are matrices of polynomials in the lag operator L, with coefficients for the various lagged values of y and x, as estimated in the structural model; and $u(t)$ is a vector of random disturbances. The solution of the model is

$$(2) \qquad y(t) = P(t) + B(L)^{-1}C(L)x(t) + B(L)^{-1}u(t)$$

where $B(L)^{-1}$ is the inverse of the matrix $B(L)$, and where $P(t)$ is a vector of functions giving the solutions to the transient part of the system in terms of initial conditions and characteristic roots.

According to equation (2), the time path of the endogenous variables depends on the structure of the model and on the nature of the forces impinging on the system. The structure of the model determines the values of the characteristic roots of $P(t)$, and it also determines the response of the system to external forces, as summarized in the matrices $B(L)^{-1}C(L)$ and $B(L)^{-1}$, which represent systems of weights to be applied to the various current and lagged values of the exogenous variables and random disturbances.

Although Howrey is primarily concerned with testing the stochastic part of the system for cyclical effects, he has also performed the arduous task of extracting more than 40 characteristic roots of the model; this work was later checked independently by Kei Mori, using a different computational algorithm. The linearized condensed version of the Wharton Model apparently yields one pair of cyclical roots with only moderate damping. Further analysis by Howrey leads to the conclusion that the complex roots do not impart discernible cyclical properties to the solution, however, since their effects are swamped by the contribution of larger positive real roots. One real root is slightly greater than unity, incidentally, implying that the system may be unstable in a growth sense, although this is uncertain because of the sampling variability to which the estimates are subject.

Thus, Howrey's results confirm the implication of the simulation studies that the Wharton Model is stable in its deterministic part, at least insofar as an endogenous cyclical mechanism is concerned. What about its response to random disturbances? To answer this question, Howrey analyzes the spectral representation of the stochastic process $B(L)^{-1}u(t)$ implied by the model. He concludes that the lag structure of the model does not impart the sort of smoothing that is required to convert a sequence of random shocks into cyclical fluctuations in the endogenous variables. "Any cyclical behavior that this model might exhibit is, therefore, due to serial correlation in the disturbance process or to business-cycle variations in the exogenous variables."

Once again, these results confirm the earlier findings. Random disturbances were not enough to generate fluctuations with cyclical properties in the stochastic simulations of the Wharton and OBE Models—rather, it was necessary to introduce serial correlation in the shocks to accomplish that result. It appears that the classical Wicksell–Slutsky–Frisch hypothesis—that business cycles are the result of a stream of erratic shocks operating on a dynamic system which otherwise would exhibit only damped oscillations—must be rejected on the evidence of this Conference. On the other hand, broader versions of the hypothesis, in which the admissible class of shocks or impulses is enlarged, cannot be rejected.

Indeed, the first possibility to be considered — that the exogenous variables may be subject to random shocks — can be regarded as falling within the classical hypothesis on erratic shocks. If the shocks were random and serially uncorrelated, the moving average process represented by $C(L)$ could, nevertheless, impart a cyclical path to the exogenous variables, and hence to the endogenous ones, even if the lag structure of the model itself were noncyclical.

Second, as Frank de Leeuw emphasizes in his discussion of the Wharton Model simulations, the impulses impinging on the economy include identifiable and measurable forces, such as wars, monetary disturbances, and exogenous changes in policy variables or parameters. Perhaps, the business cycles of experience reflect sporadic occurrences or variations in such exogenous forces, rather than truly stochastic disturbances that cannot be measured directly or isolated in time. This hypothesis would argue for systematic historical investigations of the role of identifiable exogenous impulses, and of the responses to such impulses during particular cyclical episodes or epochs. Such studies can and have been done as model simulations, but they did not fall within the purview of this Conference. Incidentally, to the extent that some external events, such as wars, have a generalized impact on the economy, allowance should be made for covariation between disturbances to exogenous variables and stochastic equations in simulation experiments.

Third, shocks to either the exogenous variables, or the equations, may be serially correlated. As we have seen, the latter possibility was extensively tested in this Conference, and the general finding is that the model simulations did exhibit "business cycles" in response to serially correlated disturbances. Moreover, the OBE group also ran five stochastic simulations in which serially correlated shocks were applied to the exogenous variables, as well as to the endogenous equations, with the result that the cycles were increased in amplitude; in addition, they frequently showed absolute declines in real GNP, lasting three to five quarters. As the authors observe, "These brief results suggest that movements commonly considered exogenous in large-scale models may play a crucial role in the determination of business cycles."

Thus, it appears that some classes of shocks may generate cycles when acting upon the models studied at this Conference. It should be emphasized, however, that broadening the class of shocks to include perturbations in exogenous variables — and to allow for serial correlation in the disturbances to equations and exogenous variables — diminishes the role of model structure as a cycle-maker. If the real roots dominate the cyclical ones and the lag structure does not convert serially independent random shocks into cycles in the endogenous variables, the model structure becomes simply a multiplier mechanism for amplifying shocks of any kind. There is still an impulse-response mechanism, but the cycles are inherent in the impulses rather than in the responses.

The question of whether serial correlation should be expected in real-world shocks to the economy naturally arises. It is easy to think of reasons why this could be so. Important political events, such as wars, may impinge on the economy for several quarters, or even years, before being reversed. Similarly, policy actions may be maintained over several quarters or more. It is well to recall, also, that Frisch suggested the Schumpeterian theory of innovations as a possible source of impulse energy, which would impinge on the economy in a sustained fashion during certain phases of the cycle, while being absent in others.

Unfortunately, it is possible, too, that the observed presence of serial correlation in the sample disturbances may merely reflect mis-specification of the econometric models. At the Conference, this position was stated most forcefully in de Leeuw's perceptive comment, where he concludes that "the principal simulation results reported in the Evans-Klein-Saito paper and some of the other Conference papers could, it seems to me, just as easily result from mis-specification as from the historical validity of the Slutsky-Frisch theory." He supports this conclusion partly by arguing that the actual errors during the sample period from a poorly specified model will tend to be larger than the true magnitude of stochastic forces and, hence, may exaggerate their power to generate fluctuations. This could happen, of course, but note should also be taken of the observation of Green, Liebenberg, and Hirsch that the sample-period errors were not rescaled to reflect the much larger size of the economy that is implied in the control-solutions for the postsample simulations, so that the shocks could be understated on that account.

One final caveat concerning the stochastic simulations is in order before we turn to other topics. The simulations prepared for the Brookings Model failed to reveal systematic cyclical periodicities in the average spectral density function for fifty stochastic runs, despite the inclusion of serial correlation in the disturbances. Hence, the simulation results are consistent with the stochastic disturbance theory only for the OBE and Wharton Models. On the present evidence, the theory would be rejected for the Brookings Model, insofar as it applies to shocks to equations rather than to exogenous variables. Finally, the theory has not yet been tested for the FMP Model.

Let us consider now another major topic that cuts across several papers in this volume—the subject of forecasting. It is convenient to organize the discussion under three headings: ex post predictions, ex ante forecasts, and forecasts of cyclical turning points. Ex post predictions provide a test of model specification and structural stability, whereas ex ante forecasts involve, as well, the skills of the forecaster in supplementing the model with extraneous predictions of such items as policy actions, changes in noncontrolled exogenous variables, strikes and political events.

The paper by Ronald L. Cooper, "The Predictive Performance of Quarterly Econometric Models of the United States," is a major effort to evaluate and compare the structural specifications of alternative econometric models. This is done in two ways: by testing the models for structural change over time, and by comparing their ex post forecasts against predictions by naive auto-regressive models. His general conclusions are that all the models tested are structurally unstable, and that none could forecast better than purely mechanical models with no economic content. Apparently skeptical of further structural model-building, he suggests that forecasting performance might be improved by combining instrumental variables from econometric models with mechanical auto-regressive schemes. These are sobering conclusions, indeed; because of their sweeping nature, they will require careful evaluation by econometricians and noneconometricians alike.

Cooper's procedure was to make a series of ex post single-period forecasts from the reduced forms of the models, given the actual values of the predetermined variables; and then, to compare them with similar predictions from auto-regressive equations fitted to the individual endogenous variables. An auto-regressive scheme is simply a mechanical regression of a variable on its own lagged values, and in the present paper, Cooper chose for each variable the best-fitting equation from among candidates with up to eight lagged quarterly values. One or another of the econometric models could predict some of the endogenous variables better than the corresponding auto-regressive equations, but the latter had the highest over-all score for both the sample and postsample forecasts. Seven econometric models were included in the tests, including earlier versions of the OBE and Wharton-EFU Models than those used in the other papers in this volume.

One important issue concerns the length of the forecast period. As already noted, Cooper's tests were restricted to single-period forecasts. All the discussants of his paper stress that this choice not only puts the auto-regressive schemes in the most favorable light — since they tend to deteriorate rapidly when forecasting more than one period ahead — but is also irrelevant to realistic forecasting situations, which usually involve forecasts of four to eight quarters ahead.

Thus, there is a presumption that structural models are capable of better multiperiod forecasts than are auto-regressive schemes. In his comment on Cooper's paper, Michael McCarthy cites results for the current Wharton Model to demonstrate that it outperforms the best auto-regression for real GNP over the sample period, when using only the initial information available at the start of the period — even though the standard deviation of one-quarter forecasts was smaller for the naive model over the same period. In similar vein, the OBE group quotes average errors for real GNP obtained over the sample period for one to six quarter forecasts, made with a later version of their model than the one tested by Cooper. In this case, the model outperforms the naive auto-regressive form even for first-period forecasts, and the improvement gets progressively larger as the forecast horizon is extended. As Cooper notes in his rejoinder, these results are for the sample period only, and it is possible that the relative performance of the structural and naive models would be reversed for multiperiod predictions beyond the sample period. Further testing will be required to settle the issue definitively, but it seems likely that structural models will prove superior to auto-regressive schemes when it comes to multiperiod ex post forecasting.

Some additional evidence on ex post forecasts is included in the paper by Michael Evans, Yoel Haitovsky, and George Treyz, "An Analysis of the Forecasting Properties of U.S. Econometric Models." Their analysis deals with newer versions of the Wharton and OBE Models than were studied by Cooper. In the case of the Wharton Model, the errors for one-quarter predictions during the sample period were generally larger than those of a naive model extrapolating the last observed quarterly change; and those for postsample forecasts were larger than a naive model of no-change. These results are consistent with Cooper's findings. On the other hand, the newer OBE Model outperforms the no-change and same-change naive models for the sample period (which — in contrast to the Wharton Model — includes the trend-dominated years, 1965–66), as distinct from Cooper's finding for the earlier version, which did, however, involve comparison with a more stringent naive model.

Evans, Haitovsky, and Treyz also made multiperiod (six-quarter) ex post predictions with both the OBE and Wharton Models, including some postsample forecasts for the latter. In general, both models outperform the naive forecasts after one or two quarters.

It appears from the preponderance of evidence, then, that the models perform better than mechanical schemes in multiperiod forecasts with known exogenous variables. This is not to say that the generally poor record on single-period ex post forecasts should be lightly dismissed. Until an econometric model is brought to a point where it can make better ex post forecasts over a short horizon than can a mechanical scheme, the structural specification or stability of the model must always be in question.

Critics and model-builders alike are agreed on the pervasiveness of structural change and the difficult problems it poses for specification and forecasting with econometric models. Cooper's study was designed to test the specifications of alternative models by refitting them through a statistically equivalent estimation technique to a common sample-period, in order to run a fair race between them. His discussants stress, however, that such a mechanical reestimation of the models meant that some of them were fitted to historically revised national-income data which differed considerably from those originally used; that others were fitted to Korean War data which had been omitted or treated with dummy variables in the original models; that tax-rate changes over the Cooper sample period were ignored by him in refitting the revenue and depreciation functions; and that other of the modifications made by Cooper in the reestimation of several of the models implicitly or explicitly changed their structures. In short, structural change is a persistent phenomenon, and econometricians attempt to deal with it as carefully and explicitly as possible when specifying and estimating a model. Cooper's negative findings, it is asserted, may stem in large part from an inadvertent introduction of structural mis-specifications due to his wholesale approach and mechanical reestimation procedure. As Stephen Goldfeld remarked in his comment: "More recent evidence such as the FRB-MIT results cited earlier, and the results with the OBE Model presented at this Conference, suggest that even for one-period forecasts, carefully estimated large econometric models outperform the auto-regressive standards."

Be that as it may, Cooper's work presents a serious challenge to model-builders to redouble their efforts to improve methods of specification, estimation, and evaluation in order to assure more accurate and stable structures. At the Conference, a number of constructive suggestions were made in this connection. A new estimation technique, suggested earlier by Dale Jorgenson and employed by Cooper, was further tested on a partial basis in the paper by Evans, Haitovsky, and Treyz. It was found to lead to estimates of the structural parameters which reduced the ex post forecast error for two quarters, and the authors suggest that an as yet untried modification of the method suggested by Klein may improve the results for longer forecast periods. The new techniques are intended to reduce the propagation of single-equation errors across equations, and to reduce error-buildup over time through the lagged endogenous variables.

In his comment on the paper by Evans, Haitovsky, and Treyz, Alvin Karchere conjectures that the principal problem is single-equation error itself, particularly as it leads to systematic bias in the postsample forecasts. He urges model-builders to choose among alternative specifications of structural equations according to their ex post error properties over the standard forecast period, rather than by their sample-period characteristics. Another suggestion for dealing with individual equations was made from the floor: namely, to use bloc simulation to isolate those equations, or sectors, contributing the most to forecast errors, and then to concentrate on improving the weak equations. Finally, as shown in several of the papers, improved ex post forecasts are obtained from the models when automatic adjustments are made to the constant terms of the normalized structural equations to take account of serial correlation in the calculated residuals.

A few comments are now in order on ex ante forecasting with econometric models. It is here that science shades into art. Anyone who has the mistaken impression that an econometric model is simply a black box used to convert ex ante predictions of exogenous variables into ex ante forecasts of endogenous variables, will find the paper by Evans, Haitovsky, and Treyz enlightening indeed. They distinguish three classes of judgmental inputs to ex ante model forecasts: (1) the selection of values for exogenous variables, including informed guesses about future monetary and fiscal policies, export developments, and so forth; (2) adjustments to the constant terms of individual structural equations to allow for known structural changes since the estimation period, to correct for substantive data revisions, to offset observed autocorrelation in the estimated residuals, and to incorporate extraneous information about future exogenous developments, such as strikes; and (3) changes in the initial decisions made about constant adjustments or exogenous variables if preliminary forecasts with these assumptions lead to a forecast for some variables that is out of the range of the forecaster's a priori concept of a reasonable forecast.

In their section on evaluation of ex ante forecasts, Evans, Haitovsky, and Treyz compare actual ex ante forecasts from the Wharton, Evans, and OBE Models with ex post forecasts, and with hypothetical ex ante forecasts using alternative mechanical schemes to adjust the constant terms of structural equations for autocorrelation. They demonstrate that the true ex ante forecasts are much better than the ex post forecasts. For example, the average forecast error for the true ex ante first-quarter forecasts of the Wharton-EFU Model for real GNP during 1966–68 was 3.0 billion dollars, as compared with

6.0 billion for a mechanically adjusted ex post forecast and 16.3 billion for unadjusted ex post forecasts. They also show that the true ex ante forecasts are better than hypothetical ex ante forecasts generated by mechanical methods for the Wharton Model, and for most of the OBE forecasts. Evidently, the use of judgmental adjustments contributes substantially to the reduction of ex ante forecast errors. On the basis of their empirical analysis of the sources of ex ante forecast error, the authors conclude that it is the third class of judgmental adjustment — changing the preliminary assumptions on exogenous variables and constants until the resulting forecast falls within the range thought to be reasonable — which is principally responsible for the improvement in ex ante forecasts. From this point of view, the model serves primarily to assess judgmentally the general implications of the forecaster's assumptions on future exogenous developments, including his ad hoc adjustments for anticipated changes in structure since the sample period, and for the correction of apparent specification errors.

In summary, Evans, Haitovsky, and Treyz recognize the current limitations of econometric forecasting techniques but are sanguine about future improvements:

> This study has shown that econometricians have had a better forecasting record to date than an analysis of the econometric models that they used would have led us to predict. Our results offer no substantive evidence that the same econometricians, forecasting without the "benefit" of an econometric model, would have done any better or any worse in their predictions. This recognition of the limitations of current models need not lead to pessimism about the future development of accurate econometric forecasting models. With a finer understanding of how changes in monetary and fiscal policy actually influence economic activity, closer attention to the short-run specifications and lag adjustments of the system, possible improvements in the National Income Accounts, and refinement of existing estimation and forecasting techniques, the next few years could offer substantial advances in the art and the science of econometric forecasting.

The discussion thus far has abstracted from the prediction of business-cycle turning points. There was no analysis of ex ante forecasting of turning points at the Conference. However, the business-cycle simulations of Part I include relevant material concerning ex post forecasts of upturns and downturns. In addition to the long-run simulations discussed earlier, these papers contain a series of short-run ex post simulations around the observed postwar cyclical peaks and troughs, as dated by the National Bureau of Economic Research. For each turning point, three sets of six-quarter simulations were prepared, beginning respectively three quarters, two quarters, and one quarter before the business-cycle peak or trough. Results are available for varying sample periods for the Wharton, OBE, FMP and Brookings Models. However, the Brookings simulations were not completed in time for analysis by the NBER team.

In the judgment of Zarnowitz, Boschan, and Moore, the Wharton, OBE, and FMP Models were fairly successful in duplicating cyclical turns, with two-thirds or more of the actual turns being matched by turns in the model simulations. The success rates were about the same at peaks and troughs. Also, there is not much to choose between the simulations started one, two, or three quarters before the business-cycle turns, despite the implied differences in the amount of fore-shadowing information included in the initial conditions. Finally, although two-thirds or more of the business-cycle turns were matched by the simulations, the simulated turns did not always coincide with the actual peaks and troughs, although a substantial majority were either coincident or within one quarter of the actuals.

It should be noted that the short-period simulations analyzed by Zarnowitz, Boschan, and Moore were made without correction for serial correlation of the residuals. However, the OBE and Wharton groups discovered that the short-term simulations were marginally improved by making automatic adjustments to the constant turns to correct for autocorrelation. The discussion of sample-period turning point behavior in the OBE paper is based on the adjusted simulations, but no comparison is attempted with the unadjusted simulations analyzed by the NBER group. It would be interesting to make such comparisons for all models.

The limited objectives of these experimental simulations should be borne in mind when appraising the results. The principal focus of the Conference was on the dynamic properties and structural stability of econometric models, rather than on forecasting technique. Hence, there was no attempt to provide a comparison of the errors of the turning point simulations with those from ex post cyclical forecasts with naive auto-regressive models. Similarly, no comparison was attempted with ex post forecasts by other methods, let alone between ex ante forecasts by persons using econometric models and those using other techniques. The paper by D. J. Daly, "Forecasting with Statistical Indicators," contains a judicious appraisal of the strengths and weaknesses of one of the principal forecasting alternatives to econometric models, but it is not intended to provide the basis for a systematic comparison of either ex ante or ex post forecasts of turning points by the two methods.

The last two papers to be introduced stand somewhat apart from the others. The first one is an attempt to model a particular literary theory of business cycles, whereas the second deals with the methodological problem of the effects of aggregation over time on the estimated lag structure of dynamic econometric models.

In "An Econometric Model of Business Cycles," Gregory Chow and Geoffrey Moore present a progress report on their efforts to specify and estimate a mathematically explicit model containing the major elements of the Mitchell-Burns theory of the business cycle. They point out that they have included many, though not all, of the important elements in Arthur F. Burns' recent article on business cycles in the *International Encyclopedia of the Social Sciences* (1968). "Hence, this is by no means a perfect translation. In general, the material we present is a simplified, aggregative version of the earlier text." The model contains 20 stochastic equations and 5 identities.

As mentioned at the outset of this Introduction, it was originally hoped that the new "NBER Model" would be completed in time for simulations to be made and analyzed on the common plan for Part I. The existing large quarterly models include many of the variables emphasized in the analytical descriptions of business-cycle processes by Burns, Mitchell, Moore, and others at the NBER. The structural hypotheses incorporating the variables in the models are generally different from those suggested in the NBER writings, however, and in some cases markedly so. Thus, even if these models were capable of simulating well the characteristics emphasized in NBER empirical studies—timing, amplitude, conformity, diffusion, and so forth—this would not be verification of the Mitchell-Burns theory of cyclical processes, since many structures are consistent with the same reduced form. It seemed desirable, therefore, to construct a model with a structural specification reflecting the Mitchell-Burns hypotheses, in order to see if it could match, or exceed, the successes of other specifications in capturing the empirical regularities isolated in the long history of NBER cycle studies.

Owing to limitations of time, this program still remains to be carried out. Meanwhile, the progress report of Chow and Moore must be evaluated in terms of its structural specification and statistical methodology. The lively debate between the authors and discussants can scarcely be summarized here, beyond noting that R. A. Gordon, especially, has questioned the extent to which this initial specification embodies the essential features of the "NBER approach" to an explanation of business cycles.

The effects of aggregation over time on the parameter estimates and dynamic properties of econometric models is a subject of great interest to model-builders. The paper by Robert Engle and Ta-Chung Liu is an important attack on this highly technical and intractable problem. Their basic approach is to assume that a given model with a particular time unit—in the empirical application, Liu's monthly model—is the true one, and then to investigate the biases that may result from aggregating the observations into longer time-periods. Unfortunately, there are several different effects working in different directions; the net result depends on the time structure of the exognous variables and cannot readily be generalized. The analytic results presented by Engle and Liu are based on a rational distributed-lag model, which is aggregated to a Koyck-Nerlove form. The predicted results are then tested by estimating quarterly and annual versions of Liu's model for comparison with the monthly estimates. The authors conclude that the empirical results are consistent with the theory and that biases are, indeed, introduced by aggregation over time.

Apart from the restrictive assumptions necessary to produce predictable outcomes, the major issue concerning the Engle-Liu results is the validity of assuming that the monthly equations are the correct ones. This assumption is questioned, especially, in the Comment by Zvi Griliches, who argues that the Koyck-Nerlove lag distribution does not make much sense for monthly time units, and that the Liu Model is a pioneering effort to test the feasibility of building a monthly model, rather than being a well-shaken-down final version. An important related point is the prevalent belief that in actual applications with calendar-year data, autocorrelation is less prevalent than when calendar time is sliced more finely. Perhaps, the annual model is the more nearly correct, and the additional "bias" resulting from the introduction of serial correlation in the disturbances by aggregation of, say, the monthly time unit, is less serious than that stemming from the serial correlation initially existing in the model estimated from monthly, instead of quarterly or calendar-year, data.

In conclusion, the papers and comments included in this volume reflect a high order of analytical insight and technical competence. Because many of the issues are both technical and controversial, the reader is urged to study the comments as carefully as the papers. As in all good conferences, the proceedings have opened as many issues as they have settled. Scientific testing of econometric models is still in its infancy, but the effort is a continuing one, and the papers in this volume have substantially advanced the subject by clarifying the issues and sharpening the methodology for future work in this important field.

Insofar as prediction is concerned, research on alternative forecasting schemes will doubtless continue and broaden. These schemes can, and should, include auto-regressive models, direct reduced-form systems and, perhaps, other methods which also eschew economic analysis and provide a forecasting standard for econometric models. Nonetheless, these methods must, it seems to me, be regarded as spurs for structural model-building, rather than as substitutes. Unless economic theory is truly a set of empty boxes, it should be possible to improve on mechanical methods by incorporating structural hypotheses into our quantitative models. In this respect, all economists have a stake in the econometricians' credo or, at least, his hopes. Moreover, structural models have much more to offer than alternative methods. In forecasting applications, they provide a framework into which extraneous information on structural changes — especially those involving fiscal and monetary policy — and predictable shocks can be incorporated. They afford, also, a vehicle for analysis of the historic causes of economic instability. It is quite possible, for example, that the postwar models are strongly damped because of the high degree of built-in flexibility which now characterizes the economy; this is a hypothesis which can be tested on a structural model by simulation experiments. Finally, structural models which have been constructed with an eye to policy analysis, and which, therefore, incorporate explicit quantitative policy instruments and parameters, can be used not only to forecast, but also to study alternative policies to change the course of the economy if the forecasted outcome is unsatisfactory.[1]

[1] For a discussion of policy uses of econometric models, the reader is referred to an earlier conference, which was also sponsored by the Social Science Research Council Committee on Economic Stability. The papers have been published in *Quantitative Planning of Economic Policy*, Bert G. Hickman, ed. (the Brookings Institution, 1965).

PART ONE

BUSINESS-CYCLE SIMULATIONS

SHORT- AND LONG-TERM SIMULATIONS WITH THE OBE ECONOMETRIC MODEL

GEORGE R. GREEN · Department of Commerce
with MAURICE LIEBENBERG
and ALBERT A. HIRSCH

1   INTRODUCTION

THIS paper reports procedures used and some results obtained from various simulations with versions of the OBE Econometric Model. The results presented are not comprehensive, some results being analyzed in another paper prepared for this Conference [21].

The section which follows provides a brief description of the OBE Model structure and a note on equation normalization for model solution. In Section 3, the procedures and results for ex post simulations over the sample period are considered. Modifications in model structure, and other procedures used for twenty-five-year simulations, are presented in Section 4. Also discussed are results obtained from simulations with stochastic shocks applied to endogenous behavioral equations. Included is a spectral analysis of real GNP series generated from these runs. A final section summarizes major results.

NOTE: All of the above are members of the Econometric Branch, Office of Business Economics, U.S. Department of Commerce. Although I [Mr. Green] assumed primary responsibility for the project and wrote this paper, I drew heavily upon the contributions of my two colleagues. We benefited greatly from the cooperation of fellow econometricians at other institutions: particularly, Lawrence Klein, Philip Howrey, and Michael McCarthy, of the University of Pennsylvania; and Gary Fromm and George Shink, of the Brookings Institution. Principal quality research assistance was provided by Judith K. Pritchard. Additional assistance was provided by Charles Alexander, Jr., and Fannie Hall. The views expressed are those of the author and do not necessarily agree with those of the U.S. Department of Commerce.

2 THE OBE ECONOMETRIC MODEL

2.1 THE STRUCTURAL EQUATIONS

The simulations reported in the next section use a quarterly econometric model of the U.S. economy developed in the Econometric Branch of the Office of Business Economics. The present model contains 56 stochastic equations and is the outgrowth of an earlier 36-equation model [17]. The present model structure follows the general scheme of the earlier version, but some parts of the model have been expanded, and many equations have been respecified. The present model includes endogenous equations for fixed nonresidential investment, an expanded financial sector, additional tax and transfer functions, and major respecification of price, wage rate, employment, and labor force equations. Appendix A defines all symbols used, and a complete list of structural equations is given in Appendix B. Alternative specifications are given for some equations. In such cases, the discussion below is confined to forms marked (*a*), which were used in the sample-period simulations. The (*b*) alternatives were used for the twenty-five-year stochastic simulations, and will be discussed in Section 4.

As in most other macroeconometric models, equations for components of GNP, on the product side, are estimated in constant dollar terms, while income items are estimated as current dollar values. The major exogenous variables are government purchases, government employment, gross exports, consumption of housing services, population, Federal Reserve member bank nonborrowed reserves, reserve requirements, the Federal Reserve discount rate, tax rates, and some transfer items.

The consumption equations relate components of consumption expenditures to relative prices, disposable income (sometimes disaggregated into transfer and nontransfer income), and measures of cyclical activity. Also, the equations for consumer durables expenditures include allowances for credit and liquidity effects and, for the automobile expenditures equation, strike effects. Taken as a whole, the consumption equations show a short-run marginal propensity to consume out of current disposable income of 0.464, which is somewhat lower than in other models [cf. 6, 7, 8, and 12], reflecting, in part, the exogenous treatment of housing services.

Equation 10, for the ratio of fixed investment in nonresidential structures and equipment (*ISE*) to capacity output, is an adaptation of research by Shirley Almon [2, 3], who estimated separately the lag between expenditures and appropriations, and that between investment determinants and appropriations. We have formed convolutions of her estimates of these lags, and have used the resulting relative weights in estimating the *ISE* equation shown. The explanatory variables in this equation—output, interest rates, and deflated cash flow—follow the determinants used by Almon.

Interest rates (with a shift of variable during the bills-only policy), a rent to cost-of-housing ratio, and the vacancy level (expressed as a deviation from a long-term trend) are used as explanatory variables in the equation for housing starts (*HS*). Housing investment (*IH*) is determined by a phase out of *HS* levels, where the phase weights are those used by the Census Bureau.

The change in business inventories (*II*) is split into two parts: change in auto inventory investment (*IIA*), and change in nonauto inventory investment (*IINA*). Each equation uses a stock adjustment mechanism to current and lagged sales levels. In addition, the lagged changes in unfilled orders and inventories are used as explanatory variables in the *IINA* equation. The implied adjustment of inventory stock to recent sales is much more rapid for autos than for the nonauto case.

Imports are divided into merchandise (*IMT*), military expenditures (*IMG*), and "other" services (*IMS*) imports. The second category is treated exogenously. *IMS* is made a function of current real disposable income and past levels of services imports. The cyclical sensitivity of *IMT* is introduced by a variable coefficient on output, the effect of which varies with domestic industrial capacity utilization (*CUW*). A relative price variable, and a dummy variable for dock strikes, are also included in this equation.

Since government purchases and housing services are treated exogenously, the broadest, essentially endogenous, measure of real productive activity in the OBE Model is real private *GNP*, excluding housing services (X). The basic price in the OBE Model is the implicit price deflator for X (P). The determinants in the P equation are unit labor costs, recent relative changes in final demand (modified by the level of capacity utilization), and a time trend. The interaction of capacity utilization and relative changes in final demand is an attempt to allow for demand effects, which are more evident at high levels of capacity utilization. Component deflators for the major categories of final demand are made dependent mainly on the over-all deflator and on the wage rate.

Since there is both an equation for P and equations, or exogenous values, for all components, the price sector is overdetermined. As a result, there are, initially, two estimates for P—one from the equation for P, and the other from a properly weighted sum of the component deflators. Any discrepancy between these two estimates of P is resolved by arbitrarily adjusting the component deflators. That is, the equation-determined over-all deflator serves as a control index to which component prices are adjusted.

The equation for wage per employee (WR) is of the Philips-curve type, in which the relative change in the wage rate is a function of the inverse of the unemployment rate. This equation is expressed as wage per employee rather than wage per man-hour because of substantial deficiencies of the aggregate hours series. In addition to the inverse of the unemployment rate, this equation includes the composition of unemployment, the rate of change in manufacturing hours, and recent rates of change in consumer prices as explanatory variables. Since unit labor costs are a key variable in the equation for P, the WR equation plays an important role in the determination of the over-all price level.

The equations for capacity output, labor force, employment, and hours are highly interrelated. The full rationale for these formulations is discussed in another paper [13]. First, a constrained Cobb-Douglas production function is estimated, along with the two equations for civilian labor force, and an equation for private weekly hours. Equations for potential private employment (EC), and for potential private weekly hours (HC), are derived from the above-mentioned equations by setting the capacity utilization index (CUW) equal to 1.0, and by setting unemployment rates at frictional levels. Values of EC and HC, together with lagged values of capital stock, are then used to solve for potential private GNP, excluding housing services (XC). The equations for private civilian employment (E) and private man-hours (H) are both partial adjustment mechanisms, constrained so that when X reaches XC, the desired employment equals EC, and the desired level of weekly hours is HC.

Corporate profits and inventory valuation adjustment (CPR) is made a multiplicative function of output, the wage share, and CUW. There are equations for two other income items: entrepreneurial income and dividends, and indirect business taxes. Other income components — interest, rent, and capital consumption allowances — are made exogenous. To avoid overdetermination, the statistical discrepancy (SD) is determined endogenously as the residual reconciliation item. However, when the full model is solved, SD is constrained to vary slowly and its absolute value is kept at a low level. This is achieved by adjusting, when necessary, other income components.

The tax and transfer equations relate tax items to tax rates and the tax base wherever possible. Most of the excise tax and transfer functions are the outgrowth of a study by Waldorf [20]. For Federal personal tax payments, different equations for sub-periods are used because of changes in tax legislation.

The set of eight stochastic equations in the monetary sector are broadly patterned after the work of the FED–MIT Model [4, 5]. Exogenous levels of nonborrowed reserves, the discount rate, and reserve requirements — together with disposable personal income — determine liquid assets, money supply, and various interest rates.

Finally, there are three equations — new orders, shipments, and unfilled orders — for manufacturing durables. The main impact of these equations on the rest of the model is through the nonauto inventory equation, which includes the lagged change in unfilled orders as an explanatory variable. We have used a direct estimate of ΔUMD, which is essentially a reduced-form equation, because of better performance over the sample period.

2.2 EQUATION NORMALIZATION FOR MODEL SOLUTION

The set of equations which comprise the OBE Model was solved using the Gauss-Seidel iterative solution method. A complete model solution required about one-fourth of a second of central processor time, using a Univac 1108 computer system. The solution method operates on normalized equation forms, with all normalized error terms set at expected values (zeros except for serial correlation adjustments).

In most cases, the normalized equation is a transformation of the estimated equation. This is most easily understood by considering some of the equations in Appendix B. Of the consumption equations, the equations for CA, COD, and CN are used without transformation, since the left-hand side of each equation consists of a single variable. The CS equation, however, is estimated with CS/N as the dependent variable; for model solution, the equation is rewritten by multiplying both sides of the equation by N, so that only CS is on the left-hand side of the equation. Similarly, the equation estimated as ISE/XC is normalized as an equation in ISE, and all equations estimated with dependent variables of the form $\ln(x)$ are converted to antilog form in the normalization process.

A discussion of constant-term procedures and the application of random shocks to the normalized model equations will be found below. It should be noted that the error properties of a normalized equation may be quite different from those of the corresponding estimated equation. In particular, if the normalization involves converting to antilogs, or multiplication of both sides of the equation by a variable, then the error term in the normalized form will be heteroscedastic if the error term in the estimated form was homoscedastic.

3 SAMPLE-PERIOD SIMULATIONS

THIS section discusses various simulations made with the model described in the previous section. All of these simulations used ex post data, revised through June, 1968, for "actual" values. (Subsequent data revisions are not reflected in the results presented.) The model equations were estimated using this same data base. For all simulations, exogenous variables were set at actual, ex post levels.

Six quarter ex post forecasts were made, using several adjustment procedures for serial correlation in the estimated endogenous equations. These procedures and brief results are presented in Section 3.1. Following this, we provide an analysis of single equation, and model forecast, errors for all endogenous variables. Section 3.3 considers, also briefly, the performance of the model as evidenced by short simulations around NBER reference-cycle turning points within the sample period. A final subsection comments on the results of a fifty-five-quarter simulation over the entire sample period.

3.1 ADJUSTMENTS FOR SERIAL CORRELATION

It has long been recognized that when serial correlation is present in a regression model, the pattern of equation residuals over prior observations contains information which is useful in prediction. Goldberger shows that in the single equation case with serially correlated residuals, the gain in predictive efficiency associated with such adjustments may be substantial [9]. We consider here appropriate adjustments for forecasts made with the OBE Model.

Six quarter ex post forecasts were made, using four different mechanical procedures for adjusting the constant terms of normalized stochastic equations.

All equations were stated in the normalized forms used to solve the model, and single equation residuals over the sample period were then calculated. A first-order serial correlation coefficient for each normalized equation was estimated from

$$(1) \qquad\qquad e_t = b_0 e_{t-1} + v$$

and second-order serial correlation coefficients were estimated from

$$(2) \qquad\qquad e_t = b_1 e_{t-1} + b_2 e_{t-2} + u$$

using least squares in both cases, where e_t refers to a residual value for a particular equation in time period t. For convenience, let t represent the jump-off quarter (i.e., one quarter before the first forecast period). Then $t + i$, $i = 1, 2, \ldots, 6$ represents one of the six forecast quarters.

Procedure 1 involves no constant-term adjustments of any kind.

Procedure 2 is a first-order serial correlation adjustment, using only the observed residual in the jump-off quarter. The adjustment for forecast period i is

(3) $$e_{t+i} = b_0^i e_t$$

Procedure 3 also employs a first-order serial correlation specification, but a weighted average of the last two residuals is used. This method guards against giving excessive weight to a large random element in the jump-off quarter residual.

The adjustment applied in the ith forecast period is

(4) $$e_{t+i} = b_0^i \left(\frac{e_t + b_0 e_{t-1}}{2} \right)$$

Procedure 4 uses a second-order serial correlation specification if the second-order serial correlation is significantly higher than the first-order serial correlation. In such cases, the adjustment for forecast period i is

(5) $$e_{t+i} = b_1 e_{t+i-1} + b_2 e_{t+i-2}$$

In equations where a first-order serial correlation was adequate, Procedure 2 was substituted.

For all procedures, no adjustment was made unless the serial correlation was significant at the 5 per cent level.

Selected summary results from using these four alternative procedures for nineteen different six-quarter model forecasts before NBER reference-cycle peaks and troughs, are presented in Tables 1 and 2. Any correction for serial correlation of residuals resulted in a substantial improvement in the average absolute errors (AAE) for the first-quarter forecasted values of the first three variables listed. Averages of forecast errors, without regard to sign, in the first four quarters of each forecast are nearly the same for all procedures, al-

TABLE 1

Average Absolute Errors in First Forecast Quarter of Nineteen Simulations, with Alternative Adjustment Procedures

Variable	No Adjustment	First-Order	First-Order Average	Second-Order
GNP	4.9	3.7	3.7	3.7
GNP58$	3.4	2.5	2.7	2.6
ISE	1.4	0.7	0.9	0.8
II	1.8	1.8	1.8	1.8

TABLE 2

*Average of Quarterly Forecast Errors Without Regard for Sign in the
First Four Quarters of Nineteen Simulations, with Alternative
Adjustment Procedures*

Variable	No Adjustment	First-Order	First-Order Average	Second-Order
GNP	5.6	5.2	5.2	5.3
GNP58$	4.2	4.3	4.3	4.3
ISE	1.6	1.3	1.3	1.3
II	2.4	2.5	2.5	2.3

though there is a slight improvement for *GNP* and *ISE* if an adjustment for serial correlation is made. It appears that any adjustment for serial correlation results in better model forecasts of real variables in the first quarter of the forecast, but somewhat larger errors in successive quarters, which to a large extent, cancel out the benefit of the smaller errors in the first forecast quarters. Also, adjustment for serial correlation results in better price forecasts over the entire forecast period.

The brief results presented above suggest that for our model, a first-order serial correlation adjustment is adequate. Of the two first-order procedures, we had a strong a priori preference for Procedure 3, which guards against large random residuals in the jump-off quarter, and which is closer to the adjustments we tend to make in ex ante forecasting. Two sets of short, six-quarter ex post forecasts were made, using first Procedure 1 (no adjustments), and then Procedure 3. All of the results for short forecasts presented below use Procedure 3. The relevant first-order serial correlation coefficients used are given in Table 3.

3.2 AN ANALYSIS OF SINGLE EQUATION AND MODEL FORECAST
     ERRORS

Econometric-model builders have devoted an overwhelming portion of their research efforts to the structural specification of single equations or small blocks of equations. Little attention has been given

TABLE 3

First-Order Serial Correlation Coefficients
(Rho Values) for Endogenous Variables

Variable	Rho	Variable	Rho	Variable	Rho
CA	.438	KC$	.922	RS	.534
CN	.364	LH	−.214	RT	.345
COD	.552	LFP	.545	RTB	.525
CPR	−.120	LFS	.633	TCF	.603
CS	.483	OMD	.429	TCRI	.744
CUW	.153	P	.573	TCSL	.448
DD	.537	PHS	.822	TD	.465
DSE	.755	PIE	−.205	TEXAV	.577
EW	.381	PIH	.548	TEXS	.727
HM	.242	PIS	.433	TISL	.851
HS	.442	PN	−.095	TPF	.643
IH	.758	POD	.482	TPSL	.535
IINA	.191	PRI	.610	TRU	.729
IMS	.953	PS	.848	TSSW	.679
IMT	.799	PWMD	.411	UMD	.310
ISE	.905	REM	.953	URP	.647
IVA	.217	RM	.686	WR	.301

NOTE: All of the above coefficients are significant at the 5 per cent level. Variables with nonsignificant serial correlations were not adjusted.

to a comparison of error statistics from full model solutions with those of the component single equations, and their possible implications for model construction. This section represents a modest attempt at such a comparison for endogenous variables of the OBE Econometric Model.

Tables 4, 5, and 6 present average errors, average absolute errors, and root mean square errors for normalized, single-equation solutions and for one- to six-quarter full model ex post forecasts. *All averages shown cover the same forty-eight observations, from 1955-I through 1966-IV.*

The sample period extended over 55 quarters (starting in 1953-II), but the automatic constant-term adjustment procedure used requires data from two previous quarters, so that 1953-IV was the first quarter

TABLE 4

Average Errors for All Endogenous Variables from Single-Equation Solutions and from One Through Six Quarter Ex Post Model Forecast Solutions: 48 Observations, 1955-I-1966-IV

Type of Solution	Variable								
	C	CA	CMP/MH	CN	COD	CPR	CS	CUW	DD
Single equation	-.15	-.01	.0000	-.08	-.11	.01	.04	-.0008	-.01
First quarter forecasts	-.11	-.03	-.0016	-.05	-.08	-.09	.04	-.0010	.01
Second quarter forecasts	-.25	-.14	-.0039	-.09	-.07	-.23	.04	-.0024	-.02
Third quarter forecasts	-.43	-.23	-.0063	-.14	-.09	-.38	.03	-.0037	-.13
Fourth quarter forecasts	-.61	-.29	-.0083	-.19	-.13	-.59	.00	-.0050	-.21
Fifth quarter forecasts	-.82	-.37	-.0105	-.24	-.19	-.88	-.02	-.0064	-.27
Sixth quarter forecasts	-1.00	-.44	-.0124	-.29	-.25	-1.12	-.04	-.0077	-.31
	DIV	DPI	DSE	EC	E	EW	FBF	FBSL	GNP
Single equation	.01	-.16	.02	.00	-.03	-.03	.10	.01	-.11
First quarter forecasts	.01	-.36	.01	.01	-.03	-.03	-.16	-.01	-.42
Second quarter forecasts	-.01	-.73	.01	.01	-.05	-.05	-.30	-.03	-1.00
Third quarter forecasts	-.04	-1.10	.01	.01	-.08	-.08	-.46	-.05	-1.58
Fourth quarter forecasts	-.06	-1.44	.01	.01	-.10	-.10	-.64	-.08	-2.13
Fifth quarter forecasts	-.10	-1.81	.01	.01	-.12	-.12	-.88	-.12	-2.80
Sixth quarter forecasts	-.13	-2.14	.01	.01	-.14	-.14	-1.08	-.17	-3.41

(continued)

TABLE 4 (continued)

Type of Solution	Variable								
	GNP58$	H	HM	HS	IE	IH	II	II$	IIA
Single equation	.15	-.01	-.04	-8.	.00	.17	.08	.00	-.019
First quarter forecasts	.04	-.01	-.04	-5.	.00	.04	.06	-.02	-.022
Second quarter forecasts	-.19	-.02	-.06	-6.	.01	.00	-.01	-.09	-.040
Third quarter forecasts	-.51	-.02	-.08	-13.	-.01	-.06	-.10	-.17	-.053
Fourth quarter forecasts	-.90	-.03	-.11	-23.	-.04	-.15	-.19	-.27	-.062
Fifth quarter forecasts	-1.35	-.03	-.13	-33.	-.06	-.27	-.29	-.37	-.070
Sixth quarter forecasts	-1.77	-.03	-.15	-43.	-.08	-.40	-.38	-.48	-.078

Type of Solution	IINA	IMS	IMT	IS	ISE	IVA	KA	KC$	KH
Single equation	.14	.32	-.01	.33	.34	.12	.08	.14	-4.
First quarter forecasts	.12	.03	-.05	.00	.00	.20	.05	-.02	-4.
Second quarter forecasts	.07	.05	-.08	.01	.02	.22	-.04	-.03	-8.
Third quarter forecasts	.00	.07	-.12	.01	.00	.24	-.21	-.05	-15.
Fourth quarter forecasts	-.08	.10	-.15	.00	-.04	.25	-.39	-.08	-21.
Fifth quarter forecasts	-.18	.12	-.20	-.01	-.07	.26	-.60	-.09	-29.
Sixth quarter forecasts	-.26	.16	-.24	-.02	-.10	.26	-.75	-.07	-39.

Type of Solution	KI	KIA	KINA	KSE	KSE$	LH	LFP	LFS	MONEY
Single equation	.00	.000	-.01	.00	-.01	.21	.00	-.01	.00
First quarter forecasts	.02	-.005	.02	-.01	-.03	.16	.00	-.02	.01
Second quarter forecasts	.03	-.010	.04	-.01	-.06	.16	.01	-.02	-.02
Third quarter forecasts	.03	-.019	.05	-.01	-.11	.03	.01	-.02	-.13
Fourth quarter forecasts	.03	-.025	.05	-.02	-.17	-.17	.00	-.03	-.21
Fifth quarter forecasts	.02	-.032	.05	-.02	-.22	-.49	.00	-.03	-.27
Sixth quarter forecasts	.00	-.039	.04	-.02	-.22	-.77	.00	-.04	-.31

	NETEXP	OMD	P	PADJ	PC	PERINC	PGNP	PHS	PIE
Single equation	−.31	−.20	−.0007	—	−.0001	.00	.00	−.0897	.0001
First quarter forecasts	.02	−.27	−.0010	−.0002	−.0009	−.44	−.09	−.0211	−.0014
Second quarter forecasts	.03	−.46	−.0019	−.0005	−.0017	−.87	−.16	−.0387	−.0028
Third quarter forecasts	.04	−.62	−.0026	−.0005	−.0023	−1.32	−.21	−.0554	−.0041
Fourth quarter forecasts	.06	−.77	−.0030	−.0005	−.0027	−1.72	−.25	−.0680	−.0052
Fifth quarter forecasts	.07	−.97	−.0036	−.0005	−.0031	−2.16	−.29	−.0792	−.0064
Sixth quarter forecasts	.08	−1.14	−.0040	−.0005	−.0035	−2.56	−.32	−.0897	−.0072

	PIH	PIS	PISE	PN	POD	PRI	PROD	PS	PWMD
Single equation	−.0008	−.0011	.0001	−.0001	−.0005	−.08	−.10	.0004	−.0004
First quarter forecasts	−.0011	−.0020	−.0016	−.0011	−.0008	−.09	.11	−.0007	−.0008
Second quarter forecasts	−.0019	−.0037	−.0031	−.0023	−.0014	−.15	.13	−.0016	−.0015
Third quarter forecasts	−.0026	−.0049	−.0043	−.0033	−.0018	−.23	.17	−.0021	−.0024
Fourth quarter forecasts	−.0032	−.0058	−.0053	−.0041	−.0019	−.31	.25	−.0021	−.0031
Fifth quarter forecasts	−.0040	−.0070	−.0063	−.0051	−.0019	−.37	.35	−.0021	−.0034
Sixth quarter forecasts	−.0046	−.0079	−.0073	−.0060	−.0020	−.45	.43	−.0020	−.0034

	REM	RESF	RL	RM	RS	RT	RTB	SD	SDADJ
Single equation	.18	.0177	.01	−.01	−.01	.00	.00	−.10	—
First quarter forecasts	.00	.0156	.00	−.01	−.02	.00	−.01	.11	−.12
Second quarter forecasts	−.01	.0222	.01	−.02	−.02	−.01	−.01	.13	−.06
Third quarter forecasts	−.02	.0387	.01	−.03	−.03	−.01	−.01	.17	−.08
Fourth quarter forecasts	−.02	.0512	.02	−.02	−.03	−.02	−.02	.25	−.12
Fifth quarter forecasts	−.03	.0631	.03	−.01	−.03	−.02	−.02	.35	−.14
Sixth quarter forecasts	−.04	.0707	.03	.00	−.03	−.02	−.02	.43	−.12

(continued)

TABLE 4 (concluded)

Type of Solution	Variable								
	SIB	SIP	SMD	SRATE	TCF	TCRI	TCSL	TD	TEXAV
Single equation	.02	.02	.95	−.0001	.07	.0000	.01	.01	−.03
First quarter forecasts	.00	.00	.76	.0002	−.08	−.0014	.00	.01	−.02
Second quarter forecasts	.00	.00	1.50	.0003	−.14	−.0015	.00	−.03	−.02
Third quarter forecasts	.00	.00	2.17	.0003	−.20	−.0014	.00	−.07	−.03
Fourth quarter forecasts	.00	.00	2.68	.0003	−.28	−.0008	.00	−.11	−.04
Fifth quarter forecasts	−.01	−.01	3.17	.0003	−.41	.0006	−.01	−.22	−.04
Sixth quarter forecasts	−.02	−.02	3.52	.0003	−.51	.0026	−.02	−.29	−.05
	TEXS	TIF	TISL	TPF	TPSL	TRP	TRU	TSSW	UMD
Single equation	.00	−.03	.10	.02	.00	.02	.02	.05	−.17
First quarter forecasts	.01	−.01	.00	−.06	−.02	.01	.01	.01	−.13
Second quarter forecasts	.01	−.02	−.01	−.12	−.02	.03	.03	.01	−.38
Third quarter forecasts	.01	−.03	−.02	−.18	−.03	.05	.05	.00	−.67
Fourth quarter forecasts	.00	−.04	−.03	−.24	−.04	.07	.07	−.01	−.99
Fifth quarter forecasts	−.01	−.05	−.06	−.30	−.06	.09	.09	−.02	−1.26
Sixth quarter forecasts	−.02	−.07	−.09	−.36	−.07	.11	.11	−.04	−1.53

	UNI-TLC	UN-RATE	URP	V	W	WR	X	XC
Single equation	.0000	.00	.0000	-4.	-.06	.0017	.14	.00
First quarter forecasts	-.0008	.03	.0002	-4.	-.37	-.0041	.03	.03
Second quarter forecasts	-.0014	.06	.0005	-8.	-.74	-.0098	-.19	.03
Third quarter forecasts	-.0019	.09	.0008	-15.	-1.11	-.0154	-.51	.03
Fourth quarter forecasts	-.0022	.11	.0010	-21.	-1.43	-.0200	-.90	.03
Fifth quarter forecasts	-.0025	.14	.0012	-29.	1.79	-.0253	-1.35	.04
Sixth quarter forecasts	-.0027	.16	.0014	-39.	2.11	-.0298	-1.77	.06

NOTE: See Appendix A for full definitions of all symbols.

TABLE 5

Average Absolute Errors for All Endogenous Variables from Single-Equation Solutions and from One Through Six Quarter Ex Post Model Forecast Solutions: 48 Observations, 1955-I–1966-IV

Type of Solution	Variable								
	C	CA	CMP/MH	CN	COD	CPR	CS	CUW	DD
Single equation	1.34	.85	.00	.81	.44	.72	.35	.0083	.52
First quarter forecasts	1.48	.82	.02	.85	.40	1.60	.35	.0117	.44
Second quarter forecasts	1.91	.94	.02	1.04	.43	2.00	.39	.0191	.76
Third quarter forecasts	2.48	1.05	.02	1.20	.50	2.48	.40	.0235	.93
Fourth quarter forecasts	2.75	1.12	.03	1.30	.60	2.85	.41	.0261	1.00
Fifth quarter forecasts	2.91	1.16	.02	1.33	.72	3.11	.42	.0285	1.09
Sixth quarter forecasts	3.06	1.21	.02	1.37	.79	3.18	.44	.0294	1.17
	DIV	DPI	DSE	EC	E	EW	FBF	FBSL	GNP
Single equation	.17	1.39	.07	.00	.16	.16	.45	.09	3.22
First quarter forecasts	.17	1.43	.04	.06	.17	.17	1.24	.25	2.84
Second quarter forecasts	.25	2.43	.05	.07	.28	.28	1.79	.36	4.54
Third quarter forecasts	.31	3.10	.06	.07	.36	.36	2.23	.45	5.93
Fourth quarter forecasts	.35	3.65	.06	.07	.44	.44	2.48	.48	6.62
Fifth quarter forecasts	.39	3.90	.07	.07	.48	.48	2.64	.51	7.01
Sixth quarter forecasts	.41	4.10	.07	.07	.50	.50	2.66	.55	7.19

	GNP58$	H	HM	HS	IE	IH	II	II$	IIA
Single equation	2.85	.12	.19	54.	.49	.42	1.51	1.51	.596
First quarter forecasts	2.35	.12	.19	48.	.87	.31	1.45	1.46	.609
Second quarter forecasts	3.58	.13	.27	52.	1.16	.43	1.75	1.77	.662
Third quarter forecasts	4.47	.14	.30	56.	1.40	.45	2.01	2.04	.670
Fourth quarter forecasts	4.92	.15	.31	62.	1.54	.52	2.06	2.12	.698
Fifth quarter forecasts	5.42	.15	.32	73.	1.63	.63	2.18	2.26	.706
Sixth quarter forecasts	5.82	.15	.34	85.	1.69	.79	2.44	2.51	.709

	IINA	IMS	IMT	IS	ISE	IVA	KA	KC$	KH
Single equation	1.21	.34	.54	1.80	1.75	.54	.25	.37	10.
First quarter forecasts	1.19	.10	.42	.48	.98	.67	.94	.31	10.
Second quarter forecasts	1.64	.13	.59	.56	1.34	.69	1.55	.60	18.
Third quarter forecasts	1.89	.17	.71	.66	1.69	.76	2.06	.94	29.
Fourth quarter forecasts	1.89	.20	.79	.72	1.96	.79	2.49	1.30	40.
Fifth quarter forecasts	1.98	.21	.85	.77	2.13	.79	2.98	1.67	53.
Sixth quarter forecasts	2.23	.24	.90	.83	2.30	.79	3.28	2.04	64.

	KI	KIA	KINA	KSE	KSE$	LH	LFP	LFS	MONEY
Single equation	.03	.000	.63	.03	.04	1.22	.07	.19	.00
First quarter forecasts	.38	.152	.87	.25	.26	1.32	.06	.15	.44
Second quarter forecasts	.64	.202	1.11	.52	.61	1.71	.07	.18	.76
Third quarter forecasts	.94	.222	1.40	.88	1.05	2.14	.07	.19	.93
Fourth quarter forecasts	1.19	.236	1.70	1.27	1.54	2.63	.07	.20	1.00
Fifth quarter forecasts	1.36	.246	1.89	1.65	2.05	3.16	.07	.21	1.09
Sixth quarter forecasts	1.45	.255	1.95	2.01	2.52	3.75	.07	.22	1.17

(continued)

TABLE 5 (concluded)

Type of Solution	Variable								
	NETEXP	OMD	P	PADJ	PC	PERINC	PGNP	PHS	PIE
Single equation	—	1.45	.0028	—	.0014	.00	.00	.2298	.0031
First quarter forecasts	.45	1.68	.0027	.0018	.0027	1.64	.22	.1507	.0047
Second quarter forecasts	.64	1.89	.0045	.0019	.0042	2.91	.37	.1973	.0084
Third quarter forecasts	.77	2.09	.0059	.0018	.0057	3.69	.49	.2295	.0113
Fourth quarter forecasts	.86	2.24	.0069	.0019	.0064	4.33	.57	.2522	.0140
Fifth quarter forecasts	.93	2.41	.0076	.0018	.0071	4.67	.62	.2699	.0160
Sixth quarter forecasts	.96	2.59	.0081	.0017	.0075	4.92	.66	.2802	.0178

Type of Solution	PIH	PIS	PISE	PN	POD	PRI	PROD	PS	PWMD
Single equation	.0043	.0049	.0031	.0023	.0022	.75	.00	.0048	.0032
First quarter forecasts	.0052	.0071	.0050	.0039	.0023	.59	.51	.0046	.0034
Second quarter forecasts	.0071	.0100	.0083	.0063	.0044	.77	.60	.0064	.0059
Third quarter forecasts	.0086	.0120	.0110	.0087	.0062	.89	.68	.0075	.0080
Fourth quarter forecasts	.0099	.0134	.0129	.0099	.0077	1.05	.71	.0088	.0101
Fifth quarter forecasts	.0108	.0141	.0144	.0111	.0094	1.16	.78	.0100	.0123
Sixth quarter forecasts	.0114	.0147	.0159	.0116	.0113	1.29	.88	.0114	.0145

Type of Solution	REM	RESF	RL	RM	RS	RT	RTB	SD	SDADJ
Single equation	.20	.0336	.05	.08	.08	.05	.20	4.04	—
First quarter forecasts	.04	.0766	.07	.07	.14	.05	.17	.98	.37
Second quarter forecasts	.06	.1130	.11	.13	.20	.08	.21	1.34	.28
Third quarter forecasts	.07	.1298	.13	.17	.21	.10	.22	1.43	.24
Fourth quarter forecasts	.09	.1425	.15	.20	.21	.12	.22	1.51	.22
Fifth quarter forecasts	.11	.1496	.16	.23	.21	.14	.22	1.54	.20
Sixth quarter forecasts	.13	.1572	.16	.25	.21	.14	.22	1.58	.18

	SIB	SIP	SMD	SRATE	TCF	TCRI	TCSL	TD	TEXAV
Single equation	.08	.08	1.52	.0006	.36	.0187	.05	.53	.16
First quarter forecasts	.06	.06	1.44	.0037	.83	.0223	.05	.50	.15
Second quarter forecasts	.08	.08	2.58	.0039	1.12	.0307	.06	.86	.17
Third quarter forecasts	.09	.09	3.33	.0042	1.38	.0365	.06	1.21	.17
Fourth quarter forecasts	.10	.10	3.98	.0045	1.56	.0430	.07	1.56	.17
Fifth quarter forecasts	.11	.11	4.80	.0048	1.64	.0524	.07	1.81	.17
Sixth quarter forecasts	.11	.11	5.25	.0049	1.64	.0614	.07	2.09	.17

	TEXS	TIF	TISL	TPF	TPSL	TRP	TRU	TSSW	UMD
Single equation	.24	.31	.36	.28	.14	.23	.23	.16	1.19
First quarter forecasts	.15	.23	.20	.35	.12	.26	.26	.13	1.13
Second quarter forecasts	.19	.27	.28	.51	.15	.34	.34	.16	2.15
Third quarter forecasts	.20	.28	.32	.60	.16	.42	.42	.18	3.10
Fourth quarter forecasts	.21	.29	.37	.66	.16	.48	.48	.20	4.05
Fifth quarter forecasts	.21	.28	.40	.67	.17	.49	.49	.21	4.91
Sixth quarter forecasts	.21	.28	.42	.72	.17	.49	.49	.22	5.34

	UNI-TLC	UN-RATE	URP	V	W	WR	X	XC
Single equation	.0000	.00	.0015	10.	1.15	.0213	2.86	.00
First quarter forecasts	.0028	.23	.0025	10.	1.73	.0280	2.34	.33
Second quarter forecasts	.0044	.37	.0035	18.	3.05	.0449	3.58	.35
Third quarter forecasts	.0055	.46	.0041	29.	3.77	.0530	4.48	.35
Fourth quarter forecasts	.0064	.49	.0044	40.	4.32	.0564	4.94	.36
Fifth quarter forecasts	.0069	.52	.0045	53.	4.43	.0579	5.43	.43
Sixth quarter forecasts	.0074	.52	.0046	64.	4.58	.0578	5.82	.54

NOTE: See Appendix A for full definitions of all symbols.

TABLE 6

Root Mean Square Errors for All Endogenous Variables from Single-Equation Solutions and from One Through Six Quarter Ex Post Model Forecast Solutions: 48 Observations, 1955-I-1966-IV

Type of Solution	Variable								
	C	CA	CMP/MH	CN	COD	CPR	CS	CUW	DD
Single equation	1.69	1.04	.0000	1.07	.54	.89	.44	.0102	.66
First quarter forecasts	1.93	1.00	.0186	1.14	.52	1.98	.43	.0154	.59
Second quarter forecasts	2.52	1.19	.0265	1.32	.58	2.53	.50	.0234	1.01
Third quarter forecasts	3.08	1.33	.0310	1.50	.68	3.03	.56	.0282	1.17
Fourth quarter forecasts	3.42	1.40	.0320	1.60	.78	3.29	.57	.0308	1.26
Fifth quarter forecasts	3.69	1.44	.0308	1.67	.96	3.52	.56	.0315	1.33
Sixth quarter forecasts	3.90	1.47	.0308	1.74	1.09	3.70	.57	.0325	1.39
	DIV	DPI	DSE	EC	E	EW	FBF	FBSL	GNP
Single equation	.24	1.76	.08	.00	.21	.21	.60	.11	3.79
First quarter forecasts	.24	1.84	.06	.07	.24	.24	1.61	.31	3.64
Second quarter forecasts	.34	2.94	.07	.08	.35	.35	2.26	.45	5.60
Third quarter forecasts	.40	3.74	.07	.08	.43	.43	2.74	.55	7.13
Fourth quarter forecasts	.45	4.30	.08	.08	.51	.51	2.94	.59	7.90
Fifth quarter forecasts	.49	4.67	.08	.08	.55	.55	3.02	.64	8.44
Sixth quarter forecasts	.52	5.08	.09	.08	.56	.56	3.11	.67	8.91

	GNP58$	H	HM	HS	IE	IH	II	II$	IIA
Single equation	3.41	.14	.23	67.	.57	.57	1.89	1.90	.764
First quarter forecasts	3.12	.15	.26	63.	1.09	.40	1.86	1.87	.782
Second quarter forecasts	4.49	.17	.35	65.	1.41	.54	2.24	2.27	.851
Third quarter forecasts	5.59	.17	.39	69.	1.64	.56	2.50	2.56	.864
Fourth quarter forecasts	6.20	.18	.39	77.	1.81	.62	2.60	2.68	.900
Fifth quarter forecasts	6.74	.18	.39	93.	1.95	.77	2.71	2.81	.902
Sixth quarter forecasts	7.34	.18	.41	109.	2.08	.96	2.94	3.05	.910

	IINA	IMS	IMT	IS	ISE	IVA	KA	KC$	KH
Single equation	1.72	.42	.67	2.32	2.24	.71	.38	.43	12.
First quarter forecasts	1.72	.14	.51	.62	1.26	.84	1.14	.39	12.
Second quarter forecasts	2.08	.18	.71	.70	1.75	.89	1.94	.77	22.
Third quarter forecasts	2.29	.21	.87	.80	2.13	.96	2.66	1.20	36.
Fourth quarter forecasts	2.37	.24	.98	.90	2.42	.98	3.28	1.68	49.
Fifth quarter forecasts	2.50	.26	1.07	.95	2.64	.99	3.78	2.15	62.
Sixth quarter forecasts	2.70	.28	1.14	1.00	2.82	.99	4.26	2.61	76.

	KI	KIA	KINA	KSE	KSE$	LH	LFP	LFS	MONEY
Single equation	.04	.000	2.90	.03	.06	1.82	.08	.25	.00
First quarter forecasts	.48	.195	2.83	.32	.33	1.85	.07	.19	.59
Second quarter forecasts	.82	.253	2.78	.69	.77	2.24	.08	.23	1.01
Third quarter forecasts	1.12	.288	2.85	1.12	1.30	2.64	.08	.25	1.17
Fourth quarter forecasts	1.35	.301	3.18	1.60	1.90	3.16	.08	.26	1.26
Fifth quarter forecasts	1.60	.312	3.34	2.08	2.50	3.81	.08	.26	1.33
Sixth quarter forecasts	1.78	.327	3.42	2.51	3.08	4.35	.08	.27	1.40

(continued)

TABLE 6 (concluded)

Type of Solution	Variable								
	NETEXP	OMD	P	PADJ	PC	PERINC	PGNP	PHS	PIE
Single equation	.00	1.80	.0033	—	.0019	.00	.00	.2887	.0044
First quarter forecasts	.54	2.10	.0035	.0022	.0036	2.15	.29	.1859	.0059
Second quarter forecasts	.78	2.37	.0057	.0024	.0055	3.50	.47	.2322	.0104
Third quarter forecasts	.97	2.61	.0074	.0024	.0071	4.44	.61	.2720	.0144
Fourth quarter forecasts	1.08	2.70	.0086	.0023	.0081	5.07	.70	.3008	.0176
Fifth quarter forecasts	1.13	2.95	.0095	.0022	.0089	5.49	.77	.3119	.0201
Sixth quarter forecasts	1.18	3.23	.0102	.0021	.0095	5.98	.83	.3251	.0228
	PIH	PIS	PISE	PN	POD	PRI	PROD	PS	PWMD
Single equation	.0052	.0064	.0041	.0027	.0027	.91	.02	.0059	.0045
First quarter forecasts	.0065	.0097	.0064	.0049	.0030	.75	.65	.0063	.0046
Second quarter forecasts	.0092	.0126	.0103	.0079	.0055	.95	.78	.0086	.0081
Third quarter forecasts	.0111	.0145	.0135	.0103	.0079	1.09	.88	.0101	.0110
Fourth quarter forecasts	.0123	.0158	.0160	.0120	.0097	1.23	.94	.0116	.0135
Fifth quarter forecasts	.0136	.0172	.0181	.0133	.0120	1.37	1.02	.0129	.0162
Sixth quarter forecasts	.0145	.0187	.0203	.0143	.0142	1.47	1.14	.0138	.0190
	REM	RESF	RL	RM	RS	RT	RTB	SD	SDADJ
Single equation	.28	.04	.07	.11	.11	.07	.26	4.76	—
First quarter forecasts	.08	.10	.09	.09	.20	.07	.23	1.15	.73
Second quarter forecasts	.10	.15	.13	.17	.26	.11	.27	1.59	.58
Third quarter forecasts	.12	.17	.15	.22	.28	.14	.28	1.78	.58
Fourth quarter forecasts	.14	.18	.18	.25	.28	.17	.28	1.80	.51
Fifth quarter forecasts	.16	.19	.20	.28	.28	.18	.28	1.84	.50
Sixth quarter forecasts	.18	.20	.20	.30	.28	.18	.28	1.91	.47

	SIB	SIP	SMD	SRATE	TCF	TCRI	TCSL	TD	TEXAV
Single equation	.12	.12	2.03	.0010	.48	.0355	.06	.67	.21
First quarter forecasts	.09	.09	1.93	.0046	1.03	.0395	.07	.67	.19
Second quarter forecasts	.11	.11	3.17	.0051	1.33	.0547	.07	1.06	.22
Third quarter forecasts	.12	.12	4.08	.0055	1.59	.0659	.08	1.42	.23
Fourth quarter forecasts	.13	.13	4.62	.0056	1.73	.0773	.08	1.85	.23
Fifth quarter forecasts	.14	.14	5.52	.0060	1.80	.0899	.09	2.13	.23
Sixth quarter forecasts	.14	.14	6.25	.0062	1.88	.1027	.09	2.42	.22

	TEXS	TIF	TISL	TPF	TPSL	TRP	TRU	TSSW	UMD
Single equation	.28	.36	.45	.37	.17	.31	.31	.24	1.59
First quarter forecasts	.20	.28	.24	.44	.16	.35	.35	.18	1.51
Second quarter forecasts	.23	.32	.33	.62	.19	.50	.50	.21	2.64
Third quarter forecasts	.24	.34	.39	.72	.21	.60	.60	.25	3.62
Fourth quarter forecasts	.25	.34	.43	.77	.21	.64	.64	.27	4.63
Fifth quarter forecasts	.25	.34	.47	.80	.22	.64	.64	.28	5.55
Sixth quarter forecasts	.25	.35	.50	.86	.23	.62	.62	.28	6.42

	UNI-TLC	UN-RATE	URP	V	W	WR	X	XC
Single equation	.0000	.00	.0019	12.	1.39	.0271	3.40	.00
First quarter forecasts	.0035	.31	.0035	12.	2.15	.0366	3.11	.39
Second quarter forecasts	.0054	.49	.0051	22.	3.71	.0571	4.50	.43
Third quarter forecasts	.0067	.60	.0060	36.	4.72	.0685	5.60	.42
Fourth quarter forecasts	.0079	.66	.0065	49.	5.28	.0722	6.21	.45
Fifth quarter forecasts	.0085	.66	.0065	62.	5.52	.0716	6.75	.53
Sixth quarter forecasts	.0093	.65	.0062	76.	5.74	.0725	7.36	.67

NOTE: See Appendix A for full definitions of all symbols.

for which a full model solution could be obtained, and 1955-I was the first quarter for which a sixth quarter forecast was available.

The single equation errors shown for each variable defined by an identity were derived by first substituting into the identity the calculated values from all stochastic variables, and then subtracting the actual value of the variable defined by the identity. The errors shown for first quarter forecasts are averages of errors (forecast minus actual values) in each of the 48 quarters. The errors shown for second quarter forecasts are average values of errors over these same 48 quarters; i.e., each quarter from 1955-I through 1966-IV is now the second quarter of an ex post forecast; and so on, through the sixth quarter. We will not attempt to discuss all of the results contained in these tables, but will concentrate on some of the more important aspects instead.

The extent and direction of bias in any variable can be ascertained from Table 4, which shows average errors. Nonzero values for single equation solutions can arise both from the normalization of equations and from the use of an analysis period which is not identical with the sample period used for equation estimation. The largest single-equation average errors for GNP components are slightly over 0.3 billion dollars for IMS and $ISE;$ most single-equation average errors are quite small. However, the patterns of average forecast errors from full model solutions reveal, for some variables, persistent biases increasing in magnitude as the forecast period is lengthened. For example, first quarter forecasts of $GNP58\$$ are, on the average, virtually free of bias, but sixth quarter forecasts of $GNP58\$$ are 1.8 billion dollars low on the average. The biases in current dollar variables are even more striking. Forecasts of GNP show an average downward bias of 0.4 billion dollars for first quarter forecasts, but this bias is enlarged to 3.4 billion dollars for sixth quarter forecasts. An examination of the average errors for P reveals a downward bias of one-tenth of an index point for first quarter forecasts, mounting to four-tenths of an index point in sixth quarter forecasts.

We cannot give definitive answers to the questions raised by the above-noted biases without additional research, but a key element seems discernible. The downward bias for major current dollar variables is about twice as large as the downward bias in constant dollar counterparts in the sixth quarter forecasts. Moreover, there is noticeable bias for current dollar magnitudes and for prices, even in the first quarter forecasts. The level of wages is a main determinant in the over-all price equation, and wages are simply the product of private employment (E) and wage rates (WR). Both E and WR show a downward bias in the first forecast quarter, and an increasing downward bias as the forecast period is lengthened. The first quarter downward bias in E is the same as the average error from a single-equation solution for E. But the average error from a single-equation solution for WR is slightly positive, while the first quarter forecast solution average error is negative. Thus, it appears that the downward bias of the WR equation when placed in a model environment, leads to low forecasts of prices, and this in turn leads to forecast biases in other variables. When the forecast period is lengthened from one quarter to four or six quarters, these biases cumulate, becoming more prominent because of the under-prediction of lagged endogenous values. This does not necessarily mean that the wage rate and price equations are the only possible culprits. Other equations may also be contributors to the over-all bias. Nevertheless, as a practical aid in forecasting, it may be advisable to introduce adjustments in the WR and/or P equations so that biases in important magnitudes are eliminated.

Two explanatory forays were made in an effort to isolate the biases noted above. First, we tested to make sure that the automatic constant term adjustment procedure was not a culprit. We made simulation runs without automatic constant term adjustments and generated average error statistics. The biases noted above were still present, and the amounts of these biases were virtually unaltered. A second set of simulations was made, using the same procedures as used to generate Table 4, except that two equation parameters were altered slightly. The constant term in the estimated form of the WR equation was increased from 0.0076 to 0.00846, an effective increase of about four dollars per man per year. Also, the constant term in the price equation was increased from 0.263 to 0.264. These two changes eliminated about 97 per cent of the price bias noted earlier. The average error in P for six-quarter forecasts became -0.0001, compared with -0.004 registered in Table 4. Similarly, the GNP bias was cut from -3.41 to -1.84 for six-quarter forecasts. While the price bias was virtually eliminated, these two parameter changes had almost no effect upon the biases in constant dollar magnitudes. These results suggest that further research along these lines may prove fruitful.

The average absolute errors (AAE) shown in Table 5 and the root mean square errors ($RMSE$) shown in Table 6 show similar patterns. For nearly all variables, the AAE or $RMSE$ for the sixth quarter forecasts is from one and a half, to two and a half, times the corresponding error measure for the first quarter forecasts. Some variables—for instance, other durables consumption, demand deposits, and all broad categories of investment—show lower AAE or $RMSE$ for first quarter forecasts than for the single-equation solutions; this apparently reflects the use of a serial correlation adjustment procedure for the model forecasts. A comparison of single-equation errors with first quarter forecast errors also brings out quite clearly the difficulty of predicting certain variables. For instance, the first quarter AAE for each of the consumption variables is not far different from the single-equation AAE, but the first quarter AAE for corporate profits of 1.6 is more than twice as large as the single-equation counterpart value of 0.72. Profits are residual in nature, and thus are sensitive to errors in the determinants of the profits equation—private output, the wage share, and the industrial capacity utilization index—while the main determinant in the consumption equations is disposable income, which is much more stable and easier to predict.

The AAE for aggregates are smaller than sums of the AAE for components of the aggregates, reflecting the partial offsetting of errors of opposite sign when aggregates are formed. To illustrate, the sum of AAE for components of consumption (C)—CA, CN, COD, CS—is 2.45 for single-equation solutions, 2.42 for first quarter forecasts, and 3.81 for sixth quarter forecasts. The corresponding AAE values for C are 1.34, 1.48, and 3.06. The same holds true for the change in inventory investment (II), where the AAE for II is always smaller than the sum of the AAE for IIA and $IINA$. A similar benefit can be noted in even broader aggregates. The AAE for $GNP58\$$ is 2.35 for first quarter forecasts and 5.82 for sixth quarter forecasts, while the corresponding sums of AAE for broad components of $GNP58\$$—C, IH, II, ISE, and $NETEXP$—are 4.67 and 9.55.

Values of AAE or $RMSE$ for broad aggregates predicted by the model are fairly small. The AAE for first quarter forecasts of X,

GNP58$, and *GNP* are 2.34, 2.35, and 2.84, respectively. Each *AAE* is only one-half of 1 per cent of the average value of the variable to which it refers. The *AAE* from sixth quarter forecasts for these same aggregates are about 1.3 per cent of mean values.

As an aid in appraising the general magnitude of these errors, a comparison can be made with results obtained using an auto-regressive equation for each variable. The *RMSE* (in billions of dollars) from first quarter model forecasts for *X*, *GNP58$*, and *GNP* are 3.11, 3.12, and 3.64, respectively. Comparable *RMSE* values for second-order auto-regressive equations are 4.64, 4.68, and 4.52, and fourth-order auto-regressive equations yield *RMSE* of 4.55, 4.58, and 4.42, respectively. The superior performance of the model is primarily due to better behavior at turning points.

3.3 SHORT SIMULATIONS AROUND TURNING POINTS

It has long been recognized that the most difficult and critical job for any forecaster is the correct indication of turning points in important series. For this reason, we will now consider the performance of short, ex post model forecasts over periods which contain NBER reference-cycle peaks and troughs. The sample period contained six of these critical periods: troughs in 1954-III, 1958-II, and 1961-I; and peaks in 1953-II, 1957-III, and 1960-II. The 1953-II peak is not included in our analysis, since its inclusion would have required solving the model for quarters prior to the sample period. Three simulations were made for each turning point, with first forecast quarters one, two, and three quarters before the one designated as a reference-cycle peak or trough. Each of these forecasts used actual data for all exogenous variables; mechanical constant term adjustments were made, based on the serial correlation in various equations, using the procedure explained above.

Model performance for selected variables over these critical periods is shown in the accompanying charts. Each chart plots actual data (revised through June, 1968) and three forecasted series. For instance, in the top panel of each chart, the dashed line shows forecasted results with 1953-IV as the first forecast quarter; the dotted line traces

CHART 1

Actual and Predicted Values for Gross National Product,
Constant (1958) Dollars, Around Five Turning Points

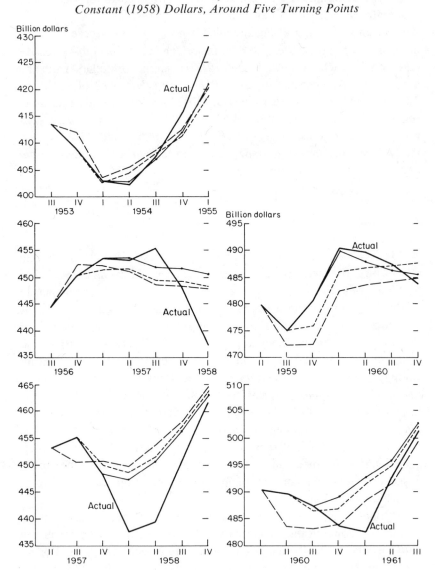

CHART 2

Actual and Predicted Values for Residential Fixed Investment,
Constant (1958) Dollars, Around Five Turning Points

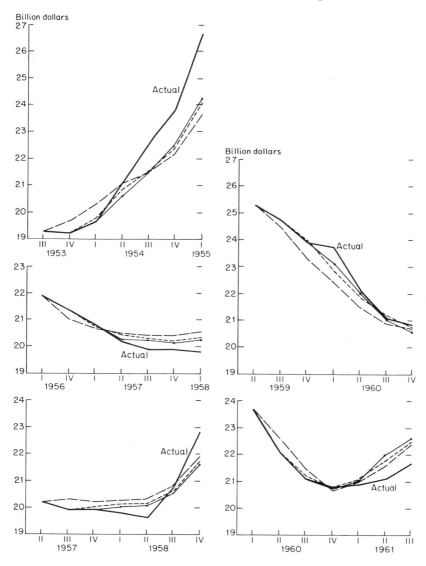

CHART 3

*Actual and Predicted Values for Nonresidential Fixed Investment,
Constant (1958) Dollars, Around Five Turning Points*

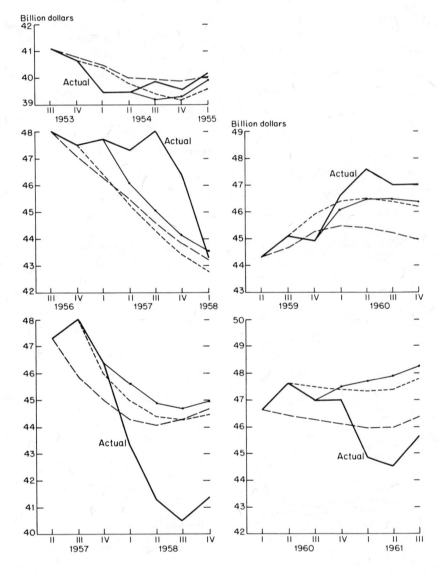

CHART 4

*Actual and Predicted Values for Change in Business Inventories,
Constant (1958) Dollars, Around Five Turning Points*

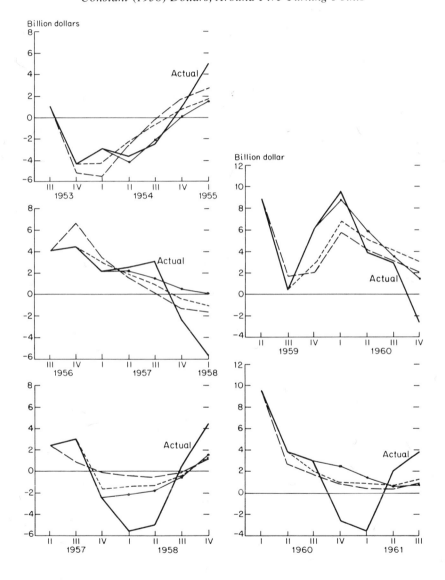

CHART 5

Actual and Predicted Values for Personal Consumption Expenditures, Constant (1958) Dollars, Around Five Turning Points

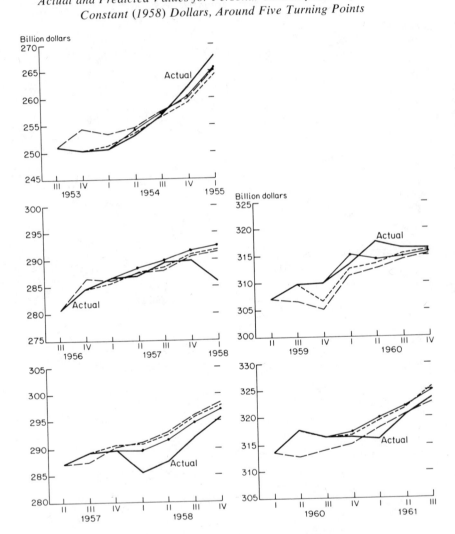

CHART 6

*Actual and Predicted Values for Private Civilian Employment
Around Five Turning Points*

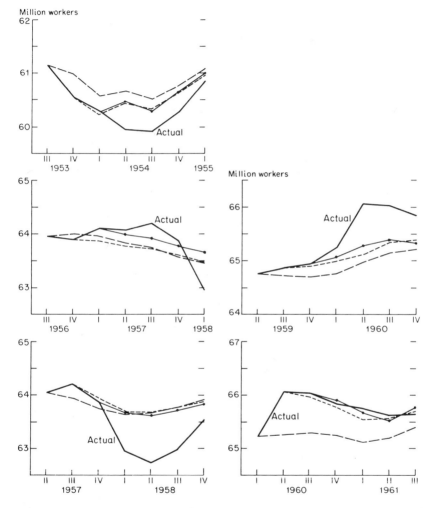

CHART 7

Actual and Predicted Values for Gross National Product, Current Dollars, Around Five Turning Points

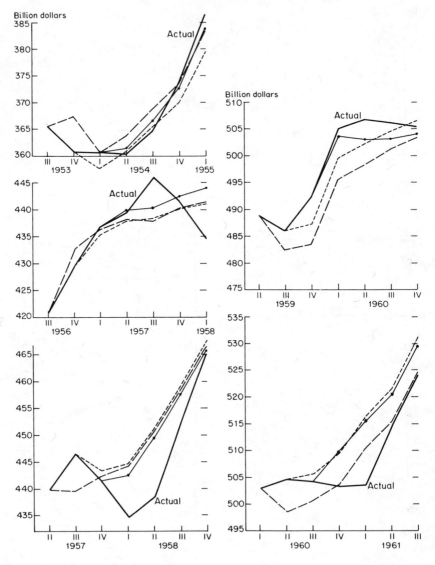

CHART 8

*Actual and Predicted Values for Corporate Profits and
Inventory Adjustment, Current Dollars, Around Five Turning Points*

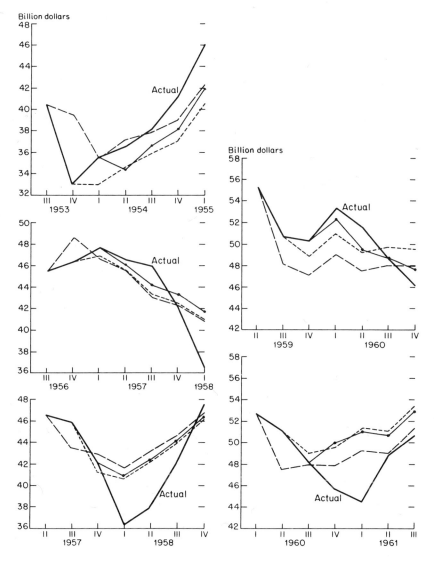

CHART 9

Actual and Predicted Values for Unemployment Rate Around Five Turning Points

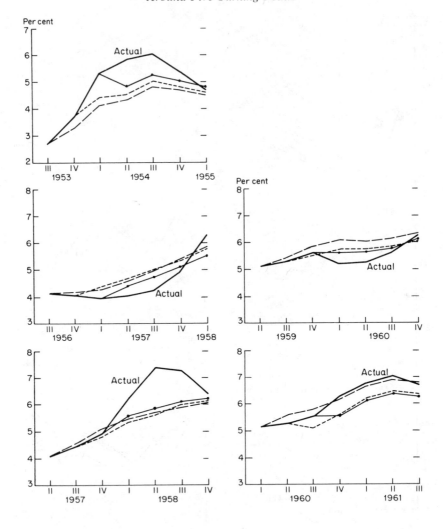

CHART 10

Actual and Predicted Values for Change in Money Supply,
Current Dollars, Around Five Turning Points

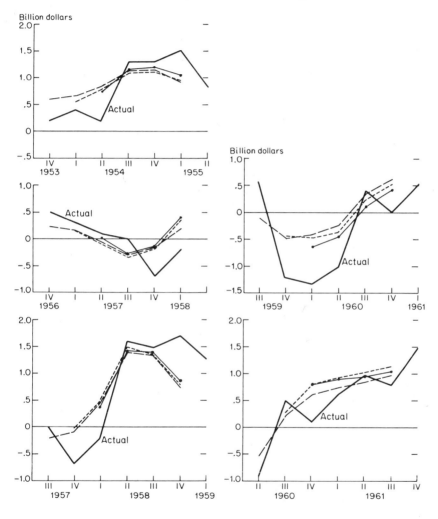

CHART 11

Actual and Computed Values for Real Gross National Product:
Fifty-five Quarter Ex Post Simulation over Sample Period,
1953-II–1966-IV

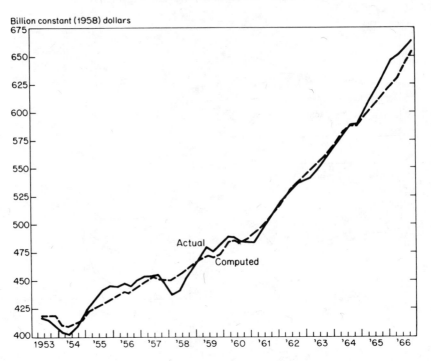

Billion constant (1958) dollars

a second simulation, using 1954-I as the first forecast quarter; and so on.

Attention here will center on real *GNP*, with only incidental reference to other magnitudes. Timing and phase relationships between variables are analyzed in another paper prepared for this Conference [*cf.* 21].

Of the five critical periods selected for the simulations, it is evident that the model behavior over the 1954 recession is the most satisfactory. As can be seen from the top panel of the first chart for real *GNP*, the general contours of the actual series are fairly well depicted. There is an obvious tendency for the model to turn up prematurely, but the downturn is pretty well revealed in all of the early simulations. The forecast using 1954-I as a jump-off (which was one quarter before the actual trough in real *GNP*) predicted the trough and subsequent upturn correctly. In all the simulations for this period the strong rise after the trough is slightly underestimated.

The next period covered includes the peak in economic activity prior to the 1957–58 recession. (It is shown in the second panel of the charts.) In this instance, each of the three simulations reveals a peak in economic activity with subsequent recession, but the timing of the peak in *GNP58$* is incorrect. The first simulation, with 1956-III as the jump-off quarter, peaks fully three quarters prior to the actual high point in activity. The next simulation, with 1956-IV as the jump-off quarter, peaks one quarter early, as does the forecast using 1957-I as the jump-off. In each instance, the depth of the recession which followed is badly underestimated. It is apparent that such a series of forecasts could be used by decision-makers to detect basic weaknesses in the economy some time prior to their occurrence, but the estimated magnitude of the drop in activity could not be similarly relied upon. A glance at the charts for inventory investment and for nonresidential fixed investment (*ISE*) shows that, in general, the former was fairly well depicted. But in each instance, *ISE* shows an early downturn with values that depart markedly from the actual series, which was maintained at fairly high levels until 1957-III.

The next panel (bottom left on the charts) shows the period both before and after the 1957–58 recession. In this case, the most obvious point is that all the simulations badly underestimate the full extent of the recession. *ISE* is again the main culprit, but inventories are at least partly to blame. The model magnitudes are, of course, interrelated, and certain series cannot easily be isolated and labeled as the primary causes of model failure. But, had *ISE* been better predicted, inventory investment would have shown a larger drop than is reported. It is noteworthy, however, that each of the three simulations, begun at various periods prior to the trough, depict the timing of the trough in *GNP58$* correctly. The first simulation, that using 1957-II as a jump-off, turns down one quarter early, but by the end of the period covered by the chart, all simulations are roughly on target.

The peak in economic activity prior to the 1960 recession (shown in the upper right-hand panels of each chart) is reasonably well recorded. Despite obvious substantial departures from the series of actual real GNP, the general contours of activity during the period are depicted in the forecasted series. The simulation with 1960-I as the first forecast quarter shows good direction and exact timing of the peak, and the subsequent downturn is also fairly well approximated. However, simulations which start in earlier quarters—covering the same period—fail to reveal the correct peak in the first quarter of 1960, although a marked flattening does occur. Except for the flattening instead of a drop in activity after the peak, the first simulation, with 1959-II as a jump-off quarter, is noteworthy; it roughly follows the contours of real GNP throughout the entire period.

The last panel depicts the period around the 1960-I trough. The most conspicuous feature is that all the simulations show too-early recoveries. The model shows declines in activity during 1960, when such declines actually occurred, but in no case is the true trough correctly timed. Again, it should be noted that ISE fails to show the drop that actually occurred in this series, and that although the estimates of inventories decline, they sadly underestimate the full extent of the drop in the actual series.

In order to set in perspective the performance of the model around turning points, Tables 7 and 8 show, respectively, average absolute errors (AAE) and root mean square errors ($RMSE$) for selected variables over a set of 53 short forecasts started in consecutive quarters beginning in 1953-IV, and over a subset of 19 forecasts which started one, two, or three quarters before reference-cycle peaks or troughs. The initial forecast quarters for these 19 runs are: 1953-IV to 1954-II; 1956-IV to 1958-I; 1959-III to 1960-IV; and 1966-I to 1966-IV. All first quarter errors lie within the sample period, but some of the second (and subsequent) quarter errors involve post-sample-period observations.

For several variables shown, the AAE or $RMSE$ from the 19 runs are larger than the comparable values from the 53 runs for most forecast quarters. The AAE or $RMSE$ values from runs made near turning points are notably larger for GNP in real and current dollars, real consumption expenditures, inventories, and corporate profits. Substantial errors in real nonresidential fixed investment are evidenced for both the periods around turning points, and for other periods as well. The fourth forecast quarter AAE and $RMSE$ values are more mixed, but this is not surprising, since for each of the 19 runs, the reference-cycle turning point occurs before the fourth quarter of forecast.

Any judgment regarding the performance of the model over the selected critical periods must depend on the stringency of the criteria imposed. If one requires exact timing and full movements in magnitudes, our model—at this stage of development—does not usually come up to such standards. The model does, however, reveal the rough contours of cyclical behavior, and in some instances, it does show correct timing.

TABLE 7

Average Absolute Errors from Short Ex Post Forecasts:
19 Runs Starting Before Cyclical Turning Points;
Runs Starting in 53 Consecutive Quarters

Variable	First Forecast Quarter		Second Forecast Quarter		Third Forecast Quarter		Fourth Forecast Quarter	
	19 Runs	53 Runs	19 Runs	53 Runs	19 Runs	53 Runs	19 Runs	53 Runs
GNP	3.7	2.9	5.6	4.5	6.3	5.9	5.8	6.5
GNP58$	2.7	2.3	4.3	3.6	5.1	4.6	5.5	5.1
C	2.0	1.5	2.3	2.0	2.8	2.6	3.3	3.0
IH	.3	.3	.5	.4	.5	.5	.8	.6
ISE	.9	.9	1.2	1.3	1.6	1.6	1.7	1.8
II	1.8	1.4	2.6	1.8	2.6	2.1	3.0	2.1
NETEXP	.6	.4	.8	.6	.7	.7	.6	.8
PERINC	1.9	1.6	3.1	2.9	3.4	3.6	3.0	4.2
PGNP	.3	.2	.4	.4	.5	.5	.6	.6
E	.2	.2	.4	.3	.5	.4	.5	.4
UNRATE	.3	.3	.5	.4	.6	.5	.5	.5
CPR	2.2	1.7	2.6	2.1	3.2	2.7	3.6	3.1
HM	.2	.2	.3	.3	.3	.3	.3	.3
OMD	1.8	1.7	2.0	1.9	2.0	2.1	2.0	2.3
UMD	1.4	1.2	2.6	2.2	3.3	3.2	4.0	4.2
RS	.2	.1	.2	.2	.2	.2	.3	.2
RL	.1	.1	.1	.1	.1	.1	.1	.1
MONEY	.6	.4	1.0	.8	1.3	1.0	1.4	1.1

TABLE 8

Root Mean Square Errors from Short Ex Post Forecasts:
19 Runs Starting Before Cyclical Turning Points;
Runs Starting in 53 Consecutive Quarters

Variable	First Forecast Quarter		Second Forecast Quarter		Third Forecast Quarter		Fourth Forecast Quarter	
	19 Runs	53 Runs	19 Runs	53 Runs	19 Runs	53 Runs	19 Runs	53 Runs
GNP	4.5	3.6	6.9	5.6	7.5	7.1	6.9	7.7
GNP58$	3.7	3.1	5.7	4.6	6.5	5.8	7.1	6.5
C	2.5	2.0	3.0	2.6	3.5	3.2	4.1	3.7
IH	.4	.4	.6	.6	.7	.6	1.1	.8
ISE	1.1	1.2	1.6	1.7	2.0	2.0	2.1	2.3
II	2.3	1.8	3.0	2.2	3.3	2.6	3.6	2.7
NETEXP	.7	.5	.9	.8	1.0	.9	.9	1.0
PERINC	2.4	2.1	3.6	3.4	4.0	4.4	3.6	4.9
PGNP	.4	.3	.5	.5	.6	.6	.7	.7
E	.3	.2	.4	.4	.5	.4	.6	.5
UNRATE	.4	.3	.7	.5	.8	.6	.7	.7
CPR	2.7	2.1	3.5	2.8	4.0	3.4	4.4	3.7
HM	.3	.2	.4	.4	.4	.4	.4	.4
OMD	2.1	2.1	2.4	2.4	2.4	2.6	2.6	2.8
UMD	1.8	1.6	3.1	2.8	4.0	3.7	4.9	4.8
RS	.3	.2	.3	.2	.3	.3	.4	.3
RL	.1	.1	.2	.1	.2	.2	.2	.2
MONEY	.8	.6	1.3	1.0	1.7	1.3	1.8	1.5

3.4 SIMULATION OVER THE ENTIRE SAMPLE PERIOD

The sample period for the OBE Model was comprised of 55 observations, starting 1953-II and ending 1966-IV. The simulation run was made without constant term adjustments over the entire period, and all exogenous variables were set at ex post actual values. Results from this simulation are summarized in Table 9, which shows maximum errors and average absolute errors for selected variables, and in Chart 11, which shows actual and computed values for *GNP58$*. As in the short simulations, the actual values used are revised through the June, 1968, *Survey of Current Business*.

Since the OBE Model was designed for short-term use, a long-run simulation of this kind is a severe strain on the underlying assumptions and rationale used to justify the model structure. It would be expected that errors would accumulate in lagged variables and cause subsequent errors in later forecast periods. Even if the model were perfectly specified, the neglect of stochastic elements would in itself give rise to errors which, due to the presence of lagged terms, would be carried forward. Under such conditions, one might expect that model results would not follow the actual course of economic magnitudes very closely.

Despite such considerations, it is evident from an examination of the accompanying chart that the simulated values of *GNP58$* follow the general pattern of the actual data quite well. The general growth path over the period is fairly well predicted, although there is an evident drifting off of predicted values in the later quarters. The simulated

TABLE 9

Maximum Error and Average Absolute Error for Selected Variables —
55-Quarter Ex Post Simulations over Sample Period,
1953-II–1966-IV

Variable	Maximum Error	Quarter	Average Absolute Error
C	−11.70	1966 I	3.21
CPR	9.07	1953 IV	3.17
EMPLOY	1.14	1954 II	.58
GNP	−36.43	1966 II	10.11
GNP58$	−21.24	1966 I	6.40
II	−8.92	1966 IV	2.58
ISE	6.57	1963 II	2.66
PERINC	−26.16	1966 II	8.24
PGNP	2.75	1966 IV	1.35
UNRATE	−2.03	1954 II	.66

series depicts the 1954 recession quite well, although it fails to reveal the entire drop in output. In that recession, the trough occurs in the same quarter in both the simulated and actual series.

The 1958 recession is much less adequately portrayed. The simulated series flattens but fails to show the full drop noted in the actual data. The 1960 recession, which is small by any criteria, is depicted with a somewhat improper timing: the trough in the simulated series occurs two quarters before the trough in the actual data.

The maximum errors for most variables occur toward the end of the 55 quarter simulation period, when some series drift away from the actual data. This is especially true for prices (not shown), and may be a reflection of cumulative bias effects discussed earlier. However, the average absolute errors over the entire 55 quarter simulation are not vastly larger than the *AAE* from sixth quarter forecasts presented in Section 3.2. The *AAE* for *GNP58$* is 5.82 for 48 sixth quarter forecasts, and 6.40 for the 55 quarter simulation.

4   TWENTY-FIVE-YEAR STOCHASTIC SIMULATIONS

EACH of the model-builders participating in this Conference was expected to carry out simulations over a twenty-five-year period under reasonable assumptions of smooth growth in the exogenous variables. The resulting control solution was not to be regarded as a serious attempt at a model forecast over such a long period; such a "true forecast" would have demanded a realistic projection of all exogenous variables, and would have required a much larger effort. Moreover, the demands placed on a short-term model, which by and large neglects demographic and other long-run factors, would make any "true forecast" highly suspect. Instead, the control solution was meant to delineate a reasonable path for subsequent operations.

The later operations required that stochastic shocks be introduced into the model on a continuous basis, and that such shocked runs be repeated many times. The results obtained provide a large number of ready-made "observations" beyond the sample period, which permit analyses of model dynamics, including the timing and amplitudes of major component series. Presumably, if NBER studies of lead and lag series reveal real-world relationships between important magnitudes, then the same analyses applied to model simulated results would also reveal such relationships, providing yet another yardstick for judging the adequacy of a model structure. The task of carrying out such analyses was placed in the hands of the NBER [cf. 21].

Another, and perhaps equally important, purpose of introducing stochastic shocks over a long time period was to determine whether business cycles with realistic characteristics — e.g., amplitude, periodicity, and phase relationships — are found in the simulated results. Such an exercise bears directly on business-cycle theory. Specifically, it is addressed to the question of whether some of the major models in operation today yield business cycles as the result of interaction of model structure with stochastic elements.

The introduction of random shocks is, of course, not new. An early and noteworthy project was carried out by Irma and Frank Adelman [1]. Using the Klein-Goldberger Model, they found that random elements introduced in the endogenous system resulted in cyclical behavior not too unlike that observed in the real world. An annual model was used and only one time path was traced; moreover, the random shocks used were drawn under the assumption of no serial correlation and zero contemporaneous covariances. One can view the results presented here as a further development of their work, under conditions where the random shock procedure allows for nonzero covariances and, in some instances, for auto-correlation of residuals.

The reported simulations cover the 100 quarters from 1966-I to 1990-IV. The starting period was selected, in part, because behavior of the U.S. economy in 1964 and 1965 was very close to that depicted by the set of equations in the model. This minimized difficulties in the transition from actual past data to the model solutions.

Modifications in the model structure are discussed in Section 4.1. All exogenous variables over the simulation period were smoothed, trendlike series; the procedures used to generate these series are presented in Section 4.2. The nature of the resulting control (nonshocked) solution is treated in Section 4.3. Following this, Section 4.4 presents the methods used to generate two types of stochastic shocks. Finally, a spectral analysis of real GNP series obtained from the various stochastic simulations is presented in Section 4.5.

4.1 MODIFICATIONS IN MODEL STRUCTURE

This section discusses all changes made in the model structure for the twenty-five-year simulations. Initial attempts to solve the OBE Model far into the future, revealed deficiencies in the longer-term properties of a few equations in the model. The forms marked (*b*) in Appendix B document all alternative equations used for the twenty-five-year simulation runs.

The (*b*) form of the equation for nonresidential fixed investment (*ISE*) is still an adaptation from the work by Almon. Preliminary runs with the (*a*) alternative resulted in steeply rising capital/output ratios over time. The only difference between the (*b*) form and that used earlier is that now the coefficient of long-term interest rates varies with the level of capacity output when the equation is stated in normalized form. The (*b*) equation reflects more precisely the structure implied by the Almon work.

In simulations over the sample period, and for short-term forecasts, we treated total and corporate capital consumption allowances as exogenous. Over a long period of time, this is clearly not satisfactory, so we have made both of these magnitudes simple functions of capital stock.

Two equations which determine final demand variables yielded preliminary results which were judged to be somewhat low by the end of the twenty-five-year simulation period. Accordingly, we added a time trend of 24.8 thousand units per quarter to the housing starts equation, and a small trend of 0.17 billion dollars per quarter to the trade imports equation. Each of these equations was adjusted so that these trends started in the initial simulation quarter.

The price of government purchases from the private sector, normally exogenous for short-term forecasts, was made endogenous and set to grow at the same percentage rate as the price for private GNP, excluding housing services (*P*).

During the sample period, small negative trends in the primary labor-force participation rate and in hours worked at capacity output levels, plus a small positive trend for the frictional unemployment rate of secondary workers, were observed. We judged that these trends were unlikely to continue, and so they were not allowed to operate over the simulation period. This slightly alters the equations for the primary labor force, capacity hours, and capacity output.

The functions used during the sample period for Federal, and for state and local, personal tax and nontax payments, and for the investment tax credit, are empirical relationships devoid of longer-run considerations. All of these functions were changed for the twenty-five-year runs. The investment tax credit was made proportional to estimated nonresidential equipment investment (in current dollars). For state and local personal tax and nontax payments, we arbitrarily assumed both a rising marginal rate of taxation and an augmented time trend (to reflect rises in nontax payment rates). The parameters selected are based, in large part, on recent observations of these payments and the tax base.

In the case of Federal personal tax and nontax payments, we thought that the best approach would be to tie payments to liabilities. Payments are predicted in three recursive equations: the first derives taxable income from personal per capita income (per capita exemptions are held constant); the second derives tax liability based on the 1965 tax structure; the third is a simple empirical relation between liabilities and payments. The first two equations were adapted from the work of Waldorf [cf. 20, pp. 26–33]. This procedure is a considerable improvement over the equation forms used during the sample period, but it is somewhat deficient for purposes of the simulations with stochastic shocks, in that it fails to incorporate the varying short-term gap between liabilities and payments which would inevitably accompany any uneven growth in income.

The equation for the interest rate on savings deposits (RT) produced absurdly low values during preliminary runs; we held RT at its value in 1965-IV over the entire simulation period.

Finally, the reduced-form equation for the change in unfilled orders produced unacceptable negative values for the level of unfilled orders during preliminary runs. We had developed a better equation for shipments of manufacturers' durables (SMD) after the short simulation runs were initiated, and this newer equation for *SMD* was used, together with a near identity for the change in unfilled orders.

4.2 TREATMENT OF EXOGENOUS VARIABLES

All tax rates and exogenous interest rates—the discount rate and the time deposit rate—were held at constant levels, and most other variables were set to grow at constant rates of change. Usually, the average rate of change used was that observed over the sample period.

Various criteria were used to adjust the growth rates of a few series. In the course of preliminary runs, various magnitudes and ratios were examined for reasonableness. For instance, we examined ratios of final demand and income items to disposable income or to *GNP*. In addition, we scrutinized the paths of government deficits, net exports, and the growth of some exogenous categories relative to related endogenous elements. Where clearly unreasonable patterns were found, we adjusted growth rates of various exogenous variables until the results seemed plausible.

Table 10 shows values in the jump-off and final quarters for each exogenous variable, and an average annual rate of change over the twenty-five-year simulation period. While space prohibits a detailed description of procedures used for all variables, a few of them deserve special comment.

Population series used were based on projections provided by the U.S. Bureau of the Census. The paths of related series (for instance, Social Security payments) were made consistent with the population assumptions. Over the twenty-five-year simulation period, the population of males aged 25 to 54 (*NP*) grows at a slightly increasing rate of change, but the population of the remaining persons aged 16 to 64 (*NS*) grows at a decreasing rate. These projections are in large part a reflection of birthrate patterns over the 1930 to 1965 period.

Nonborrowed reserves of banks (*RESNB*) were determined by forcing free reserves to zero for all periods in the control run. In all of the runs with stochastic shocks, free reserves were not restricted, and the *RESNB* series from the control run was used. The resulting implied monetary policy is accommodating with respect to growth but unresponsive to cyclical movements.

TABLE 10

Values in 1965-IV and 1990-IV; with Average Annual Rates of Change for Exogenous Variables from Twenty-Five-Year Simulations

Variable	Value for 1965-IV	Value for 1990-IV	Average Annual Rate of Change
AM58$	33.1	33.1	.00
CH	59.5	193.2	4.82
CURR	36.1	60.3	2.07
D$	61.6	273.6	6.15
DC$	37.8	141.2	5.41
DH$	10.4	54.0	6.81
EE	8.3	6.3	−1.10
EG	8.6	27.2	4.71
EXP$	40.5	206.8	6.74
G58$	117.4	342.0	4.37
GFD$	52.4	193.5	5.36
GFND$	17.4	232.1	10.92
GIA	12.2	258.4	12.99
GSL$	72.5	601.0	8.83
HH	58,208.0	90,503.0	1.78
IHF	.5	.2	--3.60
IHR	5.0	11.9	3.53
IMG$	3.0	3.8	.95
INB	18.8	74.8	5.68
INC	11.7	46.5	5.67
INGF	8.9	8.9	.00
INGSL	.5	.5	.00
MAXSS	4,800.0	12,003.0	3.73
N	195.5	273.0	1.34
NP	32.6	51.9	1.88
NS	78.4	111.3	1.41
PA	.987	1.309	1.14
PE	55.4	170.7	4.60
PE1E	53.0	162.6	4.59
PE2E	54.8	163.9	4.48
PEX	1.041	1.259	.76
PF	.252	.269	.26

(*continued*)

TABLE 10 (*concluded*)

Variable	Value for 1965-IV	Value for 1990-IV	Average Annual Rate of Change
PH	1.098	1.613	1.55
PIM	1.033	1.248	.76
PR	1.093	1.582	1.49
PWG	1.364	4.323	4.72
RDIS	4.17	4.00	−.17
RENT	19.2	38.9	2.86
RESNB	21.6	169.4	8.59
RMBD	.884	.884	.00
RMBT	.826	.826	.00
RRD	.1465	.1465	.00
RRT	.04	.04	.00
RT	3.44	3.44	.00
RTCF	.48	.48	.00
RTEXAV	.791	.791	.00
RTEXS	1.098	1.098	.00
RTQ	4.0	4.0	.00
RTRU	51.5	144.1	4.20
SGF	4.1	14.1	5.06
SGSL	−3.2	−8.2	−
SIBOF	5.3	61.4	10.30
SIBSL	2.6	28.2	10.00
SIPOF	3.1	18.1	7.31
SIPSL	2.0	17.1	8.96
TIFO	4.98	5.20	.17
TRB	2.6	16.3	7.62
TRFF	2.0	3.3	2.02
TRFP	.7	1.1	1.82
TRPOF	28.9	162.5	7.15
TRPSL	7.0	39.4	7.16
TRUEX	1.0	1.0	.00
WG$	70.9	691.9	9.54

Series for government purchases and government employment were first set at reasonable trend-levels. But these preliminary levels were then raised or lowered to produce a desired path in the control solution. Forty per cent of any alteration in real government purchases was allocated to government employment and wages, and the remainder was assigned to government purchases from the private sector. It should be noted that the resulting series for the government variables exhibit very smooth and regular behavior over the entire period.

4.3 THE NATURE OF THE CONTROL SOLUTION

We wanted a control solution which exhibited a fairly smooth pattern for all major variables. As described in the previous section, we adjusted government purchases to achieve a stipulated path. At first, we had hoped to produce a control solution with a 4 per cent unemployment rate and a constant rate of growth in real GNP. These twin objectives were inconsistent, owing to the population patterns used. A constant rate of growth in real GNP resulted in unemployment rates which fell off sharply in the later simulation periods. Similarly, a control solution forced to a constant over-all unemployment rate exhibited a sharp decline in the rate of growth of GNP.

Table 11 lists annual levels and percentage changes for a few series taken from the final control solution. The final control solution has an unemployment rate of 4.2 per cent in the initial year of simulation, which gradually declines to 3.9 per cent by 1990. Real GNP grows at a declining rate of change, while prices and productivity vary within a fairly small range. Other variables produced by the control solution (not shown) show reasonable patterns.

4.4 GENERATION OF STOCHASTIC SHOCKS

Fifty simulations were made with stochastic shocks applied to endogenous behavioral variables. Variables relating to taxes and transfers, and those explained by identities or near identities, were not shocked. The shocks were applied to the normalized equation forms.

TABLE 11

Annual Levels and Per Cent Changes for Selected Series from the Twenty-Five-Year Control Simulation

	Level			Per Cent Change			
Year	*GNP*	*GNP58$*	*UNRATE*	*GNP*	*GNP58$*	*PGNP*	*PROD*
1965ᵃ	684.1	616.6	4.5				
1966	735.6	649.3	4.2	7.52	5.31	2.11	3.03
1967	788.5	679.7	4.2	7.20	4.68	2.41	2.98
1968	847.5	713.5	4.2	7.47	4.97	2.38	3.32
1969	909.5	748.2	4.2	7.32	4.87	2.34	3.16
1970	974.7	782.9	4.2	7.17	4.63	2.43	2.97
1971	1,044.4	818.3	4.2	7.15	4.52	2.51	2.94
1972	1,119.4	855.1	4.1	7.18	4.50	2.57	2.95
1973	1,199.1	892.8	4.1	7.11	4.41	2.58	2.95
1974	1,283.4	931.5	4.1	7.04	4.34	2.59	2.87
1975	1,372.1	970.5	4.1	6.91	4.18	2.62	2.81
1976	1,466.2	1,010.4	4.1	6.85	4.11	2.63	2.81
1977	1,565.5	1,051.2	4.1	6.77	4.04	2.63	2.79
1978	1,670.1	1,092.8	4.1	6.68	3.96	2.62	2.77
1979	1,780.6	1,135.5	4.1	6.62	3.91	2.61	2.78
1980	1,898.3	1,179.9	4.0	6.61	3.91	2.59	2.83
1981	2,020.0	1,224.5	4.0	6.41	3.77	2.54	2.75
1982	2,148.0	1,269.8	4.0	6.33	3.70	2.53	2.75
1983	2,282.4	1,316.2	4.0	6.26	3.65	2.51	2.75
1984	2,423.2	1,363.6	4.0	6.17	3.60	2.48	2.76
1985	2,570.7	1,412.2	4.0	6.09	3.56	2.44	2.76
1986	2,725.1	1,461.9	3.9	6.00	3.52	2.40	2.77
1987	2,886.4	1,513.0	3.9	5.92	3.49	2.34	2.78
1988	3,054.9	1,565.5	3.9	5.84	3.47	2.29	2.80
1989	3,230.4	1,619.5	3.9	5.75	3.45	2.22	2.81
1990	3,413.4	1,675.1	3.9	5.66	3.43	2.16	2.83

ᵃ Actual values.

The forty-one variables subjected to shocks and the standard errors of estimate from normalized equations for these variables are shown in Table 12.

The procedures used for generating shocks were developed by Michael McCarthy, and are described in an Appendix to a paper prepared for this Conference [18]. The McCarthy procedures combine the sample period residuals with random normal deviates. The latter values were taken from a computer tape generated by the Rand Corporation, containing one-hundred-thousand random normal deviates. The McCarthy procedures are such that the expected value of the variance-covariance matrix of stochastic shocks over the simulation period equals the variance-covariance matrix of the observed residuals over the sample period. Moreover, one of these procedures allows for serial correlation of residuals.

These procedures differ in several respects from those applied to an annual model by Adelman and Adelman [1]. They generated shocks which assumed zero covariances and no serial correlation for all

TABLE 12

Standard Errors of Estimate over the Sample Period for Forty-One Variables Subjected to Shocks

Variable	$\overline{S}$	Variable	$\overline{S}$	Variable	$\overline{S}$
CA	1.0039	IINA	1.6825	PN	.0030
CN	1.0414	IMS	.4002	POD	.0034
COD	.5112	IMT	.6382	PRI	.9017
CPR	.9827	ISE	.9571	PS	.0058
CS	.4794	IVA	.6790	PWMD	.0047
CUW	.0108	LH	1.7452	RL	.0704
DD	.6415	LFP	.0778	RM	.1066
DIV	.2601	LFS	.2497	RS	.1190
EW	.2183	OMD	1.7628	RTB	.2527
H	.1476	P	.0034		
HM	.2168	PHS	.3789	SMD	1.2976
HS	70.7435	PIE	.0045	TD	.6618
IE	.5379	PIH	.0062	URP	.0018
IIA	.7452	PIS	.0064	WR	.0269

errors. Also, the Adelmans scaled their shocks so that the ratio of the standard deviation of residuals relative to the value of the dependent (normalized) variable observed in the sample period was maintained in the simulation period. To the extent that variances of the true normalized equation errors are heteroscedastic, with increasing size over time, the scaling aspect of the Adelmans' procedure seems preferable to that used for this Conference.

4.5 A SPECTRAL ANALYSIS OF REAL *GNP* SERIES FROM STOCHASTIC SIMULATIONS

Fifty stochastic simulations, starting in 1966-I and continuing for one-hundred quarters, were made. Twenty-five of these simulations used serially correlated random shocks, while the other twenty-five runs were made with non-serially correlated random shocks. The runs with stochastic shocks were designed to reveal the dynamic properties of the OBE Model and to determine whether the observed cyclical behavior of the economy could be replicated by the model through the interaction of model structure and stochastic elements applied to endogenous variables. We present here a summary analysis of the real *GNP* series from these fifty simulations as a supplement to the analysis presented by the NBER team [21].

Chart 12 presents the time paths of real *GNP* series taken from two arbitrarily selected runs. The heavy line depicts the time path from a run which used serially correlated shocks, while the dashed line is a series from a run in which non-serially correlated shocks were introduced. Both series are given in terms of deviations from the control solution.

It is apparent that both of these time paths reveal cyclical movements. The maximum deviation from the control solution is not far different in the two series — 19.5 billion dollars for the serially correlated case; and 16.1 billion dollars for the non-serially correlated series.

While all of the resultant series in real *GNP* exhibited the same general character as the two presented, very few of the fifty series showed downturns in the real *GNP* series. When downturns were ob-

CHART 12

Deviations Between Shocked and Control Series for Real GNP: One Simulation with Serially Correlated Shocks, One with Non-serially Correlated Shocks

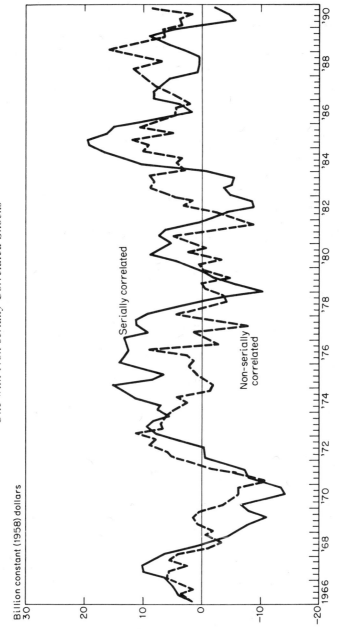

served, they were usually of very short duration with a strong tendency to rebound quickly. If the criterion for the presence of cycles is that protracted downturns must occur, then the present results do not depict cyclical behavior adequately. It should be emphasized, however, that these simulations incorporate very strong growth elements in the exogenous variables; such elements have to be overcome by the effects of stochastic shocks for actual downturns to occur. The importance of movements in exogenous variables during recent marked recessions in the United States economy is clear; both the 1953–54 and the 1957–58 recessions were accompanied by flattening or decreases in such variables as government purchases and gross exports.

The chart also shows that apart from slightly smaller amplitude, the non-serially correlated run produced a series which is quite ragged. This was, in general, true of all the runs made using this procedure. It is apparent that the ragged character of these series is not typical of recorded, real-world data. The serially correlated shocks generated series with much less ragged time paths, which are more in line with our expectations.

Spectral analysis was applied to the fifty real GNP series generated by the simulation runs in order to test for persistent periodicities in the revealed cyclical movements. The analysis presented here used forty-eight lags and a Parzen window. Since spectral analysis can only be applied to stationary series, it was first necessary to filter out any trend. Two filters were applied. Let X be the original, unfiltered series, and t be time; then the first filtered series, Y_1 is defined by

$$Y_{1,t} = X_t - X_{t-1}$$

and the second series, Y_2 is defined as

$$Y_{2,t} = X_t - \hat{X}_t$$

where $\ln (\hat{X}_t) = b_1 + b_2 t + b_3 t^2$, and b_1, b_2, and b_3 are determined by ordinary least squares. We shall call these filters a first-difference filter and a log-polynomial filter, respectively. Both filters are discussed in Jenkins and Watts [16], and in Granger [11]. The first-difference filter is applied to economic series in Howrey [14], and with some modification, in Nerlove [19]. The degree of the log-polynomial filter was chosen to allow for the declining rate of growth evidenced in the control solution.

Results from using each of the two detrending (filtering) methods are shown separately: for the series generated by serially correlated shocks; and for those obtained using non-serially correlated shocks. Charts 13 and 14 show spectral power as a function of periodicity. In preparing each panel, spectral densities from twenty-five runs were averaged. The ordinate of each panel shows logarithms of spectra, which have identical confidence interval widths; and the periodicities, shown on the abscissa, are scaled as cycle lengths in quarters. Three of the four panels show highest power at the very long cycle lengths (low frequencies), with generally lower power for shorter cycles (higher frequencies). Granger [10] has noted similar patterns for several economic time series. The remaining panel, which depicts results from series generated using non-serially correlated shocks and using a first-difference filter, shows a high power at low frequencies, but a distinct minimum of power for 24-month cycles, followed by ever increasing power at the higher frequencies. This result is not too surprising, given the ragged character of the underlying series.

Each of these panels shows some evidence of peaks. The significance of any noted peak is ascertained by an F test, which is simply the ratio of the spectral value at the peak to the spectral value at least two spectrums distant. Each summed spectrum has approximately 193 degrees of freedom, so the significant values for an F test are 1.2, 1.28, and 1.41 for the 10, 5, and 1 per cent levels, respectively.

The summed spectra from runs which use data generated by the non-serially correlated shocks, using the log-polynomial filter, show a very weak peak at 6.6 quarters, which is not significant — even at the 10 per cent level. The spectra generated by the non-serially correlated shocks, when a first-difference filter is used, do reveal a peak between 12.0 and 13.7 quarters and another between 6.0 and 6.4 quarters. The latter peak is significant at the 10 per cent level, but the two peaks are not significantly different from one another. These two peaks may be a reflection of the same basic periodicity, since one is the first harmonic of the other.

The sums of spectra from data generated by serially correlated shocks show no peak at all when the log-polynomial filter is used, but the use of a first-difference filter yields two peaks, at 8.7 and 13.7 quarters. The peak at 8.7 quarters is significant at the 5 per cent level, and the two peaks are significantly different at the 10 per cent level.

CHART 13

*Sum of Spectra for Twenty-five Real GNP Series Generated
Using Non-serially Correlated Shocks*

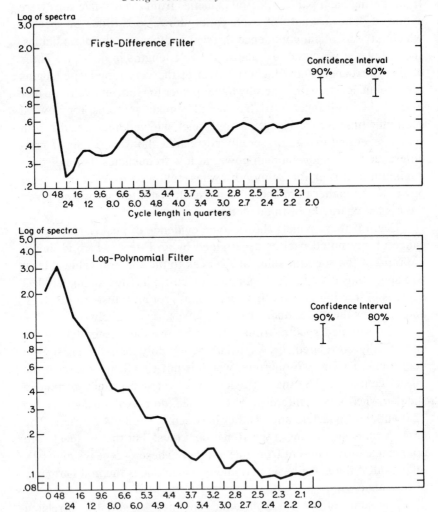

CHART 14

Sum of Spectra for Twenty-five Real GNP Series Generated Using Serially Correlated Shocks

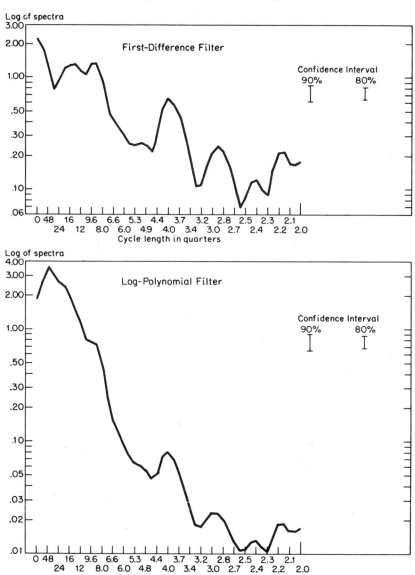

Charts 15 and 16 show frequency bar charts of the most prominent spectral peaks in the range from six to thirty-two quarters, from each of the four sets of real *GNP* series. The choice of filter has a marked effect upon the results. The spectral peaks from data generated by the non-serially correlated shocks show a concentration at 13.7 quarters when a log-polynomial filter is used; and at 6.4 quarters when a first difference filter is used. In both of the above cases, a substantial number of spectral runs yielded no peak in the 6–32 quarter range. For the spectral runs generated by serially correlated shocks, using a log-polynomial filter, a concentration of peaks at 19.2 quarters is noted; but nine of the twenty-five spectral runs show no peak in the stipulated range. Use of the first-difference filter on the data generated from serially correlated shocks reveals a marked clustering of major peaks; here all spectral runs show major peaks in the stipulated range, with equal concentrations at 8.7, 9.6, and 13.7 quarters, and with four peaks in the 4 to 5 year range.

Despite the convenience and elegant nature of spectral analysis, the results presented here are not without ambiguity. The choice of filter has a dramatic effect upon the results. We tend to place more reliance on the results which employed a first-difference filter, since its use more successfully eliminated power at the very low frequencies.

The results presented above are considerably different from those obtained in the Adelmans' study [1]. Using a modified Klein-Goldberger Model, they found that random shocks applied to endogenous equations resulted in cyclical behavior similar to that observed in the real world. Also, they found that shocks applied to exogenous variables played a very minor role. The differences between the results presented here and those obtained by the Adelmans may be the result of differences in procedures: they used a small annual model, our model is quarterly and somewhat larger; they used random shocks drawn under the assumption of no serial correlation and zero contemporaneous covariances, while our shocks take into account the intercorrelation of equation residuals, and in some cases, serial correlation properties, as well.

A comparison of the size of the shocks on endogenous equations in the Adelmans' study with those used here reveals dramatic size differences. For instance, the coefficients of error variation (ratio of

CHART 15

Frequency Bar Charts of Most Prominent Spectral Peaks from Twenty-five
Real GNP Series Generated Using Non-serially Correlated Shocks

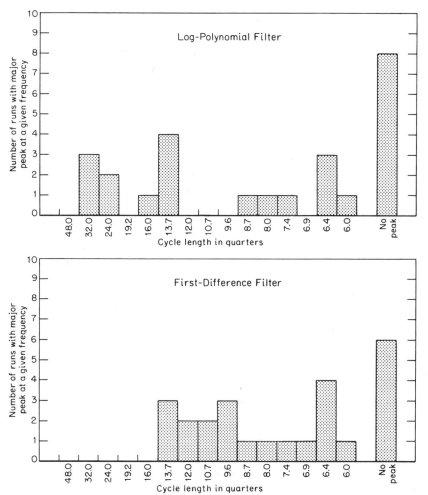

CHART 16

Frequency Bar Charts of Most Prominent Spectral Peaks from Twenty-five Real GNP Series Generated Using Serially Correlated Shocks

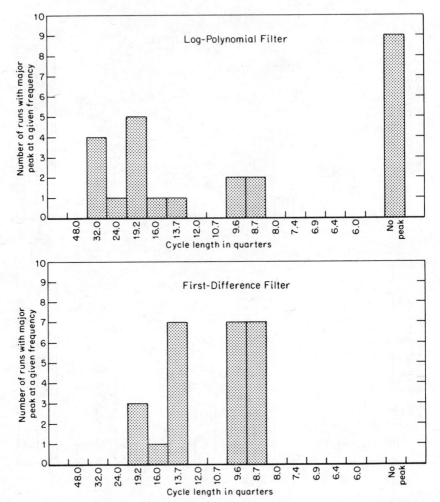

the standard error over the sample period to the mean value of the dependent variable in the simulated period) for total real investment and for corporate profits used in the Adelmans' study were 6.5 and 7.8 times as large, respectively, as those we used in this study. This suggests that exogenous variables may play a much more important role for our model, and that shocks on them may play an important role in cycle generation.

We performed some additional stochastic simulations with serially correlated shocks on the endogenous equations, and with shocks applied to five exogenous variables—government purchases from the private sector, government wages, government employment, exports, and nonborrowed reserves of the banking system. For pseudo-residuals for these exogenous variables, we used residuals from log linear trend equations, fitted over the sample period. The residuals for total real government purchases are substantial—$16.2 billion in 1953-II; and $11.3 billion in 1966-IV.

Chart 17 presents the time paths of real GNP series (shown as deviations from the control solution) taken from two arbitrarily selected runs. The same random normal deviates were used to generate the two time paths shown—but in one series, shocks were applied to endogenous equations only; while for the second series, shocks were applied to endogenous equations and to the five exogenous variables given above. The maximum deviation from the control solution is far different for the two series—21.4 billion dollars for the first series, but 51.4 billion dollars when selected exogenous variables are also shocked. Other simulation runs showed deviations of up to $60 billion when these selected exogenous variables were also shocked—a figure much larger than the $20 billion maximum deviation obtained from runs with shocks on endogenous variables only.

Moreover, unlike our earlier results, the simulations with shocked exogenous variables show sustained cycles in real GNP $levels$. In many cases, a peak in real GNP is followed by three to five quarters of lower real GNP values. These brief results suggest that movements in elements commonly considered exogenous in large-scale models may play a crucial role in the determination of business cycles.

CHART 17

Deviations Between Shocked and Control Series for Real GNP: One Simulation with Serially Correlated Shocks on Endogenous Variables, One with Serially Correlated Shocks on Both Endogenous Variables and Selected Exogenous Variables

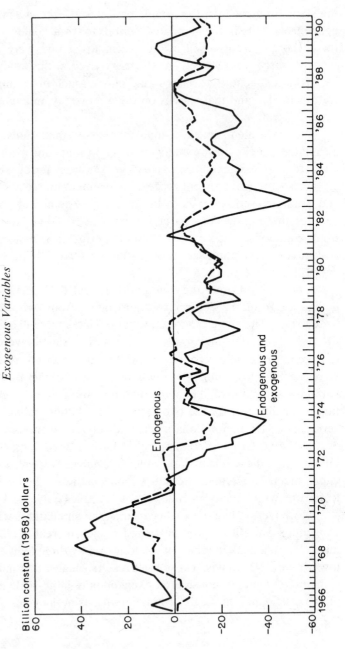

5 CONCLUDING REMARKS

WE have here reported on various simulations with the OBE Quarterly Econometric Model. Major findings are:

(1) For short ex post forecasts during the sample period, mechanical adjustments of equation constants, based on serial correlation of estimated equation residuals, lead to improved forecasts of real magnitudes in initial quarters, and to improved price forecasts over at least a six-quarter period.

(2) Average errors from six-quarter ex post model forecasts revealed biases which were tentatively traced to the wage-rate equation. As a practical aid in model forecasting, it may be advisable to introduce adjustments into selected equations so that biases in important magnitudes are eliminated.

(3) The average absolute errors for GNP and real GNP from one-quarter ex post model forecasts during the sample period were about one-half of 1 per cent of the average value for each variable.

(4) Short, ex post model forecasts near peaks and troughs revealed the rough contours of actual movements in variables. However, pronounced movements in variables were typically underestimated, and precise timing of turning points was not generally achieved.

(5) A fifty-five quarter simulation over the entire sample period generally followed the patterns in actual data, but several simulated series drifted off from the actual series toward the end of the simulation period.

(6) Real GNP series from simulations with random shocks applied to endogenous behavioral equations rarely show downturns, presumably because of the strong growth elements in exogenous variables. However, when measured as deviations from the control solution values, real GNP series from runs with stochastic shocks show definite cycles.

(7) The use of serially correlated shocks yielded real GNP series much less jagged and more in line with expectations than comparable series generated using non-serially correlated shocks.

(8) Spectral analyses using a first-difference filter on real GNP series generated by the shocked simulations revealed spectral peaks in

the range usually assigned to business cycles. Each of the twenty-five runs on data generated using serially correlated shocks showed a spectral peak in the 2 to 5 year cycle-length range. However, spectral analyses using a log-polynomial filter on these same series did not reveal significant spectral peaks.

(9) When serially correlated shocks are applied to endogenous equations and to selected exogenous variables, the resulting real *GNP* series shows sustained cycles with prolonged downturns of from three to five quarters. Maximum deviations from the control solution are about three times as large as those observed when shocks are applied to endogenous equations only.

REFERENCES

[1] Adelman, Irma, and Adelman, Frank L., "The Dynamic Properties of the Klein-Goldberger Model," *Econometrica,* Vol. 27, No. 4 (October, 1959), pp. 596–625.

[2] Almon, Shirley, "The Distributed Lag Between Capital Appropriations and Expenditures," *Econometrica,* Vol. 33, No. 1 (January, 1965), pp. 178–196.

[3] ———, "Lags Between Investment Decisions and Their Causes," *Review of Economics and Statistics,* Vol. 1, No. 20 (May, 1968), pp. 193–206.

[4] de Leeuw, Frank, and Gramlich, Edward, "The Channels of Monetary Policy: An Econometric Progress Report." Paper presented at the Annual Meeting of the American Finance Association, Chicago, Illinois, December, 1968.

[5] ———, "The Federal Reserve–MIT Econometric Model," *Federal Reserve Bulletin,* January, 1968, pp. 11–40.

[6] Evans, Michael K., "Computer Simulations of Non-Linear Econometric Models," Discussion Paper No. 97, Department of Economics, University of Pennsylvania, October, 1968.

[7] ———, and Klein, Lawrence R., "The Wharton Economic Forecasting Model," Studies in Quantitative Economics, No. 2, Department of Economics, University of Pennsylvania, 1967.

[8] Fromm, Gary, and Taubman, Paul, *Policy Simulations with an Econometric Model,* Washington, D.C., Brookings Institution, 1968.

[9] Goldberger, Arthur S., "Best Linear Unbiased Prediction in the Generalized Linear Regression Model," *Journal of the American Statistical Association,* Vol. 57, No. 2 (June, 1962), pp. 369–375.

[10] Granger, C. W. J., "The Typical Shape of an Economic Variable," *Econometrica,* Vol. 34, No. 1 (January, 1966), pp. 150–161.

[11] ———, and Hatanaka, M., *Spectral Analysis of Economic Time Series,* Princeton, New Jersey, Princeton University Press, 1964.

[12] Green, George R., "Multiplier Paths and Business Cycles: A Simulation Approach." Paper presented at the North American Meeting of the Econometric Society, Evanston, Illinois, December, 1968.

[13] Hirsch, Albert A., "Reconciliation of the Short-Run Employment Function and the Long-Run Production Function." Paper presented at the North American Meeting of the Econometric Society, Evanston, Illinois, December, 1968.

[14] Howrey, E. Philip, "Dynamic Properties of a Condensed Version of the Wharton Model." Paper prepared for the Conference on Econometric Models of Cyclical Behavior, Cambridge, Massachusetts, November, 1969.

[15] Jenkins, G. M., "General Considerations in the Analysis of Spectra," *Technometrics,* Vol. 3, No. 2 (May, 1961), pp. 133–166.

[16] ———, and Watts, Donald G., *Spectral Analysis and Its Applications,* San Francisco, Holden-Day, 1968.

[17] Liebenberg, Maurice, Hirsch, Albert A., and Popkin, Joel, "A Quarterly Econometric Model of the United States: A Progress Report," *Survey of Current Business,* May, 1966, pp. 13–39.

[18] McCarthy, Michael D., "Some Notes on the Generation of Pseudo Structural Errors for Use in Stochastic Simulation Studies," Appendix to Evans, Klein, and Saito, "Short Run Prediction and Long Run Simulation of the Wharton Model." Paper presented at the Conference on Research in Income and Wealth, November 14–15, 1969.

[19] Nerlove, Marc, "Spectral Analysis of Seasonal Adjustment Pro-

cedures," *Econometrica,* Vol. 32, No. 3 (July, 1964), pp. 241–286.

[20] Waldorf, William H., "Long-Run Federal Tax Functions: A Statistical Analysis," U.S. Department of Commerce, Office of Business Economics, Staff Working Paper on Economics and Statistics, No. 15, Washington, D.C., February, 1968.

[21] Zarnowitz, Victor, Boschan, Charlotte, and Moore, Geoffrey H., "Business Cycle Analysis of Econometric Model Simulations." Paper prepared for the Conference on Econometric Models of Cyclical Behavior, Cambridge, Massachusetts, November, 1969.

APPENDIX A

DEFINITIONS OF SYMBOLS

*AM58$	Prime contract awards, military, billions of 1958 dollars
C	Personal consumption expenditures, billions of 1958 dollars
CA	Personal consumption expenditures, automobiles and parts, billions of 1958 dollars
*CH	Personal consumption expenditures, housing, billions of 1958 dollars
CMP/MH	Private employee compensation per man-hour, dollars
CN	Personal consumption expenditures, nondurables, billions of 1958 dollars
COD	Personal consumption expenditures, durables other than automobiles and parts, billions of 1958 dollars
CPR	Corporate profits and inventory valuation adjustment, billions of dollars
CS	Personal consumption expenditures, services except housing, billions of 1958 dollars
*CURR	Currency outside banks, daily average of quarter, billions of dollars

NOTE: Asterisk indicates exogenous variable.

CUW   Utilization rate of industrial capacity for manufacturing, mining, and utilities, Wharton School index, decimal

*D$ Capital consumption allowances, billions of dollars

*DC$ Capital consumption allowances, corporate, billions of dollars

*DCA1   Strike dummy used in auto consumption function: 1953-I to 1956-II = 0.0; 1956-III = −1.0; 1956-IV = 1.0; 1957-I to 1959-III = 0.0; 1959-IV = −1.0; 1960-I = 1.0; 1960-II to 1964-III = 0.0; 1964-IV = −1.0; 1965-I = 1.0; 1965-II to 1966-I = 0.0; 1966-II = −1.0; 1966-III and on = 0.0

*DCA2   Dummy for change in auto installment credit regulations used in auto consumption function: 1953-I to 1954-IV = 0.0; 1955-I and on = 1.0

DD   Demand deposits, adjusted daily average of quarter, billions of dollars

*DH$ Capital consumption allowances, residential, billions of historical dollars

*DHS1   Dummy for shift in interest rate policy used in housing starts equation: 1953-I to 1962-I = 0.0; 1962-II to 1966-I = 1.0; 1966-II and on = 0.0

*DHS2   Dummy for interest rate shift used in housing starts equation: 1953-I to 1962-I = 1.0; 1962-II to 1966-I = 0.0; 1966-II and on = 1.0

*DII   Strike dummy used in investment equations: 1953-I to 1959-I = 0.0; 1959-II = 1.0; 1959-III = −2.0; 1959-IV = 0.0; 1960-I = 1.0; 1960-II to 1964-IV = 0.0; 1965-I = 1.0; 1965-II and on = 0.0

*DIM   Strike effects dummy used in import functions: 1953-I to 1959-II = 0.0; 1959-III = 1.0; 1959-IV to 1964-III = 0.0; 1964-IV = 0.5; 1965-I = −1.0; 1965-II = 0.5; 1965-III and on = 0.0

DIV   Dividends, billions of dollars

*DLFS   Dummy for secondary labor force transition after the Korean Conflict, used in secondary labor force and employment capacity functions: 1953-I to 1955-I = 1.0; 1955-II = 0.7; 1955-III = 0.3; 1955-IV and on = 0.0

*DPHS   Dummy for discontinuity in *PHS* series: 1953-I to 1954-III = 1.0; 1954-IV = 0.5; 1955-I and on = 0.0

DPI   Disposable personal income, billions of dollars

*DRS   Dummy for introduction of certificates of deposit used in short-term interest rate equation: 1953-I to 1962-I = 0.0; 1962-II and on = 1.0

DSE   Depreciation, structures and equipment, billions of 1958 dollars

*DSMD   Strike dummy for shipments of manufacturers' durables: 1953-I to 1959-I = 0.0; 1959-II = 1.0; 1959-III to 1959-IV = −1.0; 1960-I = 1.0; 1960-II and on = 0.0

*DTRU   Dummy for supplemental benefits for state unemployment transfer payments function: 1953-I to 1957-IV = 0.0; 1958-I to 1958-IV = 1.0; 1959-I and on = 0.0

*DTSSW   Dummy for additional coverage used in Social Security tax function: 1953-I to 1954-III = 0.0; 1954-IV and on = 1.0

*DUMD   Dummy for Korean Conflict effects used in new and unfilled manufacturers' durables orders equations: 1953-I = 0.0; 1953-II to 1953-III = 1.0; 1953-IV and on = 0.0

E   Total private civilian employment, millions

EC   Employment, potential private (capacity), millions

*EE   Self-employed, millions

*EG   Employment, general civilian government, millions

EW   Employment, civilian wage and salary, millions

*EXP$ Exports, billions of dollars

FBF   Fiscal balance, Federal net surplus (*NIA* basis), billions of dollars

FBSL   Fiscal balance, state and local net surplus (*NIA* basis), billions of dollars

*G58$ Total government purchases of goods and services, billions of 1958 dollars

*GFD$ Federal government defense purchases of goods and services, billions of dollars

*GFND$ Federal government nondefense purchases of goods and services, billions of dollars

*GIA   Federal grants-in-aid to state and local governments, billions of dollars

GNP   Gross national product, billions of dollars

GNP58$ Gross national product, billions of 1958 dollars

*GSL$ State and local government purchases of goods and services, billions of dollars

H Average weekly hours, private employment

HC Average weekly hours, capacity

*HH Households at end of quarter, thousands

HM Average weekly hours, production workers in manufacturing establishments

HS Private nonfarm housing-starts, annual rate, thousands of units

IE Fixed investment, nonresidential, producers' durable equipment, billions of 1958 dollars

IH Fixed investment, residential structures, billions of 1958 dollars

*IHF Fixed investment, residential structures, farm, billions of 1958 dollars

*IHR Fixed investment, residential construction on other than new units (additions, alterations, etc.), billions of 1958 dollars

II Change in business inventories, billions of 1958 dollars

II$ Change in business inventories, billions of dollars

IIA Change in auto inventory investment, domestic new cars, billions of 1958 dollars

IINA Change in nonauto inventory investment, billions of 1958 dollars

*IMG$ Imports, military, goods and services, billions of dollars

IMS Imports, other nonmilitary (mainly services), billions of 1958 dollars

IMT Imports, merchandise, billions of 1958 dollars

*INB Net interest, business, billions of dollars

*INC Interest paid by consumers, billions of dollars

*INGF Net interest payments, Federal, billions of dollars

*INGSL Net interest payments, state and local, billions of dollars

IS Fixed investment, nonresidential structures, billions of 1958 dollars

ISE Fixed investment, nonresidential, billions of 1958 dollars

ITER Number of iterations required for model convergence (used only during forecast periods)

IVA Inventory valuation adjustment, billions of dollars

KA   Stock, automobiles and parts, billions of 1958 dollars

KC$ Net stock of nonfarm, nonfinancial corporate plant and equipment at end of quarter, billions of historical dollars

KH   Stock of dwelling units at end of quarter, thousands

KI   Stock of inventories at end of quarter, billions of 1958 dollars

KIA   Stock of auto inventories, billions of 1958 dollars

KINA   Stock of nonauto inventories, billions of 1958 dollars

KSE   Net stock of plant and equipment at end of quarter, billions of 1958 dollars

KSE$ Net stock of plant and equipment at end of quarter, billions of historical dollars

LFP   Labor force, civilian, prime, males aged 25–54, millions

LFS   Labor force, civilian, secondary (excludes prime males), millions

LH   Liquid assets held by households at end of quarter (currency plus demand and bank savings deposits plus savings and loan shares), billions of dollars

*MAXSS   Maximum salary subject to Social Security deductions, dollars

MONEY   Total money supply, demand deposits plus currency, billions of dollars

*N   Total population, millions

NETEXP   Net exports, billions of 1958 dollars

*NP   Population, civilian resident, males aged 25–54, millions

*NS   Population, other civilian resident, aged 16–64, millions

OMD   New manufacturers' orders, durable goods, billions of dollars, deflated by *PWMD*

P   Implicit price deflator, gross private output except housing services, 1958 = 1.000

*PA   Implicit price deflator, personal consumption expenditures, automobiles and parts, 1958 = 1.000

PADJ   Implicit price deflator adjustment (nonzero only during forecast periods)

PC   Implicit price deflator, personal consumption expenditures, 1958 = 1.000

PERINC   Personal income, billions of dollars

*PEX   Implicit price deflator, exports, 1958 = 1.000

*PF   Index, prices received by farmers for all farm products, 1910–1914 = 1.000

PGG   Implicit price deflator, government purchases of goods, 1958 = 1.000

PGNP   Implicit price deflator, gross national product, 1958 = 1.000

*PH   Implicit price deflator, personal consumption expenditures, housing, 1958 = 1.000

PHS   Average cost per new private nonfarm housing unit started, thousands of dollars

PIE   Implicit price deflator, fixed investment, nonresidential, producers' durable equipment, 1958 = 1.000

PIH   Implicit price deflator, fixed investment, residential structures, 1958 = 1.000

*PIM   Implicit price deflator, imports, 1958 = 1.000

PIS   Implicit price deflator, fixed investment, nonresidential structures, 1958 = 1.000

PISE   Implicit price deflator, fixed investment, nonresidential, 1958 = 1.000

PN   Implicit price deflator, personal consumption expenditures, nondurables, 1958 = 1.000

POD   Implicit price deflator, personal consumption expenditures, durables other than automobiles and parts, 1958 = 1.000

*PR   BLS consumer rent index, 1957–1959 = 1.000

PRI   Proprietors' income, billions of dollars

PROD   Index of real private *GNP* per man-hour, 1958 = 100.0

PS   Implicit price deflator, personal consumption expenditures, services except housing, 1958 = 1.000

*PWG   Implicit price deflator, compensation of general government employees, 1958 = 1.000

PWMD   Wholesale price index, durable manufactures, 1957–1959 = 1.000

*RDIS   Federal Reserve average discount rate, per cent

REM   Net removal of private housing during quarter, thousands

*RENT   Rental income of persons, billions of dollars

RESF	Free reserves, daily average of quarter, billions of dollars
*RESNB	Nonborrowed reserves, daily average of quarter, billions of dollars
RL	Per cent yield, corporate bonds (Moody's)
RM	Per cent yield, secondary market, FHA-insured homes
*RMBD	Ratio, Federal Reserve member bank demand deposits to money supply component of demand deposits, decimal
*RMBT	Ratio, Federal Reserve member bank time deposits to total time deposits, decimal
*RRD	Average reserve requirement against member bank demand deposits, decimal
*RRT	Average reserve requirement against member bank time and savings deposits, decimal
RS	Short-run interest rate, average yield on 4–6 month commercial paper, per cent
RT	Interest rate on commercial bank savings deposits, per cent
RTB	Three-month Treasury bill yield, per cent
*RTCF	Rate, Federal corporate profits tax, decimal
*RTEXA	Index of average rates, Federal ad valorem excise taxes, 1958 = 1.00
*RTEXS	Index of average rates, Federal specific excise taxes, 1958 = 1.00
*RTQ	Maximum interest rate on Federal Reserve member bank savings deposits under Regulation Q, per cent
*RTRU	Maximum weekly benefit rate, unemployment insurance, dollars
*RTSSW	Combined employer-employee contribution rate for OASI, decimal
SD	Statistical discrepancy, billions of dollars
SDADJ	Statistical discrepancy adjustment (nonzero only during forecast periods)
*SGF	Federal subsidies less current surplus of Federal government enterprises, billions of dollars
*SGSL	Subsidies less current surplus of state and local government enterprises, billions of dollars

SIB	Social insurance, employer contributions, billions of dollars
*SIBOF	Federal social insurance programs, employer contributions, excluding OASI, billions of dollars
*SIBSL	State and local social insurance programs, employer contributions, billions of dollars
SIP	Social insurance, personal contributions, billions of dollars
*SIPOF	Federal social insurance programs, personal contributions, excluding OASI except for self-employed contributions to OASI, billions of dollars
*SIPSL	State and local social insurance programs, personal contributions, billions of dollars
SMD	Manufacturers' shipments, durable goods, billions of dollars, deflated by *PWMD*
SRATE	Personal savings as a proportion of disposable personal income, decimal
*T531	Time in quarters, 1953-I = 1.0
*T581	Time in quarters, 1958-I = 1.0; 1953-I to 1957-IV = 0.0
TCF	Corporate profits tax liability, Federal, billions of dollars
TCRI	Investment tax credit, billions of dollars
TCSL	Corporate profits tax liability, state and local, billions of dollars
TD	Time deposits, commercial banks, billions of dollars
TEXAV	Ad valorem excise tax receipts, Federal, billions of dollars
TEXS	Specific excise tax receipts, Federal, billions of dollars
TIF	Indirect business tax and nontax receipts, Federal, billions of dollars
*TIFO	Indirect tax receipts, business other than excise, Federal, billions of dollars
TISL	Indirect business tax receipts, state and local, billions of dollars
TPF	Personal tax and nontax payments, Federal, billions of dollars
*TPFS	Final personal tax and nontax settlements plus estate and gift taxes, Federal, billions of dollars

TPSL   Personal tax and nontax payments, state and local, billions of dollars

*TRB   Transfer payments, business, billions of dollars

*TRFF   Net transfer payments to foreigners, Federal, billions of dollars

*TRFP   Transfer payments to foreigners, personal, billions of dollars

TRP   Transfer payments to persons, billions of dollars

*TRPOF   Transfer payments to persons, Federal, except unemployment insurance benefits, billions of dollars

*TRPSL   Transfer payments to persons, state and local, billions of dollars

TRU   Transfers, state unemployment insurance benefits, billions of dollars

*TRUEX   Unemployment insurance factor for supplementary unemployment programs

TSSW   Personal and employer contributions for old-age and survivors' insurance (OASI) excluding self-employed and personal medical payments, but including hospital insurance, billions of dollars

UMD   Unfilled manufacturers' orders, durable goods, at end of quarter, billions of dollars, deflated by *PWMD*

UNITLC   Private employee compensation per unit of real private *GNP*, dollars

UNRATE   Unemployment rate, civilian labor force, per cent

UR   Unemployment rate, civilian labor force, decimal

URP   Unemployment rate, prime males, decimal

V   Vacant nonfarm housing units at end of quarter, thousands

W   Wages and salaries plus other labor income, billions of dollars

*WAMD   Wage accruals less disbursements, billions of dollars

*WG$ Wages, compensation of general government employees, billions of dollars

WR   Annual wage per private employee, thousands of dollars

X   Gross private output, except housing services, billions of 1958 dollars

XC   Gross private output, except housing services, capacity, billions of 1958 dollars

APPENDIX B

LIST OF STRUCTURAL EQUATIONS

I. *GNP* COMPONENTS

(1) Gross National Product (Current Dollars)

$$GNP = PC \times C + PIH \times IH + PISE \times ISE + II\$ + EXP\$$$
$$- PIM(IMT + IMS) - IMG\$ + GFD\$ + GFND\$$$
$$+ GSL\$$$

$$GNP = P \times X + PH \times CH + WG\$$$

(2) Gross National Product (Constant Dollars)

$$GNP58\$ = X + CH + \left(\frac{WG\$}{PWG}\right)$$

(3) Gross Private Output, Except Housing Services

$$X = C - CH + IH + ISE + II + \left(\frac{EXP\$}{PEX}\right)$$
$$- \left[IMT + IMS + \frac{IMG\$}{PIM}\right]$$
$$+ \left(\frac{GFD\$ + GFND\$ + GSL\$ - WG\$}{PGG}\right)$$

Consumption functions.

(4) Personal Consumption Expenditures, Autos and Parts

$$CA = -20.9 - 41.3 \frac{PA}{PC} + .117 \frac{DPI - TRP}{PC} + 1.392(HM)_{-1}$$
$$\qquad\quad (8.7) \qquad (.029) \qquad\qquad (.340)$$
$$- .0623(KA)_{-1} + 1.9DCA1 + 3.1DCA2$$
$$(.0269) \qquad (.4) \qquad\quad (.7)$$

$$TSLS \quad \bar{R}^2 = .95 \quad \bar{S} = 1.0 \quad DW = 1.2$$

(5) Stock of Autos

$$KA = \sum_{i=0}^{40} (.929)^i CA_{t-i}$$

(6) Personal Consumption Expenditures, Durables Other Than Autos and Parts

$$COD = 43.95 - \underset{(19.7)}{53.1} \frac{POD}{PC} + \underset{(.02)}{.056} \frac{DPI}{PC} + \underset{(.015)}{.103} \left(\frac{LH}{PC}\right)^{\text{dev}_t}_{-1}$$

$$+ \underset{(.00007)}{.00148} (\overline{HS})_{-2:3}$$

$$TSLS \qquad \bar{R}^2 = .99 \qquad \bar{S} = .6 \qquad DW = .96$$

where $\left(\frac{LH}{PC}\right)^{\text{dev}_t}_{-1} = \left(\frac{LH}{PC}\right)_{-1} - 129.6 - 3.39T_{531}$

(7) Personal Consumption Expenditures, Nondurables

$$CN = 16.4 + \underset{(.04)}{.216} \left(\frac{DPI - TRP}{PC}\right) + \underset{(.247)}{.282} \left(\frac{TRP}{PC}\right)$$

$$+ \underset{(.207)}{.393} (\overline{CN})_{-1:8}$$

$$TSLS \qquad \bar{R}^2 = .994 \qquad \bar{S} = 1.5 \qquad DW = .97$$

(8) Personal Consumption Expenditures, Services Except Housing

$$\frac{CS}{N} = .158 + \underset{(.014)}{.075} \left(\frac{DPI}{N \times PC}\right) + \underset{(.131)}{.555} \left(\frac{\overline{CS}}{N}\right)_{-1:8} - \underset{(7.5)}{19.2} \left(\frac{1}{N}\right)$$

$$TSLS \qquad \bar{R}^2 = .994 \qquad \bar{S} = .0021 \qquad DW = .98$$

(9) Personal Consumption Expenditures

$$C = CA + COD + CN + CS + CH$$

Fixed investment functions.

(10) Fixed Investment, Nonresidential Structures and Equipment

$$\text{a.} \quad \frac{ISE}{XC} = .02897 \left[\frac{\sum_{i=1}^{11} WT1_i X_{t-i+1}}{XC} \right]$$

$$+ .5310 \left[\frac{\sum_{i=1}^{11} WT2_i FV_{t-i+1}}{XC} \right]$$

$$+ 3.4698 \left[\frac{\sum_{i=1}^{11} WT3_i RL_{t-i+1}}{XC} \right] + .05218$$

where $FV = \dfrac{(CPR + DC\$ - TCF - TCSL) \times ISE}{PISE \times ISE - TCRI}$.

$$OLS \qquad \bar{S} = \left(\frac{ISE}{XC} \right) = .0048$$

i	$WT1$	$WT2$	$WT3$
1	.592	.024	−.135
2	1.043	.065	−.257
3	1.050	.112	−.297
4	.671	.150	−.255
5	.272	.166	−.168
6	−.104	.161	−.113
7	−.435	.137	−.028
8	−.678	.100	.049
9	−.780	.056	.105
10	−.476	.024	.072
11	−.155	.006	.028

b. $L \left(\dfrac{ISE}{XC} \right) = \underset{(.00423)}{.01608} + \underset{(.00403)}{.03151L} \left[\dfrac{\sum_{i=1}^{11} WT1_i X_{t-i+1}}{XC} \right]$

$$+ \underset{(.0362)}{.7022L} \left[\frac{\sum_{i=1}^{11} WT2_i FV_{t-i+1}}{XC} \right]$$

$$+ \underset{(.000944)}{.004214L} \left[\sum_{i=1}^{11} WT3_i RL_{t-i+1} \right]$$

where $L(X) = X_t - .8432X_{t-1}$

$$FV = \frac{(CPR + DC\$ - TCF - TCSL) \times ISE}{PISE \times ISE - TCRI}.$$

$$\bar{S}\left(\frac{ISE}{XC}\right) = .0022$$

$WT1, WT2, WT3$ same as weights in version (a).

(11) Fixed Investment, Nonresidential Equipment

$$\frac{IE}{ISE} = .563 + .033225[(CUW)_{-1} + (CUW)_{-2}]$$
$$\quad\;\; (.028) \quad (.0164)$$

$$+ 1.308 \left(\frac{TCRI}{IE \times PIE}\right)_{-1}$$
$$\;\;(.0962)$$

$OLS \qquad \bar{R}^2 = .784 \qquad \bar{S} = .011 \qquad DW = .80$

(12) Fixed Investment, Nonresidential Structures

$$IS = ISE - IE$$

(13) Net Stock of Plant and Equipment

$$KSE = (KSE)_{-1} + .25ISE - DSE$$

(14) Depreciation, Fixed Nonresidential Investment

$$DSE = -.186 + .0269(KSE)_{-1}$$
$$\qquad\qquad (.0007)$$

$OLS \qquad \bar{R}^2 = .974 \qquad \bar{S} = .22 \qquad DW = .111$

(15) Capital Consumption Allowances

    a. Exogenous

    b. $D\$ = .1995(KSE \times PIE)_{-1}$

(16) Capital Consumption Allowances, Corporate

    a. Exogenous

    b. $DC\$ = 7.83 + .0973(KSE \times PIE)_{-1}$

Housing functions.

(17) Private Investment, Residential Structures

$$IH = \underset{(.000003)}{.00102} \left(\frac{1}{PIH}\right) [.41(PHS \times HS) + .49(PHS \times HS)_{-1}$$

$$+ .10(PHS \times HS)_{-2}] + IHR + IHF$$

$$OLS \quad \bar{R}^2 = .93 \quad \bar{S} = .5 \quad DW = .81$$

(18) Private Nonfarm Housing Starts

a. $HS = \underset{(1186.)}{309.} + 3846.DHS1 + \underset{(570.)}{1493.} \left(\frac{PR}{PIH}\right)_{-1}$

$$- 118.6DHS2 \times \overline{(RTB)}_{-2:4} - \underset{(234.2)}{726.5}DHS1(RM)_{-2}$$

$$- \underset{(.072)}{.356}(V - .03HH)_{-2}$$

$$OLS \quad \bar{R}^2 = .82 \quad \bar{S} = 74.7 \quad DW = 1.10$$

b. $HS = -896.6 + 3846.DHS1 + 1493. \left(\frac{PR}{PIH}\right)_{-1}$

$$- 118.6DHS2 \times \overline{(RTB)}_{-2:4}$$

$$- 726.5DHS1 \times (RM)_{-2} - .356(V - .03HH)_{-2}$$

$$+ 356.9DHS2 + 24.8T_{531}$$

(19) Stock of Dwelling Units (End of Quarter)

$$KH = (KH)_{-1} + .25(HS)_{-2} - REM$$

(20) Vacant Nonfarm Housing Units (End of Quarter)

$$V = (V)_{-1} + .25(HS)_{-2} - \Delta HH - REM$$

(21) Net Removal of Private Housing During Quarter

$$REM = 17.5 + .0018(KH)_{-1}$$

Inventory investment functions.

(22) Change in Business Inventories (Current Dollars)

$$II\$ = PWMD \times II$$

(23) Change in Business Inventories (Constant Dollars)

$$II = IIA + IINA$$

(24) Change in Auto Inventory Investment

$$IIA = -1.46906 + .21144CA - .13171\Delta CA$$
$$ (.5177) \quad (.0456) \qquad (.1054)$$

$$- 1.363(KIA)_{-1} + .52405DCA1$$
$$(.321) \qquad\qquad (.378)$$

$$OLS \quad \bar{R}^2 = .315 \quad \bar{S} = .782 \quad DW = 1.91$$

(25) Change in Inventory Investment, Nonauto

$$IINA = 1.684 + .0811(X - II - CS - CA)$$
$$ (3.14) \quad (.039)$$

$$- .1759\Delta(X - II - CS - CA)$$
$$(.0010)$$

$$+ .3529(IINA)_{-1} - .1512(KINA)_{-1}$$
$$(.111) \qquad\qquad (.104)$$

$$+ .6675\Delta(UMD)_{-1} + 1.958DII$$
$$(.118) \qquad\qquad (.690)$$

$$OLS \quad \bar{R}^2 = .828 \quad \bar{S} = 1.8 \quad DW = 1.54$$

(26) Stock of Inventories (End of Quarter)

$$KI = (KI)_{-1} + .25II$$

(27) Stock of Auto Inventories (End of Quarter)

$$KIA = (KIA)_{-1} + .25IIA$$

(28) Stock of Nonauto Inventories (End of Quarter)

$$KINA = (KINA)_{-1} + .25IINA$$

Imports.

(29) Merchandise Imports

a. $IMT = 8.88 + (.01006 + .01578CUW) \times [X + (X)_{-1}]$
   (5.43)   (.0054)   (.0040)

$$- 12.955 \left(\frac{PIM}{P}\right)_{-1} + 1.5053DIM$$
   (3.72)   (.3948)

OLS $\bar{R}^2 = .975$ $\bar{S} = .618$ $DW = .56$

b. $IMT = .04 + (.01006 + .01578CUW) \times [X + (X)_{-1}]$

$$- 12.955 \left(\frac{PIM}{P}\right)_{-1} + 1.5053DIM + .17T_{531}$$

(30) Nonmilitary Services Imports

$$IMS = -2.8 + .019 \frac{DPI}{PIM} + .328(\overline{IMS})_{-1:4}$$
              (.004)   (.196)

TSLS $\bar{R}^2 = .991$ $\bar{S} = .1$ $DW = 1.97$

Government purchases.

(31) Government Purchases of Goods and Services, Total (Constant Dollars)

$$G58\$ = \left(\frac{GFD\$ + GFND\$ + GSL\$ - WG\$}{PGG}\right) + \left(\frac{WG\$}{PWG}\right)$$

NOTE:

$$(\bar{Z})_{-j:k} = \frac{1}{k - j + 1} \sum_{i=j}^{k} Z_{t-i}$$

II. PRICES AND WAGE RATES

(1) Implicit Price Deflator, Gross Private Output (Except Housing Services)

$$P = .263 + 1.230 \sum_{i=0}^{3} W_i \left(\frac{W - WG\$}{X}\right)_{t-1}$$
$$\quad (.053)$$

$$+ .456 CUW^{*7.1} \left(\frac{(X - II) - \overline{(X - II)}_{-1:4}}{\overline{(X - II)}_{-1:4}}\right) + .00137 T_{531}$$
$$\quad (.084) \qquad\qquad\qquad\qquad\qquad\qquad\qquad (.00013)$$

where $CUW^* = .87$ if $CUW \leq .87$ $\qquad W_0 = .4 \qquad W_1 = .3$
$W_2 = .2 \qquad W_3 = .1$

$$TSLS \qquad \bar{R}^2 = .998 \qquad \bar{S} = .0032 \qquad DW = 1.02$$

(2) Implicit Price Deflator, Consumer Durables (Excluding Autos)

$$\Delta POD = -.007 + .32 \Delta P + .00011 (UMD)_{-1}$$
$$\qquad\qquad (.12) \qquad (.000043)$$

$$OLS \qquad \bar{R}^2 = .210 \qquad \bar{S} = .003 \qquad DW = 1.12$$

(3) Implicit Price Deflator, Consumer Nondurables

$$\Delta PN = .72 \Delta P + .45 \Delta PF$$
$$\qquad (.08) \qquad (.07)$$

$$TSLS \qquad \bar{R}^2 = .58 \qquad \bar{S} = .0028 \qquad DW = 1.66$$

(4) Implicit Price Deflator, Consumer Services (Except Housing)

$$\frac{PS - \overline{(PS)}_{-1:4}}{(PS)_{-1:4}} = .0117 + .258 \left[\frac{WR - \overline{(WR)}_{-1:4}}{\overline{(WR)}_{-1:4}}\right]$$
$$\qquad\qquad\qquad\qquad (.053)$$

$$- .177 \left[\frac{HM - \overline{(HM)}_{-1:4}}{\overline{(HM)}_{-1:4}}\right]$$
$$\quad (.075)$$

$$TSLS \qquad \bar{R}^2 = .15 \qquad \bar{S} = .006 \qquad DW = .35$$

(5) Implicit Price Deflator, Residential Investment

$$PIH = -.075 + .687 \left(\frac{W - WG\$}{X}\right) + .00230 (IH + ISE)$$
$$\qquad\quad (.022) \qquad\qquad\qquad\qquad (.00024)$$

$$+ .540(\overline{PIH})_{-1:4}$$
$$(.070)$$

$$TSLS \quad \bar{R}^2 = .994 \quad \bar{S} = .007 \quad DW = .81$$

(6) Price Per New Dwelling Unit Started

$$PHS = 1.9066 + 10.472PIH - 1.2198DPHS$$
$$(.499) \quad (.471) \quad (.131)$$

$$OLS \quad \bar{R}^2 = .955 \quad \bar{S} = .257 \quad DW = .73$$

(7) Implicit Price Deflator, Nonresidential Structures

$$PIS = -.173 + .944 \left(\frac{W - WG\$}{X} \right) + .00118(IH + ISE)$$
$$(.131) \qquad\qquad (.00016)$$

$$+ .565(\overline{PIS})_{-1:4}$$
$$(.053)$$

$$TSLS \quad \bar{R}^2 = .996 \quad \bar{S} = .0065 \quad DW = 1.34$$

(8) Implicit Price Deflator, Equipment

$$\frac{PIE}{(PIE)_{-1}} = -.5005 + .80003 \frac{P}{(P)_{-1}} + .69885 \frac{PWMD}{(PWMD)_{-1}}$$
$$(.255) \quad (.308) \qquad\quad (.191)$$

$$TSLS \quad \bar{R}^2 = .449 \quad \bar{S} = .0054 \quad DW = 1.91$$

(9) Price Index, Wholesale Durables, Manufacturing

$$\frac{PWMD}{(PWMD)_{-1}} = .33272 + .02750 \left(\frac{OMD}{SMD} \right)_{-1} + .64169 \frac{P}{(P)_{-1}}$$
$$(.269) \quad (.0117) \qquad\qquad (.272)$$

$$TSLS \quad \bar{R}^2 = .227 \quad \bar{S} = .0054 \quad DW = .95$$

(10) Implicit Price Deflator, Government Purchases of Goods and Services Other Than Employment Compensation

a. Exogenous

b. $\dfrac{PGG}{(PGG)_{-1}} = \dfrac{P}{(P)_{-1}}$

(11) Implicit Price Deflator, Personal Consumption Expenditures

$$PC = \left(\frac{PA \times CA + POD \times COD + PN \times CN + PS \times CS + PH \times CH}{C}\right)$$

(12) Implicit Price Deflator, Nonresidential Fixed Investment

$$PISE = \left(\frac{PIS \times IS + PE \times IE}{ISE}\right)$$

(13) Wage Per Employee, Private Sector

$$\frac{WR - (\overline{WR})_{-1:4}}{(\overline{WR})_{-1:4}} = .0076 + \underset{(.000139)}{.000982}\left[\frac{1}{\sum_{i=0}^{3} W_i(UR)_{t-i}}\right]$$

$$-\underset{(.0196)}{.0385}\left[\frac{URP \times LFP}{LFP + LFS - EW - EG}\right]$$

$$-\underset{(.144)}{.529}[UR - (\overline{UR})_{-1:4}]$$

$$+\underset{(.103)}{.622}\left[\frac{HM - (\overline{HM})_{-1:4}}{(\overline{HM})_{-1:4}}\right]$$

$$+\underset{(.179)}{.869}\left[\frac{(PC)_{-1} - (\overline{PC})_{-2:5}}{(\overline{PC})_{-2:5}}\right]$$

where $W_0 = .4$ $\quad$ $W_1 = .3$ $\quad$ $W_2 = .2$ $\quad$ $W_3 = .1$

$\qquad$ OLS $\qquad$ $\bar{R}^2 = .757$ $\qquad$ $\bar{S} = .0061$ $\qquad$ $DW = 1.39$

NOTE:

Any discrepancy between the value of P given by Equation 1 of this section and that given by a properly weighted sum of the component deflators (P') is resolved as follows:

Let $PADJ = P - P'$

Then the component deflators are adjusted as follows:

PN adjustment $= PADJ \times .3 \times X/CN$
PS adjustment $= PADJ \times .4 \times X/CS$
PIH adjustment $= PADJ \times .07 \times X/IH$

$$PIS \text{ adjustment} = PADJ \times .15 \times X/IS$$
$$PIE \text{ adjustment} = PADJ \times .08 \times X/IE$$

After adjustment $P' = P$.

III. CAPACITY, CAPACITY UTILIZATION, AND PRODUCTIVITY

(1) Potential Private Employment

    a. $EC = .985LFP + (.97 - .000191T_{531})[NS(.2991 + .05285$

        $\ln (T_{531} + 100) - .0203DLFS)] - EG$

    b. $EC = .985LFP + .9593[NS(.2991 + .05285$

        $\ln (T_{531} + 100) - .0203DLFS)] - EG$

(2) Potential Private Weekly Hours

    a. $\log HC = 1.6319 - .000654T_{531} + .000466T_{581}$

    b. $HC = 40.9261$

derived from estimated equation

$$\log H = 1.6319 + .0855 \log CUW - .000654T_{531}$$
$$(.012) \qquad\qquad (.000066)$$

$$+ .000466T_{581}$$
$$(.000085)$$

$$OLS \qquad \bar{R}^2 = .90 \qquad \bar{S} = .00169 \qquad DW = 1.656$$

(3) Potential Private GNP (Except Housing Services)

$$\log XC = -.5506 + .002056T_{531} + .3 \log (\overline{KSE})_{-1:4}$$
$$+ .7 \log (EC \times HC)$$

derived from estimated equation

$$\log \left(\frac{X}{E \times H}\right) - .3 \log \left[\frac{.96CUW \times (\overline{KSE})_{-1:4}}{\frac{PROD}{PROD_{TR}} \times E \times H}\right]$$

$$= -.5453 + .0002056T_{531}$$
$$(.000030)$$

where $PROD_{TR}$ = the trend in productivity.

$$OLS \qquad \bar{S} = .0032 \qquad DW = .36$$

(4) Industrial Capacity Utilization, Wharton Index

$\ln CUW - \rho(\ln CUW_{-1})$

$$= -.127203 + 1.43398 \left[\ln \left(\frac{X}{XC} \right) - \rho \ln \left(\frac{X}{XC} \right)_{-1} \right]$$
$$ (.076) \qquad (.2096)$$

$$-.389164 \left[\ln \left(\frac{CS}{X} \right) - \rho \ln \left(\frac{CS}{X} \right)_{-1} \right]$$
$$(.224)$$

where $\rho = .8058$.

$$OLS \qquad \bar{R}^2 = .789 \qquad \bar{S} = .0129 \qquad DW = 1.7$$

(5) Private GNP (1958 dollars) Per Man-Hour

$$PROD = \left[\frac{X + CH}{H(EW + EE - EG)} \right] \times 563.7$$

IV. LABOR FORCE, EMPLOYMENT, AND HOURS

(1) Civilian Labor Force, Males (25–54)

a. $\dfrac{LFP}{NP} = .956 - .000068 T_{531}$
$\phantom{a. \dfrac{LFP}{NP} = .956} (.000020)$

$$OLS \qquad \bar{R}^2 = .22 \qquad \bar{S} = .0025 \qquad DW = .91$$

b. $\dfrac{LFP}{NP} = .952$

(2) Civilian Labor Force Except Males (25–54)

for $URP < 0.045$:

$$\frac{LFS}{NS} = .3123 - 1.068URP + 12.53URP^2 - .0203DLFS$$
$$\phantom{\frac{LFS}{NS} =} (.299) \qquad (3.78) \qquad (.002)$$

$$+ .05285 \ln (T_{531} + 100)$$

$$TSLS \qquad \bar{R}^2 = .924 \qquad \bar{S} = .00375 \qquad DW = .765$$

for $URP \geqslant 0.045$:

$$\frac{LFS}{NS} = .28635 + .07222URP - .0203DLFS$$

$$+ .05285 \ln (T_{531} + 100)$$

(3) Private Civilian Employment

$$\Delta \log E = b \left[\log EC + .418 \log \left(\frac{X}{XC}\right) - \log (E)_{-1} \right]$$
$$(.021)$$

$$OLS \qquad \bar{R}^2 = .651 \qquad \bar{S} = .0017 \qquad DW = 1.07$$

where $E = EW + EE - EG$

$$b = \begin{cases} .33422, \ URP \geqslant .06 \\ (.5627 - 3.808URP)(1 - e^{-224.0(URP-.01)}), \\ \qquad URP < .06 \end{cases}$$

(4) Civilian Unemployment Rate

$$UR = \left(\frac{LFP + LFS - EW - EE}{LFP + LFS}\right)$$

(5) Unemployment Rate, Males (25–54)

$$URP = -.0629 + .2816UR + 6.482(UR)^2$$
$$(.0081) \ (.1761) \qquad (1.714)$$

$$+ .1528 \left(\frac{LFP}{LFP + LFS}\right)$$
$$(.0132)$$

$$OLS \qquad \bar{R}^2 = .971 \qquad \bar{S} = .0018 \qquad DW = .806$$

where $URP \leqslant .85(UR)$

(6) Private Man-Hours

$$\Delta \log H = .661 \left[\log HC + .130 \log \left(\frac{X}{XC}\right) - \log (H)_{-1} \right]$$
$$(.105) \qquad\qquad (.020)$$

$$OLS \qquad \bar{R}^2 = .423 \qquad \bar{S} = .0016 \qquad DW = 1.96$$

(7) Average Weekly Hours, Manufacturing

$$HM = 17.35 + .0450[X - (X)_{-2}] + 4.27CUW + .469(\overline{HM})_{-1:4}$$
$$\quad\quad\quad (.0048) \quad\quad\quad\quad (1.49) \quad\quad (.119)$$

$$TSLS \quad \bar{R}^2 = .803 \quad \bar{S} = .0073 \quad DW = 1.24$$

V. INCOME

(1) Corporate Profits and Inventory Valuation Adjustment

$$\rho \log (CPR + DC\$) = -.3480 + 1.092\rho \log (P \times X)$$
$$\quad\quad\quad\quad (.00199) \quad (.0032)$$

$$- 2.165\rho \log \left(\frac{W - WG\$}{P \times X}\right)$$
$$(.0339)$$

$$+ .563\rho \log CUW$$
$$(.1014)$$

where $\rho = .762$
$\quad\quad (.0014)$

$$\bar{S} = .00659$$

(2) Dividends

$$DIV = -.19 + .034CPR + .899(DIV)_{-1}$$
$$\quad\quad\quad (.012) \quad\quad (.099)$$

$$TSLS \quad \bar{R}^2 = .994 \quad \bar{S} = .3 \quad DW = 1.64$$

(3) Inventory Valuation Adjustment

$$IVA = .14 - 134.5\Delta PWMD - .0628(II)_{-1}$$
$$\quad\quad (17.5) \quad\quad\quad\quad (.0230)$$

$$OLS \quad \bar{R}^2 = .592 \quad \bar{S} = .7 \quad DW = 1.52$$

(4) Proprietors' Income

$$PRI - (\overline{PRI})_{-1:4} = -.3 + .221[(PN \times CN + PS \times CS)$$
$$\quad\quad\quad\quad\quad (.051)$$

$$- (\overline{PN \times CN + PS \times CS})_{-1:4}]$$

$$-4.98[WR - (\overline{WR})_{-1:4}]$$
$$(3.36)$$

$$TSLS \quad \bar{R}^2 = .24 \quad \bar{S} = 1.0 \quad DW = .70$$

(5) Wages and Salaries Plus Other Labor Income

$$W = WR(EW - EG) + WG\$$$

(6) Personal Income

$$PI = W - WAMD + PRI + DIV + RENT + INB + INC$$
$$+ INGF + INGSL + TRP - SIP$$

(7) Disposable Personal Income

$$DPI = PI - TPF - TPSL$$

(8) Savings Rate

$$SRATE = \left[\frac{DPI - (PC \times C - INC + TRFP)}{DPI} \right] \times 100$$

(9) Statistical Discrepancy

$$SD = GNP - W - RENT - INB - PRI - CPR - TRB$$
$$- WAMD - SIB - D\$ - TIF - TISL$$
$$+ SGF + SGSL$$

NOTE:

During forecast periods, restrictions are placed on the level and change in SD:

(1) The absolute level of SD must be less than, or equal to, the larger of \$4.0 billion or $0.00522 \times GNP_{-1}$.

(2) The change in SD from the previous period must be no larger than \$1.0 billion.

The model is first solved without taking into account the above restrictions. Then tests are made to see whether or not the calculated value of SD from identity (9) meets the above restrictions. If the restrictions are met, then no further calculations are necessary.

If the restrictions are not met, then $SDADJ$, an amount just sufficient to bring SD into line, is calculated. Additive adjustments are then made to the equations for three income items as follows:

$$WR \text{ adjustment} = SDADJ \times .7574(EW_{-1} - EG_{-1})$$

$$CPR \text{ adjustment} = SDADJ \times .5065$$

$$PRI \text{ adjustment} = SDADJ \times .2440$$

Then the entire model is re-solved, and the above tests repeated until the calculated value of SD from identity (9) meets the two restrictions.

VI. TAXES, TRANSFERS, AND FISCAL BALANCE

(1) Personal Tax Payments, Federal

a. for 531–534:

$$(TPF - TPFS) = 1.8095 + .10031BASE$$
$$(10.2) \quad (.037)$$

$$OLS \quad \bar{R}^2 = .682 \quad \bar{S} = .122$$

where $BASE = W + DIV + PRI + RENT + INB + INC$
$$+ INGF + INGSL.$$

for 541–634:

$$(TPF - TPFS) = -9.2113 + .13047BASE$$
$$(.522) \quad (.0014)$$

$$TSLS \quad \bar{R}^2 = .995 \quad \bar{S} = .465$$

for 641:

$$(TPF - TPFS) = -12.45 + .133BASE$$

for 642–661:

$$(TPF - TPFS) = -20.3324 + .13599BASE$$
$$(1.85) \quad (.0037)$$

$$TSLS \quad \bar{R}^2 = .995 \quad \bar{S} = .231$$

for 662:

$$(TPF - TPFS) = -35.31 + .165BASE$$

for 663–674:

$$(TPF - TPFS) = -42.824 + .17951BASE$$
$$(5.33) \quad (.0091)$$

$$OLS \quad \bar{R}^2 = .987 \quad \bar{S} = .347$$

b. *TPF* is found by recursively solving the three equations below:

(1) $\log \left(1 - \dfrac{TI}{PI}\right) = .0619 - .3431 \log \left(\dfrac{PI}{N}\right)$

$$+ .3466 \log [.656(1.004)(T_{531} - 52.0)]$$

where TI = taxable personal income.

(2) $\log TPFL = -1.0038 + 1.124 \log (TI)$

where *TPFL* = personal Federal income tax liabilities.

(3) $TPF = -1.004 + 1.01TPFL + .052T_{531}$

(2) Personal Tax and Nontax Payments, State and Local

a. $TPSL = 3.5579 + .02527BASE + .01122T_{531}$
$(.496) \quad (.0018) \quad\quad (.00739)$

$$+ .06498T_{581}$$
$$(.00901)$$

[*BASE* is defined as in the *TPF* equation given above.]

$$TSLS \quad \bar{R}^2 = .997 \quad \bar{S} = .174 \quad DW = .883$$

b. $TPSL = -10.292 + [.146 + .0002T_{531}]BASE + .176T_{531}$

(3) Corporate Tax Liability, Federal

$$\log (TCF + TCRI) = -.1056 + \log RTCF$$

$$+ 1.0150 \log (CPR - IVA)$$
$$(.0092)$$

$$OLS \quad \bar{R}^2 = .996 \quad \bar{S} = .0065 \quad DW = .36$$

(4) Corporate Tax Liability, State and Local

$$TCSL = -.13203 + .02052(CPR - IVA) + .01286T_{531}$$
$$(.0629) \quad (.00177) \qquad\qquad (.00144)$$

$$TSLS \qquad \bar{R}^2 = .973 \qquad \bar{S} = .077 \qquad DW = 1.06$$

(5) Investment Tax Credit

a. $TCRI = 0$; prior to 1962-I

$$= -.97505 + .057734(IE \times PIE); \text{ after 1962-I}$$
$$(.0729) \quad (.00175)$$

$$OLS \qquad \bar{R}^2 = .983 \qquad \bar{S} = .055 \qquad DW = .57$$

b. $TCRI = .02554(IE \times PIE)$

(6) Federal Specific Excise Tax Liability

$$\log TEXS = -1.8521 + 1.5511 \log RTEXS$$
$$(.1675) \quad (.1072)$$

$$+ 1.047 \log (X - II - CS)$$
$$(.0669)$$

$$OLS \qquad \bar{R}^2 = .977 \qquad \bar{S} = .0171 \qquad DW = .720$$

(7) Federal Ad Valorem Excise Tax Liability

$$\log TEXAV = -2.8341 + 1.1641 \log RTEXAV$$
$$(.2436) \quad (.2310)$$

$$+ 1.2275 \log [P(X - II)]$$
$$(.0938)$$

$$OLS \qquad \bar{R}^2 = .799 \qquad \bar{S} = .0412 \qquad DW = .829$$

(8) Indirect Business Tax and Nontax Receipts, Federal

$$TIF = TEXS + TEXAV + TIFO$$

where $TIFO$ = other indirect business tax receipts.

(9) Indirect Tax and Nontax Liability, State and Local

$$TISL = -2.0 + .0646P(X - II) + .250T_{531}$$
$$(.0038) \qquad\qquad (.021)$$

$$TSLS \qquad \bar{R}^2 = .998 \qquad \bar{S} = .5 \qquad DW = .26$$

(10) Transfer Payments to Persons

$$TRP = TRU + TRPOF + TRPSL + TRB$$

(11) OASDI Contributions, Employer-Employee

$$\log TSSW - \log RTSSW = -1.5471 + .53062 \log MAXSS$$
$$(.035)$$

$$+ .005744DTSSW$$
$$(.0041)$$

$$+ .78495 \log (W - WG)$$
$$(.024)$$

$$OLS \quad \bar{R}^2 = .995 \quad \bar{S} = .00725 \quad DW = .67$$

(12) State Unemployment Insurance Benefits

$$\log TRU - \log (1 + TRUEX) = -.9644 + .33551 \log RTRU$$
$$(.0944)$$

$$+ 1.4238 \log (LFP + LFS$$
$$(.0714)$$

$$- EW - EE)$$

$$+ .066773DTRU$$
$$(.0243)$$

$$OLS \quad \bar{R}^2 = .942 \quad \bar{S} = .041 \quad DW = .832$$

(13) Social Insurance, Personal Contributions

$$SIP = .5TSSW + SIPOF + SIPSL$$

(14) Social Insurance, Employer Contributions

$$SIB = .5TSSW + SIBOF + SIBSL$$

(15) Fiscal Balance, Federal Net Surplus or Deficit

$$FBF = TPF + TCF + TIF + TSSW + SIPOF + SIBOF$$

$$- GFD\$ - GFND\$ - TRU - TRPOF - TRFF$$

$$- GIA - INGF - SGF$$

(16) Fiscal Balance, State and Local Net Surplus or Deficit

$$FBSL = TPSL + TCSL + TISL + SIPSL + SIBSL + GIA$$
$$- GSL\$ - TRPSL - INGSL - SGSL$$

VII. INTEREST RATES AND MONEY SUPPLY

(1) Free Reserves Identity

$$RESF = RESNB - (RMBD \times RRD \times DD + RMBT$$
$$\times RRT \times TD)$$

(2) Liquid Assets, Households

$$LH = -6.34 + .8599(LH)_{-1} + .142DPI - 3.82(RL - RT)$$
$$(.0633) \qquad (.057) \qquad (.95)$$

$$OLS \qquad \bar{R}^2 = .999 \qquad \bar{S} = 1.82 \qquad DW = 2.433$$

(3) Demand Deposits (Adjusted) Plus Currency (Money Stock)

$$DD + CURR = .9 + .9617(DD + CURR)_{-1} - .9122RT$$
$$(.0923) \qquad\qquad (.5460)$$

$$- .7180RTB + .0269DPI$$
$$(.1787) \qquad (.0170)$$

$$OLS \qquad \bar{R}^2 = .997 \qquad \bar{S} = .67 \qquad DW = .914$$

(4) Time Deposits

$$TD = -1.5 + .9935(TD)_{-1} - .7140(RTB - RT)$$
$$(.0191) \qquad (.1734)$$

$$- .8808(RL - RT) + .0170DPI$$
$$(.3594) \qquad\qquad (.0079)$$

$$OLS \qquad \bar{R}^2 = 1.00 \qquad \bar{S} = .7 \qquad DW = 1.02$$

(5) Interest Rate, 3 Month Treasury Bills

$$RTB = -.35163 + 1.0723RDIS$$
$$(.1582) \quad (.0495)$$

$$- \underset{(23.67)}{126.12} \left[\frac{RESF}{(DD + CURR)_{-1}} \right] - \underset{(3.865)}{7.06} \left[\frac{FBF}{(GNP\$)_{-1}} \right]$$

$$OLS \qquad \bar{R}^2 = .94 \qquad \bar{S} = .262 \qquad DW = .95$$

(6) Interest Rate, 4–6 Month Commercial Paper

$$RS = .45 + \underset{(.044)}{.750}RTB + \underset{(.045)}{.317}(RTB)_{-1} - \underset{(.050)}{.189}DRS$$

$$OLS \qquad \bar{R}^2 = .985 \qquad \bar{S} = .12 \qquad DW = .88$$

(7) Interest Rate, Savings Deposits

a. $RT = \underset{(.096)}{-.189} + \underset{(.0488)}{.9322}(RT)_{-1} + \underset{(.0559)}{.128}(RTQ)$

$$- \underset{(.0008)}{.00168}(TD)_{-1} + \underset{(.0315)}{.0686} \times [(1.0 - RRD)(-.57)$$

$$+ (1.0 - RRT)] \times RS$$

$$OLS \qquad \bar{R}^2 = .992 \qquad \bar{S} = .07 \qquad DW = 1.3$$

b. $RT = 3.44$

(8) Interest Rate, Corporate Bonds (Term Structure)

$$(RL - RS) = \underset{(.0849)}{.05891} - \underset{(.0329)}{.67679}RS + \underset{(.0381)}{.68793}(RS)_{-1}$$

$$+ \underset{(.0433)}{1.13338}(RL - RS)_{-1} - \underset{(.0421)}{.20604}(RL - RS)_{-2}$$

$$OLS \qquad \bar{R}^2 = .98 \qquad \bar{S} = .0878 \qquad DW = 1.828$$

(9) Mortgage Yield, FHA Secondary Market

$$RM = .59 + \underset{(.070)}{.198}RL + \underset{(.077)}{.739}(RM)_{-1}$$

$$OLS \qquad \bar{R}^2 = .96 \qquad \bar{S} = .10 \qquad DW = .97$$

VIII. NEW ORDERS, SHIPMENTS, AND UNFILLED ORDERS

(1) New Orders, Manufacturing Durables

$$OMD = 42.3 + 1.101(CA + COD) + .134\Delta X$$
$$\quad\quad\quad (.123) \quad\quad\quad\quad\quad (.067)$$

$$+ .0647[(X)_{-1} - (X)_{-3}] - .3951(KI)_{-1}$$
$$(.0266) \quad\quad\quad\quad\quad (.0843)$$

$$+ .2515(AM58\$)_{-1} - 4.96DUMD$$
$$(.0762) \quad\quad\quad\quad (1.58)$$

$$OLS \quad \bar{R}^2 = .957 \quad \bar{S} = 1.9 \quad DW = 1.14$$

(2) Shipments, Manufacturing Durables

a. $$\frac{SMD}{(UMD)_{-1}} = .419 - .3973CUW + .9271\frac{(SMD)_{-1}}{(UMD)_{-2}}$$
$$\quad\quad\quad\quad (.0896) \ (.0958) \quad\quad\quad (.0236)$$

$$OLS \quad \bar{R}^2 = .97 \quad \bar{S} = .034 \quad DW = 1.73$$

b. $$SMD = \left[.637 - .153\left(\frac{UMD}{SMD}\right)_{-1}\right]OMD$$

$$+ \left[.324 - .078\left(\frac{UMD}{SMD}\right)_{-2}\right](OMD)_{-1}$$

$$+ \left[.104 + .002\left(\frac{UMD}{SMD}\right)_{-3}\right](OMD)_{-2}$$

$$+ \left[-.023 + .079\left(\frac{UMD}{SMD}\right)_{-4}\right](OMD)_{-3}$$

$$+ \left[-.058 + .157\left(\frac{UMD}{SMD}\right)_{-5}\right](OMD)_{-4}$$

$$- 1.52DSMD$$

$$OLS \quad \bar{R}^2 = .972 \quad \bar{S} = .132 \quad DW = 1.264$$

(3) Unfilled Orders, Manufacturing Durables

a. $$\Delta UMD = 22.187 + .145(AM58\$)_{-1} - 6.564DUMD$$
$$(8.214) \ (.064) \quad\quad\quad\quad (1.426)$$

$$+ \sum_{i=1}^{5} WT1_i(KI)_{t-i} + \sum_{i=1}^{5} WT2_i X_{t-i+1}$$

where

i	$WT1$	$WT2$
1	−.9285	.06143
2	−.4035	.07257
3	−.0485	.07200
4	1.375	.05972
5	.1536	.03572

$$OLS \quad \bar{R}^2 = .656 \quad \bar{S} = 1.79 \quad DW = 1.36$$

b. $\Delta UMD = -.299 + .949(OMD - SMD)$
$\quad\quad\quad (.0798) \quad (.0255)$

$$TSLS \quad \bar{R}^2 = .962 \quad \bar{S} = .592 \quad DW = 1.85$$

DISCUSSION

GUY H. ORCUTT

URBAN INSTITUTE

1. INTRODUCTION

My task is to comment on the paper prepared by George Green and his associates. This I am pleased to do, since they have provided us with an excellent report on an interesting body of simulations, carried out with an important and sizeable econometric model (over 90 equations). Interest in their study is heightened by the fact that both the model, and the simulations with it, were developed and carried out by government employees within the U.S. Department of Commerce. Except for what are, perhaps, minor points, I will not find fault with what they have done. Rather, my primary contribution—if I have one to make—will be to point out additional simulation studies that they or others might find useful in complementing what has already been achieved.

In thinking about simulation studies that should be done with models of this type, I believe it helpful to focus attention on the objectives which simulation studies might help us reach. To this end, I have grouped my remarks under the following headings: forecasting, prediction of policy implications, evaluation of predictive ability, and research guidance. I shall treat these topics in turn, concluding with some general observations.

2. FORECASTING

By forecasting, I mean use of a model in predicting future—and thus, unobserved—values of endogenous variables of the model. This I take to be the primary objective of the model. In practice, it must be carried out employing only that information available at the time of prediction. Two points cause me some concern.

First, how are values to be assigned to unlagged input variables? In the sample-period simulations of this paper, actual values have been assigned, but where are the values of these variables to come from in real forecasting? Should not whatever procedures are to be used in practice be presented and tested to see how they work? A concern with values of predetermined variables which—although they have already occurred at the point of forecasting—have not yet resulted in available measurements also seems reasonable.

A second, and perhaps negligible, point which I would like to raise, relates to the use of—or, rather, failure to use—stochastic simulation in forecasting applications of the model. Except for special cases, which do not appear to include this model, even the expected values of endogenous variables will depend on the stochastic specification of a model. Setting all error terms equal to zero and running a model *may* produce reasonably close approximations to expected values, but this is not guaranteed, in general. Thus, some concern on this score is warranted; particularly so, since there is a reasonably straightforward way to explore the matter.

Stochastic shocks could be introduced, much as they are in the twenty-five-year simulations for the spectral analysis found in Part 4 of Green's paper. Repeated simulations could be carried out over the periods to be forecast. For any given variable and time period, the mean for these repeated simulations with independent sets of shocks would provide estimates of expected values which could be compared with results obtained by setting all error terms equal to zero when simulating. The sampling variances of means could be estimated, of course, from the samples of values averaged to obtain the means. These would facilitate the provision of interval forecasts, as well as serving as a check to see whether or not neglecting stochastic terms resulted in significant biases.

3. PREDICTION OF POLICY IMPLICATIONS

An important use of models is in exploring the implications of hypothetical uses of policy instruments. Prediction is involved here, as well as in forecasting, but the focus of attention is on predicting the *dependence* of endogenous variables on the level of policy variables, rather than on predicting the level of endogenous variables.

Forecasts of the level of endogenous variables have an obvious utility, since policy-makers need warning if the effects of their actions are to be timely. Nevertheless, knowledge about how the future depends on policy choices is even more important than forecasting ability. After all, many physical control systems work very well by adjusting corrective actions to observed past discrepancies between actual and desired. These systems count on limited continuity and have no built-in forecasting devices. Their design, nevertheless, did require an approximate knowledge of the way endogenous variables respond to control or policy variables.

In my opinion, policy implications of the OBE Model could, and should, be explored by simulation techniques. Perhaps this has been done adequately elsewhere. If so, it would have been helpful to have such a fact footnoted, at least, in the paper under discussion. If such simulations are carried out, special attention should be given to the treatment of stochastic inputs. It would be desirable to explore policy implications with different sets of stochastic shocks. Nevertheless, in

comparing the implication of different policies, whatever set of stochastic shocks are used should be held constant. A policy-maker does
not know what shocks are in store for him—but he does not expect the
error terms of a model to be systematically dependent on his actions.

4. EVALUATION OF PREDICTIVE ABILITY

One of the many fine features of Green's paper is the extensive
investigation of how the OBE Model works in the neighborhood of
turning points which it reports. Another of its fine features is the exploration of the effects on forecast errors of the alternative adjustment
procedures aimed at taking advantage of the substantial auto-correlation found in residuals. For me, this part struck a particularly respon-
sive note. In some early papers in the forties, I pointed out that many
models generated residuals which implied highly auto-correlated error
terms, that this fact could be used in improving forecasts, and, in addition, might be used in improving parameter estimation.

The primary weakness of the approach used by Green and his
associates in exploring predictive ability is the fact that the same data
is used both for estimating the model and for judging the model's forecasting utility. Unfortunately, experience shows that residuals obtained from within-sample forecasting may be poor guides as to how
well a model will predict beyond the time span used in estimation. In
addition to the excellent paper prepared for this Conference by Ronald
Cooper, which uses forecasting outside of the sample period to good
effect in comparing models, I would like to draw attention to a paper by
John Edwards and myself. It is entitled "The Reliability of Statistical
Indicators of Forecasting Ability," and is available on request to me.
Our paper presents some evidence of how misleading within-sample
fits can be, both in guiding selection of variables to be retained, and in
anticipating errors to be made.

5. RESEARCH GUIDANCE

The paper by Green and his associates uses two simulation approaches to obtain results which would be useful in planning research
strategy. In the first, an analysis of single-equation forecast errors is

made; this would be useful in localizing the origin of forecast errors down to the level of particular equations. In this approach, actual rather than generated values of all except a single output variable are used for each equation. This would not be very useful in actual forecasting, but it does help to sort out errors resulting from incorrect values of equation inputs from errors which arise as a consequence of poor equations.

The second use of simulation in bringing forth results that might help guide subsequent research lies in obtaining the set of 50 twenty-five-year stochastic simulations for a hypothetical specification of policy and exogenous variables. These, along with the spectral analysis of outputs, might throw some useful light on whether or not the model needs to be adjusted to achieve outputs of acceptable time-series properties. Of course, to be useful in this connection, some information about the spectral properties of real economic time-series would be essential. In addition, there are some difficult problems of estimation and testing which require careful consideration.

Another type of simulation analysis which might be useful in providing research guidance is sensitivity experimentation. By finding out how sensitive results were to parameter specification, the researcher could better determine where to direct his efforts.

Still another type of simulation study which might be informative in guiding research effort is the following: having estimated a model, treat it as though it were an exact representation of the world. Use it to generate repeated sets of data, and then see how well the estimating techniques (used in obtaining the model from real-world data) would work in estimating the model from the data obtained by running it. The objective would be to find out how well the estimating techniques used would work if the world were really like the model. If the techniques do not work well under these circumstances, it is hard to see why they should be expected to work well when applied to real-world data.

6. CONCLUDING COMMENTS

I do not know whether or not to accept fully Cooper's remark at the end of his paper: "It is as true now as it was at the time of Christ's study that mechanical forecasting models can be constructed which predict economic variables about as well as econometric models." In any case, I find it very sobering. Nor was I greatly reassured by Daly's paper on the forecasting value of statistical indicators.

Gains made in improving the quality and timeliness of measures describing past behavior of the economy are important. Ascertainment of expectations, intentions, and plans of consumers and businessmen are helpful in peering a little way into the future. However, on two fronts the situation is disappointing. Not only does our ability to predict the future seem inadequate relative to our perceived needs, but I find no evidence, in the papers presented at this Conference, of how successful econometric models are in predicting policy implications. Since I believe that models for predicting policy implications are far more necessary than models for forecasting the future, I am sorry that the problem of building and testing policy-response models has not received more attention.

If econometric models had shown more spectacular results in terms of forecasting, I am sure that this success would have led to their wider use in predicting policy implications. Nevertheless, any connection between success in these two types of prediction may be extremely weak. Econometric models have policy implications, and the predictive value of the models in this area may be more, or may be less, than the predictive value of these models for forecasting the level of economic variables. But, at present, we don't seem to know. My own view is that we never will know with even modest assurance if we restrict our analyses to data of the United States national-accounts type.

THOMAS H. NAYLOR

DUKE UNIVERSITY

INTRODUCTION

A carefully designed computer simulation experiment with a model of an economic system requires that special attention be given to the following activities: (1) definition of the problem, (2) formulation of an econometric model, (3) formulation of a computer program,

(4) validation, (5) experimental design, and (6) data analysis [9]. In evaluating Dr. Green's simulation experiments with the OBE Model, we shall focus on these six activities.

DEFINITION OF THE PROBLEM

I found Dr. Green's paper particularly difficult to evaluate, because his procedure, generally, was a simple description of his simulation results and his conclusions. Nowhere did he state explicitly why he conducted the simulation experiments in the first place. However, from his concluding remarks [3, pp. 89–90], it is possible to work backward and gain some insight into what the experimental objectives may have been. As near as I can tell, the objectives were:

(1) To test the effects of four different mechanical procedures for adjusting the constant terms of the model on the historical performance of the model over the sample period [3, pp. 31–33].

(2) To compare the error statistics of the complete model solutions with the error statistics of the single equation components [3, pp. 33–51].

(3) To evaluate the short-run historical performance of ex post simulations over periods which contain NBER reference-cycle peaks and troughs [3, pp. 51–66].

(4) To compare the simulated time paths of the endogenous variables of the model with the actual observed values of these variables over the entire sample period [3, pp. 66–68].

(5) To determine the cyclical properties of the model over the twenty-five-year period beginning in the first quarter of 1966 [3, pp. 68–88].

FORMULATION OF AN ECONOMETRIC MODEL

Since the structure of the model described in Dr. Green's paper "follows the general scheme of the earlier version" of the OBE Model—which is well known to this audience—I shall limit my comments on the model per se and focus attention on the simulation experiments. It goes without saying that the performance of the OBE Model might benefit from the expansion of some of its sectors along the lines of the more recent versions of the Brookings and Wharton models. Furthermore, I question the treatment of population as an exogenous variable for a twenty-five-year period. One could certainly argue that over a twenty-five-year period, population size and the behavior of the economy of the United States may be jointly determined, and that, therefore, population should be treated endogenously.

FORMULATION OF A COMPUTER PROGRAM

I have only one comment regarding the computer programming techniques used in conducting the simulation experiments. It seems incongruous to use such an "old-fashioned" technique as the Rand Table to generate random variables with such a sophisticated model. To be sure, there is nothing wrong with the numbers in the Rand Table, but reading numbers from a magnetic tape is not a particularly efficient way to use a third-generation computer, when there exist a number of fully tested computer sub-routines [6, 7] for generating pseudo-random numbers internally, and these can be easily transformed into normal deviates by suitable transformations. Perhaps, unlike the situation at most universities today, computer time is still a free gift of nature at the Department of Commerce. If that is the case, I wonder if I could have an hour or two of time on your computer next month?

VALIDATION

The validity of an econometric model depends on the ability of the model to predict the behavior of the actual economic system on which the model is based. To test the degree to which data generated by simulation experiments with econometric models conform to observed data, two alternatives are available: historical verification, and verification by forecasting. The essence of these procedures is prediction, for historical verification is concerned with retrospective predictions (ex post simulations over the sample period), while forecasting is concerned with prospective predictions (ex ante simulations beyond the sample period).

Sections 3.3 and 3.4 of Dr. Green's paper describe his attempts to validate the OBE Model through the use of ex post simulations over the sample period. Although Dr. Green conducted ex ante simulations beyond the sample period, he did not use these simulations for validation purposes. Therefore, I shall restrict my comments to the ex post simulations over the sample period.

In Section 3.3, Dr. Green describes short-run ex post simulations over periods which contain NBER reference-cycle peaks and troughs. In Section 3.4, he describes ex post simulations over the entire sample period. In comparing the simulated time paths of the endogenous variables of the model with the actual time paths, Dr. Green makes use of average absolute errors, root mean square errors, maximum errors, and graphical observation. On the basis of these criteria, Dr. Green concludes that

> it is evident . . . that the simulated values of *GNP* follow the general pattern of the actual data quite well. The general growth path over the period is fairly well predicted, although there is an evident drifting off of predicted values in later quarters [3, p. 67].

In the paper by Naylor and Finger [10] several other criteria are suggested for deciding when the time paths generated by a simulation experiment agree sufficiently with the observed time paths so that agreement cannot be attributed merely to chance. Several specific measures and techniques are suggested for testing the "goodness-of-fit" of simulation results, i.e., the degree of conformity of simulated time series to observed data.

EXPERIMENTAL DESIGN

In a computer simulation experiment, as in any experiment, careful thought should be given to the problem of experimental design. Among the important considerations in the design of computer simulation experiments are: (1) factor selection, (2) method of randomization, (3) number of replications, (4) length of simulation runs, and (5) multiple responses [9].

Factor selection. In a factorial design for several factors, the number of design points required is the product of the number of levels for each of the factors in the experiment. It is clear that a full factorial design can require an unmanageably large number of design points if more than a few factors are to be investigated. Given the limited number of design points considered by Dr. Green in his experiments, the problem of factor selection is not a relevant consideration in the evaluation of his work.

Method of randomization. Two different types of simulation experiments are described by Dr. Green: deterministic simulations and stochastic simulations. The ex post simulations reported in Section 3 are all deterministic. The ex ante simulations in Section 4 are stochastic. The reasons given by Dr. Green [3, pp. 69] for using stochastic simulations are somewhat obscure.

There are at least three reasons why one might want to include stochastic shocks in simulation experiments with simultaneous, non-linear, difference-equation models. First, as Philip Howrey has pointed out in an unpublished paper entitled "Dynamic Properties of Stochastic Linear Econometric Models," if the long-term properties of an econometric model are to be investigated

> . . . it may not be reasonable to disregard the impact of the disturbance terms on the time paths of the endogenous variables. Neither the characteristic roots nor the dynamic multipliers provide information about the magnitude or correlation properties of deviations from the expected value of the time path.

Secondly, Howrey and Kelejian [4] have demonstrated that "the application of nonstochastic simulation procedures to econometric models that contain nonlinearities in the endogenous variables yields results that are not consistent with the properties of the reduced form of the model."

Thirdly, by including stochastic error terms, one can then replicate the simulation experiment and make statistical inferences and test hypotheses about the behavior of the system being simulated, based on the output data generated by the simulation experiment.

Number of replications. If one is going to make inferences of the type made by Dr. Green in his concluding remarks [3, pp. 89–90], then the optimal sample size (number of replications) depends on the answers one gives to the following questions: (1) How large a shift in population parameters do you wish to detect? (2) How much variability is present in the population? (3) What size risks are you willing to take? Dr. Green has arbitrarily used a sample size of fifty replications without providing us with a clue as to how he would answer these questions. The paper by Gilman [2] describes several rules for determining the number of replications of a simulation experiment when the observations are independent. (Observations obtained by replicating a simulation experiment will be independent, provided that one uses a random-number generator which yields independent random numbers.)

Length of simulation runs. Another consideration in the design of simulation experiments is the length of a given simulation run. This problem is more complicated than the question of the number of replications, because the observations generated by a given simulation rule will, typically, be auto-correlated, and the application of "stopping rules" based on classical statistical techniques may underestimate the variance substantially, leading to incorrect inferences about the behavior of the system being simulated.

In the large majority of current simulations, the required sample record length is guessed at by using some rule such as "stop sampling when the parameter to be estimated does not change in the second decimal place when 1000 more samples are taken." The analyst must realize that makeshift rules such as this are very dangerous, since he may be dealing with a parameter whose sample values converge to a steady state solution very slowly. Indeed, his estimate may be several hundred per cent in error. Therefore it is necessary that adequate stopping rules be used in all simulations [2, p. 1].

The paper by Gilman [2] describes several "stopping rules" for determining the length of simulation runs with auto-correlated output data.

Dr. Green's paper does not provide any information on how he decided on the particular simulation-run lengths used in his experiments.

Multiple-response problem. The multiple-response problem arises when we wish to observe and evaluate many different response variables in a given experiment. Dr. Green's simulation experiment contains approximately one hundred response variables. A question arises as to how one goes about validating multiple-response simulation experiments, and how one evaluates the results of the use of alternative policies in the case of policy-simulation experiments. To solve the validation problem, the analyst must devise some technique for assigning weights to the different response variables before applying specific "goodness-of-fit" tests. Gary Fromm [1, p. 8] has proposed the use of utility theory to evaluate the results of policy-simulation experiments with the Brookings Model. Dr. Green's approach to the multiple-response problem is simply to present the results of his experiments, letting the policy-maker assign his own weights to the different output variables. Given the practical and theoretical problems involved in assigning weights or utilities to different response variables, Dr. Green's approach is likely to remain the most popular answer to the multiple-response problem.

DATA ANALYSIS

Given the fact that Dr. Green's ex post simulations: (1) consist of a single replication, (2) involve a small number of observations, and (3) yield output data with a high degree of auto-correlation present, not a great deal more can be said about the analysis of the data generated by these simulation experiments. About all one can do is to observe the graphical output of the simulation experiment—and, perhaps, calculate average errors, average absolute errors, and root mean square errors.

If Dr. Green had chosen to replicate his ex post simulation experiments, several other options would have been open to him. First, he could have given statistical precision to some of the inferences which he made in his concluding remarks [3, p. 89]. Second, he could have applied a conventional analysis of variance to test errors. Third, he could have used multiple-comparison procedures to show how average errors and root mean square errors differ among alternative simulation runs. Fourth, he could have used multiple-ranking procedures to rank the sample means of the errors associated with a single output variable, like GNP, for different simulation runs. For example, Dr. Green might have used multiple-ranking procedures to rank the average quarterly forecast errors of GNP associated with the four procedures for adjusting the constant terms. With what probability can we say that a ranking of sample means represents the true ranking of the population means? Basically, it is this question which multiple-ranking procedures attempt to answer [5].

The paper by Naylor, Wertz, and Wonnacott [11] describes the application of the F test, multiple comparisons, and multiple-ranking procedures to the analysis of national income data generated by policy-simulation experiments with an econometric model.

Finally, Dr. Green has computed the power spectra for the GNP series generated by his ex ante, stochastic-simulation experiments, using serially correlated shocks, non-serially correlated shocks, and two different filters. He then tested the statistical significance of the spectral peaks of these series. Having gone so far as to calculate the power spectra of these GNP series with different types of shocks and filters, he could have said rather more about his results than he reported in his concluding remarks. For example, with spectral analysis it is relatively easy to construct confidence bands and to test hypotheses for the purpose of comparing the simulated output for two or more series. The paper by Naylor, Wertz, and Wonnacott [12] describes several procedures of this type and applies them to national income series generated by an econometric model.

REFERENCES

[1] Fromm, Gary, and Taubman, Paul, *Policy Simulations with an Econometric Model.* Washington, D.C., The Brookings Institution, 1968.

[2] Gilman, Michael J., "A Brief Survey of Stopping Rules in Monte Carlo Simulations," *Digest of the Second Conference on Applications of Simulation* (Dec. 2–4, 1968).

[3] Green, George, "Short- and Long-Term Simulations with the OBE Econometric Model." Paper prepared for the Conference on Econometric Models of Cyclical Behavior, and printed in this volume.

[4] Howrey, Philip, and Kelejian, H. H., "Computer Simulation Versus Analytical Solutions," *The Design of Computer Simulation Experiments,* Thomas H. Naylor, ed. Durham, N.C., Duke University Press, 1969.

[5] Kleijnen, Jack P., and Naylor, Thomas H., "The Use of Multiple Ranking Procedures to Analyze Business and Economic Systems," *Proceedings of the American Statistical Association,* Aug. 1969.

[6] Lewis, P. W. W., Goodman, A. S., and Miller, J. M., "A Pseudo-Random Number Generator for the System/360," *IBM Systems Journal,* VIII (Nov. 2, 1969), 136–146.

[7] Marsaglia, George, and Bray, T. A., "One-Line Random Number Generators and Their Use in Combinations," *Communications of the ACM,* XI (Nov., 1968), 757–759.

[8] Naylor, Thomas H., *Computer Simulation Experiments.* New York, John Wiley, 1971.

[9] ——, Burdick, Donald S., and Sasser, W. Earl, "Computer Simulation Experiments with Economic Systems: The Problem of Experimental Design," *Journal of the American Statistical Association,* LXII (Dec., 1967), 1315–1337.

[10] ——, and Finger, J. M., "Verification of Computer Simulation Models," *Management Science,* XIV (Oct., 1967), 92–101.

[11] ——, Wertz, Kenneth, and Wonnacott, Thomas H., "Some Methods for Evaluating the Effects of Economic Policies Using Simulation Experiments," *Review of the International Statistical Institute,* XXXVI (1968), 184–200.

[12] ——, Wertz, Kenneth, and Wonnacott, Thomas H., "Spectral Analysis of Data Generated by Simulation Experiments with Econometric Models," *Econometrica,* XXXVII (April, 1969), 333–352.

REPLY

GREEN

Both discussants suggest many additional simulations which one might undertake. Some of these projects are indeed worthy of study, while others are not directly relevant to the main theme of this Conference. Some of the suggested projects have been completed and are reported elsewhere. An analysis of ex ante forecasting performance is contained in the paper by Evans, Haitovsky, and Treyz, prepared for this Conference. I reported on some policy simulations at last winter's meetings of the Econometric Society.

Two of the suggestions made by Professor Orcutt seem of special interest to us, and we hope to undertake efforts in this direction in the future. One is the use of stochastic shocks in short-term forecasts to see if the mean of these results agrees with results obtained when shocks are not introduced. In the case of the twenty-five-year simulations reported here, the mean of the stochastic runs is very close to the control solution.

A second suggestion concerns use of the results from the twenty-five-year shocked simulations with different estimating techniques, to try to recapture the "true" parameters. The payoff from this study might well be quite high. Our present estimation methods leave open a lot of questions, especially where the model is to be used for multi-period forecasts.

Concerning the use of the Rand tape of random normal deviates instead of a pseudo-random number generator, I disagree with most of Professor Naylor's comments. First, several pseudo-random number generators do exist, but most of them are too "pseudo" – i.e., tests by Fromm and Nagar at Brookings, and by the staff at the National Bureau of Standards, have shown that the generated series are not very random in several respects. Relatively speaking, the Rand numbers are much better. Second, the same random number generator, used on different computers, can result in far different degrees of accuracy and adequacy. Third, some other participants in this Conference had elected to use the Rand tape, and we conformed – in part, to standardize procedures. Finally, the amount of computer time required is not, as Professor Naylor suggests, a matter of hours, but a matter of a few minutes. The computer time required to generate shocks for twenty-five stochastic runs over twenty-five years, plus twenty-five stochastic simulations (each solving the model for one-hundred quarters) was about fifteen minutes.

SHORT-RUN PREDICTION AND LONG-RUN SIMULATION OF THE WHARTON MODEL

MICHAEL K. EVANS · Chase Econometric Associates, Inc.

LAWRENCE R. KLEIN · Wharton School

MITSUO SAITO · Osaka University

ANALYSIS OF THE MODEL AT TURNING POINTS

THE version of the Wharton Model used for the sample-period simulations is the one contained in the first edition of the Wharton Econometric Forecasting Model; i.e., with the two-equation monetary sector. This model contains 47 stochastic equations and was estimated for the sample period 1948.1 to 1964.4, using two-stage least squares with twelve principal components. In performing these short-period simulations we used data including revisions of the July, 1967, national income accounts; the model was estimated with data revised through July, 1965. Thus, most of the 1963 and 1964 data are slightly changed between estimation and application; in addition, a few series were revised from earlier years. The general direction of the revision of the national income accounts since 1963 has been in an upward direction. Accordingly, the results of the performance of the model using different methods of constant adjustment are slightly biased against the no-adjustments forecasts ($b_k = 0$) at the 1966 peak. None of the other turning point comparisons is affected by the data revisions.

In using the Wharton-EFU Model for ex ante forecasting, we always adjust some of the constant terms of the stochastic equations to take into account revisions in the data, exogenous information not included in the equations (such as strikes), shifts in the institutional framework, or errors in the equations. However, for the sample period and ex post forecasts summarized here, no such adjustments were

NOTE: The authors are deeply indebted to Mr. Koji Shinjo for his research assistance.

139

made. The only change from the published version of the model was the substitution of different tax and transfer equations during periods of divergent tax laws. These equations, used for the complete sample, are as follows:

Direct Business Taxes (T_b)

$T_b = 14.02 + 0.0250NI + 0.3949t$	1948.1–1953.4
$T_b = -2.90 + 0.0721NI + 0.3839t$	1954.1–1965.1
$T_b = -3.40 + 0.0721NI + 0.3839t$	1965.2
$T_b = -4.65 + 0.0721NI + 0.3839t$	1965.3–1967.4

Corporate Income Taxes (T_c)

$T_c = -1.38 + 0.40(P_{cb} - IVA)$	1948.1–1949.4
$T_c = -1.38 + 0.45(P_{cb} - IVA)$	1950.1–1950.4
$T_c = -1.58 + 0.54(P_{cb} - IVA)$	1951.1–1953.4
$T_c = -2.25 + 0.50(P_{cb} - IVA)$	1954.1–1961.4
$T_c = -3.40 + 0.50(P_{cb} - IVA)$	1962.1–1963.4
$T_c = -3.50 + 0.48(P_{cb} - IVA)$	1964.1–1967.4

Transfer Payments (T_r)

$T_r = 9.84 + 0.400N_{Un} + 0.1369t$	1948.1–1949.4, 1950.3–1953.4
$T_r = 18.54 + 0.400N_{Un} + 0.1369t$	1950.1
$T_r = 12.54 + 0.400N_{Un} + 0.1369t$	1950.2
$T_r = -2.95 + 1.565N_{Un} + 0.5069t$	1954.1–1965.2
$T_r = -0.75 + 1.565N_{Un} + 0.5069t$	1965.3–1966.2
$T_r = 0.25 + 1.565N_{Un} + 0.5069t$	1966.3
$T_r = 3.25 + 1.565N_{Un} + 0.5069t$	1966.4
$T_r = 6.55 + 1.565N_{Un} + 0.5069t$	1967.1–1967.4

Personal Income Tax (T_p)

$T_p = -4.41 + .142(PI + SCI - T_r)$	1948.1
$T_p = -3.92 + .125(PI + SCI - T_r)$	1948.2
$T_p = -3.53 + .113(PI + SCI - T_r)$	1948.3–1950.4
$T_p = -22.26 + .210(PI + SCI - T_r)$	1951.1–1953.4
$T_p = -16.91 + .176(PI + SCI - T_r)$	1954.1–1963.4
$T_p = -16.02 + .167(PI + SCI - T_r)$	1964.1
$T_p = -14.91 + .155(PI + SCI - T_r)$	1964.2–1967.4

where:

NI = national income, billions of current dollars

t = time trend, 1948.1 = 1

P_{cb} = corporate profits before taxes, billions of current dollars

IVA = inventory valuation adjustment, billions of current dollars

N_{Un} = number of unemployed, millions

PI = personal income, billions of current dollars

SCI = social insurance contributions by individuals, billions of current dollars

Several different methods were used to adjust the constant terms of the stochastic equations. In all cases, the rules were mechanical and no attempt was made to incorporate extraneous information, as is done in the actual ex ante forecasts. If the single-equation residual of the kth equation at time t is denoted by r_{kt}, then calculate the regression

$$r_{kt} = \rho_k r_{k,t-1} + u_{kt} \qquad\qquad k = 1, \ldots , 47$$

If the estimates of ρ_k are denoted by $\hat{\rho}_k$, then the constant adjustments were calculated in the following manner:

Shorthand notation

(1) $r_{k,t+i} = 0$ $\qquad\qquad\qquad\qquad\qquad b_k = 0$

(2) $r_{k,t+i} = r_{kt}$ $\qquad\qquad\qquad\qquad\qquad b_k = 1$

(3) $r_{k,t+i} = (\hat{\rho}_k)^i r_{kt}$ $\qquad\qquad\qquad\qquad b_k = \hat{\rho}_k$

(4) $r_{k,t+i} = (\hat{\rho}_k)^i r_{kt}$ for $i = 1,2$

$\qquad r_{k,t+i} = 0$ for $i = 3, \ldots ,6$ $\qquad\qquad b_k = \hat{\rho}_k, 0$

(5) $r_{k,t+i} = r_{kt}$ for $i = 1,2$

$\qquad r_{k,t+i} = (\hat{\rho}_k)^i r_{k,t+i}$ for $i = 3, \ldots ,6$ $\qquad b_k = 1, \hat{\rho}_k$

The first two methods state that no constant adjustment was made at all, or that it was equal to the previous period's residual, respectively. Case (2) is, of course, the assumption made implicitly in first-difference forecasting for linear systems. Case (3) stems from a suggestion made by Goldberger;[1] it assumes that the serial correlation present in

[1] A. S. Goldberger, "Best Linear Unbiased Prediction in the Generalized Linear Regression Model," *Journal of the American Statistical Association,* Vol. 57, No. 2 (June, 1962), pp. 369–375.

the sample period will continue into the forecast period. Cases (4) and (5) were added to test the possibility that though errors for the first two periods were rather large, the model tends to get back on the track for spans of three periods or longer. They represent the natural extension of methods (1)–(3).

We now turn to the actual performance of the model at the turning points. If the figures for constant-dollar GNP (symbol X) are compared with the summary statistics given in Evans, Haitovsky, and Treyz, Table 3, it becomes apparent that when no mechanical constant adjustments are used, the model performs much more poorly at turning points than it does for the average of the sample period. The sample-period statistics for the period 1953.1–1964.4 show that with no constant adjustments, the average absolute errors of X for 1, 2, and 3 quarters from solution starting point are $6.9, $7.6, and $7.3 billion, respectively. At the turning points, the figures are $9.9, $10.3, and $10.2 billion. Furthermore, even if the "best" method of adjustment, $b_k = \hat{\rho}_k$, is used, the errors are still $9.8, $9.9, and $9.9 billion, respectively.

In the post-sample period only one turning point observation is available, that of 1966.4. The errors in the ex post forecast of X for that quarter—1, 2, and 3 periods ahead—are $18.5, $18.6, and $18.6 billion; the comparable errors for the 1965.1–1967.4 period are $8.5, $9.8, and $12.9 billion, respectively. In contrast, the ex ante forecasting record of the various Wharton models for the period 1965.1–1967.4 shows errors of $2.8, $4.9, and $5.2 billion, respectively.[2] A further examination of the relevant tables reveals that this comparison is not limited to X but, in fact, extends to almost all of the components of aggregate demand and supply catalogued in these tables.

We now examine the individual tables for the various methods in order to see whether a particular method of constant adjustment yields improved results at peaks compared to troughs, or for certain variables. The over-all summary statistics are given in Tables 1–3. These tables show the number of times a given adjustment method (column designation) makes the best forecasts for the 17 variables being predicted; these 17 variables are the ones being studied for all the models at this

---

[2] This comparison is examined further in Evans, Haitovsky, and Treyz.

TABLE 1

Number of Best Forecasts for Different Adjustment Methods: 17 Variables
(One Quarter Before Turning Points)

b_k	0	1	$\hat{\rho}_k$	$\hat{\rho}_k,0$	$1,\hat{\rho}_k$
All turning points	32	34	31	17	22
1949 T	2	6	0	5	4
1953	2	1	11	1	2
1954 T	6	1	6	2	2
1957	1	13	3	0	0
1958 T	4	1	2	4	6
1960	10	3	1	2	1
1961 T	7	1	6	1	2
1966	0	8	2	2	5
Troughs	19	9	14	12	14
Peaks	13	25	17	5	8

TABLE 2

Number of Best Forecasts for Different Adjustment Methods: 17 Variables
(Two Quarters Before Turning Points)

b_k	0	1	$\hat{\rho}_k$	$\hat{\rho}_k,0$	$1,\hat{\rho}_k$
All turning points	29	19	48	21	19
1949 T	3	1	4	6	3
1953	6	3	7	0	1
1954 T	1	3	9	2	2
1957	2	1	9	3	2
1958 T	11	2	2	1	1
1960	4	0	7	3	3
1961 T	1	1	9	5	1
1966	1	8	1	1	6
Troughs	16	7	24	14	7
Peaks	13	12	24	7	12

TABLE 3

*Number of Best Forecasts for Different Adjustment Methods: 17 Variables
(Three Quarters Before Turning Points)*

b_k	0	1	$\hat{\rho}_k$	$\hat{\rho}_k,0$	$1,\hat{\rho}_k$
All turning points	28	28	45	13	22
1949 T	2	2	12	1	0
1953	3	3	11	0	0
1954 T	2	3	11	1	0
1957	8	2	2	2	3
1958 T	6	5	1	3	2
1960	1	2	5	2	7
1961 T	4	5	2	2	4
1966	2	6	1	2	6
Troughs	14	15	26	7	6
Peaks	14	13	19	6	16

Conference.[3] The scores are given for each turning point (row designation). For the entire sample and ex post forecast period (hereafter referred to as the extended sample period), the methods $b_k = 0$, 1, or $\hat{\rho}_k$ appear to be roughly equal in their predictive efficacy and somewhat superior to methods 4 or 5. It might seem that the $b_k = \hat{\rho}_k$ method is somewhat superior for the forecasts 2 and 3 quarters ahead. However, its superiority is registered only for the first three turning points, which fall before, and immediately after, the Korean War. Since many of the equations of the latest version of the Wharton-EFU Model are estimated for the post-Korean War period alone, it might be reasonable to focus our attention on the post-1954 results.

For that period, it would seem that there is little difference between the first three methods, and that, in fact, only the fourth ($b_k = \hat{\rho}_k,0$) is definitely inferior. It is hard to apply much meaning to standard statistical tests for five observations; the statistics, in any case, show no significant deviation from normality in distributions of any of the summary totals. Similarly, categorizing the methods into performance at peaks and troughs does not yield clear-cut superiority

[3] Six-quarter simulations, starting 1, 2, and 3 quarters before each turning point, were made for each peak or trough. The "best" forecast is the one with the lowest root-mean-squared error in the turning point calculations.

for any of the methods. For the 1-quarter solutions, it appears that $b_k = 1$ does better at the peaks, but this is not supported by the other quarters. Similarly, the $1,\hat{\rho}_k$ method does well at troughs for the 1-quarter solutions but performs poorly for 2 and 3 quarters ahead. The tendency for the "best" method to shift over time is shown in Table 4, where it can be seen that the method $b_k = \hat{\rho}_k$ does better for almost every variable during the first three turning points but is somewhat worse than the no-adjustment assumption for the rest of the sample, and than the $b_k = 1$ assumption for the extended sample. This would suggest that choosing a given method on the basis of extended-sample-period results might lead to some difficulties when applying the material to ex ante forecasting. If there is any conclusion to be drawn from these results, it is that for the methods tried, no one mechanical method seemed to have much to recommend it over any other.

It should be stressed that these results are based on complete system solutions rather than on single-equation results. Thus, the large error for, say, consumption, might be due not to large errors in the consumption function itself but to poor predictions of disposable income. In the limiting case, there is no stochastic equation for X at all, since it

TABLE 4

Aggregation of Best Forecasts for All Three Periods Before Turning Points

b_k	0	1	$\hat{\rho}_k$	$\hat{\rho}_k,0$	$1,\hat{\rho}_k$
All turning points	89	81	124	51	63
First four turning points	38	39	85	23	19
Second four turning points	51	42	39	28	44
First three turning points	27	23	71	18	14
Next four turning points	59	36	49	28	32
Last turning point	3	22	4	5	17

NOTE: Two or more different methods are assumed to have done equally well if the difference in the error is less than 0.1 per cent of the actual value. Ties were calculated as $\frac{1}{2}$, $\frac{1}{3}$, $\frac{1}{4}$, or $\frac{1}{5}$ of a point, but in these tables, all results have been rounded to the nearest integer.

is merely identical to the sum of all components of aggregate demand. Yet, it may still be of interest to compare the size of the errors for individual variables, using different adjustment methods. In the first place, the statistics of Tables 1–4 may obscure the results for over-all important summary variables, such as output, prices, or unemployment. Second, some equations, such as those for interest rates or net foreign balance, are not so closely tied to the over-all structure; thus we might be able to improve over-all forecasts by adjusting the equations in these semi-exogenous sectors with a method different from that used in other equations. The evidence for this suggestion is given in Table 5. In order to conserve space, we list only the combined statistics for 1–3 periods ahead of each turning point. The results are not substantially changed by this aggregation.

The results presented in Table 5 suggest that for over-all summary variables (personal income, GNP, and unemployment) the method

TABLE 5

Best Adjustment Method for Each of 17 Variables: All Turning Points (All Three Periods Before Turning Points)

b_k	0	1	$\hat\rho_k$	$\hat\rho_k,0$	$1,\hat\rho_k$
i_s	7	7	4	4	2
i_L	6	7	8	1	2
I_p	5	4	9	1	5
p	4	7	6	5	2
U	10	2	6	4	2
I_h	2	3	4	13	2
PI	4	5	13	0	2
P_{cb}	5	4	8	2	5
$GNP\$$	7	2	10	1	4
X	7	3	7	2	5
Un	2	2	8	3	9
C	12	4	3	5	0
ΔI_i	4	4	9	3	4
B	1	8	9	1	5
E	3	6	8	3	4
H	6	5	6	1	6
w_r	4	8	6	2	4
	89	81	124	51	63

$b_k = \hat{\rho}_k$ gives somewhat superior results. However, among individual components, some of the other methods do much better. For example, unfilled orders — which category contains a large exogenous component determined mainly by spending needs of the military — is predicted best by using $b_k = 0$, and worst by $b_k = 1$, or $b_k = 1,\hat{\rho}_k$. Somewhat more surprising is the fact that consumption seems to be predicted best with $b_k = 0$, even though it is a relatively smooth series, and income is predicted best by the method $b_k = \hat{\rho}_k$. The $b_k = \hat{\rho}_k,0$ method works poorly for all variables except residential construction, and this may be due to the built-in serial correlation for two periods in that series, caused by the method OBE uses to convert housing starts to actual investment.

It should be pointed out that while $b_k = \hat{\rho}_k$ does seem to perform better for the extended sample period, problems mentioned at the beginning of this section (such as data revision) may mean that methods closer to $b_k = 1$ could prove to be more reasonable. However, these results tentatively suggest that for those equations where there have been no noticeable shifts in data or structure, an adjustment based on the auto-correlation coefficients of the individual equations may improve forecast accuracy.

LONG-RUN SIMULATIONS

ALTHOUGH the Wharton-EFU Model is primarily designed for short-run forecasting (as are the other models being considered at this Conference), and is primarily subjected to the tests or applications considered in the previous section, it is both worthwhile and interesting to simulate the model over longer periods of time.

In short-run testing, both ex post and ex ante forecasts have been considered. For the longer-run simulations, we have, in a sense, made ex post forecasts by simulating the model over the extended-sample period. In this case, we have actual performance data with which to check the model results. Equally interesting from the viewpoint of business-cycle analysis, however, is the simulation of the model over a hypothetical stretch of future time. Although it would be possible to view this long-run simulation as an ex ante forecast, we would prefer to regard it purely as a hypothetical simulation for the purpose of studying cyclical response characteristics of the system, inasmuch as the exogenous input was not carefully considered for true prediction purposes. It was simply extrapolated along reasonable trend paths from its own history, or so as to smooth approaches to targets for endogenous variables.

The major difference, of course, between the long- and short-run extrapolations is in the treatment of initial conditions. The short-run extrapolations (either ex post or ex ante) are *re-initialized* before every six- or eight-quarter extrapolation. Lagged values of endogenous variables are set at observed levels (ex post) or most recently observed levels (ex ante). Exogenous variables are retrospectively put at observed levels, and prospectively put at levels determined by judgments of future developments.

For the longer-run simulation over the historical sample period, lagged values are set initially at conditions prevailing before 1948.3, and are not adjusted during the course of the simulation exercise. Lagged inputs for subsequent periods are developed as needed by the solution of the system. As in the case of the short-run solutions over the sample period, exogenous variables are assigned observed values. Pre-1948.3 variables and exogenous variables are given; the model accounts for the rest of the solution. The end of the sample occurs in 1964.4, but the solution is extended until 1968.1.

The other longer-run simulation begins in 1968.3 and runs forward for one-hundred quarters. It is entirely outside sample experience, and is largely in the future, as we perceive it now. This solution is programmed for realistic initial (lagged) inputs as of 1968.3, and starts with initial exogenous variables that have realistic values. For the rest, exogenous inputs, mainly reflecting fiscal and monetary policy of central authorities, are fixed at values that attempt to keep the economy on a long-run growth path of approximately 4 per cent unemployment, with interest rates between 4 and 5 per cent.

Two special situations must be dealt with in the longer-run simulations. Over the sample period, there must be an attempt to deal with the dislocations caused by the Korean War; while over the future period, there must be some final settlement of the Vietnam War. Both these wars are major economic disturbances. To some extent, the

Korean episode is accounted for by special variables in the model, introduced for estimation purposes; but these are inadequate to handle the extreme movements that occurred in import demand and inventory investment. Stockpiling of basic materials and speculation distorted these magnitudes. We have, accordingly, adjusted inventory and trade equations upward and downward at strategic quarters, in order to account for the largest disturbances appearing as equation residuals. There is a similar adjustment needed for the export equation in late 1949 and 1950, because of the ineffectiveness of the devaluation of September, 1949.[4] There are no other adjustments to the model equations for the sample-period simulation, except to reflect changes in tax-transfer laws; or where explicitly introduced, through dummy variables that are listed with the model estimates.

The economic implications of a Vietnam settlement are more problematical. We have made the following assumptions: (1) A cease-fire and demobilization would begin in 1970.1. Over a period of six quarters, the military establishment would be cut back by 350,000 men. Military spending would be reduced by $11.1 billion at 1958 prices, spread over six quarters. Taxes would be reduced by the ending of the surcharge. Correspondingly, civilian expenditures would gradually increase, so that total spending falls only slightly for two quarters in real terms and never drops in current prices. This fiscal policy counteracts the decline in military expenditures, and monetary policy becomes easier through a drop in the discount rate of 0.5 percentage points. Net free reserves are held steady at $200 million.

The outcome produced by these assumptions is a pause in growth during the 1970 transition phase, allowing unemployment to reach 5.5 per cent, but an actual recession, such as the one that occurred after the Korean War, does not take place. The dimensions of the demobilization and peace settlement are nearly as great in absolute (not in percentage) terms as those that followed Korea, but it is assumed that wise government policy will enable us to avoid a similar recession. The temporary rise in unemployment is quickly corrected. Then there is a

[4] Our export equation, through relative price effects, suggests that U.S. exports should have dropped considerably after the devaluation, but this did not happen, because European nations could not increase supply at that time, and because U.S. exports were being used to reconstruct Europe.

movement toward the long-run growth trajectory of the economy. Steady taxes, steady monetary controls, growth in government spending, normal population growth, and normal growth in world trade all make a long-run growth in real GNP that keeps the economy at an unemployment rate of approximately 4 per cent.

In order to produce this result, however, we must go beyond our usual range of short-run assumptions about productivity, labor force growth, and length of the work week. Trends are introduced in the equations associated with these variables so that the unemployment rate does not fall below 3.77 per cent. Some of the equations explaining hours worked, or labor-force participation, would not produce reasonable long-term results unless they were adjusted throughout the solution period. The hours equations depend negatively on the wage rate, which rises steadily over the rest of the century. These equations are short-run equations in the model, and are not particularly well suited to such long-run exercises. The number of self-employed, farm and nonfarm, must be placed on a long-run time path (exogenously) so as to yield the desired unemployment rate. These are difficulties that arise in programming a short-run model for a long-run study. It is by no means a simple mechanical exercise.

These considerations are relevant for the deterministic solutions. In the hypothetical future simulation, we regard the deterministic case as a *base-line* solution. We then produced fifty replications of stochastic versions of this solution. Each equation of the model is written as

$$y_{it} = g_i(y_{1,t}, \ldots, y_{nt} y_{1,t-1}, \ldots, y_{n,t-p} x_{1t}, \ldots, x_{mt}) + e_{1t}$$

$$i = 1, 2, \ldots, n$$

There are n dependent (endogenous) variables and m independent (exogenous) variables. Lags of up to the pth order occur in the dependent variables. The system is written in a somewhat arbitrary way, with one (different) dependent variable isolated on the left-hand side. In general, the equations are nonlinear and are specified by parameters that have been estimated from sample data. The expected value of each e_{it} is zero, and the deterministic solutions are obtained by using point estimates of the parameters of the g_i functions, together with zero values for e_{it}. In stochastic solutions, we substitute random drawings for each of the e_{it}. The random numbers are normally distributed variates that have the same variance-covariance matrix as the sample residuals. This variance-covariance matrix is an estimate of

$$\Sigma = [Ee_{it}e_{jt}]$$

The method of drawing the random numbers is that suggested by Michael D. McCarthy.[5] It consists of forming the matrix

$$R = \begin{bmatrix} r_{11} & \cdots & r_{1G} \\ \cdot & & \cdot \\ \cdot & & \cdot \\ \cdot & & \cdot \\ r_{T1} & \cdots & r_{TG} \end{bmatrix}$$

of residuals in each of G equations for a sample period of length T. Thus, each column of R is a T-element vector of residuals from one of the structural equations. The next step is to draw random numbers from a normal distribution with zero mean and unit variance.

$$N = \begin{bmatrix} n_{11} & \cdots & n_{1T} \\ \cdot & & \cdot \\ \cdot & & \cdot \\ \cdot & & \cdot \\ n_{S1} & \cdots & n_{ST} \end{bmatrix}$$

Each row of N is a vector of independent unit normal deviates of length equal to the sample span, T. There are as many rows in N as there are future periods of simulation. Thus we provide for one-hundred periods of stochastic simulation. The matrix product

$$V = \frac{1}{\sqrt{T}} NR$$

provides an $S \times G$ matrix of disturbances that have the same variance-covariance matrix as the sample estimate of Σ. This is the McCarthy

[5] See the Appendix by Michael D. McCarthy, pp. 185–191.

technique. It is essentially a scrambling of the sample residuals that preserves their variance-covariance matrix.

The random numbers in N are taken from the Rand Corporation table of random numbers.[6] In the fifty replications of this procedure, we enter the table (or tape) each time at a random position and draw ST successive numbers. For the Wharton-EFU Model, $G = 51$, and $T = 44$. We do not use the whole sample length, since some of the equations introduced at a later stage — in model estimation of an enlarged financial sector — were based on a shorter sample, from 1954.1 to 1964.4.[7]

Some of the equations are identities, and we did not shock these equations in the stochastic simulations. We shocked only the 51 behavioral, institutional, and technological equations.

Another detail requires explanation. In some of the equations, different normalizations were used for estimation and for solution. In the equation for consumer expenditures on nondurables and services, C_{ns}/Y is the normalized variable for *estimation,* while C_{ns} is the normalized variable for *solution.* Similarly, in the production functions, we normalized on log X_m, or log X_n, for estimation, but on N_m, or N_n, for solution. Since our solution program is written in such a way that it is easy to perturb, period by period, the constant term of each equation in the form that is normalized for solution, we have not shocked each equation in exactly the form that we assume random components for estimation theory. This has the effect of introducing some heteroscedasticity into the stochastic simulations.

If the random numbers are independently drawn, the successive elements within columns of V will be independent

$$Ev_{ti}v_{t-j,i} = 0 \qquad j \neq 0$$

The shock procedure preserves variances and unlagged correlations across equation residuals; it does not preserve serial properties, either within, or across, equation residuals. McCarthy has shown how serial properties can be preserved if we modify his procedure as follows: the rows of N should not be independent in this case. The first row will

[6] Rand Corporation, *A Million Random Digits with 100,000 Normal Deviates* (Glencoe, The Free Press, 1955).

[7] In the short-run solutions, the revised and extended monetary equations were not used, as explained in the previous section.

consist of a T-element series of independent unit normal deviates. The second row will consist of the first T-1 elements of the first row shifted one place to the right, and a new independent drawing will be made for the vacant first position. The third row will consist of the first T-1 elements of the second row, shifted one place to the right and an independent drawing, and so on. The whole matrix will be

$$
N^* = \begin{pmatrix}
n_1 & n_2 & n_3 & \cdots & n_T \\
n_{T+1} & n_1 & n_2 & & n_{T-1} \\
n_{t+2} & n_{T+1} & n_1 & & n_{T-2} \\
& \cdot & & & \cdot \\
& \cdot & & & \cdot \\
& \cdot & & & \\
n_{T+S-1} & n_{T+S-2} & n_{T+S-3} & \cdots & n_S
\end{pmatrix}
$$

In this case

$$
V^* = \frac{1}{\sqrt{T}} N^* R
$$

will have the expected variances, covariances, and lag correlations (within and between disturbance series) equal to corresponding sample values obtained from the residual matrix.

Our stochastic simulation differs from the well-known stochastic simulation of the Klein-Goldberger Model by I. and F. Adelman in the following four respects:[8]

(*i*) Our simulations are quarterly; theirs are annual.

(*ii*) Our covariance matrix of errors has nonzero (sample) covariances; theirs has zero covariances.

(*iii*) Our covariance matrix of errors permits nonzero serial correlations; their errors are serially uncorrelated.

(*iv*) Our stochastic simulations are replicated (fifty times); theirs is a single run.

[8] Irma Adelman and Frank L. Adelman, "The Dynamic Properties of the Klein-Goldberger Model," *Econometrica*, 27 (October, 1959), pp. 596–625.

DISCUSSION OF THE RESULTS

The first simulations from the longer-run solutions are like those from the first short-run solutions. The historical simulations begin in 1948.3 and continue beyond the end of the sample (1964.4) until 1968.1. The results are graphed in Charts 1–8 for some leading variables. The downturn of 1953 and the recovery of 1954 provide the first relevant cyclical test period for the model, beginning from initial conditions in 1948.3. The recession-recovery period of 1953 is generally well represented by the model. In the case of 1957–58 and 1960–61, many of the relevant calculated series do not actually turn down and then turn up. At best, they slow down, or pause, in these recession phases. Cyclical performance, however, is mixed. Many of the estimated series are smoother than observed series. Major deviations (either shocks or cyclical swings) are often missed in amplitude, and sometimes in direction. The computed series show steady growth, right through periods of wide actual movement up and down.

Apart from the behavior at turning points, many of the series start from approximately the correct position in 1948.3 and end at the right value for 1964.4. Some residual variables, such as net exports and corporate profits, are exceptions. They start to drift substantially at the end of the sample run and continue on a divergent course. The correspondence for personal income, GNP, and other aggregates is remarkably good. Although the computed general price level does not rise fast enough during the 1960's, the estimate of real GNP turns out to have the general drift of the actual series. It rises more than actually occurred after 1960, but the price deflator rises a few points below observed index values. These compensating errors leave GNP in current prices on the right trend path for the whole extended sample period. Although GNP and other very broad aggregates are projected fairly closely throughout the historical simulation, some of the components show bigger discrepancies. Total consumer expenditures, for example, are biased upward for the whole calculation.

Associated with the under-prediction of inflation is a low projection of wage rates. At the end of the sample and beyond, computed wage rates are below actual wage values. On the other hand, interest

CHART 1

GNP (*Current Prices*)

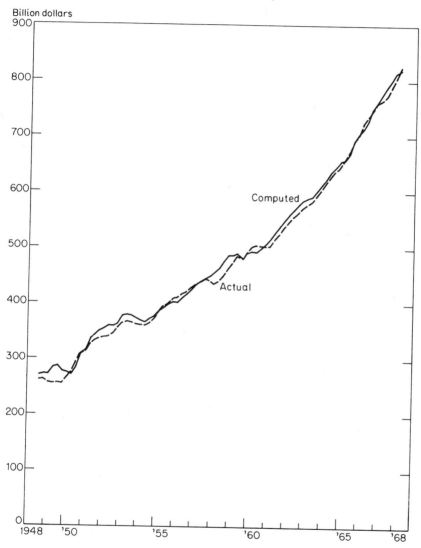

CHART 2

GNP (1958 Prices)

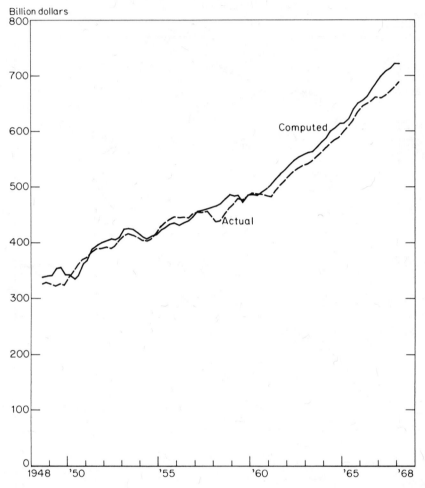

rates, which are strongly influenced by exogenous variables, are closely projected for the entire period.

The correspondence is closer for most series during the sample period than in the ex post extrapolations from 1964.4 to 1968.1. It should be remarked that the better extrapolations in the sample period are not based on a resetting of the initial conditions, and that many of the basic series have undergone extensive revision for the period since 1964.4. Some of the series have been revised for the last three sample-years, as well.

Noteworthy features of the longer-run simulation starting from 1968.3 are the persistent, steady growth of the economy (real GNP grows from \$703 billion in 1968.3 to \$1,663 billion in 1993.2), just under 4 per cent annually; the divergent movement of prices (consumer durable goods come down in price after about six years, while services grow on a steady uptrend); and the eventual transition from government deficits to surpluses during the final third of the calculation. The economy is not cycle-free in this period. Capacity utilization, unemployment, inventory change, and other strongly cyclical variables show much rhythmic variation, but aggregate output stays close to its trend growth path. The implied management of the economy is responsible for the better results.

The stochastic solutions do, however, exhibit discernible cyclical

CHART 3

P (GNP Deflator)

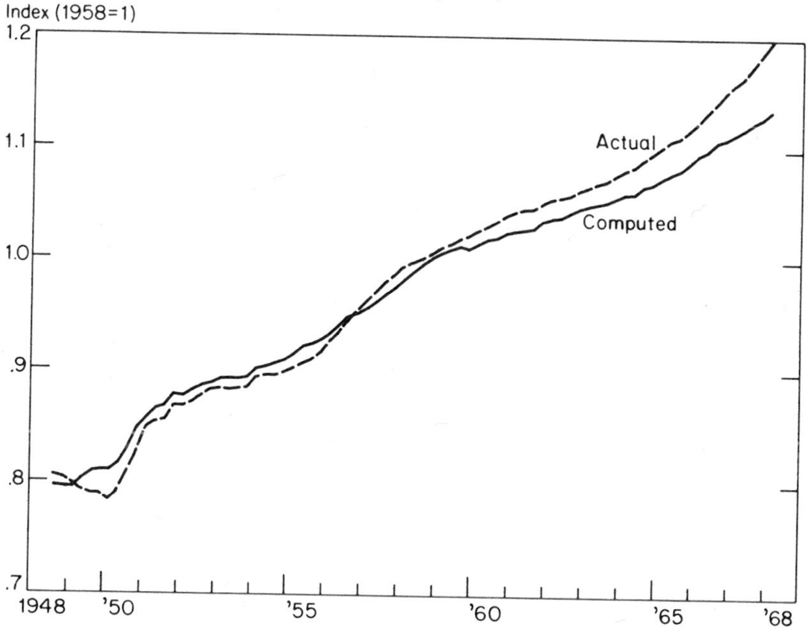

Index (1958=1)

CHART 4

I_p *(Fixed Investment)*

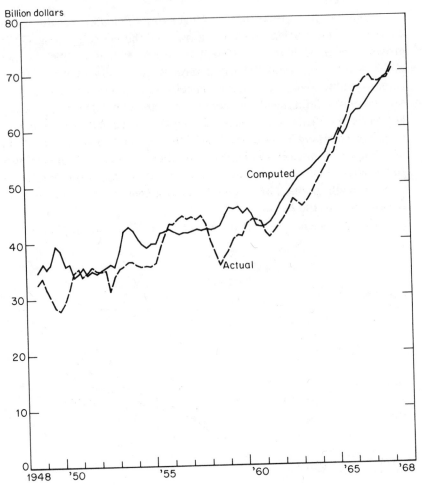

behavior. In the fifty replications, there is much variability in cyclical performance, but the time chart of real *GNP* from a single one of the stochastic simulations of one-hundred quarters shows that there is cyclical movement (see Chart 9). This particular movement appears to oscillate about its trend approximately every ten quarters. This is a comparatively short cycle, but if the implied fiscal and monetary policies are being used to keep the economy on a 4 per cent unemployment course for twenty-five years, it is not unreasonable to find that the only evident cycle is the true inventory cycle of no more than two and a half years.

Two of the more cyclical variables of the model are the unemployment rate and residential construction expenditures; these are graphed in Charts 10 and 11. Even at the nonstochastic level, they show some cyclical variation, and this becomes more pronounced when random errors are introduced into the solution.

While the cyclical behavior of most variables in the system became more measurable in the stochastic, than in the nonstochastic, simulations, they seem to improve (in the sense of being more like the textbook case) when the random shocks to the system are programmed

CHART 5

I_s (Short-Term Interest Rate)

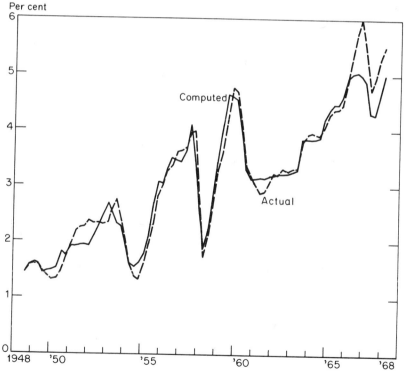

CHART 6

W_r (Wage Rate)

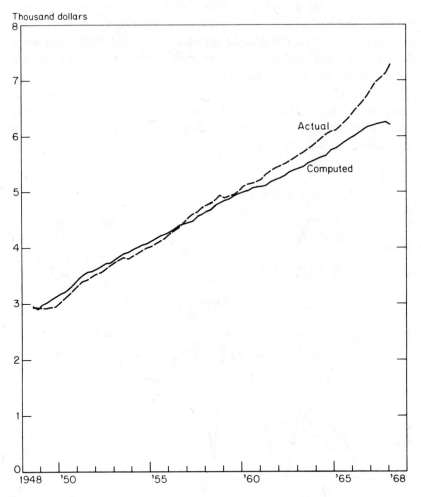

CHART 7
E (*Employment*)

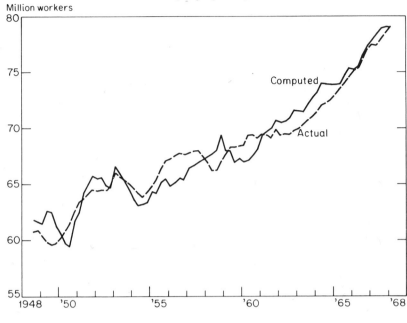

Million workers

Computed

Actual

CHART 8
U_n (*Unemployment Rate*)

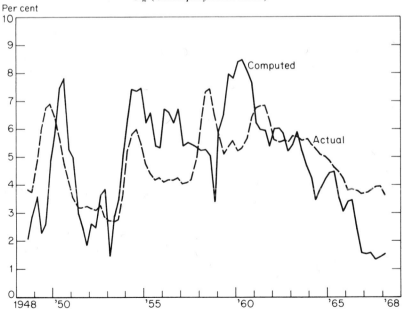

Per cent

Computed

Actual

CHART 9

GNP: Stochastic Simulations (1958 Prices)

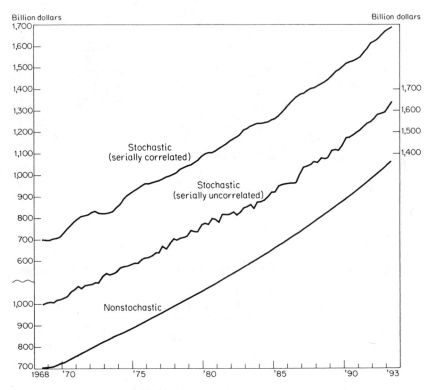

with the same serial dependence found in the sample residuals. For these variants of the stochastic simulations, the cycles are smoother and longer. In a corresponding simulation of one-hundred quarters, where we previously observed a ten-quarter cycle in real *GNP*, we now observe a more discernible cycle of close to sixteen quarters. This is the established average cycle-length put forward by the National Bureau of Economic Research.

Not only in the particular series plotted are smooth cycles exhibited in the serially correlated stochastic simulations, but throughout the whole model solution. The most satisfying simulation, from the point of view of business-cycle analysis, appears to be a stochastic simulation with serially dependent random errors.

A SPECTRAL ANALYSIS OF THE STOCHASTIC SIMULATIONS

A MORE careful analysis of cyclical characteristics can be evolved from the spectral density functions for such variables as real *GNP*, consumer expenditures, fixed capital formation, residential construction, inventory change, material imports, and the unemployment rate. For all fifty replications, we have made spectral analyses of leading variables, and will report, selectively, those listed above.

CHART 10

U_n (*Unemployment Rate*)

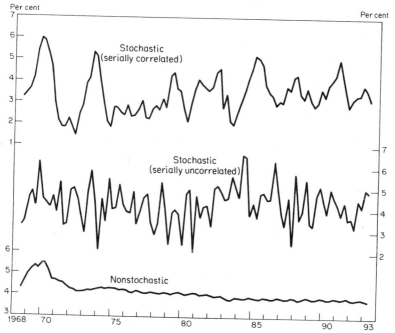

CHART 11

I_h (*Residential Construction, 1958 Prices*)

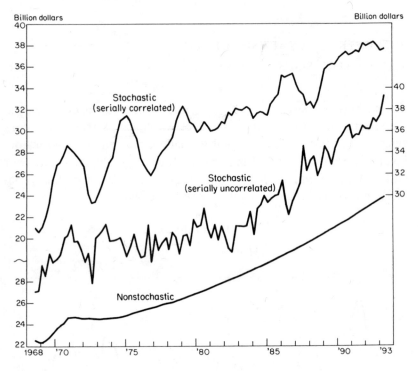

Before presenting the results, the procedure of calculation may be stated:

(1) All the spectra are estimated by

$$f(w_j) = \tfrac{1}{2}\lambda_o R_o + \sum_{k=1}^{m} \lambda_k R_k \cos (w_j k),$$

$$w_j = \frac{\pi_j}{N} \quad \text{and} \quad j = 0,1, \ldots ,N,$$

where R_k is the estimate of the auto-correlation coefficient, and λ_k is the weight of the filter using a Parzen window, i.e.,

$$\lambda_k = 1 - \frac{6k^2}{m^2}\left(1 - \frac{k}{m}\right), \qquad 0 \leqslant k \leqslant m/2,$$

$$= 2\left(1 - \frac{k}{m}\right)^3, \qquad m/2 \leqslant k \leqslant m$$

The m and N stand respectively for the number of lags and the number of points at which the spectrum is evaluated.

(2) The spectra are calculated for the deviations of the variables from fitted semilog trends, except for inventory investment. The presence of growth trends obscures the cyclical characteristics that would be revealed in the spectral density function. In the stochastic simulation, inventory investment sometimes takes a negative value; thus, an exponential trend cannot be estimated for this variable.

(3) The (nonstochastic) projected values of the first several quarters are obtained by taking into consideration the effect of demobilization, and provide relatively large fluctuations, compared with the values of the later period; therefore, the first ten quarters are dropped in the computation of the spectra. The spectrum is evaluated at 40 points.

STOCHASTIC SIMULATION WITH SERIALLY UNCORRELATED ERROR TERMS

GNP IN CONSTANT DOLLARS (X)

Spectral density functions of real GNP in the fifty replications of stochastic simulations may be grouped by the number of peaks. For each case of one, two, and three peaks, typical examples of the spectral histogram are given in Chart 12, where the period is measured horizontally; and the percentage spectrum, vertically. In picking out peaks of the spectrum cycles, we may exclude periods in excess of forty quarters from consideration, since ninety observations are not enough to warrant definite decisions. With this consideration, the peak

CHART 12

Spectral Densities GNP (1958 Dollars)

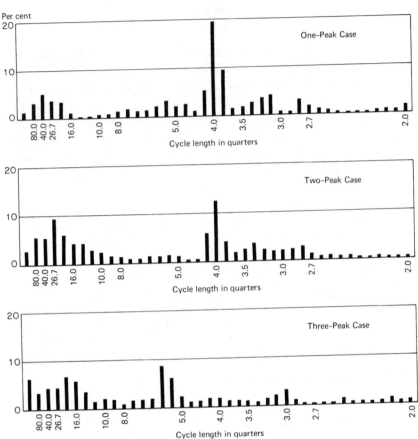

of the first diagram occurs at 4.0 quarters only. Similarly, it is seen from the other two diagrams that peaks occur at 4.0 and 26.7 quarters in a two-peak example; and at 3.0, 5.7, and 20.0 quarters in a three-peak case. Although the procedure of counting the peaks is to some degree subjective, it is useful for describing the general features of the results. Table 6 presents the number of runs of each case. The two-peak case occurs in about 40 per cent of total runs; one- and three-peak cases each occur in about 20 per cent; while other cases occur in

TABLE 6

Frequency of Peaks
(Serially Uncorrelated)

Variable	Number of Peaks				
	0	1	2	3	Over 4
(1) X	6	10	19	10	5
(2) C	14	19	14	3	0
(3) I_p	19	15	11	5	0
(4) I_h	18	2	14	11	5
(5) ΔI_i	4	14	12	9	11
(6) F_{im}	10	9	16	11	4
(7) Un	2	18	13	14	3

the remaining 20 per cent. Chart 13 shows the frequency histogram of the position of the peak for each case. It is seen that there is a concentration of peaks at approximately 4.0 quarters in the one-peak and three-peak cases, and, though less distinct, near 16.0 and 4.0 quarters in the two-peak case.

Chart 14a shows the frequency histogram of the GNP peak positions for all those included in the one- to four-peak cases. From the diagram we find four types of cycles in the behavior of GNP:

	Range of Period (Quarters)	Peak in Each Range (Quarters)	Frequency
(1)	26.7–10.0	26.7	29
(2)	8.9–5.3	5.7	20
(3)	5.0–3.5	4.0	38
(4)	3.3–2.0	3.0	11

Here, frequency implies the number of times that the GNP peak positions fall in each range. The 5.0–3.5 range has the highest frequency, and the 26.7–10.0 range the second highest. Chart 14b is the frequency histogram of the peak position for the highest peak of each run. Simi-

CHART 13

Spectrum Cycles GNP: One to Three Peaks

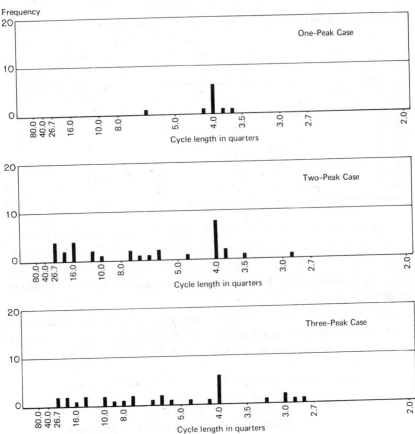

lar to Chart 14*a*, there are concentrations in the 26.7–10.0, and 5.0–3.5, ranges, while the highest peak appears less frequently in the 8.9–5.3, and 3.3–2.0, ranges.

I. and F. Adelman found the average length of a cycle in *one* stochastic simulation of 93 years to be 4.0 years.[9] In our *fifty* replications, the peaks of the spectrum in the range of 26.7–13.3 quarters (or 6.6–3.3 years) occur in 24 out of 50 cases (48 per cent of all trials), and 16 of these 24 peaks are the largest peak of each run. In addition, our results,

[9] Adelman and Adelman, *op. cit.*

based on the quarterly model, disclose that shorter cycles (11.4–6.2 quarters) occur with a lower probability, while 4-quarter cycles occur with a higher probability.

CONSUMPTION (*C*)

As shown in Table 6, the one-peak case is more frequent in the spectral histogram of consumption than in that of *GNP*, while the case of three or more peaks occurs infrequently. Charts 15*a* and 15*b* present the histogram of the peak position of the consumption spectrum for all peaks, and for the highest peak, respectively. Comparison between consumption and *GNP* (or other variables, as shown later) reveals that concentration of the peak on 4.0 quarters is much more striking in consumption than in *GNP* (or other variables), while both

CHART 14

Spectrum Cycles GNP: One to Four Peaks

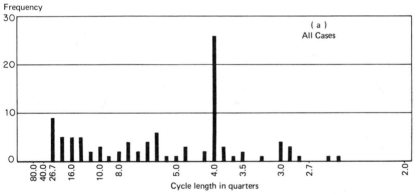

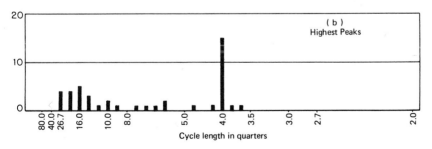

CHART 15

Consumption: Serially Uncorrelated Error Terms
(Histogram of Peaks)

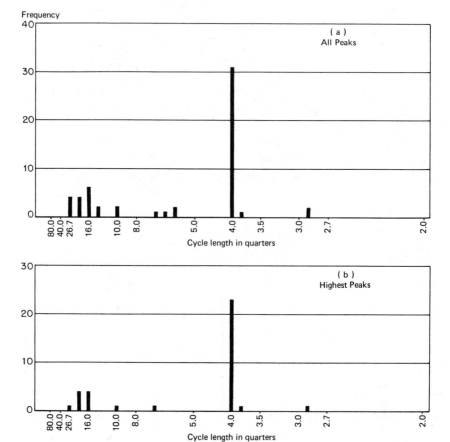

indicate similar patterns in the distribution of cycles of the other quarters. This suggests that the consumption and related equations with stochastic terms tend to generate a cyclical movement of 4.0 quarters.[10] This cycle might be ascribed to the wage-determination

[10] Since seasonally adjusted series were used in estimating the equations, it is very unlikely that the seasonality of consumption causes the four-quarter cycle in our model. If the simulation path of each variable is seasonally adjusted, the spectral diagrams reveal no presence of the yearly cycle, but the computed seasonal patterns vary greatly for any variable among the fifty replications. This suggests that seasonal movement, in the usual sense, is not responsible for the four-quarter cycles found in our simulation.

process. Since the wage equations in the manufacturing and non-manufacturing sectors have a four-quarter lag, a four-quarter cycle may occur in wage rates and, thus, in income and consumption.

The basis for the yearly cycle may be deduced from the following considerations. In an approximation to our wage equation

$$w - w_{-4} = \alpha_1 Un + \alpha_o + e$$

we may disregard fluctuations in Un, since the simulation is designed to keep the unemployment rate nearly steady at 4 per cent over the long-run equilibrium growth-path. The characteristic roots of the homogeneous equation are ± 1.0 and $\pm i$. The complex roots will provide a maintained cycle of four quarters. If we extend our equation to the form

$$w - w_{-4} = \alpha_1 Un + \alpha_2(w_{-4} - w_{-8}) + \alpha_o + e,$$

the corresponding characteristic roots are

$$\pm 1, \pm i, \left(\frac{\alpha_2}{4}\right)^{1/4}(1 \pm i), > \left(\frac{\alpha_2}{4}\right)^{1/4}(1 \pm i)$$

If α_2 is small (0.2 in our model for the manufacturing sector), the dominant cyclical roots will still be $\pm i$.

It is interesting to note that the wage-price subsector of a model of the U.K., where this form of four-quarter wage adjustment was introduced some time ago, also has a yearly cycle.[11]

PRIVATE FIXED INVESTMENT (I_p)

As shown in Table 6, there is no distinct peak in the investment spectrum in 19 out of 50 runs, while the one- and two-peak cases occur with frequencies of 15 and 11, respectively. Chart 16a provides the distribution of the peak position for all the peaks of 50 runs. This diagram bears a closer similarity to that of GNP than to any other variable, suggesting a close relationship between investment and general economic fluctuations.

Chart 16b describes the distribution of the largest peak. Here, we find a concentration in the region of 26.7–10.0 quarters (or 6.6–2.5 years), which corresponds to the standard business-cycle.

[11] See L. R. Klein, R. J. Ball, A. Hazlewood, and P. Vandome, *An Econometric Model of the U.K.* (Oxford, Blackwell, 1961). Appendix III, p. 269.

CHART 16

Fixed Investment (Histogram of Peaks)

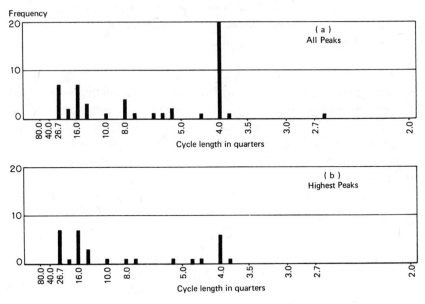

RESIDENTIAL CONSTRUCTION (I_h)

Charts 17*a* and 17*b* present the histogram of the peak positions of the spectrum for all peaks, and for the largest peak, respectively. The latter shows that the greater part of the largest peaks are concentrated in the range in excess of 7.3 quarters, indicating a longer period for construction cycles. Further, it should be noted that the former, unlike the diagrams of the other variables, has very few peaks in the range 4.4–3.6 quarters.

INVENTORY INVESTMENT (ΔI_i)

Charts 18*a* and 18*b* refer to inventory investment. When compared with the corresponding figure of the other variables, Chart 18*a* indicates that the number of cases in which the peak of the spectrum falls in the range 10.0–5.0 quarters is relatively large in inventory

CHART 17

Residential Construction (*Histogram of Peaks*)

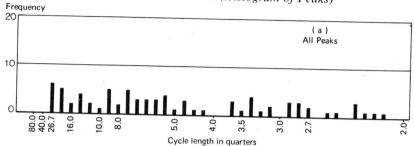

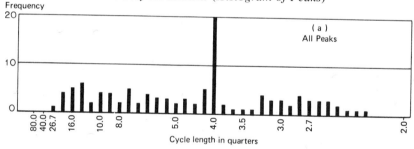

CHART 18

Inventory Investment (*Histogram of Peaks*)

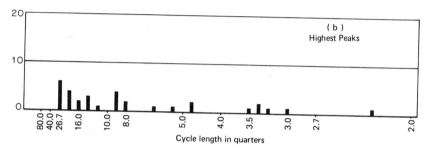

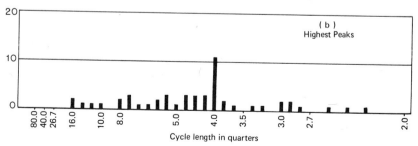

173

investment. Chart 18*b*, relating to the largest peak, gives some support to this finding. This is the time-honored distinction in business-cycle theory between the *business cycle* (Juglar) and *inventory cycles.*

IMPORTS OF MATERIALS (F_{im})

Charts 19*a* and 19*b* suggest that the patterns of the spectral distribution of material imports, apart from the frequency of the 4-quarter cycle, are similar to those of inventory investment. The cycles of 8.9–5.0 periods are relatively frequent in both figures.

THE UNEMPLOYMENT RATE (Un)

It can be seen from Charts 20*a* and 20*b* that there is a large concentration at 4.0 quarters in the diagrams, both for all peaks, and for the highest peaks. Their patterns are similar to those for consumption.

CHART 19

Material Imports (Histogram of Peaks)

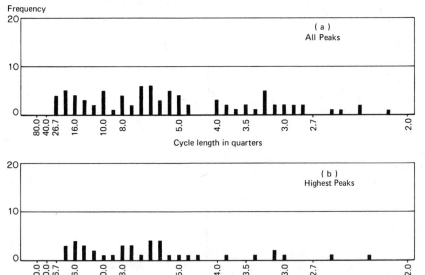

CHART 20

Unemployment Rate (Histogram of Peaks)

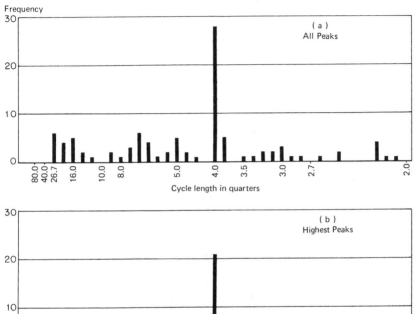

STOCHASTIC SIMULATIONS WITH SERIALLY CORRELATED ERROR TERMS

THE stochastic solutions with serially *correlated* random terms present outcomes substantially different from those with serially *uncorrelated* errors. First, the movements of each variable of the serially correlated scheme are much smoother. As a result, their cyclical patterns are much more distinct. Second, the period of the dominant cycle of all the variables treated here lies in the range of 26.7–10.0 quarters.

TABLE 7

Frequency of Peaks
(Serially Correlated)

	Number of Peaks				
Variable	0	1	2	3	Over 4
(1) X	3	25	16	6	0
(2) C	8	17	12	13	0
(3) I_p	3	32	11	3	1
(4) I_h	2	42	5	1	0
(5) ΔI_i	1	15	15	12	7
(6) F_{im}	0	8	22	13	7
(7) Un	0	8	26	14	2

In most of 50 replications, the spectra of real GNP present either the one-peak case, with a peak around 16.0 quarters; or the two-peak case, with two peaks around 16.0 and 4.0 quarters (see Table 7). As shown in Charts 21a and 21b, the position of the highest peak of each run occurs in the range of 26.7–10.0 quarters in 46 out of 50 replications; another concentration of the peak positions, though less frequent and less strong, is found in the range of 5.0–3.5 quarters. The results for consumption, fixed investment, and residential construction, as shown in Charts 22 to 24, are quite similar to those for real GNP. However, the peak positions of fixed investment and residential construction reveal more distinct concentration in 16.0 quarters; in particular, the highest peaks for residential construction—in all cases but one—occur in the range 20.0–13.3 quarters.

The highest peak of inventory investment is also strongly concentrated at 26.7–10.0 quarters, while the frequency diagram covering all peaks shows some concentration in the range of 8.9–5.0 quarters, with a peak of 7.3 quarters. Finally, it should be noted that the mode of the frequency diagrams of material imports and of the unemployment rate are found, respectively, at 7.3 and 11.4 quarters, instead of the 16.0 quarters for real GNP and other variables mentioned above (see Charts 25–27).

Another way of looking at the spectral density functions in fifty replications is to graph the averages of the density functions at each frequency. In contrast to the diagrams of Figure 12, which are presented for single cases of one, two, and three peaks, in Chart 28 we show the average spectral densities for seven variables in the case of serially correlated disturbances. The results portray a preponderance of distinct peaks for all variables. The corresponding "average" spectral density functions for the case of serially independent errors does not have distinct peaks, except for some accumulation at 4 quarters.

These findings suggest that the stochastic simulations with serially correlated disturbances are more consistent with the historical facts on business cycles than those with serially uncorrelated disturbances.

CHART 21

Gross National Product (Histogram of Peaks)

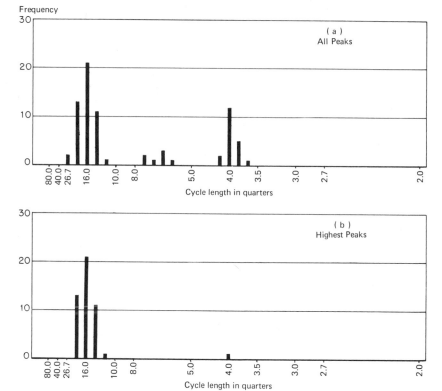

CHART 22

Consumption: Serially Correlated Error Terms
(Histogram of Peaks)

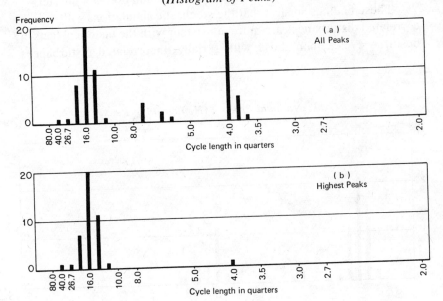

CHART 23

Fixed Investment (Histogram of Peaks)

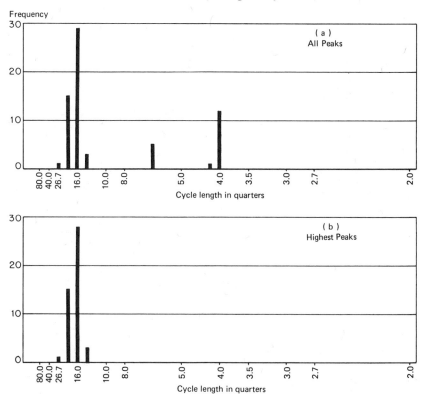

CHART 24

Residential Construction (*Histogram of Peaks*)

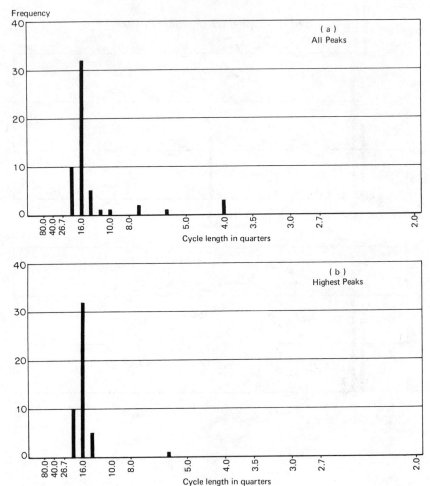

CHART 25

Inventory Investment (Histogram of Peaks)

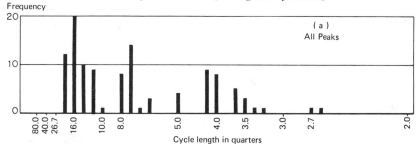

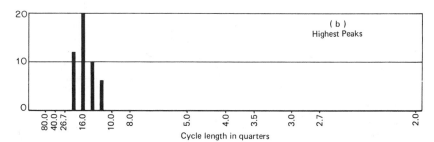

CHART 26

Material Imports (Histogram of Peaks)

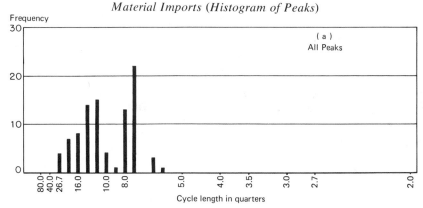

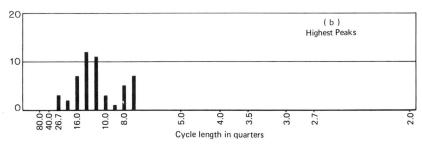

CHART 27

Unemployment Rate (Histogram of Peaks)

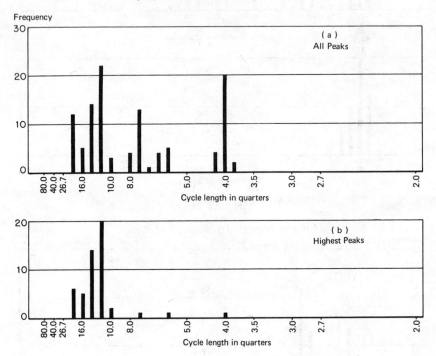

Cycle length in quarters

(a)
All Peaks

(b)
Highest Peaks

Cycle length in quarters

CHART 28

Average Spectral Densities: Serially Correlated Errors

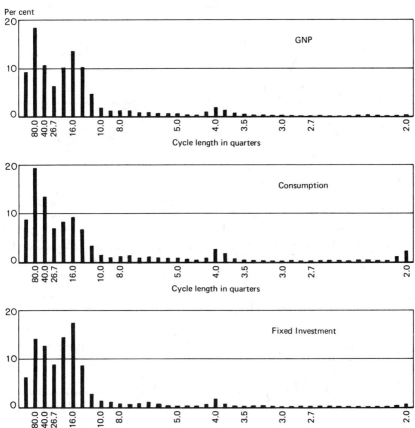

Average Spectral Densities: Serially Correlated Errors (concluded)

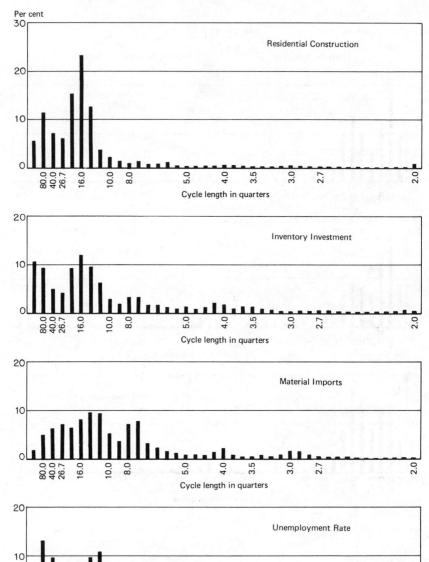

Thus, we conclude that the results of our research are favorable for the former scheme, not only in the efficacy of short-run predictions by non-stochastic simulations, but also in the experimental generation of cyclical movements by the stochastic simulations.

APPENDIX

SOME NOTES ON THE GENERATION OF PSEUDO-STRUCTURAL ERRORS
FOR USE IN STOCHASTIC SIMULATION STUDIES

MICHAEL D. McCARTHY
WHARTON SCHOOL

It has been claimed that in order to achieve a realistic simulation of an econometric model of a society—a simulation in which business cycles might be exhibited—it is necessary to simulate the model in such a way that its equations are subject to random stochastic errors (or shocks).[1] The idea here, put forward by Slutzky,[2] is that economic fluctuations may be due simply to random shocks. Another, perhaps more appropriate, reason for undertaking stochastic simulation is that the device provides a way of studying the statistical distribution of the endogenous variables and of policy predictions.[3]

Whatever the reason for simulating econometric models subject to stochastic shocks, one would presumably want to undertake the simulation using the "appropriate" types of shocks—shocks which exhibited the same statistical properties as those which affect the economic system.

In the material that follows, a method is described for generating disturbances for use in the stochastic simulation of an estimated econometric model. One advantage of the method is that it can be used

[1] See Irma Adelman and Frank L. Adelman, "The Dynamic Properties of the Klein-Goldberger Model," *Econometrica*, XXVII (October, 1959), pp. 596–625. For a more recent study, see A. L. Nagar, "Simulation of the Brookings Econometric Model," presented at the December, 1966 meetings of the Econometric Society, San Francisco.

[2] E. Slutzky, "The Summation of Random Causes as the Source of Cyclical Processes," *Econometrica*, V (1937), p. 105.

[3] See Nagar, *op. cit.*

regardless of the number of observations available for estimating the model. However, the statistical properties of the generated errors will, of course, depend on this number. It will be shown that for a large number of observations, if the true structural errors are jointly normally distributed, and have expected values of zero, the generated structural disturbances will be distributed in the same manner as the structural disturbances of the model. A method is also described for deriving disturbances with suitable auto-regressive properties, assuming that the number of observations is sufficiently large. It will be assumed that the true disturbances are generated by a stationary stochastic process.

1. Let S be a $1 \times M$ matrix of pseudo-structural disturbances.
2. Let r be a $1 \times T$ matrix of random errors, assumed to be distributed $N(0,1)$.
3. Let U be any $T \times M$ matrix of disturbances from T observations of M true structural equations. We shall derive S as follows:

$$S = T^{-1/2}rU$$

4. Let $1/T\ EU'U = \Sigma$, where Σ is the $M \times M$ covariance matrix of the system, which is assumed constant over time. The term E is an expectations operator.
5. Let r be independent of U and consider the expected value of the covariance matrix of S

$$\Sigma_S = T^{-1}EU'r'rU = ES'S$$

The typical element in Σ_S is given by

(1) $$\Sigma_{S_{ij}} = T^{-1}EU'_i r'rU_j$$

where U_i is the ith column of U and U'_i is its transpose. The term U_j is similarly defined.

Equation (1) may be rewritten:

(1a) $$\Sigma_{S_{ij}} = T^{-1}E \sum_{b=1}^{T} \sum_{a=1}^{T} (r_a r_b)(U_{ia} U_{jb})$$

where r_a is the ath element in the row vector r, and U_{ia} is the ath element in the column vector U_i. Again, the terms r_b and U_{jb} are similarly defined.

Since r is independent of U and $Er_a r_b = 0$, $a \neq b$ and $Er_a r_b = 1$, $a = b$, it follows that

$$\Sigma_{S_{ij}} = T^{-1}E \sum_{a=1}^{T} r_a^2 U_{ia} U_{ja}$$

$$= T^{-1}E \sum_{a=1}^{T} U_{ia} U_{ja}$$

$$= \Sigma_{ij}$$

Thus, $\Sigma_S = \Sigma$.

This property holds as long as U is derived from a known structural form. This result suggests that if we are given a sample set of errors, $\hat{U}$, derived from an estimated model, we might use as pseudo-disturbances the following:

$$(2) \qquad \hat{S} = T^{-1/2} r \hat{U}$$

For models estimated by consistent methods, the covariance matrix of $\hat{S}$ will be asymptotically equal to the true covariance matrix of the system.

For small samples, if we take the $\hat{U}$ as given, it will be true that the conditional expected value of $\hat{S}$ will be equal to the sample variance-covariance matrix of the system, calculated as

$$\hat{\Sigma} = T^{-1} \hat{U}' \hat{U}$$

To obtain pseudo-errors that have suitable auto-regressive properties, we might define

$$S_t = T^{-1/2} \bar{r}_t U, \text{ and } S_{t-1} = T^{-1/2} \bar{r}_{t-1} U$$

where $\qquad \bar{r}_t = [r_t r_{t-1} r_{t-2} \ldots r_{t-T+1}]$

and $\qquad \bar{r}_{t-1} = [r_{t-1} r_{t-2} r_{t-3} \ldots r_{t-T}]$

and t is a time subscript.

In what follows, we examine the first-order auto-regressive properties of S. Form

$$(3) \qquad ES_t' S_{t-1} = T^{-1} EU' \bar{r}_t' \bar{r}_{t-1} U$$

The typical element in (3) is given by

$$Z_{ij} = T^{-1} E U_i \bar{r}'_t \bar{r}_{t-1} U_j$$

$$= T^{-1} E U'_i \begin{bmatrix} r_t \\ r_{t-1} \\ r_{t-2} \\ \cdot \\ \cdot \\ \cdot \\ r_{t-T+1} \end{bmatrix} \begin{bmatrix} r_{t-1} r_{t-2} & \cdots & r_{t-T} \end{bmatrix} U_j$$

$$= T^{-1} E U'_i \begin{bmatrix} r_t r_{t-1} r_t r_{t-2} & & & r_t r_{t-T} \\ (r_{t-1})^2 r_{t-1} r_{t-2} & & & r_{t-1} r_{t-T} \\ r_{t-2} r_{t-1} (r_{t-2})^2 & & & r_{t-2} r_{t-T} \\ \cdot & & & \\ \cdot & & & \\ \cdot & & & \\ r_{t-T+1} r_{t-1} r_{t-T+1} r_{t-2} & \cdots & (r_{t-T+1})^2 r_{t-T+1} r_{t-T} \end{bmatrix} U_j$$

Since $\bar{r}$ is independent of U, and $E r_a r_b = 0$, $a \neq b$, and finally $E r_a^2 = 1$, we have:

$$Z_{ij} = T^{-1} E \sum_{k=t-T+1}^{t-1} U_{ik} U_{jk+1}$$

$$= \frac{T-1}{T} E U_{jt} U_{it-1}$$

where U_{jt} is the tth error of the jth equation, and $U_{i_{t-1}}$ is the $t - 1$th error for the ith equation.

Returning to equation (3), we have:

$$Z = E S'_t S_{t-1} = \frac{T-1}{T} E U^{t'} U^{t-1}$$

where $U^{t'}$ is the transpose of the tth row of U, and U^{t-1} is similarly defined.

In the case of kth-order auto-regression, we would find

$$ES'_tS_{t-k} = \frac{T-k}{T} EU^{t'}U^{t-k}$$

If T is sufficiently large, this suggests that we use as pseudo-structural errors:

$$\hat{S}_t = T^{-1/2}\bar{r}_t\hat{U} \text{ and } \hat{S}_{t-1} = T^{-1/2}\bar{r}_{t-1}\hat{U}$$

where $\hat{U}$ is a set of sample structural errors and $\bar{r}_t$ and $\bar{r}_{t-1}$ are defined as above. Hopefully, $\hat{U}$ will be derived from a model estimated by consistent methods.

In what follows, we examine the asymptotic distribution of S in the absence of auto-regression. It will be shown that if r is a vector of random numbers distributed $N(0,1)$, and if the structural disturbances are jointly normally distributed, the asymptotic distribution of S will be the same as the distribution of the structural errors.

PROOF: Let U^i be the ith observation of the structural disturbances. We assume that U^i is distributed $N(0,V)$ for all i; that is, the frequency function is given by

$$F(U^i) = (2_\pi)^{-M/2}|V|^{-1/2}e^{-1/2U^iV^{-1}U^{i'}}$$

for all i. (Note that U^i is a row vector containing M elements.)

The joint moment generating function of U^i is

(4) $$M(U^i) = e^{1/2t'Vt}$$

where t is now a $M \times 1$ column vector of constants, with elements t_i, $i = 1, 2, \ldots, M$.

In the following demonstration we show that as the number of observations approaches ∞, the joint moment generating function of S is the same as (4).

The moment generating function of S is given by

$$M(S) = (2_\pi)^{-MT/2}|V|^{-T/2} \int \cdots \int e^{T^{-1/2}} \sum_{j=1}^{M} t_j r U_j$$

$$-\frac{1}{2} \sum_{i=1}^{T} U^iV^{-1}U^{i'} - \frac{1}{2} \sum_{i=1}^{T} r_i^2 \cdot \prod_i \prod_j dU_j^i \cdot \prod_i dr_i$$

where U_j is the jth column of U.

This may be rewritten

$$M(S) = (2_\pi)^{-MT/2}|V|^{-T/2} \int \cdots \int e^{T^{-1/2} \sum_{i=1}^{T} r_i U^i t - \frac{1}{2} \sum_{i=1}^{T} U^i V^{-1} U^{i'}}$$

$$-\frac{1}{2} \sum_{i=1}^{T} r_i^2 \cdot \prod_i \prod_j dU_j^i \prod_i dr_i$$

The term $T^{-1/2} r_i U^i t$ can be interpreted as a linear combination of the terms in U^i. It can be verified that $M(S)$ may be written

$$M(S) = (2_\pi)^{-MT/2}|V|^{-T/2} \int \cdots \int e^{1/2 \sum_{i=1}^{T} r_i^2/T \ t'Vt}$$

$$\cdot \ e^{-1/2 \sum_{i=1}^{T} (U^i - r_i T^{-1/2} t'V)V^{-1}(U^i - r_i T^{-1/2} t'V)'}$$

$$-\frac{1}{2} \sum_{i=1}^{T} r_i^2 \cdot \prod_i \prod_j dU_j^i \prod_i dr_i$$

$$= (2_\pi)^{-MT/2}|V|^{-T/2} \int \cdots \int e^{1/2 \sum_{i=1}^{T} r_i^2/T \ t'Vt - \frac{1}{2} \sum_{i=1}^{T} Z^i V^{-1} Z^{i'}}$$

$$\cdot \ e^{-1/2 \sum_{i=1}^{T} r_i^2} \cdot \prod_i \prod_j dZ_j^i \prod_i dr_i$$

where $Z^i = U^i - r_i T^{-1/2} t'V$. The Jacobian of the transformation equals one.

We first integrate $M(S)$ with respect to Z^i, taking the r_i as given. The result is

$$(5) \quad M(S) = (2_\pi)^{-T/2} \int \cdots \int e^{1/2 \sum_{i=1}^{T} r_i^2/T \ t'Vt - \frac{1}{2} \sum_{i=1}^{T} r_i^2} \cdot \prod_i dr_i$$

$$= (2_\pi)^{-T/2} \int \cdots \int e^{1/2t'Vt \sum_{i=1}^{T} r_i^2/T - \frac{1}{2} \sum_{i=1}^{T} r_i^2} \cdot \prod_i dr_i$$

Next, integrate (5), taking T as given, and then take the limit. The result is

$$M(S) = \left(1 - \frac{t'Vt}{T}\right)^{-T/2}, \text{ and}$$

$$\lim_{T \to \infty} M(S) = e^{1/2t'Vt}$$

In the case of consistently estimated models, the pseudo-structural errors

$$\hat{S} = T^{-1/2}r\hat{U}$$

will have the same asymptotic distribution as U^i, if r and U^i are distributed in the manner assumed above. Generalization of the proof about asymptotic distribution to the case where errors exhibit autocorrelation is not difficult.

DISCUSSION

FRANK DE LEEUW

URBAN INSTITUTE

One way to classify theories of economic fluctuations is by which forces they identify as the underlying ones setting an economy's dynamic responses in motion. The Slutsky-Frisch theory emphasizes stochastic disturbances—forces of the kind we often cannot measure directly or pinpoint in time. Many textbooks on macroeconomics emphasize measurable and relatively autonomous injections, or withdrawals, from the income-expenditure process: government spending, exports, tax laws, and so on. Monetarists emphasize exogenous disturbances affecting the quantity of money: changes in monetary policy, gold discoveries, bank runs, and so on. The theories have to do with which one, or ones, of these forces have been the prime movers in the past, or are likely to be dominant in the future.

The classification is useful here, since the Conference appears to have been designed with the stochastic-disturbance view exclusively in mind. There has been much attention as to how the models behave under different short-run error-term adjustments, and how they respond to simulated "typical" stochastic shocks. These are characteristics concerning which the Slutsky-Frisch theory has strong implications. In contrast, no attention has been given to which kinds of exogenous variables the models are sensitive, or to what kinds of fluctuations "typical" patterns of change in exogenous variables produce.[1] Outside of this Conference, the emphasis is largely reversed; current discussion of economic fluctuations centers mainly around which exogenous forces matter, and how they work, to the virtual exclusion of discussion of the role of stochastic disturbances.

What I would like to do here is look at the Evans-Klein-Saito paper, and some of the other papers, from the point of view of the light they shed on these alternative explanations of economic fluctuations. First, I shall discuss the question of whether the simulation results tell us anything about the validity or strength of the stochastic-disturbance theory. My conclusion is that the simulation results tell us very little, since we would expect the same kind of results if: (a) the stochastic-disturbance theory is valid; or (b) the theory isn't valid, but the models are mis-specified. The next section takes up the question of whether the models — mainly, the Wharton and OBE Models — are mis-specified, and attempts to use some comparisons of model results with single-equation "reduced-form" explanations of GNP fluctuations to make headway on this question. The conclusion stresses the likelihood that there are important mis-specifications in the models.

1. THE SIMULATION RESULTS

From the many simulations of the models under investigation at this Conference, three generalizations find support (though not unanimous support by each investigator of each model). First, both within and beyond the sample period, forecasts one quarter ahead are better than forecasts two or more quarters ahead. Second, forecasts which take some account of serial correlation in error terms are better than forecasts which do not. Third, simulations of the model when it is subjected to serially correlated stochastic shocks whose distribution is based on equation errors during the sample period, succeed in reproducing mild fluctuations; exactly how mild seems to be a matter of controversy. This third generalization is somewhat ambiguous in the case of the Wharton Model simulations, because the exogenous variables are not set at perfectly smooth growth rates for the stochastic simulation runs but include at least half a cycle due to an assumed

---

[1] In his oral presentation, George Green referred to some simulation results produced by "typical" patterns of change in exogenous variables in the OBE Model. I hope that these interesting results will be made available in written form.

Vietnam War settlement. For the OBE Model simulations, in which exogenous variables *are* set at perfectly smooth growth rates, the cycles generated by stochastic simulations are very mild. The first two generalizations hold for the OBE Model, and also for a version of the FRB-MIT Model that I worked with in late 1968.

Now, if economic fluctuations are largely the economy's response to stochastic disturbances which interact over time, then we would expect all of these generalizations to hold true for a well-specified econometric model. Predictions should improve, the shorter the prediction period; because a short prediction-period enables us to capture, in the initial conditions, the effect of past stochastic forces. Predictions should improve when account is taken of intercorrelations of error terms, because the error terms, including their intercorrelation properties, are the basic force driving the economy. Finally, stochastic simulation should reproduce the characteristics of historical fluctuations, because they reproduce the kind of impulses which, in fact, give rise to historical fluctuations. Thus, the reported simulation results might seem at first glance to provide strong support for the stochastic-disturbance theory — at least, as far as mild cycles are concerned.

Unfortunately, another set of conditions can just as easily account for these reported simulation results. Suppose that an economy responds to the forces which drive it by effects which develop gradually over time; but suppose, further, that a particular model mis-specifies the path by which these effects develop. This mis-specification could result from incorrect lag distributions, from bias in estimating the initial impact effect of some exogenous variable, or from other problems. Whatever the cause, one result ought to be better predictions one quarter ahead than two or more quarters ahead, since much of the effect of the mis-specification ought to be undone by inserting actual initial conditions of the endogenous variables in one-quarter forecasts. Another result ought to be serially correlated residuals in the sample period; taking account of this correlation ought to correct for some of the model's error and improve forecasts.

As for stochastic simulation, it might, on first thought, seem unlikely that random shocks could result in anything like historical fluctuations unless the stochastic-disturbance theory has validity. But when we remember that the simulations are based on the model's actual errors during the historical sample-period, I think success in matching the characteristics of historical fluctuations is not so surprising. The actual errors from a poorly specified model will tend to be larger than the true magnitude of stochastic forces. These large actual errors would, in themselves, lead to exaggeration of the power of stochastic forces to generate fluctuations. But if a model happens to understate the economy's response to stochastic forces, this understatement will work in the opposite direction. It is, therefore, hard to form any clear expectation of how stochastic simulation results should turn out if a model is mis-specified.

In summary, the principal simulation results reported in the Evans-Klein-Saito paper and in some of the other Conference papers could, it seems to me, just as easily result from mis-specification as from the historical validity of the Slutsky-Frisch theory.

2. COMPARISONS WITH REDUCED-FORM GNP EQUATIONS

Another way of stating the conclusion of the previous analysis is to remark that much of what we can say about the simulations prepared for this Conference depends on what we are willing to assume about the specification accuracy of the models. One way to form an impression of the specification accuracy of the models is to compare them with simpler, reduced-form relationships between GNP and major exogenous variables, such as the recently publicized relationship of GNP to monetary and fiscal policy variables. If these simple relationships catch certain features of historical fluctuations that a model misses, then, I think, there is some support for the proposition that the model is mis-specified. These reduced-form relationships are crude in their fixed-weight distributed lags, and in their ignoring of initial conditions; but it seems to me that these and other shortcomings put the reduced-form method under a handicap, making any indication of superiority over models all the more impressive.

The reduced-form equations I will use are those estimated by Edward Gramlich and reported in his paper, "The Usefulness of Monetary and Fiscal Policy as Discretionary Stabilization Tools."[2] He has

[2] Gramlich's paper was presented at the Conference of University Professors, sponsored by the American Bankers' Association, Milwaukee, September, 1969.

improved on earlier reduced-form equations: (1) by separating Federal government transactions into those which affect final demand directly (purchases plus grants-in-aid); those which affect household income directly; and those which operate through other channels (representing these by dummy variables)—instead of employing the usual classification into disbursements and receipts; (2) by adding exports to Federal purchases and grants-in-aid; (3) by adjusting defense expenditures to a value-added basis (that is, adding in changes in inventories of defense products); and (4) by adding a variable to represent major strikes.

Like previous investigators, Gramlich has estimated his equations in first-difference form, using the Almon polynomial-weight technique to reduce the lag problem to manageable proportions. He has tried out several monetary policy variables; I shall report on results using the monetary base, and on those using unborrowed reserves—the residuals of which he has kindly made available to me.

Since these equations take no account of initial conditions—that is, initial capacity utilization, initial unemployment rates, recent residuals, and so forth—they are most directly comparable to the "long-period" historical simulations for the Wharton and OBE Models, which also make GNP depend only on current and lagged exogenous variables. However, I will, in addition, compare the equations with the shorter-span simulations for the OBE Model. Unfortunately, the shorter-period simulations of the Wharton Model have not been reported in detail, so I cannot comment on them. The summary statistics presented indicate that the Wharton Model is less satisfactory than the OBE Model in these short-period simulations.

In the two recession-recovery periods of the 1950's—the 1953–54 cycle and the 1957–58 cycle—reduced-form equations do no better than the models. In fact, in the 1953–54 cycle, the models mirror the actual GNP path quite closely, proving slightly better than the reduced-form equations. The Wharton Model misses the 1957–58 cycle completely, and the OBE Model (both long-period and short-period simulations) indicates only the mildest of slowdowns; the reduced-form equations likewise indicate a very mild slowdown for this period.

In the 1960's, however, the reduced-form equations do capture some fluctuations that the models tend to miss. The models do not capture the 1960 decline, apart from slight declines in the second quarter of 1960, which followed the post-steel-strike inventory jump. The reduced-form equations do better — especially the one using unborrowed reserves, which correctly estimates practically no change in *GNP* from the second through the fourth quarter of 1960. The Wharton Model completely misses the 1967 slowdown; the reduced-form equations indicate, at least, a reduction in *GNP* growth, though not as much of a reduction as actually took place. Model calculations for 1968, as reported in the Evans-Haitovsky-Treyz paper, indicate a severe understatement in the second half of that year. Reduced-form equations also understate that period, but I would guess that their understatement of about $2 billion per quarterly change in *GNP* is not so severe. (Perhaps, however, the inclusion of 1968 in the reduced-form sample period heavily affects these results.)

Thus, there does seem to be some evidence in the 1960's supporting the view that the models are mis-specified. The evidence is not dramatic but, I think, it is enough to raise serious doubts as to how to interpret the simulations prepared for this Conference. Furthermore, the periods in which the reduced-form equations do better than the models suggest that it may be in the representation of the effects of monetary policy that these models are weak.

As a final point, let me note that these comments bear on only one possible contribution of this Conference; namely, its assistance in understanding the underlying causes of economic fluctuations. There are other contributions, as well; not the least of which is simple tabulation of the average errors models make when unaided by forecaster judgment. Any negative remarks about the area I have chosen to discuss are not meant to belittle these additional contributions.

BRIDGER M. MITCHELL

STANFORD UNIVERSITY

For purposes of long-run simulation, the structure of the Wharton Model can be considered as a set of 47 stochastic equations

$$y_i = G(y,x) + \epsilon_i, \quad i = 1, \dots, 47$$

where the vectors of the endogenous variables y and exogenous variables x include both current and lagged values.

If G is a set of linear difference equations in the endogenous variables, the model can be solved to yield the values of the endogenous variables as rational lag functions of both the exogenous variables and the disturbances. The stochastic behavior of current y, given the values of the exogenous x, is then determined by the distribution of the errors ϵ_i and the estimated lag structure. In particular, for fixed exogenous values, such a model can be viewed as a linear filter operating on the random errors. In the frequency domain, the spectral densities of the output of this filter completely characterize the model's response to random shocks, obeying the assumed probability distribution, and the presence of peaks in the spectra of the outputs indicates the tendency of endogenous variables to reflect a cycle at the corresponding frequencies.

When the model contains *nonlinear* functions of the endogenous variables, this approach is not directly available. Since virtually all interesting macroeconomic models will include both real and monetary variables with endogenously determined prices, nonlinearity is the general case. One line of attack has been taken in another paper prepared for this Conference by Howrey; namely, to linearize the model around sample means and to evaluate the spectra of the endogenous variables as computed from this linear approximation.

The present paper by Evans, Klein, and Saito preserves the nonlinear features of the model by fixing the exogenous variables at the values of a control solution, drawing random numbers for values of the disturbances, and solving the model for 100 successive quarters. Fifty such experiments yield an equal number of time series for each of the endogenous variables. The authors then *estimate* the spectra of the nonlinear filter applied to the random process, treating each experiment as a random sample from that process.

Unfortunately, the paper is marred by a technical deficiency at this point. The authors have produced 50 separate estimates of the power spectrum of each of the important endogenous variables. However, as the experiments are designed to generate independent drawings from the same stochastic process with fixed initial conditions, it will be efficient to average the estimated auto-covariances from the 50 experiments, each of about 100 observations, and then compute a single estimate of the spectrum. For estimation purposes this must approach the ideal large sample in economics, and will certainly allow asymptotic confidence limits to be used to test hypotheses regarding spectral peaks at business-cycle frequencies.[1]

In lieu of this, the authors have tabulated the relative frequency of occurrence in the 50 experiments of various characteristics of the estimated spectra, such as the number of experiments having one, two, or three peaks. It is difficult to use these statistics to draw inferences about the probability of occurrence of periodic fluctuations of different frequencies in the model, since the spectrum of a particular endogenous variable has a determinate number of peaks, whereas the occurrence of estimated spectra with different numbers of peaks, or peaks at different frequencies, is an indication of the sampling variation of the estimate. In any event, the probability of a cycle of a given period occurring in a 100-quarter run of the model is not related in a simple way to the existence of significant power at the corresponding frequency. A direct estimate, of course, would be to count the number of occurrences in the time domain of cycles of the given period over the 50 experimental series.

Turning to the evidence which is tabulated for these runs, there appears to be substantial variance in the GNP series at a three-and-one-half- to seven-year band of frequencies. This is in striking contrast to the results from Howrey's linearized condensed version of the model, since in the latter, the longest period is only a year and a half (apart from a very low frequency component).[2]

The makings of an equally interesting difference between the linearized and simulated results appear when one is considering the stability of the model for constant values of the exogenous variables. The simulated nonlinear model's stability — in the range of appropriate values of the variables — is somewhat uncertain and calls for further investigation. To achieve a desirable base line, or nonstochastic path, for the endogenous variables required that equations relating to labor markets be more-or-less continually adjusted to keep the control solu-

---

[1] In estimating the spectra, the particular trend removal technique can have a major effect on the final results. In stochastic simulations of this sort, a natural procedure would be to take deviations from the nonstochastic control solution.

[2] The quantitative results from Howrey's study are based on his first-circulated computations, whose numerical accuracy he later questioned.

tion close to the target values for long-run steady growth.[3] On the other hand, the solutions as plotted on the charts, which show only one of the 50 stochastic simulation runs, do not appear to exhibit increasing variance with time. Not readjusting the labor equations for the different shocks in different experiments may account for the rather large variability seen in the chart, as compared with the nonstochastic run. The fact that this does not lead to explosive behavior may be due to damping effects of some nonlinear relations, when values depart sufficiently far from the base-line solution.

By way of comparison, Howrey has analyzed the linearized model both with, and without, the monetary sector. Both versions display explosive behavior, but the presence of the monetary equations has a decided effect in making the model more nearly stable. This, too, suggests that the stabilizing role of prices and interest rates at values away from their sample means may be stronger than one measured by purely linear equations.

I have suggested the possible role of nonlinearities as the key to the different dynamics found by these two papers, for uncovering such a structural explanation would be most interesting. However, other differences between the papers obscure such a finding. First, the linearized model is a somewhat reduced version of the full Wharton Model. Secondly, Howrey appears to assume that the shocks are independent both over time and across equations, whereas the Evans-Klein-Saito results I have referred to are based on disturbances independent over time, but having the contemporary covariances estimated from the sample. The effects of this relatively greater interdependence of the model on the cyclical behavior of the endogenous variables are uncertain a priori but could be established.

I would urge the authors of these two papers to collaborate in order to obtain comparative results from their different approaches. By use of the same model and parameter estimates, constant values for all exogenous variables, and identical assumptions about the distribution of disturbances, any differences due to nonlinearities can be isolated, and the adequacy of linear approximations in analyzing dynamic responses assessed.

---

[3] The emphasis on the short-run nature of the model suggests that the authors would not draw policy implications from this behavior.

McCarthy's suggested method of calculating Monte Carlo shocks, having the covariance structure estimated from the sample, provides a useful addition to our computational techniques, as one simply uses disturbances calculated as linear combinations of independent random variables, with the sample residuals as weights. I question, however, whether one wants to employ this method for generating auto-correlated disturbances in the manner that Evans, Klein, and Saito have adopted in their second set of stochastic experiments. In those runs, the generating mechanism reproduces auto-correlations up to the forty-fourth order. Most of the smoothing effects and longer cyclical periods are likely to be obtained from merely first- or second-order auto-correlation, and it is straining the data rather fine to estimate auto-correlation coefficients of all orders, as well as the structural parameters of the model.

The authors found no clear gain from using first-order auto-correlation corrections in making their short-run forecasts of the historical period. However, in view of the abundant evidence of auto-correlated data in quarterly models, it would be interesting to experiment further with this approach, employing asymptotically more efficient estimators of both the structural and auto-correlation parameters.

SHORT- AND LONG-TERM SIMULATIONS WITH THE BROOKINGS MODEL

GARY FROMM · American University and
     Brookings Institution
LAWRENCE R. KLEIN · Wharton School
GEORGE R. SCHINK · Brookings Institution and
     University of Maryland

PREDICTIONS with econometric models, even thirty years after Tinbergen's initial attempt, still involve art as well as science. The present version of the Brookings Model is an advance over its predecessors. Yet much remains to be done to improve the specification of certain sectors and to reduce the predictive error of the system as a whole. The equations of the present system, the 1969 BUSEM, are similar to those presented previously in the Fromm-Taubman simulations,[1] but there are a few significant differences.

1 STRUCTURE OF THE MODEL

TO begin, the sample period for earlier versions of the model was 1948–60. Thus, it included the waning years of readjustment to World War II and the Korean War experience. Analysis of covariance tests run for the periods 1948–53, 1954–60, and 1948–60 revealed significant shifts in many coefficients between the earlier and later years of these intervals. It was decided to select a sample period germane to the analysis of current economic problems. Therefore, the present version of the model is estimated over the post–Korean War years, 1954–65. The data employed also are taken from different sources: revised na-

---

[1] Gary Fromm and Paul Taubman, *Policy Simulations with an Econometric Model* (the Brookings Institution, 1968).

tional income and product accounts and later revisions of unpublished statistics.[2]

The theory underlying some of the equations of the model has been modified as well. Consequently, it is not surprising that certain variables in specific functions no longer have statistically significant coefficients, and these variables have been eliminated. In other instances, new variables or better measures of previous ones have been included.

The 1969 version of the model, for which solutions are presented below, contains 230 equations (118 of which are stochastic) and 104 exogenous variables or parameters. Most of the exogenous variables are of minor importance. The model is estimated using ordinary least squares. Two-stage least squares estimates of a somewhat larger and improved version of the model also have been prepared and will be the basis of complete system solutions to be released in 1970.

A description of the difference in specification of the 1969 BUSEM from the 1968 BUSEM follows. Equations for the 1969 and 1968 models are shown in the appendixes of this paper and in the Fromm and Taubman book, respectively.

CONSUMER DEMAND

The present consumption functions depart from the earlier versions primarily in that they are estimated on a real per capita rather than on a real absolute basis. The principal explanatory variables are real disposable income per capita and relative prices. A credit dummy variable has been added to the consumption of durables other than automobiles. The autos equation now includes a capital stock of autos variable and a dummy variable (scaled by per capita disposable income) to reflect auto strikes. The two nondurables consumption equations (foods and beverages, and other nondurables) are unchanged, while the liquid assets term has been deleted from the services equation.

[2] The National Income and Product Accounts of the United States, 1929–1965, Statistical Tables and Survey of Current Business, July 1966, July 1967, and July 1968.

RESIDENTIAL CONSTRUCTION

Because of compositional shifts in the late 1950's, housing unit starts have now been disaggregated into three categories: single units, double units, and three or more units. All of the original variables appear in the various starts functions, but in different equations. Single unit starts are dependent on cost and the availability of funds in financial markets (short-term interest rates are used as a proxy), real disposable income per household, and the real market price of the average home. (The latter price is also a function of real disposable income per household.) Lagged single unit starts, together with three-quarter moving averages (lagged one-quarter) of the other variables give a modified Koyck lag effect to the impact of the explanatory factors. The same type of lag distribution is used in the other starts and price equations.

Housing starts of dual units are a function of interest rates, disposable income per household, a time trend and lagged starts. Presumably, a market price variable might be significant but data on dual unit prices are not available separately from other multi-unit prices. Multi-unit starts (three or more units) are mainly dependent on supply conditions and are strongly influenced by interest rates and housing unit vacancies. Vacancies also have a significant influence on the market price of multiple units.

Due to the above disaggregation, the price-quantity identity that defines housing unit expenditures is, of course, slightly modified. The equation for other residential expenditures is unchanged, except now the coefficient of the price of such outlays is significant and bears the correct negative sign. Expenditures for new private nonfarm, non-residential, nonbusiness construction also are included in this sector; here, the lagged dependent variable has been added as an explanatory factor.

INVENTORY INVESTMENT

The inventory investment equations for durable and nondurable manufacturing are nearly identical to those used previously. Real inventory change is a function of real final sales, beginning of period inventory stocks and unfilled orders, and the previous period's inventory investment. (The lagged real change in unfilled orders also appears in the durables equation.) The one exception is that a change in final sales of nondurable goods has been deleted from the nondurable function.

Trade inventories, because of requirements elsewhere in the model, have been separated into investment in car inventories and in trade inventories other than cars. The latter is made a function of the final sale of goods and the beginning of period stock of such inventories.

By definition, car inventories are held only by the trade sector and not by manufacturers. Therefore, the change in the value of dealer stocks is hypothesized to be dependent on the level and first difference of personal consumption expenditures on automobiles and the value of the stock of cars at the beginning of the period.

For the residual sector, real inventory investment is a function of real final sales, the beginning of period stock, and lagged inventory change. Price changes and interest rate terms have been dropped from this equation.

ORDERS

A few modifications have been made in the orders sector. For durable manufacturing, speculative price changes and lagged final sales terms have been dropped from the real new orders equation. A two-quarter lagged moving average of Department of Defense military prime contract awards has been substituted for current government military expenditures (both variables in real terms). The reciprocal of the rate of capacity utilization has been added to reflect the impact of capacity constraints. The remaining key explanatory variables are real final sales of durables, construction expenditures, and the level of unfilled orders at the beginning of the period.

The level of real unfilled orders in durables manufacturing is given by an identity between the beginning of period level, price changes (the identity is only valid in current dollar terms), real new orders, and real sales. A linear function relating real sales to real output originating is substituted for the sales term in the identity.

The approach for nondurables manufacturing, suggested by Gerald Childs, is somewhat different.[3] Here, using inventory decision rules, the real change in unfilled orders is hypothesized to depend on real values of the first difference in new orders, lagged new orders, the lagged level of unfilled orders, inventory stocks, the level and rate of change in the wholesale price index of nondurables, and the reciprocal of capacity utilization in the industry. New orders are then given by an identity similar to that for unfilled orders for durables manufacturing.

INVESTMENT IN NONFARM BUSINESS PLANT AND EQUIPMENT

The real fixed business investment equations include nearly the same variables as previous formulations. Expenditures are functions of real output originating, long-term interest rates, and beginning of period real capital stocks. Rather than including explicit lag terms of various explanatory factors, as was done previously, Almon lag distributions have been used instead. Also, lagged capacity utilization rates (in the form of real actual to potential output) have been included as an indicator of short-term modification of investment plans. Finally, dummy variables and truncated time-trend variables have been added to act as proxies for the effects of the investment tax credit.

FOREIGN TRADE

Due to modifications in the basic data, equations have been estimated for nondurables and services, and for durables imports rather than for finished and unfinished imports. Real nondurables and services expenditures are a function of the price of these imports relative to the price of consumption, as well as real disposable income, lagged imports, and a dummy variable for dock strikes.

The equation for real export expenditures is unchanged except for the additions of a dock strike dummy. Exports are dependent on the volume of world trade and the price of U.S. exports relative to world export prices.

[3] This is based on his *Unfilled Orders and Inventories: A Structural Analysis* (North-Holland, 1967).

GOVERNMENT TAXES AND TRANSFER PAYMENTS

There are four tax functions for total Federal, state, and local receipts of personal, excise, corporate profits and social insurance taxes. In each of the equations, as before, a variable which corresponds to the tax base is included. Now, however, given the changes in rates after 1960, profits before taxes are multiplied by the normal corporate rate plus surtax. (The elasticity of this combined variable is less than unity because of the lower rate that applies to low income corporations and because of carry-forward and carry-back averaging of losses.) Similarly, the social insurance equation now includes terms which reflect the contribution rate, the percentage of employees covered, and the maximum individual tax base. There is also a term to reflect employers' contribution rates for unemployment insurance. Finally, dummy variables are utilized to capture the cut in tax liabilities of the 1964 and 1965 personal and excise tax reductions and the 1962 investment tax credit.

Government transfer payments are predicted by the same equations used previously. Transfers of unemployment benefits are a function of the number of persons unemployed and a *GNP* potential gap valued in current dollars. The remaining categories of government transfers, social security, veterans', and miscellaneous payments, are treated exogenously.

PRODUCTION FUNCTIONS

Rather than utilize linear employment functions, this version of the model contains a restructuring of the production functions in accord with more recent theoretical developments. Starting with a Cobb-Douglas function, and an inertial adjustment process, Michael McCarthy developed logarithmic equations for man-hour requirements for production workers in the durables manufacturing, nondurables manufacturing, and trade sectors. The explanatory variables are real output originating and real capital stocks. Time trends are included to account for technological change; dummy variables are introduced in the 1960's to reflect apparent shifts in production functions and reductions in manufacturing production labor requirements. Further study is needed to validate the justification for use of the latter dummies.

Data are not available on hours worked by nonproduction workers in the manufacturing and trade sectors. Therefore, employment of these workers is made the dependent variable in logarithmic equations with real output originating and lagged employment as the explanatory elements.

Logarithmic functions also are used to explain total man-hour requirements for the contract construction, regulated, and residual sectors. Again, aside from an inertial adjustment process, the principal explanatory variables are real output originating and a time trend for technological change. Because the residuals of these equations were highly serially correlated, Cochrane-Orcutt corrections were applied.

In the previous model, average weekly hours of production workers in the manufacturing and trade sectors and of all workers in the contract construction and regulated sectors were explained by equations of the form:

$$H = \beta_0 + \beta_1 \frac{\Delta X^{58}}{X^{58}_{-1}} + \beta_2 H_{-1}$$

where

H = average weekly hours
X^{58} = gross product originating in 1958 dollars

In specifying the present model an attempt was made to include the real product wage per man-hour (wage rates divided by the price of output) as an explanatory variable measuring labor substitution effects. Unfortunately, statistically significant coefficients were not found. One member of the project staff estimated an hour's equation using the level and change in real output and the level of wage rates as explanatory variables. This produced statistically significant coefficients and the equations were incorporated in the present model. The complete system solutions for the period 1957–65 for hours of all workers are extremely accurate; the root mean square error is only 0.15 hours per week and the mean error is 0.02 hours (on a base of 40 hours per week).

Given the equations for man-hours and average weekly hours, it is then possible to calculate employment by sector from identities of the form $E = MH/H$.

INDUSTRY PRICES

In the earlier model, prices of output originating in durables and nondurables manufacturing were determined as a function of the level of normal unit labor costs (current wage rates divided by a twelve-quarter average of output per man-hour), the difference between actual and normal unit labor costs and, as an indicator of demand pressures, the deviation of real inventory stocks per dollar of real output from its three-year trend. Wholesale price indexes for these industries then simply were made linear functions of the prices of output originating.

The present model defines normal unit labor costs as a four-quarter average of wage rates divided by normal productivity (the above output per man-hour average). Following Eckstein and Fromm, wholesale prices then were made dependent on normal unit labor costs, actual from normal unit labor cost deviations, capacity utilization, and the prices of materials inputs from other sectors.[4]

The price of output originating for durables manufacturing then was related (in a linear equation) to the wholesale price index for this sector and input materials prices (the latter has a negative sign). Output originating prices for nondurables manufacturing were better predicted by using a function similar to that for its wholesale prices (without the raw materials term) than by relating them to wholesale prices. (The marginally significant average weekly hours term—ceteris paribus, an inefficiency indicator—probably should be deleted from the equation.)

With the exception that normal unit labor costs have been slightly redefined, equation specifications for the prices of output originating for the remaining sectors—trade, contract construction, regulated, and other—are identical to those used previously. The primary explanatory variables are normal unit labor costs and actual from normal unit labor cost deviations. For the trade sector, a ratio of an inventory-stock-to-output variable, see above, is included. For the regulated sector, normal (and the deviation of actual from normal) unit capital consumption allowances are important additional determinants of prices.

---

[4] O. Eckstein and G. Fromm, "The Price Equation," *American Economic Review*, Vol. 58 (December 1968), pp. 1159–83.

WAGE RATES

The four-quarter percentage change in wage rates previously had been explained by four-quarter percentage changes in the consumer price index and profits per dollar of real output, the reciprocal of an average of unemployment rates, and the dependent variable lagged four quarters. Basically, the same form still applies. The equations have been altered slightly by dropping the profits per unit of output term (which is no longer significant), by taking the reciprocal of a four-quarter, unweighted average of unemployment rates (instead of a five-quarter weighted average), and by adding, as a distributed lag adjustment, the dependent variable lagged one quarter.

Also, the sample period for the present model encompasses the guidepost era from 1962–65, when the government attempted to restrain wage and price movements by moral suasion. Inclusion of guidepost dummy variables in the equations yielded significant negative coefficients for the durables and nondurables manufacturing, regulated, and residual sectors.

FINAL DEMAND AND PRICE CONVERSION

The format for relating the final demands and outputs of industry to GNP component demands, and GNP component prices to industry prices, was originally presented in the first volume on the model.[5] There, as in the Fromm-Taubman solutions, coefficients in equations relating final demands to GNP expenditures were constrained to sum to unity. In further analysis, it was hypothesized that changing mixes within the industry and expenditure aggregates would vitiate the homogeneity constraints.[6] The latter approach has been applied in the present model.

Real final demands by industry are related to real GNP com-

[5] F. M. Fisher, L. R. Klein, and Y. Shinkai, "Price and Output Aggregation in the Brookings Econometric Model," in *The Brookings Quarterly Econometric Model of the United States*, J. S. Duesenberry, G. Fromm, L. R. Klein, and E. Kuh, eds. (Rand McNally—North Holland, 1965), pp. 652–79.

[6] G. Fromm and L. R. Klein, "Solutions of the Complete System" in *The Brookings Model: Some Further Results*, J. S. Duesenberry, G. Fromm, L. R. Klein, and E. Kuh, eds. (Rand McNally—North-Holland, 1968), pp. 382–408.

ponent expenditures, which correspond most closely to the output of the industry. For example, for durables manufacturing, the components, in real terms, are inventory change of durables and trade, exports, consumption of durables, producers' durables equipment expenditures, and government purchases of durables. Dummy variables are added in selected periods to account for dock strikes and other unusual phenomena that are imperfectly reflected in the explanatory variables. For sectors other than durables manufacturing, auto-regressive transformations are used to eliminate strong serial correlation of residuals.

As in the past, industry gross product originating is predicted using the input-output relationship:

$$X_t^{58} = D_t^{-1}(I - A)^{-1}F_t^{58}$$

where

X^{58} = a vector of industry gross product originating in 1958 dollars
D^{-1} = the inverse of a diagonal matrix of the ratio of real gross output to real gross product originating for each industry
A = a fixed coefficient input-output matrix
F^{58} = a vector of industry final demands in 1958 dollars.

Previously, the 1947 input-output matrix had been used for complete model solutions; the 1958 table is employed for the current runs. The D matrix bears a time subscript because the ratio of gross output to gross product originating in the case of two industries, agriculture and contract construction, has been shifting over the sample period.

In previous solutions, auto-regressive transformations were applied to the output calculations as the next step. These were not done here because final demands are now corrected for serial correlation of residuals prior to the input-output conversion. Also, previously, the sum of real industry gross product originating was constrained to equal real gross national product. A trial calculation indicated that this discrepancy was small (on the order of one to two billion dollars) and the constraint was not imposed. However, it will be applied in future solutions and, if past experience is a guide, should result in improved accuracy.

The conversion of industry prices into GNP component prices has been refined for the present solutions. Previously, GNP prices were related directly to industry prices of gross product originating using the same combined matrix as for the conversion of real GNP expenditures into industry gross product originating. Now, industry prices of gross product originating (PX) are first transformed into prices of industry final demands (PF) using

$$PF = (I - A)^{-1}D^{-1}PX$$

Then the prices of GNP components (such as the implicit price deflator for personal consumption expenditures on durables automobiles, P_{CDA}) are derived from regressions of these prices on the prices of the relevant industry final demands. For example, P_{CDA} is a function of PF in the durables manufacturing and trade sectors. As previously, autoregressive transformations are needed for some GNP component prices to correct for serial correlation of residuals.

An expenditure weighted combination of these prices yields the over-all implicit deflator for total personal consumption expenditures, P_C. The consumer price index, which appears in the wage rate equations, is then predicted as a linear function of P_C.

FINANCIAL SECTOR

The specification of the financial sector retains the essential features and structure of de Leeuw's condensed simultaneous submodel, which was employed in previous solutions.[7] There have been a few changes.

First, equations for both currency and demand deposits and for demand deposits alone appear in the model. This makes currency an endogenous rather than exogenous variable (unborrowed reserves remain the principal Federal Reserve exogenous policy instrument). In each of these equations, the lagged disposable income and business investment variables have been dropped as explanatory variables. Those that remain are time deposit yields, government bill rates, disposable income, and the beginning of quarter level of the dependent variable. The functions are homogeneous in wealth, which now is de-

---

[7] F. de Leeuw, "A Condensed Model of Financial Behavior," *ibid.*, pp. 270–316.

fined as the sum of a twenty-quarter exponentially distributed lag of real GNP multiplied by the current price of GNP. (Previously, the distributed lag was taken on current dollar GNP.)

The time deposits equation also remains homogeneous in wealth with the primary explanatory variables being time deposit yields, Treasury bill rates, and the prior level of deposits. An alternative first-difference type specification shows a weak influence of disposable income. However, the t-statistic of this variable was only slightly greater than unity, so the simpler version of the equation was used for the present model solutions.

In de Leeuw's original formulation, banks' demand for free reserves as a percentage of demand and time deposits was made a function of government bill rates, the Federal Reserve discount rate, and short-run percentage changes in deposits less required reserves. For the present model, the equation was renormalized and the bill rate was made the dependent variable. The discount rate and the level and changes in free reserves relative to deposits became the principal explanatory factors of bill rate changes; government deficits (which have a negative sign) as a percentage of wealth also are found to have an effect and, other things being equal, exert upward pressure on short-term money rates.

The term structure equation relating bill rates and long-term bond yields also has been modified along lines suggested by Modigliani and Sutch.[8] The bond yield now is a function of the level and change in bill rates and the prior level of bond yields.

The yield paid on time deposits equation has been altered, too. It is assumed that quarterly changes in the time deposit rate, RM_{BDT}, cover a fraction of the gap between desired and actual rates subject to the Federal Reserve's Regulation Q ceiling limit (RM_{BDTM}):

$$\Delta RM_{BDT} = \beta_0 (RM_{BDT}^* - RM_{BDT_{-1}}) + \beta_1 RM_{BDTM}$$

The desired rate RM_{BDT}^* is obtained by maximizing banks' profits on deposits (net of reserve requirements with government bills as the mar-

[8] F. Modigliani and R. Sutch, "Innovations in Interest Rate Policy," *American Economic Review*, Vol. 56 (May 1966), pp. 178–97.

ginal investment outlet) less the yield paid on time deposits. Finally, a dummy variable is included to reflect the issuance of certificates of deposit (CD's) in the early 1960's.

NONWAGE INCOME

There has been no change in specification of the nonwage income equations. Government interest payments are a function of levels and changes in government bill rates and the amount of public debt. Dividend payments, following the work of Lintner and Brittain, depend on profits after taxes and capital consumption allowances and lagged dividends. Entrepreneurial income is related to labor compensation and corporate profits in the private sector other than agriculture. Net interest paid by consumers is dependent on a moving average of bond yields multiplied by the sum of personal consumption expenditures on durables and nonfarm residual construction.

CAPITAL CONSUMPTION ALLOWANCES

These equations are identical in form to those in the previous model. Quarterly changes in capital consumption allowances depend on recent investment and on prior allowances and various dummy variables to account for the transitions between the use of different depreciation methods.

LABOR FORCE

The equation for estimating the number of persons in the civilian labor force remains unchanged. The explanatory elements are the number of persons employed, last quarter's level and change in unemployment, and a time trend to approximate the trend toward higher labor force participation rates of working age women.

IDENTITIES, FIXED PROPORTIONS, AND MISCELLANEOUS
RELATIONSHIPS

Most of these equations comprise the aggregation of the national
income and product accounts and have not been modified. A few
changes have been occasioned by redefinition of data or better approximations to splits in an aggregate quantity.

For example, previously, real producers' durables equipment investment, I^{58}_{PDE}, was taken as a fixed proportion of real business investment. Now the split is made a function of time and dummy variables to
reflect the impact of the investment tax credit on desired proportions
of plant to equipment.

Several additions have been made for the purpose of defining potential GNP and both capacity output and capacity utilization in manufacturing. Potential real GNP and real capacity output is estimated to
have grown by 3.5 per cent per year from the third quarter of 1953
through 1965 and by 4 per cent thereafter. The model uses the Wharton capacity utilization rates for durables and nondurables manufacturing as explanatory variables. These, in turn, are related to previous
utilization rates and changes in the real actual- to capacity-output
ratios.

2   TURNING POINT ANALYSIS

A DISTINCTIVE feature of the Brookings Model, among the others
being considered at this Conference, is its size and detail. The model
generates dynamic solutions of 230 variables every quarter. There is a
rich analysis waiting to be undertaken in the study of many individual
variables or groups of variables. Nevertheless, in the light of the Conference format, the principal analysis is conducted in terms of solutions
for seventeen standardized variables. (See Table 1.)

The sample period for parameter estimation begins after the
Korean War; therefore, the first cycle analyzed is the 1953–54 reces-
sion. The 1957–58, and 1960–61 recessions are then considered.
Given the need for lagged values, the first solution is for the trough of

the recession in the third quarter of 1954. The first of the successive six-quarter simulations begins in 1954, in the first quarter or two quarters before the trough. The other turning points have simulations beginning one, two, and three quarters before the peak or trough. A way of evaluating performance at peaks and troughs is to compare root mean square (*RMS*) errors at the turning point, near the turning point, or over the whole six-quarter span with root mean square errors from the whole sample period (which includes steady growth

TABLE 1

Long-Run Simulation Errors, 1957–65
(*billions of dollars or billions of 1958 dollars unless otherwise indicated*)

Variable	Root Mean Square Error
Short-term Treasury bill rate (RM_{GBS3}), per cent	0.226
Long-term Treasury bond yield (RM_{GBL}), per cent	0.177
Real nonagricultural gross capital formation ($I^{58}_{BUS_{EAF}}$)	0.946
GNP delator (P_{GNP}), index, 1958 equals 1.0	0.0072
Unfilled orders (O^{58}_U)	4.155
Real nonfarm residential construction expenditures (I^{58}_{CNFR})	1.006
Personal income (YP)	3.384
Corporate profits before tax (ZB)	3.650
GNP in current dollars (GNP)	5.841
GNP in 1958 dollars (GNP^{58})	4.998
Unemployment rate (RU), proportion	0.00622
Consumer expenditures in 1958 dollars (C^{58})	2.429
Nonfarm inventory investment in 1958 dollars (INV^{58}_{EAF})	2.653
Net foreign balance (B)	1.350
Employment (EHH), millions of persons	0.534
Hours worked per week (H), hours	0.150
Money wage rate ($RWSS$), dollars per hour	0.0397

NOTE: These are quite favorable results. *GNP* solutions with root mean square errors of approximately $5.0 billion are good for ex post solutions. Interest rates are estimated with root mean square errors of approximately 20 basis points. Price level errors are approximately ¾ of a point movement in the index based on 100. Similarly, the error in the unemployment rate, RU, is about ⅔ of a point in the third decimal place when the rate is expressed as a per cent.

phases between the lower and the succeeding upper turning points). The longer dynamic simulation from given initial values begins in the first quarter of 1957 and runs through the fourth quarter of 1965. Given the small size of the variable, the root mean square error of real inventory investment is large. Similarly, corporate profits before taxes and the net foreign balance are estimated subject to a fair size error.

Simulations of eleven variables around the five sample-period turning points are depicted in Charts 1–11. In general, the pattern of predicted values follows actual experience reasonably well. However, solutions tend to run within the actual cycles, understating peak and overstating trough values. Furthermore, predicted turning points often occur either too early or too late. These phenomena have been found in other studies.[9] In the following discussion of the individual turning points, emphasis is placed primarily on the accuracy of GNP and real GNP predictions. The reader is encouraged, however, to examine all the charts in conjunction with the text discussion.

THE 1954 TROUGH

Most variables show a substantial negative residual (actual minus computed) at the trough, the third quarter of 1954. In some cases the negative residual is one quarter on either side of the trough. In the case of the unemployment rate, the small negative residual at the trough does not indicate underestimation of amplitude; the residual is much smaller than the root mean square value for RU in Table 1. For the other variables, the root mean square values are both larger and smaller than the reference values; but the residuals almost all have the same sign, supporting the view that when the economy makes a large movement in either direction, model solutions vary with lower amplitude. The nonstochastic solution is often a smooth series compared to the actual data and cuts off extreme peak and trough fluctuations.

On the whole, performance is good at this turning point. The errors in the solution are frequently lower than those in Table 1. Several

---

[9] George R. Green in association with Maurice Liebenberg and Albert A. Hirsch, "Short- and Long-Term Simulations with the OBE Econometric Model," this volume, pp. 25–123.

CHART 1

GNP^{58}
Gross National Product in 1958 Dollars

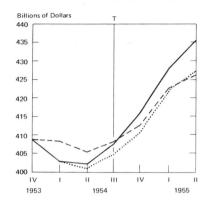

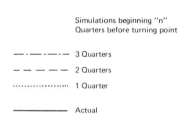

Simulations beginning "n"
Quarters before turning point

—·—·—·— 3 Quarters

— — — — 2 Quarters

·················· 1 Quarter

———————— Actual

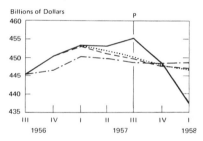

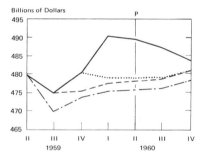

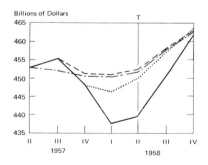

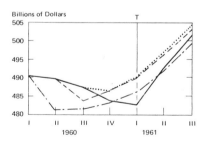

CHART 2

P_{GNP}
Implicit Price Deflator for Gross National Product
(1958 = 100)

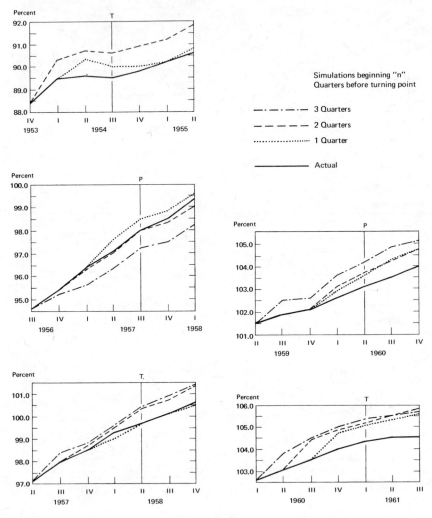

Simulations beginning "n"
Quarters before turning point

— · — · — 3 Quarters

— — — — 2 Quarters

· · · · · · · · · · 1 Quarter

———————— Actual

CHART 3

$I^{58}_{BUS_{EAF}}$

Nonagricultural Business Gross Investment

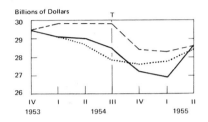

Billions of Dollars

Simulations beginning "n"
Quarters before turning point

—·—·—·— 3 Quarters

— — — — 2 Quarters

·················· 1 Quarter

——————— Actual

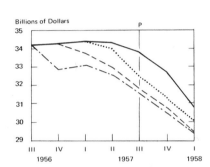

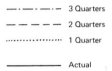

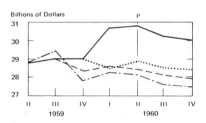

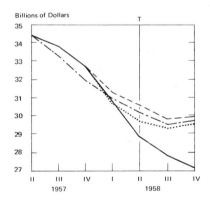

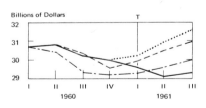

CHART 4

I_{CNFR}^{58}

New Private Nonfarm Residential Construction in 1958 Dollars

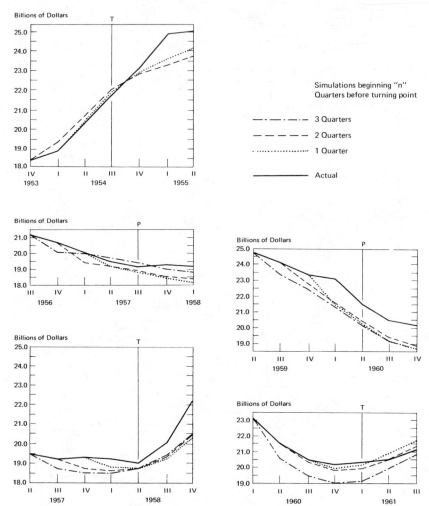

CHART 5

$$\Delta INV_{EAF}^{58}$$

Nonfarm Inventory Investment in 1958 Dollars

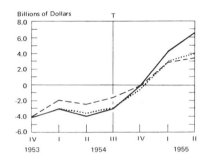

Simulations beginning "n"
Quarters before turning point

——·——·—— 3 Quarters

— — — — 2 Quarters

·················· 1 Quarter

———————— Actual

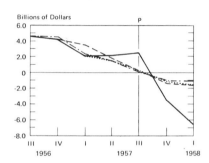

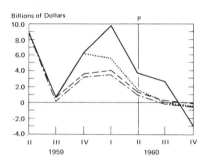

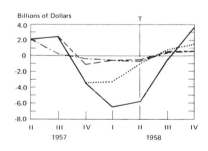

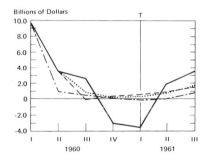

CHART 6

C^{58}

Personal Consumption Expenditures in 1958 Dollars

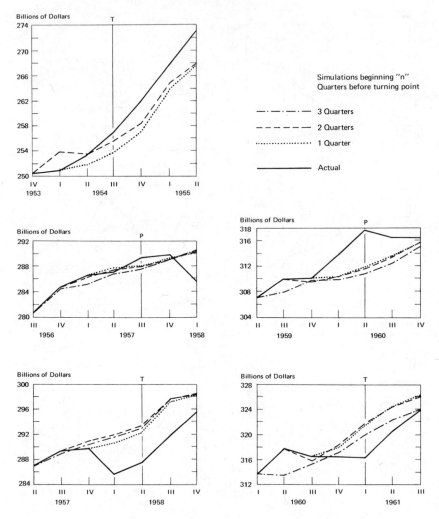

CHART 7

RU
Unemployment Rate

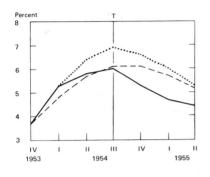

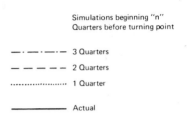

Simulations beginning "n"
Quarters before turning point

—·—·—·— 3 Quarters

— — — — 2 Quarters

················· 1 Quarter

———————— Actual

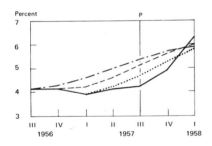

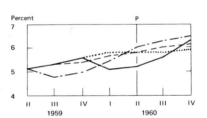

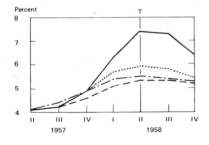

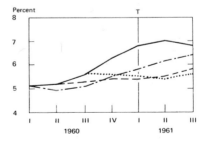

CHART 8

EHH
Civilian Employment

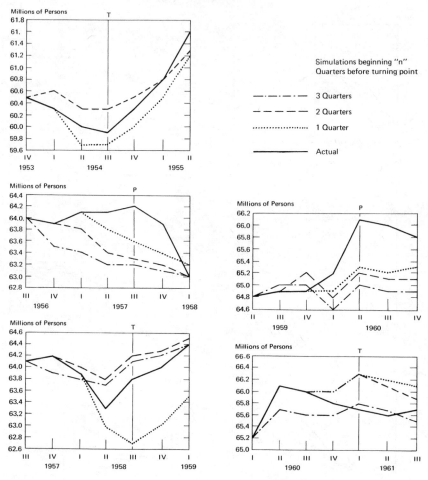

CHART 9

RM_{GBS3}
Short-Term Treasury Bill Rate

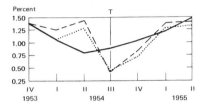

Simulations beginning "n"
Quarters before turning point

—·—·—·— 3 Quarters

— — — — — 2 Quarters

················· 1 Quarter

——————— Actual

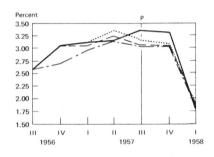

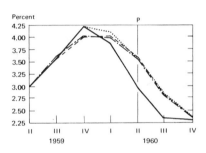

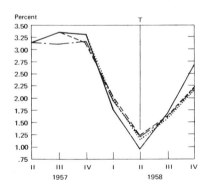

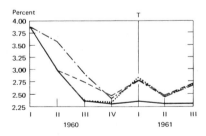

CHART 10

RWSS
Hourly Wage Rate Including Supplements

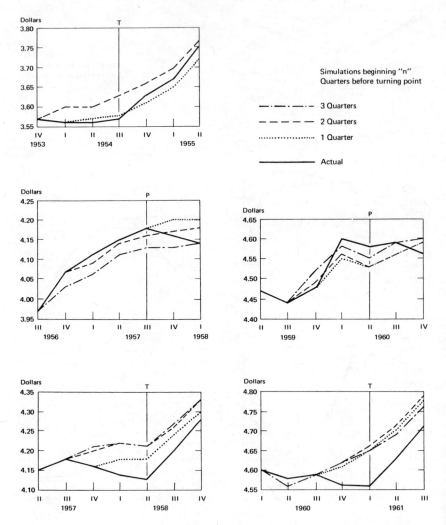

CHART 11

Z_B
Corporate Profits Before Taxes Including Inventory Valuation Adjustment

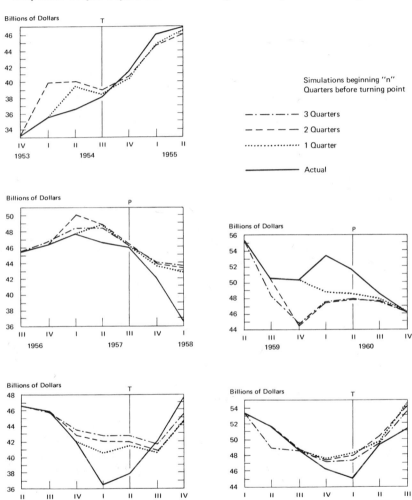

TABLE 2

1954 Recovery: Root Mean Square Errors, Trough
(billions of dollars)

	Starting from 1954:1		Starting from 1954:2	
	Six Quarters	1954:3	Six Quarters	1954:3
GNP	4.958	−5.058	4.239	0.615
GNP58	5.184	−0.738	5.079	2.639

turning point errors improve when we start up the solution one instead of two quarters before the trough. (See Table 2.)

1957–58 RECESSION

In this case the peak is in the third quarter of 1957 and the trough is in the second quarter of 1958. At the peak, the performance appears to be good. Many cyclical variables have the correct quarter-to-quarter movements, and the root mean square errors are either smaller or not significantly larger than the sample average values either at the peak point or over an entire six-quarter solution period. There is a tendency, however, for underestimation to occur at the peak.

Usually, models such as the present one do better at business cycle troughs than at peaks. (See Table 3.) This does not seem to be the case for the Brookings Model in the 1957–58 recession. Corresponding to the comparatively good performance at the peak, the root mean square errors are mostly larger for the trough calculations, both at the trough point and for the whole six-quarter simulation period.

With the two *GNP* series, there is consistent underestimation at peaks and overestimation at troughs. The timing and change-of-sign correspondence was good at the troughs in spite of large errors.

THE 1960–61 RECESSION

One of the mildest sets of actual turning points of the economy is the 1960–61 recession. The movement is so slight that it is more difficult to predict this recession than other postwar downturns. At both the peak and trough, there are discrepancies in the movement of principal series. The inability to deal with 1960–61 does not necessarily mean that the model has serious defects; fluctuations in narrow ranges are difficult to project. Some variables, however, perform well in this set of solutions (1960–61). The GNP series generally misses the turning point, a defect that needs to be corrected. (See Table 4.)

Generally speaking, there are large errors in comparison with root mean square values for the whole sample period. This is true for both measures of GNP at peaks. Behavior near the trough is better. The root mean square errors for GNP^{58} in six quarters covering the trough are low and the error for trough quarters are not excessive. At the peak quarters, observations exceed computed values of GNP and GNP^{58}. This again is a failure to reach the complete range of the observed amplitude. At troughs, the reverse result holds, and the model fails to fall enough, leaving negative errors.

TABLE 3

1957–58 Recession — Recovery: Root Mean Square Errors
(billions of dollars)

	Peak Starting from 1956:4		Peak Starting from 1957:1		Peak Starting from 1957:2	
	Six Quarters	1957:3	Six Quarters	1957:3	Six Quarters	1957:3
GNP	6.180	8.904	5.582	5.573	6.993	2.781
$GNP58$	5.488	5.339	5.850	5.405	5.808	5.092

	Trough Starting from 1957:3		Trough Starting from 1957:4		Trough Starting from 1958:1	
	Six Quarters	1958:2	Six Quarters	1958:2	Six Quarters	1958:2
GNP	9.741	−15.213	9.635	−15.266	6.423	−10.374
$GNP58$	7.928	−12.100	8.235	−12.750	7.025	−10.544

TABLE 4

1960–61 Recession—Recovery: Root Mean Square Errors
(billions of dollars)

	Peak Starting from 1959:3		Peak Starting from 1959:4		Peak Starting from 1960:1	
	Six Quarters	1960:2	Six Quarters	1960:2	Six Quarters	1960:2
GNP	6.517	9.339	6.661	9.144	5.838	8.465
GNP58	10.356	14.118	8.334	11.801	7.433	10.939

	Trough Starting from 1960:2		Trough Starting from 1960:3		Trough Starting from 1960:4	
	Six Quarters	1961:1	Six Quarters	1961:1	Six Quarters	1961:1
GNP	4.929	−8.538	7.472	−11.911	8.364	−11.245
GNP58	4.467	−3.557	3.850	−7.289	3.877	−7.407

3 LONGER-RUN SIMULATIONS

THERE are two basic ways of generating long-run solutions of the model. One approach is limited to the sample period, with possibly a few post-sample-period observations added. The other approach extrapolates the series entirely beyond the sample. There is no limit, in principle, to the time duration of simulations outside the sample period. First, sample period simulations for thirty-six quarters are examined, starting in the first quarter of 1957 and ending with the fourth quarter of 1965.

The general impression of these thirty-six-quarter dynamic simulations is that computed values track the course of observed values rather closely, especially at the beginning and end of the period. This point is supported by the relatively small residuals shown in Table 1 and Charts 12–15.

CHART 12

GNP[58]
Gross National Product in 1958 Dollars

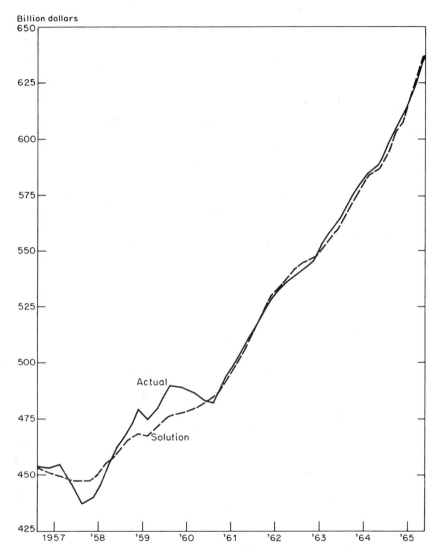

CHART 13

P_{GNP}
Implicit Price Deflator for Gross National Product

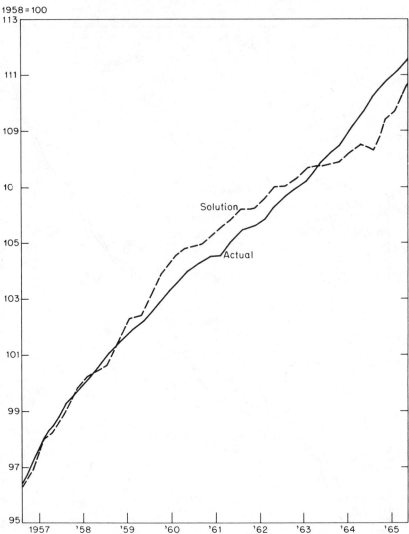

CHART 14

$I^{58}_{BUS_{EAF}}$

Nonagricultural Business Gross Investment

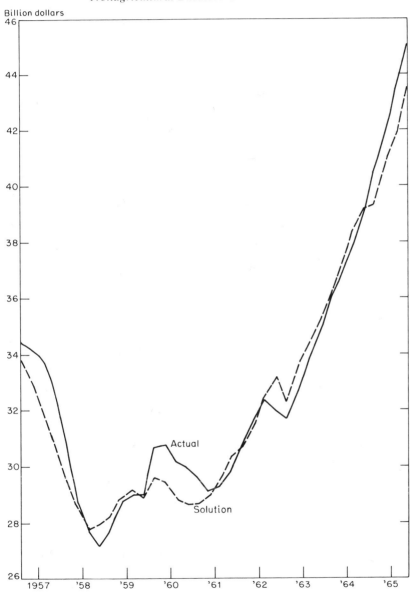

CHART 15

I^{58}_{CNFR}

New Private Nonfarm Residential Construction in 1958 Dollars

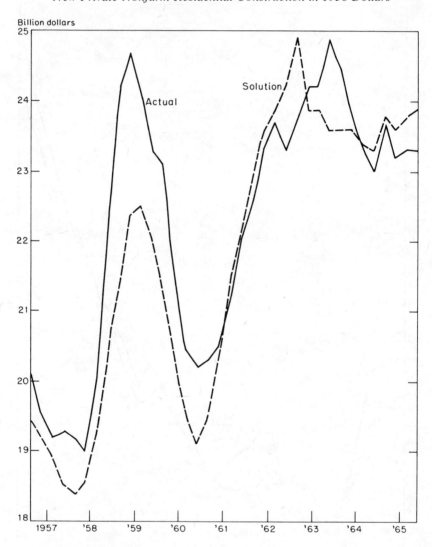

Some larger errors occur in the middle ranges of the simulation. The model picks up the trend component very well. Cyclical behavior is mixed. The solution for real GNP, however, does follow the 1957–58 period, but it fails to decline in 1960–61. Current dollar GNP, reflecting steady price inflation, has only one quarterly decline in the whole nine-year period. It misses the peak and trough points.

The quantitative nature of the solution, however, is good. Among the seventeen simulated variables, the quarterly sign change is correct in most instances. The percentage of correct signs estimated for quarterly changes exceeds 75 per cent in all except four cases.

Some strong trend variables and some highly cyclical variables are displayed in Charts 12–15. Real GNP and the GNP deflator both have the appropriate trend growth corresponding to the actual data. In addition, real GNP has some of the appropriate cyclical content. Price projections are one or two points low at the end of the calculation, but this is not a large error. In the case of the capital formation series — both business investment and residential construction — the main cyclical swings are well delineated by the computed values. Conformity is acceptable not only at the reference cycle peaks and troughs, but also at the specific cycle peaks and troughs. In 1959–60, the amplitudes of the peak and trough in residential construction are underestimated, but the timing is approximately correct.

In comparison with the previous version of the Brookings Model, these results represent improvement. Earlier, there were biases that gave rise to a regular discrepancy between estimated and actual GNP. Also, the older model implied more price inflation than actually occurred in the early part of the 1960's. The absolute errors in the present simulation, though for a different time span, are generally one-third to one-half of those reported by Nagar in his study of stochastic and nonstochastic simulations over the sample period.[10]

Two methodological points are highlighted by these results: (1) the estimates of the model at the present time have been computed only by ordinary least squares (OLS); (2) some of the estimated structural equations have serially correlated errors.

Although the OLS estimates appear to be functioning very well in

[10] A. L. Nagar, "Stochastic Simulation of the Brookings Model" in *The Brookings Model: Some Further Results, op. cit.,* pp. 423–56.

these exercises on complete system performance, other studies have found that least squares bias sometimes appears to be more significant in complete system solutions than in separate equations, and that biases tend to accumulate as simulations are conducted over long time periods.[11] Consistent estimates of the new Brookings Model will be forthcoming.

In the paper on the OBE Model, and also on the Wharton Model, it was found that auto-regressive transformations of individual equations (to take account of the presence of serial correlation in calculated residuals) brought modest improvement to sample period simulations. That technique was not used for solution of the Brookings Model, but some of the equations were originally estimated with second-order auto-regressive corrections. For a relationship

$$y_t = \alpha_0 + \alpha_1 x_t + e_t$$

$$e_t = \rho_1 e_{t-1} + \rho_2 e_{t-2} + u_t$$

the estimated form was

$$(y_t - r_1 y_{t-1} - r_2 y_{t-2}) = a_0(1 - r_1 - r_2) + a_1(x_t - r_1 x_{t-1} - r_2 x_{t-2})$$

$$a_i = \text{est } \alpha_i, \qquad r_i = \text{est } \rho_i$$

These estimates were made for investment functions, where it was found that second-order corrections were needed in order to eliminate serial correlation of residuals. Although the estimates of α_0 and α_1 should be more efficient by this correction, the transformed equations gave very poor results in the complete system simulations. The alternative of solving the system using

$$y_t = a_0 + a_1 x_t$$

admitting serial correlations in residuals was not undertaken. Instead,

$$y_t = a_0^* + a_1^* x_t$$

was re-estimated in the presence of serially correlated errors. Although a_i^* should be less efficient than a_i, the equations with a_i^* coefficients gave better system solution results than the transformed set using a_i.

[11] L. R. Klein, "The Estimation of Interdependent Systems in Macroeconometrics," *Econometrica* (April, 1969), pp. 171–192.

The transformed equation uses more lagged values, and probably goes astray through error build-up in the process of dynamic solution. At present, we are experimenting with other estimates of investment equations using a combination of new lag distributions and first-order autoregressive transformations to see if they perform better in simulations.

It should be pointed out that the complete system dynamic simulations all have serially correlated residuals (between computed and actual values). This serial correlation is part of the complete solution of the finite difference equation system and arises through the solution process.

4 TWENTY-FIVE-YEAR SIMULATIONS

THE Brookings Model is essentially a short-run forecasting model and as such is not designed for simulations over a twenty-five year period. Therefore, certain adjustments, discussed below, were necessary in order to produce a reasonable control solution. The control solution is a hypothetical growth path over the period from the first quarter of 1966 through the fourth quarter of 1990. However, actual values of some of the exogenous variables were used for the first three and one-half years.[12] Also, government spending and employment were adjusted to reflect the possible slowdown of the Vietnam War during 1970.

Shocked simulations were produced by introducing random additive disturbances to the stochastic equations of the model. These disturbances are selected so that they have the same asymptotic variance-covariance properties, of all orders, as the original single equation residuals. The procedure used to generate these shocks is discussed in the paper by Michael D. McCarthy.[13] A slight change from McCarthy's procedure was necessary because residuals from the equation estimates were not available. The residuals were computed over the

---

[12] The variables set to exact values were G, G^{58}, WSS_G, WS_G, E_G, DOD_{MPCA}, WSS_A, and E_A. The components of G^{58} were adjusted to add up to G^{58}.

[13] M. D. McCarthy, "Some Notes on the Generation of Pseudo Structural Errors for Use in Stochastic Simulation Studies," Appendix to "Short-Run Prediction and Long-Run Simulation of the Wharton Model," this volume, pp. 185–191.

sample period using the simulation program, which leads to different results in cases where equations are renormalized. For example, the man-hours equations were estimated in log form but the residuals for the man-hours equations as computed in the simulation program were in man-hours.

The exogenous variables for the twenty-five year simulation were generated mainly by extrapolation along their actual trends over the period from 1954 through 1965. In cases where actual data were used through the second quarter of 1969, the trend was extended from that point. The government sector exogenous variables were lowered in 1970 to simulate the end of the Vietnam War and then raised to their trend levels during 1971. The beginning and ending values along with annual percentage rates of change are shown for the principal exogenous variables in Table 5.

As is mentioned above, certain equations had to be modified in

TABLE 5

Exogenous Variables for the Twenty-five Year Simulation

	Principal Exogenous Assumptions		Annual Rate of Change
	1965:4	1990:4	
G^{58}	118.4	286.6	3.6
G	143.3	694.9	6.5
E_G	10.26	19.86	2.7
WSS_G	78.5	283.9	5.3
$V_{OASI_{GF}}$	18.6	100.1	7.0
V_{VET}	5.7	13.1	3.4
V_{OG}	11.5	47.0	5.8
$IBUS_{AF}^{58}$	4.6	9.6	3.0
WSS_A	3.6	5.2	1.5
E_A	4.20	1.81	−3.3
PEX_W	1.030	1.065	0.1
EX_W^{58}	164.8	356.5	3.1
PM	1.047	1.537	1.5
INT_{BUS}	6.9	17.70	3.8
INT_{CON}	11.7	26.75	3.4
N^R	194.73	267.67	1.3

order to arrive at a reasonable growth path over the twenty-five year period. The two sets of functions where modifications were necessary were the tax, man-hours and hours equations. The modified tax functions are presented in Table 6. The personal income tax function was adjusted to approximate actual tax yields from 1966 through the second quarter of 1969. The surcharge was cut in half for the first two quarters of 1970 and then terminated. The tax rate was raised gradually through 1976 and then held constant in order to keep disposable income from growing too rapidly and also to limit government deficits.

The corporate profits tax function was adjusted so as to yield an approximately correct value given the actual data over the initial three and one-half years. The suspension of the investment tax credit in the fourth quarter of 1966 and first quarter of 1967 was accounted for by setting the tax credit dummy (DMY_{ITC}) to zero. The expected termination of the credit in the third quarter of 1970 was simulated by both a change in DMY_{ITC} and the corporate tax rate TC_{RT}. The corporate tax surcharge was cut in half in the first quarter of 1970 and terminated in the third quarter.

The indirect business tax function was adjusted, through changes in DMY_{TX}, to approximate actual excise tax collections from the first quarter of 1966 through the second quarter of 1969. The value of DMY_{TX} was held constant from that point onwards. The contributions for social insurance function was similarly adjusted.

Assumptions about old age and survivors insurance (OASI) contribution rates, and maximum individual wage and salary tax bases, and unemployment insurance contribution rates are taken from Pechman, Aaron and Taussig, and from Pechman, respectively.[14] The percentage of employees covered by OASI was raised over the period from 89 to 93 per cent.

The rate of productivity increase implicit in the production man-hours equations for the manufacturing nondurables, trade, and other sectors was too moderate, so the time trends and constant terms in these equations were appropriately adjusted. The long-term rate of productivity increase in the construction sector was also negligible,

[14] Joseph A. Pechman, Henry J. Aaron, and Michael K. Taussig, *Social Security: Perspectives for Reform* (Brookings, 1968), p. 272; and Joseph A. Pechman, *Federal Tax Policy* (Brookings, 1966), p. 251.

TABLE 6

Tax Function Assumptions
(by year and quarter, unless otherwise indicated)

I. Personal Income Tax

$$TP = -5.8DMY_{TP} + 0.14DMY_{TP}Y_P$$

$$(DMY_{TP})$$

Year	1	2	3	4
1966	0.923	0.950	0.975	1.000
1967	1.000	1.000	1.010	1.020
1968	1.020	1.030	1.120	1.140
1969	1.150	1.150	1.150	1.150
1970	1.100	1.100	1.050	1.050
1971	1.060	1.070	1.080	1.090
1972	1.100	1.110	1.120	1.130
1973	1.140	1.150	1.160	1.170
1974	1.180	1.190	1.200	1.210
1975	1.220	1.230	1.240	1.250
1976	1.250	1.250	1.250	1.250
1990	1.250	1.250	1.250	1.250

II. Corporate Profits Tax

$$TC = 0.9303 - 0.6567DMY_{ITC} + 0.8360(TC_{RT})(Z_{BU})$$

$$(DMY_{ITC})$$

Year	1	2	3	4
1966	1.000	1.000	1.000	0.000
1967	0.000	1.000	1.000	1.000
1968	0.949	0.949	0.950	0.948
1969	0.945	0.945	0.945	0.945
1970	0.967	0.967	0.988	0.988
1971	0.988	0.988	0.988	0.988
1990	0.988	0.988	0.988	0.988

$$(TC_{RT})$$

Year	1	2	3	4
1966	0.480	0.480	0.480	0.480
1967	0.480	0.480	0.480	0.480
1968	0.539	0.539	0.539	0.539
1969	0.543	0.543	0.543	0.543
1970	0.518	0.518	0.493	0.493
1971	0.493	0.493	0.493	0.493
1990	0.493	0.493	0.493	0.493

TABLE 6 (concluded)

III. Indirect Business Tax

$$TX = -7.5578 + 2.1879DMY_{TX} + 0.1014GNP$$

(DMY_{TX})

Year	1	2	3	4
1966	-1.37	-1.23	-1.10	-1.42
1967	-1.37	-1.23	-1.28	-1.14
1968	-1.46	-1.14	-0.87	-0.69
1969	-0.70	-0.70	-0.70	-0.70
1990	-0.70	-0.70	-0.70	-0.70

IV. Contributions for Social Insurance

$$TW = -5.8424 + 0.1552(t-4) + 0.0286UINS_{RT}EHH$$
$$-0.2765OASI_{PR-RT}(OASI_{BA}EHH - WSS)$$
$$+ 0.7199OASI_{PR-RT}OASI_{BA}EHH + DMY_{CR}$$

Years	$OASI_{PR-RT}$	$OASI_{BA}$	$UINS_{RT}$
1966	0.075	6.6	3.1
1967	0.079	6.6	3.1
1968	0.079	7.8	3.1
1969	0.086	7.8	3.1
1970	0.087	7.8	3.1
1971-72	0.094	7.8	3.1
1973-75	0.103	7.8	3.1
1976-77	0.104	7.8	3.1
1978-79	0.105	7.8	3.1
1980-82	0.107	7.8	3.1
1983-86	0.108	7.8	3.1
1987	0.110	7.8	3.1
1988-90	0.111	7.8	3.1

(DMY_{CR})

Year	1	2	3	4
1966	-1.1	-0.9	0.1	0.2
1967	0.1	0.8	1.0	1.3
1968	-0.6	-0.1	0.4	0.9
1969	1.0	1.0	1.0	1.0
1990	1.0	1.0	1.0	1.0

241

TABLE 7

Productivity Changes, Control Solution

	1965:4	1990:4	Annual Rate of Change (per cent)
$X_{MD}^{58}/MH_{P_{MD}}$	6.7804	16.3988	3.6
$X_{MD}^{58}/E_{O_{MD}}$	42.7671	92.0779	3.1
$X_{MN}^{58}/MH_{P_{MN}}$	6.4520	18.5101	4.3
$X_{MN}^{58}/E_{O_{MN}}$	39.9040	59.5704	1.6
X_T^{58}/MH_{P_T}	5.7309	15.1120	4.0
X_T^{58}/E_{O_T}	34.4419	45.9639	1.2
X_R^{58}/MH_R	6.8742	21.0194	4.6
X_C^{58}/MH_C	3.7652	3.9542	0.2
X_O^{58}/MH_O	5.9058	10.0364	2.1
GNP^{58}/EHH	8.8653	16.1126	2.4

but was modified only slightly. Productivity was adjusted upward in the overhead employment functions. All the hours functions showed a consistent upward bias and were adjusted to maintain an approximately constant workweek. Productivity figures at the start and end of the twenty-five year control simulation and average annual rates of change are shown in Table 7.

Over the 1966–90 period the control solution exhibited very little fluctuation, especially after 1970. Smooth extrapolation of the exogenous variables most likely caused this steady growth. Fluctuations over the first four years are due largely to the use of some actual exogenous data and to the initial conditions.

Simulation of the slowdown attributable to the end of the Vietnam War and its aftermath resulted in fluctuations in 1970–71. Only a slowdown in growth, and no actual downturn, resulted with the unemployment rate rising to only 4.4 per cent.

Control solution time paths over the full twenty-five year simulation period for P_{GNP}, GNP^{58}, $I_{BUS_{EAF}}^{58}$, and I_{CNFR}^{58} are shown in Charts 16–19, respectively. Values for the seventeen variables considered in this study are presented in Table 8 for the fourth quarters of 1965 and 1990, together with their annual rates of change (where relevant).

Fifty stochastic simulations were run over the period from the first quarter of 1966 through the fourth quarter of 1990. In computing these simulations, random disturbance terms were introduced having the same variance-covariance and serial correlation properties as the residuals from the sample period equation estimates. While some of the stochastic simulations drifted, the majority fluctuated about the control path. The means of the stochastic simulation values were almost identical to their control solution values. Charts 16–19 show the control solution, a representative stochastic simulation, and the control solution plus and minus two standard errors for real gross national product (GNP^{58}), the implicit deflator for GNP (P_{GNP}), real nonfarm business gross fixed investment ($I^{58}_{BUS_{EAF}}$), and real new private nonfarm residential construction (I^{58}_{CNFR}).

In order to determine whether the stochastic simulations produced

TABLE 8

Summary of Control Solution

	1965:4	1990:4	Annual Rate of Change (per cent)
RM_{GBS3}	4.160	6.942	—
RM_{GBL}	4.350	5.155	—
$IBUS^{58}_{EAF}$	45.2	141.0	4.7
P_{GNP}	1.115	1.709	1.7
O^{58}_{U}	63.4	114.6	2.4
I^{58}_{CNFR}	23.3	55.4	3.5
Y_P	558.4	2088.0	5.4
Z_B	80.3	372.3	6.3
GNP	710.0	2779.8	5.6
GNP^{58}	636.6	1626.9	3.8
RU	0.041	0.039	—
C^{58}	409.2	1075.9	3.9
ΔINV^{58}_{EAF}	8.1	10.1	—
B	5.7	−0.3	—
EHH	71.81	100.97	1.4
H	39.93	38.59	—
$RWSS$	5.691	16.283	4.3

CHART 16

GNP[58]

Gross National Product in 1958 Dollars

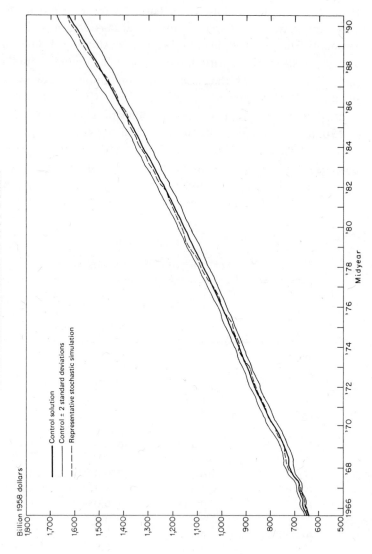

CHART 11

P_{GNP}

Implicit Price Deflator for Gross National Product

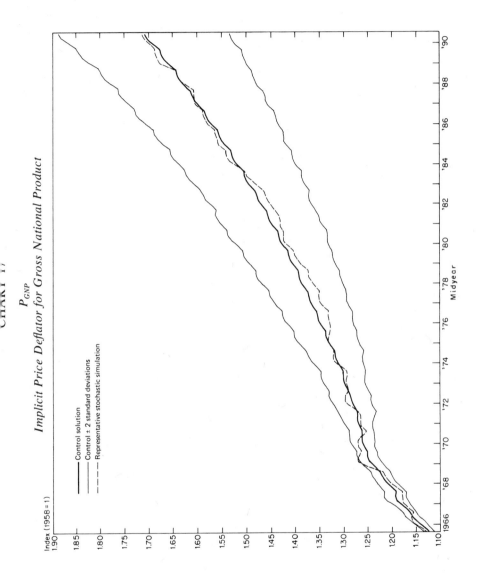

Index (1958 = 1)

Control solution
Control ± 2 standard deviations
Representative stochastic simulation

Midyear

CHART 18

$I^{58}_{BUS_{EAF}}$

Nonagricultural Business Gross Investment

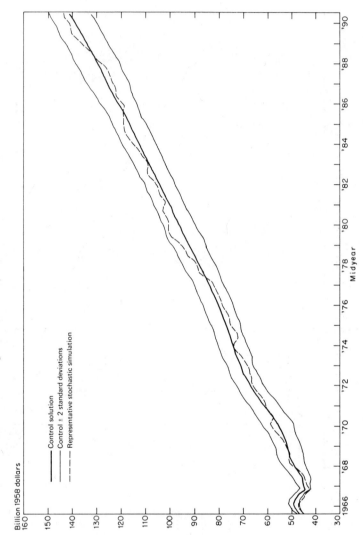

Billion 1958 dollars

——— Control solution
——— Control ± 2 standard deviations
– – – Representative stochastic simulation

Midyear

CHART 19

I_{CNFR}^{58}

New Private Nonfarm Residential Construction in 1958 Dollars

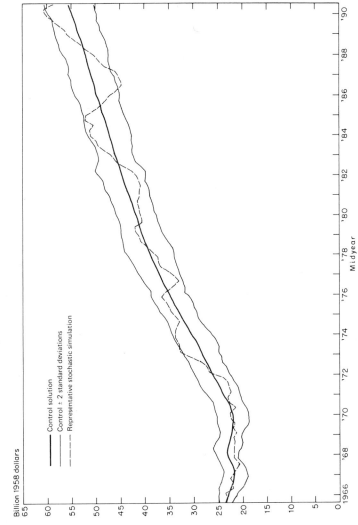

cyclical movements similar to those observed in historical data, spectral analysis was applied to the fifty series generated for each of these four variables. This required the removal of trends in the series. Denoting the original stochastically generated series as Y_S, the control solution as Y_C, and t as a time index, the detrended series, X, may be represented by

$$X_t = Y_{S,t} - a - bY_{C,t} - ct, \text{ for } t = 1966{:}1, \ldots, 1990{:}4$$

where a, b and c are determined by ordinary least squares regressions of $Y_{S,t}$ on $Y_{C,t}$ and t. The effectiveness of this detrending procedure was tested by comparing the means and variances of X_t computed over the first and second halves of the period first quarter of 1966

CHART 20

Average Spectra for Fifty Real National Product Series

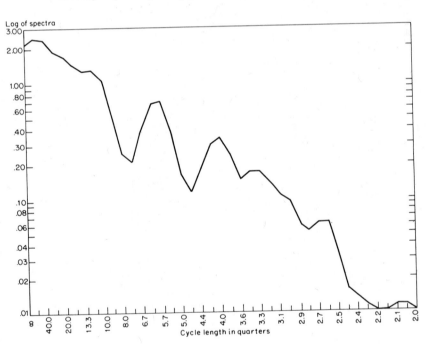

Log of spectra

Cycle length in quarters

CHART 21

Average Spectra for Fifty GNP Implicit Price Deflator Series

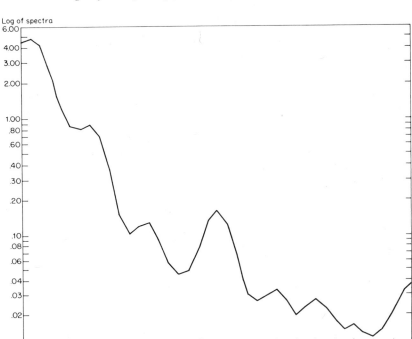

through the fourth quarter of 1990. In almost all cases, the two sub-sample means and variances were not significantly different.[15]

Average spectral densities are shown for each of the four series in Charts 20–23. Chart 24 shows frequency counts of the most prominent spectral peaks in the fifty series. A Parzen window and a lag length of 40 were used for all spectral calculations.[16] All the average

---

[15] The *t*- and *F*-tests were used to test equality of the means and variances, respectively. Even though an implicit normality assumption was required, especially for the *F*-test, no test for normality was made.

[16] C. W. J. Granger and M. Hatanaka, *Spectral Analysis of Economic Time Series* (Princeton University Press, 1964), pp. 52–73.

CHART 22

Average Spectra for Fifty Nonfarm Business Gross Fixed Investment Series

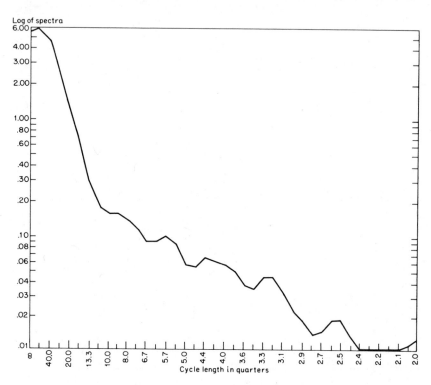

CHART 23

*Average Spectra for Fifty Real New Private Nonfarm Residential
Construction Series*

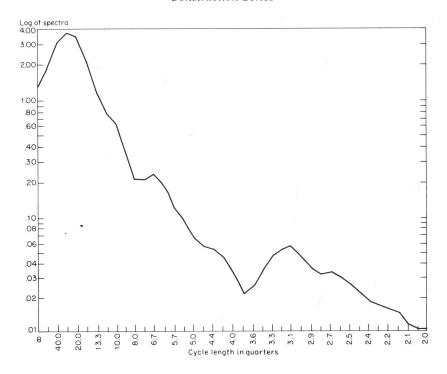

CHART 24

Frequency Bar Charts of the Most Prominent Spectral Peaks for Fifty Series Generated Using Serially Correlated Random Disturbances

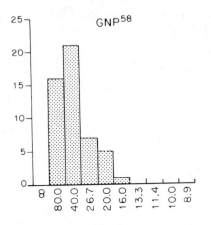

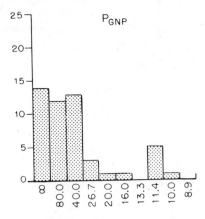

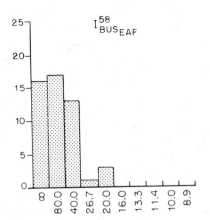

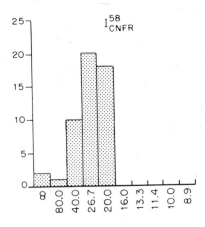

spectra have their highest power at low frequencies (long cycle length) and all exhibit minor cyclical movements at the highest frequencies (less than one year cycle length). These latter movements probably reflect seasonal fluctuations. The average spectra for real GNP also exhibits peaks at approximately four and six quarters. P_{GNP} tends to exhibit both six quarter and three year cycles. While the three year cycle is not obvious in its average spectra, examination of the individual spectra shows that the cycle occurs in twenty-six of the fifty series – in six series the three year cycle was most prominent (see Chart 24). Real fixed nonfarm business investment ($I^{58}_{BUS_{EAF}}$) does not exhibit any significant cycles of intermediate length. The most prominent spectral peaks for real private nonfarm residential construction (I^{58}_{CNFR}) almost all lie in the five to ten year cycle length range – five to seven year cycle lengths are the most common. For the average spectra of I^{58}_{CNFR}, the most prominent spectral peak also occurs in the five to seven year range.

5   CONCLUSION

THE present, 1969 version of the Brookings Model exhibits sample period properties similar to the earlier Fromm-Taubman version. The model tracks trends quite well. Also, although leads and lags at turning points and cyclical amplitudes are not always predicted accurately, the model portrays the actual cyclical fluctuations.

Judging by root mean square errors, the 1969 version exhibits improved complete system performance over earlier versions. Problem areas basically remain the same, notably inventories, wage rates, and prices. But even here differences between predicted and actual values have been reduced to some extent.

Twenty-five year nonstochastic and stochastic simulations beyond the sample period were run with the model for the first time. It was found that the nonstochastic path of the solution depends primarily on the values chosen for principal exogenous variables but that, given these, endogenous variables take values that accord well with prior historical experience. Although some had trend deviations, stochastic solutions generally fluctuated about the nonstochastic control. A spectral analysis of these results revealed a general pattern of falling spectral densities from low to high frequencies without much evidence of distinct peaks except in isolated cases of highly cyclical variables. It might be said that the average spectral diagram exhibited the typical spectral shape of economic variables suggested by Granger.[17] Analysis of the frequency distribution of spectral peaks did, however, reveal some short-run cyclical content for many of the variables.

APPENDIX A

CONSUMER DEMAND

(A.1)
$$\frac{C_{DEA}^{58}}{N_R} = \underset{(2.5)}{-0.1378} + \underset{(11.6)}{0.2004} \frac{Y_D^{58}}{N_R} - \underset{(0.4)}{0.0150} \frac{P_{CDEA}}{P_C}$$

$$- \underset{(1.8)}{0.1499} \left[\frac{K_{CDEA}^{58}}{N_R}\right]_{-1} + \underset{(0.8)}{0.0014} DMY_{55}$$

$$\bar{R}^2 = 0.986 \qquad SE = 0.0028 \qquad DW = 0.94$$

(A.2)
$$\frac{C_{DA}^{58}}{N_R} = \underset{(1.4)}{0.0430} + \underset{(7.5)}{0.0913} \frac{Y_D^{58}}{N_R} - \underset{(2.5)}{0.0723} \frac{P_{CDA}}{P_C}$$

$$- \underset{(1.3)}{0.0903} \left[\frac{K_{CDA}^{58}}{N_R}\right]_{-1} - \underset{(6.3)}{0.5262} RU + \underset{(6.8)}{0.0214} DMY_{55}$$

$$+ \underset{(1.3)}{0.0039} [DMY_{STR}] \left[\frac{Y_D^{58}}{N_R}\right]$$

$$\bar{R}^2 = 0.893 \qquad SE = 0.0053 \qquad DW = 1.77$$

(A.3)
$$\frac{C_{NFB}^{58}}{N_R} = \underset{(5.5)}{0.4180} + \underset{(8.0)}{0.0655} \frac{Y_D^{58}}{N_R} - \underset{(2.9)}{0.1332} \frac{P_{CNFB}}{P_C}$$

[17] Ibid., pp. 55–59.

$$+ 0.0796 \left(\frac{1}{4}\right) \sum_{i=1}^{4} \left[\frac{C_{NFB}^{58}}{N_R}\right]_{-i}$$

$$\bar{R}^2 = 0.923 \qquad SE = 0.0032 \qquad DW = 0.94$$

(A.4) $\quad \dfrac{C_{NEFB}^{58}}{N_R} = 0.3053 + 0.1451 \dfrac{Y_D^{58}}{N_R} - 0.2636 \dfrac{P_{CNEFB}}{P_C}$
$\qquad\qquad\qquad\quad$ (4.4) $\qquad$ (9.8) $\qquad\qquad$ (4.6)

$$+ 0.1710 \left(\frac{1}{4}\right) \sum_{i=1}^{4} \left[\frac{C_{NEFB}^{58}}{N_R}\right]_{-i}$$
$$(1.4)$$

$$\bar{R}^2 = 0.989 \qquad SE = 0.0030 \qquad DW = 1.92$$

(A.5) $\quad \dfrac{C_S^{58}}{N_R} = 0.0422 + 0.0529 \dfrac{Y_D^{58}}{N_R} + 0.9272 \left(\dfrac{1}{4}\right) \sum_{i=1}^{4} \left[\dfrac{C_S^{58}}{N_R}\right]_{-i}$
$\qquad\qquad\quad$ (7.0) $\qquad$ (4.9) $\qquad\qquad$ (33.6)

$$\bar{R}^2 = 0.998 \qquad SE = 0.0030 \qquad DW = 0.82$$

RESIDENTIAL CONSTRUCTION

(A.6) $\quad \Delta HU_{AVL_{EAF}} = -\,0.0035 - 0.0019[HU_{AVL_{EAF}}]_{-1}$
$\qquad\qquad\qquad\qquad$ (0.2) $\qquad\quad$ (5.6)

$$+ 0.2620[.25(HU_{STS_{EAF}})_{-1} + .50(HU_{STS_{EAF}})_{-2}$$
$$(28.9)$$

$$+ .25(HU_{STS_{EAF}})_{-3}]$$

$$\bar{R}^2 = 0.944 \qquad SE = 0.0093 \qquad DW = 0.93$$

(A.7) $\quad HU_{VAC_{EAF}} = [HU_{VAC_{EAF}}]_{-1} + \Delta HU_{AVL_{EAF}} - \Delta HH_{EAF}$

(A.8) $\quad HU_{STS_{EAF}}^1 = 0.7343 + 0.6413[HU_{STS_{EAF}}^1]_{-1}$
$\qquad\qquad\qquad\quad$ (2.4) $\qquad$ (9.7)

$$- 0.0740 \left(\frac{1}{3}\right) \sum_{i=1}^{3} [RM_{GBS3}]_{-i}$$
$$(4.6)$$

$$+ 0.0957 \left(\frac{1}{3}\right) \sum_{i=1}^{3} \left[\frac{Y_D}{(P_C)(HH_{EAF})}\right]_{-i}$$
$$(2.2)$$

$$- 0.0624 \ \frac{PM^1_{ICRD}}{P_{ICNFR}}$$
$$(2.3)$$

$$\bar{R}^2 = 0.924 \qquad SE = 0.0469 \qquad DW = 1.65$$

(A.9) $\quad HU^2_{STS_{EAF}} = 0.6223[HU^2_{STS_{EAF}}]_{-1} - 0.0045 \left(\frac{1}{3}\right) \sum\limits_{i=1}^{3} [RM_{GBS3}]_{-i}$
$\qquad\qquad\qquad (6.4) \qquad\qquad\qquad\qquad (3.4)$

$$+ 0.0002[\text{time-8}] + 0.0024 \left(\frac{1}{3}\right) \sum\limits_{i=1}^{3} \left[\frac{Y_D}{P_C HH_{EAF}}\right]_{-1}$$
$$(3.0) \qquad\qquad\qquad (1.5)$$

$$\bar{R}^2 = 0.682 \qquad SE = 0.0044 \qquad DW = 1.85$$

(A.10) $\quad HU^{3+}_{STS_{EAF}} = 0.1682 + 0.7796[HU^{3+}_{STS_{EAF}}]_{-1}$
$\qquad\qquad\qquad\quad (2.6) \qquad (13.7)$

$$- 0.0207 \left(\frac{1}{3}\right) \sum\limits_{i=1}^{3} [RM_{GBS3}]_{-i}$$
$$(2.8)$$

$$+ 0.0031[\text{time-8}] - 0.0118 \left[\frac{PM^{2+}_{ICRD}}{P_{ICNFR}}\right]_{-1}$$
$$(3.9) \qquad\qquad\qquad (2.2)$$

$$- 0.0596[HU_{VAC_{EAF}}]_{-1}$$
$$(3.1)$$

$$\bar{R}^2 = 0.983 \qquad SE = 0.0193 \qquad DW = 1.74$$

(A.11) $\qquad\qquad HU^{2+}_{STS_{EAF}} = HU^2_{STS_{EAF}} + HU^{3+}_{STS_{EAF}}$

(A.12) $\qquad\qquad HU_{STS_{EAF}} = HU^1_{STS_{EAF}} + HU^{2+}_{STS_{EAF}}$

(A.13) $\quad \dfrac{PM^1_{ICRD}}{P_{ICNFR}} = 1.1205 + 0.7296 \left[\dfrac{PM^1_{ICRD}}{P_{ICNFR}}\right]_{-1}$
$\qquad\qquad\qquad\quad (2.1) \qquad (10.3)$

$$+ 0.3559 \left(\frac{1}{3}\right) \sum\limits_{i=1}^{3} \left[\frac{Y_D}{P_C HH_{EAF}}\right]_{-i}$$
$$(2.6)$$

$$\bar{R}^2 = 0.918 \qquad SE = 0.1730 \qquad DW = 2.82$$

(A.14) $\quad \dfrac{PM^{2+}_{ICRD}}{P_{ICNFR}} = 4.3574 + 0.6390 \left[\dfrac{PM^{2+}_{ICRD}}{P_{ICNFR}}\right]_{-1}$
$\qquad\qquad\qquad\qquad (3.2) \qquad (5.9)$

$$- 0.7727[HU_{VAC_{EAF}}]_{-1}$$
$$(2.0)$$

$$\bar{R}^2 = 0.558 \qquad SE = 0.4480 \qquad DW = 1.80$$

(A.15) $\dfrac{PM_{ICRD}}{P_{ICNFR}}$

$$= \left[\frac{PM^1_{ICRD}}{P_{ICNFR}} (HU^1_{STS_{EAF}}) + \frac{PM^{2+}_{ICRD}}{P_{ICNFR}} (HU^{2+}_{STS_{EAF}}) \right] \frac{1}{HU_{STS_{EAF}}}$$

(A.16) $$I^{58}_{CNFRH} = 0.41 \left[\frac{PM_{ICRD}}{P_{ICNFR}} HU_{STS_{EAF}} \right]$$

$$+ 0.49 \left[\frac{PM_{ICRD}}{P_{ICNFR}} HU_{STS_{EAF}} \right]_{-1}$$

$$+ 0.10 \left[\frac{PM_{ICRD}}{P_{ICNFR}} HU_{STS_{EAF}} \right]_{-2}$$

(A.17) $$I^{58}_{CNFREH} = 2.6589 + .1773[HU_{AVL_{EAF}}]_{-1}$$
$$(1.5) \qquad (16.7)$$

$$- 6.9202 \left[\frac{P_{ICNFR}}{P_C} \right]_{-2}$$
$$(3.3)$$

$$\bar{R}^2 = 0.891 \qquad SE = 0.2080 \qquad DW = 0.49$$

(A.18) $$I^{58}_{CNFR*} = I^{58}_{CNFRH} + I^{58}_{CNFREH}$$

(A.19) $$I^{58}_{CNFR} = (DMY_{15})I^{58}_{CNFR*}$$

(A.20) $$I^{58}_{CO} = -2.2879 + 0.4240 \left(\frac{1}{8} \right) \sum_{i=1}^{8} \left[\frac{Y_D}{(P_C)(HH_{EAF})} \right]_{-i}$$
$$(3.7) \qquad (3.6)$$

$$+ 0.8148[I^{58}_{CO}]_{-1}$$
$$(12.8)$$

$$\bar{R}^2 = 0.976 \qquad SE = 0.0913 \qquad DW = 1.77$$

INVENTORY INVESTMENT

(A.21) $\quad \Delta INV_{MD}^{58} = -0.8912 + 0.0613[SF_D^{58} + GNP_{IC}^{58}]$
$\qquad\qquad\quad (0.3) \qquad (1.9)$

$\qquad\qquad\quad - 0.2922[INV_{MD}^{58}]_{-1} + 0.2846\Delta[INV_{MD}^{58}]_{-1}$
$\qquad\qquad\qquad (1.7) \qquad\qquad\qquad (2.7)$

$\qquad\qquad\quad + 0.1090\Delta[O_{U\,MD}^{58}]_{-1} + 0.0427[O_{U\,MD}^{58}]_{-1}$
$\qquad\qquad\qquad (4.8) \qquad\qquad\qquad (1.9)$

$\qquad\qquad\qquad\qquad \bar{R}^2 = 0.725 \qquad SE = 1.2391 \qquad DW = 1.93$

(A.22) $\quad \Delta INV_{MN}^{58} = -0.2809 + 0.0747SF_N^{58} - 0.5350[INV_{MN}^{58}]_{-1}$
$\qquad\qquad\qquad (0.1) \qquad (2.7) \qquad\qquad (2.2)$

$\qquad\qquad\quad + 0.2480\Delta[INV_{MN}^{58}]_{-1} + .7117[O_{U\,MN}^{58}]_{-1}$
$\qquad\qquad\qquad (2.1) \qquad\qquad\qquad (3.0)$

$\qquad\qquad\qquad\qquad \bar{R}^2 = 0.310 \qquad SE = 0.7103 \qquad DW = 1.94$

(A.23) $\quad \Delta[INV_T^{58} - INV_{CAR}^{58}] = -5.659 + 0.0750\left[SF^{58} - \dfrac{WS_G}{P_G} - C_S^{58}\right]$
$\qquad\qquad\qquad\qquad\qquad\quad (2.9) \qquad (2.7)$

$\qquad\qquad\qquad\quad - 0.4559[INV_T^{58} - INV_{CAR}^{58}]_{-1}$
$\qquad\qquad\qquad\qquad (2.2)$

$\qquad\qquad\qquad\qquad \bar{R}^2 = 0.182 \qquad SE = 1.3300 \qquad DW = 1.69$

(A.24) $\qquad \Delta INV_{CAR}^{58} = 0.9420 + 0.3642C_{DA}^{58} - 0.1649[C_{DA}^{58}]_{-1}$
$\qquad\qquad\qquad (1.0) \qquad (4.3) \qquad\qquad (1.6)$

$\qquad\qquad\quad - 1.019[INV_{CAR}^{58}]_{-1}$
$\qquad\qquad\quad (2.8)$

$\qquad\qquad\qquad\qquad \bar{R}^2 = 0.366 \qquad SE = 0.8516 \qquad DW = 1.93$

(A.25) $\quad \Delta INV_{O*4}^{58} = -0.6917 + 0.0071\left[SF^{58} - \dfrac{WS_G}{P_G}\right]$
$\qquad\qquad\qquad (2.0) \qquad (2.5)$

$\qquad\qquad\quad - 0.3209[INV_{O*4}^{58}]_{-1} + 0.4485\Delta[INV_{O*4}^{58}]_{-1}$
$\qquad\qquad\qquad (2.0) \qquad\qquad\qquad (4.0)$

$\qquad\qquad\qquad\qquad \bar{R}^2 = 0.435 \qquad SE = 0.2616 \qquad DW = 2.20$

(A.26)
$$INV_j^{58} = \frac{1}{4}\Delta INV_j^{58} + [INV_j^{58}]_{-1}$$

$$j = MD, MN, T\text{-}CAR, CAR, O*4$$

ORDERS

(A.27) $O_{MD}^{58} = 264.692 + 0.9950[SF_D^{58} + GNP_{IC}^{58}]$
$\qquad\qquad\quad$ (6.2) $\qquad$ (10.1)

$$+ 4.0568\,\frac{1}{2}\sum_{i=0}^{1}\left[\frac{DOD_{MPCA}}{P_{GF}}\right]_{-i} - 160.57\left[\frac{1}{JCAP_{MD}}\right]$$
$\qquad$ (2.6) $\qquad\qquad\qquad\qquad\qquad\qquad$ (8.3)

$$- 1.0381[O_{U_{MD}}^{58}]_{-1}$$
$\qquad$ (4.4)

$$\bar{R}^2 = 0.936 \qquad SE = 7.5083 \qquad DW = 0.96$$

(A.28) $O_{MN}^{58} = 4\left[O_{U_{MN}}^{58} - [O_{U_{MN}}^{58}]_{-1}\left\{\frac{[WPI_{MN}]_{-1}}{WPI_{MN}}\right\}\right] + 2.5650X_{MN}^{58}$

$$- 0.6959\Delta INV_{MN}^{58} + 0.3478[\text{time-4}] + 7.1606$$

(A.29) $\qquad O_{U_{MD}}^{58} = [O_{U_{MD}}^{58}]_{-1}\left\{\frac{[WPI_{MD}]_{-1}}{WPI_{MD}}\right\} + 0.25O_{MD}^{58}$

$$- 0.25[37.1023 + 1.8387X_{MD}^{58}]$$

(A.30) $\Delta O_{U_{MN}}^{58} = 17.4029 + 0.0255\Delta O_{MN}^{58} + 0.0106[O_{MN}^{58}]_{-1}$
$\qquad\qquad\qquad$ (3.6) $\qquad$ (1.8) $\qquad\qquad$ (2.2)

$$- 0.6090[O_{U_{MN}}^{58}]_{-1} - 0.1892[INV_{MN}^{58}]_{-1}$$
$\qquad$ (6.1) $\qquad\qquad\qquad$ (3.9)

$$+ 3.0671[WPI_{MN}]_{-1} - 9.9576\left\{\frac{WPI_{MN}}{[WPI_{MN}]_{-1}}\right\}$$
$\qquad$ (1.3) $\qquad\qquad\qquad$ (2.3)

$$- 5.2507\left[\frac{1}{J_{CAP_{MN}}}\right]$$
$\qquad$ (3.5)

$$\bar{R}^2 = 0.557 \qquad SE = 0.1360 \qquad DW = 2.10$$

INVESTMENT IN NONFARM BUSINESS PLANT AND EQUIPMENT

(A.31) $I_{BUSE_{MD}}^{58} = -19.8370 + 7.7521[DMY_{23} - DMY_{22}]$
 (5.1)   (2.0)

$+ [10.3800 - 0.1567t]DMY_{22}$
 (0.6)   (0.7)

$+ [0.2300 - 0.110(DMY_{23} - DMY_{22})] \sum_{i=0}^{7} A_i[X_{MD}^{58}]_{-i-2}$
 (6.5)   (2.3)

$- 0.3066 \sum_{i=0}^{7} A_i[RM_{GBL}]_{-i-2} + 10.4768 \left[\dfrac{X_{MD}^{58}}{X_{K_{MD}}^{58}}\right]_{-1}$
 (1.1)   (5.3)

$\bar{R}^2 = 0.817 \qquad SE = 0.5051 \qquad DW = 0.56$

(A.32) $I_{BUSE_{MN}}^{58}$

$= 3.9778 - 11.2909[DMY_{23} - DMY_{22}]$
 (3.3)   (5.9)

$+ [9.6082 - 0.1369t]DMY_{22}$
 (1.5)   (1.5)

$+ [0.3332 + 0.1641(DMY_{23} - DMY_{22})] \sum_{i=0}^{7} A_i[X_{MN}^{58}]_{-i-2}$
 (9.1)   (5.3)

$- 1.4847 \sum_{i=0}^{7} A_i[RM_{GBL}]_{-2} - 0.3533[K_{E_{MN}}^{58}]_{-1}$
 (7.2)   (5.8)

$\bar{R}^2 = 0.931 \qquad SE = 0.2068 \qquad DW = 1.10$

(A.33) $I_{BUS_R}^{58} = -14.0539 - 2.1526[DMY_{23} - DMY_{22}]$
 (5.4)   (6.8)

$+ [19.0730 - 0.2533t]DMY_{22}$
 (1.5)   (1.5)

$+ 0.5494 \sum_{i=0}^{7} A_i[X_R^{58}]_{-i-2} - 1.5925 \sum_{i=0}^{7} A_i[RM_{GBL}]_{-i-2}$
 (7.3)   (3.1)

$$+ 15.0179 \left[\frac{X_R^{58}}{X_{KR}^{58}}\right]_{-1} - 0.0627[K_R^{58}]_{-1}$$
$$(4.7) \qquad\qquad\qquad (1.5)$$

$$\bar{R}^2 = 0.937 \qquad SE = 0.3862 \qquad DW = 0.87$$

(A.34) $\quad I_{BUS_{O*2}}^{58} = 7.1978 + 0.0672 \sum_{i=0}^{7} A_i [X_{O*6}^{58}]_{-i-2}$
$$\qquad\qquad\quad (0.9) \qquad (1.5)$$

$$- 1.4991 \sum_{i=0}^{7} A_i [RM_{GBL}]_{-i-2} + 21.4221 \left[\frac{X_{O*6}^{58}}{X_{K_{O*6}}^{58}}\right]_{-1}$$
$$(4.0) \qquad\qquad\qquad\qquad\qquad (2.1)$$

$$- 0.7015[K_{O*2}^{58}]_{-1} + 0.0971 \frac{1}{2}\sum_{i=1}^{2} [X_{O*6}^{58}]_{-i}$$
$$(6.0) \qquad\qquad\qquad (3.0)$$

$$\bar{R}^2 = 0.930 \qquad SE = 0.3189 \qquad DW = 0.85$$

FOREIGN TRADE

(A.35) $\quad [M_N^{58} + M_S^{58}] = 4.9227 - 5.0961 \frac{PM_{N+S}}{P_C} + 0.0229 Y_D^{58}$
$$\qquad\qquad\qquad (1.7) \qquad (2.2) \qquad\qquad\qquad (4.4)$$

$$+ 0.5508[M_N^{58} + M_S^{58}]_{-1} + 0.5789 DMY_{DKSTR1}$$
$$(4.8) \qquad\qquad\qquad\qquad (5.4)$$

$$\bar{R}^2 = 0.983 \qquad SE = 0.3521 \qquad DW = 1.91$$

(A.36) $\quad M_D^{58} = 1.9971 + 0.569 X_{MD}^{58} - 3.5042 \frac{PM_D}{PX_{MD}} + 0.4622[M_D^{58}]_{-1}$
$$\qquad\quad (3.1) \qquad (9.8) \qquad\quad (5.9) \qquad\qquad\qquad (7.7)$$

$$+ 0.3438 DMY_{DKSTR} + 0.5395 DMY_{STLWT2}$$
$$(4.2) \qquad\qquad\qquad (7.8)$$

$$\bar{R}^2 = 0.987 \qquad SE = 0.1966 \qquad DW = 1.95$$

(A.37) $\quad EX^{58} = 19.9535 - 20.5046 \frac{P_{EX}}{P_{EXW}} + 0.6204[EX^{58}]_{-1}$
$$\qquad\quad (2.7) \qquad (2.6) \qquad\qquad\qquad (7.0)$$

$$+ 0.1303[EX_W^{58} - EX^{58}] + 1.3051DMY_{DKSTR1}$$
$$(4.7) \qquad\qquad (4.6)$$

$$\bar{R}^2 = 0.972 \qquad SE = 0.9543 \qquad DW = 2.13$$

GOVERNMENT TAXES AND TRANSFER PAYMENTS

(A.38) $\quad TP = -14.5008 + 13.7186DMY_{TP} + 0.1613Y_P$
$\qquad\qquad (12.3) \qquad (1.7) \qquad\qquad (51.7)$

$\qquad\qquad - 0.0392[DMY_{TP}Y_P]$
$\qquad\qquad (2.5)$

$$\bar{R}^2 = 0.989 \qquad SE = 1.0715 \qquad DW = 1.08$$

(A.39) $\quad TX = -7.5578 + 2.1879DMY_{TX} + 0.1014GNP$
$\qquad\qquad (15.9) \qquad (11.3) \qquad\qquad (100.4)$

$$\bar{R}^2 = 0.997 \qquad SE = 0.5355 \qquad DW = 1.10$$

(A.40) $\quad TC = 0.9303 - 0.6567DMY_{IC} + 0.8360[TC_{RT}Z_{BU}]$
$\qquad\qquad (2.5) \qquad (4.1) \qquad\qquad (54.5)$

$$\bar{R}^2 = 0.993 \qquad SE = 0.3176 \qquad DW = 0.45$$

(A.41) $\quad TW = -5.8424 + 0.1552[t - 4]$
$\qquad\qquad (8.7) \qquad (11.0)$

$\qquad\qquad + 0.7199[OASI_{RT}OASI_{PR}OASI_{BA}]EHH$
$\qquad\qquad (20.1)$

$\qquad\qquad - 0.2765[OASI_{RT}OASI_{PR}][OASI_{BA}EHH - WSS]$
$\qquad\qquad (8.0)$

$\qquad\qquad + 0.0286UINS_{RT}[EHH]$
$\qquad\qquad (7.2)$

$$R^2 = 0.999 \qquad SE = 0.2233 \qquad DW = 0.71$$

(A.42) $\quad V_{USGF} = -1.3555 + 0.9403U + 0.0127[GNP_K^{58} - GNP^{58}]P_{GNP}$
$\qquad\qquad (5.4) \qquad (8.7) \qquad\quad (2.6)$

$$\bar{R}^2 = 0.930 \qquad SE = 0.2379 \qquad DW = 1.04$$

(A.43) $V_G = V_{US_{GF}} + V_{OASI_{GF}} + V_{VET} + V_{OG}$

PRODUCTION FUNCTIONS

(A.44) $\Delta \ln MH_{P_{MD}} = 0.3246 + 0.7085 \ln X^{58}_{MD}$
               (1.2)   (18.5)

$- 0.1426 \ln [K^{58}_{E_{MD}}]_{-1}$
(4.7)

$- 0.3963 \ln [MH_{P_{MD}}]_{-1}$
(6.4)

$- 0.2749 \ln [X^{58}_{MD}]_{-1}$
(4.2)

$- 0.270 DMY_1 - 0.0046 DMY_1[t - 61]$
(4.2)   (4.9)

$- 0.0094 DMY_2 + 0.0037 DMY_2[t - 74]$
(3.2)   (3.1)

$\bar{R}^2 = 0.941$ $SE = 0.0078$ $DW = 1.52$

(A.45) $\Delta \ln MH_{P_{MN}} = 0.5880 + 0.7264 \ln X^{58}_{MN} - 0.3283 \ln [K^{58}_{E_{MN}}]_{-1}$
               (1.7)   (15.4)   (4.1)

$- 0.0050[t - 8] - 0.8675 \ln [MH_{P_{MN}}]_{-1}$
(16.9)   (15.7)

$+ DMY_3[3.8371 - 0.1102(t - 8)$
          (2.4)   (2.5)

$+ 0.0007881(t - 8)^2]$
(2.5)

$\bar{R}^2 = 0.861$ $SE = 0.0052$ $DW = 1.61$

(A.46) $\ln MH_{P_T} = 0.2195 + 0.1780 \ln X^{58}_T + 0.1659 \ln [X^{58}_T]_{-1}$
               (1.1)   (3.4)   (2.5)

$$-0.0022t + 0.4412 \ln [MH_{P_T}]_{-1}$$
$$\quad (4.8) \qquad (4.5)$$

$$\bar{R}^2 = 0.984 \qquad SE = 0.0040 \qquad DW = 2.19 \qquad \rho_1 = 0.5940$$

(A.47) $\quad \ln MH_C = -1.0240 + 0.6899 \ln X_C^{58} - 0.00044t$
$$\qquad\qquad (3.5) \qquad (5.2) \qquad\qquad (1.1)$$

$$+ 0.3848 \ln [MH_C]_{-1}$$
$$\quad (3.5)$$

$$\bar{R}^2 = 0.899 \qquad SE = 0.0185 \qquad DW = 1.90 \qquad \rho_1 = 0.2574$$

(A.48) $\quad \ln MH_R = -0.4213 + 0.4172 \ln X_R^{58} + 0.1157 \ln [X_R^{58}]_{-1}$
$$\qquad\qquad (1.5) \qquad (10.5) \qquad\qquad (1.9)$$

$$- 0.00603t + 0.4226 \ln [MH_R]_{-1}$$
$$\quad (8.7) \qquad (5.1)$$

$$\bar{R}^2 = 0.982 \qquad SE = 0.0092 \qquad DW = 2.46 \qquad \rho_1 = 0.7326$$

(A.49) $\quad \ln MH_O = -0.7940 + 0.4788 \ln X_O^{58} + 0.1260 \ln [X_O^{58}]_{-1}$
$$\qquad\qquad (3.0) \qquad (4.9) \qquad\qquad (0.9)$$

$$- 0.00131t + 0.3445 \ln [MH_O]_{-1}$$
$$\quad (2.1) \qquad (2.0)$$

$$\bar{R}^2 = 0.999 \qquad SE = 0.0028 \qquad DW = 1.80 \qquad \rho_1 = 0.4653$$

(A.50) $\ln E_{O_{MD}} = -0.1553 + 0.0461 \ln X_{MD}^{58} + 0.9495 \ln [E_{O_{MD}}]_{-1}$
$$\qquad\qquad (3.3) \qquad (3.7) \qquad\qquad (41.3)$$

$$\bar{R}^2 = 0.993 \qquad SE = 0.0084 \qquad DW = 0.36$$

(A.51) $\ln E_{O_{MN}} = -0.1363 + 0.0473 \ln X_{MN}^{58} + 0.9046 \ln [E_{O_{MN}}]_{-1}$
$$\qquad\qquad (4.2) \qquad (4.5) \qquad\qquad (43.3)$$

$$\bar{R}^2 = 0.998 \qquad SE = 0.0026 \qquad DW = 1.85$$

(A.52) $\quad \ln E_{O_T} = -0.6613 + 0.2262 \ln X_T^{58} + 0.0011t$
$$\qquad\qquad (5.2) \qquad (6.6) \qquad\qquad (2.5)$$

$$+ 0.5801 \ln [E_{OT}]_{-1}$$
(8.1)

$$\bar{R}^2 = 0.998 \qquad SE = 0.0053 \qquad DW = 2.12$$

(A.53) $\qquad H_{PMD} = 37.5601 + 0.0744X_{MD}^{58} + 0.0416\Delta X_{MD}^{58}$
$\qquad\qquad$ (125.8) $\quad$ (14.0) $\qquad\qquad$ (3.3)

$$- 1.0769RWSS_{MD}$$
(7.5)

$$\bar{R}^2 = 0.859 \qquad SE = 0.2770 \qquad DW = 0.96$$

(A.54) $\qquad H_{PMN} = 37.6692 + 0.1319X_{MN}^{58} + 0.1190\Delta X_{MN}^{58}$
$\qquad\qquad$ (178.7) $\quad$ (10.3) $\qquad\qquad$ (3.8)

$$- 2.4588RWSS_{MN}$$
(8.8)

$$\bar{R}^2 = 0.803 \qquad SE = 0.185 \qquad DW = 1.13$$

(A.55) $\qquad H_{PT} = 42.8931 + 0.0170X_T^{58} + 0.0108\Delta X_T^{58} - 2.5898RWSS_T$
$\qquad\qquad$ (379.5) $\quad$ (2.5) $\qquad\quad$ (0.6) $\qquad\qquad$ (9.7)

$$\bar{R}^2 = 0.965 \qquad SE = 0.1069 \qquad DW = 0.79$$

(A.56) $\qquad H_C = 36.0767 + 0.0764X_C^{58} + 0.2181\Delta X_C^{58} - 0.2527RWSS_C$
$\qquad\qquad$ (30.1) $\quad$ (1.0) $\qquad\quad$ (1.5) $\qquad\qquad$ (1.3)

$$\bar{R}^2 = 0.053 \qquad SE = 0.3891 \qquad DW = 1.50$$

(A.57) $\qquad H_R = 39.7580 + 0.0816X_R^{58} + 0.0657\Delta X_R^{58} - 0.8953RWSS_R$
$\qquad\qquad$ (541.7) $\quad$ (13.5) $\qquad\quad$ (4.0) $\qquad\qquad$ (9.6)

$$\bar{R}^2 = 0.915 \qquad SE = 0.0760 \qquad DW = 1.85$$

(A.58) $\qquad MH_{Oj} = (40)(.052)E_{Oj} \qquad j = MD, MN, T$

(A.59) $\qquad\qquad MH_j = MH_{Pj} + MH_{Oj}$
$$j = MD, MN, T$$

$$(A.60) \qquad E_{P_j} = \frac{MH_{P_j}}{(0.052)H_{P_j}}$$

$$j = MD, MN, T$$

$$(A.61) \qquad E_j = \frac{MH_j}{(0.052)H_j}$$

$$j = C, R, O$$

PRICES AND WAGE RATES

$$(A.62) \qquad ULC_j^N = \frac{\frac{1}{4}\sum_{i=0}^{3}[RWSS_j]_{-i}}{\frac{1}{12}\sum_{i=0}^{11}\left[\frac{X_j^{58}}{MH_j}\right]_{-i}}$$

$$j = MD, MN, T, C, R, O$$

$$(A.63) \qquad ULC_j = \frac{WSS_j}{X_j^{58}}$$

$$j = MD, MN, T, C, R, O$$

$$(A.64) \quad WPI_{MD} = -0.1632 + 0.6688[ULC_{MD} - ULC_{MD}^N]$$
$$\phantom{(A.64) \quad WPI_{MD} = } (5.2) \qquad (7.5)$$

$$+ 1.1594 ULC_{MD}^N + 0.2314 J_{CAP_{MD}} + 0.1393 PR_{MD}$$
$$(38.7) \qquad\qquad (7.0) \qquad\qquad (3.6)$$

$$\bar{R}^2 = 0.982 \qquad SE = 0.0074 \qquad DW = 0.61$$

$$(A.65) \quad WPI_{MN} = -0.0228 + 0.6418[ULC_{MN} - ULC_{MN}^N]$$
$$\phantom{(A.65) \quad WPI_{MN} = } (0.3) \qquad (4.9)$$

$$+ 0.6844 ULC_{MN}^N + 0.3118 J_{CAP_{MN}} + 0.2995 PR_{MN}$$
$$(18.3) \qquad\qquad (6.6) \qquad\qquad (9.8)$$

$$\bar{R}^2 = 0.917 \qquad SE = 0.0048 \qquad DW = 0.77$$

(A.66) $\quad PX_{MD} = 0.0443 + 1.0987WPI_{MD} - 0.1507PR_{MD}$
$\qquad\qquad (1.2)\qquad (40.2)\qquad\qquad (4.9)$

$$\bar{R}^2 = 0.972 \qquad SE = 0.0103 \qquad SW = 1.85$$

(A.67) $\quad PX_{MN} = -0.7470 + 0.9675[ULC_{MN} - ULC_{MN}^N]$
$\qquad\qquad\quad (3.6)\qquad (3.7)$

$\qquad\qquad + 1.7518ULC_{MN}^N + 0.2225J_{CAP_{MN}} + 0.0108H_{PMN}$
$\qquad\qquad\quad (25.1)\qquad\qquad (2.1)\qquad\qquad (1.6)$

$$\bar{R}^2 = 0.947 \qquad SE = 0.0087 \qquad DW = 0.71$$

(A.68) $\quad PX_T = 0.1809 + 0.9021[ULC_T - ULC_T^N] + 1.4527ULC_T^N$
$\qquad\qquad (6.5)\qquad (3.4)\qquad\qquad\qquad\qquad (28.7)$

$$- 0.4160 \left[\frac{INV_T^{58}}{X_T^{58}} - \frac{1}{12}\sum_{i=0}^{11}\left(\frac{INV_T^{58}}{X_T^{58}}\right)_{-i}\right]_{-1}$$
$\qquad\quad (1.7)$

$$\bar{R}^2 = 0.953 \qquad SE = 0.0104 \qquad DW = 0.94$$

(A.69) $\quad PX_C = 0.1046 + 1.4501[ULC_C - ULC_C^N] + 1.2301ULC_C^N$
$\qquad\qquad (11.2)\qquad (24.7)\qquad\qquad\qquad\qquad (99.3)$

$$\bar{R}^2 = 0.997 \qquad SE = 0.0076 \qquad DW = 0.39$$

(A.70) $$UCCA_R^N = \frac{1}{12}\sum_{i=0}^{11}\left[\frac{CCA_R}{X_R^{58}}\right]_{-i}$$

(A.71) $$UCCA_R = \frac{CCA_R}{X_R^{58}}$$

(A.72) $\quad PX_R = 0.2699 + 0.8097[ULC_R - ULC_R^N] + 0.7517ULC_R^N$
$\qquad\qquad (6.7)\qquad (7.2)\qquad\qquad\qquad\qquad (10.2)$

$\qquad\qquad + 1.5635[UCCA_R - UCCA_R^N] + 2.3607UCCA_R^N$
$\qquad\qquad\quad (5.8)\qquad\qquad\qquad\qquad (27.4)$

$$\bar{R}^2 = 0.972 \qquad SE = 0.0064 \qquad DW = 1.03$$

(A.73) $PX_O = 0.1483 + 1.2332[ULC_O - ULC_O^N] + 2.3036 ULC_O^N$
                (20.1)   (4.3)   (119.9)

$$\bar{R}^2 = 0.997 \qquad SE = 0.0046 \qquad DW = 0.62$$

(A.74)

$$\left[\frac{RWSS_{MD} - RWSS_{MD-4}}{RWSS_{MD-4}}\right] = 0.0124 + 0.00073 \,\frac{4}{\sum\limits_{i=0}^{3} [RU]_{-i}}$$
                                                    (1.4)   (1.7)

$$- 0.0069 DMY_{GP}$$
$$(2.2)$$

$$+ 0.2010 \,\frac{1}{4}\sum_{i=0}^{3}\left[\frac{CPI - CPI_{-4}}{CPI_{-4}}\right]_{-i}$$
$$(1.3)$$

$$- 0.2918 \left[\frac{RWSS_{MD-4} - RWSS_{MD-8}}{RWSS_{MD-8}}\right]$$
$$(2.4)$$

$$+ 0.6821 \left[\frac{RWSS_{MD-1} - RWSS_{MD-5}}{RWSS_{MD-5}}\right]$$
$$(6.4)$$

$$\bar{R}^2 = 0.649 \qquad SE = 0.0084 \qquad DW = 1.21$$

(A.75)

$$\left[\frac{RWSS_{MN} - RWSS_{MN-4}}{RWSS_{MN-4}}\right] = 0.0084 + 0.0012 \,\frac{4}{\sum\limits_{i=0}^{3} [RU]_{-i}}$$
                                                    (2.1)   (5.2)

$$- 0.0055 DMY_{GP}$$
$$(3.9)$$

$$+ 0.2309 \,\frac{1}{4}\sum_{i=0}^{3}\left[\frac{CPI - CPI_{-4}}{CPI_{-4}}\right]_{-i}$$
$$(2.9)$$

$$- 0.4551 \left[\frac{RWSS_{MN} - RWSS_{MN-8}}{RWSS_{MN-8}}\right]$$
$$(7.6)$$

$$+ 0.6463 \left[\frac{RWSS_{MN-4} - RWSS_{MN-5}}{RWSS_{MN-5}}\right]$$
$$(9.3)$$

$$\bar{R}^2 = 0.898 \qquad SE = 0.0039 \qquad DW = 2.41$$

(A.76)

$$\left[\frac{RWSS_T - RWSS_{T-4}}{RWSS_{T-4}}\right] = \underset{(0.7)}{0.0040} + \underset{(6.1)}{0.0016} \frac{1}{RU} - \underset{(0.70)}{0.0011}DMY_{GP}$$

$$+ \underset{(4.2)}{0.5628} \frac{1}{4}\sum_{i=0}^{3}\left[\frac{CPI - CPI_{-4}}{CPI_{-4}}\right]_{-i}$$

$$- \underset{(4.7)}{0.4628}\left[\frac{RWSS_{T-4} - RWSS_{T-8}}{RWSS_{T-8}}\right]$$

$$+ \underset{(4.7)}{0.4239}\left[\frac{RWSS_{T-1} - RWSS_{T-5}}{RWSS_{T-5}}\right]$$

$$\bar{R}^2 = 0.794 \qquad SE = 0.0049 \qquad DW = 1.77$$

(A.77) $\quad\left[\dfrac{RWSS_C - RWSS_{C-4}}{RWSS_{C-4}}\right] = \underset{(4.2)}{0.0277} - \underset{(0.4)}{0.0020}DMY_{GP}$

$$+ \underset{(2.9)}{0.9016} \frac{1}{4}\sum_{i=0}^{3}\left[\frac{CPI - CPI_{-4}}{CPI_{-4}}\right]_{-i}$$

$$- \underset{(3.6)}{0.3480}\left[\frac{RWSS_{C-4} - RWSS_{C-8}}{RWSS_{C-8}}\right]$$

$$+ \underset{(3.2)}{0.4060}\left[\frac{RWSS_{C-1} - RWSS_{C-5}}{RWSS_{C-5}}\right]$$

$$\bar{R}^2 = 0.511 \qquad SE = 0.0164 \qquad DW = 2.15$$

(A.78) $\quad\left[\dfrac{RWSS_R - RWSS_{R-4}}{RWSS_{R-4}}\right] = \underset{(3.6)}{0.0283}$

$$+ \underset{(3.1)}{0.0008} \frac{1}{RU} - \underset{(4.2)}{0.0097}DMY_{GP}$$

$$+ \underset{(4.4)}{0.5999} \frac{1}{4}\sum_{i=0}^{3}\left[\frac{CPI - CPI_{-4}}{CPI_{-4}}\right]_{-i}$$

$$- 0.5782 \left[\frac{RWSS_{R-4} - RWSS_{R-8}}{RWSS_{R-8}} \right]$$
$$(4.9)$$

$$+ 0.4718 \left[\frac{RWSS_{R-1} - RWSS_{R-5}}{RWSS_{R-5}} \right]$$
$$(4.3)$$

$$\bar{R}^2 = 0.731 \qquad SE = 0.0055 \qquad DW = 2.03$$

(A.79) $\quad \left[\dfrac{RWSS_0 - RWSS_{0-4}}{RWSS_{0-4}} \right] = 0.0071$
$$(1.0)$$

$$+ 0.0014 \frac{1}{RU} - 0.0049 DMY_{GP}$$
$$(3.2) \qquad\qquad (2.0)$$

$$+ 0.2674 \frac{1}{4} \sum_{i=0}^{3} \left[\frac{CPI - CPI_{-4}}{CPI_{-4}} \right]_{-i}$$
$$(1.7)$$

$$- 0.3346 \left[\frac{RWSS_{0-4} - RWSS_{0-8}}{RWSS_{0-8}} \right]$$
$$(2.6)$$

$$+ 0.3914 \left[\frac{RWSS_{0-1} - RWSS_{0-5}}{RWSS_{0-5}} \right]$$
$$(2.8)$$

$$\bar{R}^2 = 0.587 \qquad SE = 0.0068 \qquad DW = 1.45$$

FINAL DEMAND AND GROSS PRODUCT ORIGINATING

(A.80) $\quad F_{MD}^{58} = -29.1841 + 1.2973 \Delta INV_{MD}^{58} + 0.4711 \Delta INV_T^{58}$
$$(4.3) \qquad (7.2) \qquad\qquad (2.0)$$

$$+ 0.6235 EX^{58} + 0.8437 [C_D^{58} + I_{PDE}^{58}]$$
$$(2.3) \qquad\qquad (9.2)$$

$$+ 1.3531 G_{CD}^{58} + 9.6516 DMY_{24} - 2.8153 DMY_{25}$$
$$(4.8) \qquad\qquad (7.2) \qquad\qquad (2.5)$$

$$- 1.3382 DMY_{DKSTR1}$$
$$(1.5)$$

$$\bar{R}^2 = 0.979 \qquad SE = 2.1390 \qquad DW = 1.26$$

(A.81) $F_{MN}^{58} = -11.8126 + 0.6936[C_{NFB}^{58} + C_{NEFB}^{58} + G_{CN}^{58}]$
$\qquad\qquad$ (2.2) $\qquad$ (20.8)

$\qquad\qquad + 0.2670[\Delta INV_T^{58} - \Delta INV_{CAR}^{58}] + 0.5848\Delta INV_{MN}^{58}$
$\qquad\qquad\quad$ (1.7) $\qquad\qquad\qquad\qquad\qquad$ (2.0)

$\qquad \bar{R}^2 = 0.985 \qquad SE = 1.6287 \qquad DW = 1.62 \qquad \rho_1 = 0.6534$

(A.82) $F_T^{58} = -17.0536 + 0.2087C_{DA}^{58} + 0.4179C_{DEA}^{58}$
$\qquad\qquad\qquad$ (3.1) $\qquad$ (3.7) $\qquad\qquad$ (3.8)

$\qquad\qquad + 0.4726C_{NFB}^{58} + 0.5676C_{NEFB}^{58}$
$\qquad\qquad\quad$ (4.3) $\qquad\qquad$ (5.7)

$\qquad \bar{R}^2 = 0.998 \qquad SE = 0.5325 \qquad DW = 1.93 \qquad \rho_1 = 0.3960$

(A.83) $F_C^{58} = -1.9315 + 1.0547[I_{CNFR}^{58} + I_{CER}^{58} + I_{CRAF}^{58} + G_{IC}^{58}]$
$\qquad\qquad$ (0.3) $\qquad$ (10.2)

$\qquad \bar{R}^2 = 0.970 \qquad SE = 0.7993 \qquad DW = 0.8365 \qquad \rho_1 = 0.9603$

(A.84) $F_R^{58} = -7.9821 + 0.2624C_S^{58} + 0.1316G_{CS}^{58}$
$\qquad\qquad\qquad$ (3.1) $\qquad$ (7.3) $\qquad\qquad$ (1.2)

$\qquad \bar{R}^2 = 0.988 \qquad SE = 0.6182 \qquad DW = 1.92 \qquad \rho_1 = 0.6930$

(A.85) $F_O^{58} = 14.9166 + 0.7141C_S^{58} + 0.0545G_{CS}^{58}$
$\qquad\qquad\qquad$ (3.4) $\qquad$ (7.9) $\qquad\qquad$ (3.6)

$\qquad \bar{R}^2 = 0.997 \qquad SE = 0.9096 \qquad DW = 1.69 \qquad \rho_1 = 0.9900$

OUTPUT CONVERSION

$$
\begin{array}{ll}
\text{(A.86)} & \hat{X}_A^{58} \\
\text{(A.87)} & \hat{X}_C^{58} \\
\text{(A.88)} & \hat{X}_T^{58} \\
\text{(A.89)} & \hat{X}_R^{58} \\
\text{(A.90)} & \hat{X}_O^{58} \\
\text{(A.91)} & \hat{X}_{MD}^{58} \\
\text{(A.92)} & \hat{X}_{MN}^{58} \\
\text{(A.93)} & \hat{X}_{GE}^{58}
\end{array}
=
\begin{bmatrix}
1.46397 & 0.04525 & 0.02645 & 0.03357 \\
0.02976 & 1.01411 & 0.02154 & 0.05480 \\
0.07616 & 0.12910 & 1.03212 & 0.04237 \\
0.06969 & 0.09119 & 0.06838 & 1.15032 \\
0.19137 & 0.16668 & 0.19038 & 0.16624 \\
0.07864 & 0.55824 & 0.06445 & 0.09801 \\
0.25868 & 0.15821 & 0.08993 & 0.10977 \\
0.00811 & 0.01037 & 0.02080 & 0.07036
\end{bmatrix}
$$

$$
\text{(A.94)} \qquad X_A^{58} = \frac{1}{d_{A_t}} \hat{X}_A^{58}
$$

$$
\text{(A.95)} \qquad X_C^{58} = \frac{1}{d_{C_t}} \hat{X}_C^{58}
$$

$$
\text{(A.96)} \qquad X_T^{58} = \frac{1}{1.281} \hat{X}_T^{58}
$$

$$
\text{(A.97)} \qquad X_R^{58} = \frac{1}{1.604} \hat{X}_R^{58}
$$

PRICE CONVERSION

$$
\begin{array}{ll}
\text{(A.102)} & PF_A \\
\text{(A.103)} & PF_C \\
\text{(A.104)} & PF_T \\
\text{(A.105)} & PF_R \\
\text{(A.106)} & PF_O \\
\text{(A.107)} & PF_{MD} \\
\text{(A.108)} & PF_{MN} \\
\text{(A.109)} & PF_{GE}
\end{array}
=
\begin{bmatrix}
1.46397 & 0.04525 & 0.02645 & 0.03357 \\
0.02976 & 1.01411 & 0.02154 & 0.05480 \\
0.07616 & 0.12910 & 1.03212 & 0.04237 \\
0.06969 & 0.09119 & 0.06838 & 1.15032 \\
0.19137 & 0.16668 & 0.19038 & 0.16624 \\
0.07864 & 0.55824 & 0.06445 & 0.09801 \\
0.25868 & 0.15821 & 0.08993 & 0.10977 \\
0.00811 & 0.01037 & 0.02080 & 0.07036
\end{bmatrix}
$$

where T superscript stands for the transpose operator.

$$\begin{bmatrix} 0.05342 & 0.05061 & 0.29911 & 0.13344 \\ 0.05363 & 0.01562 & 0.02295 & 0.15350 \\ 0.04555 & 0.07743 & 0.07501 & 0.04890 \\ 0.07312 & 0.09810 & 0.10622 & 0.19775 \\ 1.21264 & 0.15223 & 0.24717 & 0.14496 \\ 0.14863 & 1.61022 & 0.13512 & 0.12618 \\ 0.14432 & 0.16316 & 1.50119 & 0.14877 \\ 0.01795 & 0.01142 & 0.01331 & 1.01571 \end{bmatrix} \begin{bmatrix} F_A^{58} \\ F_C^{58} \\ F_T^{58} \\ F_R^{58} \\ F_O^{58} \\ F_{MD}^{58} \\ F_{MN}^{58} \\ F_{GE}^{58} \end{bmatrix}$$

(A.98) $$X_O^{58} = \frac{1}{1.589} \hat{X}_O^{58}$$

(A.99) $$X_{MD}^{58} = \frac{1}{2.354} \hat{X}_{MD}^{58}$$

(A.100) $$X_{MN}^{58} = \frac{1}{3.255} \hat{X}_{MN}^{58}$$

(A.101) $$X_{GE}^{58} = \frac{1}{1.741} \hat{X}_{GE}^{58}$$

$$\begin{bmatrix} 0.05342 & 0.05061 & 0.29911 & 0.13344 \\ 0.05363 & 0.01562 & 0.02295 & 0.15350 \\ 0.04555 & 0.07743 & 0.07501 & 0.04890 \\ 0.07312 & 0.09810 & 0.10622 & 0.19775 \\ 1.21264 & 0.15223 & 0.24717 & 0.14496 \\ 0.14863 & 1.61022 & 0.13512 & 0.12618 \\ 0.14432 & 0.16316 & 1.50119 & 0.14877 \\ 0.01795 & 0.01142 & 0.01331 & 1.01571 \end{bmatrix}^T \begin{bmatrix} 0.43880 & PX_A \\ 0.41873 & PX_C \\ 0.72587 & PX_T \\ 0.61871 & PX_R \\ 0.62026 & PX_O \\ 0.43317 & PX_{MD} \\ 0.34656 & PX_{MN} \\ 0.51510 & PX_{GE} \end{bmatrix}$$

(A.110) $\quad P_{CDA} = 0.1394 + 0.6925PF_{MD} + 0.1480PF_T$
$\qquad\qquad (0.9) \qquad (4.2) \qquad\qquad (0.7)$

$\qquad\qquad \bar{R}^2 = 0.954 \qquad SE = 0.0143 \qquad DW = 1.98 \qquad \rho_1 = 0.8316$

(A.111) $\quad P_{CDEA} = \left[0.0522 + 0.9472\left(\dfrac{P_{CDEA}}{P_{CDA}}\right)_{-1} \right] P_{CDA}$

(A.112) $\quad P_{CNEFB} = 0.1779 + 0.5023PF_{MN} + 0.3254PF_T$
$\qquad\qquad (8.5) \qquad (5.2) \qquad\qquad (3.9)$

$\qquad\qquad\qquad \bar{R}^2 = 0.981 \qquad SE = 0.0058 \qquad DW = 0.69$

(A.113) $\qquad P_{CNFB} = 0.8301PF_{MN} + 0.1710PF_T$
$\qquad\qquad\qquad (9.8) \qquad\qquad (2.0)$

$\qquad\qquad \bar{R}^2 = 0.983 \qquad SE = 0.0059 \qquad DW = 1.85 \qquad \rho_1 = 0.9504$

(A.114) $\qquad\qquad P_{CS} = 0.9667PF_O + 0.0456PF_R$
$\qquad\qquad\qquad\qquad (20.6) \qquad\qquad (1.0)$

$\qquad\qquad \bar{R}^2 = 0.999 \qquad SE = 0.0030 \qquad DW = 2.06 \qquad \rho_1 = 0.9504$

(A.115) $\quad P_{IBUS} = -0.1400 + 0.9733PF_{MD} + 0.1673PF_C$
$\qquad\qquad (5.7) \qquad (16.8) \qquad\qquad (4.2)$

$\qquad\qquad\qquad \bar{R}^2 = 0.985 \qquad SE = 0.0095 \qquad DW = 1.44$

(A.116) $\qquad\qquad P_{ICNFR} = 0.2059 + 0.8074PF_C$
$\qquad\qquad\qquad\qquad (8.9) \qquad (35.6)$

$\qquad\qquad\qquad \bar{R}^2 = 0.963 \qquad SE = 0.0147 \qquad DW = 0.35$

(A.117) $\quad P_{EX} = 0.5719 + 0.3353PF_{MD} + 0.0943PF_{MN}$
$\qquad\qquad (5.4) \qquad (2.7) \qquad\qquad (0.5)$

$\qquad\qquad \bar{R}^2 = 0.920 \qquad SE = 0.0085 \qquad DW = 1.55 \qquad \rho_1 = 0.8118$

(A.118) $\quad P_G = -0.3385 + 0.2667PF_{MD} + 0.3462PF_{MN}$
$\qquad\qquad (3.4) \qquad (2.8) \qquad\qquad (1.9)$

$$+ 0.1430PF_C + 0.0951\,\frac{WSS_G}{E_G}$$
$\qquad\qquad (1.4) \qquad\qquad (7.0)$

$\qquad\qquad \bar{R}^2 = 0.997 \qquad SE = 0.0060 \qquad DW = 1.52 \qquad \rho_1 = 0.9009$

(A.119) $\qquad P_{GF} = \left[0.0587 + 0.940 \left(\dfrac{P_{GF}}{P_G} \right)_{-1} \right] P_G$

(A.120) $\quad P_C = \left[\dfrac{\sum\limits_{j} P_{Cj} C_j^{58}}{\sum\limits_{j} C_j^{58}} \right] \quad j = DA, DEA, NFB, NEFB, S$

(A.121) $\qquad \Delta CPI = -0.0003 + 1.0626 \Delta P_C$
$\qquad\qquad\qquad (0.6) \qquad (8.8)$

$\qquad\qquad \bar{R}^2 = 0.620 \qquad SE = 0.0022 \qquad DW = 2.61$

FINANCIAL SECTOR

(A.122) $\qquad RES_F = RES_{NB} - RES_R$

(A.123) $\quad RES_R = \left[\dfrac{DD_{MB}}{DD_{CB}} \right] RRR_D [DD + DD_{GF}]_{CB}$

$\qquad\qquad + \left[\dfrac{DT_{MB}}{DT_{CB}} \right] RRR_T DT_{CB}$

(A.124) $\qquad WLTH^{58} = .114 \sum\limits_{i=1}^{20} (0.9)^{i-1} [GNP^{58}]_{-i}$

(A.125) $\qquad WLTH = [P_{GNP}]_{-1} WLTH^{58}$

(A.126) $\quad DEF_G = TP + TX + TC + TW - G - V_G$

$\qquad\qquad - SUB_G - INT_G - V_{FOR_{GF}}$

(A.127) $\quad \dfrac{CURR + DD}{WLTH} = -0.0232 + 0.8703 \left[\dfrac{CURR + DD}{WLTH} \right]_{-1}$
$\qquad\qquad\qquad\qquad (1.2) \qquad (30.7)$

$\qquad\qquad - 0.0039 RM_{BDT} - 0.0026 RM_{GBS3}$
$\qquad\qquad\quad (2.8) \qquad\qquad\quad (6.6)$

$\qquad\qquad + 0.1047 \dfrac{Y_D}{WLTH}$
$\qquad\qquad\quad (3.4)$

$\qquad\qquad \bar{R}^2 = 0.998 \qquad SE = 0.0016 \qquad DW = 1.18$

(A.128)
$$\frac{DD}{WLTH} = -0.0124 + 0.8522 \left[\frac{DD}{WLTH}\right]_{-1}$$
$$(0.7) \quad (26.6)$$

$$- 0.0039 RM_{BDT} - 0.0023 RM_{GBS3}$$
$$(3.1) \qquad\qquad (6.6)$$

$$+ 0.0845 \frac{Y_D}{WLTH}$$
$$(3.2)$$

$$\bar{R}^2 = 0.997 \qquad SE = 0.0014 \qquad DW = 1.19$$

(A.129)
$$\frac{DT}{WLTH} = -0.0015 + 1.0023 \left[\frac{DT}{WLTH}\right]_{-1}$$
$$(1.3) \quad (72.6)$$

$$+ 0.0036 RM_{BDT} - 0.0020 RM_{GBS3}$$
$$(6.0) \qquad\qquad (7.1)$$

$$\bar{R}^2 = 0.998 \qquad SE = 0.0013 \qquad DW = 0.75$$

(A.130)
$$RM_{GBS3} = -0.4580 + 0.0860[RM_{GBS3}]_{-1} + 1.0050 RM_{FRB}$$
$$(2.6) \quad (0.7) \qquad\qquad (6.8)$$

$$- 78.1320 \left[\frac{RES_F}{(DD + DT)_{-1}}\right]$$
$$(3.3)$$

$$- 167.9075 \left[\frac{RES_F - RES_{F-1}}{(DD + DT)_{-1}}\right]$$
$$(4.6)$$

$$- 3.9087 \frac{DEF_G}{WLTH}$$
$$(1.2)$$

$$\bar{R}^2 = 0.942 \qquad SE = 0.2195 \qquad DW = 1.46$$

(A.131)
$$RM_{GBL} = 0.1933 + 0.2035 RM_{GBS3} - 0.1890[RM_{GBS3}]_{-1}$$
$$(1.7) \quad (5.6) \qquad\qquad (4.9)$$

$$+ 0.9431[RM_{GBL}]_{-1}$$
$$(21.3)$$

$$\bar{R}^2 = 0.966 \qquad SE = 0.0958 \qquad DW = 2.19$$

(A.132) $RM_{BDT} = 0.2261 + 0.9052[RM_{BDT}]_{-1}$
           (1.6)   (15.0)

$$+ 0.0351[(1 - RRR_{DD})(.65)$$
$$(2.9)$$

$$+ (1 - RRR_{DT})]RM_{GBS3}$$

$$- 1.1181 \left[\frac{DT}{DD + DT}\right]_{-1}$$
$$(1.5)$$

$$+ 0.1405 DMY_{CD} + 0.0882 RM_{BDTM}$$
$$(2.5) \qquad\qquad (1.3)$$

$$\bar{R}^2 = 0.990 \qquad SE = 0.0742 \qquad DW = 1.49$$

NONWAGE INCOME

(A.133) $\Delta INT_G = 0.0515 + 0.0152(RM_{GBS3})\Delta BF_{PUB}$
           (2.6)   (3.2)

$$+ 0.0008(BF_{PUB})\Delta RM_{GBS3}$$
$$(2.7)$$

$$\bar{R}^2 = 0.293 \qquad SE = 0.1240 \qquad DW = 1.62$$

(A.134) $\Delta DIV = -0.0045 + 0.0671[Z_A + CCA_{CORP}] - 0.2511[DIV]_{-1}$
           (1.5)   (6.1)   (5.1)

$$\bar{R}^2 = 0.514 \qquad SE = 0.2000 \qquad DW = 2.70$$

(A.135)

$$\Delta Y_{ENT_{EAF}} = 0.1727 + 0.0245\Delta \left[\sum_j WSS_j\right] + 0.0752\Delta \left[\sum_j Z_{Bj}\right]$$
$$(2.5) \qquad (1.2) \qquad\qquad\qquad (3.6)$$

$$j = MD, MN, T, C, R, O$$

$$\bar{R}^2 = 0.409 \qquad SE = 0.3000 \qquad DW = 1.48$$

(A.136) $\Delta INT_{BUS_O} = -0.0763 + 0.00059 \sum_{i=0}^{1} [RM_{GBL}(C_D + I_{CNFR})]_{-i}$
          (1.8)   (2.8)

$$\bar{R}^2 = 0.268 \qquad SE = 0.1390 \qquad DW = 1.43$$

CAPITAL CONSUMPTION ALLOWANCES

(A.137)

$$\Delta CCA_{MD} = 0.1157 + 0.0318 \left[\frac{1}{2} \sum_{i=0}^{1} (I_{BUSE_{MD}})_{-i} - CCA_{MD-1} \right]$$
$$+ 0.1053 DMY_{22} + 0.1059 DMY_{23}$$

(A.138) $\quad \Delta CCA_{MN} = 0.1146 + 0.0328 \left[\frac{1}{2} \sum_{i=0}^{1} (I_{BUSE_{MN}})_{-i} - CCA_{MN-1} \right]$
$$+ 0.0722 DMY_{22} + 0.0827 DMY_{23}$$

(A.139) $\quad \Delta CCA_R = 0.0807 + 0.0170 \left[\frac{1}{2} \sum_{i=0}^{1} (I_{BUS_R})_{-i} - CCA_{R-1} \right]$
$$+ 0.1231 DMY_{22} + 0.0474 DMY_{23} + 0.0698 DMY_{21}$$

(A.140) $\quad \Delta CCA_{O*6} = 0.3031 + 0.0183 \left[\frac{1}{2} \sum_{i=0}^{1} (I_{BUS_{O*2}})_{i} - CCA_{O*6-1} \right]$
$$+ 0.0681 \frac{1}{2} \sum_{i=0}^{1} [I_{BUS_{O*2}}]_{-i} + 0.1144 DMY_{23}$$

LABOR FORCE

(A.141)

$$L = 15.371 + 0.740 EHH + 0.520[U]_{-1} + 0.594\Delta[U]_{-1} + 0.064t$$
$$\quad (3.6) \quad\quad (14.3) \quad\quad\quad (7.4) \quad\quad\quad\quad (7.0) \quad\quad\quad\quad (5.1)$$

$$\bar{R}^2 = 0.997 \quad\quad SE = 0.1890 \quad\quad DW = 1.57$$

(A.142) $\quad EHH = E_A + E_{P_{MD}} + E_{O_{MD}} + E_{P_{MN}} + E_{O_{MN}} + E_{P_T} + E_{O_T}$
$$+ E_C + E_R + E_O + E_G + \epsilon_E$$

(A.143)
$$U = L - EHH$$

(A.144)
$$RU = \frac{U}{L}$$

IDENTITIES AND FIXED PROPORTIONS

Gross national product or expenditures.

(A.145) $$GNP^{58} = SF^{58} + \Delta INV^{58}$$

(A.146) $$SF^{58} = C^{58} + I^{58}_{CNFR} + I^{58}_{CO} + I^{58}_{CRAF} + I^{58}_{BUS}$$
$$+ EX^{58} - M^{58} + G^{58} + \epsilon_{IBUS58}$$

(A.147) $$C^{58} = C^{58}_{DA} + C^{58}_{DEA} + C^{58}_{NFB} + C^{58}_{NEFB} + C^{58}_{S}$$

(A.148) $$C^{58}_{D} = C^{58}_{DA} + C^{58}_{DEA}$$

(A.149) $$\Delta INV^{58}_{EAF} = \Delta INV^{58}_{MD} + \Delta INV^{58}_{MN} + \Delta INV^{58}_{T} + \Delta INV^{58}_{O*4}$$

(A.150) $$\Delta INV^{58} = \Delta INV^{58}_{EAF} + \Delta INV^{58}_{AF}$$

(A.151) $$I^{58}_{BUS} = I^{58}_{BUS_{AF}} + I^{58}_{BUSE_{MD}} + I^{58}_{BUSE_{MN}} + I^{58}_{BUS_{O*2}}$$

(A.152) $$M^{58} = [M^{58}_{N} + M^{58}_{S}] + M^{58}_{D}$$

(A.153) $$I^{58}_{PDE} = [0.6047 + 0.0007t - 0.6943DMY_{IC}$$
$$+ 0.0067DMY_{IC}t](I^{58}_{BUS} + \epsilon_{IBUS58})$$
$$+ 11.0393DMY_{IC} + 0.7895$$

(A.154) $$I^{58}_{CER} = [I^{58}_{BUS} + \epsilon_{IBUS58}] - I^{58}_{PDE} + I^{58}_{CO}$$

(A.155) $$[I^{58}_{CPL_{EAF}} + I^{58}_{C_{AF}}] = I^{58}_{CER} + I^{58}_{CRAF} - I^{58}_{CO}$$

(A.156) $$\epsilon_{IBUS58} = I^{58}_{CER} + I^{58}_{PDE} - I^{58}_{BUS} - I^{58}_{CO}$$

(A.157) $$I^{58}_{C} = I^{58}_{CNFR} + I^{58}_{CO} + [I^{58}_{CPL_{EAF}} + I^{58}_{C_{AF}}]$$

(A.158) $$GNP^{58}_{IC} = I^{58}_{C} + G^{58}_{IC}$$

(A.159) $$C_{D} = [P^{58}_{CDA}][C_{DA}] + [P_{CDEA}][C^{58}_{DEA}]$$

(A.160) $$EX^{58}_{D} = (0.4189 - 0.0011t)EX^{58}$$

(A.161) $$SF^{58}_{D} = C^{58}_{D} + I^{58}_{PDE} + G^{58}_{CD} + EX^{58}_{D} - M^{58}_{D}$$

(A.162) $$EX^{58}_{N} = (0.3897 - 0.0008t)EX^{58}$$

(A.163) $$M^{58}_{N} = (0.5422 - 0.0002t)(M^{58}_{N} + M^{58}_{D})$$

(A.164) $$SF^{58}_{N} = C^{58}_{NFB} + C^{58}_{NEFB} + G^{58}_{CN} + EX^{58}_{N} - M^{58}_{N}$$

(A.165)
$$I_{BUS_j} = [P_{IBUS}][I^{58}_{BUS_j}]$$
$$j = MD, MN, R, O*2, AF$$

(A.166)
$$\Delta INV = [PM_{AF}][\Delta INV^{58}_{AF}] + [WPI_{MD}][\Delta INV^{58}_{MD}]$$
$$+ [WPI_{MN}][\Delta INV^{58}_{MN}] + [.5462 WPI_{MD}$$
$$+ .3722 WPI_{MN} + .0816 P_{MAF}][\Delta INV^{58}_{O*4}]$$
$$+ \epsilon_{\Delta INV}$$

(A.167)
$$I_{CO} = [PICNFR][I^{58}_{CO}] + \epsilon_{ICO}$$

(A.168)
$$I_{CNFR} = [PICNFR][I^{58}_{CNFR}]$$

(A.169)
$$I_{FIXER} = \sum_j I_{BUS_j} + [P_{IBUS}][\epsilon_{IBUS58}] + \epsilon_{IBUS} + I_{CO}$$
$$j = MD, MN, R, O*2, AF$$

(A.170)
$$I^{58}_{BUS_{EAF}} = I^{58}_{BUS} - I^{58}_{BUS_{AF}}$$

(A.171)
$$GNP = [P_C][C^{58}] + I_{CNFR} + \Delta INV + I_{FIXER}$$
$$+ [P_{EX}][EX^{58}] - [P_M][M^{58}] + G + I_{CRAF}$$

(A.172)
$$P_{GNP} = \frac{GNP}{GNP^{58}}$$

(A.173)
$$M^{58} = [M^{58}_N + M^{58}_S] + M^{58}_D$$

Relations among gross national product, national income, personal income and disposable personal income.

(A.174) $\quad Y_N = GNP - CCA - TX - V_{BUS} - STAT + SUB_G$

(A.175)
$$CCA = \sum_j CCA_j + \epsilon_{CCA}$$
$$j = A, MD, MN, R, O*6$$

(A.176)
$$CCA_{CORP} = 0.6086 CCA$$

(A.177) $\quad Z_B = Y_N - WSS - Y_{ENT} - Y_{RENT} - INT_{BUS} + WALD$

(A.178)
$$WSS = \sum_j WSS_j + \epsilon_{WSS}$$
$$j = A, G, W, MD, MN, T, C, R, O$$

(A.179)
$$WSS_j = [RWSS_j][MH_j]$$
$$j = MD, MN, T, C, R, O$$

(A.180)
$$INT_{BUS} = \sum_j INT_{BUS_j}$$
$$j = A, C, T, R, O, MD, MN, W$$

(A.181)
$$Z_{BU} = Z_B - IVA_{CORP}$$

(A.182)
$$Z_{AU} = Z_{BU} - TC$$

(A.183)
$$Z_A = Z_{AU} + IVA_{CORP}$$

(A.184)
$$RE = Z_{AU} - DIV$$

(A.185)
$$Y_P = Y_N - RE - TC - IVA_{CORP} - TW - WALD$$
$$+ V_G + INT_G + V_{BUS} + INT_{CON}$$

(A.186)
$$Y_D = Y_P - TP$$

(A.187)
$$Y_D^{58} = Y_D/P_C$$

(A.188)
$$T = TP + TC + TX + TW$$

Miscellaneous relationships.

(A.189)
$$X_{K_j}^{58} = [X_j^{58}]_{1953.2}\left[1.0 + \frac{r}{4}\right]^{t-34}$$
$$j = MD, MN, R, O*6$$
$$r = 0.035 \text{ in } 1953{:}3{-}1965{:}4$$
$$r = 0.040 \text{ in } 1966{:}1{-}1990{:}4$$

(A.190)
$$K_{MD}^{58} = K_{MD-1}^{58} + .25[I_{BUS_{MD}}^{58} - .1638K_{MD-1}^{58}]$$

(A.191)
$$K_{MN}^{58} = K_{MN-1}^{58} + .25[I_{BUS_{MN}}^{58} - .1118K_{MN-1}^{58}]$$

(A.192)
$$K_R^{58} = K_{R-1}^{58} + .25[I_{BUS_R}^{58} - 0.778K_{R-1}^{58}]$$

(A.193)
$$K_{O*2}^{58} = K_{O*2-1}^{58} + .25[I_{BUS_R}^{58} - .1575K_{O*2-1}]$$

(A.194)
$$GNP_K^{58} = [GNP_K^{58}]_{1953.2}\left[1.0 + \frac{r}{4}\right]^{t-34}$$
$$r = 0.035 \text{ in } 1953{:}3{-}1965{:}4$$
$$r = 0.040 \text{ in } 1966{:}1{-}1990{:}4$$

(A.195) $\quad J_{CAP_{MD}} = 0.000673 + 0.99[J_{CAP_{MD}}]_{-1}$

$$+ 1.0461 \left[\frac{X_{MD}^{58}}{X_{K_{MD}}^{58}} - 0.99 \left(\frac{X_{MD}^{58}}{X_{K_{MD}}^{58}} \right)_{-1} \right]$$

(A.196) $\quad J_{CAP_{MN}} = 0.00176 + .9682[J_{CAP_{MN}}]_{-1}$

$$+ .9012 \left[\frac{X_{MN}^{58}}{X_{K_{MN}}^{58}} - 0.9682 \left(\frac{X_{MN}^{58}}{X_{K_{MN}}^{58}} \right)_{-1} \right]$$

(A.197) $\quad K_{CDEA}^{58} = .25 C_{DEA}^{58} + .92784[K_{CDEA}^{58}]_{-1}$

(A.198) $\quad K_{CDA}^{58} = .25 C_{DA}^{58} + .925[K_{CDA}^{58}]_{-1}$

(A.199) $\quad X_M^{58} = X_{MD}^{58} + X_{MN}^{58}$

(A.200) $\quad O_{UM}^{58} = O_{UMD}^{58} + O_{UMN}^{58}$

(A.201) $\quad B^{58} = EX^{58} - M^{58}$

(A.202) $\quad H = \dfrac{\left[\begin{array}{c} H_{P_{MD}}E_{P_{MD}} + H_{P_{MN}}E_{P_{MN}} + H_{P_T}E_{P_T} \\ + H_R E_R + H_C E_C + H_O E_O \end{array} \right]}{[E_{P_{MD}} + E_{P_{MN}} + E_{P_T} + E_R + E_C + E_O]}$

(A.203) $\quad RWSS = \dfrac{[WSS - WSS_A - WSS_G]}{[EHH - E_A - E_G]}$

LIST OF VARIABLES AND DEFINITIONS

MONETARY variables are in billions of dollars, seasonally adjusted. Monetary stock variables are, unless otherwise indicated, end-of-period; and monetary flow variables, including changes in stocks between ends of periods, are at annual rates. In the definitions, the variables are generally defined as if they are in current dollars. In the equations, the distinction is made between current and constant 1958 dollars. Variables in the latter units are superscripted 58. Other modifiers of the variables are:

1. Sector subscripts. These refer only to producing sectors and government; those that appear in the system of equations presented here are as follows:

A	Agriculture, forestry, and fisheries
AF	Farming
C	Contract construction
EAF	Nonfarm business
F	Federal government (used only as a subscript for government expenditure variables)
G	Government and government enterprises
GE	Government enterprises
GF	Federal government
GSL	State and local government
M	Manufacturing
MD	Durables manufacturing
MN	Nondurables manufacturing
O	Residual industries: mining; finance, insurance, and real estate; and services
O∗2*	Mining, wholesale and retail, services, finance, and contract construction
O∗4*	All industries except manufacturing, wholesale and retail trade, and farming
O∗6*	Wholesale and retail trade and contract construction plus residual industries (mining; finance, insurance, and real estate; and services)
R	Regulated industries: railroad and nonrail transportation, communications, and public utilities
T	Wholesale and retail trade

2. *Other subscripts are defined with the variables to which they apply.* The variables in alphabetical order are:

A_i Almon weights for investment equations

$$A_0 = .074 \quad A_{-1} = .132 \quad A_{-2} = .170 \quad A_{-3} = .183$$

$$A_{-4} = .171 \quad A_{-5} = .138 \quad A_{-6} = .091 \quad A_{-7} = .041$$

B Net exports of goods and services

BF_{PUB} Marketable Federal debt held outside the Federal Reserve and U.S. government agencies and trust funds, average during quarter

C	Personal consumption expenditures on goods and services
CCA	Capital consumption allowances
C_D	Personal consumption expenditures on durable goods
C_{DA}	Personal consumption expenditures on new and net used automobiles
C_{DEA}	Personal consumption expenditures on durable goods other than automobiles
C_{NEFB}	Personal consumption expenditures on nondurable goods other than food and beverages
C_{NFB}	Personal consumption expenditures on food and beverages
CPI	Consumer price index, $1958 = 1.00$
C_S	Personal consumption expenditures on services including imputations
$CURR$	Currency in the hands of the nonbank public, average during quarter
d	Ratio of gross output to output originating
DD_{CB}	Private demand deposit liabilities of commercial banks less interbank deposits, cash items in process of collection, and Federal Reserve float, average during quarter
DD_{GFCB}	Federal government demand deposits at commercial banks, average during quarter
DD_{MB}	Demand deposits subject to reserve requirements at Federal Reserve System member banks, average during quarter
DEF_G	Government surplus or deficit on income and product accounts
DIV	Dividends
DMY_1	Dummy variable representing a productivity shift, 0.0 in 1954.1 through 1960.1, 1.0 thereafter
DMY_2	Dummy variable representing a productivity shift, 0.0 in 1954.1 through 1963.1, 1.0 thereafter
DMY_3	Dummy variable representing a productivity shift, 0.0 in 1954.1 through 1963.3, 1.0 thereafter
DMY_{15}	Dummy variable to convert from Bureau of the Census value of new private nonfarm residential

buildings put in place to GNP expenditures on private residential nonfarm new construction, both in 1958 dollars

DMY_{21} Dummy variable representing the investment boom in 1955, 1.0 in 1955.1 through 1955.4, 0.0 elsewhere

DMY_{22} Dummy variable representing a change in the investment tax credit, 1.0 in 1962.1 through 1962.4, 0.0 elsewhere.

DMY_{23} Dummy variable representing the investment tax credit, 0.0 in 1954.1 through 1961.4, 1.0 elsewhere

DMY_{24} Dummy variable, 0.0 in 1954.1 through 1960.1, 1.0 thereafter

DMY_{55} Dummy variable representing the 1955 easing of consumer credit, 1.0 in 1955.1 through 1955.4, 0.0 elsewhere

DMY_{CD} Dummy variable representing the establishment of the market for certificates of deposit, 0.0 in 1954.1 through 1960.4, .82 in 1961, 1.0 in 1962, .96 in 1963, .74 in 1964, and 1.0 thereafter

DMY_{DKSTR} Dummy variable representing longshoremen's strikes, −1.0 in 1954.1, 1956.4, 1957.1, 1959.4, 1962.4, 1963.1, 1965.1, 0.0 elsewhere

DMY_{DKSTR1} Dummy variable representing longshoremen's strikes and incorporating anticipatory and make-up effects, −1.0 in 1954.1, 1.0 in 1954.2, 1.0 in 1956.3, −1.0 in 1956.4, 0.5 in 1957.1, 1.0 in 1959.3, −1.5 in 1959.4, 0.5 in 1960.1, 0.5 in 1962.3, −0.5 in 1962.4, −1.0 in 1963.1, 0.5 in 1963.2, −1.0 in 1965.1, 1.0 in 1965.2, 0.0 elsewhere

DMY_{GP} Dummy variable representing the wage guide posts, 0.0 in 1954.1 through 1961.4, 1.0 in 1962.1 through 1965.4

DMY_{ITC} Dummy variable representing the investment tax credit, 0.0 from 1954.1 through 1961.4, 1.0 in 1962.1 through 1965.4

DMY_{STLWT2} Dummy variable representing anticipation of steel strikes occurring after foreign producers became competitive in the U.S. market, 1.0 in 1959.2, 2.0

in 1959.3, 2.0 in 1959.4, 1.0 in 1965.1, and 0.0 elsewhere

DMY_{STR} Dummy variable representing strikes in the automobile industry and incorporating make-up effects, −1.0 in 1958.4, 1.0 in 1959.1, −1.0 in 1961.3, −1.0 in 1961.4, −1.0 in 1967.3, −1.0 in 1967.4, 1.0 in 1968.1, 0.0 elsewhere

DMY_{TP} Dummy variable representing the 1964 tax cut, 0.0 in 1954.1 through 1963.4, 1.0 in 1964.1 through 1965.4

DMY_{TX} Dummy variable representing a change in the excise tax rate, 0.0 in 1954.1 through 1960.1, 1.0 in 1960.2 through 1965.4

$DODMPCA$ Department of Defense military prime contract awards for work performed in the U.S.

DT_{CB} Time deposits at all commercial banks other than those due to domestic commercial banks and the U.S. government, average during quarter

DT_{MB} Time deposits at Federal Reserve System member banks other than those due to domestic commercial banks and the U.S. government, average during quarter

EHH Employment, as reported in the household survey, millions of persons, average during quarter

E_O Employment of nonproduction workers, as reported in the payroll survey, millions of persons, average during quarter

E_P Employment of production workers, as reported in the payroll survey, millions of persons, average during quarter

EX U.S. exports of goods and services

EX_D U.S. exports of durable goods

EX_N U.S. exports of nondurable goods

EX_W World exports excluding U.S. exports

ϵ_{CCA} Capital consumption allowances epsilon: the difference between capital consumption allowances in the national income accounts and the sum of the same concept by industry from quarterly interpolations of annual data (on an establishment basis)

$\epsilon_{\Delta INV}$ Inventory investment epsilon: the difference between current dollar inventory investment in the gross national product accounts and the sum of real inventory investment inflated

ϵ_E Employment epsilon: the difference between employment estimates based on the Bureau of Labor Statistics' household survey, from which unemployment estimates are derived, and the sum of employment by industry from BLS's establishment survey

ϵ_{IBUS} Business investment epsilon: the difference between the sum of expenditures on producers' durable equipment and business construction expenditures as reported in the GNP accounts and the sum of such investment by industry

ϵ_{ICO} The difference between the current dollar balance of new private nonfarm, nonresidential, nonbusiness construction put in place and the real value of such construction, inflated by the implicit price deflator for nonfarm residential construction

F Estimated final demand

G Government purchases of goods and services

G_{CD} Government purchases of durable goods

G_{CN} Government purchases of nondurable goods

G_{CS} Government purchases of services

G_{IC} Government expenditures on new construction

GNP Gross national product

GNP_{IC} Construction component of gross national product

GNP_K Potential gross national product

H Average weekly hours of all workers, hours

HH Number of households, millions

H_P Average weekly hours of production or nonsupervisory workers, hours

HU_{AVL} Number of housing units available, millions

HU^1_{STS} Number of single-family housing units started, millions

HU_{STS}^2	Number of two-family housing units started, millions
HU_{STS}^3	Number of multiple-family housing units started, millions
HU_{VAC}	Vacant available housing units, millions
I_{BUS}	Business gross investment in plant and equipment
I_C	New construction component of gross private domestic investment
I_{CER}	Gross private domestic investment in nonresidential structures
I_{CNFR}	New private nonfarm residential construction, GNP basis
I_{CNFREH}	Value of new private nonfarm residential construction excluding housing units put in place (additions and alterations plus nonhousekeeping buildings)
I_{CNFRH}	Value of new private nonfarm housing units put in place
I_{CNFR*}	Value of new private nonfarm residential buildings put in place, Bureau of the Census basis
I_{CO}	Value of new private nonfarm, nonresidential, nonbusiness construction put in place, billions of dollars
I_{CPL}	Business construction
I_{CRAF}	New farm residential construction
I_{FIXER}	Gross private domestic investment in nonresidential structures and producers' durable equipment
INT_{BUS}	Personal interest income paid by business
INT_{CON}	Personal interest income paid by consumers
INT_G	Personal interest income paid by government
INV	The stock of business inventories
INV_{CAR}	Dealers' automobile inventories
I_{PDE}	Investment in producers' durable equipment
IVA	Corporate and unincorporated enterprises' inventory valuation adjustment
K	Stock of business fixed capital
K_{CDA}	Stock of consumers' automobiles
K_{CDEA}	Stock of consumers' durable goods other than automobiles
L	Civilian labor force, millions of persons

M	Imports of goods and services
M_D	Imports of durable goods
M_N	Imports of nondurable goods
M_S	Imports of services
MH	Total man-hours, billions per year
MH_O	Man-hours of nonproduction workers, billions per year
MH_P	Man-hours of production or nonsupervisory workers, billions per year
NR	Total resident population, millions of persons, average during quarter
O	Manufacturers' net new orders
$OASI_{BA}$	Salary base for determining payments to the Old-Age, Survivors, and Disability Insurance program (OASDI), thousands of dollars
$OASI_{PR}$	Percentage of employees covered by the OASDI program
$OASI_{RT}$	Percentage of base salary paid into OASDI, sum of employees' and employers' contributions
O_U	Manufacturers' unfilled orders
P_C	Implicit price deflator for personal consumption expenditures, 1958 = 1.0
P_{CDA}	Implicit price deflator for personal consumption expenditures on new and used automobiles, 1958 = 1.0
P_{CDEA}	Implicit price deflator for personal consumption expenditures on durable goods other than new and used automobiles, 1958 = 1.0
P_{CNEFB}	Implicit price deflator for personal consumption expenditures on nondurable goods other than food and beverages, 1958 = 1.0
P_{CNFB}	Implicit price deflator for personal consumption expenditures on foods and beverages, 1958 = 1.0
P_{EX}	Implicit price deflator for exports of goods and services, 1958 = 1.0
P_{EXW}	Unit value index of world exports excluding U.S. components, 1958 = 1.0

P_F Implicit price deflators for the final demand sectors, 1958 = 1.0

P_G Implicit price deflator for total government purchases of goods and services, 1958 = 1.0

P_{GF} Implicit price deflator for Federal government purchases of goods and services, 1958 = 1.0

P_{GNP} Implicit price deflator for gross national product, 1958 = 1.0

P_{IBUS} Implicit price deflator for business gross investment in plant and equipment, 1958 = 1.0

P_{ICNFR} Implicit price deflator for new private nonfarm residential construction, 1958 = 1.0

P_M Implicit price deflator for imports

PM_{AF} Implicit price deflator for value of cash receipts from farm marketing and CCC loans plus value of farm products consumed directly in farm households

PM_{ICRD} Average cost per unit of private housing starts, thousands of dollars

$PM_{(N+S)}$ Implicit price deflator for imports of nondurable goods and services, 1958 = 1.0

PR Index of prices of raw materials in manufacturing, 1958 = 1.0

PX Implicit price deflator for gross product originating, 1958 = 1.0

RE Undistributed corporate profits

RES_F Free reserves of Federal Reserve member banks, average during quarter

RES_{NB} Nonborrowed reserves of Federal Reserve member banks, average during quarter

RES_R Required reserves of Federal Reserve member banks, average during quarter

RM_{BDT} Yield on commercial bank time deposits, per cent

RM_{BDTM} Maximum rate payable on time deposits under Regulation Q

RM_{FRB} Federal Reserve Bank of New York discount rate, average during quarter, per cent

RM_{GBL} Yield on U.S. government securities maturing or

	callable in ten years or more, average during quarter, per cent
RM_{GBS3}	Market yield on three-month U.S. Treasury bills, average during quarter, per cent
RRR_D	Effective required reserves ratio for demand deposits at Federal Reserve member banks, average during quarter
RRR_T	Effective required reserves ratio for time deposits at Federal Reserve member banks, average during quarter
RU	Rate of unemployment
$RWSS$	Compensation of employees per man-hour including supplements, dollars
SF	Final sales, gross national product less change in inventories
SF_D	Final sales of durable goods
SF_N	Final sales of nondurable goods
$STAT$	Statistical discrepancy in the reconciliation of gross national product with national income
SUB	Subsidies less current surplus of government enterprises
t	Time trend where 1946:1 = 1 and 1954:1 = 37
T	Government receipts
TC	Corporate profits tax liability
TC_{RT}	Corporate profits tax rate
TP	Personal tax and nontax receipts (or payments)
TW	Contributions for social insurance
TX	Indirect business tax and nontax accruals
U	Unemployed in the civilian labor force
$UCCA$	Unit capital consumption allowances (capital consumption allowances per unit of real gross product originating), dollars per dollar of real product
$UCCA^N$	Normal unit capital consumption allowances
$UINS_{RT}$	The unemployment insurance tax rate
ULC	Unit labor cost (compensation of employees per unit of gross product originating), dollars per dollar of real product

ULC^N	Normal unit labor costs
V_{FORG}	Net government transfer payments to foreigners
V_G	Government transfer payments to persons
V_{OASIGF}	Old age and survivors insurance benefits
V_{OG}	Government transfer payments to persons other than old age and survivors insurance benefits, state unemployment insurance benefits and veterans' benefits
V_{USGF}	State unemployment insurance benefits
V_{VET}	Veterans' benefits
$WLTH$	Wealth, a weighted moving average of GNP
WPI	Wholesale price index, 1958 = 1.0
WS_G	Wages and salaries in government
WSS	Total compensation of employees (wages, salaries, and supplements)
X	Gross product originating, by sector
X_K	Potential gross product in the producing sector
Y_D	Disposable personal income
Y_{ENT}	Proprietors' income
Y_N	National income
Y_P	Personal income
Z_A	Corporate profits after taxes, including inventory valuation adjustment
Z_{AU}	Corporate profits after taxes, excluding inventory valuation adjustment
Z_B	Corporate profits before taxes, including inventory valuation adjustment
Z_{BU}	Corporate profits before taxes, excluding inventory valuation adjustment

DISCUSSION

RALPH B. BRISTOL, JR.

U.S. TREASURY DEPARTMENT

The Brookings Model, née the SSRC Model, has now been in existence for over ten years, which is a long enough period of time to establish some trends. For one thing, the model, formerly the biggest one of all, seems to get a little smaller at each appearance. The government sector originally contained some thirty-odd equations, with at least a dozen for state and local receipts and expenditures. Now the model is down to one transfer and four tax equations, and state and local government receipts have vanished entirely. Furthermore, the tax functions themselves look pretty scruffy, which is particularly surprising in light of all the tax research that has been conducted at Brookings. One of the boasts of the original model was that it used tax rates and tax bases, but the present model uses neither. The tax rate, of course, has little meaning if we combine federal receipts with state and local receipts. The tax base or income variable used for estimating personal taxes is the national income accounts variable, personal income. This variable includes transfer payments and excludes personal contributions for social insurance, just the opposite of the Internal Revenue Service definition of taxable income. Indirect taxes are a straight percentage of GNP, minus a constant, with a dummy variable apparently intended to reflect changes in federal excise tax rates. Corporate tax liabilities are regressed on the product of corporate profits and "the tax rate" (federal plus state and local, presumably). An advantage claimed for the original model was the endogeneity of many government expenditures. Now we have just one equation: state unemployment insurance payments.

Another area of shrinkage in the model involves the estimation of the labor force. Originally there were thirty or forty equations explaining participation rates and even marriage rates. Now we have one equation making the labor force a function of employment, lagged unemployment, and a time trend. While it may be unreasonable to expect an econometric model to predict the marriage rate, I do think that demographic factors should have some influence on the labor force.

Another trend that I think I observe in the model is an increased willingness to use dummy variables. This is the way the investment credit is handled, for example. I am rather surprised that the credit is estimated to reduce corporate taxes by only $0.7 billion. That is a lot lower than Treasury estimates. The impact of the investment credit on business expenditures shows up as three additive and multiplicative dummy terms. Other variables determining business investment are the long-term interest rate on government bonds and capacity utilization or capital stock or both, depending on the sector being examined. Some of Dale Jorgenson's pioneering work on investment functions was done in connection with this model, and I question whether the present formulations are an advance over his work.

Dummy variables used for personal tax changes yield curious results. The 1964 tax cut is represented by a dummy that serves both as a constant term and as a multiplier of personal income. I have two observations to make on this procedure. First, only two-thirds of the tax cut was effective in 1964; the rest came in 1965. Second, even at 1965 income levels, the implied estimate of the tax cut is only $7 billion, about three-fourths of the Treasury estimate.

Perhaps the ultimate in dummy variables is shown in the equation for consumer expenditure on durables excluding automobiles, where a dummy variable is included even though its coefficient is less than its standard error!

Another difference between this and earlier versions of the model is the sample period. Formerly, the equations were fit to 1948–60, but the authors state that analysis of covariance tests indicated significant shifts in many coefficients between 1948–53 and 1954–60, so the present model was fit to 1954–65 "to select a sample period germane to the analysis of current economic problems" (page 201). This seems to me a mistaken procedure. Granted that the Korean War period was one of great instability, with horrifying effects on correlation coefficients and standard errors, I think we should hesitate before restricting ourselves to more homogeneous observations. Limiting the sample period to 1954–65, for example, means that we have *no* observations in which unemployment was below 4 per cent! Is this sample really "germane to the analysis of current economic problems"? I am not surprised that statistically significant shifts occurred in the period after 1953. The economy entered a period of stagnation from which it did not emerge until it reached its potential again in 1966. Is this the experience most germane to an analysis of the current inflationary situation? In light of the relative homogeneity of the sample period, it seems a shame the authors did not make use of observations after 1965. In addition to different unemployment levels and price movements, we have experienced large swings in residential construction since 1965 and reached the end of the strong upward trend in nonresidential construction in the fourth quarter of 1965. I would be willing to bet that the model failed to pick up either of these last two phenomena.

Turning to applications of the model, there are three analyses in the present paper, the simulation of five National Bureau "turning points"; a sample period simulation covering 1957–65; and a post-sample, twenty-five-year simulation extending from 1966 to 1990. The format of this conference provided no criteria for the performance of models at turning points, so it is difficult, if not impossible, to evaluate them. For example, is it better to forecast the precise timing of a turning point but badly miss the numerical magnitude, or to be close to the correct magnitude even if the direction of movement is wrong? Past disagreements between econometricians and adherents of the indicators approach have been based on just this distinction. The econometric model builder has concerned himself with minimizing squared residuals, be they dollars, unemployment percentages, or interest rates. The sign of the derivative of a variable with respect to time does not really matter to him, and a change in this sign is important only if it affects the error of the equation or model. Given this approach, it is hardly surprising that most econometric models move much more smoothly than the economy, lagging behind turning points, underestimating amplitudes (both high and low), but "on the average" being not far off.

A "business cycles indicator" researcher, on the contrary, is concerned with dating and forecasting turning points. Less interested in the magnitude of a series than in the sign of its first difference, he deals with indexes of economic performance that are aggregated differently from those of econometric models (e.g., diffusion indexes). It is, therefore, hardly surprising that forecasts based on this approach tend to be qualitative, focusing on the probability that a turning point will or will not occur. The quantitative aspects of such a forecast tend to be adjectival ("vigorous," "weak") rather than numerical.

We cannot label either of these approaches the "correct" one. If we are at, or think we are at, a turning point, a leading indicator's analysis may be of more interest to us; otherwise, we may prefer to focus on the output of an econometric model. As long as the two approaches remain as different from one another as they are at present, the one to which we turn depends on what information we have at hand and what questions we are asking.

In line with this, the Brookings Model simulations turn out to have root mean square errors that are larger for turning points than for non-turning point periods, but not very much larger. While the magnitude of the variables is forecast rather well, the turning points are not, and the peaks and troughs are underestimated.

The "longer-run simulations" cover the last three-fourths of the sample period. Charts 12–15 indicate that the model tracked real GNP and business investment rather well for the post-1960 expansion, but did not perform very well during the earlier, less stable years. The price estimates appear subject to severe serial correlation errors, and the residential construction simulation does not seem particularly good. Attempts to simulate the 1966 "credit crunch," which was outside the period of fit, might have been instructive.

For the purposes of the twenty-five-year simulation (1966–90), certain adjustments were necessary in tax rates and productivity equations. Specifically, after expiration of the surcharge, the personal tax rate was *increased* each quarter until 1976, then held constant. The authors state that this was done "in order to keep disposable income from growing too rapidly and also to limit government deficits." This result is certainly different from most long-run projections, which typically show the necessity of periodic tax *cuts* to reduce what used to be referred to as "fiscal drag." The model's low personal tax elasticity, combined with the assumed rising government share of current dollar GNP, changes projections of "fiscal dividends" to "fiscal deficits," and certainly warrants further discussion by the authors.

The authors also felt it necessary to alter some of the time trends in the production man-hour equations in order to raise productivity increases to what they considered more "reasonable" levels. Since the productivity equations seem to be influenced mainly by various "shift" dummy variables during the sample period, I wonder if productivity should really be considered an endogenous variable in this model.

The control solution produced very smooth paths to 1990, presumably the result of smooth extrapolation of the exogenous variables. None of the variables in Charts 16–19 seems to display any cyclical behavior after 1970 in the control solution, although there seems to be considerably more variation in the "representative stochastic simulation." In fact, the residential construction series (Chart 19) exhibits strong cycles that look as if they would become explosive in the late 1980's.

In conclusion, let me say that I approach econometric models as both a producer and a consumer. As a producer who has spent some years attempting to develop improved forecasts, I am filled with humility for my own efforts and admiration for the success of others in building models. As a consumer of models, who is supposed to provide technical assistance to policymakers in the government, I am often appalled at how inappropriate models can be. Consider the economic policy issues that agitated the government during the last ten years: the investment credit and its suspension and revocation, the 1964 tax cut, the 1965 excise cuts, and the 1968 surcharge with its extensions. To be honest, I think the only time econometric models had a major impact on policy decisions came in 1968. At that time, everyone's model showed that the Federal Reserve should ease up on monetary policy to avoid a recession in 1969. I am afraid we still have quite a way to go. If I have seemed critical of the Brookings Model, it is because I was speaking as a consumer of econometric models. Speaking as a producer, I will confess that I agree with the opening sentence of the paper: "Predictions with econometric models, even thirty years after Tinbergen's initial attempt, still involve art as well as science."

ROBERT J. GORDON

THE UNIVERSITY OF CHICAGO AND NATIONAL BUREAU OF
ECONOMIC RESEARCH

The paper by Fromm, Klein, and Schink (hereafter FKS) is the fourth version of the Brookings Model to appear in print. Version I, the set of equations presented in the individual chapters of the 1965 Brookings volume [7], has been extensively criticized [16] but never solved nor simulated. Version II was the abbreviated version presented at the end of the 1965 volume, which was solved but never simulated. The equations of version III are presented by Fromm and Taubman in an appendix of [13] and have been used to derive dynamic policy multipliers, but the transition from version II to version III has never been rigorously justified and the equations of the latter are presented in [13] denuded of all measures of goodness of fit or other statistical information.

Version IV replaces version III, as version III replaced version II, with scarcely a word of explanation. Old variables are dropped and new ones appear, with goodness of fit or a "structural change" during the sample period as virtually the only criteria for replacement offered in the cursory explanation by FKS. During the span of roughly six years since the articles in the original Brookings volume were written, almost no published or unpublished articles have been written to justify either theoretically or econometrically the changes made from version to version. In contrast with the MIT-FRB and Wharton Models, which are both supported by a considerable body of theoretical and econometric literature, the Brookings Model has been transformed so many times since its inception that it is now a model almost devoid of theory, with equations altered and dummy variables added wherever necessary to maximize the model's ability to produce a control solution that accurately tracks GNP during the sample period.[1] In version IV many vari-

---

[1] Despite the recent publication of a second set of econometric papers by the Brookings project [8], none of the equations in version IV has incorporated any of the results of the new papers. In contrast, the equations of the Wharton-EFU Model have been copiously justified and defended ([9] [11] and other references cited there). The MIT-FRB Model is based on several well-known theoretical models [1] [3] [19], and the specific assumptions underlying the financial sectors and monetary channels are described in [5] and [6].

ables are included in the equations and thus influence the simulation results even if their coefficients are not significant (there are thirty-six coefficients with "t" ratios below 2.0 in the first seventy-nine equations). As the specification of the model becomes more arbitrary in successive versions, the less one is likely to trust its policy multipliers or secular simulations, yet richness of simulation detail has always been an important justification for the continuation of research on a model as large as Brookings. And even the details are gradually being sacrificed as the model shrinks in over-all size between successive versions. In light of these developments, which continually reduce the model's margin of disaggregation over competing models with no offsetting theoretical or statistical innovations, one is left with the impression that the model project has lost its sense of direction.

A natural point of departure for these comments is the "menu of revisions" suggested in my recent critical review [15] of version III. To what extent have the major weaknesses of that version been corrected in the new version IV used for the present simulations? Are any important weaknesses introduced in version IV that were absent in the previous version? Do the simulation results appear to be accurate representations of the cyclical and secular features of the real world, or are some of the results of questionable validity due to the particular assumptions made in specifying the model?

1. THE MODEL

Final Expenditure Equations. As in previous versions, consumption is disaggregated into five components. In version III the absence of a flexible accelerator in the auto equation contributed to the sluggishness of the model in simulations. This defect has now been cured, since the lagged stock of automobiles appears with a negative coefficient in the auto equation as well as that for nonauto durables. Previous critics [9] [16] noted that in earlier versions the long-run marginal propensity to consume implied by the five equations taken together was much lower than the average postwar propensity to consume of about .92. Version IV appears to err in the opposite direction, with a long-run marginal propensity to consume of 1.175. This high propensity will cause long-run policy multipliers to be misleadingly high when these

TABLE 1

Propensity to Consume

| | Brookings Marginal Propensity to Consume | | Actual Average Propensity to Consume, 1969 |
	Impact (1)	Long-Run (2)	(3)
Autos	.2204	.1322	.0786
Nonauto durables	.0913	.0700	.0640
Food and beverages	.0655	.0710	.1910
Other nondurables	.1451	.1755	.1964
Services	.0529	.7260	.3890
	.5752	1.1747	.9190

Source by column: Columns 1 and 2 — Calculated from equations (A.1)–(A.5), (A.197), and (A.198) in appendix to FKS paper; *Column 3 — Survey of Current Business* (April 1970), Table 11, p. 9.

are eventually calculated for version IV, and it is responsible for the increase in the ratio of real consumption to *GNP* in the 1965–90 simulations presented in the FKS paper. Table 1 suggests that the equation for services is the primary culprit responsible for the excessively high long-run marginal propensity to consume.

The present set of consumption equations, as in previous versions, fails to allow for any direct influence of monetary policy on consumption. Thus monetary policy multipliers calculated for the Brookings Model are likely to be smaller than those for the MIT-FRB Model, where total consumption is a function of real wealth (which is influenced by monetary policy via stock prices) and where durables consumption depends on interest rates.[2] And we might expect overpredic-

[2] Although econometric evidence is preferable to anecdotes, direct monetary influence on consumption is supported by frequent reports in the financial press in 1969–70 of reduced consumption of luxury goods, attributed to the drop in stock prices. One also notes the marked decline in the average propensity to consume between the first and last halves of 1966, and the first and last halves of 1969, both of which were years characterized by much slower rates of growth of monetary aggregates in the last half than in the first half.

tions of *GNP* in simulations following periods of monetary tightness. The residential construction equations suffer from a failure to distinguish between the separate influence of monetary factors on the demand for housing and the supply of credit for housing. One would expect demand to be a function of the mortgage rate, which is much less volatile than the Treasury bill used by Brookings. (Housing demand would also be expected to depend on household formations, tax rates and the expected rate of capital gains.) The supply of housing credit, on the other hand, depends on the gap between short-term market interest rates and deposit rates at banks and savings institutions. The Brookings Model would probably underpredict housing expenditures for periods like 1967 and the last half of 1968, when the Treasury bill rate was relatively high compared to the 1954–65 sample period but the supply of credit to the housing market was ample because deposit rates were high relative to the Treasury bill rate. Another weakness, which the housing equations have in common with many others, is that lags on interest rates and other variables are fixed arbitrarily rather than estimated statistically by the numerous methods now available.

The change in inventories causes difficulties in all models, but the Brookings equations do an unusually poor job of fitting the sample period in all sectors but manufacturing durables. This is unfortunate, since inventory change has been the main contributor to the timing pattern of postwar recessions, and models which explain inventories badly are likely to track badly in simulations of recession. Because of the difficulty of explaining inventory change, it is suggested below that the ability to track final sales rather than *GNP* should be the criterion for judging dynamic simulations of alternative models.

The investment equations were extremely weak in version III, but version IV is even worse. The new equations repeat the earlier error of representing the cost of capital with a nominal rather than a real interest rate. The previous arbitrary "spiked" lag distributions (in which virtually all of the influence of a change in output and interest rates occurs in the fifth quarter after the change, rather than being spread out over several quarters) have been replaced by a smooth distributed lag pattern. But these new lag weights should have been estimated by the Almon technique separately for the output and interest rate variables in each of the four sectors. Instead, however, the authors have used a *single* set of weights for output and interest rates in each sector, and these weights were not estimated for the Brookings sectors, variables, or sample period but were simply copied from weights estimated by Shirley Almon for a different variable (the lag of expenditures behind appropriations), a different sector (all of manufacturing) and a different sample period (1954–61). Why create a disaggregated model if a single inappropriate lag pattern is going to be imposed on all sectors?[3]

The extension of the end of the sample period of version IV from 1960 to 1965 forces the authors to deal with the investment tax credit and liberalized depreciation allowances introduced in 1962. The approach is a completely ad hoc use of dummy variables and stands in contrast to numerous recent articles [3] [4] [17] [18], one of which was written by an author of the FKS paper, that attempt to base the treatment of investment incentives on theoretical considerations. And the effect of the dummy variables is very peculiar. They raise the constant and reduce the output elasticity of investment in durable manufacturing, but lower the constant and raise the elasticity in nondurables and lower the constant and leave the elasticity unaffected in the regulated sector. The most dubious feature of the equations is the result that, ceteris paribus, investment incentives *reduced* real investment spending between 1961 and 1963 by about $7 billion![4] Very little confidence should be placed in the long-run simulations calculated with these equations.

Other equations. In general, the equations outside of the final expenditures sector are not as weak as other models and require less extended comment that the expenditure equations. The production functions warrant attention, since they determine how rapidly productivity will grow in the twenty-five-year simulations. The durables manufac-

---

[3] Exactly the same use of nonestimated weights is employed in the Wharton-EFU Model (see [9]).

[4] To perform the ceteris paribus experiment, fix the interest rate at 4.0; durables output originating at the approximate 1963 figure of $90 billion; nondurables output at $60 billion; and the durables utilization rate at .85. The equations then predict durables investment of $13.3 billion with 1961 values of the dummy variables and $8.9 billion with 1963 values; $10.1 billion in 1961 and $9.3 billion in 1963 for nondurables; and a straight $2.1 billion reduction in the regulated sector.

turing equation calls for reexamination, since its steady-state version has an unreasonably high degree of increasing returns (1.26) and erratic fluctuations in the rate of disembodied technical change (a zero annual rate before 1960:1, a 4.6 per cent annual rate between 1960:2 and 1963:1, and 0.9 per cent annual rate thereafter). The degree of increasing returns is even stronger in nondurables (1.65).

The hours equations introduce a novel theory of money illusion in the long-run labor supply curve. An increase in the nominal wage rate reduces hours per week, no matter how rapidly prices are rising. An increase in nominal wages of $1.00 due entirely to inflation would reduce hours by 2.5 hours per man per week. The coefficients in these equations are influenced by the slow rate of inflation during the sample period and will overestimate the secular decline in hours during periods of faster inflation.

In the twenty-five-year simulation the price-wage sector generates a remarkably low 1.7 per cent steady-state annual rate of inflation at a 3.9 per cent unemployment rate, a much lower rate of inflation than is implied in other econometric work (for my own simulation results see [14]). In the price equation the elasticity of prices to changes in unit labor cost is between 1.27 and 1.75, implying an increasing secular ratio of profits to wages. If corporations are so aggressive in raising the profit share, why is the rate of inflation so slow in the long-run simulations? The coefficients in the wage equation suggest implausibly docile behavior by workers. The wage equations of the old version III imply a plausible annual rate of wage increase of 6.7 per cent at a steady 4 per cent unemployment rate [15, Table 2], but in version IV workers have become more timid. The steady-state rate of increase of wages can be calculated for a 4 per cent unemployment rate on the assumption of a unitary elasticity of product prices to changes in unit labor cost, a rate of productivity growth of 3.0 per cent per annum in each sector, and an increase in consumer prices at the same rate as in product prices.[5] The resulting figures are extremely low: 6.0 per cent in durables, 3.8 per cent in nondurables, 3.4 per cent in trade, 4.8 per

---

[5] These assumptions are the same as those used in [16] and [15, Table 2], except for the arbitrary assumption of a unitary elasticity of prices to changes in unit labor cost, which is introduced here to judge the coefficients of the wage equations in combination with a "more reasonable" set of price equations than those in version IV.

cent in regulated, 3.6 per cent in the residual sector, and approximately zero in contract construction. These low estimates in version IV compared to version III may be due to the exclusion from the sample period of any years with an unemployment rate below 4.0 per cent, to the ending of the sample period in 1965:4 before the falling unemployment rate of 1964–65 had much time to influence wage rates, and perhaps to the arbitrary lag distributions. These weak equations also ignore the recent emphasis in the literature on price expectations and disguised unemployment as determinants of wage rates (e.g., [12] [20]).

An improvement in the financial sector of version IV compared to version III is the elimination of the investment variable in the demand for money equation, the coefficient of which in earlier versions was negative and caused the model to generate misleading policy multipliers (see [15]). But the model will still predict that a cut in personal tax revenues will increase interest rates more than an equal increase in government expenditures, due to the use in the demand for money equations of disposable income rather than some broader income concept. Finally, an extremely important flaw in the financial sector is the failure to incorporate any influence on interest rates of changes in the expected price level. In 1968 and 1969 an increase in the rate of expected inflation was a major factor causing a rapid rise in nominal interest rates, and by ignoring inflationary expectations the Brookings Model in a prediction experiment would presumably have underpredicted nominal interest rates. As noted above, the model makes no distinction between the nominal interest rates that enter the demand for money function and the real interest rates that should influence the demand for commodities.

2. THE SIMULATIONS

Turning points. On what criteria should we judge the turning point simulations? A one- or two-quarter error in predicting the exact timing of peaks and troughs is not serious if the order of magnitude of the boom or recession is tracked accurately. And the FKS criterion of comparing six-quarter simulation errors around turning points with errors in a nine-year simulation is uninformative, since a good performance by this criterion might be due to the shorter time span of the turning point simulations rather than a relatively accurate performance of the model at turning points. Instead, I would ask of these simulations whether a policy maker having confidence in the model and using it for forecasting postwar recessions would have been misled into making an incorrect policy decision. The simulations of the 1958 and 1961 troughs shown in Charts 1–11 are pessimistic on this score. For instance, the trough unemployment rate in 1958:2 (Chart 7) is estimated to be 5 per cent instead of 7 per cent, and the rate of inflation (Chart 2) is overestimated by almost 1 per cent per annum between 1957:2 and 1958:2. These forecasts would have thus supported the arguments of those like Secretary Humphrey who stood against a stimulative monetary and fiscal policy during the Eisenhower recessions.

Once simulation errors have been judged to be serious, the equations that make the largest contributions to the errors should be sought out, a task not attempted by FKS. One first notes that the unemployment error is only about half due to the error in tracking real GNP.[6] At the 1958 trough, for instance, the overestimate of real GNP is about 3 per cent of real GNP, which by application of Okun's law should cause an underestimate of the unemployment rate by one percentage point.[7] Since the unemployment rate is actually underestimated by about two percentage points, about half of the unemployment error is contributed not by the expenditure equations but on the supply side by the productivity-hours-participation equations. The small employment errors (Chart 8) relative to the unemployment errors suggest that the participation equation is an important source of the trouble. Until the supply equations in this and other large-scale econometric models are improved, model builders would be well advised to rely on a simple Okun's law equation to minimize errors in estimating unemployment for a given estimate of real GNP.

Considering the large underestimates of unemployment in the 1958 and 1961 troughs, the overestimate of wage and price changes is

[6] To simplify the following discussion, we consider only the simulations starting four quarters before the 1958 and 1961 troughs.

[7] For recent statistical evidence that Okun's law is valid for the 1951–69 period, see [14, Appendix B, equation (2)].

surprisingly small. The slight response of wage changes to unemployment errors is consistent with comments on the wage equations made above, and with the impossibly low rates of inflation generated by the model in the twenty-five-year secular simulation.

Turning now to the real GNP errors at troughs, these appear to be about half due to incorrect predictions of inventory change. The model seems to generate a flat and smooth, rather than cyclical, pattern of inventory change in all postwar recessions (Chart 5), and it would be interesting to know whether the same is true of the residuals in the underlying inventory equations. The model does a much better job of tracking real final sales than real GNP and large-scale models will make a much better impression on readers of simulation reports if increased emphasis is placed on the ability to track final sales. Of the components of final sales, residential construction is tracked very closely, and the nonresidential investment predictions behave quite well except at the 1960 peak. Consumption contributes most (in absolute, not relative terms) to final sales errors, due to the model's inability to predict a drop in the propensity to consume in 1958 and a marked increase in 1960. These results cannot fail to give support to the monetarist argument that velocity is relatively more stable than the Keynesian multiplier.

1957–65 simulation. The $5.0 billion root mean square error in tracking real GNP during a nine-year simulation between 1957:1 and 1965:4 appears quite impressive. By contrast the MIT-FRB Model in a similar simulation for 1958:1 through 1967:2 generates a $7.0 billion error [2]. But the lustre of the Brookings achievement dims somewhat when we consider the heavy dependence of the results on dummy variables. Excluding all strike and tax rate dummies, the remaining dummy variables change values in eight of the thirty-six quarters included in the simulation. The dummy variables in the investment equations, which change in 1962:1 and 1963:1 are particularly important in keeping the model on target in the 1961–65 period.

But even without dummy variables most models fitted to the post-Korea era do well in simulations of 1961–65, simply because most of the variance of expenditure components between 1954 and 1965 occurs during 1961–1965, so that these years play a dominant role in determining the coefficients in the underlying expenditure equations. A much more challenging test would have been an extension to 1966–69, an experiment in which the Wharton Model goes completely off the rails [10].

The long-term 1966–90 simulations. The authors introduce this section with the puzzling statement: "The Brookings Model is essentially a short-run forecasting model and as such is not designed for simulation over a twenty-five-year period." Whatever its original intent, however, the model has never been used as a forecasting device (to my knowledge no *ex ante* forecasts have ever been released), partly because the large size of the model inhibits the maintenance of an up-to-date data file. Thus the only possible justification for the Brookings Model is that its large scale yields superior representation of the true structure of the economy than smaller models. If so, a secular simulation is one of the few experiments in which the Brookings Model should have a comparative advantage.

One is tempted to apply a microscope to the graphs of the 1966–69 portion of the 1966–90 simulation values depicted in Charts 16–19 to test the model's ability to track outside of its sample period. Lacking a microscope, I shall eschew comment on this aspect of the simulations, except to remark that the Brookings Model exhibits the universal failing—common to all large-scale econometric models which misspecify the channels by which monetary policy influences real spending—of predicting an economic slowdown in late 1968 and speed-up in the last half of 1969.

Given the extrapolations of steady growth in government spending, it is not surprising that the economy is relatively stable after 1972. Tax rates are manipulated to maintain the economy at full employment, so we would expect a stabler economy than occurred with the highly unstable full-employment surplus of 1953–69. As one looks down the list of exogenous variables, however, it is apparent that Hamlet is missing. Nowhere do FKS mention the assumption made about the secular behavior of unborrowed reserves, the major exogenous monetary variable, although I am told privately that a constant growth rate was assumed. The assumed stability of monetary growth compared to the instability of 1953–69 makes a contribution to the steadiness of the economic advance of 1970–90, even in a model like Brookings where money plays a marginal role.

In their discussion of exogenous assumptions, the authors state that tax rates are raised steadily through 1976 "to keep disposable income from growing too rapidly." At first glance this appears to conflict with the widespread assumption that steady economic growth yields a "fiscal dividend" that allows a reduction in tax rates. But in this secular simulation the fiscal dividend is negative, since an assumption of a roughly constant ratio of real government spending to real GNP combined with a rising relative price of government requires an increase in the G/GNP ratio in current dollars from 20.2 per cent in 1965:4 to 25.0 per cent in 1990:4, and revenues must also increase the same relative amount to maintain a balanced full-employment budget. This increase in tax revenues could be attained over a twenty-five-year period with income-elasticity of tax revenues of only 1.16, but the Brookings tax equations understate the income elasticity of the U.S. tax system, forcing an increase in the "dummy" coefficients in the tax equations.[8]

Do the secular rates of growth in Table 8 tell us anything about what is likely to occur in the real world? Virtually all of the results can be traced to some of the peculiar features of the model, described in Part I above. For instance, the ratio of profits to GNP (both in current prices) increases from the already high level of .113 in 1965:4 to .134 in 1990:4 (as compared to .101 in the prosperous year of 1968). This is caused by the unreasonably high elasticity of changes in prices to changes in unit labor cost in the price equations. The low rate of wage increase and low rate of inflation originate in a very weak set of wage equations. The increase in the ratio of consumption to GNP is due to the long-run marginal propensity to consume of greater than 1.0 in the consumption equations. A surprising result is the rapid increase in the ratio of business nonresidential investment to GNP in light of the predicted increase in interest rates. An increase in this ratio would imply a reversal of the secular decline in the capital-output ratio which has continued in the United States since 1919. In fact the behavior of this ratio tells us more about the effect of dummy variables in the investment equations than it tells us about the real world.

[8] The ad hoc adjustment that FKS apply to the hours and productivity equations confirm the critical comments made above about the supply sector of the model.

All in all, version IV of the Brookings Model does not appear to be a net improvement over previous versions. Its improved performance in sample-period simulations rests on a shortening of the sample period, the widespread adoption of dummy variables, and ad hoc techniques for specifying equations to maximize simulation performance and goodness of fit. The long-run implications of the resulting equations are questionable in many cases, but the creation of a plausible set of long-run implications is a basic test which must be passed by any model, and this is particularly true of a model like Brookings, which is so unwieldy that it has never been used to fulfill its primary purpose of short-term forecasting. My unhappy conclusion is that, rather than attempt to move on to another version, the Brookings Model builders should merge the best features of their equations into the MIT-FRB Model, which in my judgment is the only large-scale model robust enough to withstand the onslaught of the St. Louis monetarists on either the simulation or forecasting front.

REFERENCES

[1] Ando, A., and Modigliani, F., "The Life Cycle Hypothesis of Saving: Aggregate Implications and Tests," *American Economic Review* (March 1963), *53*, pp. 55–84.
[2] ———, "Econometric Analysis of Stabilization Policies," *American Economic Review* (May 1969), *59*, pp. 296–314.
[3] Bischoff, D. W., "Lags in Fiscal and Monetary Impacts on Investment in Producers' Durable Equipment," in Fromm, G., ed., *Tax Incentives and Investment Behavior.* Washington, Brookings, 1971.
[4] Coen, R. M., "Tax Policy and Investment in Manufacturing, 1954–66," in Fromm, G., ed., *Tax Incentives and Investment Behavior.* Washington, Brookings, 1971.
[5] De Leeuw, F., and Gramlich, E., "The Federal Reserve–MIT Econometric Model," *Federal Reserve Bulletin* (January 1968), *54*, pp. 11–40.
[6] ———, "The Channels of Monetary Policy," *Federal Reserve Bulletin* (June 1969), *55*, pp. 472–91.

[7] Duesenberry, J., et al., The Brookings Quarterly Econometric Model of the United States. Chicago, Rand McNally, 1965.

[8] ———, The Brookings Model: Some Further Results. Chicago, Rand McNally, 1969.

[9] Evans, M. K., Macroeconomic Activity. New York, Harper and Row, 1969.

[10] ———, Haitovsky, Y., and Treyz, G. I., "An Analysis of the Forecasting Properties of U.S. Econometric Models," this volume.

[11] ———, and Klein, L., The Wharton Econometric Forecasting Model. Philadelphia, Wharton School, 1968.

[12] Friedman, M., "The Role of Monetary Policy," American Economic Review (March 1968), 58, pp. 1–17.

[13] Fromm, G., and Taubman, P., Policy Simulations with an Econometric Model. Washington, Brookings, 1968.

[14] Gordon, R. J., "The Recent Acceleration of Inflation and Its Lessons for the Future," Brookings Papers on Economic Activity (May 1970), 1, pp. 8–41.

[15] ———, "The Brookings Model in Action: A Review Article," Journal of Political Economy (May/June 1970), 78, pp. 489–525.

[16] Griliches, Z., "The Brookings Model Volume: A Review Article," Review of Economics and Statistics (May 1968), 50, pp. 215–34.

[17] Hall, R. E., and Jorgenson, D. W., "Tax Policy and Investment Behavior," American Economic Review (June 1967), 57, pp. 391–414.

[18] Klein, L. R., and Taubman, P., "Impact of Accelerated Depreciation and Investment Tax Credit on Investment and General Economic Activity," in Fromm, G., ed., Tax Incentives and Investment Behavior. Washington, Brookings, 1971.

[19] Modigliani, F., "The Monetary Mechanism and Its Interaction with Real Phenomena," Review of Economics and Statistics (February 1963, Part 2), 45, pp. 79–107.

[20] Vroman, W., "Manufacturing Wage Behavior with Special Reference to the Period, 1962–1966," The Review of Economics and Statistics (May 1970), 52, pp. 160–7.

BUSINESS CYCLE ANALYSIS OF ECONOMETRIC MODEL SIMULATIONS

VICTOR ZARNOWITZ · University of Chicago
CHARLOTTE BOSCHAN · National Bureau of
Economic Research
GEOFFREY H. MOORE · Bureau of Labor
Statistics
assisted by JOSEPHINE SU

1 INTRODUCTION

1.1 BACKGROUND AND PURPOSE

IN A pioneering study published ten years ago, Irma Adelman and Frank L. Adelman [2] calculated and analyzed the time paths of the main endogenous variables from the 1955 Klein-Goldberger (KG) econometric model of the United States [22]. They examined several forms of hypothetical long-term development of this system: (1) non-stochastic simulations based on smooth extrapolations of the exogenous variables; (2) stochastic simulations of "Type I," with random shocks superimposed upon the extrapolated values of the exogenous quantities; and (3) stochastic simulations of "Type II," with random shocks introduced into each of the fitted equations. Each of these different solutions was dynamic, in that it related current values of endogenous variables to their lagged values generated by the model from earlier data; each also involved some tentative assumptions about secular economic trends, in that it projected the exogenous variables far beyond the sample-period base of the KG estimates (1929–52) over one hundred years of the "future." The Adelmans were primarily interested in learning whether the KG Model can, internally, generate cyclical movements resembling cycles found historically in the United States economy. The nonstochastic simulations and those using the Type I shocks did not produce such movements, but the stochastic

311

simulations with shocks of Type II did, as the Adelmans concluded from comparisons of the time paths computed for the KG Model with the NBER "reference cycle" measures for the series involved.

Since then—in the 1960's—increasingly ambitious efforts have been made to estimate economic relationships with more detailed and complex econometric models, and the simulation experiments performed upon these models have grown correspondingly in size and scope. Simulations of a quarterly model by Duesenberry, Eckstein, and Fromm [8] were designed to test the proneness to recession of the U.S. economy and the effectiveness of automatic stabilizers. Later, several quarterly models of the postwar U.S. economy were unveiled in quick succession, notably those by L. R. Klein [22], Klein and M. K. Evans [13], M. Liebenberg, A. A. Hirsch, and J. Popkin for the Office of Business Economics of the Department of Commerce (OBE) [23], the Brookings Model [9], and most recently, the FRB-MIT Model [3], [11], [27]. The last two systems represent efforts by sizable groups of economists, and each consists of a very large number of equations. At the NBER, an econometric model of business cycles was formulated in the last few years by G. C. Chow and G. H. Moore: its early sets of estimates are currently being evaluated [6].

The present Conference is concerned with these recent models, viewed as instruments for the analysis and prediction of general economic fluctuations. Our study, in particular, deals with experiments performed on some of these systems in a search for answers to the type of question which Irma and Frank Adelman asked with respect to the KG system. Do these models endogenously generate cyclical behavior, and, if so, to what extent, how, in which sectors, and over what predictive span? To what degree are the fluctuations produced by external impulses? How do such cycles as may originate in the nonstochastic and stochastic simulations compare with the relationships observed in the NBER business cycle studies? How do the models differ from each other in these respects?

The materials that can now be analyzed with a view to clarifying these issues are clearly much richer than those available in the late 1950's. It has long been recognized, for instance, that annual data are far less adequate in business cycle analysis than are quarterly or monthly data. The new quarterly models, therefore, should definitely be more appropriate for the purposes at hand than are the older annual models (such as the KG equation system). Furthermore, the present models draw on longer experience with, and better knowledge of, econometric estimation methods; and they cover larger data samples and a much greater number and variety of macroeconomic relations. These data were hardly tapped for studies of cyclical behavior before the present Conference. Such simulations as were made with these models were used primarily for general evaluation and for analyzing the effects of specific postulated policy changes [10], [17].

Although simulation is a powerful tool of economic analysis, its inherent limitations are substantial and should be recognized. As noted by Irma Adelman, "Any simulation experiment produces no more than a specific numerical case history of the system whose properties are to be investigated" [1, p. 272]. Hence, the inferences drawn from simulation results concerning the properties of the economic system are only as good as the model which is used as the analogue of that system. For example, the Adelmans' study has shown that the cyclical fluctuations in the KG Model are due to random shocks of a certain type; to what extent this study has verified the hypothesis that random perturbations were the major cause of business cycles of experience, depends essentially on the quality of the KG equation system as a representation of basic relationships in the U.S. economy.

While no simulation study can avoid being limited in this sense, evidence from studies based on different models, applications to different periods, and so forth, may to some extent cumulate and help reduce this weakness. This would be so if the different applications and models were complementary in their substantially valid parts, and if the evidence based on them were internally consistent. For example, should the simulations for a variety of differently structured quarterly models yield similar indications of the importance of exogenous erratic impulses, we would regard this as additional support for the random-shock hypothesis of cyclical behavior. In the light of possibilities of this sort, a plausible argument can be made in favor of comprehensive and diversified coverage of econometric model simulations in business cycle analysis.

1.2 PROGRAM AND DATA

According to the original plan for the Conference, the study was to cover five models: Brookings, Wharton-EFU, OBE, FRB-MIT-PENN, and Chow-NBER.[1] However, no simulation data were received for the Brookings Model before the time scheduled for delivery of the Conference papers, and the estimates for the Chow-NBER Model are still incomplete. The Wharton, OBE, and FMP model-builders have supplied us with the large amounts of required data, and have given us excellent cooperation. In its present version, therefore, our study covers the estimates produced by the current versions of these three quarterly models of the postwar U.S. economy.[2]

Twenty-two variables were selected for the cyclical simulations. The list includes GNP in constant (1958) dollars and five of its components: consumption, residential construction, nonresidential fixed investment, change in business inventories, and net exports. Also specified for the investigation were data on GNP, personal income, and corporate profit in current dollars, employment and the unemployment rate, average workweek, new and unfilled orders, construction contracts and housing starts, the implicit price deflator for GNP, labor compensation per man-hour and unit of output, money supply, and the short- and long-term interest rates. These variables were selected because of their importance for macroeconomic theory in general, and business cycle analysis in particular, and in view of their cyclical sensitivity and timing. With some exceptions and modifications, they appear in most of the recent econometric models of intermediate or large size.

[1] See references in previous section. For brevity, the Wharton Econometric Forecasting Unit (EFU) Model and the FRB-MIT-PENN Model will henceforth be referred to as the Wharton and FMP Models, respectively.

[2] In the process of being developed and revised, each model has been undergoing changes of varying importance and frequency. Models with relatively long histories, such as the Wharton Model, have passed through several distinguishable versions, as described in the paper by Evans, Haitovsky, and Treyz [12]. The OBE Model, as used in this report and identified by the list of its equations in the paper by George Green and associates [18], differs from the earlier version introduced in 1966 [23]. The model variants on which our analysis is based are those developed by the spring and summer seasons of 1969, prior to the time when the simulation data were supplied to us by the model-builders. These models are explained in considerable detail in other reports prepared for this Conference [12], [14], [18]; we shall refer to this information as needed, without reproducing it at length.

Table 1.1 gives some descriptive detail and sources for the data actually used to represent the selected variables in each of the cooperating systems. It shows that, on the whole, the models agree rather well with each other in regard to coverage of the specified items. However, there are several differences among models, and some variables have been omitted. Thus, none of the three systems includes construction contracts. Only the OBE Model estimates housing starts, and labor costs per unit of real private GNP; only OBE and FMP have endogenous components of money supply. Also, the concepts and industrial coverage differ among the models for certain variables. For example, OBE uses both new and unfilled orders for durable-goods manufactures in real terms; Wharton, deflated unfilled orders for all manufacturing; and FMP, unfilled orders for machinery and equipment industries, in current dollars.

Most of the important differences in data definitions and coverage are brought out in Table 1.1, and some minor discrepancies in units of measurement are also annotated, but we do not claim to have identified all factors that impair comparisons across the models. Such factors are undoubtedly numerous and some are difficult to detect, notably the differences in the vintage of data used, which can be quite significant, as in the case of the frequently revised series for GNP and components.

For each of the models, three types of complete-model simulations were examined, namely: (a) nonstochastic simulations over selected six-quarter periods which include the dates of the turning points of recent fluctuations in aggregate economic activity; (b) nonstochastic simulations over the entire period covered by the models; (c) stochastic simulations projecting the models for a period of twenty-five years, starting at the end of the sample period.

Each set of simulations of a particular type consists of discontinuous sequences (for a), or continuous time-series (for b and c) of estimates for as many of the selected endogenous variables as are included in the given model. One set per model is sufficient to produce the simulations of type a; and one run, for those of type b; but for the stochastic simulations (c), as many as fifty runs per model were requested, with one hundred quarterly terms in each run. This was done to examine the variability of responses of a given system to different configurations of random shocks, and to avoid excessive reliance on

TABLE 1.1

List of Variables and Data Definitions for Business-Cycle Simulations of Three Econometric Models
(x indicates simulated series available)

Line	Symbol	Variable and Units	Wharton Model[a] (1)	OBE Model[a] (2)	FMP Model[a] (3)
1	GNP[a]	Gross national product, annual rate, billions of dollars	x	x	x
2	$GNP58$[a]	Gross national product, annual rate, billions of 1958 dollars	x	x	x
3	C[a]	Personal consumption expenditures, annual rate, billions of 1958 dollars	x	x	x
4	IH[a]	Investment in nonfarm residential structures, annual rate, billions of 1958 dollars	x	x	x
5	ISE[a]	Investment in nonfarm nonresidential structures and producers' durable equipment, annual rate, billions of 1958 dollars	x	x	x
6	II[a]	Change in nonfarm business inventories, annual rate, billions of 1958 dollars	x	x	x
7	NE[a]	Net exports, annual rate, billions of 1958 dollars	x	x	x
8	YP[a]	Personal income, annual rate, billions of dollars	x	x	x
9	P[b]	Implicit price deflator for GNP, 1958 = 100	x	x	x
10	LE[b]	Total civilian employment, millions of persons	x	x	x

11	UN^b	Unemployment rate, per cent of labor force	x	x	x
12	CPR^b	Corporate profits and inventory valuation adjustment, annual rate, billions of dollars	x	x	x
13	AWW^b	Average workweek, private employment, hours per week	x	x	x
14	LH^a	Total hours per man in nonfarm private domestic sector, thousands of hours per year	x	x	
15	OMD^b	New orders, durable manufacturers' goods, billions of 1958 dollars			x
16	UMD^b	Unfilled orders, durable manufacturers' goods, at end of quarter, billions of 1958 dollars		x	
17	$OUME^b$	Unfilled orders, machinery and equipment industry, end of quarter, billions of dollars	x	x	x
18	HS^b	Private nonfarm housing starts, annual rate, thousands			
19	RS	Average yield, 4–6 month prime commercial paper, per cent per annum	x	x	
20	RL	Average yield, corporate bonds, Moody's, per cent per annum	x	x	x
21	W	Private wage and salary compensation per man-hour, dollars	x	x	x
22	LC/O^b	Private employee compensation per unit of constant dollar private GNP, dollars	x	x	x
23	M	Demand deposits, adjusted, and currency outside banks, daily average of quarter, billions of dollars		x	
				x	x

Source Notes for Table 1.1
Line
 1. OBE definition. National Income Accounts (NIA) Table 1.1, line 1.
 2. NIA Table 1.2, line 1.
 3. *Ibid.,* line 2.
 4. *Ibid.,* line 11. In FMP Model, hundred billion 1958 dollars.
 5. *Ibid.,* line 8.
 6. *Ibid.,* line 15.
 7. *Ibid.,* line 17.
 8. NIA Table 2.1, line 1.
 9. NIA Table 8.1, line 1.
 10. Based on monthly BLS figures. In Wharton Model, includes armed forces.
 11. *Ibid.* In FMP Model, labor-force base includes armed forces.
 12. Corporate profits before taxes, including inventory valuation adjustment.
 13. Based on monthly BLS figures. OBE: 1957–59 = 1.00. Wharton: 40 hours = 1.00 (manufacturing and nonmanufacturing).
 14. Unpublished BLS series.
 15. Based on monthly Census figures. Deflated by Wholesale Price Index for durable-goods manufactures.
 16. *Ibid.* In Wharton Model, equals unfilled orders for all manufacturing. Deflated by corresponding Wholesale Price Index series.
 17. *Ibid.*
 18. *Ibid.*
 19. Based on monthly Federal Reserve System data.
 20. Based on monthly Moody's Investors Service series. In FRB-MIT Model, the A bond yield.
 21. Based on monthly BLS labor income and man-hours data. In Wharton Model, wage rate (quarterly earnings at annual rate), weighted average for manufacturing and nonmanufacturing. In FMP Model, rate of compensation in nonfarm private domestic sector.
 22. Based on monthly OBE data.
 23. Based on monthly Federal Reserve System data.

[a] Seasonally adjusted.
[b] Quarterly, seasonally adjusted.

the results of any particular distribution of the shocks that could well be highly idiosyncratic.

The sections that follow deal successively with these three types of simulations, thus proceeding from the shortest to the longest ones. The six-quarter simulations (*a*) can be viewed as conditional predictions over selected, relatively short periods. They are conditioned on the ex post values of the exogenous factors, and on the structure of the model estimated from the sample-period data, which include the turning point episodes covered here. Being reinitiated from actual base-period values in each new run, they predict six successive quarters. The sample-period simulations (*b*) are conditional, or ex post, in the same sense, but they have much longer predictive spans: up to (approximately) 11, 14, and 20 years, for the FMP, OBE, and Wharton Models, respectively. Finally, the stochastic simulations (*c*) start from initial conditions as of the end of the sample-period, and look into the future: a period which is for the most part unknown and—for a long time yet—unknowable. These simulations are based on nonstochastic projections (control solutions) of each of the models, which embody various assumptions—some, reasonably well founded; others, made for working purposes only. In a purely formal sense, these simulations are ex ante model forecasts over a long stretch of time, but they were not intended, or constructed, to serve any practical forecasting purposes. Instead, their function is to help us evaluate some important characteristics of the models and to compare the evolution charted in these experiments with the historical movements of the economy.

1.3 SOME PROBLEMS OF MEASUREMENT AND INTERPRETATION

Different types and aspects of simulations require different analytical methods and measures. For the six-quarter simulations around business cycle turning points (Part 2), the emphasis is on the reproduction of turning points, the timing of these turns, and the amplitudes of cyclical swings—all in comparison with the corresponding segments of the actual series. The measures applied to the sample-period simulations (Part 3) range widely, from the NBER reference-cycle patterns, cyclical timing and amplitude comparisons, through some results of time-series decomposition and correlation and regression analysis, to selected summary measures of absolute and relative accuracy of prediction. For the long stochastic simulations extending into the future (Part 4), broad comparisons with the sample-period actuals are made in terms of the average frequencies, durations, and relative size of movements. The relative timing of the various simulated variables is analyzed, and an attempt is made to find out whether the simulated series can be classified as leaders, coinciders, and laggers— in the same way in which the historical indicators were classified.

This diversification of the techniques and tools used (still understated in the above summary) reflects the difficulty of any attempt to establish the degree of verisimilitude of a model as an analogue of the economic system in motion. The task is necessarily intricate, for it involves study of relationships of various kinds, between different economic processes and over time. Incomplete knowledge of the past, and ignorance of the future, reduce the potential attainments of the analysis. Recurrent, diverse, cumulative, and widely diffused expansions and contractions in economic activities, which underlie aggregative cyclical fluctuations, have been a persistent feature of highly developed capitalistic economies of the modern era. To what extent they will continue in this role in the future, no one can predict with confidence: it depends on structural changes in the economy, the success of economic policies (and of the underlying forecasts), international developments, and so on. All we have as a measurable criterion for evaluating the model-results is the past evolution of the economy. This compels a particularly cautious interpretation of any findings for the long-term simulations.

The results for the different models are not directly comparable for at least two reasons. First, there are differences between the sample periods (e.g., the simulations start late in 1948 for the Wharton Model, in 1953 for OBE, and in 1956 for FMP). This can strongly affect the relative performance of the models. As a task for the future, it would be most desirable to recalculate the simulations with one common sample period for all included models. Secondly, models differ in coverage: in particular, what is endogenous in one model may be exogenous in another. This is a major problem for comparing models of different scope, with respect to their predictive performance [7, Sec. E-1], but it is not so serious for our study, which concentrates on a subset of selected variables that are basically common to, and endogenous in, all of the models covered. However, some points of difference ought to be noted. Comprehensive aggregates, such as GNP, include certain exogenous components in each case, but they are not always exactly the same across the models. Thus, in the Wharton Model, the parts of real GNP originating in the farm sector, and in the government sector, are exogenous; in the OBE Model, in addition to government purchases of goods and services, and investment in farm structures, housing services are treated exogenously; and in the FMP Model, only the federal part of government expenditures is exogenous, while the state and local government purchases are handled essentially as endogenous [13], [18], [25]. Furthermore, exports and imports are endogenous for Wharton, while exports are exogenous for OBE and FMP (as are military imports). Of variables other than real expenditure components, the money supply (M) deserves attention. In the OBE Model, M consists of currency outside banks (exogenous) and demand deposits (endogenous). The FMP Model, which is particularly concerned with monetary factors and financial markets, also adopts this differential treatment of the two components of M. The variable does not appear in the Wharton Model.

Because of these differences in sample-periods and scope, large parts of this report deal with each of the models separately. However, comparisons between the models will inevitably be made, and some of them may be justified if they are framed with caution. We shall have something to say on this subject in summarizing the results of the different types of simulation.

2 SIX-QUARTER SIMULATIONS AROUND REFERENCE TURNS

BUILDERS of cyclical models have stressed—correctly—that their models are short-term models, that cumulations of short-run errors would tend to distort the results of simulations which are run continuously for many quarters, and that, therefore, it would be inappropriate to test the efficacy of the models by long-run simulations only. Another rationale for this contention is the argument that dynamic relationships, such as consumption responses to cyclical swings of income, may be structurally different in the short run and in the long run. Thus, this type of model should be tested for its efficacy over relatively short time-spans. Since such tests may not be very interesting over stretches without any cyclical turns, we tested the models by a more stringent criterion; that is, by their performance during six-quarter periods which include cyclical turns in general business conditions. Specifically, simulations were carried out for six-quarter periods beginning, alternatively, three quarters, two quarters, and one quarter before each business cycle turn. In these simulations, the endogenous variables were derived by using actual values for the quarter preceding the simulation and letting the model determine subsequent values; exogenous variables were used throughout the simulation period at their historical levels. The resulting configurations of twenty specified variables were compared with the actual behavior of these variables during the corresponding periods. The following three behavioral characteristics of the simulated and actual series were investigated: (*a*) Did cyclical turns occur in simulated and actual behavior? (*b*) If so, what were the timing relations between simulated and actual turns? (*c*) What were the comparative amplitudes of simulated and actual cycle phases?

2.1 INCIDENCE OF TURNING POINTS

For the Wharton Model, the sample period starts in the third quarter of 1948 and ends in the fourth quarter of 1964, but the simulations are extended through the first quarter of 1968. Thus, they include four reference troughs (1949-IV, 1954-III, 1958-II, and 1961-I) and three reference peaks (1953-II, 1957-III, and 1960-II). The Office of Business Economics (OBE) sample period starts in 1953-II and ends in 1966-IV, including three troughs and two peaks. The Federal Reserve-MIT-PENN (FMP) Model has the shortest sample period, extending from 1956 to 1966 and covering two troughs and two peaks only.

For each variable and for each turning point covered by a given model, we compared the simulated behavior produced in the three simulation runs with the actual behavior of the particular variable. Chart 2.1 contains a selection of these comparisons. We reproduced charts only for those variables and turning points which were common to the three models. The charts are arranged in such a way that the Wharton Model is on the left, the OBE in the middle, and the FMP on the right. The top panel shows comparisons for the 1957 peak; the second panel, for the 1958 trough; and so on. In each diagram, the

CHART 2.1

Nonstochastic Six-Quarter Simulations

Gross National Product

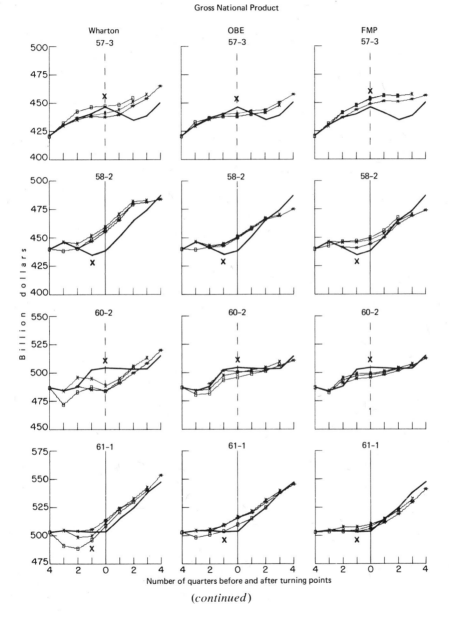

Number of quarters before and after turning points

(*continued*)

CHART 2.1 (*continued*)

Gross National Product, 1958 Dollars

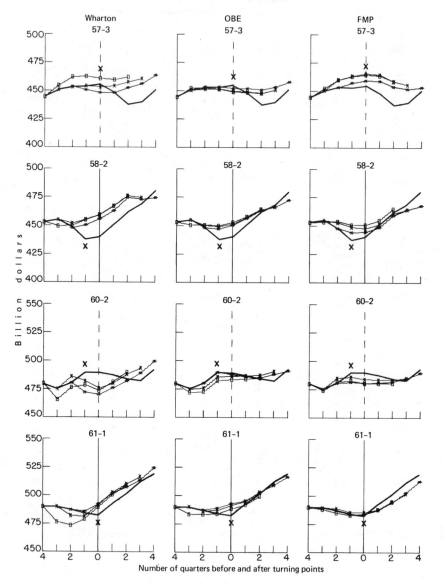

Number of quarters before and after turning points

CHART 2.1 *(continued)*

Investment in Nonfarm Residential Structures

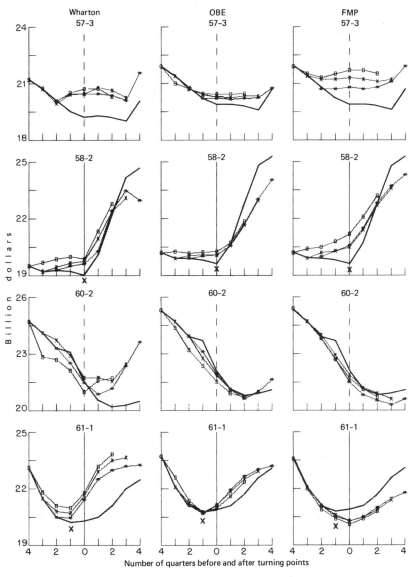

Number of quarters before and after turning points

(continued)

CHART 2.1 (*continued*)

Investment in Plant and Equipment

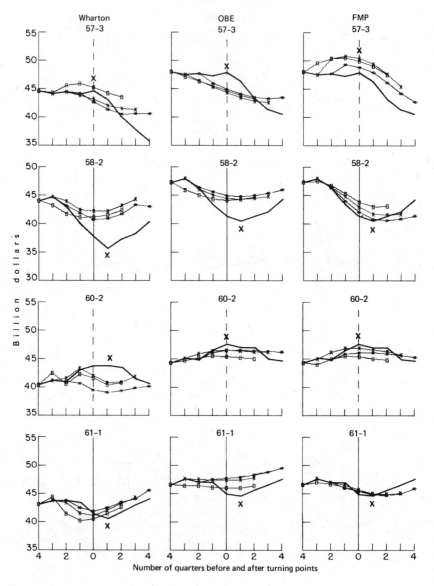

Number of quarters before and after turning points

CHART 2.1 (continued)

Change in Business Inventories

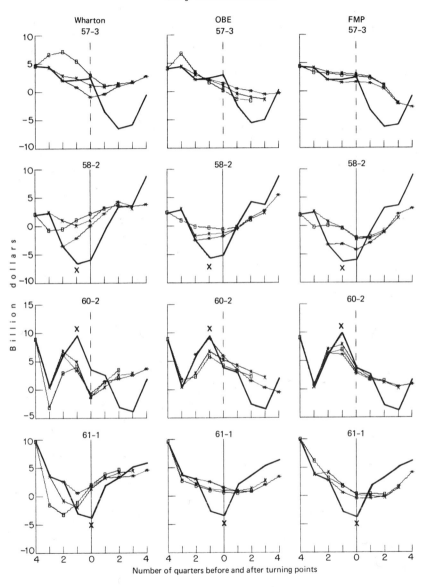

Number of quarters before and after turning points

(continued)

CHART 2.1 (*continued*)

Total Civilian Employment

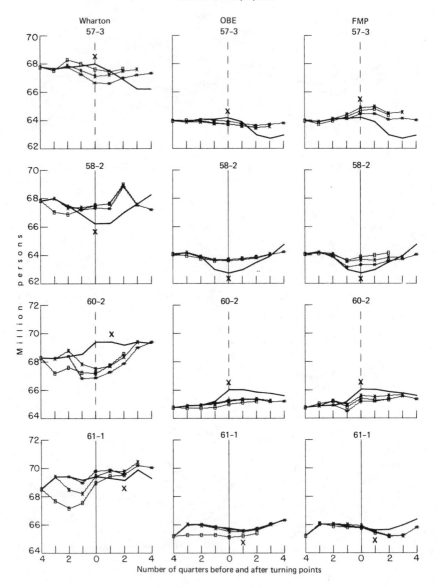

Number of quarters before and after turning points

CHART 2.1 (*continued*)

Unemployment Rate

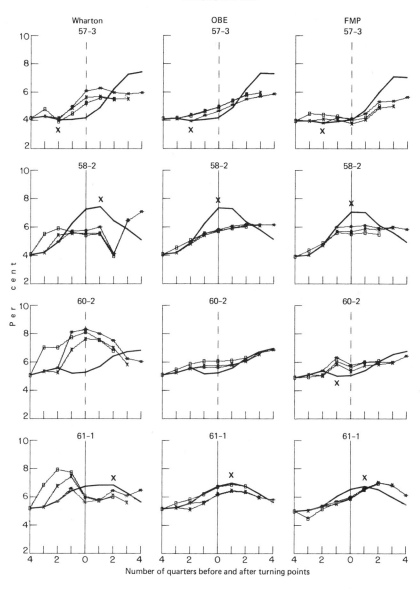

Number of quarters before and after turning points

(*continued*)

CHART 2.1 (*continued*)

Corporate Profits and Inventory Valuation Adjustment

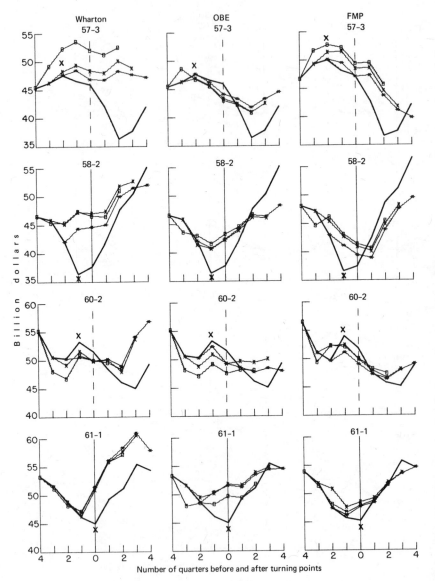

Number of quarters before and after turning points

CHART 2.1 (*continued*)

Average Yield, Short Term

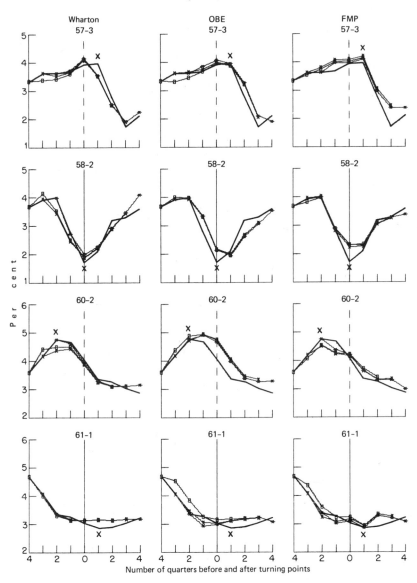

Number of quarters before and after turning points

(*continued*)

CHART 2.1 (concluded)

Average Yield, Long Term

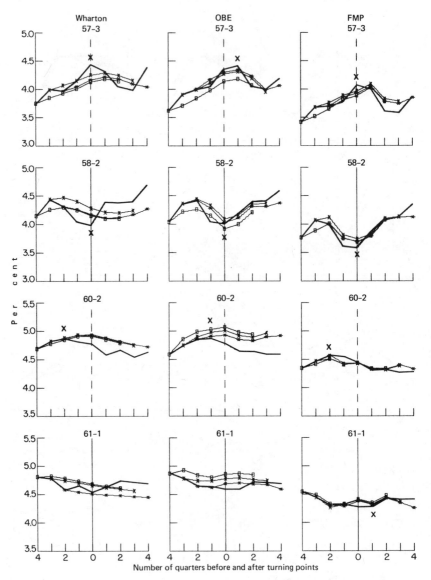

Number of quarters before and after turning points

actual is shown as a solid line; the simulation starting three quarters before the turn is delineated by boxes (□); the simulation starting two quarters before the turn by x's; and the simulation starting one quarter before the turn by asterisks. In each case, the simulation results are connected to the last available actual observation. Turning points in the actuals are marked by X's.

Our investigation of the incidence of successfully simulated turns must begin with the determination of cyclical turning points. This task, never an easy one, is complicated by several circumstances. First, the data refer to short, nonconnected periods, making it impossible to use existing computer programs. Second, the shortness of the simulation period makes it difficult to decide whether observed changes in direction are cyclically significant or merely reflect random movements of short duration. This is particularly difficult whenever the suspected turns fall close to the beginning or the end of the six-quarter period, causing the observable part of one of the phases to become very short indeed. Third, it is difficult to determine whether the observable part of the amplitude of a particular movement is large enough for it to qualify as a cyclical phase. We resolved these problems largely by deciding in favor of recognizing turns if this seemed at all reasonable.

The determination of turning points for the six-quarter simulations may require consideration of events outside this period. This gives rise to a puzzling problem: if actual series experience turning points before or after the six-quarter period chosen for simulation, should a simulation be considered successful when it shows a turn because the actual series experiences a turn—albeit not within the six-quarter period? Or should it be considered successful when it does not show a turn, because during the simulation period the actual shows no turn either? We circumvented this problem by using two types of counts: the simplest way is to take only those instances of the actual series where cyclical turns occurred in the six-quarter period under observation and match them with turns in the simulations. Alternatively, we used an increased sample by utilizing our knowledge of the behavior of the actual series shortly before and after the simulation period. Thus, if the actual series showed a peak shortly before the beginning of the simulation period and the simulated series continued downward, the simulation was presumed to have produced a peak.[3] Unfortunately, this procedure has to be modified for series with long lags extending beyond the end of the simulation period. In such situations, only those simulations which still showed a turn in the sample period could be recognized as successful. No assumptions could be made about simulated turns that might occur beyond the sample period. The incidence of successfully simulated turns is summarized in Table 2.1. The upper panel refers to the larger sample, including the inferred prior turning points; the lower panel refers only to those turns which actually occurred in the six-quarter period.

On the whole, all three models were fairly successful in reproducing cyclical turns in the neighborhood of business cycle turns, particularly when the more liberal definition — which includes inferred turning points — was used. In almost all cases, the simulated series successfully showed "no turns" whenever there were no turns in the actual series. We, therefore, based the "attainment rate" for the simulation of cyclical reversals on the number of actual turning points.

We expected simulations starting one quarter before reference turns to reproduce more turning points than those starting two or more quarters before. We had this expectation because we thought that one quarter before a reference turn the cumulative strains before peaks, and the gradual restoration of profits before troughs, are included in the data used in the simulation. Conversely, data truncated as much as

---

[3] Take, for example, the unemployment rate at the 1957 reference peak (Chart 2.1). The actual series has a trough in the first quarter of 1957, i.e., two quarters before the reference peak. For the Wharton Model (furthest left in the chart) the simulation starting in 1956-IV, i.e., three quarters before the turn, also shows a trough in 1957-I. This is unproblematic. For the simulation starting two quarters before the reference turn, a trough can be found in the first simulated observation if we connect the simulations with the last available actual before the start of the simulation. This trough is still located within the six-quarter simulation period and is counted as a turn in the larger, as well as in the more restrictive, sample. The last simulation, however, starts in 1957-II, i.e., one quarter after the trough in the actual. Although one can infer the existence of a trough from the upward direction of the simulated series, it did not occur during the simulation period. Hence, this simulation is counted as having successfully reproduced a turning point in the larger sample, but neither the actual nor the simulated turn is counted in the sample which is restricted to the six-quarter period.

The case is still more complicated for a configuration like that of the OBE simulations of this series at the same turning point (upper panel, middle row). Here all three of the simulations are higher than the last actual, so that in each case the inferred trough occurs in the quarter before the simulation starts. All are counted in the extended sample; none of the simulations and only the first two actuals are counted in the smaller sample.

TABLE 2.1

Nonstochastic Six-Quarter Simulations: Frequencies of Actual and Simulated Turning Points

	Wharton (1949–61)			OBE (1954–61)			FMP (1957–61)		
	Actual	Simulation		Actual	Simulation		Actual	Simulation	
Start of Simulations	Num- ber	Num- ber	Per Cent of Actual	Num- ber	Num- ber	Per Cent of Actual	Num- ber	Num- ber	Per Cent of Actual
	(1)	(2)	(3)	(4)	(5)	(6)	(7)	(8)	(9)
				All turns[a]					
1 3 Q before reference turns	95	64	67	85	57	67	50	38	76
2 2 Q before reference turns	95	62	65	85	59	69	50	44	88
3 1 Q before reference turns	95	57	60	85	63	74	50	45	90
			Turns occurring in 6-quarter periods						
4 3 Q before reference turns	83	59	71	71	45	63	47	33	70
5 2 Q before reference turns	79	53	67	64	43	67	46	37	80
6 1 Q before reference turns	73	35	48	60	37	62	41	32	78

[a] Including the inferred prior turning points in simulations, corresponding to the known actual turns that occurred outside the simulation period. (*See text.*)

three quarters before changing business conditions should not be expected to reflect, to the same extent, the dynamic processes preceding cyclical turns. As it turns out, these expectations have not generally been met, either by the six-quarter periods (lower panel), or by the extended sample periods (upper panel). The reason may be as follows: as the beginning of the six-quarter period approaches the reference turn, fewer specific turning points occur, both in the actual series and in the simulated ones. This is because more specific turns occur two quarters before reference turns (the quarter omitted as we go from the second to the third simulation) than four quarters after reference turns (the quarter added). This is true for the actual series (see Table 2.1, second panel, columns 1, 4, and 7), as well as for the simulated series (columns 2, 5, and 8). Whenever the simulated series lead the actuals, as seems to be the prevailing tendency for the Wharton Model (see Section 2.2 below), more turns get lost in the simulations than in the actual. For the extended sample period, no turns are actually cut off in the beginning by shifting the sample period. All the same, it seems that for the Wharton Model, simulations starting one quarter before peaks showed fewer turns (actual or imputed) than those starting two quarters before. One series for which this happens rather consistently is the average workweek, which is known to be a leading series.

We also expected the simulations to be more successful in reproducing troughs than in reproducing peaks. The reasons for this expectation are basically that the contours of troughs are often more sharply defined, and that the turning points are more closely clustered around reference troughs than around reference peaks. This can be observed particularly during the postwar period and is largely due to long-term upward trends, government intervention to end recessions, the absence of "drag" factors (such as backlogs, contractual obligations, gestation periods—as they exist at peaks), and the rapid expectational changes, based on these elements. We thought that these characteristics might be reflected in the structure of the models and would certainly be imposed upon the simulations by actual reversals in the exogenous variables—much more decisively than in the neighborhood of reference peaks. We expected that all of these elements would increase the likelihood of reversals in the neighborhood of troughs falling within our six-quarter simulation period.

TABLE 2.2

Nonstochastic Six-Quarter Simulations: Incidence of Successfully Simulated Peaks and Troughs
(frequencies as per cent of actual turns)

Start of Simulations	Wharton Model			OBE Model			FMP Model		
	Troughs	Peaks	All Turns	Troughs	Peaks	All Turns	Troughs	Peaks	All Turns
	All turns[a]								
1 3 Q before reference turns	65	71	67	69	65	67	65	88	76
2 2 Q before reference turns	65	66	65	69	71	69	92	83	88
3 1 Q before reference turns	70	46	60	75	74	74	100	79	90
	Turns occurring in 6-quarter periods								
4 3 Q before reference turns	64	83	71	69	50	63	62	81	70
5 2 Q before reference turns	61	77	67	79	57	67	85	75	80
6 1 Q before reference turns	50	44	48	55	81	62	92	53	78

[a] Including the inferred prior turning points in simulations corresponding to the known actual turns that occurred outside the simulation period. (*See text.*)

TABLE 2.3

Nonstochastic Six-Quarter Simulations: Relative Frequency
of Inferred Prior Peaks and Troughs
(as per cent of all turns)[a]

Start of Simulations		Wharton Model (1)	OBE Model (2)	FMP Model (3)
	At reference troughs			
1	3 Q before troughs	3	3	6
2	2 Q before troughs	14	11	8
3	1 Q before troughs	37	37	8
	At reference peaks			
4	3 Q before peaks	14	50	19
5	2 Q before peaks	15	50	25
6	1 Q before peaks	42	48	58
	At all reference turns			
7	3 Q before turns	8	21	13
8	2 Q before turns	15	27	16
9	1 Q before turns	39	41	29

[a] The inferred prior turning points in simulations (*see text and Table 2.1, note a*) are expressed as percentages of all turning points in the simulations (as listed in Table 2.1, lines 1 to 3, columns 2, 5, and 8).

However, the evidence summarized in Table 2.2 does not show any systematic difference between successful duplication of peaks and of troughs.[4] Perhaps we should investigate to what extent this may reflect the failure of the models to distinguish the difference in cyclical dynamics in the neighborhood of peaks and troughs; and to what extent it portrays the relative weakness of the exogenous variables in imposing characteristic cyclical behavior on the simulation patterns.

[4] There is a facet of this experiment where the wider spread of turning points in the neighborhood of peaks does cause the six-quarter periods before troughs to differ from the six-quarter periods before peaks: for the actual, as well as the simulated, series more turns had to be inferred before peaks than before troughs, relative to the turns actually occurring in the six-quarter period. (*See Table 2.3.*)

Although the three models cannot be directly compared—for the reasons stated in Section 1.3 above—it must be noted that in the matter of reproducing turning points, the FMP Model has higher attainment rates. The reason for this is not that fluctuations are more easily simulated for the period 1957–61, since the better performance of the FMP Model is retained even when comparisons for the three models are based on this shorter period. Nevertheless, it is possible that the better performance is caused, at least partly, by the better fits associated with a shorter sample period.

2.2 TIMING COMPARISONS

For Tables 2.4 and 2.5, timing comparisons between the turning points in the actual and the simulated time-series are based on observed cyclical turns falling into the six-quarter periods only. That is, we neglect the instances in which turns falling outside those periods were inferred.

The majority of turns in the simulated series occurred within one quarter of those in the actual series. Table 2.4 shows the percentages of turns of the simulated series which coincided with turns in the actual series, those one quarter away, and those yet further away from turns in the actual series.

The relative frequency of simulated turns outside the three-quarter span—centered around the turn in the actual—is lowest in the FMP simulations and highest in the Wharton Model, both for peaks and for troughs.

Given the smaller dispersion of turning points in the neighborhood of troughs, we would have expected simulated turns at troughs to be closer to the actual ones than simulated peaks are to actual peaks. The evidence does not show any systematic difference in performance, perhaps because the simulation period is so short that long leads and lags (which are more frequent at peaks) fall outside the span of observation. Alternatively, the unexpected similarity of behavior at peaks and troughs may be a consequence of the constancy of the lag structure used by the models.

The incidence of leads and of lags is different for the three models.

TABLE 2.4

Nonstochastic Six-Quarter Simulations, Timing Relationship of Cyclical Turns in Simulated Relative to Actual Series, Per Cent of Leads, Lags and Coincidences[a]

	Troughs			Peaks			All Turns		
Start of Simulations	Coincidences (1)	Leads & Lags of 1 Q (2)	Longer Leads & Lags (3)	Coincidences (4)	Leads & Lags of 1 Q (5)	Longer Leads & Lags (6)	Coincidences (7)	Leads & Lags of 1 Q (8)	Longer Leads & Lags (9)
	Wharton Model, 1949–1961								
1 3 Q before turn	21	32	47	14	50	36	18	39	43
2 2 Q before turn	14	57	39	20	55	25	17	56	27
3 1 Q before turn	21	54	25	55	27	18	31	46	32
	OBE Model, 1954–1961								
4 3 Q before turn	34	49	17	18	46	36	30	48	22
5 2 Q before turn	41	47	12	31	46	23	38	47	15
6 1 Q before turn	59	30	11	34	60	6	50	40	10
	FMP Model, 1957–1961								
7 3 Q before turn	44	50	6	50	38	12	47	44	9
8 2 Q before turn	46	45	9	57	36	7	50	42	8
9 1 Q before turn	33	63	4	50	38	12	38	56	6

[a] In each line, figures add up to 100 in columns 1–3, 4–6, and 7–9 (subject to rounding errors).

The Wharton Model shows a clear preponderance of leads in the turns of simulated series compared to those in the actual ones; the FMP Model shows more lags than leads; and the OBE Model does not show any systematic preference for leads or lags (leads being more frequent in the simulations starting three quarters and two quarters before reference turns, with lags predominating in the simulations starting one quarter before). The numerical findings are given in Table 2.5.

One important question is whether the models generate simulated time-series which exhibit the same general timing characteristics as those shown by the actual variables. In other words, do turning points in the simulated leading series lead business-cycle turning points? Do coinciders coincide and laggers lag? The series included in each model were classified into leaders, coinciders, and laggers, according to their historical performance.[5] For each group, leads (including inferred leads), coincidences, and lags — expressed as a percentage of all turns that can be matched with business-cycle turns — are shown in Table 2.6. The evidence reveals a distinct bias toward early turns in the simulated series. For the Wharton Model, the majority of the simulated series in all three groups lead at reference turns. In the OBE Model, most of the simulated leading and coinciding series lead, while lagging series show a tendency to coincide. The FMP Model generally produces more leads than lags, but the bias is a little less strong. The percentage of leaders in the simulated leading series is actually smaller than that in the actual leading series.

The bias toward leads is substantially reduced if we exclude turns before the start of the six-quarter period (actual turns as well as inferred turns of the simulations). The evidence, presented in Table 2.7, shows that for the actual series only those classified as leaders are seriously affected by this exclusion. The proportion of leads for this group is reduced from about two-thirds (if all turns are considered) to about half (if only those in the six-quarter period are counted). Since few long leads — i.e., turns before the start of the six-quarter simulation

[5] Wharton Model, leading series: IH, II, CPR, AWW, UMD; coinciding series: GNP, $GNP58, C, YP, LE, UN$; lagging series: ISE, RS, RL. OBE Model, leading series: same as Wharton, plus OMD, HS, and M; coinciding series: same as Wharton; lagging series: same as Wharton plus LC/O. FMP Model, leading series: IH, II, CPR, LH and $OUME$; coinciding series: $GNP, GNP58, C, Y, LE, UN$; lagging series: same as Wharton.

TABLE 2.5

Nonstochastic Six-Quarter Simulations: Leads, Coincidences, and Lags of Cyclical Turns in Simulated Series Relative to Those in Actual Series

Start of Simulations	Total, All Compa- rable Turns[a] (1)	Leads		Coincidences		Lags	
		Number (2)	Per Cent of Total (3)	Number (4)	Per Cent of Total (5)	Number (6)	Per Cent of Total (7)
Wharton Model, 1949–1961							
1 3 Q before turn	56	33	59	10	18	13	23
2 2 Q before turn	48	27	56	8	17	13	27
3 1 Q before turn	35	15	43	11	31	9	26
OBE Model, 1954–1961							
4 3 Q before turn	46	21	46	14	30	11	24
5 2 Q before turn	45	18	40	17	38	10	22
6 1 Q before turn	42	9	21	21	50	12	29
FMP Model, 1957–1961							
7 3 Q before turn	32	8	25	15	47	9	28
8 2 Q before turn	36	5	14	18	50	13	36
9 1 Q before turn	32	6	19	12	37	14	44

[a] Refers to number of turning points in the six-quarter periods which occurred in the actual series as well as in the simulated series. It may be less than the total number of simulated turns shown in Table 2.1, since some turns in the simulated series cannot be matched with actual turns, either because there was no turn in the actual series, or because the turn occurred outside the six-quarter period.

TABLE 2.6

Nonstochastic Six-Quarter Simulations: Timing Relative to Business-Cycle Turns in Leading, Coinciding, and Lagging Series; Actuals and Simulations (per cent of all turns)[a]

	Wharton Model			OBE Model			FMP Model		
	Leads	Coincidences	Lags	Leads	Coincidences	Lags	Leads	Coincidences	Lags
Leading series									
Actuals	67	27	6	74	21	5	59	23	18
Simulations starting:									
1 3 Q before reference turn	88	4	8	80	10	10	60	27	13
2 2 Q before reference turn	83	4	13	90	3	7	50	22	28
3 1 Q before reference turn	87	0	13	81	3	16	59	12	29
Coinciding series									
Actuals	41	46	13	42	46	12	33	52	15
Simulations starting:									
4 3 Q before reference turn	96	0	4	69	23	8	58	17	25
5 2 Q before reference turn	90	5	5	67	13	20	42	29	29
6 1 Q before reference turn	84	11	5	65	12	23	56	6	38
Lagging series									
Actuals	14	29	57	20	20	60	17	50	33
Simulations starting:									
7 3 Q before reference turn	50	37	13	20	47	33	46	18	36
8 2 Q before reference turn	42	29	29	13	47	40	42	16	42
9 1 Q before reference turn	20	53	27	21	36	43	33	17	50

NOTE: For classification of series see text.

[a] Includes inferred prior turns in simulations (see text), and turns occurring outside the 6-quarter simulation period in actuals.

TABLE 2.7

Nonstochastic Six-Quarter Simulations: Timing Relative to Business-Cycle Turns in Leading, Coinciding and Lagging Series; for All Turns and for Turns Occurring in 6-Quarter Period Actuals and Simulations

	Wharton Model			OBE Model			FMP Model		
	Leads	Coincidences	Lags	Leads	Coincidences	Lags	Leads	Coincidences	Lags
All turns[a]									
Leading series									
Actuals	67	27	6	74	21	5	59	23	18
Simulations	86	3	11	83	6	11	56	20	24
Coinciding series									
Actuals	41	46	13	42	46	12	33	52	15
Simulations	90	5	5	66	16	18	52	17	31
Lagging series									
Actuals	14	29	57	20	20	60	17	50	33
Simulations	37	40	23	18	43	39	40	17	43
Turns in 6-quarter period									
Leading series									
Actuals	46	44	10	55	36	9	45	31	24
Simulations	79	4	17	70	10	20	33	30	37
Coinciding series									
Actuals	37	49	14	38	50	12	32	53	15
Simulations	88	6	6	55	21	24	47	18	34
Lagging series									
Actuals	12	31	57	15	21	64	12	53	35
Simulations	36	40	24	12	46	42	32	19	49

[a] Includes inferred prior turns in simulations and turns occurring outside the 6-quarter period in actuals.

period—occur in the actual coinciding and lagging series, the percentage distributions for those two groups are not much affected. For the simulated series, on the other hand, long leads were inferred for coincident series, as well as for some lagging ones. Thus, the bias toward leads is somewhat reduced by eliminating the inferred turns from the count. However, even for turns occurring in the six-quarter period only, leads are relatively more frequent in the simulations than in the actuals for all groups except the laggers in the OBE Model and the leaders in the FMP Model.

On the whole, then, the simulations discriminate only very weakly between the historically leading, coinciding, and lagging variables. In view of the importance of lead-lag relationships in economic dynamics, it should be worthwhile to investigate whether there exists any connection between the model formulations and the timing biases observed in the simulations.

2.3 AMPLITUDES

Amplitude measures—in the framework of the present investigation—can obviously describe only those segments of expansions and contractions which occur during the six-quarter simulation periods. In spite of this truncation, it is of interest to establish whether there are systematic differences between the observable portions of simulated and actual amplitudes: among different variables, cyclical phases, and variously timed simulations.

A glance at the charts shows one fact quite clearly: in most cases, the patterns of the simulated series are flatter—i.e., they have amplitudes which are more shallow than those of the actual series. A related finding is that the patterns of simulated phases are more similar to each other than to the actual ones. This is particularly striking for the three time-staggered simulations produced by the same model; but it is also often true across models. The similarity among the time-staggered simulations may be explained by the fact that cyclical conditions vary relatively slowly and, therefore, the initial conditions for the three simulations are fairly similar. Furthermore, forecasts for the first quarter are typically more successful than those for later quarters. The family resemblance of simulations produced by different models may be due to the fact that all models reflect only the systematic portion of cyclical interactions, which during any historical period, represent only a part of economic reality. It is, of course, also possible that the three models have some common biases and that this is the reason why they resemble each other more than they resemble reality.

In order to give some precision to these impressions, amplitudes were computed for the observable part of expansions and contractions in the actual and the simulated series for each simulation that contained a cyclical turning point.[6] As a first step in the analysis, we determined the frequencies with which simulated amplitudes were smaller than, similar to, or larger than, those of the actual series. Differences of one percentage point and less (for UN, II, RS, and RL, differences of 10 per cent and less in the absolute differences) were regarded as negligible, and the amplitudes were tabulated as similar. The frequencies are summarized in Table 2.8. For each model, for each type of time-staggered simulation, and for all expansions and all contractions, the frequencies are expressed as a percentage of all comparisons feasible in that class.

On the whole, simulated amplitudes underestimate actual amplitudes more often than they overstate or equal actual amplitudes. As the table shows, this is equally true for expansions and contractions, for each of the time-staggered simulations, and for each model.[7] The one exception occurred in the Wharton Model, for which this tendency is generally somewhat less pronounced. The incidence of underestimation amounts usually to more than half of all cases, except in the Wharton Model, where the incidence of underestimating expansions is only about 40 per cent.

Let us turn from the analysis of incidences to that of measured amplitudes. Table 2.9 presents average expansion and average contrac-

---

[6] Since no direct comparisons between expansion and contraction amplitudes were intended, the percentage-base bias of amplitude measures could be neglected, and relative amplitudes could simply be measured as percentage changes from initial levels. In case of rates and differences (for UN, II, RS, and RL), absolute changes rather than percentage changes were computed.

[7] It is also true for each cycle, for phases before and after the turn, and for most activities. A minor exception, not shown in the summary table, is the expansion preceding the 1958 peak for the FMP Model, where the simulations overestimated amplitudes for almost all variables.

tion amplitudes of all variables included, irrespective of comparability. The average amplitude measures presented for each variable in each model cover all incidents for which amplitudes could be measured; thus, the composition of the measures is not strictly comparable among the different variables or models. Comparability exists only insofar as there is a corresponding expansion for each contraction, and a corresponding actual phase for each simulation phase. The number of simulations included in each average amplitude is indicated in the table. The comparisons show that for a large majority of variables, the averages of the simulated amplitudes are smaller than those of the actual amplitudes; for about 60 per cent of the possible comparisons, they are more than 20 per cent below the actuals. The Wharton Model simulations seem to underestimate less than the others, but comparisons are difficult to make, because of the heterogeneous composition of the amplitude averages.

In order to increase comparability, we present comparisons only of those cycle phases which could be measured for the same time period and the same well-defined economic process in all models. This attempt to increase comparability from model to model brought about a sharp reduction in sample size. Furthermore, for the sake of simplicity, and in view of the observed similarity among the time-staggered simulations, we used only the simulations starting two quarters before reference turns. The results appear in Table 2.10. Again we find that the incidence of underestimation of amplitudes by the simulations is pervasive, particularly for contractions. The magnitudes of underestimation vary widely. In spite of problems of summarization, due to the large variation in size among the amplitudes themselves, Table 2.11 provides averages for simulated and actual amplitudes, and for absolute and relative differences.[8] Again, the summary measures show the smaller amplitudes of the simulations. Intermodel comparison shows that for the simulations included, the Wharton Model comes very close to actual amplitudes during expansions. During contractions the FMP Model gives closer approximations than do the other two

---

[8] Since the average of percentage differences gives a large weight to large percentage differences which may be based on very small amplitudes (see, for instance, the last expansion phase in Table 2.10), we also provide the percentage difference of the average amplitudes (which gives larger weight to large amplitudes, e.g., corporate profits).

models. However, comparisons among models remain very uncertain, even for this less heterogeneous selection, since the sample is small and the differences not very pronounced.

A major analytical interest concerns the reasons for the sweeping tendency toward underestimation of amplitudes shown by most simulations. It has been argued that most of the explanation can be found in

TABLE

Nonstochastic Six-Quarter Simulations: Amplitude Incidence of Underestimation

		All Phases			
		Number of Phases Compared (1)	Per Cent of All Phases Compared		
	Start of Simulations		$S < A$ (2)	$S \approx A$ (3)	$S > A$ (4)
	Wharton Model, 1949-1961				
1	3 Q before turn	104	36	28	36
2	2 Q before turn	96	51	27	22
3	1 Q before turn	70	44	34	22
4	All simulations	270	44	29	27
	OBE Model				
5	3 Q before turn	90	64	29	7
6	2 Q before turn	84	67	27	6
7	1 Q before turn	76	59	30	11
8	All simulations	250	63	29	8
	FMP Model				
9	3 Q before turn	62	62	19	19
10	2 Q before turn	72	67	15	18
11	1 Q before turn	66	61	27	12
12	All simulations	200	63	21	16

NOTE: S and A denote amplitudes of simulated and actual series, respectively. For *UN, II, RS,* and *RL,* amplitudes were computed as absolute changes between two turning points; for all other series, as percentage changes from initial levels.

the systemic tendency of regression techniques to underestimate changes. Also, there is some bias inherent in the method used for selecting turning points. Randomly high observations tend to be selected as peaks; and randomly low ones, as troughs — leading to an overstatement of the cyclical component of actual amplitudes. The simulated series, on the other hand, are constructed without imposition of

2.8

*Comparisons Between Actual and Simulated Series;
and Overestimation*

	Expansions				Contractions		
Number of Phases Compared (5)	Per Cent of All Compared Phases			Number of Phases Compared (9)	Per Cent of All Compared Phases		
	$S < A$ (6)	$S \approx A$ (7)	$S > A$ (8)		$S < A$ (10)	$S \approx A$ (11)	$S > A$ (12)
52	33	29	39	52	40	27	33
48	52	19	29	48	50	35	15
35	40	37	23	35	49	31	20
135	42	27	31	135	46	31	23
45	65	24	11	45	65	33	21
42	72	21	7	42	62	33	5
38	66	24	10	38	53	37	10
125	67	23	10	125	60	34	6
31	49	19	32	31	75	19	6
36	64	14	22	36	69	17	14
33	67	21	12	33	55	33	12
100	60	18	22	100	66	23	11

TABLE 2.9

Nonstochastic Six-Quarter Simulations: Simulated and Actual Amplitudes for All Simulations with Turning Points; Averages by Variable, Cycle Phase, and Model

I. Wharton Model

Variable	Number of Observations	Expansions[a]				Contractions[a]			
		S	A	S/A	S-A	S	A	S/A	S-A
GNP	8	7.2	7.2	1.00	0	-1.2	-1.1	1.09	-0.1
GNP58	12	5.6	6.0	0.93	-0.4	-2.1	-3.9	0.54	+1.8
Consumption	2	7.6	3.7	2.05	+3.9	-0.9	-0.6	1.50	-0.3
Investment in housing	4	9.9	10.4	0.95	-0.5	-5.0	-5.7	0.88	+0.7
Investment in plant and equipment	15	7.2	8.6	0.84	-1.4	-4.9	-7.1	0.69	+2.2
Change in inventory investment	9	6.8	9.6	0.71	-2.8	-5.2	-7.2	0.72	+2.0
Personal income	6	6.0	6.2	0.97	-0.2	-0.9	-0.5	1.80	-0.4
Employment	10	2.4	2.0	1.20	+0.4	-2.4	-1.9	1.26	-0.5
Unemployment (inverted)	11	3.2	2.3	1.39	+0.9	-1.4	-0.7	2.00	+.7
Corporate profits	9	18.0	22.0	0.82	-4.0	-9.1	-18.4	0.49	+9.3
Workweek	4	0.7	0.7	1.00	0	-0.9	-1.2	0.75	+.3
New orders	8	15.3	28.4	0.54	-13.1	-4.6	-9.2	0.50	+4.6
Unfilled orders	9	3.4	9.8	0.35	-6.4	-16.4	-20.6	0.80	+4.2
Interest rate, short	14	0.7	0.8	0.88	-0.1	-0.7	-1.6	0.47	+0.9
Interest rate, long	16	0.1	0.3	0.33	-0.2	-0.1	-.3	0.35	+0.2

II. OBE Model

Variable	Number of Observations	Expansions[a]				Contractions[a]			
		S	A	S/A	S-A	S	A	S/A	S-A
GNP	4	6.8	7.8	0.87	-1.0	-0.6	-0.5	1.20	-0.1
GNP58	12	3.5	5.3	0.66	-1.8	-1.0	-2.6	0.38	+1.6
Investment in housing	4	9.7	10.1	0.96	-0.4	-5.2	-5.6	0.93	+0.4
Investment in plant and equipment	11	2.9	6.1	0.48	-3.2	-2.8	-7.0	0.40	+4.2
Change in inventory investment	9	3.6	8.5	0.42	-4.9	-5.1	-9.7	0.53	+4.6
Employment	12	1.0	2.7	0.37	-1.7	-0.6	-1.3	0.46	+0.7
Unemployment (inverted)	6	0.3	1.2	0.25	-0.9	-1.4	-2.2	0.65	+0.8
Corporate profits	9	12.6	27.2	0.46	-14.6	-9.0	-14.9	0.60	+5.9
Workweek	4	0.1	0.6	0.17	-0.5	-0.9	-1.7	0.53	+0.8
New orders	6	1.9	4.5	0.42	-2.6	-18.1	-15.4	1.18	-2.7
Housing starts	4	18.4	23.8	0.77	-5.4	-5.9	-9.6	0.61	+3.7
Interest rates, short	15	0.6	0.7	0.86	-0.1	-1.5	-1.6	0.94	+0.1
Interest rates, long	12	2.7	3.2	0.84	-0.5	-2.5	-3.4	0.74	+0.9
Labor cost per unit of output	3	1.5	3.0	0.50	-1.5	-0.6	-0.3	2.00	-0.3
Money	3	2.9	3.3	0.88	-0.4	-0.2	-0.7	0.29	+0.5

(continued)

TABLE 2.9 (concluded)

III. FMP Model

Variable	Number of Observations	Expansions[a]				Contractions[a]			
		S	A	S/A	S-A	S	A	S/A	S-A
GNP	5	6.5	8.0	0.81	-1.5	-.6	-1.4	0.43	+0.8
GNP58	11	3.4	4.5	0.76	-1.1	-1.1	-2.6	0.42	+1.5
Consumption	8	4.0	4.0	1.00	0	-.4	-1.1	0.36	+0.7
Investment in housing	3	5.4	8.5	0.64	-3.1	-8.9	-6.8	1.31	-2.1
Investment in plant and equipment	11	2.9	4.7	0.62	-1.8	-7.4	-9.9	0.75	+2.5
Change in inventory investment	7	4.6	10.4	0.44	-5.8	-4.3	-8.7	0.49	+4.4
Employment	9	1.0	1.2	0.83	-0.2	-.9	-1.6	0.56	+0.7
Unemployment (inverted)	5	.4	1.3	0.31	-0.9	-2.8	-2.2	1.27	-0.6
Corporate profits	8	14.7	24.6	0.60	-9.9	-12.0	-18.6	0.65	+6.6
Workweek	6	.4	.8	0.50	-0.4	-.8	-1.0	0.80	+0.2
Unfilled orders	7	3.0	5.3	0.57	-2.3	-9.5	-12.2	0.78	2.7
Interest rates, short	11	.6	.8	0.75	-0.13	-1.4	-1.8	0.78	+0.4
Interest rates, long	9	.3	.4	0.75	-0.08	-.3	-.4	0.75	+0.1

[a] S and A denote amplitudes of simulated and actual series respectively. For II, UN, RS and RL, amplitudes were computed as absolute changes between two turning points; for all other series, as percentage changes from initial levels.

TABLE 2.10

Simulated and Actual Amplitudes, Comparable Phases Only

Variable	Turn	Wharton Model				OBE Model				FMP Model			
		S	A	S/A	S-A	S	A	S/A	S-A	S	A	S/A	S-A
Expansions													
Investment in housing (IH)	T 61-II	14.5	8.9	1.63	+5.6	10.1	8.7	1.16	+1.4	5.4	9.2	0.59	-3.8
Investment in plant and equipment (IP)	T 58-II	5.0	7.3	0.68	-2.3	1.1	4.2	0.26	-3.1	0.2	4.2	0.05	-4.0
	P 60-III	5.1	6.8	0.75	-1.7	3.1	5.5	0.56	-2.4	4.2	6.2	0.68	-2.0
Change in inventory investment (II)	T 61-II	7.8	6.2	1.26	+1.6	1.7	4.5	0.38	-2.8	0.5	4.7	0.11	-4.2
	T 58-II	4.7	10.2	0.46	-5.5	4.0	9.9	0.40	-5.9	3.7	10.1	0.37	-6.4
	P 60-III	6.3	9.2	0.68	-2.9	6.2	9.1	0.68	-2.9	7.4	9.5	0.78	-2.1
Employment (LE)	T 61-II	6.4	9.1	0.70	-2.7	1.8	8.9	0.20	-7.1	1.7	9.0	0.19	-7.3
	T 58-II	2.4	2.1	1.14	+0.3	0.6	1.9	0.31	-1.3	0.4	1.9	0.21	-1.5
Corporate profits (PCB)	T 58-II	16.6	38.5	0.43	-21.9	13.5	38.5	0.35	-25.0	20.2	39.9	0.51	-19.7
	T 61-II	30.6	23.1	1.32	+7.5	10.7	23.1	0.46	-12.4	12.6	23.5	0.54	-10.9
Interest rates, short (RS)	P 57-III	0.59	0.36	1.64	+0.23	0.37	0.36	1.03	+0.01	0.56	0.36	1.56	+0.26
	T 58-II	1.57	1.58	0.99	-0.01	1.11	1.64	0.68	-0.53	1.03	1.59	0.65	-0.50
	P 60-II	0.26	0.58	0.46	-0.31	0.73	0.57	1.28	+0.16	0.34	0.57	0.60	-0.23
Interest rates, long (RL)	P 57-III	0.30	0.47	0.64	-0.17	0.41	0.52	0.79	-0.11	0.41	0.39	1.05	+0.02
	T 58-II	0.04	0.42	0.10	-0.38	0.27	0.41	0.66	-0.14	0.40	0.55	0.73	-0.15
	P 60-II	0.11	0.05	2.20	+0.06	0.26	0.12	2.17	+0.14	0.04	0.10	0.40	-0.16

(continued)

TABLE 2.10 (concluded)

Variable	Turn	Wharton Model				OBE Model				FMP Model			
		S	A	S/A	S-A	S	A	S/A	S-A	S	A	S/A	S-A
					Contractions								
Investment in housing (IH)	T 61-II	-3.7	-6.0	0.62	+2.3	-5.9	-5.9	1.00	0	-8.1	-6.3	1.29	-1.2
Investment in plant and equipment (IP)	T 58-II	-5.6	-20.1	0.28	+14.5	-7.7	-15.6	0.49	+7.9	-13.3	-15.6	0.85	+2.3
	T 60-III	-5.8	-5.5	1.05	-0.3	-0.6	-5.7	0.11	+5.1	-2.6	-5.9	0.44	+3.3
	T 61-II	-6.2	-7.3	0.85	+1.1	-0.4	-6.3	0.06	+5.9	-6.0	-6.5	0.92	+0.5
Change in inventory investment (II)	T 58-II	-3.4	-8.9	0.38	+5.5	-4.7	-8.6	0.55	+3.9	-4.8	-8.8	0.55	+4.0
	P 60-III	-8.0	-13.5	0.59	+5.5	-4.6	-13.0	0.35	+8.4	-7.7	-13.7	0.56	+6.0
	T 61-II	-5.5	-7.4	0.74	+1.9	-2.9	-7.2	0.40	+4.3	-4.4	-7.5	0.59	+3.1
Employment (LE)	T 58-II	-1.0	-2.6	0.38	+1.6	-0.8	-2.3	0.35	+0.5	-1.0	-2.3	0.43	+1.3
Corporate profits (PCB)	T 58-II	-1.5	-20.7	0.07	+19.2	-11.3	-20.7	0.55	+9.6	-15.0	-22.5	0.67	+7.5
	T 61-II	-10.1	-12.8	0.79	+2.7	-4.1	-12.8	0.32	+8.7	-8.1	-12.9	0.63	+4.8
Interest rate, short (RS)	P 57-III	-2.22	-2.27	0.98	+0.05	-1.93	-2.27	0.85	+0.34	-1.73	-2.27	0.76	+0.54
	T 58-II	-2.07	-2.27	0.91	+0.20	-1.96	-2.27	0.86	+0.31	-1.78	-2.28	0.78	+0.50
	P 60-II	-1.34	-1.74	0.77	+0.40	-1.58	-1.75	0.90	+0.17	-1.18	-1.75	0.67	+0.57
Interest rate, long (RL)	P 57-III	-0.14	-0.46	0.30	+0.32	-0.36	-0.43	0.86	+0.06	-0.31	-0.49	0.63	+0.18
	T 58-II	-0.27	-0.46	0.59	+0.19	-0.35	-0.42	0.83	+0.07	-0.39	-0.49	0.86	+0.10
	P 60-II	-0.18	-0.33	0.55	+0.15	-0.12	-0.28	0.43	+0.16	-0.19	-0.30	0.63	+0.11

NOTE: _S_ and _A_ denote amplitudes for simulated and actual series respectively. For _RS_ and _RL_, amplitudes are computed as absolute changes between two turning points; for all other series, as percentage changes from initial levels.

TABLE 2.11

Nonstochastic Six-Quarter Simulations: Summary Amplitude Comparisons Between Simulated and Actual Series; 16 Comparable Phases Only

	Simulations	Actuals	$\dfrac{\text{Avg } S}{\text{Avg } A}$	$\text{Avg}\left(\dfrac{S}{A}\right)$
Expansions				
Wharton	6.39	7.80	0.81	0.99
OBE	3.50	7.37	0.47	0.71
FMP	3.69	7.61	0.48	0.56
Contractions				
Wharton	−3.56	−7.02	0.50	0.61
OBE	−3.08	−6.59	0.47	0.55
FMP	−4.78	−6.48	0.74	0.70

NOTE: For explanation of symbols, see footnote to Table 2.10.
SOURCE: Table 2.9.

random factors and thus their cyclical highs and lows are not "exaggerated" by such components.[9] It is true, however, that the described distortion of amplitudes by random elements is weaker for quarterly series than for monthly series, and is, perhaps, not likely to constitute a major part of the explanation of the observed underestimation of amplitudes.

In view of the weakness of the suggested explanation, the tendency of the models to underestimate amplitudes requires further investigation.

[9] The effect of random factors on amplitude measures could be tested by imposition of random elements.

3 NONSTOCHASTIC SIMULATIONS FOR THE SAMPLE PERIODS

THERE are three main sections in this part of our report, one for each of the models covered. The same general format is used in each section, the material being organized around four tables that show respectively: (1) the average absolute and relative errors of the simulated series; (2) selected regression and correlation statistics summarizing the relations between the simulated and the actual changes; (3) comparisons of average cyclical amplitudes; and (4), comparisons of the cyclical timing of the simulated and actual series. A summary section concludes this analysis.

To compile the measures included in (3) and (4), dates of cyclical turning points had to be identified in all of the simulated series. For the sample-period data, this was done by the NBER computer program for the determination of cyclical turning points, and checked independently by at least two of the co-authors of this paper, who then jointly resolved any judgmental discrepancies involved. The process involved a careful examination of time-series charts. These charts, although very useful for the analysis that follows, are too numerous to be fully reproduced here; however, we do show them for a subset of selected variables at the beginning of each of the three main sections.

In addition, individual and average reference-cycle patterns are discussed for all of the actual (A) and simulated (S) series. Again, illustrations are provided in charts for the selected variables.

3.1 THE WHARTON MODEL

3.1.1   The extended sample-period simulations for this model embrace 79 quarters (from 1948-III through 1968-I) and include all four of the postwar contractions, as well as such milder retardations as those of 1962–63 and 1966–67.

As shown in Chart 3.1, the simulated GNP series runs more often above than below the actual series; but such differences are much less systematic here than they are for the series in constant dollars. The

CHART 3.1

Nonstochastic Simulations for the Sample Period, Wharton Model:
Simulated and Actual Series for Selected Variables
(1948-III–1968-I)

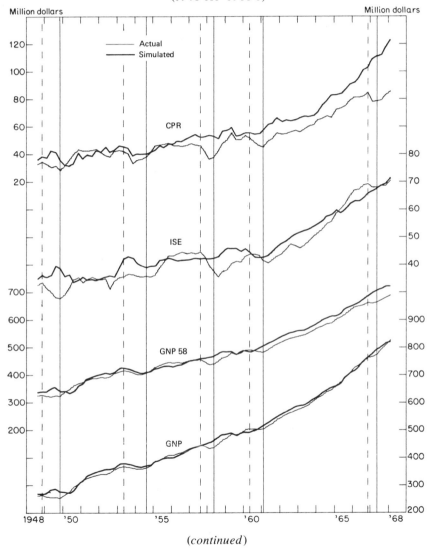

(*continued*)

CHART 3.1 (*concluded*)

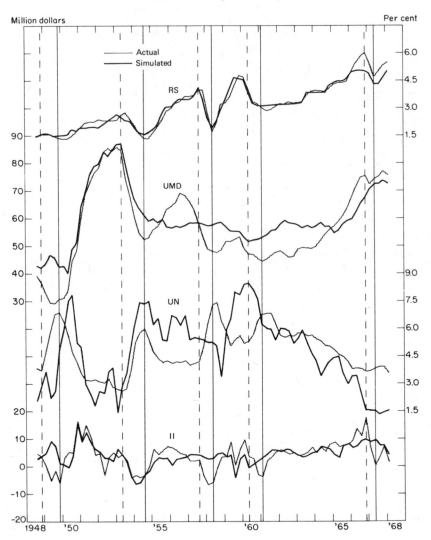

simulated $GNP58$ figures exceed the corresponding actual levels, except for relatively brief stretches of time in 1950–51, 1955–56, and 1960. For real consumption (not shown in Chart 3.1), the levels of S exceed those of A throughout. Consistent with these results, the S series for the GNP price deflator (also not shown) runs first slightly above the A series in 1949–56, and then increasingly below it in 1957–68. Substantial and persistent level discrepancies of a similar sort can also be observed for such other "real" variables as plant and equipment investment (ISE), net exports (NE), and employment (LE).

For several variables with large cyclical and irregular fluctuations and relatively weaker trends, the outstanding feature of the charts is that the variations in S tend to be smaller than those in A, often by large amounts. The best examples of this are furnished by the investment series, particularly in housing and inventories, and by profits and unfilled orders (IH, ISE, II, CPR, UMD). On the other hand, opposite or mixed results are obtained in this respect for the unemployment rate and the hours worked in industry (UN, AWW). There is a very satisfactory, close comovement of S and A for the short-term interest rate (RS), except only in 1966–67 when S underestimated both the level and change of A. (RS is determined only by exogenous variables which describe the policy of the FRB.) For the long-term rate (RL), however, S looks very much like a heavily smoothed and lagged version of A, a frequent effect of relating a series to its own previous value (which is done here via the familiar Koyck transformation, with the aim of making RL a function of present and past values of RS).

On the average, of course, variations in S must be expected to be smaller than those in A, because the (nonstochastic) simulations do not include the component of random disturbances that is present in the actuals. Single-equation estimates for the sample period would be entirely consistent with this expectation; the complete-model simulations need not conform to it quite as well, because here the errors from different equations can interact, becoming magnified in various ways, both across the model and over time. For the same reason, the model simulations can show persistent drifts away from the course of the actual series, in contrast to the single-equation short-period "predictions," in which such bias is precluded by the estimation method itself. (This point applies only to the sample-period simulations.)

3.1.2 The prevalence of positive mean errors of levels (MEL) shown in Table 3.1, column 1, suggests that, on the average, over-estimates outweigh underestimates in the Wharton simulations for the sample period 1948–68 (the errors are defined as differences $S_t - A_t$). The opposite errors of level underestimation prevail for the price, wage, and interest variables, as well as for personal income and unemployment (P, W, RS, RL, YP, and UN).

The MEC figures in column 2 of Table 3.1 suggest that increases in GNP, P, and LE (employment) were on the average underestimated, and that increases in $GNP58$, C, and YP were on the average over-estimated. For variables with less pronounced trends and strong fluctuations, however, the signs of the MEC's cannot be interpreted so simply.[10] A very conspicuous and uniform characteristic of the MEC statistics is that they are much smaller absolutely than the corresponding MEL figures (compare columns 1 and 2). This reflects two facts: (1) the errors of change are typically much smaller than the errors of levels; (2) the errors of change vary in sign more than the errors of levels. Consequently, the cancellation of positive against negative figures has stronger effects on MEC than on MEL.

As usual, the mean absolute errors of levels and changes (MAEL and MAEC) are generally much larger (disregarding sign) than the corresponding mean errors, for here the positive and negative errors are not permitted to cancel each other (compare column 1 with column 3, and column 2 with column 4).[11] For all variables, the MAE figures are larger for levels than for changes; that is, MAEL > MAEC (see

[10] Errors of absolute change (defined as $\Delta S_t - \Delta A_t$) are negative when: (1) increases are underestimated; (2) decreases are overestimated; or (3) the actual change is positive and the predicted one is negative. They are positive in the three converse cases (cf. [29, p. 51]). Thus the sign of the mean change error (MEC in column 2) does not in itself indicate whether changes have been under- or overestimated. For example, if both A and S were positive and rising, a negative MEC would denote understatement of the actual increases by the simulated series, while a positive MEC would indicate overstatement. Should both A and S be positive and declining, then the situation would be precisely the reverse. For series that fluctuate, the outcome will depend on the relative timing, durations, and amplitudes of rises and falls in A and S; for series that assume negative as well as positive values, it will also depend on the extent to which S and A agree in sign.

[11] Arithmetic means tell us something about the bias which occurs when a set of predictions typically understates or overstates the corresponding actual values. A set S, for example, is unbiased if the mean error ($\bar{E} = \bar{S} - \bar{A}$, where $\bar{S}$ and $\bar{A}$ are the simple averages of S_t and A_t, respectively, over the entire period covered) is not significantly different from zero (cf. [24, pp. 8–10]). If $\bar{E} \neq 0$, then there is a constant, common ele-

columns 3 and 4). Of the two factors that were identified above as accounting for an analogous relationship between the mean errors ($|MEL| > |MEC|$), only the first one applies here: the absolute errors of changes are typically much smaller than the absolute errors of levels.

The fact that the average errors are larger for levels than for changes is a familiar result from the analysis of forecasts, having a twofold explanation: (*a*) the error of each level forecast is the algebraic sum of the error in the base of the forecast (in the estimate of the preceding level of the series) and the error of the predicted change; (*b*) on the average, errors of the base have the same signs as the errors of the succeeding levels (e.g., if the prediction for period t is too low, that for period ($t + 1$) is likely to be so, too). It is therefore not the common finding that $|MEL| > |MEC|$ and $MAEL > MAEC$ that is particularly interesting but, rather, the fact that the differences involved are as large and pervasive as Table 3.1 shows them to be. The explanation is again simple but also important. When forecasts are made frequently over short spans, the errors of base values can be, and usually are, kept relatively small, so that the level errors are not very much larger than the change errors. In multiperiod forecasts made over long spans of time, however, errors for successive periods can cumulate and the predictions can be increasingly off base. Complete-model simulations over entire sample-periods, in which the errors of lagged dependent variables can cumulate, are comparable to very long multiperiod forecasts in this respect.

For most of the aggregative variables under study, quarterly changes are typically small relative to the levels of the series; hence, simulation errors may well be small when compared with the levels, but large when compared with the changes in the realizations. Typi-

---

ment in all errors for the given set. When $\bar{E}$ is subtracted from each observed error, the remainder reflects the variation among the errors measured from this average. The mean square error, which is the sum of the bias component ($\bar{E}^2$) and the variance of error (S_e^2), offers a comprehensive and mathematically convenient summary measure, which has been computed, and could be used here. (By taking the root of this MSE figure, an average is obtained which has the proper dimension, being expressed in the same units as the errors to be summarized.) However, for present purposes, it will be sufficient to use the simpler measure of the mean absolute error (MAE). The MAE figures are as a rule smaller than the root mean-square errors (RMSE) statistics for the same samples, since RMSE gives more than proportionate weight to large, as compared with small, errors.

TABLE 3.1

Nonstochastic Simulations for the Sample Period, Wharton Model: Average Errors and Their Ratios to Average Actual Values (1948-III–1968-I)

	Variable		Mean Error (ME)		Mean Absolute Error (MAE)			Ratio of MAE to Mean Absolute Actual Values (MAA)		
Line	Symbol[a]	Unit[b]	Level (MEL)	Change (MEC)	Level (MAEL)	Change (MAEC)	Relative Change[c] (MAERC)	Level $\left(\frac{MAEL}{MAAL}\right)$	Change $\left(\frac{MAEC}{MAAC}\right)$	Relative Change[d] $\left(\frac{MAERC}{MAARC}\right)$
			(1)	(2)	(3)	(4)	(5)	(6)	(7)	(8)
1	GNP	billion $	6.34	−0.15	9.298	4.901	1.171	.019	.604	.681
2	GNP58	billion 58$	11.75	0.26	15.093	5.069	1.125	.032	.818	.852
3	C	billion 58$	22.81	0.20	22.812	2.963	1.028	.079	.975	.985
4	IH	billion 58$	0.15	0.01	1.465	0.721	3.477	.070	.901	.898
5	ISE	billion 58$	1.99	−0.02	3.192	1.266	3.118	.072	1.013	1.036
6	II	billion 58$	0.11	0.06	3.054	2.752	e	.568	.894	e
7	NE	billion 58$	1.92	0.32	5.906	0.994	e	1.366	1.079	e
8	YP	billion $	−3.70	0.81	9.486	3.207	0.935	.025	.537	.600
9	P	1958 = 100	−0.01	−0.001	0.017	0.002	0.269	.018	.439	.453
10	LE	million	0.13	−0.01	1.101	0.500	0.745	.016	1.214	1.238
11	UN	per cent	−0.02	−0.004	1.411	0.755	17.795	.293	2.199	2.502
12	CPR	billion $	7.70	0.43	8.541	2.365	4.905	.166	1.058	1.037
13	AWW	40 hrs. = 1.000	0.01	0.0003	0.007	0.005	0.448	.007	1.484	1.436
14	UMD	billion 58$	2.97	−0.09	6.093	2.007	3.712	.106	.780	.802
15	RS	% per annum	−0.05	−0.01	0.209	0.163	5.808	.066	.677	.702
16	RL	% per annum	−0.04	0.01	0.191	0.096	2.339	.047	.924	.935
17	W	dollars	−0.10	0.02	0.207	0.063	1.107	.044	.714	.678

ᵃ For meaning of symbols, see Table 1.1.

ᵇ The average errors, with and without regard to sign (ME and MAE), which are listed in columns 1 through 4, are expressed in these units, and so are the average actual values (MAA); hence the figures for MAE/MAA, in columns 6 and 7, are pure ratios.

ᶜ In percentage points. Mean of the differences: quarterly per cent change in the simulated series minus quarterly per cent change in the actual series, all taken without regard to sign.

ᵈ Ratio of the figure in column 5 to the corresponding mean of actual percentage changes.

ᵉ Not applicable: since net change in inventories and net foreign investment can assume negative values, these series can be analyzed only in absolute, not in relative, terms.

cally, then, the ratios of mean absolute errors of simulations to mean absolute actual values (MAE/MAA) are quite small fractions for the level measures and considerably larger for the changes. That is, $\frac{MAEL}{MAAL} < \frac{MAEC}{MAAC}$ (columns 6 and 7), although MAEL > MAEC (implying that the MAAL figures exceed the corresponding values of MAAC by very large amounts). As elsewhere in the analysis of predictive accuracy, the comparisons with changes are on the whole much more meaningful than those with levels. Because the series have different units and levels, it is useful to express changes in the simulated series in relative terms, and to compute their errors, correspondingly, as deviations from the actual relative changes. The averages of the absolute errors of relative changes (in percentage points) are listed in column 5. They vary between 0.9 and 1.2 for the comprehensive income and consumption aggregates, and for the wage series (GNP, $GNP58$, C, YP, and W), but are considerably larger for most of the other variables (fixed investment, profits, and, particularly, unemployment) and smaller for only a few (P, LE, AWW).

Since the series also differ greatly in variability, the most meaningful comparisons are probably those that relate the average size of errors to the average size of actual changes. The ratios of the relative-change measures are generally quite similar to the ratios of the absolute-change measures for the same variables (columns 7 and 8). The lowest ratios (most favorable to the simulations) are those for current-dollar GNP, YP, P, RS, and W; they fall in the range of 0.4 to 0.7. The ratios for $GNP58$, C, IH, II, UMD, and RL exceed 0.75 but are smaller than one. Ratios in excess of unity signify that errors are on the average larger than the recorded changes, an adverse finding applying to the simulations of *ISE, NE, LE, UN, CPR*, and *AWW*. On the whole, the ratios tend to be relatively low for the more stable trend-dominated variables and high (unfavorable) for the more volatile and fluctuating ones.

3.1.3   The correlations between the actual and simulated *levels* of the series are, in general, quite high, as would be expected; they exceed .90 for thirteen, and .95 for eleven, of the seventeen variables. The lower r-coefficients, ranging from .331 to .659, are those for the volatile series *NE, UN, II*, and *IH*. However, the high correlations of levels reflect mainly common trends, rather than good agreement between the shorter movements in simulations and realizations. Correlations between the relative or absolute *changes* in S and A are drastically lower than those between levels. They vary from practically zero for *ISE* to .777 ($\bar{r}^2 = .598$) for *RS* (Table 3.2, columns 1 and 2). Nine of these r-coefficients are smaller than .4; five (*GNP, IH, II, NE*, and *YP*) are larger than .4 but smaller than .6; and only three (*P, UMD*, and *RS*) exceed .6.

Simple linear least-square regressions of actual on simulated changes yield the statistics on the constant intercept a and the slope coefficient b, listed in columns 3 and 4 of Table 3.2. Ideally, the true population parameters for the constant (α) and for the slope (β) should equal zero and one, respectively, in order for the simulation to be both unbiased and efficient. In terms of the limited-sample statistics available, this means that a and b should not be statistically different from zero and one, respectively. Tests of the corresponding null hypotheses (that $\alpha = 0$ and $\beta = 1$, jointly or separately) are summarized in columns 5 and 6.

The results are fair or good for some of the variables whose changes were relatively well simulated, judging from the correlation statistics: *IH, II, P, UMD, RS*, and *RL*. Here the constants are very small fractions, while the slope coefficients range from .72 to 1.06 and do not appear to be significantly different from one, using the conventional probability levels. Elsewhere, the intercepts are still generally small and—what is more meaningful—the differences between the means of simulated and actual changes are for the most part small. But

TABLE 3.2

Nonstochastic Simulations for the Sample Period, Wharton Model: Correlation, Regression, and Test Statistics (1948-III–1968-I)

Line	Variable Symbol[a]	Correlation of Simulated with Actual Changes[b]		Regression of Actual on Simulated Changes[c]			
		r (1)	$\bar{r}^2$ (2)	Constant (a) (3)	Slope (b) (4)	F-ratio for $(\alpha = 0, \beta = 1)$[d] (5)	t-test for $\beta = 1$[e] (6)
1	GNP	.409	.156	.010	.355	25.27	7.10
2	GNP58	.328	.096	.007	.278	31.07	7.88
3	C	.159	.012	.010	−.122	84.09	12.97
4	IH	.450	.192	.001	.808	0.56	1.04
5	ISE	.016	g	.010	.021	21.54	6.56
6	II[f]	.503	.243	−.052	.724	1.88	1.93
7	NE[f]	.407	.155	−.177	.458	13.86	4.60
8	YP	.538	.280	.009	.447	24.44	6.89
9	P	.666	.436	.001	.938	0.72	0.52
10	LE	.342	.105	.003	.208	72.73	12.06
11	UN[f]	.115	.0002	−.003	.060	125.07	15.81
12	CPR	.336	.102	−.008	.356	16.02	5.64
13	AWW	.132	.004	−.001	.114	40.88	9.02
14	UMD	.637	.398	−.004	.827	1.23	1.51
15	RS[f]	.777	.598	.011	.902	1.5	0.3
16	RL[f]	.343	.106	.010	1.065	0.5	1.0
17	W	.330	.097	−1.336	2.097	1.45	1.59

NOTES TO TABLE 3.2

ᵃ For meaning of symbols, see Table 1.1.

ᵇ Based on relative changes in the simulated series S_t, defined as $(\Delta S/S)_t = (S_t - S_{t-1})/S_{t-1}$, and on relative changes in the actual series A_t, defined as $(\Delta A/A)_t = (A_t - A_{t-1})/A_{t-1}$, except as noted in footnote f. Correlation coefficients r are listed in column 1, adjusted determination coefficients $\bar{r}^2$ in column 2.

ᶜ The regressions are of the form $(\Delta A/A)_t = a + b(\Delta S/S)_t + u_t$, except as noted in footnote f.

ᵈ See text. Some of the relevant percentage points of the F-distributions (for $n_1 = 2$, $n_2 = 77$) are: $F_{0.01} = 4.93$, $F_{0.05} = 3.12$, $F_{0.10} = 2.38$, and $F_{0.25} = 1.41$.

ᵉ See text. Some of the relevant percentage points of the t-distribution ($n = 77$, two-tailed test) are 2.65, 1.99, 1.67, and 1.16 (for 1, 5, 10 and 25 per cent significance levels, respectively).

ᶠ Based on absolute changes in S_t and A_t; that is, these regressions are of the form: $\Delta A_t = a + b(\Delta S_t) + u_t$.

ᵍ Correlation too low to give a meaningful adjusted coefficient $\bar{r}^2$ (unadjusted $r^2 = .00026$).

the regression coefficients b are much too low for comfort: they not only definitely differ from one (in the downward direction), but in several cases they are not significantly different from zero according to the standard t-test. (This is so for ISE, UN, AWW, and C where the slope coefficient is negative.) For these series, then, changes in S and A are apparently uncorrelated.

Among the probable reasons for these rather disappointing results is the effect of the "base errors" that were noted before, in connection with the large differences between the accuracy of the level and that of the change predictions, based on the S series. These base errors are likely to act as errors of observation in independent variables; that is, they would tend to lower the regression, as well as the correlation coefficients. Whatever their source, large deviations of the slope coefficients from unity indicate that the simulated series provide inefficient estimates of the actual changes.

3.1.4 Confirming and quantifying what has been broadly observed with the aid of our basic charts of the A and S series, Table 3.3 shows that the simulations understate the fluctuations of the actuals in most cases. The averages listed in columns 1 to 6 are based on amplitudes measured for both A and S over successive business-cycle expansions and contractions in the sample period. These amplitude meas-

TABLE 3.3

Nonstochastic Simulations for the Sample Period, Wharton Model:
Average Amplitudes of Cyclical and Trend Movements
(1948-III-1968-I)

Line	Variable Symbol[a]	Average Change Per Month in Reference-Cycle Relatives[b] During:						Mean Absolute Per Cent Change Trend-Cycle Component[c]	
		Expansions		Contractions		Full Cycle			
		Simulated (1)	Actual (2)	Simulated (3)	Actual (4)	Simulated (1)−(3) (5)	Actual (2)−(4) (6)	Simulated (7)	Actual (8)
1	GNP	.57	.67	.17	−.12	.40	.79	1.67	1.66
2	GNP58	.48	.40	−.18	.04	.66	.36	1.20	1.26
3	C	.34	.35	.22	.12	.12	.23	0.99	0.93
4	IH	−.01	−.09	.48	.48	−.49	−.57	1.78	3.59
5	ISE	.38	.67	−.10	−.87	.48	1.54	1.78	2.44
6	II	.08	.27	−.16	−.72	.24	.99	1.79	1.88
7	NE	.16	−.01	−.17	−.01	.33	0	1.28	0.76
8	YP	.52	.63	.19	−.03	.33	.66	0.76	1.56
9	P	.18	.20	.14	.06	.04	.14	1.42	.5
10	LE	.14	.18	−.01	−.16	.15	.34	0.46	0.53
11	UN	−.09	−.25	.03	.07	−.11	−.32	0.65	6.51
12	CPR	.70	.85	−.36	−1.16	1.06	2.01	11.53	3.59
13	AWW	−.02	−.01	−.06	−.11	.04	.10	2.10	0.23
14	UMD	.48	.93	−.91	−1.92	1.39	2.85	0.22	4.37
15	RS	.04	.05	−.11	−.09	.15	.14	2.67	7.33
16	RL	.014	.02	−.004	−.03	.018	.05	6.39	2.04
17	W	.35	.44	.34	.20	.01	.24	1.05	1.35

NOTES TO TABLE 3.3

The period covered by the measures in columns 1 through 6 extends from the 1948-IV peak to the assumed 1966-IV peak.

ᵃ For meaning of symbols, consult Table 1.1.

ᵇ Based on quarterly data but expressed as rate per month (quarterly rates would be three times as large). Figures for all series except *II, NE, UN, RS* and *RL* are expressed as reference-cycle relatives; that is, as a percentage of the average level of the series during each business ("reference") cycle. Figures for *II, NE, UN, RS* and *RL* are expressed in absolute units. (*See Table 1.1 for units.*)

ᶜ Average quarter-to-quarter percentage change, without regard to sign, in the trend-cyclical component: a smooth, flexible moving-average of the seasonally adjusted series.

ures refer to per month rates of change between standings at business-cycle peaks and at business-cycle troughs, both expressed in per cent of the average level of the respective series during the particular business cycle.[12] The differences between amplitudes of *A* and *S* depend not only on the relative size of the cyclical swings ("specific cycles") in the paired series, but also on the differences in their timing and conformity to business cycles. Thus, it is conceivable that, say, *A* showed systematically larger specific-cycle amplitudes than did *S*, while no such regular relationship applied to the reference-cycle amplitudes of the same two series. For this to be possible, *A* and *S* would have to have sufficiently different timing at the peaks and troughs of the business cycle, and *S* would have to conform more closely to the general business cycle than *A* does. Actually, substantial differences in timing and conformity are not uncommon for the compared *A* and *S* series.

The simulations for *GNP* and *YP* show small positive, instead of small negative, changes during contractions, while the reverse applies to *GNP58*. Also, for net exports, the expansion amplitude is negative in *A*, positive in *S*. In all other cases, the average amplitudes of *A* and *S* agree in sign (compare columns 1 and 2, 3 and 4). This includes eight series that show definite procyclical changes (positive in expansions and negative in contractions, except for the unemployment rate, where an inverted pattern is, of course, expected); three series that experienced only retardations of growth rather than declines during business contractions (*C, P,* and *W*); one series that moved downward

[12] See below, Section 3.1.6.

throughout, though less so in expansions (AWW); and one whose movements were on the average countercyclical (IH). In most instances, the average changes per month are larger for A than for S in both expansion and contraction periods. In all but two cases—$GNP58$ and NE—the full-cycle amplitudes (i.e., expansion amplitude minus contraction amplitude) are larger for A than for S. This is strong evidence for the tendency of these simulations to underestimate the observed cyclical movements.[13]

As another average amplitude measure, one that disregards the difference between rises and falls, and does not depend on the relative cyclical timing and conformity of the series, we use the mean absolute percentage change per quarter in the trend-cycle component of the series. This is based on changes in a weighted moving average, which contains practically all of the trend and cyclical movements and little, if any, of the seasonal and short irregular movements in the data.[14] Here the amplitude of S is smaller than that of A for twelve of the seventeen variables; and in most of the remaining cases, the differences between the paired measures are very small (columns 7 and 8).

The simulations, although usually underestimating the average changes in the series, rank the variables very well according to their typical amplitudes. The ranks based on the expansion averages (columns 1 and 2) show a positive correlation of .934; those based on the contraction averages (columns 3 and 4), a correlation of .919. The correlation between the ranks based on the mean absolute percentage changes in the trend-cycle components of S and A (columns 7 and 8) is .950. (These Spearman coefficients adjusted for tied ranks—r_s—are all high enough not to be attributable to chance.)

3.1.5   The Wharton series cover four business-cycle peaks (1948-IV, 1953-II, 1957-III, and 1960-II) and four troughs (1949-IV, 1954-III, 1958-II, and 1961-I) but in some cases their timing at the beginning of the sample period—that is, at the 1948 peak—could not

---

[13] However, let us remember that these amplitude differences still reflect in some unknown degree the fact that the variance of A includes the random disturbance component, while the variance of S does not.

[14] This is a quarterly equivalent of "Spencer's graduation" (a weighted fifteen-term formula used as an estimate of the trend-cycle component of a series in the Census Bureau computer program of seasonal adjustment and time-series decomposition). See Julius Shiskin, "Electronic Computers and Business Indicators" [26, Chapter 17].

be determined. In addition, some of these series, notably those for inventory investment and short-term interest rates, show strong contractions in 1966–67 in both the actual and simulated values. These movements correspond to the business retardation that can be dated as having occurred in the period 1966-IV–1967-II, and they have been so treated here.

Table 3.4 summarizes the record of cyclical timing of the A and S series for fourteen variables. The price-level series show only one cyclical decline in A (in 1948–49) and none in S; the wage-rate series have no contractions at all, in either A or S. Net exports data conform poorly to business cycles, so that of the nine turning points in the A series for this variable, only four can be matched with reference dates; but the S series reproduced fairly well six of these episodes in the years 1948–58. (Afterward, its fit to A became quite inadequate, however.) Because so few comparisons of business revivals and recessions can be made for these data, the variables P, W, and NE are not included in Table 3.4.

The simulations for $GNP, GNP58, C, LE, AWW$, and UMD failed to match the contractions of 1957–58 and 1960–61; thus, each of these six series "skipped" four of the business-cycle turns that occurred in the Wharton sample period (Table 3.4, column 1). The corresponding A series, in contrast, did turn in conformity with these general economic reversals. The simulation for personal income matched only the 1953–54 contraction and missed six reference dates at other times, while the actual YP skipped only the two turning points marking the 1960–61 recession. For each of the other variables included in the table, the S series skipped two turning points (typically either in 1957–58 or in 1960–61), except that the RS simulation declined at each peak, and rose at each trough, of the business cycles covered. The corresponding actuals, on the other hand, matched these turns on practically all occasions.

Another manifestation of lapses from conformity is found in "extra turns," which occur when a series shows a specific-cycle peak or trough which cannot be matched with a business-cycle recession or revival. For a few variables — $GNP58, LE, UMD$ — the simulations do show such extra turns, where the actuals have none; while in two cases — C and ISE — the opposite applies (Table 3.4, column 2). On the

Nonstochastic Simulations for the Sample Period, Wharton Model: Timing at Business-Cycle Turns and Corresponding Measures for the Actual Values (1948-III–1968-I)

Frequencies of Timing Observations for Series S and A

Line	Variable Symbol[a]	Business Cycle Turns Skipped[b] (1)	Extra Turns[b] (2)	Leads (3)	Exact Coincidences (4)	Lags (5)	Long Leads or Lags[c] (6)	Dominant Type of Timing[b] (7)
1	GNP S	4	0	1	1	2	1*	n.i.[i]
2	A	0	0	3	5	0	0	coincident
3	GNP58 S	4	2	1	1	2	1*	n.i.
4	A	0	0	4	4	0	0	coincident
5	C S	4	0	2	0	2	1	n.i.
6	A	2	2	2	3	1	1	coincident
7	IH S	2	4	3	2	0	3	leading-irregular
8	A	2	4	4	2	0	3	leading-irregular
9	ISE S	2	0	2	1	3	3[d]	coincident-lagging
10	A	0	2	0	4	4	0	coincident-lagging
11	II S	2	2	4	1[e]	1	3	leading-irregular
12	A	0	2	6	4[f]	0	3	leading-irregular
13	YP S	6	0	1	0	1	0	n.i.
14	A	2	0	2	3	1	0	coincident
15	LE S	4	2	2	0	2	1*	n.i.
16	A	0	0	2	4	2	0	coincident
17	UN[g] S	2	0	3	0	2	4[h]	n.i.-irregular

(continued)

TABLE 3.4 (concluded)

Frequencies of Timing Observations for Series S and A

Line	Variable Symbol[a]	Business Cycle Turns Skipped[b] (1)	Extra Turns[b] (2)	Leads (3)	Exact Coincidences (4)	Lags (5)	Long Leads or Lags[c] (6)	Dominant Type of Timing[b] (7)
18	A	0	0	2	3	2	1	coincident
19	CPR S	2	0	3	0	2	1	leading-irregular
20	A	0	0	5	2	0	3	leading
21	AWW S	4	2	3	0	1	2	leading-irregular
22	A	0	1	4	2	1	3	leading
23	UMD S	4	4	0	1	2	1*	n.i.-irregular
24	A	0	0	4	2	1	1	leading-coincident
25	RS S	0	0	5e	3	2c	1	coincident-leading
26	A	0	0	1	3f	6	0	lagging
27	RL S	2	0	0	1	5	1*	lagging
28	A	0	0	1	4	3	1*	coincident-lagging

a For meaning of symbols, see Table 1.1. S refers to simulations, A to actuals.

b See explanation in text.

c Leads or lags of three or more quarters. Numbers marked by asterisks refer to lags, others refer to leads at business-cycle turns (see also notes d and h below).

d Includes two lags and one lead.

e Includes one observation relating to the 1966-67 retardation.

f Includes two observations relating to the 1966-67 retardation.

g Treated on the inverted plan: peaks in UN are matched with business-cycle troughs, troughs in UN with business-cycle peaks.

h Includes one lag and three leads.

i Not identified.

whole, however, extra turns are not an important source of discrepancies between S and A.

The frequencies of leads, coincidences, and lags, and also of those leads or lags that are longer than two quarters, are listed in columns 3 to 6 of Table 3.4 for each of the paired A and S series. It is often easier to identify the presence of a lead or lag than to measure its duration with adequate precision, especially at the beginning and end of a series; and the shortness of the simulated series makes this a fairly important consideration. Moreover, we are here interested mainly in whether the simulations agree with the actuals regarding the type of timing that is predominant for the given variable — not in comparisons of the length of leads and lags, which would be needlessly ambitious and could only be spuriously precise for the available data. For these reasons, the timing measures proper are not presented here; we show only the frequency distributions that are based on them. However, the entire evidence is used to determine the "dominant type of timing" of A and S in column 7.

For some variables, the paucity of the timing comparisons at turning points, or the varied composition of these observations, or both, make it impossible to identify the series as a leader, coincider, or lagger. This applies to the simulations of GNP, $GNP58$, C, YP, and LE: all cases in which the label "not identified" (n.i.) had to be used for the S series, whereas the actuals, as shown by the historical evidence, are clearly coincident. In addition, the simulations for the unemployment rate and unfilled orders are best described as "n.i.-irregular," while the actual data show UN as typically coincident and UMD as leading at peaks and coincident at troughs. For the other variables in Table 3.4, there is a good or fair correspondence between the timing of S and A, except that leads are more frequent in the simulated data for RS and lags more important in the actual data. For example, leads, often of long duration, prevail in both A and S for investment in housing (IH), and in inventories (II), while lags are more characteristic of A and S for business investment in plant and equipment (ISE).

3.1.6 One way of evaluating the models' capacity to simulate cyclical characteristics is the use of NBER reference-cycle patterns for simulated and actual series. These reference-cycle patterns represent the condensation of time-series data for each business cycle into nine cyclical stages, covering standings at business-cycle turning points, and average standings for thirds of expansions and contractions. In trough-peak-trough cycles, the initial, middle, and terminal turns are designated as Stages I, V, and IX respectively. Average standings during successive thirds of business expansions are Stages II, III, and IV; those of contractions, VI, VII, and VIII. Stage relatives are constructed by expressing these average stage standings as percentages of the average value of the series over the full cycle.

In the graphic presentation, the time scale can reflect chronological time or it can be standardized to represent all cycle phases (expansions and contractions) as equal time-spans before and after the central turn. A third possibility, the one used in this study, is to represent expansions and contractions in proportion to the average duration of these phases during the whole period covered by the series.[15]

The Wharton sample-period series cover three complete trough-peak-trough cycles: 1949–53–54, 1954–57–58, and 1958–60–61; but acceptance of the proxy dates for a peak in 1966-IV, and for a trough in 1967-II (actually, these dates identify a definite retardation in general economic activity), enables us to use the subsequent data in a fourth pattern for the period 1961–66–67. Similarly, with the aid of the same pair of extra reference dates, four successive peak-trough-peak patterns can be computed for each series: 1948–49–53, 1953–54–57, 1957–58–60, and 1960–61–66. Each set of computations inevitably fails to cover some of the data at the beginning and end of the sample period: in particular, the trough-to-trough patterns miss the 1948–49 contraction, and the peak-to-peak patterns miss the declines or retardation of 1966–67. In order to maximize the informational potential of this approach, we have computed, plotted, and inspected all the T-to-T and P-to-P patterns that the data allow, including a pair of average patterns for each series. For economy in presentation, the patterns have then been combined so as to show in one diagram the behavior of the series on both sides of each of three turns, T-P-T. Chart 3.2

---

[15] Since this time period is different for each of the three models, the time-scales of the charts vary among models. In the present case of quarterly data, interpolations had to be used in dividing up the contraction phase when this phase was short.

For a full discussion of the reference-cycle patterns and their application to quarterly data, see [5, pp. 160–70, 200–202]. For a condensed discussion of the approach, description of related computer programs, and interpretation of output measures see [4, Part III].

CHART 3.2

*Nonstochastic Simulations for the Sample Period, Wharton
Model: Reference-Cycle Patterns for Simulated and
Actual Series, Selected Variables
(1949–1967)*

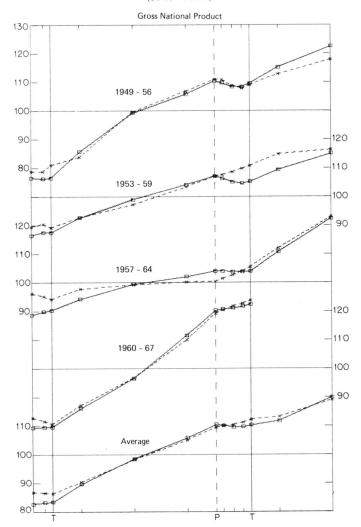

NOTE: Scale in reference-cycle relatives or (for unemployment rate and short-term interest rate) in absolute deviations from cycle base. *P* and *T* stand for peaks and troughs, respectively.

(continued)

375

CHART 3.2 (*continued*)

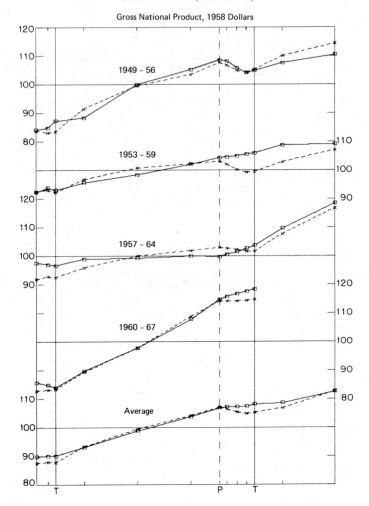

Gross National Product, 1958 Dollars

CHART 3.2 *(continued)*

Investment in Housing

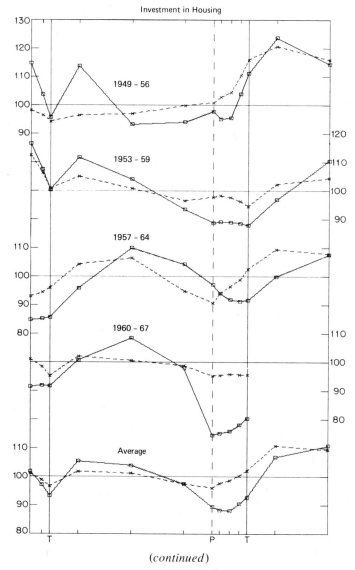

(continued)

CHART 3.2 (*continued*)

Investment in Plant and Equipment

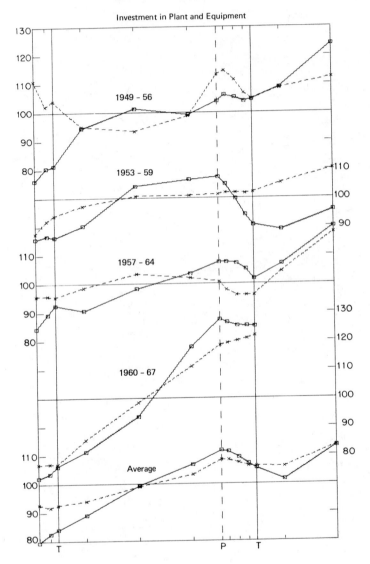

CHART 3.2 (*continued*)

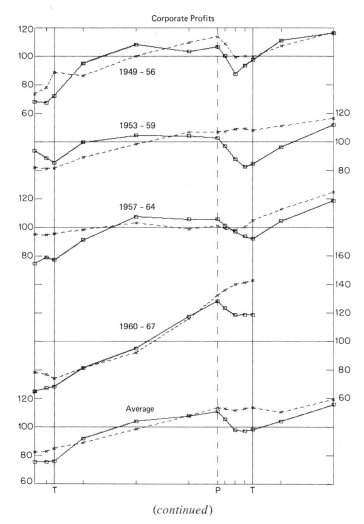

Corporate Profits

(*continued*)

CHART 3.2 (*continued*)

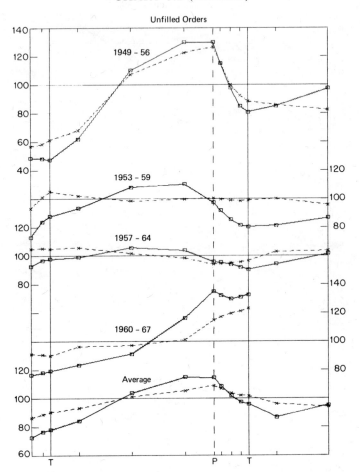

CHART 3.2 *(continued)*

Short-Term Interest Rate

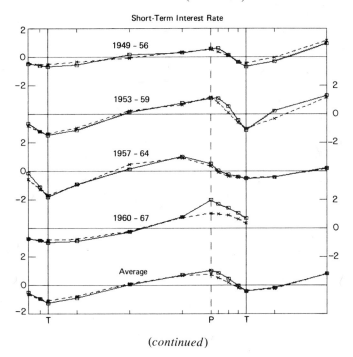

(continued)

CHART 3.2 (*concluded*)

Unemployment Rate

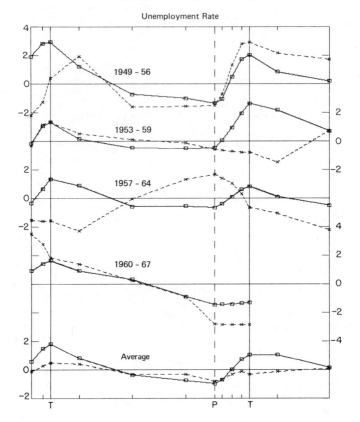

presents a sample of these diagrams for selected variables, while the discussion that follows is based on the entire material.

The method of measurement employed is such as to eliminate the intercycle trends and to smooth out much of the short "irregular" movements of the series within the stages of the business cycle. The apparent effect of this detrending and smoothing is, in many cases, to make S and A resemble each other much better than they do in terms of the original data (*cf.* Charts 3.1 and 3.2). The evidence of the patterns is also, in general, more favorable to the simulations than are some of the sets of measures discussed before, notably the average errors and correlations based on quarterly changes in S and A.

For the variables dominated by strong growth tendencies — *GNP*, *GNP58*, *C*, *YP*, *P*, *LE*, and *W* — the patterns show clearly that *S* decreased less often and by smaller relative amounts during business recessions than did *A*. Frequently, small cyclical declines in *A* are matched by reduced rates of increase in *S*; but then, in most such cases, the retardations of growth in *S* are so pronounced as to make the contrast between the patterns of behavior in expansions and contractions nearly as marked for *S* as for *A*. However, it is also true that the correspondence between the patterns for the paired series was, on the whole, considerably closer during expansions than during contractions. The agreement between *S* and *A* was, by and large, appreciably better during the 1953–54 recession than in the other three periods of contraction (including the 1966–67 retardation).

For the variables with large fluctuations and relatively weak trends, much greater discrepancies are observed between the patterns for the paired *A* and *S* series. Some of the largest discrepancies are found for the investment series (*IH*, *ISE*, *II*), the unemployment rate, unfilled orders, and net exports. The amplitudes of the *S* patterns tend to be smaller than those of the corresponding *A* patterns (only for *NE* is the opposite clearly indicated). The correspondence between the *A* and *S* patterns is particularly good for the short-term interest rate, *RS*.

3.2 THE OBE MODEL

3.2.1 The sample period for this model is 1953-II through 1966-IV (55 quarterly observations). It includes three business-cycle contractions and two minor retardations.

Chart 3.3 shows that the simulated *GNP* series declined only briefly in the first quarter of 1954. Because of the relatively large amplitude of the decline and the slowness of the subsequent recovery, this movement is considered to be cyclical, although one-quarter declines are usually thought to be too short for such consideration. Only one other interruption of the upward trend is observed in this series: it occurred in 1959-III, a reflection of the major steel strike, which similarly affected the actual *GNP* series. During the 1957–58 and 1960–61 recessions, the simulated *GNP* fails to show downward

CHART 3.3

Nonstochastic Simulations for the Sample Period,
OBE Model: Simulated and Actual Series for
Selected Variables
(1953–1966)

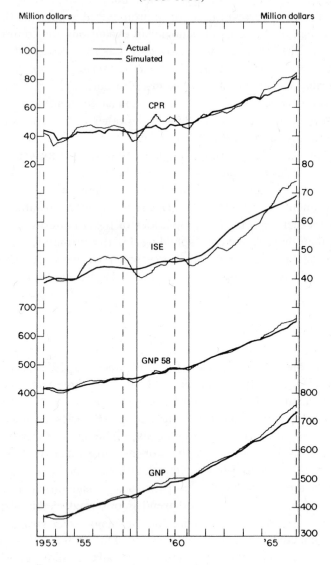

CHART 3.3 (*concluded*)

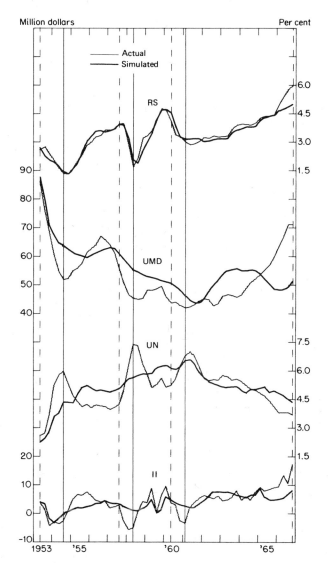

movements corresponding to those in actual GNP. The values of simulated GNP exceed the recorded values only during the recession years 1953–54 and 1958. At other times, i.e., in eleven out of the fourteen years covered, the level of GNP was persistently underestimated in the simulation. The amount of this underestimation is shown to have increased at the end of the sample period, in 1965–66.

Much the same can be said about the simulation of personal income in current dollars, except that, here, the 1953–54 decline lasted two quarters. Considerably less underestimation, however, is observed in the simulations of GNP in 1958 dollars, and of personal consumption expenditures in 1958 dollars; in particular, the fits here are very close for the years 1961–64.

The story is quite similar for other variables with strong upward trends and relatively small fluctuations, such as the GNP price deflator, private wage and salary compensation per man-hour, and private labor costs per unit of output; except for the first three or four years after the "initial shock" of starting the simulation, the levels of these series are consistently underestimated. On the other hand, for the more volatile variables with large fluctuations and much weaker, or less consistent, trends, the tendency for the simulated series to run below the levels of the actuals is not so apparent. What the charts do clearly indicate for these series is the tendency to underestimate *changes:* the curves for simulated values show fewer and smaller fluctuations than do their counterparts for the actuals.

3.2.2   Table 3.5 confirms the prevalence of underestimation errors in the OBE Model simulations for the sample period 1953–66. For all but four of the twenty-one variables used, the average level of the simulated series is lower than that of the actual series, $\bar{S} < \bar{A}$, as indicated by the negative signs of the mean level errors (MEL) in column 1. (The errors of simulation are defined as the difference, simulated minus actual value.) For all but five of the variables, the mean change errors (MEC) are negative (column 2). As noted above, in Section 3.1.2, the sign of MEC can mean different things under different circumstances; but where both A and S are positive and show predominantly rises rather than declines, negative MEC indicates that changes were, on the average, underestimated. This is the case for most of the variables covered by the OBE data. The variables with

TABLE 3.5

Nonstochastic Simulations for the Sample Period, OBE Model: Average Errors and Their Ratios to Average Actual Values (1953-II–1966-IV)

Line	Variable Symbol[a]	Unit[b]	Mean Error (ME) Level (MEL) (1)	Change (MEC) (2)	Mean Absolute Error (MAE) Level (MAEL) (3)	Change (MAEC) (4)	Relative Change[c] (MAERC) (5)	Ratio of MAE to Mean Absolute Actual Values (MAA) Level $\left(\frac{MAEL}{MAAL}\right)$ (6)	Change $\left(\frac{MAEC}{MAAC}\right)$ (7)	Relative Change[d] $\left(\frac{MAERC}{MAARC}\right)$ (8)
1	GNP	billion $	-7.51	-0.48	9.991	3.340	0.701	.020	.421	.459
2	GNP58	billion 58$	-1.95	-0.14	6.291	3.101	0.644	.013	.502	.518
3	C	billion 58$	-1.57	-0.02	3.153	1.926	0.612	.010	.578	.595
4	IH	billion 58$	-0.16	0.07	1.196	0.537	2.436	.053	.794	.794
5	ISE	billion 58$	0.16	-0.09	2.616	0.916	1.896	.053	.793	.812
6	II	billion 58$	-0.49	-0.16	2.540	1.928	e	.470	.846	e
7	NE	billion 58$	0.09	0.05	0.894	0.449	e	.208	.529	e
8	YP	billion $	-5.87	-0.40	8.106	1.774	0.460	.020	.308	.334
9	P	1958 = 100	-0.96	-0.05	1.353	0.234	0.239	.013	.469	.488
10	LE	million	-0.07	-0.01	0.570	0.220	0.348	.009	.418	.430
11	UN	per cent	0.02	0.01	0.657	0.297	6.000	.131	.909	.890
12	CPR	billion $	-1.16	-0.05	3.064	1.903	3.949	.057	.868	.881
13	AWW	hours/week	-0.01	0.002	0.170	0.148	0.359	.004	.938	.046

(continued)

TABLE 3.5 (concluded)

Line	Variable Symbol[a]	Unit[b]	Mean Error (ME) Level (MEL) (1)	Change (MEC) (2)	Mean Absolute Error (MAE) Level (MAEL) (3)	Change (MAEC) (4)	Relative Change[c] (MAERC) (5)	Ratio of MAE to Mean Absolute Actual Values (MAA) Level $\left(\frac{MAEL}{MAAL}\right)$ (6)	Change $\left(\frac{MAEC}{MAAC}\right)$ (7)	Relative Change[d] $\left(\frac{MAERC}{MAARC}\right)$ (8)
14	OMD	billion 58$	−2.05	−0.03	3.279	2.053	4.403	.066	1.035	1.033
15	UMD	billion 58$	2.04	−0.36	6.158	2.008	3.674	.113	.922	.976
16	HS	thousand/year	−16.48	7.01	109.642	64.837	4.723	.079	.925	.925
17	RS	% per annum	−0.07	−0.02	0.212	0.149	4.797	.062	.556	.512
18	RL	% per annum	−0.01	−0.002	0.145	0.074	1.828	.033	.778	.802
19	W	dollars	−0.05	−0.002	0.054	0.015	0.674	.022	.667	.579
20	LC/O	dollars	−0.01	−0.0005	0.013	0.003	0.552	.002	.784	.784
21	M	billion $	−1.02	−0.02	1.359	0.493	0.336	.001	.533	.532

[a] For explanation of symbols, see Table 1.1.

[b] The average errors, with and without regard to sign (ME and MAE), which are listed in columns 1 to 4 are expressed in these units, and so are the average actual values (MAA); hence the figures for MAE/MAA, in columns 6 and 7, are pure ratios.

[c] In percentage points. Mean of the differences: quarterly per cent change in the simulated series, minus quarterly per cent change in the actual series, all taken without regard to sign.

[d] Ratio of figure in column 5 to the corresponding mean of actual percentage changes.

[e] Not applicable: Since net change in inventories and net foreign investment can assume negative values, these series can be analyzed only in absolute, not in relative terms.

positive average errors (ISE and UMD for levels; IH, AWW, and HS for changes; and NE and UN for both levels and changes) all have large cyclical and irregular fluctuations in actual values. The differences between the average levels of A and S are relatively small in most of these cases and not very important. Furthermore, measures of average changes taken without regard to sign, or separately, for periods of expansion and contraction (Table 3.7), suggest that the fluctuations of S are usually smaller than those of A, even for these variables.

Table 3.5 shows that for all variables $|MEL| > |MEC|$ and $MAEL > MAEC$; also $MAEL > |MEL|$ and $MAEC > |MEC|$ (see columns 1 to 4). These relationships and the underlying causes are already familiar. (They were discussed for the Wharton Model in Section 3.1.2, above.) The fact that the level errors exceed the corresponding change errors by relatively large amounts must again be attributed to the cumulation of errors over time, which throws the S predictions increasingly off base.

The mean absolute errors of relative change in S, as compared with A, vary from 0.2 to 0.7 percentage points for the comprehensive income, consumption, and employment aggregates, and also for prices, wages, and money. (See the entries in column 5, lines 1 to 3, 8 to 10, 13, and 19 to 21.) The errors for the other variables – investment outlays and commitments, unemployment, corporate profits, and interest rates – are substantially larger in these terms, ranging from 1.8 to 6.0 percentage points.

Another relationship that is confirmed by the figures in Table 3.5 is that $\dfrac{MAEL}{MAAL} < \dfrac{MAEC}{MAAC}$ (columns 6 and 7). It is the ratios for the absolute and relative changes in the last two columns of the table (the two values are generally close to each other) that, here as elsewhere, deserve our particular attention. These figures are of the order of .3 to .6 for the most comprehensive aggregates, as well as for money supply and the price, wage, and short-term interest series. They are much higher (.8 to .9) for the more volatile investment series, such as ISE, II, and HS and for various – mainly leading – indicators, such as UN, CPR, AWW, UMD, RL, and LC/O. Only for one variable, new orders for durables, do the ratios exceed one; that is, the average errors slightly exceed the average actual changes.

3.2.3 The correlations between the actual and simulated levels of the series exceed .86 for sixteen, and .95 for twelve, of the twenty-one variables. For the volatile series *HS, UMD, UN, II,* and *IH*, the *r*-coefficients are significantly lower, varying from .597 to .721. Again, it is principally the common trends in *A* and *S* that explain the high correlations of levels, as there is much less agreement between the shorter movements in these series. Correlations between changes in *S* and *A* are much lower than those between levels, although they vary a great deal, from .185 to .980. (See Table 3.6, column 1.) The lowest correlations, between .1 and .4, are for the price, wage, profits, and a few other series, notably on investment (*ISE, HS,* and *AWW*). The highest correlations, exceeding .7, are for real *GNP*, net exports, short-term interest rate, and employment.

The regression results are favorable, in the sense that the intercepts are small (near zero) and the slope coefficients are not clearly different from one, for most of the variables. This is true even for some variables for which the correlations of simulated with actual changes are relatively low, notably *UN* and *AWW*. (See columns 3 and 4 and also the tests in columns 5 and 6.) As these cases illustrate, a simulation *S* (viewed as a set of predictions) can be unbiased and efficient (i.e., have errors that are unsystematic and uncorrelated with the values of the *S* series itself), although it is only weakly correlated with the realizations *A*. (That is, the residual variance in the regression of *A* on *S* is large, relative to the variance of *A*.) On the other hand, some of the estimates are clearly unsatisfactory if these criteria are accepted. For the series *P, OMD, W,* and *LC/O*, for example, the intercepts are too large and the slope coefficients, too small.

3.2.4 Table 3.7 shows the average amplitudes of rises and falls in the actual and simulated series, per month, in reference-cycle relatives (columns 1 to 4).[16] During the sample period, several actual series with particularly dominant trends grew on the average in both expansions and contractions, though at higher rates in the former than in the latter (*cf.* entries in columns 2 and 4 for *C, YP, P, W, LC/O,* and

---

[16] There are only two complete trough-to-trough reference cycles in the period 1953–66 (1954–57–58 and 1958–60–61); but, if the proxy date for a "peak" in 1966-IV is accepted, three peak-to-peak cycles can be distinguished in the same period, namely 1953–54–57, 1957–58–60, and 1960–61–66. We chose the second rather than the first alternative in order to utilize as much of the available information as possible.

TABLE 3.6

Nonstochastic Simulations for the Sample Period, OBE Model: Correlation, Regression, and Test Statistics
(1953-II–1966-IV)

Line	Variable Symbol[a]	Correlation of Simulated With Actual Changes[b]		Regression of Actual on Simulated Changes[c]				
		r (1)	r̄² (2)	Constant (a) (3)	Slope (b) (4)	F-ratio for ($\alpha = 0$, $\beta = 1$)[d] (5)	t-test for $\beta = 1$[e] (6)	
1	GNP	.617	.369	.266	.847	0.70	1.03	
2	GNP58	.710	.494	−.032	1.068	0.14	0.47	
3	C	.478	.214	.314	.674	1.83	1.91	
4	IH	.500	.236	−.295	.747	1.24	1.43	
5	ISE	.368	.120	.325	.828	0.28	0.60	
6	II[f]	.581	.326	.146	1.175	0.41	0.78	
7	NE[f]	.862	.738	−.036	.871	1.88	1.83	
8	YP	.635	.392	.349	.786	1.75	1.63	
9	P	.185	.016	.334	.342	4.00	2.64	
10	LE	.980	.960	.014	1.089	4.43	2.97	
11	UN[f]	.501	.237	−.013	1.022	0.03	0.09	
12	CPR	.388	.135	.626	.630	1.64	1.80	

(continued)

TABLE 3.6 (concluded)

Line	Variable Symbol[a]	Correlation of Simulated With Actual Changes[b]		Regression of Actual on Simulated Changes[c]			
		r (1)	$\bar{r}^2$ (2)	Constant (a) (3)	Slope (b) (4)	F-ratio for ($\alpha = 0, \beta = 1$)[d] (5)	t-test for $\beta = 1$[e] (6)
13	AWW	.294	.069	.005	1.097	0.02	0.20
14	OMD	.435	.174	.383	.531	4.84	3.11
15	UMD	.482	.217	.474	.792	1.21	1.05
16	HS	.375	.125	−.483	.930	0.18	0.22
17	RS[f]	.829	.681	.022	.928	0.54	0.84
18	RL[f]	.626	.380	.004	.941	0.08	0.37
19	W	.273	.057	.606	.493	2.56	2.12
20	LC/O	.412	.154	.245	.602	2.86	2.18
21	M	.665	.432	.040	.951	0.09	0.33

[a] For meaning of symbols, see Table 1.1.

[b,c,f] See the corresponding footnotes in Table 3.2.

[d] Some of the relevant percentage points of the F-distribution (for $n_1 = 2$, $n_2 = 53$) are: $F_{0.01} = 5.05$, $F_{0.05} = 3.19$, $F_{0.10} = 2.40$, and $F_{0.25} = 1.43$.

[e] Some of the relevant percentage points of the t-distribution ($n = 53$, two-tailed test) are: 2.68, 2.01, 1.68, and 1.16 (for 1, 5, 10, and 25 per cent significance levels, respectively).

TABLE 3.7

Nonstochastic Simulations for the Sample Period, OBE Model: Average Amplitudes of
Cyclical and Trend Movements
(1953-II–1966-IV)

Line	Variable Symbol[a]	Average Change Per Month in Reference-Cycle Relatives[b] During:						Mean Absolute Per Cent Change Trend-Cycle Component[c]	
		Expansions		Contractions		Full Cycle			
		Simulated	Actual	Simulated	Actual	Simulated (1) − (3)	Actual (2) − (4)	Simulated	Actual
		(1)	(2)	(3)	(4)	(5)	(6)	(7)	(8)
1	GNP	.50	.60	.16	−.08	.34	.68	1.30	1.48
2	GNP58	.34	.42	.02	−.21	.32	.63	.91	1.14
3	C	.35	.39	.21	.03	.14	.36	.93	1.00
4	IH	−.02	−.14	−.13	.16	.11	−.30	1.58	2.82
5	ISE	.42	.66	.12	−.64	.30	1.30	1.14	2.12
6	II	.10	.27	−.27	−.68	.37	.92	.70	1.41
7	NE	.054	.007	−.061	.054	.115	−.44	.58	.65
8	YP	.48	.57	.23	.06	.25	.51	1.26	1.36
9	P	.15	.18	.14	.13	.01	.05	.43	.48
10	LE	.13	.18	−.02	−.15	.15	.33	.34	.52

(continued)

TABLE 3.7 (concluded)

		Average Change Per Month in Reference-Cycle Relatives[b] During:						Mean Absolute Per Cent Change Trend-Cycle Component[c]	
		Expansions		Contractions		Full Cycle			
		Simulated	Actual	Simulated	Actual	Simulated $(1)-(3)$	Actual $(2)-(4)$	Simulated	Actual
Line	Variable Symbol[a]	(1)	(2)	(3)	(4)	(5)	(6)	(7)	(8)
11	UN	−.096	−.24	.008	.05	−.104	−.29	3.25	5.97
12	CPR	.55	.86	.23	−1.10	.32	1.96	2.03	3.47
13	AWW	−.02	0	−.07	−.13	.05	.13	.10	.24
14	OMD	.36	.53	−.44	−1.08	.80	1.61	2.22	3.79
15	UMD	−.01	.47	−1.74	−2.45	1.73	2.92	2.25	3.59
16	HS	−.15	−.38	.18	.32	−.33	−.70	1.88	4.08
17	RS	.05	.06	−.14	−.14	.19	.20	7.81	8.23
18	RL	.022	.024	−.019	−.028	.041	.52	1.56	2.06
19	W	.36	.42	.26	.15	.10	.27	1.00	1.06
20	LC/O	.13	.19	.11	.04	.02	.15	.39	.62
21	M	.17	.20	.18	.09	−.01	.11	.55	.60

NOTE: The period covered by the measures in columns 1 through 6 is from the peak in 1953-II to the assumed peak in 1966-IV (see text).

[a] For meaning of symbols, see Table 1.1.

[b,c] See the corresponding footnotes to Table 3.3.

M). The housing series, IH and HS, responded perversely; they show negative amplitude figures during expansions and positive ones during contractions (lines 4 and 16). Net exports increase more in contractions than in expansions (line 7). For all other variables—including the unemployment rate, which is treated on the inverted plan—a strong procyclical response is observed, with the average amplitudes in the actuals being positive in expansions and negative in contractions.

For business-cycle expansions, the average amplitudes of S and A agree in sign, with but two exceptions. (The figures for AWW and UMD are negative in the simulations.) For contractions, there are six cases of directional disagreement, relating to GNP, $GNP58$, ISE, CPR, IH, and NE. (All but the last two of these involve positive changes in S.)

During business-cycle expansions, the average amplitudes of the S series are smaller than those of the A series, except only for NE and AWW, where changes are very small (columns 1 and 2). The comparison of amplitudes, however, is less easily summarized for business-cycle contractions. In the eight cases where declines prevailed in the average contraction amplitudes of both S and A (including the inverted unemployment rate), average declines of A exceeded those of S in seven instances, the only exception being RS, where the declines are of the same magnitude. When both S and A showed retardations rather than actual declines (C, YP, P, W, LC/O, and M), A increased less than S throughout. In addition, as mentioned above, four series show average contraction amplitudes which are negative for A and positive for S. The two construction series (IH and HS), whose behavior seems to be countercyclical for A, are somewhat less countercyclical in S. The resulting full-cycle amplitudes (expansion amplitudes minus contraction amplitudes) are larger for A than for S in all cases except net exports and the two construction series. All of this constitutes strong evidence for the existence of a general tendency of simulations to underestimate fluctuations during historical business cycles.

When the amplitudes are measured independently of the timing of cyclical turns in the series, as the mean absolute percentage changes in trend-cycle components (columns 7 and 8), the tendency for S to underestimate the variability of A is again very strongly in evidence. Here the figure for S is in each case smaller than that for A.

The ranks of the variables based on the average reference-cycle amplitudes of S and A are positively correlated for both rises and falls, with Spearman coefficients (adjusted for tied ranks) of .937 and .714, respectively. The correlation between the ranks based on the mean absolute percentage changes in the trend-cycle components of S and A is .962.

3.2.5 The simulated series for nominal and real GNP fail to reproduce the contractions of the actual series in 1957–58 and 1960–61, which means that they skip four of the six business-cycle turns in the OBE sample period (Table 3.8, column 1). For consumption, S skips all six turns; and the simulations for eight other variables omit four or two turns each, while the actuals omit none. By this criterion, the A series conform to business cycles better than do the S series for twelve of the eighteen variables.

Turning points that are unconnected with general economic revivals and recessions constitute another class of indicators of nonconforming behavior. Only a few of the OBE simulations show such episodes where the actual series have none. (See the entries for UN, OMD, and UMD in column 2.)

A summary of the frequency distributions of leads, coincidences, and lags is followed here by an attempt to indicate the prevalent type of timing for each of the series (Table 3.8, columns 3 to 7). For eight variables, including GNP and several comprehensive, mostly coincident, indicators, the absence or paucity of turning points, or the heterogeneity of such timing observations as can be made, prohibit such a determination for the S series, and the labels used in these cases are "no turns" (n.t.) or "not identified" (n.i.). For the unemployment rate, the timing of S, instead of being coincident, is rather irregular but mostly lagging. However, for the nine remaining variables, the correspondence between the timing of S and A is, on the whole, good. And these comparisons cover a variety of timing patterns, including some with prevalent leads, as in housing starts and new orders; and others with prevalent lags, as in unit labor costs and interest rates.[17]

[17] It must be recognized that the determination of the timing patterns is necessarily more uncertain for the S series than it is for the A series, because there is some additional evidence on A but not on S. Wherever possible, we have checked the timing of the A series in the sample period against the timing of longer series for the same variables (to cover, at least, the entire postwar period). In some cases, such comparisons could only

Table 3.8 does not include three variables: P, W, and NE. No cyclical turning points in either the actual or the simulated series can be identified for the price level and the wage rate. Net exports show five major turns in the period 1953–66 (or seven if one includes a short decline in 1955). Only two of these can be matched with the reference dates (relating to the 1957–58 recession), but all were reproduced in the S series, and rather well at that.

3.2.6 Chart 3.4 shows the reference-cycle patterns of S and A for selected variables. The patterns, again extended to show both sides of each turn, cover the two T-to-T cycles between 1954 and 1961, the last curve in each set representing the average of the two.

In general, the patterns show the simulations in better light than do the measures previously discussed, probably because they involve considerable smoothing and detrending of the data. They demonstrate that the S series often underwent marked retardations during business contractions, corresponding to mild declines in the A series: this is so for each of the comprehensive indicators of production, income, consumption, and employment—GNP, $GNP58$, C, YP, and LE. In this situation, amplitude figures have different signs for S and A, and the timing comparisons show skipped turns for S, so that a somewhat exaggerated impression of simulation errors may be created by these measures, which the patterns help to correct.

For most variables, the S patterns have smaller amplitudes than the A patterns, reflecting the underestimation of cyclical movements in the S series. The relatives for S are usually higher than those for A in contractions, and lower in expansions. However, apart from these differences (which, although apparently systematic, are not always pronounced), many of the S patterns resemble rather well the corresponding patterns for A, even where the latter show large fluctuations with diverse timing. Good illustrations of this statement are provided by the diagrams for corporate profits, CPR (except in 1960–61), and, particularly, for the interest series RS and RL. On the other hand, there are also some cases of drastic dissimilarity between the paired

be very tentative or approximate, being based on fairly short records, or on data for related, rather than the same, variables (for example, different interest-rate series or undeflated GNP components). However, allowing for such discrepancies as are likely to arise in some of these cases, it is possible to conclude that our identifications for A generally do agree with those historical classifications that are applicable.

TABLE 3.8

Nonstochastic Simulations for the Sample Period, OBE Model: Timing at Business-Cycle Turns and Corresponding Measures for the Actual Values (1953–1966)

Line	Variable Symbol[a]	Frequencies of Timing Observations for Series S and A						
		Business Cycle Turns Skipped[b] (1)	Extra Turns[b] (2)	Leads (3)	Exact Coincidences (4)	Lags (5)	Long Leads or Lags[c] (6)	Dominant Type of Timing[b] (7)
1	GNP S	4	0	1	0	1	0	n.i.
2	A	0	0	3	3	0	0	coincident
3	GNP58 S	4	0	1	0	1	0	n.i.
4	A	0	0	3	3	0	0	coincident
5	C S	6	0	0	0	0	0	n.i.
6	A	0	0	2	3	1	1	coincident
7	IH S	2	2	4	0	0	3	leading-irregular
8	A	2	2	3	1	0	2	leading-irregular
9	ISE S	2	0	1	1	2	2[d]	n.i.
10	A	0	2	0	3	3	0	coincident-lagging
11	II S	0	4	3	2	1	1	leading-irregular
12	A	0	4	4	2	0	2	leading-irregular
13	YP S	4	0	1	0	1	0	n.i.
14	A	2	0	2	1	1	0	coincident
15	LE S	4	0	1	1	0	0	n.i.

No.	Symbol							Classification
16	UN^e S	0	0	1	4	1	0	coincident
17	A	2	2	1	1	2	1*	lagging-irregular
18	CPR S	0	0	2	3	1	0	coincident
19	A	2	0	3	1	0	1	leading-irregular
20	AWW S	0	2	5	1	1	2	leading
21	A	4	3	0	1	2	0	n.i.
22	OMD S	0	2	3	1	0	2	leading
23	A	0	0	5	1	0	1	leading
24		0	0	5	1	0	3	leading
25	UMD S	2	2	2	0	2	2*	n.i.-irregular
26	A	0	0	3	2	1	1	leading-coincident
27	HS S	2	2	4	0	0	3	leading
28	A	0	0	6	0	0	3	leading
29	RS S	0	0	1	2	3	1*	lagging
30	A	0	0	1	1	4	0	lagging
31	RL S	0	0	0	2	4	2*	lagging
32	A	0	0	1	1	4	1*	lagging
33	LC/O S	4	0	0	0	2	1*	n.i.-lagging
34	A	0	0	0	0	6	2*	lagging
35	M S	2	0	4	0	0	2	leading
36	A	2	0	3	1	0	2	leading

[a] For meaning of symbols, see Table 1.1.

[b] See explanation in text.

[c] Leads or lags of three or more quarters. Numbers marked by asterisk refer to lags, others refer to leads at business-cycle turns.

[d] Includes one lead and one lag.

[e] Treated on the inverted plan (see Table 3.4).

CHART 3.4

Nonstochastic Simulations for the Sample Period,
OBE Model: Reference-Cycle Patterns for Simulated
and Actual Series, Selected Variables
(1953–1964)

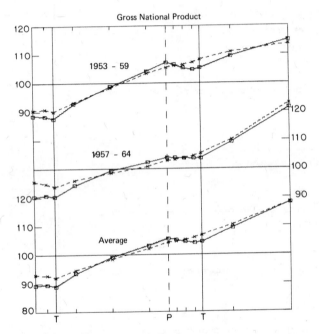

Gross National Product

NOTE: Scale in reference-cycle relatives or (for unemployment rate and short-term interest rate) in absolute deviations from cycle base. *P* and *T* stand for
peaks and troughs, respectively.

CHART 3.4 (*continued*)

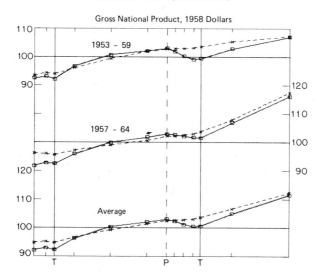

Gross National Product, 1958 Dollars

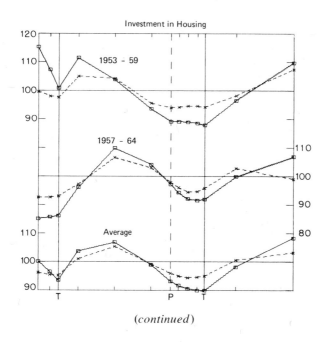

Investment in Housing

(*continued*)

CHART 3.4 (*continued*)

Investment in Plant and Equipment

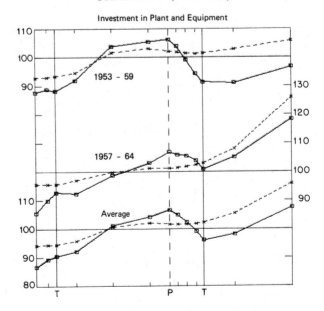

Corporate Profits

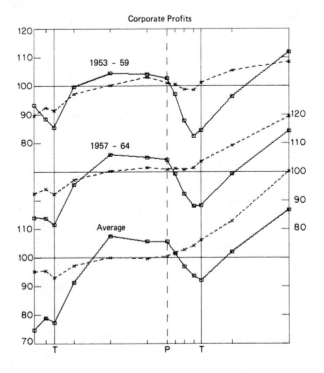

CHART 3.4 *(continued)*

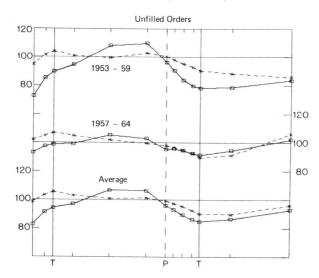

Unfilled Orders

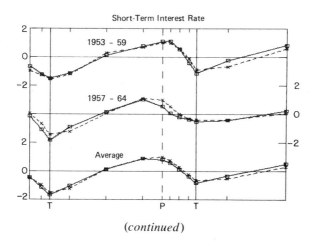

Short-Term Interest Rate

(continued)

CHART 3.4 (*concluded*)

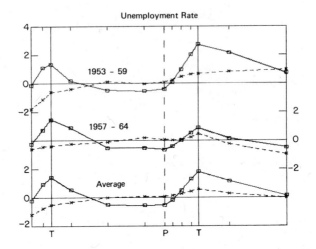

patterns, notably for the inventory change, unemployment, and unfilled orders.

3.3 THE FRB-MIT-PENN (FMP) MODEL

3.3.1 The sample period for this model is relatively short: it begins only in 1956 and covers the eleven years through 1966, or 44 quarterly observations. Thus, the contractions and retardations included are those that are also covered by the OBE sample-period simulations, except for the 1953–54 recession.

Chart 3.5 shows that the simulated GNP series declined only once for one quarter: in 1959-III, during the major steel strike. Recorded GNP also had two two-quarter declines in 1957–58 and 1960–61, but the S series continued to move upward during these recessions, although at lower rates. Through mid-1957, the levels of S and A are very close, and then, in 1957–58, A falls below S; but thereafter, in 1959–66—for nearly eight years—the levels of GNP are consistently underestimated; i.e., $S_t < A_t$.

The simulation of GNP in 1958 dollars looks better, in that here S declined along with A in 1957–58 and 1960 (as well as briefly in 1959). The level comparisons give similar results to those for GNP

CHART 3.5

*Nonstochastic Simulations for the Sample
Period, FRB-MIT-PENN Model:
Simulated and Actual Series
for Selected Variables
(1956–1966)*

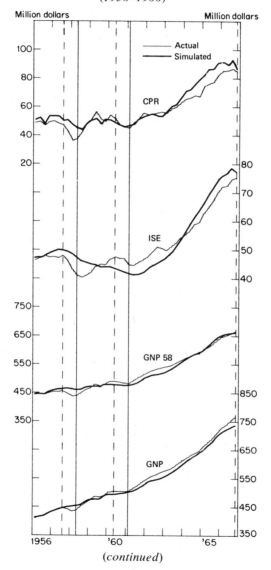

(*continued*)

CHART 3.5 (*concluded*)

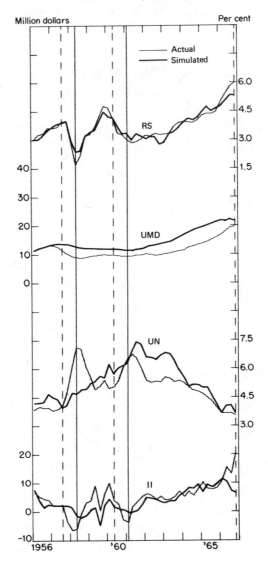

in current dollars in the period 1956–63; but in 1964–66, the S series rises above A, so that there is less underestimation for real, than for nominal, GNP. The A and S series for consumption in real terms are similarly related, except that here S shows only a retardation, not a decline, in 1960.

There are some analogous features in the graphs for the other trend-dominated, relatively smooth and stable variables. The one mild decline of personal income, in 1957–58, is not reproduced in the simulated series; also, $S_t < A_t$ persistently in 1959–66 for this aggregate. Simulated employment, too, fails to match the recorded contraction in 1957–58 and underestimates actual employment, except between mid-1957 and mid-1959; but here S does move down along with A in 1960–61. No turning points occurred in either A or S for the price index and the wage rate. The price level was underestimated in 1956–59, and again, more strongly, in 1963–66. The wage level was underestimated throughout and, again, more so in the last three or four years of the sample period.

For the more cyclical variables, trends are generally weaker and less consistent, and so are any differences between trends in S and A and the resulting discrepancies in levels. Once more, the striking feature of these graphs is that some fluctuations in A are entirely skipped by S (for example, the 1957–59 cycle in unemployment; the 1958–61 cycle in man-hours) and others are heavily muted (e.g., the 1958–61 movements in inventory investment). For one variable in this group—unfilled orders for machinery and equipment—a persistent difference in levels of the two series is observed, with S exceeding A throughout the period 1957–66. Rather close fits to A are provided by the S series for the short- and long-term interest rates.

3.3.2 The MEL figures are negative for most variables, indicating that the actual levels tend to be underestimated in the sample-period simulations (Table 3.9, column 1).[18] There is more variation in sign among the MEC statistics, but they, too, are negative for most of the series with strong upward trends, reflecting the tendency of S to have smaller rates of growth than A (column 2). As elsewhere, the

---

[18] The values of MEL are positive for ISE, NE, UN, CPR, and $OUME$—all variables that had relatively weak trends and marked fluctuations in the period covered by these simulations.

TABLE 3.9

Nonstochastic Simulations for the Sample Period, FRB-MIT-PENN Model:
Average Errors and Their Ratios to Average Actual Values
(1956–1966)

Line	Symbol[a]	Unit[b]	Mean Error (ME)		Mean Absolute Error (MAE)			Ratio of MAE to Mean Absolute Actual Values (MAA)		
			Level (MEL) (1)	Change (MEC) (2)	Level (MAEL) (3)	Change (MAEC) (4)	Relative Change[c] (MAERC) (5)	Level $\left(\frac{MAEL}{MAAL}\right)$ (6)	Change $\left(\frac{MAEC}{MAAC}\right)$ (7)	Relative Change[d] $\left(\frac{MAERC}{MAARC}\right)$ (8)
1	GNP	billion $	-7.31	-0.70	10.034	3.159	0.609	.018	.357	.377
2	GNP58	billion 58$	-2.02	-0.13	8.807	3.235	0.652	.017	.497	.524
3	C	billion 58$	-1.18	0.10	4.839	1.618	0.493	.14	.463	.480
4	IH	100 billion 58$	-0.003	0.002	0.010	0.004	2.000	.044	.698	.733
5	ISE	billion 58$	0.30	0.03	3.057	0.876	1.792	.059	.704	.746
6	II	billion 58$	-1.17	-0.34	2.794	2.129	e	.469	.874	e
7	NE	billion 58$	0.23	-0.04	0.947	0.352	e	.196	1.017	e
8	YP	billion $	-7.57	-0.47	8.769	1.425	0.355	.020	.223	.245
9	P	1958 = 100	-0.84	-0.08	1.203	0.228	0.218	.012	.443	.429
10	LE	million	-0.33	-0.01	0.755	0.222	0.341	.011	.694	.723
11	UN	per cent	0.29	-0.004	0.670	0.338	6.256	.133	1.194	1.155
12	CPR	billion $	4.27	-0.02	5.490	5.513	12.174	.095	.141	0.928
13	LH	thousand hours/year	-0.0004	0.0002	0.007	0.005	0.251	.004	.962	.962
14	OUME	billion $	3.01	0.04	3.021	0.334	2.661	.258	.768	.741
15	RS	per cent	-0.03	-0.02	0.219	0.196	6.002	.059	.741	.761
16	RL	per cent	-0.04	-0.004	0.092	0.078	1.913	.022	.764	.767
17	W	dollar	-6.38	-0.36	6.378	0.795	0.309	.025	.294	.280
18	M	billion $	-1.14	0.0006	1.398	0.562	0.386	.001	.555	.570

a For meaning of symbols, see Table 1.1

b,c,d,e See corresponding footnotes to Table 3.1

change errors are on the average much smaller than the level errors; i.e., $|MEL| > |MEC|$ and $MAEL > MAEC$, which again is largely attributable to the cumulation of errors over time (columns 1 through 4). The absolute means of the relative change errors, MAERC, range from 0.2 percentage points for P to 12.2 percentage points for CPR, and are somewhat larger than 0.6 for GNP in current and constant dollars (column 5).

The relative accuracy analysis once more shows the level ratios, MAEL/MAAL, to be quite low, and much smaller than the corresponding change ratios, MAEC/MAAC and MAERC/MAARC, which tend to be similar (columns 6 through 8). The ratios of the average change errors fall in the range between .2 and .4 for GNP, YP, and W, and in the range .4 to .6 for $GNP58$, C, P, and M; and they exceed .6, but are less than one, for the other variables, except UN and NE where they are alone in exceeding unity (columns 7 and 8).

3.3.3   The correlations between the simulated and actual levels are very high for this model, exceeding .95 for twelve variables and .7 for fifteen variables; the lowest of these coefficients is that for the unemployment rate (.67). Correlations between the changes, ΔS_t and ΔA_t, are substantially lower, though still generally respectable; they vary from .27 to .95, but all except three exceed .5, while the correlations between the relative changes, $(\Delta S/S)_t$, and $(\Delta A/A)_t$, shown in Table 3.10, are in most instances lower still, but not by much. The highest of the change correlations, ranging from .6 to .8, are recorded for the two GNP series, C, IH, YP, P, NE, M, and the two interest rates. The lowest are those for UN and hours per man, LH, which are close to .3 (Table 3.10, columns 1 and 2).

The regressions of actual on simulated changes give encouraging results. For most variables, the hypothesis that $\alpha = 0$ and $\beta = 1$ cannot be rejected on any of the considered significance levels (columns 3 to 6). However, there are good grounds for rejection in the cases of P, LE, UN, and M, and for at least some doubts concerning ISE and CPR. Quite generally, there is little indication of bias here, and such problems as are suggested by the tests relate principally to inefficiency; i.e., deviations of the slope coefficients from unity (as a rule in the downward direction).

3.3.4   Peak-to-peak reference cycles are used for the measure-

TABLE 3.10

Nonstochastic Simulations for the Sample Period, FRB-MIT-PENN Model:
Correlation, Regression, and Test Statistics
(1956–1966)

Line	Variable Symbol[a]	Correlation of Simulated With Actual Changes[b]		Regression of Actual on Simulated Changes[c]			
		r (1)	$\bar{r}^2$ (2)	Constant (a) (3)	Slope (b) (4)	F-ratio for ($\alpha=0$, $\beta=1$)[d] (5)	t-test for $\beta=1$[e] (6)
1	GNP	.633	.387	.003	.848	0.78	0.94
2	GNP58	.652	.411	.002	.772	1.34	1.63
3	C	.674	.440	.002	.802	1.06	1.44
4	IH	.740	.536	.0002	1.196	0.67	1.15
5	ISE	.573	.312	.004	.655	2.78	2.36
6	II[f]	.488	.219	.337	.742	1.07	1.24
7	NE[f]	.905	.813	.043	.979	0.18	0.25
8	YP	.690	.464	.004	.805	1.66	1.48
9	P	.601	.346	.003	.564	9.44	3.72
10	LE	.535	.269	.002	.586	4.14	2.87

TABLE 3.10 (concluded)

Line	Variable Symbol[a]	Correlation of Simulated With Actual Changes[b]		Regression of Actual on Simulated Changes[c]			
		r (1)	$\bar{r}^2$ (2)	Constant (a) (3)	Slope (b) (4)	F-ratio for $(\alpha = 0, \beta = 1)$[d] (5)	t-test for $\beta = 1$[e] (6)
11	UN[f]	.275	.053	−.004	.341	6.26	3.54
12	CPR	.556	.292	.006	.675	2.13	2.06
13	LH	.328	.086	−.0003	.577	1.34	1.63
14	$OUME$	.578	.318	−.002	.954	0.14	0.22
15	RS^t	.799	.630	.013	.975	0.08	0.21
16	RL^t	.676	.444	.009	.901	0.25	0.65
17	W	.565	.302	.002	.876	1.76	0.62
18	M	.729	.520	.204	.613	9.24	4.30

a For meaning of symbols, see Table 1.1.

b,c,f See the corresponding footnotes in Table 3.2.

d Some of the relevant percentage points of the F-distribution (for $n_1 = 2$, $n_2 = 42$) are: $F_{0.01} = 5.16$, $F_{0.05} = 3.21$, $F_{0.10} = 2.44$, and $F_{0.25} = 1.44$.

e Some of the relevant percentage points of the t-distribution ($n = 42$, two-tailed test) are: 2.70, 2.02, 1.68, and 1.17 (for 1, 5, 10, and 25 per cent significance levels, respectively).

ment of the average amplitudes in Table 3.11 because, assuming a peak in 1966, there are two such complete cycles in the sample period of the FMP Model (1957–58–60 and 1960–61–66), whereas there is only one complete trough-to-trough cycle (1958–60–61).

During expansions, S rose on the average less than A for fourteen variables, and declined less than A for the unemployment rate, whose movement is typically countercyclical. In the single case of RL, S increased more than A. Both A and S had negative signs for investment in housing and net exports, and their signs differed for hours per man in the private nonfarm sector, LH. However, the average changes per month were exceedingly small in each of these cases.

During contractions, S tended to decline less than A for seven variables and to increase less than A for the unemployment rate. The net exports, personal income, price level, wage-rate, and money-supply series continued to rise, and the corresponding simulations had still larger average increases. For $GNP58$, consumption, and employment the A series show small declines and the S series show small rises. Finally, both A and S fell by about equal average amounts in the case of IH, while for RL the decline in S was somewhat larger than that in A.

When amplitudes for the full cycle (expansion minus contraction) are compared for simulated and actual series, actual amplitudes exceed simulated ones in all but four cases: net exports, long term interest rates, and the two perversely behaving series, prices and money supply. These measures confirm the fact that cyclical fluctuations in the actual series tend to be underestimated by those in the simulations.

The strongest expression of the tendency for the S series to vary over time less than the actuals is provided by the mean absolute percentage changes in the trend-cycle components (columns 7 and 8). According to these measures, S had a smaller average amplitude than A for each of the included variables.

The differences in average variability across the series are reproduced very well in the simulations. The ranks based on the expansion measures in columns 1 and 2 show a correlation of .967; those based on the contraction measures in columns 3 and 4 have a correlation of .991; and those based on the trend-cycle component measures in columns 7 and 8 have a correlation of .991.

TABLE 3.11

Nonstochastic Simulations for the Sample Period, FRB-MIT-PENN Model:
Average Amplitudes of Cyclical and Trend Movements
(1956–1966)

| Line | Variable Symbol[a] | Average Change Per Month in Reference-Cycle Relatives[b] During: | | | | | | Mean Absolute Per Cent Change Trend-Cycle Component[c] | |
| | | Expansions | | Contractions | | Full Cycle | | | |
		Simu-lated (1)	Actual (2)	Simu-lated (3)	Actual (4)	Simu-lated (5)	Actual (6)	Simu-lated (7)	Actual (8)
1	GNP	.52	.62	.14	.11	.38	.51	1.36	1.55
2	GNP58	.40	.47	-.07	-.26	.47	.73	1.02	1.16
3	C	.40	.42	.03	-.06	.37	.48	.97	1.01
4	IH	-.07	-.00	-.40	-.39	.33	.39	1.94	2.47
5	ISE	.60	.74	-.50	-1.12	1.10	1.86	2.07	2.23
6	II	.10	.36	-.31	-.88	.41	1.24	.91	1.47
7	NE	-.05	-.07	.28	.13	-.33	-.20	.56	.64
8	YP	.50	.57	.25	.08	.25	.49	1.34	1.42
9	P	.11	.14	.23	.16	-.12	-.02	.42	.49
10	LE	.13	.18	.01	-.15	.12	.33	.37	.46
11	UN	-.07	-.25	.02	.05	.09	.30	3.65	4.71

(continued)

TABLE 3.11 (concluded)

Line	Variable symbol[a]	Average Change Per Month in Reference-Cycle Relatives[b] During:						Mean Absolute Per Cent Change Trend-Cycle Component	
		Expansions		Contractions		Full cycle			
		Simulated (1)	Actual (2)	Simulated (3)	Actual (4)	Simulated (5)	Actual (6)	Simulated (7)	Actual (8)
12	CPR	.72	1.00	-.79	-1.72	1.51	2.72	2.94	3.61
13	LH	-.00	.01	-.07	-.11	.07	.12	.13	.21
14	OUME	.61	.99	-.70	-1.74	1.31	2.73	2.40	3.49
15	RS	.04	.06	-.13	-.18	.17	.24	5.98	6.80
16	RL	.021	.018	-.037	-.010	.058	.028	1.78	2.36
17	W	.32	.38	.29	.18	.03	.20	.95	1.05
18	M	.19	.21	.29	.13	-.10	.08	.66	.66

NOTE: The period covered by the measures in columns 1 through 6 from the peak in 1957-III to the assumed peak in 1966-IV (see text).

[a] For meaning of symbols, see Table 1.1.

[b] Based on quarterly data but expressed as rate per month (quarterly rates would be three times as large). Figures for all series except II, NE, UN, RS, and RL are expressed as reference-cycle relatives; that is, as a percentage of the average level of the series during each business (reference) cycle. Figures for II, NE, UN, RS, and RL are expressed in absolute units. (See Table 1.1 for units.)

[c] Average quarter-to-quarter percentage change, without regard to sign, in the trend-cyclical component—a smooth, flexible moving average of the seasonally adjusted series.

3.3.5   Table 3.12 represents an attempt to identify the timing characteristics of twelve S series produced by the FMP Model, and to compare them with the record of the corresponding A series.

The simulated series in current dollars for GNP and YP show no declines corresponding to those in actual GNP during the 1957–58 and 1960–61 recessions. For the price level and the wage rate, neither A nor S shows any cyclical contractions during the period covered. Hence these variables are omitted from the timing comparisons of Table 3.12. Also excluded is net exports, for which the series show pronounced and well correlated fluctuations but poor conformity to business cycles.

Because of the shortness of the sample period and scarcity of observations at turning points, it has been particularly difficult to infer the timing properties of the S series for this model. For six of the twelve variables included in Table 3.12 – C, ISE, LE, UN, LH, and $OUME$ – our verdict in column 7 had to be "not identified." However, this is due primarily to the relatively weak conformity of these simulated series, which is shown by the frequency with which they skipped the business-cycle turns (column 1). It does not necessarily follow that the timing of S was very different from that of A for the variables concerned; in fact, where comparisons can be made, similarities definitely prevail. Thus, of the 38 comparisons (there were 38 turns in S and 50 in A for the data covered in Table 3.12, including the "extra" turns), 21 indicate complete agreement; i.e., coincident timing of matched turning points for the paired series, 10 consist of leads or lags of one quarter, and only 7 involve larger timing discrepancies. Also, the average leads or lags of A and S at the reference turns are not greatly different, being not more than 1.5 quarters apart in any case, and less than one quarter apart for all but three variables.

3.3.6   This section summarizes what can be learned from the reference-cycle patterns for the FMP sample-period simulations. Chart 3.6 presents a selection of such diagrams for the two peak-trough-peak cycles covered (1957–58–60 and 1960–61–66) and the corresponding average patterns; as before, each graph matches the pattern for S against that for A.

On the whole, the patterns for the S series resemble those for the A series rather well, but the differences between them tend, again, to be systematic, in that the S patterns are "flatter"; i.e., have the smaller

TABLE 3.12

Nonstochastic Simulations for the Sample Period, FRB-MIT-PENN Model: Timing at Business-Cycle Turns and Corresponding Measures for the Actual Values (1956–1966)

Line	Variable Symbol[a]	Frequencies of Timing Observations for Series S and A						Dominant Type of Timing (7)
		Business-Cycle Turns Skipped[b] (1)	Extra Turns[b] (2)	Leads (3)	Exact Coincidences (4)	Lags (5)	Long Leads or Lags[c] (6)	
1	GNP58 S	0	0	2	1	1	0	coincident?
2	A	0	0	2	2	0	0	coincident
3	C S	2	0	1	0	1	0	n.i.
4	A	0	0	1	2	1	0	coincident
5	IH S	0	1	2	1	0	2	leading-irregular
6	A	0	1	2	1	0	1	leading-irregular
7	ISE S	2	0	1	0	1	0	n.i.
8	A	0	2	0	2	2	0	coincident-lagging
9	II S	0	2	1	1	1	0	coincident?
10	A	0	2	2	1	0	0	leading-coincident
11	LE S	2	0	0	1	1	0	n.i.
12	A	0	0	0	3	1	0	coincident
13	UN[d] S	2	0	0	1	1	0	n.i.

TABLE 3.12 (concluded)

Frequencies of Timing Observations for Series S and A

Line	Variable Symbol[a]	Business-Cycle Turns Skipped[b] (1)	Extra Turns[b] (2)	Leads (3)	Exact Coincidences (4)	Lags (5)	Long Leads or Lags[c] (6)	Dominant Type of Timing (7)
14	A	0	0	2	1	1	0	coincident-leading
15	CPR S	0	0	3	1	0	0	leading
16	A	0	0	3	0	1	0	leading-irregular
17	LH S	2	1	1	0	1	1	n.i.
18	A	0	1	2	1	1	2	leading-coincident
19	OUME S	2	0	1	0	1	0	n.i.
20	A	0	0	2	0	2	1	leading-lagging
21	RS S	0	0	1	1	2	1	lagging-coincident
22	A	0	0	1	1	2	0	lagging-coincident
23	RL S	0	0	1	1	2	1	lagging-coincident
24	A	0	0	1	2	1	1	coincident-lagging
25	M S	0	0	4	0	0	2	leading
26	A	0	0	4	0	0	2	leading

[a] For meaning of symbols, see Table 1.1. S refers to simulations, A to actuals.
[b] See explanation in text.
[c] Leads or lags of three or more quarters. All figures here refer to leads.
[d] Treated on the inverted plan; see Table 3.4.

CHART 3.6

Nonstochastic Simulations for the Sample Period, FRB-MIT-PENN Model: Reference-Cycle Patterns for Simulated and Actual Series, Selected Variables
(1957–1964)

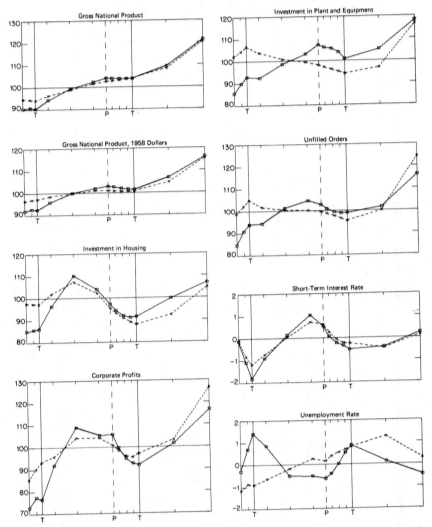

NOTE: Scale in reference-cycle relatives or (for unemployment rate and short-term interest rate) in absolute deviations from cycle base. *P* and *T* stand for peaks and troughs, respectively.

amplitudes. For series that declined very mildly during the contractions of 1957–58 and 1960–61, the S patterns show still smaller declines (as for $GNP58$), or virtually no change (C), or very small rises (GNP, YP). Yet these discrepancies are generally small, and the expansion-contraction contrasts brought out in the A patterns reappear nearly as strongly in the corresponding S patterns. The diagrams for employment, LE, present a similar picture, except for poorer correspondence between S and A in the 1957–60 cycle. Prices and wages show less retardation of growth during the two recessions covered, and this is broadly reflected in the S patterns for these variables, too. The patterns for total hours per man, LH, show very little change in terms of reference-cycle relatives during any of the episodes covered, for S as well as for A.

Some impressive similarities between the cyclical movements of S and A can be observed in the patterns for several variables that are subject to large fluctuations with diverse timing. This can certainly be said about the difficult to estimate investment in housing IH, particularly with reference to the expansion periods 1958–60 and 1961–66. (Interestingly, the fit in the early 1957–58 phase is appreciably less satisfactory.) For plant and equipment ISE, the patterns of A and S also bear good family resemblance, except for the 1958–60 expansion, during which A rose but S fell. Even for inventory investment, the agreement between the patterns is good as regards the direction of change and the timing of the turning points, although the diagram for the 1957–60 cycle shows large discrepancies between the reference-cycle relatives for A and S in all except the trough stage. A remarkably close agreement is disclosed by the patterns for net exports. There is much less conformity among the patterns for the unemployment rate and the unfilled orders for machinery and equipment industries, but, interestingly, it is again the early-1957–60 cycle (and particularly its expansion phase, 1958–60) that accounts for the largest divergencies between the simulated and the actual patterns in these variables (UN and $OUME$). The general shape of the cyclical movements in corporate profits is rather well reproduced in the S patterns, but the deviations of the relatives for simulated CPR from their counterparts for the recorded values are large during the 1957–60 cycle. Finally, very good agreement exists between the S and A patterns for both the short-term and the long-term interest rate.

3.4 SUMMARY INTERPRETATIONS AND COMPARISONS

3.4.1   The cyclical aspects of the nonstochastic sample-period simulations reviewed in this part of our study can be summarized briefly by concentrating on the behavior of the simulations for real *GNP* during each of the general business recessions covered. (See Charts 3.1, 3.3, and 3.5.) These comparisons indicate that each model reflects cyclical behavior substantially better in the early part of its simulation period than in the later part. Each of the models shows the economy (measured by real *GNP*) as declining during the first recession period covered (1948–49 for Wharton, 1953–54 for OBE, and 1957–58 for FMP), or at least during part of this period. The three models also have *GNP58* contracting, or at least flattening out, during the contractions in 1953–54, 1957–58, and 1960–61, respectively. The Wharton Model does not produce a fall in *GNP58* during the recession of 1957–58, and neither the Wharton nor the OBE Model produces one in the 1960–61 recession. Although the FMP Model does produce such declines in these two periods, it would be wrong to conclude that it is better, inasmuch as the initial conditions for this model, being as of 1956-I are much closer to these episodes than are the initial conditions for Wharton and OBE. Had the FMP Model been started in 1948 or 1953, its results for the 1957–58 and 1960–61 declines might have been similar to those obtained for the other models. Or, to put it the other way around, if the initial conditions were selected as of a late date (say 1956) for Wharton and OBE, then it is likely that these models would perform better in the last two recessions, perhaps in a way similar to the FMP predictions.[19]

The important conclusion is that there appears to be a progressive *dampening* of the fluctuations the further away a model's simulation proceeds from its initial-conditions period. This type of movement would be characteristic of a hypothetical economy representing a stable macro-dynamic system insulated from external disturbances. The diminishing oscillations in such a model originate in the divergencies

---

[19] According to A. L. Nagar, "Stochastic Simulation of the Brookings Econometric Model" [10, Chapter 12; see in particular, pp. 443–44]. "Better predictions of 1957–58 and 1960–61 would have been observed [in the Brookings simulations] if initial conditions closer to those dates had been selected." As evidence on this point, Nagar cites results obtained in [10, Chapter 11] and [17].

from equilibrium that are likely to exist in any initial state of the system; they tend to disappear as the system approaches its equilibrium rate of growth.

The hypothesis is then naturally completed by the notion that external disturbances, or "erratic shocks," do, in fact, impinge upon the economy continually. The response of the system to these irregular but persistent shocks is such that the damped fluctuations are converted into a maintained movement of the type historically observed as the recurrent business cycles. Following an important paper by Ragnar Frisch [16], this hypothesis gained a strong foothold in business-cycle theory, and became particularly influential in regard to aggregate econometric model-building.[20]

It is possible for a simple macroeconomic model to produce a heavily damped time-path of aggregate real income (output) when solved deterministically (i.e., without random disturbances), but to produce a maintained quasi-cyclical movement when solved stochastically (i.e., with addition of random disturbances).[21] It might appear, therefore, that the failure of nonstochastic sample-period simulations to re-create the continuous cyclical developments that did occur at the time need not, under the above hypothesis, constitute any adverse evidence about the structure of the underlying model. Instead, such results could be due to the suppression of the disturbance terms.

However, it must be noted that the simulations here reviewed use ex post values of exogenous variables and incorporate the effects of any changes in these variables. The latter include a large subset of "autonomous" shocks, such as changes in government defense and nondefense expenditures on goods and services, transfer payments, tax rates, monetary base, reserve requirements, population, exports, and so on.[22] This class of disturbances covers the major impact of monetary and fiscal policy changes, and is presumably very important,

[20] Frisch, writing in 1933, credits a 1907 Swedish address by Knut Wicksell with the first formulation of this hypothesis. Another important antecedent here is the 1927 paper by Slutsky [28].

[21] For hypothetical examples, see the 1940 paper by Haavelmo [19] and the 1952 article by G. H. Fisher [15]. The 1959 study by Irma and Frank L. Adelman [2] provides an empirical illustration.

[22] The models differ with respect to the identity and contents of exogenous variables, as noted in Section 1.3, but it seems safe to view the autonomous shocks as generally important.

particularly since these (partly nonstochastic) shocks may often cause relatively prolonged repercussions within the economic system. What the sample-period simulations suppress, then, is not these exogenous factors but rather the stochastic components of the endogenous variables. The nondefinitional structural relationships among these variables involve disturbance terms that reflect the impact of a variety of "unique" events, as well as errors of sampling, aggregation, and other aspects of measurement and specification.[23]

We cannot be certain that it is the disregarding of these sources of irregularity that is predominantly responsible for the errors (deviations from A) of the nonstochastic sample-period simulations. It can hardly be doubted that there are mis-specification errors in the models, which could be just as important. The autocorrelations of the disturbance terms in some of the original structural equations are high enough to be disturbing. The failure of the simulations to track major cyclical movements can often be traced to certain specific relations that seem weak; e.g., those for inventory investment or the price levels. Under an alternative hypothesis that business cycles are generated endogenously by a deterministic economic system, the absence of confluent specific cycles in the S series would have to be judged as indicative of serious specification errors in the given model. (Hypotheses in this class may well be, to a large extent, implausible or unsubstantiated, but to dismiss all of them a priori would be illegitimate, just begging the issue.)

The point of the argument is simply that the evidence of the nonstochastic sample-period simulations alone is inadequate as a basis for discriminating between the different hypotheses. If the performance of these simulations is deemed unsatisfactory, the next logical step is to construct and examine stochastic simulations — which could prove considerably more realistic, thereby lending support to the random-shock hypothesis. On the other hand, it is possible to give more emphasis to the similarities between the nonstochastic S series and the actuals; that is, to the capacity of the model to reproduce the economy's short-term movements even when the random error terms in the

---

[23] It is the existence of the random error terms in the behavioral equations of the KG Model that explains the introduction of shocks of Type II by the Adelmans. See [2, Section 8].

determination of the endogenous variables are omitted. But then one must remember that these similarities are rather short-lived and must ask next whether nonstochastic simulations beyond the sample period reflect the expected type of fluctuations in any substantial measure. And, since no one can seriously deny that models of the economy must be treated as stochastic because of the importance of random elements of behavior, gaps in knowledge, and inevitability of aggregation, it would still be necessary to study stochastic simulations in an effort to learn what difference the disturbances make or how much they matter.

Another pertinent consideration is that we are dealing here with long-run simulations, whereas the models on which these calculations are based were designed to serve primarily as short-term predictive and analytical devices. Simulations of this kind, therefore, may impose "a severe strain on the underlying assumptions and rationale used to justify the model structure," according to another paper prepared for this Conference.[24] Errors in lagged dependent variables may well cumulate, causing increasing errors at later points of time in the sample period. This argument, of course, relates to stochastic as well as to nonstochastic simulations; but, in the latter, the disregard of disturbance terms is an additional source of errors, which are subject to interaction and cumulation over time through the effects of the lagged variables. This factor must be recognized as a potentially severe handicap for the nonstochastic simulations, which is likely to counteract the favorable factors that tend to cause overstatement of the closeness of fit for simulations which cover, or largely overlap, the sample period. (Such simulations, of course, benefit from the fact that the coefficients of the model have been estimated from data for the same period, as well as from being based on ex post values of the exogenous variables.)

3.4.2 How do the models compare with one another in terms of the relative accuracy of their simulations? For reasons already noted (Section 1.3 above), this question cannot be answered with confidence on the basis of the available materials. Table 3.13 collects some measures of the kind that would be helpful in this context, but it is not conclusive because of the differences in coverage among the models.

The table lists first the mean absolute errors of relative change, in

---

[24] See [18, p. 67]; also [14, p. 147].

TABLE 3.13

Nonstochastic Sample-Period Simulations for Three Models: Average Errors of Relative Change and Their Ratios to Average Values of Actual Relative Change

Model and Period	Simulations for the Variables[a]				
	GNP (1)	*GNP58* (2)	*P* (3)	*ISE* (4)	*UN* (5)
Mean Absolute Error of Relative Change (MAERC), in percentage points[b]					
1 Wharton, 1948-III–1968-I	1.17	1.12	0.27	3.12	17.80
2 OBE, 1953-II–1966-IV	0.70	0.64	0.24	1.90	6.00
3 FMP, 1956-I–1966-IV	0.61	0.65	0.22	1.79	6.26
Ratio of MAERC to Mean Absolute Relative Change in Actuals $\left(\frac{MAERC}{MAARC}\right)$[c]					
4 Wharton, 1948-III–1968-I	0.681	0.852	0.453	1.036	2.502
5 OBE, 1953-II–1966-IV	0.459	0.518	0.488	0.812	0.890
6 FMP, 1956-I–1966-IV	0.377	0.524	0.429	0.746	1.155

[a] For meaning of symbols, see text or Table 1.1.
[b] Source: Tables 3.1, 3.5, and 3.9 (*see column 5 in each table*).
[c] Source: Tables 3.1, 3.5, and 3.9 (*see column 8 in each table*).

percentage points, for five selected variables: *GNP* in current and constant dollars, the price level, business expenditures on plant and equipment, and the unemployment rate (*GNP, GNP58, P, ISE, UN*). According to these figures, the errors of the Wharton simulations are on the average considerably larger than those of either the OBE or the FMP simulations, except for *P*, where the differences are small (compare lines 1, 2, and 3). The MAERC measures for the OBE Model are not very different from those for the FMP Model. However, the Wharton simulations cover a much longer period than the others, including the unsettled and difficult to fit developments of the late 1940's and the Korean War, which could account for the larger deviations between *S* and *A* for this model.

Dividing MAERC by the mean absolute values of actual relative change (MAARC) is a standardizing procedure which probably tends to correct for the differences in the sample periods but does not guarantee an unbiased comparison. The ratios MAERC/MAARC (lines 4 to 6) show smaller differences between the models than do the MAERC figures, but the models would be ranked very similarly according to the two measures. The FMP simulations show the smallest ratios, except for *GNP58* and *UN*, where the ratios for the OBE Model are lower. The differences between the simulations for OBE and FMP are still small according to the MAERC/MAARC figures; and for the price-level simulations, the differences remain small among all three models.

3.4.3 Finally, it is also instructive to compare the models with respect to their ability to simulate the diverse timing characteristics of selected endogenous variables. Table 3.14 assembles the relevant evidence, which indicates that the simulations do discriminate broadly between the groups of series that are typically leading or lagging at business-cycle turns, but that they do not carry this differentiation nearly as far as the actual timing distributions do. For example, among the five leading variables in the Wharton Model, leads outnumber lags by 23 to 2, according to the actuals; and by 13 to 6, according to the simulations (in percentage terms, 62 to 5 and 56 to 26, respectively). See Table 3.14, lines 1 and 2. Similarly, among the three lagging variables, actual lags outnumber leads 13 to 2; whereas in the simulations, there are 10 lags and 7 leads (the corresponding proportions here being 50 to 8 per cent for the actual, and 46 to 32 per cent for the simulated, scores). See lines 5 and 6. The worst results are obtained for the six roughly coincident indicators, where exact coincidences make up 51 per cent of the timing observations for the actual series, but only 9 per cent of those for the simulated series. (The leads and lags are nearly balanced for the latter, as shown in lines 3 and 4.)

The results for the other two models point to the same general conclusion. The OBE Model differentiates between the leaders and laggers better than does the Wharton Model but still not as well as the historical series (lines 9 and 10, 13 and 14). For the coinciders, the performance of the OBE Model is poor in that coincidences constitute a small minority of the timing comparisons for the simulated series, while the proportions of leads and lags are both large (lines 11 and 12). As for the FMP Model, it gives good results for the leaders, while overstating somewhat the proportion of lags among the laggers (lines 17 and 18, 21 and 22). But the FMP simulations, too, are disappointing on the group of roughly coincident series, where they show lags to

TABLE 3.14

Nonstochastic Sample-Period Simulations for Three Models; Absolute and Relative Frequency Distributions of Leads and Lags at Business-Cycle Turns

Line	Group of Variables[a] (number and symbols in parentheses) (1)	Number or Percentage (1)	Actuals				Simulations			
			Total (2)	Leads (3)	Exact Coincidences (4)	Lags (5)	Total (6)	Leads (7)	Exact Coincidences (8)	Lags (9)
			Wharton Model (1948–68)[b]							
1	Leading (5: IH, II, CPR, AWW, UMD)	number	37	23	12	2	23	13	4	6
2		per cent	100.0	62.2	32.4	5.4	100.0	56.5	17.4	26.1
3	Coincident (6: GNP, GNP58, C, YP, LE, UN)	number	43	15	22	6	23	10	2	11
4		per cent	100.0	34.9	51.2	14.0	100.0	43.5	8.7	47.8
5	Lagging (3: ISE, RS, RL)	number	26	2	11	13	22	7	5	10
6		per cent	100.0	7.7	42.3	50.0	100.0	31.8	22.7	45.5
7	All (14)	number	106	40	45	21	68	30	11	27
8		per cent	100.0	37.7	42.5	19.8	100.0	44.1	16.2	34.7

OBE Model (1953–66)[c]

9	Leading (8: IH, II, M, CPR, AWW, OMD, UMD, HS)	number	44	32	9	3	34	25	5	4
10		per cent	100.0	72.7	20.5	6.8	100.0	73.5	14.7	11.8
11	Coincident (6: GNP, GNP58, C, YP, LE, UN)	number	34	13	17	4	12	5	2	5
12		per cent	100.0	38.2	50.0	11.8	100.0	41.7	16.7	41.7
13	Lagging (4: ISE, RS, RL, LC/O)	number	24	2	5	17	18	2	5	11
14		per cent	100.0	8.3	20.8	70.8	100.0	11.1	27.8	61.1
15	All (18)	number	102	47	31	24	64	32	12	20
16		per cent	100.0	46.1	30.4	23.5	100.0	50.0	18.8	31.2

FMP Model (1956–66)[d]

17	Leading (6: IH, II, CPR, OUME, LH)	number	22	15	3	4	18	12	3	3
18		per cent	100.0	68.2	13.6	18.2	100.0	66.7	16.7	16.7
19	Coincident (4: GNP58, C, LE, UN)	number	16	5	8	3	10	3	3	4
20		per cent	100.0	31.2	50.0	18.8	100.0	30.0	30.0	40.0
21	Lagging (3: ISE, RS, RL)	number	12	2	5	5	10	3	2	5
22		per cent	100.0	16.7	41.7	41.7	100.0	30.0	20.0	50.0
23	All (13)	number	50	22	16	12	38	18	8	12
24		per cent	100.0	44.0	32.0	24.0	100.0	47.4	21.1	31.6

[a] Classified according to the timing of the historical data.
[b] Based on Table 3.4.
[c] Based on Table 3.8.
[d] Based on Table 3.12.

be more frequent than coincidences, and leads to be as frequent (lines 19 and 20).

For each model and in each timing category, the simulated series offer fewer observations than do the actual series, as can be seen by comparing columns 2 and 6 in Table 3.14. This reflects our finding that the S series "skipped" business-cycle turns more frequently than did the A series, particularly for the roughly coincident indicators.[25]

When all the variables included in the comparisons for a given model are combined, without regard to their historical timing, the resulting summary distributions show that the proportion of coincidences was heavily underestimated in the simulations; the proportion of leads somewhat overestimated; and that of lags, strongly overestimated. This is observed for each of the three models (lines 7 and 8, 15 and 16, and 23 and 24).

These findings suggest that the models are wanting in ability to identify the leaders and laggers, and to separate them from the coinciders. It is true that the procedure favors the actuals somewhat, in that they were used in classifying the variables according to timing, but the importance of this factor should not be exaggerated. The classification was, in fact, based to a large extent on historical information other than that contained in the sample-period actuals (e.g., GNP, C, or YP would always be treated as coinciders, although leads were more, or at least not less, frequent than coincidences in some of the periods covered).

Neither does it appear that the results are attributable to the exclusion of the stochastic elements from the simulated series. Suppose that the true timing of a variable is coincident but that this is obscured by erratic movements which cause some turning points to be misdated in the direction of extremes — leads or lags. Given small-sample data — evidence limited to short time-series — misclassification could result. Had this happened often enough, however, we should have found the proportion of coincidences to be greater in the nonstochastic simulations than in the actuals; yet, in point of fact, the opposite is found to apply. Actually, the distinctions between the leaders and laggers are in

---

[25] It should be noted that Table 3.14 covers only the series listed in the underlying Tables 3.4, 3.8, and 3.12. These tables omitted a few variables for which too few — or no — timing observations could be made for either S alone or for both S and A. GNP and YP (both coincident) were excluded from the comparisons for the FMP Model because of the lack of turning points in the S series.

large part based on sound a priori or theoretical considerations, and on substantial empirical evidence of business-cycle history—such as recurrent, and presumably typical, timing sequences. To this extent, then, the timing classifications represent systematic differences not random phenomena.

The greater frequency of laggers among the S series could be due to some induced smoothing effects; in particular, the use of distributed lag equations. In future work, it may prove interesting to check out this possibility.[26]

4 HUNDRED-QUARTER EX ANTE STOCHASTIC SIMULATIONS

THIS part of our report presents an analysis of replicated simulations in which random shocks are applied on a continued basis to estimated equations of selected systems. Such simulations were received for two models only, Wharton and OBE. As proposed in the plans for this Conference, each of these simulations covers twenty-five years beyond the model's sample period. For the Wharton Model, fifty simulations use serially uncorrelated random shocks, and fifty use serially correlated shocks. For the OBE Model, there are twenty-five runs with nonautocorrelated shocks and twenty-five runs with autocorrelated shocks.

The random shocks used in the stochastic simulations for both models were generated according to a procedure developed by Michael McCarthy.[27] The method is such that the expected value of the var-

[26] Note that ordinary smoothing of a time-series by means of moving averages can shift the timing of the turns in the series in either direction, and in random or systematic ways; the outcome depends on the statistical structure of the series and the smoothing formula applied. (See A. F. Burns and W. C. Mitchell, *Measuring Business Cycles,* pp. 316–326.) Lags will often be produced at terminal turns of brief but large cyclical movements, especially at troughs, while leads of smoothed data may be more frequent at peaks. However, it is important to recognize that smoothing does not eliminate the irregular component movements of a series; it merely redistributes them over time in successive values of that series. In contrast, stochastic elements are presumably excluded from the S series here considered.

[27] See M. D. McCarthy, "Some Notes on the Generation of Pseudo Structural Errors for Use in Stochastic Simulation Studies" [14, Appendix].

iance-covariance matrix of the shocks over the simulation period is equal to the variance-covariance matrix of the observed residuals over the sample period. In those runs where the shocks are serially correlated, such lag correlations are also, for a sufficiently large number of observations, equal to the corresponding sample values obtained for the residual matrix.

It will be noted that these procedures differ in several respects from the approach adopted in the Adelmans' study, where the simulations are annual, unreplicated (from a single run), and based only on serially uncorrelated shocks, on the assumption of zero covariance of errors. On the whole, the innovations enrich the potential of the simulations and their analysis. But doubt has been expressed about another deviation from the Adelmans' method [18, p. 77]. They used the ratio of the standard deviation of the residuals to the average value of the normalized dependent variable in the sample period as the basis for scaling their shocks in the simulation period, whereas, here, the basis is the standard deviation of the sample-period residuals itself. The latter standard could result in unduly small shocks if the variances of the true normalized equation errors were heteroscedastic — increasing over time with the levels of the simulated series.

For each model, the initial topic of discussion will be the major properties of the nonstochastic simulations beyond the sample period; that is, of the "control solution." This is necessary in order to introduce the main body of our analysis, which is concerned with the stochastic simulations. We shall present measures relating to the frequency, duration, and relative size of (a) rises and declines and (b) cyclical expansions and contractions in the stochastically simulated series. The difference between the two sets is that in (a) any upward movement, however short or small, is treated as a rise, with downward movements of any magnitude being treated as a decline, while in (b) movements must be sufficiently long and pronounced to qualify as "specific cycle" expansions or contractions, under the rules of NBER cyclical analysis. Thus in (a) any directional change in a series separates a rise from a decline, which permits an entirely objective identification of these movements; whereas in (b), the selection of the turning points between expansions and contractions is in principle a matter for trained judgment, although computer procedures for a mechanical approximation to this task have recently been designed and tested with generally good results [4].

The distributions of both the (*a*) and (*b*) measures should be compared with those of their counterparts for the sample-period actuals. But in some of the simulated series, there are very few declines and no cyclical contractions. This leads us to apply the measures not only to the shocked series proper, but also to the relative deviations of these series from the corresponding control series. The analysis is carried out for simulations with serially uncorrelated shocks, as well as for those with serially correlated shocks, so that the two sets can be compared at each point with respect to their relative performance.

Finally, the relative timing of the simulated series is analyzed with the aid of the cyclical turning points, as determined in (*b*), to see whether the typical sequence of leading, coinciding, and lagging indicators tends to be reproduced in these measures. This phase of the analysis is also applied to both types of simulation and, as required by the nature of the data, to either the levels or the deviations from trend or both.

It would have been excessively costly to execute this full program for all the simulation runs of each model, but it would also be undesirable to discard much of the potentially useful information. As a compromise, therefore, all runs were used in the analysis of the periodicities in the *GNP* and *GNP58* series; but elsewhere, measures were compiled and interpreted for random samples of a few simulation runs of a given type.

4.1 THE WHARTON MODEL

4.1.1 These simulations start in 1968-III, which is already beyond the space of sample experience, and run for one-hundred quarters into the future, to end in 1993-II. Initial values of predetermined variables were set at levels assumed to be realistic, and the further course of the exogenous factors during the entire simulation period was determined so as to keep the unemployment rate within the narrow range of 3.7 to 4.7 per cent, and the short-term and long-term interest rates within the narrow ranges of 4.4 to 4.6 per cent, and 5.3 to 5.9 per cent, respectively, beginning in 1971. In other words, the exogenous variables are assumed to take on values that would keep the model economy moving along a steady long-run growth path, at least as far as the overall aggregates of national income and output are concerned. The exogenous variables reflect primarily U.S. fiscal and monetary policies.

In the first few years of the simulation period, some of the generated series show substantial disturbances, due mainly to the repercussions of the anticipated settlement of the war in Vietnam. In 1970 and the first half of 1971, reductions of military personnel by 350,000 men and of spending by $11.1 billion in 1958 prices are assumed—to follow a cease-fire.[28] The tax surcharge is discontinued and civilian expenditures are gradually increased, so that total government spending in current prices does not decline (though in real terms it does decline slightly for two quarters). The discount rate is reduced by 1/2 of 1 percentage point and net free reserves are maintained at $200 million.

The main consequence of the postulated changes is that the unemployment rate increases sharply from 4.3 to 5.5 per cent in 1969 and early 1970, only to fall again to nearly 4.1 per cent in mid-1972. The short-term interest rate declines from 5.8 to 4.6 per cent; and the long-term rate, from 6.5 to 5.7 per cent. Corporate profits wobble briefly in 1968–70, as do unfilled orders for durable manufactures and investment expenditures on plant and equipment; also, investment in housing pauses somewhat later, in 1971–73. But no general recession develops as personal income, consumption, and GNP in both current and constant dollars all rise steadily throughout the simulation period.

In fact, apart from the mild effects of the initial shock and transition, none of the nonstochastic simulation series that represent the "control solution" of the model display any significant fluctuations. There are some minor oscillations in variables such as profits and net exports, which are in the nature of residuals; and in the average workweek, unemployment, and interest rates. (These last-named series— simulated AWW, UN, RS, and RL—differ from all others in showing downward rather than upward drifts.) But the dominant feature of any and all of these series is simply persistent trends representing the simulated long-term growth of the economy. GNP grows from about $850

---

[28] See the section on "Long Run Simulations" in [14] for more detail on the assumptions discussed at this point and in the rest of the paragraph.

billion to $3,160 billion, or approximately 3.7 times; *GNP58*, from $700 billion to $1,660 billion, or nearly 2.4 times. These figures suggest that the projected rates of growth are, on the average, about 5.5 per cent per annum for *GNP* and 3.5 per cent per annum for *GNP58*.

It is important to recall that for the 1948–68 period, the nonstochastic simulations of the Wharton Model did show a considerable degree of cyclical response in several variables, including the most comprehensive aggregates, such as *GNP*, which had, at least, substantial retardations at the time of recessions in general economic activity. This is in marked contrast to the long post-sample-period nonstochastic simulations now considered, which are virtually cycle free, particularly for the over-all aggregates of national output, employment, and so on. Now, the main difference between the two sets of simulations lies in the treatment of the exogenous variables. In the 1948–68 calculations, these variables take on their "true" (i.e., ex post) recorded values, which include some large and long fluctuations. In the 1968–93 control solution, exogenous variables are constrained to assume pure trend values consistent with a long-run growth path in real *GNP* that keeps the unemployment rate at close to four per cent. It is, therefore, tempting to speculate that stronger cyclical elements might have been obtained had the exogenous variables been subjected to shocks or somehow made to fluctuate. It should be very interesting to test this hypothesis by means of experiments with shocked or auto-regressively fluctuating exogenous variables.[29] To be sure, there are other feasible explanations of the obtained results. It is possible, for example, that specification errors in the model account largely for the differences between the sample-period, and the post-sample-period, nonstochastic simulations.

In any event, since the latter simulations are based on very tentative projections of exogenous variables, they should be regarded merely as a "base-line solution," to be used for subsequent experiments with stochastic shocks, not as preferred long-period model predictions. This is stressed by the authors of both the Wharton Model and the OBE Model [14, p. 150], [18, p. 68]. But it is also necessary to empha-

[29] That is, we advocate (here, as well as for the simulations of other models) the addition of "shocks of Type I" to the "shocks of Type II," to use the Adelmans' terminology [2].

size two other facts: (1) it appears to be quite difficult, for either model, to produce reasonable behavior over long stretches of time in the chosen time-series included in the control solution; (2) at least, in the solutions here adopted, what seemed to be a satisfactory over-all course for the most comprehensive indicators of economic activity, such as *GNP*, was "purchased" at the expense of rather implausible behavior patterns for some other variables, notably unemployment and the interest rates. (This second point, too, applies to both the Wharton Model and the OBE Model. See Section 4.2.1 below.)

4.1.2   Chart 4.1 shows two randomly selected pairs of stochastic simulations for *GNP* and *GNP58*: one drawn from the fifty runs with non-autocorrelated shocks, and the other from the fifty runs with autocorrelated shocks. These curves are clearly dominated by growth trends. Inspection of similar charts for all runs discloses no important differences among the individual simulations in this respect.

The trends in the simulated series simply reflect the assumptions about the smooth growth in the exogenous variables that underlie the nonstochastic control solution of the model. They represent the common component of the series, whereas the effects of the random shocks show up in the oscillations of the series around the trends. As illustrated in Chart 4.1, there is considerable variation in the rates of change in the *GNP* and *GNP58* simulations from quarter to quarter. In the series with serially uncorrelated random shocks, growth is frequently interrupted by declines. The declines are generally short and relatively small, but they appear to be larger and more frequent in the constant-dollar *GNP* series than in the current-dollar *GNP* series.

In the *GNP* simulations with autocorrelated shocks, there are few declines and virtually none of more than one-quarter duration; many of these series show no downward movements at all. Fluctuations are again more frequent, and not quite so small, in the *GNP58* series, but here, too, the use of serially correlated shocks results in a reduction of both the number and the size of the declines.

The impressions conveyed by the charts are confirmed and quantified in Table 4.1, which summarizes several distributional measures. In each of the fifty runs with serially uncorrelated random shocks (S_u), there are one-quarter declines in the *GNP* series; in eighteen of the runs, one or two declines of two quarters each are also observed, but

CHART 4.1

*A Random Sample of Stochastic 100-Quarter Simulations for GNP
in Current and Constant Dollars, Wharton Model
(1968-III–1993-II)*

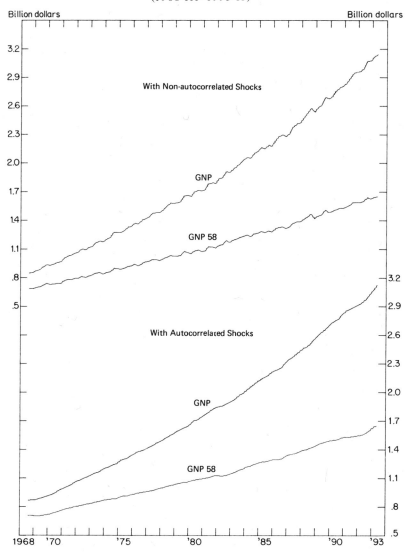

TABLE 4.1

Stochastic 100-Quarter Simulations, Wharton Model, and the Corresponding Sample-Period Actuals: Summary Statistics on Frequency, Duration, and Relative Size of Rises and Declines in Series for GNP and GNP58

Line	Type of Series and Movement	Frequency (number)		Duration (quarters)			Amplitude (per cent)	
		Mean or Total[a] (1)	Standard Deviation (S.D.)[b] (2)	Mean (per run)[c] (3)	S.D. (between runs)[b] (4)	S.D. (within runs)[d] (5)	Mean (per run)[e] (6)	S.D. (between runs)[b] (7)
				GNP in Current Dollars				
	Simulations with non-autocorrelated shocks: S_u							
1	Rises	10.71	2.87	9.02	3.05	7.53	1.88	0.20
2	Declines	9.94	2.82	1.05	0.07	0.12	0.55	0.16
	Simulations with autocorrelated shocks: S_c							
3	Rises	1.61	0.76	73.75	28.66	13.61	2.28	0.48
4	Declines	0.69	0.82	0.51	0.54	0.00	0.14	0.23
	Sample-period actuals: A							
5	Rises	8		8.12		9.69	1.85	
6	Declines	7		1.86		0.31	0.71	

TABLE 4.1 (concluded)

Line	Type of Series and Movement	Frequency (number)		Duration (quarters)			Amplitude (per cent)	
		Mean or Total[a] (1)	Standard Deviation (S.D.)[b] (2)	Mean (per run)[c] (3)	S.D. (between runs)[b] (4)	S.D. (within runs)[d] (5)	Mean (per run)[e] (6)	S.D. (between runs)[b] (7)
				GNP in Constant Dollars (GNP58)				
	S_u simulations							
7	Rises	21.35	2.83	3.60	0.65	2.43	1.64	0.16
8	Declines	21.02	2.68	1.14	0.08	0.33	0.75	0.15
	S_c simulations							
9	Rises	7.04	2.25	15.00	7.33	12.11	1.06	0.10
10	Declines	6.41	2.33	1.17	0.17	0.30	0.31	0.10
	A: actuals							
11	Rises	13		4.46		2.31	1.33	
12	Declines	11		1.73		1.19	0.68	

NOTE: All simulations refer to the 25-year period, 1968-III–1993-II; each average covers 50 runs. The actuals refer to the sample period, 1948-III–1968-I.

[a] For simulations: mean number per run; for actuals: total number (of rises or declines).

[b] Standard deviation of means per run (standard deviation between runs).

[c] For simulations: mean duration per run; for actuals: mean duration (of rises or declines).

[d] For simulations: mean standard deviation of the durations of rises or declines (standard deviation within runs); for actuals: standard deviation of the observed durations.

[e] For simulations: mean amplitude per run; for actuals: mean amplitude (of rises or declines). In per cent, at quarterly rate.

there are no longer contractions. Almost the reverse applies to the rises, among which one- or two-quarter movements are relatively few, movements of five or more quarters representing a majority. The mean durations are approximately one and nine quarters for falls and rises, respectively. However, there is no such contrast between the frequencies of occurrence per run, which average 10.7 for rises and 9.9 for declines (and range from 5 to 16 or 17 in either subset). Finally, the average amplitude per quarter is 1.9 per cent for the upward movements and 0.6 per cent for the downward ones (Table 4.1, lines 1 and 2).

In comparing such statistics for the simulations with figures on the corresponding attributes of historical series, it seems appropriate to stress the measures of frequency and duration, rather than those of amplitude. The random-shock hypothesis here considered asserts, in the formulation by Frisch [16, p. 171], that "the majority of the economic oscillations . . . seem to be explained most plausibly as free oscillations. . . . The most important feature of the free oscillations is that the length of the cycles and the tendency towards dampening are determined by the intrinsic structure of the swinging system, while the intensity (the amplitude) of the fluctuations is determined primarily by the exterior impulse." This suggests that the amplitudes of movements in the stochastic S series would depend mainly on the simulator's decision as to the magnitude of the shocks applied; they may be quite different from the amplitudes of the actuals, not because of any failure of the model to reproduce the basic structure of the economy, but because the impulses or shocks have not been properly scaled.

We have only one "run" that history has performed to produce the recorded "actuals"; we can compare its outcome with the over-all average from many experimental runs relating to the hypothetical future, allowing for the dispersion of the components of that average (the means of the individual runs). For example, the number of rises in GNP during the sample period is confronted with the mean frequency per run of rises in the simulated GNP series; i.e., of the corresponding averages for the individual runs. The declines are treated similarly. Accordingly, in Table 4.1, the entries for the S series in columns 1 and 2 are to be compared with those for A in column 1, and analogously for the duration and amplitude measures (columns 3 and 4, 6 and 7, respectively).

In addition, Table 4.1 shows the standard deviations of the durations of rises and declines in the sample-period actuals. These figures should be related to the mean standard deviations of the durations of rises and declines in the S series (that is, to the averages of the corresponding S.D. measures for the individual runs; see column 5).

During the period of nearly twenty years (1948-III–1968-I) used for the Wharton Model calculations in Part 3 of this report, seven declines occurred in the recorded quarterly GNP series. This does not appear inconsistent with the mean frequency of declines per run of 9.9 in the twenty-five year S_u simulations, with a standard deviation of 2.8 (Table 4.1, columns 1 and 2). However, the downward movements lasted on the average 1.86 quarters in the sample-period data and only 1.05 quarters (with a very small S.D.) in the S_u series for GNP (columns 3 and 4). The "within run" dispersion of the durations of movement in S_u is smaller than the dispersion of the actual duration figures (column 5). One-quarter declines account for over 95 per cent of all declines in these simulations; in contrast, GNP in 1948–68 underwent three contractions of two quarters each and one of four quarters, in addition to three one-quarter declines. As the simulated falls are shorter, so the simulated rises are longer than the actual ones (9.0 vs. 8.1 quarters; see column 3).

The mean percentage amplitudes of the declines are 0.71 for actuals and 0.55 for the S_u series. For the rises, the corresponding amplitudes are virtually identical— 1.85 and 1.88 per cent for A and S_u, respectively (column 6).

To conclude, the simulations with serially uncorrelated random shocks produce declines that are somewhat shorter and smaller than the declines observed in the postwar GNP series. But the differences are not really large. The declines are about as frequent in S_u as in A (the average length of rise-plus-decline is approximately the same in both cases, 10 quarters). The amplitude differences could, perhaps, be reduced to negligible size by the use of somewhat stronger shocks.

On the other hand, there can be no doubt that the GNP simulations with autocorrelated shocks (S_c) differ drastically from the actual data in that they show no recurrent fluctuations in levels. Half of these projections show no downturns at all, only continuous rises, so that the S_c series have very long expansions and just a few very short declines

(Table 4.1, lines 3 and 4, columns 1–5). The upward movements, also, are considerably larger, and the downward movements smaller, in S_c than in S_u (columns 6 and 7). The use of autocorrelated shocks has a powerful smoothing effect, eliminating many declines and reducing others. The behavior patterns represented by the S_c simulations seem implausible in the light of historical experience.

Turning next to the simulations for $GNP58$, we observe that they are subject to much more frequent directional changes than are the simulations for GNP: the numbers per run of both rises and falls are greater here, and the expansions are much shorter and smaller. Differences of the same kind also exist between the actuals for GNP and $GNP58$. (All this can be seen by comparing the corresponding measures in Table 4.1, lines 1–6 and 7–12.) However, in the simulated series these differences are exaggerated. The simulations for $GNP58$ deviate from the sample-period actuals in several respects.

First, the mean frequencies per run of rises and falls are too large for the S_u series (with non-autocorrelated shocks) and too small for the S_c series (with autocorrelated shocks), as compared with the numbers for the recorded $GNP58$ (columns 1 and 2). Second, the movements in S_u are shorter than those in A: the mean duration of rises and declines are 3.6 and 1.1 for these simulations, 4.5 and 1.7 quarters for the actuals. In the S_c runs, the declines are similarly short, but the expansions are much longer, averaging 15 quarters (columns 3–5). Finally, the relative amplitudes in S_u exceed, and those in S_c fall short of, their counterparts in the real GNP series for the sample period. But the differences are not large, except that the declines in the S_c series are apparently less than half the size of the declines in S_u or A (columns 6 and 7).

Thus, the pattern of movement in $GNP58$ is not reproduced closely in simulations of either type. The S_u series are rather too erratic and the S_c series too smooth; i.e., the fluctuations are too frequent and short in the former, and too infrequent and long—because of long rises —in the latter. However, the simulations are not very far off the mark on the average, according to some of the criteria applied. In general, the S_u series come out better in these comparisons than the S_c series. It is true (as noted in [14, p. 159]) that the average length of the rise-and-decline sequence in the S_c series—about 16 quarters—is approximately equal to the average length of business cycles in the United States (50 months in 1854–1958, or 52 months in 1945–58, for example; see [26, p. 671]). But we are dealing here with rises and declines of any duration rather than with the expansions and contractions of the NBER chronology (where one-quarter declines, in particular, would generally fail to qualify as cyclical contractions). In terms of the present measures, the average duration of movements is much shorter in the actuals and better approximated by the S_u than by the S_c simulations (Table 4.1, lines 7–12, columns 3 and 4).

   4.1.3   Stochastic simulations of the components of GNP in constant dollars and other indicators, when based on the equations of the Wharton Model with non-autocorrelated shocks (S_u), tend to show frequent directional changes, from rather short rises to still shorter declines, and so on. Many of these series are highly erratic, with very large up and down movements of short duration; others show relatively smaller short oscillations superimposed upon longer waves; in still others, trends are more important. There are large differences between series for different variables. When autocorrelated shocks are used, the resulting series (S_c) are generally much smoother, though no less differentiated. Chart 4.2 shows some randomly drawn examples of these S_u and S_c simulations.

   Table 4.2 lists the frequencies and average durations (AD) of rises and declines for one set of the S_u series and for two sets of the S_c series. There are no apparent reasons to suspect that the selection of these particular runs tends to bias our results, but it may be desirable to check up on this point with measures based on larger numbers of different runs. The table also contains comparable data on the number and AD of rises and declines in the recorded series for the same variables, using the sample period 1948-III–1968-I.

   Given that the actual data cover less than twenty years and the simulated series, twenty-five years, Table 4.2 suggests that rises and declines alternate much more frequently in S_u than in A (columns 1 and 3). Consequently, both rises and declines are virtually all shorter in the S_u series than in the corresponding actuals (columns 2 and 4).[30]

   The S_c series have smaller frequencies of both rises and declines

---

[30] The only exceptions are for rises in GNP, P, and declines in RL (lines 1, 17, and 32).

CHART 4.2

*A Random Sample of Stochastic 100-Quarter Simulations for
Selected Variables, Wharton Model
(1968-III–1993-II)*

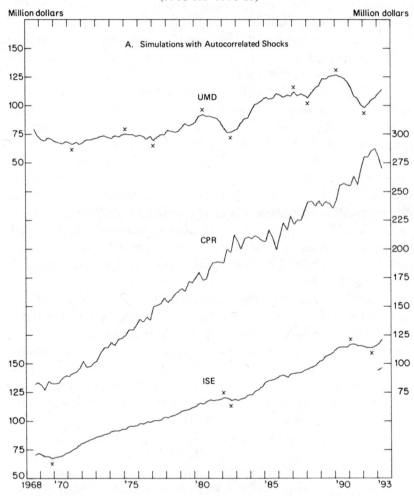

CHART 4.2 (*continued*)

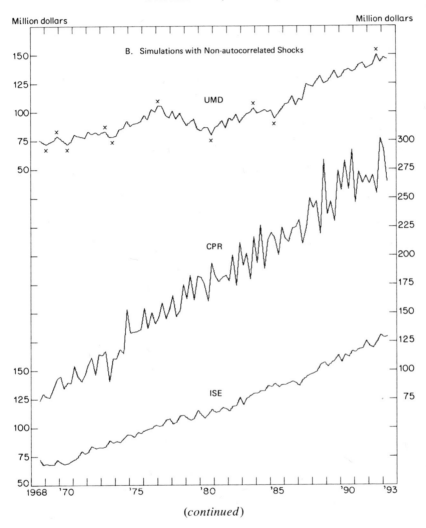

(*continued*)

CHART 4.2 (*continued*)

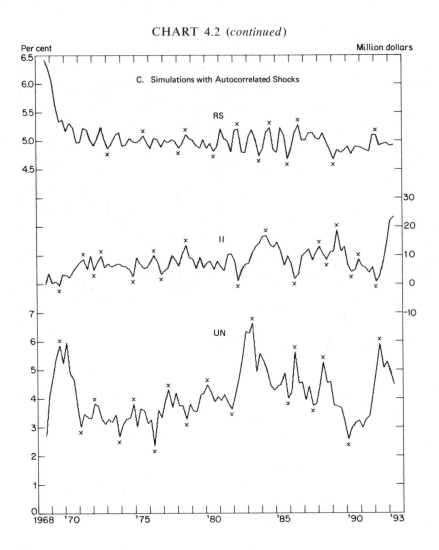

CHART 4.2 (concluded)

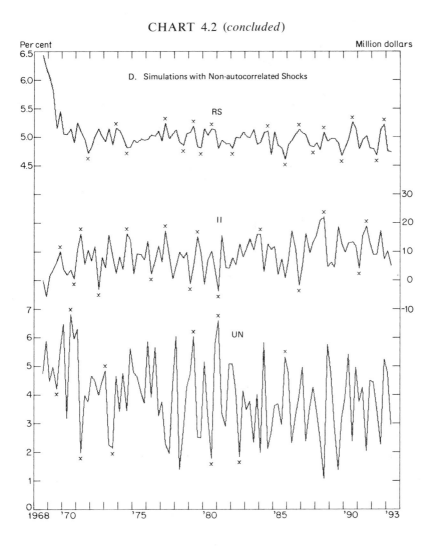

TABLE 4.2

Stochastic 100-Quarter Simulations, Wharton Model: Frequency and Average Duration of Rises and Declines in Seventeen Variables, Comparison of Three Simulation Runs and Actuals

Line	Variable Symbol[a]	Rise (R) or Decline (D)	Actuals for the Sample Period 1948-III–1968-I		Stochastic Simulations (Three Runs)					
					With Uncorrelated Shocks (Run 31)		With Serially Correlated Shocks			
							(Run 14)		(Run 26)	
			Number[b] (1)	AD[c] (quarters) (2)	Number[b] (3)	AD[c] (quarters) (4)	Number[b] (5)	AD[c] (quarters) (6)	Number[b] (7)	AD[c] (quarters) (8)
1	GNP	R	8	8.1	4	23.8	1	99.0	1	99.0
2		D	7	1.9	3	1.3	0	0	0	0
3	GNP58	R	12	4.9	20	3.7	4	23.8	7	12.9
4		D	11	1.7	20	1.3	3	1.3	6	1.5
5	C	R	7	9.9	22	3.5	5	18.8	11	8.0
6		D	6	1.1	21	1.0	5	1.0	10	1.1
7	IH	R	11	3.7	29	1.9	22	2.9	20	3.1
8		D	11	3.4	29	1.6	22	1.6	19	1.9
9	ISE	R	14	3.7	26	2.6	12	6.8	16	5.0
10		D	13	2.0	26	1.2	11	1.6	16	1.2
11	II	R	21	2.0	34	1.5	26	2.2	23	2.4
12		D	22	1.6	35	1.4	25	1.7	22	2.0
13	NE	R	14	2.6	31	1.7	30	1.9	24	2.0
14		D	15	2.7	30	1.5	30	1.4	23	2.1

			No.[b]	Dur.[c]	No.[b]	Dur.[c]	No.[b]	Dur.[c]	No.[b]	Dur.[c]
15	*YP*	R	5	13.5	23	3.3	3	32.2	5	18.8
16		D	4	2.2	22	1.0	2	1.0	4	1.2
17	*P*	R	4	17.8	4	24.0	2	49.0	1	99.0
18		D	4	1.8	3	1.0	1	1.0	0	0
19	*LE*	R	13	4.3	32	2.0	7	13.3	7	13.3
20		D	12	1.8	31	1.2	6	1.0	6	1.0
21	*UN*	R	15	2.3	33	1.4	29	1.8	25	2.2
22		D	16	2.6	33	1.5	29	1.6	25	1.7
23	*CPR*	R	15	3.4	38	1.4	30	2.2	28	2.2
24		D	14	1.9	38	1.2	29	1.1	28	1.3
25	*AWW*	R	15	3.0	28	1.9	25	1.5	23	1.7
26		D	16	2.0	29	1.6	25	2.4	22	2.7
27	*UMD*	R	8	6.0	28	2.1	20	2.7	18	3.1
28		D	9	3.3	29	1.4	20	2.2	17	2.6
29	*RS*	R	10	5.2	28	1.6	27	1.6	24	1.7
30		D	9	2.9	29	1.9	27	1.9	24	2.4
31	*RL*	R	17	2.5	26	1.7	25	1.6	26	1.7
32		D	17	2.0	25	2.2	26	2.3	27	2.0
33	*W*	R	4	18.5	25	3.0	9	10.0	12	7.2
34		D	3	1.3	24	1.0	8	1.1	12	1.0

[a] For meaning of symbols, see Table 1.1.
[b] Number of rises (R) or declines (D).
[c] Average duration, in quarters, of rises (R) or declines (D).

(fewer directional reversals) than the corresponding S_u series (compare columns 3, 5, and 7). There are only three exceptions to this among the sixty-eight comparisons that can be made.[31] Accordingly, movements in either direction, but particularly rises, tend to be longer in the S_c than in the S_u simulations. For rises, AD figures are larger for S_u than for S_c in only three of the thirty-four comparisons; for declines, they are larger in seven instances.[32]

There are nineteen instances in which the average length of rises is larger for the actuals than for the S_c series, and fifteen instances in which the reverse applies. For the most part, the upward movements in S_c, being longer than those in S_u, approximate better the duration of such movements in A. However, large deviations in either direction are apparently not uncommon in these comparisons (see the R lines for YP, P, LE, and W, for example). As for the AD of declines, the S_c series still underestimate this dimension in most cases (26 out of 34), according to the yardstick of the sample-period actuals, but the differences here are often small. (See the D lines, columns 2, 6, and 8.)

Table 4.3 compares the average percentage amplitudes (APA) of quarterly rises and declines in the actuals and in the selected S_u and S_c series. It shows a distinct tendency for the simulations with uncorrelated shocks to have larger APA than the sample-period realizations. (There are only a few exceptions here, notably for GNP, ISE and the interest-rate series; see columns 1 and 2.) In contrast, the relative changes in the simulations with serially correlated shocks tend, just as strongly, to be smaller than the APA for the actuals. (The only exceptions to this rule are found for GNP, UN, AWW, and the declines in P. See columns 1 and 3 and 4.)[33]

To sum up, the evidence for the selected variables seems on the whole more favorable to the S_c than to the S_u simulations, mainly because the latter are too erratic and have much smaller AD of rises than those observed in the historical series. The corresponding figures for S_c often differ by large margins from those of A, but apparently not in any strongly systematic fashion. The changes in S_u are too large, and the changes in S_c are too small, when compared with A. This criterion,

---

[31] All exceptions occur in the long-term interest rate RL. See lines 27 and 28.

[32] However, there are eight cases in which the AD of declines are equal for S_u and S_c. For rises, there are only two such cases.

[33] Table 4.3 omits the variables II and NE, which can, and do, assume negative values.

TABLE 4.3

Stochastic 100-Quarter Simulations, Wharton Model: Average Percentage Amplitudes, Per Quarter, of Rises and Declines in Fifteen Variables, Comparison of Three Simulation Runs and Actuals

Line	Variable Symbol[a]	Rise (R) or Decline (D)	Average Amplitude of Movement Per Quarter[b]			
			Actuals for the Sample Period 1948-III– 1968-I (1)	Stochastic Simulations (Three Runs)		
				Uncorrelated Shocks (Run 31) (2)	Serially Correlated Shocks	
					(Run 14) (3)	(Run 26) (4)
1	GNP	R	1.85	0.80	2.63	2.71
2		D	0.71	0.28	c	c
3	GNP58	R	1.33	1.68	.80	1.10
4		D	0.68	1.18	.28	0.28
5	C	R	1.32	1.83	1.14	1.09
6		D	0.87	1.34	0.25	0.21
7	IH	R	3.50	6.06	1.67	1.65
8		D	3.27	5.26	1.46	1.48
9	ISE	R	2.83	2.51	1.28	1.13
10		D	2.74	2.02	0.66	0.60
11	YP	R	1.96	2.78	1.63	1.56
12		D	1.11	2.02	0.10	0.20
13	P	R	0.55	0.84	0.35	0.58
14		D	0.39	0.60	0.53	c
15	LE	R	0.59	1.35	0.45	0.48
16		D	0.36	0.77	0.08	0.19
17	UN	R	6.25	78.19	12.22	14.35
18		D	4.97	32.18	11.15	12.11
19	CPR	R	4.85	11.55	3.34	3.52
20		D	4.48	8.05	2.59	1.80
21	AWW	R	0.31	0.99	0.59	0.63
22		D	0.33	1.33	0.58	0.56
23	UMD	R	4.45	4.55	2.67	2.52
24		D	3.33	3.78	1.97	1.90
25	RS	R	9.10	3.93	3.17	4.08
26		D	7.23	3.38	2.99	3.03
27	RL	R	3.27	1.82	1.85	1.39
28		D	1.57	1.76	1.51	1.57
29	W	R	1.31	1.82	1.12	1.05
30		D	0.64	2.17	0.41	0.38

[a] For meaning of symbols, see Table 1.1. [c] No declines.
[b] All figures are at quarterly rates.

the APA comparisons, is given less weight in our judgment than the criterion of the AD comparisons. If the projections for exogenous variables were shocked, these additional disturbances could well increase the APA figures for the simulations. This would then tend to reduce the amplitude discrepancies between S_c and A, but it would tend to increase such discrepancies between S_u and A.

4.1.4 Arguments have been made in favor of analyzing the long ex ante simulations in the form of deviations from trend as represented by ratios of the shocked series to the control series [18, pp. 78–80]. Examples of such ratio series for GNP and $GNP58$ are shown in Chart 4.3. The series with non-autocorrelated shocks, like those in Part A of the chart, are highly erratic; the series with autocorrelated shocks, in Part B, are much smoother. Movements with the attributes of "specific cycles" of the NBER analysis can be identified in both groups of the ratio series, though they are much more distinct in the runs with autocorrelated disturbances. The turning points in these movements were determined by the computer method of dating and are identified on the chart.

The series shown have been picked randomly from the fifty runs in either category. Inspection of charts for all runs discloses numerous and large differences of detail, but no systematic deviations from the general characteristics noted in the previous paragraph. Any of the ratio series is likely to show fluctuations that vary greatly in size and duration, but these variations appear to be randomly distributed over the simulation period, with no tendency either to decrease or increase.

Table 4.4 presents the summary measures of frequency, duration, and relative amplitude of movements in these series, using all of the experimental runs for GNP and $GNP58$. This table, which has the same format as Table 4.1, shows that the rises in the ratio series are on the average very close to the declines — in terms of frequency and duration, as well as in relative size. This applies to the simulations with non-autocorrelated and with autocorrelated shocks; to GNP and $GNP58$; and to the averages and the standard deviations (compare, column by column, the paired entries in lines 1 and 2, 3 and 4, and so forth). This aspect of strong symmetry suggests that the control solution provides workable estimates of the trends in GNP and $GNP58$ for both the S_u set and that of the S_c simulations.

CHART 4.3

*A Random Sample of Stochastic 100-Quarter Simulations for GNP
in Current and Constant Dollars, Ratios to Control Solutions,
Wharton Model
(1968-III–1993-II)*

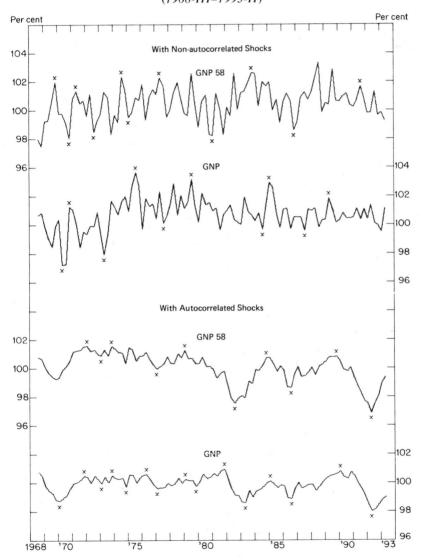

TABLE 4.4

Stochastic 100-Quarter Simulations, Wharton Model, and the Corresponding Sample-Period Actuals:
Summary Statistics on Frequency, Duration, and Relative Size of Rises and Declines in Relative
Deviations from Trend in GNP and GNP58

Line	Type of Series and Movement	Frequency (number)		Duration (quarters)			Amplitude (per cent)	
		Mean or Total[a] (1)	Standard Deviation (S.D.)[b] (2)	Mean (per run)[c] (3)	S.D. (between runs)[b] (4)	S.D. (within runs)[d] (5)	Mean (per run)[e] (6)	S.D. (between runs) (7)
				GNP: Ratio to Control Solution (S) or Trend (A)[f]				
	Simulations with non-autocorrelated shocks: S_u							
1	Rises	29.50	1.82	1.67	0.14	0.79	0.93	0.14
2	Declines	29.54	1.85	1.68	0.15	0.79	0.90	0.11
	Simulations with autocorrelated shocks: S_c							
3	Rises	21.86	2.51	2.25	0.28	1.41	0.36	0.05
4	Declines	21.82	2.27	2.29	0.29	1.49	0.36	0.05
	Sample-period actuals: A							
5	Rises	13		3.38		2.07	0.92	
6	Declines	13		2.62		1.64	0.95	

TABLE 4.4 (concluded)

Line	Type of Series and Movement	Frequency (number)		Duration (quarters)			Amplitude (per cent)	
		Mean or Total[a] (1)	Standard Deviation (S.D.)[b] (2)	Mean (per run)[c] (3)	S.D. (between runs)[b] (4)	S.D. (within runs)[d] (5)	Mean (per run)[e] (6)	S.D. (between runs)[e] (7)
		GNP58: Ratio to Control Solution (S) or Trend (A)[f]						
	S_u simulations							
7	Rises	30.02	1.80	1.64	0.15	0.80	1.11	0.15
8	Declines	29.98	1.80	1.66	0.14	0.80	1.07	0.13
	S_c simulations							
9	Rises	22.80	2.37	2.18	0.27	1.33	0.46	0.06
10	Declines	22.80	2.39	2.18	0.29	1.32	0.46	0.08
	A: actuals							
11	Rises	12		3.83		1.93	0.73	
12	Declines	12		2.67		1.43	1.02	

NOTE: See note to Table 4.1.

a,b,c,d,e See corresponding footnotes to Table 4.1.

[f] The nonstochastic control solution series for GNP and GNP58 are taken to represent the trend components of the corresponding stochastic series, S_u and S_c. Exponential trends have been fitted to the A series for GNP and GNP58.

Ratios of the quarterly *GNP* and *GNP58* values to their exponential trends in the sample period of the Wharton Model (1948–68) were computed to provide measures for actuals that correspond to those for the *S*-ratios. As would be expected, the results show the declines in the recorded deviations from trend to be as frequent as — but on the average, shorter and larger than — the rises (Table 4.4, lines 5 and 6, and 11 and 12). Compared with the fluctuations in these reference series, the rises and falls in the S_u ratios are much more frequent and shorter, but of similar relative size (*cf.* lines 1 and 2, and 5 and 6; also, lines 7 and 8, and 11 and 12). The S_c ratio series still overestimate the frequency — and underestimate the average duration — of movements in the *A* series, but by much smaller margins; on the other hand, the amplitudes of these ratios are much smaller than the corresponding measures for S_u and *A* (*cf.* lines 3 and 4, and 5 and 6; also, 9 and 10, and 11 and 12).

4.1.5   Chart 4.4 illustrates the behavior of the simulated ratio series for selected variables. The series that incorporate serially uncorrelated random shocks, S_u, are generally very erratic; those that incorporate autocorrelated shocks, S_c, are considerably less so. The large irregular up-and-down variations in S_u often obscure any longer movements that may exist in these series. In S_c, the longer movements of specific-cycle duration are more readily discernible.

As shown in Table 4.5, both rises and declines in the S_u ratios are short, varying from 1.1 to 2.1 quarters, but concentrated heavily in the range of 1.3 to 1.7 quarters (column 2). In a stationary random series, the expected value of the "average duration of run" would be 1.5 unit periods, for rises and falls alike.[34] In the S_u ratios, the rises are often longer than the declines, but the differences between these AD statistics are, in general, very small.

Upward and downward movements in the S_c series are predominantly longer than their counterparts in the S_u series. The AD figures for S_c exceed those for S_u in over 80 per cent of cases (as seen by comparing the entries in column 2 with those in columns 3 and 4). Nevertheless, both rises and declines are still, for the most part, shorter in the S_c simulations than in the corresponding actuals. In fact, the op-

[34] A run in this context denotes an uninterrupted movement in one direction (rise or decline).

CHART 4.4

A Random Sample of Stochastic 100-Quarter Simulations for Selected Variables, Ratios to Control Solutions, Wharton Model (1968-III–1993-II)

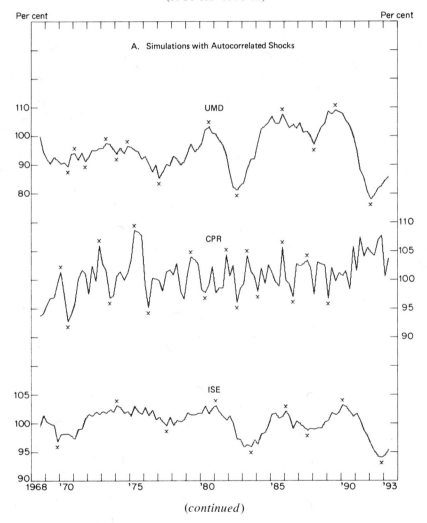

(*continued*)

CHART 4.4 (*continued*)

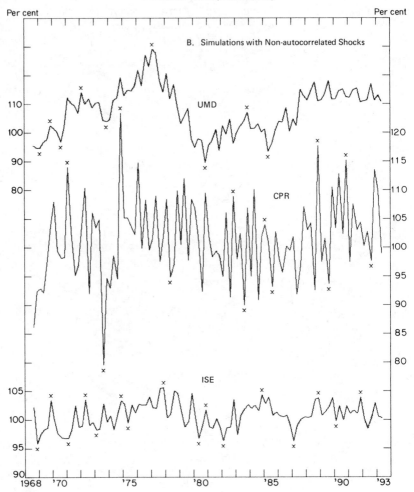

B. Simulations with Non-autocorrelated Shocks

CHART 4.4 (*continued*)

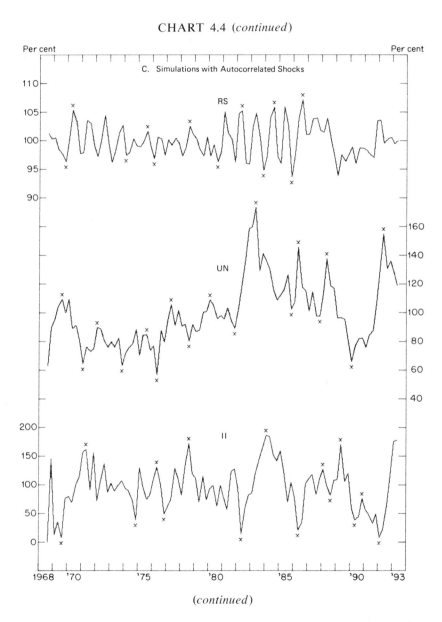

C. Simulations with Autocorrelated Shocks

(*continued*)

CHART 4.4 (*concluded*)

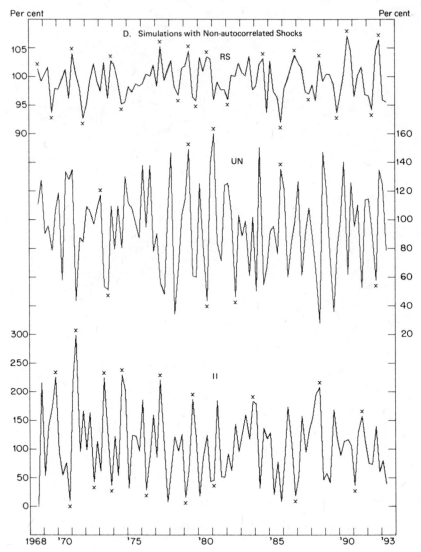

TABLE 4.5

Stochastic 100-Quarter Simulations, Wharton Model: Average Duration of Rises and Declines in Relative Deviations from Trend in Quarters, Seventeen Variables, Actuals and Three Simulation Runs

Line	Variable Symbol[a]	Rise (R) or Decline (D)	Actuals: Ratio to Exponential Trend 1948-III– 1968-I (1)	Stochastic Simulations: Ratio to Control Solution		
				Uncor-related Shocks (Run 31) (2)	Serially Cor-related Shocks (Run 14) (3)	(Run 26) (4)
1	GNP	R	3.4	1.7	2.4	2.2
2		D	2.6	1.5	2.2	2.3
3	GNP58	R	3.8	1.7	2.3	2.1
4		D	2.7	1.5	2.4	2.0
5	C	R	2.2	1.7	1.5	1.5
6		D	1.9	1.3	1.5	1.7
7	IH	R	3.2	1.7	2.2	2.1
8		D	3.0	1.6	1.8	2.1
9	ISE	R	2.9	1.7	1.6	1.7
10		D	2.5	1.5	1.9	2.0
11	II	R	3.5	1.5	2.2	2.3
12		D	3.2	1.4	1.7	2.1
13	NE	R	2.5	1.7	2.1	2.2
14		D	4.8	1.5	1.4	1.9
15	YP	R	3.2	1.6	2.5	1.7
16		D	2.4	1.4	2.0	1.8
17	P	R	2.8	1.9	3.0	2.4
18		D	3.8	1.4	1.5	1.3
19	LE	R	3.5	1.5	1.9	2.6
20		D	3.0	1.5	1.8	2.4
21	UN	R	2.3	1.5	2.0	2.2
22		D	2.8	1.5	1.6	1.8
23	CPR	R	2.5	1.3	1.8	1.5
24		D	2.2	1.3	1.9	1.6
25	AWW	R	1.9	1.8	1.9	2.3
26		D	1.7	1.5	1.5	2.3
27	UMD	R	5.2	1.8	2.2	3.0
28		D	3.1	1.5	2.3	3.6
29	RS	R	3.1	1.6	1.8	1.7
30		D	3.2	1.6	1.9	2.1
31	RL	R	2.4	1.8	1.7	2.0
32		D	3.6	2.1	2.0	1.8
33	W	R	2.4	1.8	1.7	1.9
34		D	1.6	1.1	1.4	1.6

[a] For meaning of symbols, see Table 1.1.

460 · ECONOMETRIC MODELS OF CYCLICAL BEHAVIOR

posite applies in only four instances in Table 4.5 (where sixty-eight comparisons can be made between columns 1, and 3 and 4). However, the deviations between the AD measures for S_c and the actuals are, in about one-third of the comparisons, fairly small.[35]

The average percentage amplitudes (APA) of quarterly rises and declines are systematically larger for the S_u than for the S_c simulations, as would be expected; this is shown in Table 4.6, columns 2 to 4. There is only one contrary case among all the comparisons here, and the amplitude differences between the two sets of series are often large.

The relative size of movements in S_u is sometimes considerably smaller than the relative size of movements in the sample-period deviations from trend (A), as illustrated by the figures for C, ISE, RS, and RL; but frequently the opposite applies as well, e.g., in the cases of $GNP58$, IH, P, LE, UN, CPR, and AWW (compare columns 1 and 2). Elsewhere the differences between the APA figures for S_u and A are mostly small and of either sign (as for GNP, YP, UMD, and W).

The average percentage changes in the S_c series are, with few exceptions, smaller than those in A, mostly by relatively large margins (columns 1, and 3 and 4). The exceptions are concentrated in the measures for AWW, P (declines only), and W (rises only).

On the whole, the evidence for ratio-to-trend series conforms and complements the evidence for the level series. The major conclusion to be reached is that the stochastic simulations of the Wharton Model generally understate both the average durations and the average relative amplitudes of the sample-period actuals. There are considerable differences among the results for the different variables, which for the most part cannot be readily explained. On the other hand, the differences between the S_u and the S_c simulations are, for the most part, systematic as well as pronounced, and have clear technical reasons.

4.1.6 We proceed with the analysis of specific-cycle movements in the three sets of simulated series (Run 31 for S_u, and Runs 14 and 26 for S_c; see Sections 4.1.3 and 4.1.5 above for charts of some of these series in level and ratio form, with identification of their cyclical turning

[35] There are ten cases in which the differences between the corresponding entries in columns 1 and 3 equal one-half of one quarter or less, and the same statement can be made about the differences between columns 1 and 4. On the other hand, only four deviations so small are found in comparing columns 1 and 2 (for S_u).

TABLE 4.6

Stochastic 100-Quarter Simulations, Wharton Model: Average Percentage Amplitudes Per Quarter of Rises and Declines in Relative Deviations from Trend, Fifteen Variables, Actuals and Three Simulation Runs

Line	Variable Symbol[a]	Rise (R) or Decline (D)	Actuals: Ratio to Exponential Trend 1948-III– 1968-I (1)	Uncor-related Shocks (Run 31) (2)	Serially Cor-related Shocks (Run 14) (3)	(Run 26) (4)
1	GNP	R	0.92	1.01	0.32	0.38
2		D	0.95	0.95	0.33	0.35
3	GNP58	R	0.73	1.25	0.47	0.45
4		D	1.02	1.21	0.36	0.49
5	C	R	4.57	1.16	0.46	0.85
6		D	2.95	1.42	0.47	0.81
7	IH	R	3.31	5.66	1.32	1.50
8		D	2.96	5.38	1.44	1.55
9	ISE	R	2.35	1.81	0.82	0.84
10		D	3.10	2.24	0.70	0.72
11	YP	R	0.90	0.77	0.35	0.55
12		D	0.59	0.59	0.44	0.51
13	P	R	0.34	0.45	0.20	0.23
14		D	0.28	0.48	0.45	0.40
15	LE	R	0.54	1.08	0.22	0.23
16		D	0.40	0.98	0.23	0.26
17	UN	R	6.25	76.57	11.72	14.69
18		D	4.66	32.07	11.49	11.42
19	CPR	R	4.00	9.76	3.37	2.83
20		D	4.19	8.47	2.59	2.42
21	AWW	R	0.32	1.03	0.54	0.63
22		D	0.34	1.21	0.57	0.58
23	UMD	R	3.94	3.93	2.17	2.84
24		D	3.23	3.87	2.09	2.10
25	RS	R	7.80	3.66	2.96	3.90
26		D	5.39	3.21	2.73	2.90
27	RL	R	3.56	1.94	1.94	1.52
28		D	2.34	1.61	1.36	1.46
29	W	R	0.44	1.31	0.49	0.55
30		D	2.23	2.06	0.58	0.64

[a] For meaning of symbols, see Table 1.1.

points). Of particular interest here is the relative timing of these series for variables that have historically typified the sequence of cyclical leaders, coinciders, and laggers.

Measuring this timing efficiently requires that a "reference chronology" be established for each simulation run. Some analysts of current business conditions would use a single, comprehensive aggregate such as $GNP58$ as a basis for dating the business cycle (requiring, perhaps, a two-quarter decline, or lack of growth, in that series as a minimum condition for identifying a business recession). However, even in historical situations this criterion is not always available or reliable.[36] In dealing with simulations, the problem is aggravated by the paucity of cyclical turns in the levels of the S series for GNP in current and constant dollars. It is, therefore, desirable to use more information in determining the reference dates, namely the evidence on the bunching in time of the specific-cycle peaks and troughs in the S series for different variables.[37]

The so-called "historical" diffusion indexes provide a suitable method for organizing this evidence. After the cyclical turning points have been identified in each of the S series in a given set, the percentage of the series undergoing specific-cycle expansion is calculated for each successive quarter.[38] The deviations of these percentage figures from 50 are cumulated, to give a relatively smooth series—the so-called cumulated diffusion index (CDI)—whose peaks (troughs) would be centered on the periods with the greatest concentration of specific cycle peaks (troughs) in the component S series.[39]

Two CDI series have been computed for each of the three randomly chosen sets of Wharton Model simulations: namely, an index

---

[36] For a critique of using GNP data alone in the dating of business cycles, see [30] and the references therein.

[37] It should be noted that this traditional NBER approach was also used in [1, Sec. 9].

[38] This implies that all movements contrary in direction to the cyclical phases of the series are ignored. A positively conforming series is treated as expanding in each quarter that falls between a specific trough and a specific peak in the data; it is treated as contracting in each quarter situated between a peak and a trough.

[39] At the culmination of business expansion, peaks tend to be most frequent and troughs least frequent. As the contraction begins, the proportion of series expanding falls below 50 per cent; the deviations from 50 that are cumulated in our index shift from + to − and the index passes through a peak. Analogous statements apply *mutatis mutandis* to the situation at the trough. For more information on measurements of cyclical diffusion, see [26, Chapters 8, 9, and 20].

based on the S series proper, and an index based on the ratios of these shocked series to the corresponding nonstochastic (control) series. However, only the indexes of the second type include all seventeen variables covered by the Wharton simulations. Unlike the simulated ratio series (all of which are divisible into specific cycles), the levels of the S series for some variables show only prolonged growth trends, sporadically interrupted by a very few short — predominantly one-quarter — declines (see Table 4.2). Series of this kind have no specific cycles and therefore cannot be included in diffusion indexes based on specific cycles. Thus, only ten of the seventeen variables are represented in the cumulated diffusion index (CDI) for the simulated series of Run 14. The series included are the more volatile ones, relating to types of investment, corporate profits, average workweek, unemployment, unfilled orders, and interest rates; excluded are the comprehensive aggregates for national output, income, and consumption, and the indicators of the general price and wage levels. The diffusion indexes for the level series of Runs 26 and 31 have the same composition.

According to these summary diffusion measures for the simulations with autocorrelated shocks (Runs 14 and 26), the average duration of expansions would be about 9 to 11 quarters; that of contractions, more than 5 quarters. In the postwar period, the mean actual duration was approximately 12 to 16 quarters for expansions (the latter figure includes the long expansion of the 1960's up to the end of the Wharton sample-period), and 3 to 4 quarters for contractions. The figures for the S_c series are, at least, of a similar order of magnitude.[40] However, because the simulations of the comprehensive income and product aggregates cannot be included in this analysis, no further use will be made of the cyclical diffusion and other measures based on the S series proper in this paper; instead, we shall concentrate on the corresponding measures for the ratios of shocked to control series.

Chart 4.5 shows that the indexes of cumulated percentage expanding (CDI) for the ratio series have well-defined cyclical movements, with contractions that are relatively long — often as long as the expansions. There are some upward drifts in these indexes, but they

[40] The average duration of expansions in the index for the S_u series (Run 31) is considerably larger: 20.2 quarters. The average duration of contractions in this index is again similar, 4.5 quarters.

CHART 4.5

*Cumulated Historical Diffusion Indexes for Selected Sets of Simulated
Series, Ratios to Control Solutions, Wharton Model
(1968-III–1993-II)*

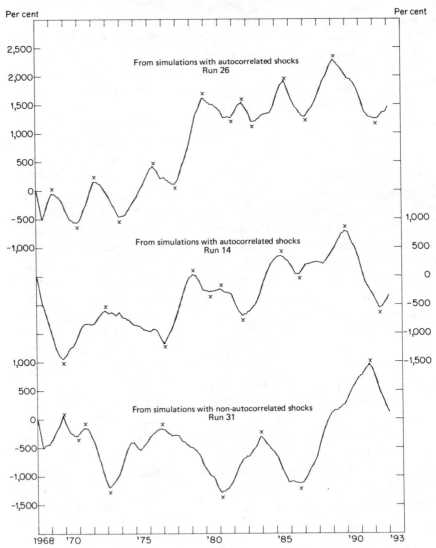

are small and not persistent (except in the first half of the simulation period for Run 26). In contrast, the indexes for the S series proper have relatively short and weak contractions and strong upward trends (cumulation due to the prevalence of expansions over contractions). This contrast reflects differences of the same kind between the movements in the levels of the simulated series on the one hand; and the movements in the ratio series, on the other.

The diffusion indexes vary greatly with respect to the timing and amplitudes of fluctuations, but this merely reflects fortuitous differences among the runs in the incidence of large and small shocks. What matters, again, is the *presence* in these composite series of reasonably smooth movements of cyclical dimensions. The main criterion is duration, and the averages in the accompanying tabulation show that the fluctuations in the cumulated diffusion indexes (CDI) for the ratio series are not very different in this respect from cycles in trend-adjusted GNP data for the postwar period.[41]

	Ratios to Control Solution, Wharton Model: Indexes of Cumulated Per Cent, Expanding			Ratios to Exponential Trend, Actual Data, 1948–68	
	Run 14	Run 26	Run 31	GNP	$GNP58$
	(1)	(2)	(3)	(4)	(5)
	Average Duration of Movement, in Quarters				
Expansions	9.4	7.2	12.0	12.5	11.0
Contractions	8.6	7.0	9.8	7.0	6.5
Full cycle	18.0	14.2	21.8	19.5	17.5

4.1.7 This section summarizes the results obtained by comparing the timing of the CDI for the Wharton Runs 31, 14, and 26, with the timing of each of the component series in the same run. In the process, measures of conformity are also computed, in the form of the fre-

[41] The figures for the historical data are sensitive to the choice of the sample period and the figures for simulations depend on the idiosyncrasies of the given run. The deviations between the tabulated measures fall comfortably within the range of such sampling variations. Other related duration measures, based on average historical "growth cycles" in sets of selected indicators, confirm the above conclusion.

quencies of those turns in CDI and the simulated ratio-series that cannot be matched (Table 4.7, columns 1 to 4). The distributions of leads and lags of the simulated series at the reference (CDI) peaks and troughs are given in Table 4.7, columns 5 to 12. The means and medians of these distributions are listed in Table 4.8.

The frequencies of specific-cycle movements and turning points that have no counterparts in the over-all reference index are much greater for the series in Run 31 than for those in either of the other sets (Table 4.7, columns 3 and 4).[42] This might have been expected, since series with autocorrelated shocks (S_c) are generally much smoother than the series with serially noncorrelated shocks (S_u). On the other hand, there is no reason why S_u should score systematically worse (or better) than S_c in matching the reference turns, and there is no evidence that they do.[43] The over-all conformity record tends to be better for the S_c than for the S_u series, because the former show fewer extra turns and no greater rate of failures to match the reference turns.

Comprehensive aggregates of national product and income should naturally be among the best conformers, with approximately coincident timing, and the historical record fully confirms this presumption.[44] Thus, it is good to find that the simulations of these variables (GNP, $GNP58$, and YP) are among those with the lowest proportions of unmatched turns in columns 2 and 4 of Table 4.7. Also in this group are the series for two large real-expenditure components, C and ISE, and unfilled orders, UMD (a well-behaved, cyclical "stock" aggregate). Business investment in plant and equipment, a lagging series, has had an excellent historical record of moving with the general business cycle. Personal income and consumption (both coinciders) have conformed less well in that they underwent merely retardations of growth

[42] All but one of the component series of Run 31 have some extra turns, while there are four series in Run 14 with no extra turns and four again in Run 26. The average percentages of such turns are 36.9, 19.4, and 13.6 for Runs 31, 14, and 26, respectively.

[43] There are eight series that fail to match all reference turns in Run 31, eleven such series in Run 14, and six in Run 26 (which, here as elsewhere, happens to yield particularly favorable results). The average percentages of unmatched reference turns are 10.4, 16.5, and 4.5 for the three runs listed in the same order (Table 4.7, columns 1 and 2).

[44] See [26, Chapters 3 and 7]. For the latest review of the performance of these and other indicators, see Geoffrey H. Moore and Julius Shiskin, *Indicators of Business Expansions and Contractions*. Occasional Paper 103. New York, Columbia University Press for the National Bureau of Economic Research, 1967.

TABLE 4.7

Cyclical Conformity and Timing of Simulated Ratio-Series, with Reference Chronologies Based on Cumulated Diffusion Indexes, Wharton Model, Three Runs

Line	Variable Symbol[a]	Reference Turns Not Matched[b]		Extra Specific Turns[c]		Number of Timing Observations							
						At Reference Peaks				At Reference Troughs			
		Number (1)	Per Cent (2)	Number (3)	Per Cent (4)	Leads (5)	Coincidences (6)	Lags (7)	Long Leads and Lags[d] (8)	Leads (9)	Coincidences (10)	Lags (11)	Long Leads and Lags[d] (12)
						Run 31: with non-autocorrelated shocks[e]							
1	GNP	2	22.2	3	30.0	2	0	2	3	1	0	2	2
2	GNP58	0	0	2	18.2	0	4	1	0	1	2	1	0
3	C	0	0	3	25.0	0	2	3	1	1	1	2	1
4	IH	2	22.2	6	46.2	4	1	2	2	1	0	2	3
5	ISE	0	0	7	43.8	0	1	4	3	1	1	2	1
6	II	0	0	8	47.1	0	4	1	0	1	2	2	0
7	YP	0	0	1	10.0	0	2	3	1	2	1	1	0
8	P	1	11.1	3	27.3	0	0	4	3	1	1	2	3
9	LE	0	0	10	52.6	0	3	2	0	2	1	1	1
10	UN[h]	2	22.2	4	36.4	1	1	2	3	1	2	0	1
11	CPR	2	22.2	7	50.0	3	0	1	3	1	0	2	2
12	AWW	2	22.2	8	53.3	1	2	1	1	0	1	2	1
13	UMD	0	0	0	0	0	3	2	1	3	0	1	2
14	RS	1	11.1	12	60.0	2	0	2	2	3	0	1	4
15	RL	2	22.2	8	53.3	1	1	2	2	0	2	1	0

(continued)

TABLE 4.7 (continued)

| Line | Variable Symbol[a] | Reference Turns Not Matched[b] | | Extra Specific Turns[c] | | Number of Timing Observations | | | | | | | |
| | | | | | | At Reference Peaks | | | | At Reference Troughs | | | |
		Number (1)	Per Cent (2)	Number (3)	Per Cent (4)	Leads (5)	Coincidences (6)	Lags (7)	Long Leads and Lags[d] (8)	Leads (9)	Coincidences (10)	Lags (11)	Long Leads and Lags[d] (12)
						Run 14: with autocorrelated shocks[f]							
16	GNP	0	0	4	26.7	2	1	2	2	1	3	2	1
17	GNP58	2	18.2	0	0	2	2	0	1	0	5	0	0
18	C	2	18.2	2	18.2	2	1	1	1	1	3	1	0
19	IH	2	18.2	4	30.8	4	0	0	3	3	1	1	3
20	ISE	2	18.2	0	0	0	1	3	2	0	1	4	2
21	II	2	18.2	2	18.2	4	0	0	2	5	0	0	0
22	YP	0	0	4	26.7	1	1	3	1	2	2	2	0
23	P	4	36.4	2	22.2	1	0	3	4	1	0	2	3
24	LE	2	18.2	3	25.0	1	1	2	1	1	1	3	2
25	UN[h]	0	0	6	35.3	1	0	4	2	3	1	2	1
26	CPR	1	9.1	4	28.6	1	1	3	2	2	3	0	2
27	AWW	0	0	2	15.4	2	2	1	0	4	1	1	0
28	UMD	2	18.2	0	0	0	0	2	0	1	2	2	2
29	RS	0	0	3	23.1	0	0	1	4	2	1	3	3
30	RL	5	45.4	4	40.0	1	1	2	1	1	0	2	2
31	W	5	45.4	0	0	0	0	2	2	1	0	2	3

TABLE 4.7 (concluded)

Line	Variable Symbol[a]	Reference Turns Not Matched[b]		Extra Specific Turns[c]		Number of Timing Observations							
						At Reference Peaks				At Reference Troughs			
		Number	Per Cent	Number	Per Cent	Leads	Coincidences	Lags	Long Leads and Lags[d]	Leads	Coincidences	Lags	Long Leads and Lags[d]
		(1)	(2)	(3)	(4)	(5)	(6)	(7)	(8)	(9)	(10)	(11)	(12)
						Run 26: with autocorrelated shocks[g]							
32	GNP	0	0	0	0	1	4	2	0	2	3	2	2
33	GNP58	0	0	0	0	1	6	0	0	4	3	0	2
34	C	0	0	2	12.5	2	4	1	0	2	3	2	2
35	IH	0	0	3	17.6	3	2	2	1	4	1	2	2
36	ISE	0	0	2	12.5	0	1	6	3	0	7	0	3
37	II	0	0	5	26.3	4	3	0	1	5	1	1	1
38	YP	0	0	1	6.7	0	5	2	0	1	4	2	0
39	P	2	14.3	0	0	0	0	6	4	0	0	6	5
40	LE	2	14.3	3	20.0	0	1	5	3	1	3	2	2
41	UN[h]	0	0	2	12.5	0	6	1	0	3	0	4	2
42	CPR	1	7.1	2	13.3	2	1	3	2	5	0	2	5
43	AWW	0	0	8	36.4	3	3	1	2	2	2	3	0
44	UMD	0	0	0	0	4	3	0	1	2	3	2	2
45	RS	1	7.1	6	31.6	4	1	2	2	2	1	3	2
46	RL	3	21.4	2	15.4	2	0	4	4	2	0	3	5
47	W	1	7.1	2	13.3	2	0	4	4	5	0	2	2

NOTES TO TABLE 4.7.

ᵃ For meaning of symbols, see Table 1.1.
ᵇ Turns in the cumulated diffusion index (CDI) not matched by turns in the simulated series. For numbers of the reference turns (in CDI), see notes e, f, and g.
ᶜ Turns in the simulated series that have no matching turns in CDI.
ᵈ Leads and lags of three or more quarters.
ᵉ Nine reference turns (5 peaks and 4 troughs).
ᶠ Eleven reference turns (5 peaks and 6 troughs).
ᵍ Fourteen reference turns (7 peaks and 7 troughs).
ʰ Inverted (peaks matched with reference troughs; troughs, with reference peaks).

rather than absolute declines in some of the recent mild recessions. Total employment (*LE*) should have a very good conformity record but does not (it has relatively large combined percentages in columns 2 and 4, which we have ranked for each run in making these comparisons). On the other hand, the unemployment simulations score fairly well here, particularly for the S_c runs, 14 and 26. The series for profits, interest rates, and wages rank lowest for conformity; i.e., have the largest total proportions of unmatched and extra turns. Actually, price and wage levels have been poor conformers in recent business fluctuations, although considerably better results would be obtained for these variables in trend-adjusted or first-difference form. Profits and, even more, interest rates (average corporate bond yields and rates on 4- to 6-month commercial paper) have been very sensitive, not only to major cyclical movements but to minor retardations and speedups as well.

4.1.8   The evidence on timing of the simulated series is substantially more difficult to summarize than that on their conformity. In an attempt to determine what, if any, are the typical timing characteristics of these experimental data, one must take into account the relative frequencies of leads, coincidences, and lags generated by the comparison of turns in the individual *S* series with turns in CDI (Table 4.7, columns 5 to 12), as well as the length of the resulting average leads or lags (Table 4.8). The timing at peaks and at troughs must be compared, and the consensus (or lack of it) between the corresponding measures for the different runs must be noted. Finally, one ought to consider any additional uncertainties due to the paucity of timing comparisons per run and the frequency of lapses from conformity.

Where leads and lags are in balance or (better) where coincidences

TABLE 4.8

Average Timing of Simulated Series (Ratios to Control Solutions) at Reference Dates
Based on Cumulated Diffusion Indexes, Wharton Model, Three Runs
(Mean (M) and Median (Md) Lead (−) or Lag (+) in Months)

Line	Variable Symbol[a]	Peaks M (1)	Peaks Md (2)	Troughs M (3)	Troughs Md (4)	All Turns M (5)	Peaks M (6)	Peaks Md (7)	Troughs M (8)	Troughs Md (9)	All Turns M (10)	Peaks M (11)	Peaks Md (12)	Troughs M (13)	Troughs Md (14)	All Turns M (15)
		Run 31[b]					Run 14[c]					Run 26[c]				
1	GNP	+0.8	+1.5	+3.0	+3	+1.7	−0.6	0	+1.0	0	+0.2	+0.9	0	+0.4	0	+0.6
2	GNP58	+1.2	0	−0.8	0	+0.3	−3.7	−3	0	0	−1.7	−0.4	0	−4.2	−3	−2.3
3	C	+3.0	+3	+2.2	+1.5	+2.7	+0.7	−1.5	−0.7	0	0	−0.4	0	+0.4	0	0
4	IH	−9.7	−7.5	+4.0	+9	−3.8	−10.5	−12	−3.6	−6	−6.7	−1.7	0	−1.7	−3	−1.7
5	ISE	+7.8	+12	0	+1.5	+4.3	+6.7	+6	+7.2	+6	+7.0	+6.9	+3	+6.5	+3	+6.6
6	II	+1.2	0	−0.7	0	+0.3	−11.2	−10.5	−3.0	−3	−6.7	−3.4	−3	−3.9	−3	−3.6
7	YP	+5.4	+3	−0.7	−1.5	+2.7	+3.0	+3	−0.5	0	+1.1	+1.3	0	+1.0	0	+1.1
8	P	+17.2	+15	+7.5	+7.5	+12.4	+7.8	+15.5	+12.0	+24	+9.6	+13.0	+12	+12.0	+9	+12.5
9	LE	+1.8	+4.5	−4.5	−3	−1.0	+3.0	+1.5	+5.4	+3	+4.8	+7.5	+7.5	+3.0	0	+5.2
10	UN[d]	+1.5	−6	−3.0	0	−0.4	+4.8	+6	+0.5	−1.5	+2.4	+0.4	0	0	+3	+0.2
11	CPR	−5.2	−6	+2.0	+6	−2.1	−1.8	+3	−6.0	0	−3.9	+0.5	+1.5	−10.3	−12	−5.4
12	AWW	−0.7	0	+5.0	+6	+1.7	−1.2	0	−5.5	−3	−3.5	−1.3	0	−0.4	0	−0.9
13	UMD	+2.4	0	−3.0	−3	0	+0.8	+1.5	+4.8	0	+3.0	−3.0	−3	−3.4	0	−3.2
14	RS	0	+1.5	−6.8	−12	−3.4	−9.0	−6	−4.0	+1.5	−6.3	−0.9	−3	+1.5	+1.5	+0.2
15	RL	+4.5	+1.5	+1.0	0	+3.0	+5.0	+3	+6.0	+6	+5.5	+8.5	+12	−0.6	+9	+4.4
16	W[e]						+11.0	+18	+9.0	+9	+10.0	+4.0	+6	−2.6	−3	+0.5

471

Notes to Table 4.8.

The average leads and lags listed in this table cover the timing observations that are included in the frequency distributions of columns 5 to 12 of Table 4.7.

ᵃ For meaning of symbols, see Table 1.1.

ᵇ With non-autocorrelated shocks.

ᶜ With autocorrelated shocks.

ᵈ Inverted. (*See note h in Table 4.7.*)

ᵉ Not computed for Run 31 because the series is highly erratic, and its specific cycles (if any) could not be reliably identified.

prevail, the timing may be classified as *roughly coincident* (*RC*). The timing averages in this class should fall in the range from −3 to +3 months (leads or lags of one quarter or less, and exact coincidences). The medians are often more reliable than the means of the timing observations, because the latter are sensitive to extremely long individual leads or lags, which are sometimes particularly uncertain.[45] Where leads prevail and the averages exceed 3 months with minus signs, the timing is classified as *leading* (*L*). Where lags prevail and the averages are similarly large, but with plus signs, the series is called *lagging* (*Lg*). The determinations were made separately for peaks and troughs, and for each of the runs, and they are not always the same for a given variable.

The following can be classified with a relatively high degree of assurance:

(1) *GNP, GNP58, C, YP,* and *UMD.* These five variables all belong to the *RC* (roughly coincident) group. In the means for *GNP* and *YP*, lags prevail slightly, while in those for *GNP58*, leads prevail, but the figures are small. The distributions in Table 4.7 and the medians in Table 4.8 clearly indicate the *RC* classification at both peaks and troughs. The same applies to *C*, where some short lags appear in Run 31, which, however, is entirely compatible with the *RC* classification). As for *UMD*, lags are somewhat more frequent in one of the runs (14), and leads in another (26), but they are on the whole short and the entire evidence, including the averages, argues for inclusion of this variable in the *RC* category.

(2) *ISE, P,* and *RL.* These must be included in group *Lg* (laggers).

[45] It is for this reason that we include the counts of "long leads and lags" (of three or more quarters) in Table 4.7, columns 8 and 12.

Lags dominate the distributions for business fixed-investment in every case, and they are intermediate or long, except for troughs in Run 31. Long lags prevail throughout in the timing of the price-level simulations. For the long-term interest rates, the lags are more variable and, on the average, much shorter.

For the remaining variables, the evidence is rather mixed, but it indicates these additional groupings:

(3) *IH, II, CPR*. Predominantly *L, leaders*. For housing investment, there are long, or intermediate, leads at peaks in Run 31; and at both peaks and troughs in Run 14. However, the average leads are small in Run 26 and *IH* can be included in the *RC* group there; and at troughs in Run 31, there are lags. Inventory investment is definitely a leader in Run 14, a short leader in Run 26, but a rough coincider in Run 31. Corporate profits have over-all mean leads in every case, but closer inspection shows them to be definitely leading only at peaks in Run 31 and at troughs in Run 26; elsewhere, *CPR* is better described as a rough coincider, with some short lags in the averages.

(4) *UN, AWW*. For the most part, *RC* (roughly coincident). Unemployment simulations show some tendency to lag, particularly at peaks in Runs 31 and 14. The series for the average workweek frequently lead, but mostly by short intervals (and *AWW* lags at troughs in Run 31).

(5) *LE*. Would be classified as *RC* in Run 31 but as *Lg* in Runs 14 and 26. These lags of the employment series, however, are on the whole not long, except at peaks in Run 26.

(6) *RS* and *W*. The simulated ratio-series for these variables are particularly erratic, and it is difficult to identify, let alone date, their specific-cycle movements. Hence, our results here are quite uncertain; moreover, they vary considerably for the different episodes and sets of data. For the short-term interest rates, coincident timing prevails at peaks in Run 31, and at either turn in Run 26, but leads are dominant elsewhere. For the wage rate, there are long lags in one run; offsetting lags and leads at peaks and troughs, respectively, in another.

There is much evidence on the historical timing-patterns of the important economic variables under study, but it generally refers to the series proper (usually after seasonal adjustment), rather than to their deviations from trend or other similar transformations. Adjusting for a rising trend would often tend to shift peaks in the series backward — and troughs, forward — in time; adjusting for a declining trend would have opposite effects. But such shifts seldom appear to be large [5, Chapter 7]; and in particular, very seldom large enough to alter the typical timing sequence of the indicator series. Also, diffusion indexes, which are highly correlated with the rates of change in the corresponding aggregates, have timing sequences that tend to parallel those between the aggregates for the same variables (see, e.g., [26, Chapter 9]). We shall proceed on the assumption that series of relative deviations from trends (or control solutions) should have the same relative timing properties as the corresponding series without any trend adjustments. This should be, at least, a justifiable first approximation, but it will deserve some checking in further research.

Historically, then, most of our variables are readily classifiable as either "rough coinciders," such as $GNP, GNP58, YP, LE,$ and UN; or "leaders," such as $II, CPR,$ and AWW; or "laggers," such as ISE. The above nine series are, indeed, all so designated in the basic list of the NBER business-cycle indicators. (See reference in footnote 18.) Real consumption expenditures, C, represent, as far as one can tell, another series in the RC group (as does the related indicator of retail sales). Unfilled orders for durables tended to lead at peaks and roughly coincide, often with short lags, at troughs [26, Chapter 14]. However, in less vigorous expansions, the lead of UMD at peaks may not be long, and the over-all timing of this series has been denoted as roughly coincident in the recently compiled comprehensive list of the NBER indicators.

The timing of the simulated series reviewed earlier in this section conforms to the historical over-all patterns for nine of these eleven variables (counting UMD simply as in the RC group). According to the measures in Tables 4.7 and 4.8, LE would be classified as lagging (instead of RC), and AWW as roughly coincident (instead of L).

Residential construction, IH, has led at each of the four postwar business-cycle peaks, at the last two of them by very long intervals; it has led by one or two quarters, or coincided, at troughs. Its conformity record was not very good. The prevalent leading patterns of the *IH* simulations, including the long leads at peaks in Runs 31 and 14, are not in conflict with this experience.

The implicit price deflator, *P*, has failed to decline in any of the three recessions since 1953, but did show retardations during each of these episodes. Historically, the wholesale price-index (except farm products and foods) has been a roughly coincident series. While many prices react sluggishly, the very long lags of the *P* simulations appear rather dubious when judged by past price-level behavior.

Compensation per man-hour, *W*, is even more dominated by upward trend and resistant to cyclical declines than *P*. In trend-adjusted form, this series could show a coincident-lagging timing broadly similar to that recorded for Run 26.

The Treasury-bill rate has been classified as roughly coincident in the comprehensive list of NBER indicators (1967), and the commercial-paper rate (*RS*) has a very similar timing. However, according to recent studies by Phillip Cagan, both *RS* and the high-grade bond yield have tended to lag.[46] The leading tendencies of the *RS* simulations are at variance with the historical pattern. The simulations show the average corporate bond yield (*RL*) as lagging, which agrees with the evidence of the long series studied by Cagan (but the NBER 1967 list classifies corporate bond yields as *RC* on the basis of data gathered since 1948).

To sum up, the timing of the simulations for *LE*, *AWW*, *P*, and *RS* seems definitely at odds with the historical patterns; but for the twelve other variables included in Tables 4.7 and 4.8, this is not the case—according to the above comparisons. We are inclined to regard this as a rather good total score, and would find it encouraging if confirmed by further testing. The latter is necessary, however, because there are many pitfalls in this kind of analysis. Perhaps the major one is that some of the simulated ratio-series are so erratic that it is difficult to identify their specific cycles, and the selection of a particular turning point date may involve considerable error. Averaging presum-

[46] See P. Cagan, "The Influence of Interest Rates on the Duration of Business Cycles," *Essays on Interest Rates,* Volume I (J. M. Guttentag and P. Cagan, editors). New York, Columbia University Press for the National Bureau of Economic Research, 1969, p. 7 (with a reference to Cagan's earlier work).

ably helps here, but we cannot count on all individual errors to offset each other neatly. High proportions of unmatched turns and extra turns, and of very long leads or lags, provide danger signals. Inspection of charts confirms that the series for CPR, AWW, W, and the interest rates (particularly RS) are especially volatile; hence, all generalizations based on their behavior are most uncertain. The series with non-auto-correlated shocks (Run 31) are generally more irregular than the others, and include some additional items for which the results are similarly dubious. Moreover, for one variable—net exports (NE)—it was impossible to make any meaningful cyclical measurements at all.[47]

4.2 THE OBE MODEL

4.2.1 The post-sample-period simulations for this model begin in 1966-I and end in 1990-IV. Several modifications in the model structure were made for the purpose of these simulations.[48] As for the treatment of exogenous variables, all tax rates, the discount rate, and the time deposit rate were held at constant levels, while most of the other factors were set to grow at the average rates of change observed for them during the sample period. However, the growth rates of several series, including government purchases and government employment, were adjusted to produce results deemed to be plausible. Census population projections were used in determining the time-paths of some series. In the control solution, free reserves were kept at zero throughout. The resulting series of unborrowed reserves of banks was used

[47] This series, it should be noted, conformed poorly in the past, which is not surprising; however, the Wharton simulated ratio-series for NE have a different and rather arbitrary appearance.

[48] Capital consumption allowances were made dependent on the value of the net stock of plant and equipment, instead of being treated as exogenous. Constant trend-increments were added to the equations for housing starts and merchandise imports, while negative trend expressions were eliminated from the equations for labor force participation and hours worked. The price level of government purchases from the private sector was made endogenous, to grow at the same percentage rate as the price level of private GNP, excluding housing services. The empirical tax and transfer relationships used during the sample period were replaced by equations linking taxable income to personal per capita income, and tax payments to liabilities; for state and local payments, some arbitrary assumptions about rising marginal rates and time trends had to be made. Improved equations for manufacturers' shipments and unfilled orders were adopted, as well as certain relatively minor changes affecting investment in plant and equipment, and some interest rates. For more detail, see [18, Sec. 4.1].

in the runs with stochastic shocks, where free reserves were not restricted. This implies that the money stock increases smoothly throughout in the OBE control solution: monetary policy is apparently growth-oriented rather than cyclical [18, pp. 72–75].

The control solution of the thus modified OBE Model shows GNP growing at annual rates varying from 7.5 to 5.7 per cent, and $GNP58$ growing at rates varying from 5.3 to 3.4 per cent. The rates tend to fall off from year to year. Had they been held constant, given the projected growth patterns for the population and labor force, the unemployment rate would have exhibited a sharp decline. Actually, it is unemployment that is held within a narrow range of variation (it decreases from 4.2 to 3.9 per cent).

Unlike the Wharton Model control-solution, apparently no special assumptions were made here about the transition period involving the Vietnam War. (The starting point of these OBE simulations is 1966-I — seven quarters earlier than the beginning of the Wharton run — and its selection is said to have "minimized difficulties in the transition from actual data to the model solutions" [18, pp. 69–70].) There are, indeed, still fewer movements other than trends in the OBE control-solution series than in those for the Wharton Model. GNP grows persistently from $736 billion in 1966 to $3,413 billion in 1990, or more than 4.6 times. $GNP58$ increases likewise from $649 billion to $1,675 billion, or nearly 2.6 times. The implied rates of growth are significantly higher here than in the solution of the Wharton Model (see Sec. 4.1.1 above), so that the GNP series reach higher levels sooner.

Of the twenty-one variables covered, all but seven have continuous upward trends in the OBE simulations. The others are: II and OMD (which show slight initial declines and a few minor, sporadic irregularities superimposed on their basic growth-trends); NE (which declines smoothly in the first eight years, then rises smoothly for the rest of the simulation period); UN (which trends downward, with a few discontinuities); AWW (which shows a short dip in 1966–68, then a rise in the 1970's, and a smoother decline in the 1980's); and finally, the interest rates RS and RL (which, like AWW, but still more smoothly, increase in the first half and decrease in the second half of the simulation period). The behavior patterns of these seven series are for the most part quite different for the OBE Model than for the Wharton

Model, but they all seem rather arbitrary when compared with the historical movements and, perhaps, may best be viewed as concomitants of the search for broadly satisfactory end results in terms of the control solution for the over-all aggregates.

In short, the conclusion reached in Sec. 4.1.1 for the Wharton Model applies here at least as strongly: the nonstochastic simulations for the sample period (1953–66 for the OBE Model) contain substantial cyclical elements, whereas the corresponding simulations for the subsequent (largely future) period of twenty-five years contain practically no such elements. One likely reason for this is that the exogenous variables are not permitted to fluctuate but are assumed, in many cases, to grow strongly throughout the simulation period. Notably, the federal defense purchases and total government nondefense expenditures on goods and services are set to increase persistently at average annual rates of 5.4 and 10.9 per cent, respectively [18, Sec. 4.2].

4.2.2   Against this background of growth, the GNP series that are derived by stochastic simulations of the OBE Model show, primarily, strong upward trends and very few declines (as illustrated by some randomly chosen runs in Chart 4.6). Indeed, only three of the twenty-five runs with non-autocorrelated random shocks, S_u, produce any downward movements at all in the GNP series (Table 4.9, column 1). Declines are much more frequent in the $GNP58$ series computed from these runs (column 2), but they are very rare in both GNP and $GNP58$ for the simulations with autocorrelated disturbances, S_c (columns 3 and 4). In all of the one-hundred series of 100 quarters each that are covered in Table 4.9, we count only 31 declines, none longer than one quarter (lines 2 to 4). Moreover, the few downturns that do show up are quite small, averaging from 0.15 to 0.24 per cent per quarter for the four sets of simulations (line 7). Being seldom interrupted, the expansions in the S_u series for GNP and in the S_c series for both GNP and $GNP58$ account for nearly the whole length of the simulation period, averaging from 91 to 99 quarters; and in the S_u series for $GNP58$ their mean duration is still not less than 59 quarters (line 5).[49]

These results contrast sharply with the observations for actual

---

[49] In a series with no declines, the expansion lasts 99 quarters; in one with a single one-quarter decline and two expansions, the average length of the latter is 49 quarters. These are the most frequent outcomes for the runs considered here.

CHART 4.6

A Random Sample of Stochastic 100-Quarter Simulations for GNP in Current and Constant Dollars, OBE Model (1966-I–1990-IV)

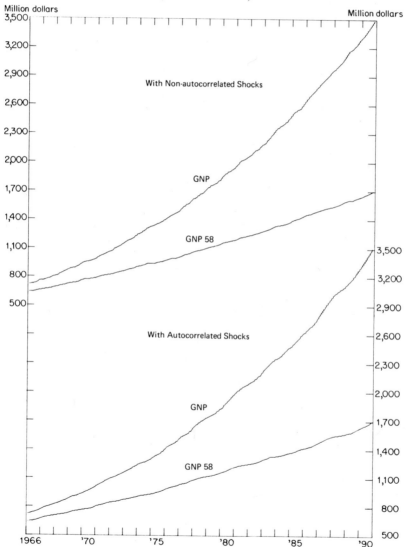

TABLE 4.9

Stochastic Simulations for 100 Quarters Beyond the Sample Period, OBE Model: Frequency, Duration, and Relative Size of Movements in GNP in Current and Constant Dollars
(1966-I–1990-IV)

Number of Series Showing—	Simulations With Serially Uncorrelated Shocks (S_u)		Simulations With Serially Correlated Shocks (S_c)	
	GNP (1)	GNP58 (2)	GNP (3)	GNP58 (4)
	Distribution of series by frequency of declines[a]			
1 No declines	22	6	24	20
2 One decline of one quarter each	3	17	1	5
3 Two declines of one quarter each	0	1	0	0
4 Three declines of one quarter each	0	1	0	0
	Average duration and amplitude[b]			
5 Mean duration of rises[c]	93.0	59.3	99.0	91.0
6 Mean size of rises[d]	3.8	1.5	3.9	1.6
7 Mean size of declines[d]	0.15	0.18	0.24	0.17

[a] Twenty-five stochastic simulation runs of each type were made; hence the entries in lines 1 to 4 of each column add up to 25.

[b] Each entry represents a mean of the averages for the given set of simulations. The averages in lines 5 and 6 include 25 figures each (means for all twenty-five runs in every case). The averages in line 7 exclude all runs with no declines; if all runs were included, the entries in this line (from left to right) would read: 0.02, 0.14, 0.01, and 0.03.

[c] In quarters.

[d] Per cent per quarter at quarterly rates.

GNP and GNP58 in the postwar period (see Table 4.1, lines 5 and 6, 11 and 12). The differences are smaller, but are still significant, when the basis of the comparison is the sample period for the OBE Model (1953-III–1966-IV). During these 54 quarterly intervals, recorded GNP had two one-quarter declines with average amplitude of 1.33 per cent per quarter. GNP58 had six declines (one of them of three quarters), averaging 1.3 quarters in duration and 0.32 per cent in amplitude. The mean duration of rises was 17.3 quarters for GNP and 6.6 quarters for $GNP58$.

It is clear that the simulated time-series for gross national income and output that result from shocked solutions of the OBE Model do not contain movements of the kind represented by the historically observed cyclical fluctuations in nominal and real GNP. However, the following two questions are pertinent: (1) Are cyclical elements also absent in simulations of various components of GNP and other sectoral indicators or—if they are present—do they tend to offset each other so as to disappear in the most comprehensive aggregates? (2) To what extent do our results for GNP reflect a state in which cyclical forces are latent but are overwhelmed by the strength of the assumed growth trends? To shed some light on (1), we present an analysis of simulations for variables other than GNP and $GNP58$. To attempt an answer to (2), we shall then turn to an evaluation of ratios of the shocked series to the control series for all variables covered by the OBE simulations.

4.2.3   Inspection of charts indicates that frequent and relatively large fluctuations are common in the stochastic simulations of the OBE Model for most of the variables covered. However, there are several variables to which this statement definitely does not apply, notably consumption, personal income, the price level, the annual wage rate per private employee, and the money supply (currency and demand deposits). The simulated series for these indicators (C, YP, P, W, and M), like those for GNP and $GNP58$, either show no declines at all or very few small and short declines. In addition, the projections for employment and labor costs per unit of output (LE and LC/O) also contain relatively few downward movements. It will be noted that these are all variables for which the recorded series have been particularly smooth and dominated by strong trends. In contrast, the simulated series with large and frequent fluctuations all refer to indicators that have varied greatly in past business cycles, such as investment in plant and equipment, housing, and inventories; unemployment, average workweek, manufacturers' orders for durable goods, net exports, and interest rates.

Simulations from three runs have been included in the complete analysis of the results for all variables. These randomly chosen runs are: 205 (with serially uncorrelated shocks) and 107 and 110 (both with serially correlated shocks).[50] Chart 4.7 illustrates the behavior of some of these series (including, for future reference, the identification of such specific-cycle turning points as can be identified).

Since the simulation period is almost twice as long as the sample period for the OBE Model, the frequencies of rises and declines would have to be about twice as large in the former as in the latter in order for the average durations (AD) of rises and declines to be approximately equal in the corresponding S and A series. Several cases of this sort are found in Table 4.10, relating to net exports, corporate profits, new orders, inventory investment (Run 107), employment (Run 205), the unemployment rate (Run 110), and the wage rate (Run 205). However, simulations for series that are typically rather volatile generally show much more numerous alterations of rises and declines than do the actual data in the sample period—often three and more times as many. Accordingly, the average durations of upward and downward movements are, as a rule, smaller in these simulations than in the actual series for the same variables—relating to investment, unemployment, the average workweek, unfilled orders, and interest rates. On the other hand, the simulations for consumption, personal income, employment, the price and wage levels, unit labor costs, and money generally have much longer expansions than those observed in the corresponding historical series. Indeed, nearly half of these simulations show monotonic growth, i.e., no declines at all. This includes all examined S series for GNP, $GNP58$, YP, and M. However, except in these extreme cases, the average durations of declines are not particularly underestimated for the variables in this set, where declines are infrequent and short in the actual series.

Thus the simulations can be divided into two groups: (1) the series with persistent expansions and few (or no) declines; and (2) the series in which both rises and falls are relatively frequent and short. Of the variables listed in Table 4.10, GNP, $GNP58$, C, YP, P, LE, W, LC/O, and M belong to Group 1, the others belong to Group 2. For the for-

[50] If and when more time and resources become available, a larger sample of simulated series of both types should be analyzed to check on the results reported in the sections that follow. Data collected and calculations made for this study will make such replications possible.

CHART 4.7

A Random Sample of Stochastic 100-Quarter Simulations for
Selected Variables, OBE Model
(1966-I–1900-IV)

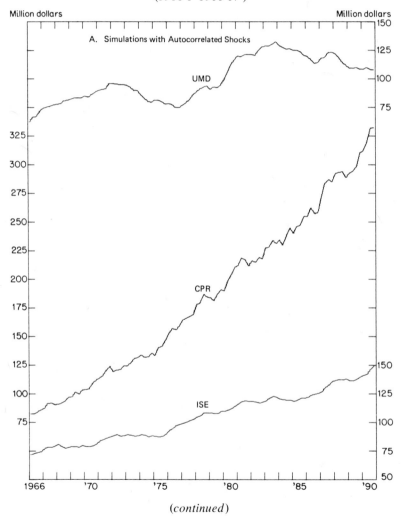

(*continued*)

CHART 4.7 (*continued*)

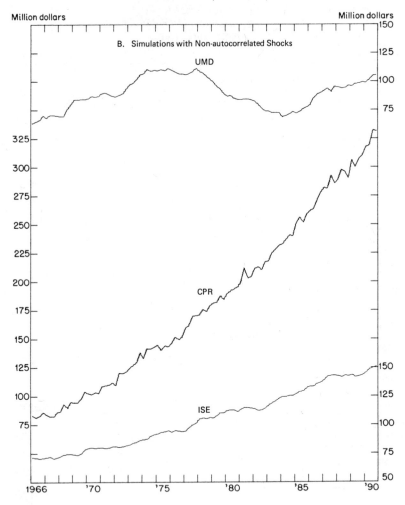

Million dollars   Million dollars

B. Simulations with Non-autocorrelated Shocks

UMD

CPR

ISE

CHART 4.7 (*continued*)

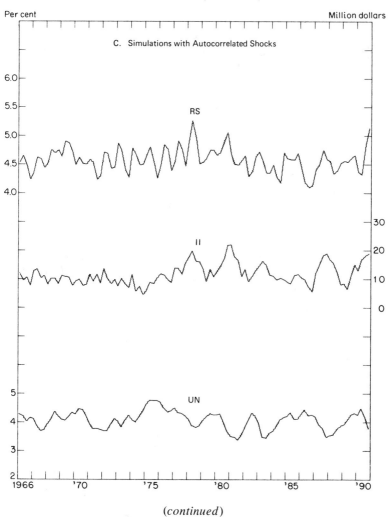

(*continued*)

CHART 4.7 (*concluded*)

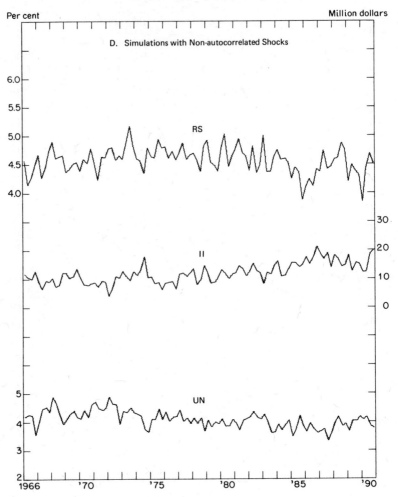

TABLE 4.10

Stochastic 100-Quarter Simulations, OBE Model: Frequency and Average Duration of Rises and Declines in Quarters for Twenty-One Variables, Comparison of Three Simulation Runs and Actuals

Line	Variable Symbol[a]	Rise (R) or Decline (D)	Actuals for the Sample Period 1953-II–1966-IV		Stochastic Simulations (Three Runs)					
					With Uncorrelated Shocks		With Serially Correlated Shocks			
					(Run 205)		(Run 107)		(Run 110)	
			Num-ber[b] (1)	AD[c] (2)	Num-ber[b] (3)	AD[c] (4)	Num-ber[b] (5)	AD[c] (6)	Num-ber[b] (7)	AD[c] (8)
1	GNP	R	3	17.3	1	99.0	1	99.0	1	99.0
2		D	2	1.0	0	0	0	0	0	0
3	GNP58	R	7	6.7	2	49.0	1	99.0	1	99.0
4		D	6	1.3	1.0	1.0	0	0	0	0
5	C	R	3	17.3	2	49.0	1	99.0	2	49.0
6		D	2	1.0	1	1.0	0	0	1	1.0
7	IH	R	5	4.0	22	2.8	18	3.7	17	4.0
8		D	6	5.7	21	1.8	17	1.8	16	1.9
9	ISE	R	4	11.0	16	4.8	18	4.2	12	6.1
10		D	3	3.3	16	1.4	17	1.4	11	2.4

(continued)

TABLE 4.10 (concluded)

Line	Variable Symbol[a]	Rise (R) or Decline (D)	Actuals for the Sample Period 1953-II–1966-IV		Stochastic Simulations (Three Runs)					
					With Uncorrelated Shocks (Run 205)		With Serially Correlated Shocks			
							(Run 107)		(Run 110)	
			Number[b] (1)	AD[c] (2)	Number[b] (3)	AD[c] (4)	Number[b] (5)	AD[c] (6)	Number[b] (7)	AD[c] (8)
11	II	R	10	2.9	30	1.8	23	2.2	27	1.9
12		D	10	2.5	30	1.5	24	2.0	27	1.8
13	NE	R	11	2.5	23	2.7	23	2.6	21	2.9
14		D	12	2.2	22	1.6	23	1.7	21	1.8
15	YP	R	2	26.0	1	99.0	1	99.0	1	99.0
16		D	1	2.0	0	0	0	0	0	0
17	P	R	1	54.0	2	49.0	1	99.0	1	99.0
18		D	0	0	1	1.0	0	0	0	0
19	LE	R	5	9.2	8	11.5	5	19.0	4	24.0
20		D	5	1.6	7	1.0	4	1.0	3	1.0
21	UN	R	10	3.0	32	1.6	22	2.1	17	2.9
22		D	10	2.4	32	1.5	23	2.3	18	2.8

23	CPR	R	12	3.0	23	3.1	23	3.1	20	3.8
24		D	12	1.5	24	1.2	22	1.2	19	1.2
25	AWW	R	7	2.0	28	1.8	34	1.6	32	1.4
26		D	7	5.7	27	1.9	33	1.4	31	1.7
27	OMD	R	15	1.9	25	2.2	24	2.3	24	2.2
28		D	15	1.7	26	1.7	23	1.9	23	2.0
29	UMD	R	4	4.8	20	2.9	20	3.0	15	3.6
30		D	4	8.8	19	2.2	19	2.0	14	3.1
31	HS	R	6	3.8	32	1.8	29	1.8	28	2.0
32		D	5	6.2	32	1.3	29	1.6	28	1.5
33	RS	R	7	5.1	30	1.7	24	2.0	25	2.0
34		D	7	2.6	31	1.5	25	2.1	24	2.1
35	RL	R	6	6.5	25	1.9	21	2.5	21	2.4
36		D	6	2.5	26	2.0	21	2.2	21	2.3
37	W	R	3	17.3	6	15.7	3	31.7	2	49.0
38		D	2	1.0	5	1.0	3	1.3	1	1.0
39	LC/O	R	11	3.7	12	7.2	5	18.6	1	99.0
40		D	10	1.3	11	1.0	4	1.5	0	0
41	M	R	4	11.2	1	99.0	1	99.0	1	99.0
42		D	3	3.0	0	0	0	0	0	0

a For meaning of symbols, see Table 1.1.
b Number of rises (R) or declines (D).
c Average duration, in quarters, of rises (R) or declines (D).

mer, the average durations of rises are heavily overestimated when compared with sample-period actuals; for the latter, they are for the most part underestimated. The average durations of declines tend to be underestimated in both groups of the simulated series, but particularly in Group 2. The frequencies are as follows:

Number of cases where—	Group 1 Rises	Group 1 De-clines	Group 2 Rises	Group 2 De-clines
AD is larger for S than for A	25	3	9	3
AD is equal for S and A	0	6	1	1
AD is smaller for S than for A	2	18	26	32
Total	27	27	36	36

For the most part, the simulations with serially uncorrelated shocks (S_u) have more frequent turning points and shorter rises and falls than the simulations with serially correlated shocks (S_c); the use of autocorrelated shocks, then, has the usual effects of smoothing (compare columns 3 and 4 with columns 5 and 6 and 7 and 8 in Table 4.10). The tabulation below shows the average durations of rises and declines in S_u and S_c for the two groups of series identified in the previous paragraph.

Number of cases where—	Group 1 Rises	Group 1 De-clines	Group 2 Rises	Group 2 De-clines
AD is smaller for S_u than for S_c	11	3	17	17
AD is equal for S_u and S_c	7	10	3	4
AD is larger for S_u than for S_c	0	5	4	3
Total	18	18	24	24

The S_u series in Group 1, having less persistent upward movements than the S_c series, overestimate the average durations of rises less in the actuals. However, they still show much longer expansions than those observed in these variables during the sample period, except for P, LE, and W (lines 17, 19, and 37; compare columns 2 and 4). With regard to the duration of declines, there is little difference between the S_u and S_c series of this group. In Group 2, where the length of both rises and declines in A tends to be underestimated, the relative advantage is often on the side of the series with autocorrelated shocks. That is, the movements in S_c — being on the average longer than those in S_u — differ less in duration from the movements in the actuals.

Table 4.11 shows the average per cent change per quarter of rises and declines in actuals and in the selected S series. It covers the same data as Table 4.10, except that II and NE, which can assume negative values, are omitted. For the relatively smooth, trend-dominated variables of Group 1, the average percentage amplitudes (APA) of rises are all larger in S than in A. In contrast, the APA of declines are here smaller in S than in A, with only two exceptions. The results are quite different for the more volatile variables in Group 2, where the average percentage changes are smaller in S than in A for both rises and falls in about 60 per cent of the cases, as shown by the accompanying figures.

Number of cases where —	Group 1		Group 2	
	Rises	De-clines	Rises	De-clines
APA is larger for S than for A	27	8	12	13
APA is smaller for S than for A	0	19	18	17
Total	27	27	30	30

In more than half of the comparisons for Group 1, the simulations with non-autocorrelated shocks, S_u, show smaller rises but larger declines than their counterparts with autocorrelated shocks, S_c. On the other hand, for the variables in Group 2, both upward and downward movements tend to be larger in the S_u than in the S_c series, as would be expected of a procedure with smoothing effects (see the tabulation on the following page).

The S_u series, having on the average larger percentage amplitudes than the S_c series, often underestimate less the relative size of movements in the actuals. By the same token, in those cases where the sim-

	Group 1		Group 2	
Number of cases where —	Rises	De-clines	Rises	De-clines
APA is smaller for S_u than for S_c	12	2	4	3
APA is equal for S_u and S_c	1	6	0	0
APA is larger for S_u than for S_c	5	10	16	17
Total	18	18	20	20

ulations overestimate the relative amplitudes of the actuals, the S_c series often differ less from A than do the S_u series. Although our sample permits twice as many comparisons for S_c as for S_u, the outcomes favor S_u about as often as S_c. Hence, the S_u series appear to have an edge over the S_c series in this respect, but this is so far merely a tentative inference from limited and rather mixed evidence.

A few general conclusions can, however, be reached with considerable confidence. The "errors" in the GNP and $GNP58$ simulations reflect, to a large extent, similar differences vis-à-vis the actuals that are observed for the simulations of real consumption expenditures. Simulations of other comprehensive aggregates and indexes — personal income, employment, the general price and wage levels, the money stock — also consist mainly of upward trends. Rises are predominantly longer and larger for S than for A, and declines are shorter and smaller. Indeed, the behavior of the S series here (Group 1) contains very few cyclical elements of the type recorded in the past. In contrast, frequent fluctuations are characteristic of the simulations for the investment variables, net exports, profits, orders, and interest rates (Group 2). These fluctuations tend to be shorter than their sample-period counterparts but are otherwise very diversified. The differences in relative size between the S and A series in Group 2 vary greatly, but not in any clearly systematic fashion: the average percentage changes in S fall short of those in A in 35 cases and exceed them in 25 cases.

4.2.4 We now turn to the analysis of ratios of the shocked to the control series for GNP in current and constant dollars. Chart 4.8 illustrates the behavior of these ratio-series. It shows that they contain frequent fluctuations, which tend to be shorter and more irregular for

TABLE 4.11

Stochastic 100-Quarter Simulations, OBE Model: Average Per Cent Amplitudes, Per Quarter, of Rises and Declines in Nineteen Variables, Comparison of Three Simulation Runs and Actuals

ne	Variable Symbol[a]	Rise (R) or Decline (D)	Actuals for the Sample Period 1953-II– 1966-IV (1)	Stochastic Simulations (Three Runs)		
				Uncor-related Shocks (Run 205) (2)	Serially Corre-lated Shocks	
					(Run 107) (3)	(Run 110) (4)
1	GNP	R	1.36	3.86	3.98	3.90
2		D	1.33	c	c	c
3	GNP58	R	0.88	1.32	1.73	1.66
4		D	0.32	0.01	c	c
5	C	R	1.17	1.39	1.77	1.39
6		D	0.46	0.02	c	0.12
7	IH	R	2.03	1.74	1.10	1.19
8		D	1.30	1.15	0.69	0.81
9	ISE	R	1.41	1.14	1.04	1.28
10		D	0.24	0.71	0.51	0.87
11	YP	R	1.71	3.89	3.95	3.94
12		D	0.46	c	c	c
13	P	R	0.50	0.65	0.82	0.85
14		D	c	0.07	c	c
15	LE	R	0.28	0.50	0.44	0.43
16		D	0.17	0.20	0.06	0.04
17	UN	R	4.09	5.84	2.91	3.34
18		D	2.32	5.45	3.02	3.22
19	CPR	R	3.72	3.32	2.51	2.22
20		D	2.10	1.52	1.09	1.22
21	AWW	R	0.04	0.35	0.37	0.43
22		D	0.07	0.36	0.42	0.40
23	OMD	R	4.56	3.21	2.53	3.07
24		D	2.70	3.05	2.34	1.98
25	UMD	R	1.67	1.81	1.72	1.87
26		D	2.12	1.50	1.17	1.27
27	HS	R	1.80	5.01	3.58	2.95
28		D	1.58	4.26	2.22	2.28
29	RS	R	9.29	4.98	4.63	4.44
30		D	5.52	4.73	3.69	3.35
31	RL	R	1.44	2.11	1.43	1.56
32		D	1.98	1.64	1.24	1.13
33	W	R	1.22	1.50	1.69	1.95
34		D	0.04	0.39	0.12	0.31
35	LC/O	R	0.59	0.81	0.68	0.89
36		D	0.27	0.12	0.16	c
37	M	R	0.52	5.12	5.15	5.11
38		D	0.15	c	c	c

or meaning of symbols, see Table 1.1.   [b] All figures are at quarterly rate.   [c] No declines.

CHART 4.8

A Random Sample of Stochastic 100-Quarter Simulations for GNP in Current and Constant Dollars, Ratios to Control Solutions, OBE Model (1966-I–1990-IV)

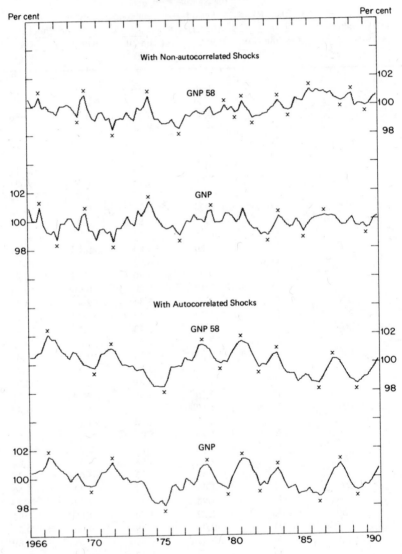

the simulations with serially uncorrelated random shocks than for the simulations with serially correlated shocks. The less erratic time-paths produced by the autocorrelated runs have been assessed by the OBE Model builders themselves as being "more in line with our expectations." This would indicate a preference for these simulations over the ones with non-autocorrelated disturbances.[51]

Since the runs used were chosen arbitrarily, there is no reason to suspect that the general observations do not apply to all runs. The ratio-series contain fluctuations that are broadly comparable to specific-cycle movements of the NBER analysis. They highlight the irregularities in the growth rates of the corresponding S series proper. The persistent upward trends that clearly dominate these simulations (see Chart 4.6) apparently conceal a great deal of variability in the deviations of the S series from the growth paths of the hypothetical shock-free solution.

The rises in the ratio series for GNP and $GNP58$ are about as long and as large as those in the corresponding declines. As shown in Table 4.12, this near-equality of upward and downward movements in the ratios applies to the simulations with non-autocorrelated shocks, S_u, as well as to those with autocorrelated shocks, S_c (compare columns 1 and 2 and 3 and 4). The symmetry extends not only to the averages, but also to the dispersion of the means for the different runs in each of the four sets.

The rises and declines in the S_u series are, on the average, more frequent, shorter, and larger than the corresponding movements in the S_c series. This, too, is a firm finding to which there are no exceptions in Table 4.12 (compare columns 1 and 3, and 5). Using serially correlated

---

[51] See [18, p. 80]. Messrs. George R. Green *et al.* also stress the contrast between the presence of "cyclical movements" in the deviations of shocked from control series for $GNP58$ and the absence of such movements in the shocked series themselves. They note that "if the criterion for the presence of cycles is that protracted downturns must occur, then the present results do not depict cyclical behavior adequately." This, however, is associated with the fact that "these simulations incorporate very strong growth elements in the exogenous variables, and such elements have to be overcome by the effects of stochastic shocks for actual downturns to occur."

It should be noted that absolute deviations (differences) are used in [18], whereas we analyze relative deviations, i.e., ratios of shocked to control series, in per cent. Our approach has some advantages in terms of standardization of measurement units and with respect to heteroscedasticity problems.

TABLE 4.12

Stochastic 100-Quarter Simulations, OBE Model, and the Corresponding Sample-Period Actuals: Summary Statistics on Frequency, Duration, and Relative Size of Rises and Declines in Relative Deviations from Trend of GNP and GNP58 (Duration in Quarters, Amplitude in Per Cent)

Line	Type of Series and Movement	Frequency		Duration			Amplitude	
		Mean or Total[a] (1)	Standard Deviation (S.D.)[b] (2)	Mean (per run)[c] (3)	S.D. (between runs)[d] (4)	S.D. (within runs)[a] (5)	Mean (per run)[e] (6)	S.D. (between runs)[b] (7)
		GNP: Ratio to Control Solution (S) or Trend (A)[f]						
	Simulations with non-autocorrelated shocks: S_u							
1	Rises	26.72	2.07	1.86	0.21	1.09	0.39	0.05
2	Declines	26.72	2.05	1.87	0.17	1.09	0.38	0.05
	Simulations with auto-correlated shocks: S_c							
3	Rises	19.16	2.37	2.70	0.43	1.93	0.30	0.04
4	Declines	19.04	2.57	2.56	0.25	1.82	0.31	0.05
	Sample period actuals: A							
5	Rises	10		3.10		3.44	0.61	
6	Declines	10		2.30		1.85	0.61	

TABLE 4.12 (concluded)

GNP58: Ratio to Control Solution (S) or Trend (A)[f]

Line	Type of Series and Movement	Frequency — Mean or Total[a] (1)	Frequency — Standard Deviation (S.D.)[b] (2)	Duration — Mean (per run)[c] (3)	Duration — S.D. (between runs)[d] (4)	Duration — S.D. (within runs)[a] (5)	Amplitude — Mean (per run)[e] (6)	Amplitude — S.D. (between runs)[b] (7)
	S_u simulations							
7	Rises	28.40	2.36	1.74	0.16	1.00	0.34	0.05
8	Declines	28.28	2.37	1.77	0.23	1.03	0.34	0.04
	S_c simulations							
9	Rises	17.42	1.93	2.92	0.38	2.00	0.28	0.14
10	Declines	17.42	2.02	2.83	0.35	1.99	0.26	0.04
	A: actuals							
11	Rises	12		2.33		3.27	0.60	
12	Declines	12		2.17		1.83	0.50	

NOTE: All simulations refer to the 25-year period, 1966-I–1990-IV; each average covers 25 runs. The actuals refer to the sample period, 1953-III–1966-IV.

[a,b,c,d,e] See the corresponding footnotes in Table 4.1.

[f] See footnote f in Table 4.4.

shocks has simply, here as elsewhere, the effects associated with smoothing.

In an attempt to construct comparable measures for the actuals, ratios of the recorded values to their exponential trends were computed from the quarterly *GNP* and *GNP58* data for the sample period of the OBE Model (1953–66). The average frequencies, durations, and amplitudes of movements in the resulting series are listed in the last two lines of the table.

Allowing for the difference in length between the sample period and the simulation period, we observe that rises and declines in *GNP* are, on the average, about as frequent in the S_c series as they actually were in 1953–66 (lines 3 to 6, columns 1 and 2). The mean duration of rises is somewhat smaller for these simulated series than for the actuals, and the mean duration of declines is slightly larger, but the differences are small. On the other hand, both the upward and downward movements in the simulated ratios with uncorrelated shocks, S_u (lines 1 and 2), are much shorter than the corresponding movements in the actual ratios (columns 3 to 4). In terms of the size of quarterly percentage changes, rises and declines in the *A* ratios are underestimated a little less in the S_u ratios than in the S_c ratios (columns 5 and 6).

The comparisons for *GNP58* yield results of the same general nature, with one exception. Unlike the case of current dollar *GNP*, S_c is here not clearly superior to S_u with regard to approximating the frequency and average duration of rises and declines in the *A* ratios. When judged by this criterion, the movements in S_c are too long in about the same measure as those in S_u are too short (columns 1 and 3, lines 7 to 12).

Because of the shortness of the OBE sample-period, one might also wish to consider the actual ratios for the Wharton sample-period, which starts in 1948 and ends early in 1968; the measures for these ratios are given in Table 4.4, lines 5, 6, 11, and 12. The trend estimates are better for the longer Wharton period, but otherwise the measures for the OBE period are more appropriate in the present context. The average duration and amplitude figures for 1948–68 are larger than those for 1953–66, and the measures for the OBE simulated ratios generally underestimate the former. Comparison with the longer sample-period results, for the most part, in larger discrepancies between the averages for the S and A ratios.

4.2.5 For most of the variables covered, the stochastic simulations for the OBE Model, in their original form, do show fluctuations; that is, declines as well as rises. (See Section 4.2.3 above.) For these variables, therefore, it is less important to use transformations of the simulated series. Nevertheless, the analysis of relative deviations from trend has been extended to variables other than GNP and $GNP58$, for the same reasons that suggested this approach earlier on. The data came from the three stochastic simulation runs which supplied the basic measures of Tables 4.10 and 4.11. The method is the same as that used in the preceding section for the GNP data. Cost-benefit considerations argued against application of more refined and diversified techniques.[52]

Chart 4.9 shows the behavior of the simulated ratio-series for selected variables. The runs using uncorrelated random shocks, S_u, produce more ragged series than those using serially correlated shocks, S_c, as elsewhere. There is a good deal of variation even in the ratios derived from those simulations that show almost no declines in levels (as, e.g., in the ratio series for C, YP, or P). Again, the specific-cycle turns marked on these graphs were selected by the computer method.

According to the information summarized in Table 4.13, movements in the ratios of shocked to control series (S) tend to be shorter than movements in the actual ratio-to-trend series (A). This applies to rises and declines alike. The average durations (AD) are smaller for S than for A in over four-fifths of the comparisons.

Both rises and declines tend to be longer in the ratio-series involving autocorrelated shocks (S_c) than in the ratio-series involving uncorrelated shocks (S_u). The AD figures are larger for S_c than S_u in about 82 per cent of the cases. Accordingly, the S_c series underestimate the length of the movements in the A ratios less than the S_u series, and even overestimate it in a few cases (notably for GNP, $GNP58$, CPR and LC/O).

Table 4.14 includes 68 instances in which the average percentage

---

[52] Different types of fitted trends are likely to be appropriate for variables with diverse characteristics, but the benefits of such selections are uncertain, and the costs would exceed the available time and resources.

CHART 4.9

A Random Sample of Stochastic 100-Quarter Simulations for Selected
Variables, Ratios to Control Solutions, OBE Model
(1966-I–1990-IV)

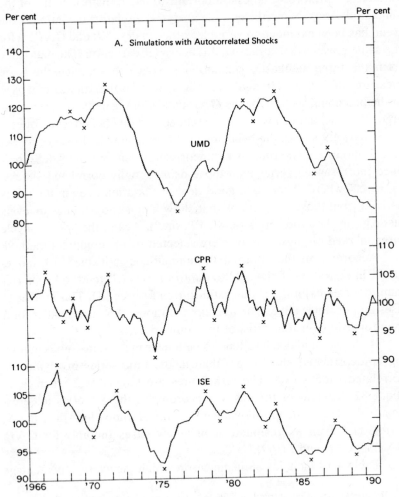

CHART 4.9 (*continued*)

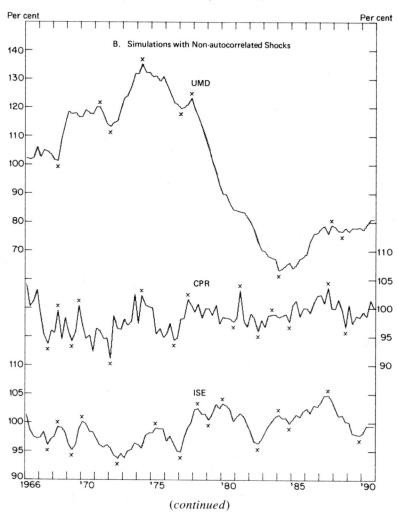

B. Simulations with Non-autocorrelated Shocks

(*continued*)

CHART 4.9 (*continued*)

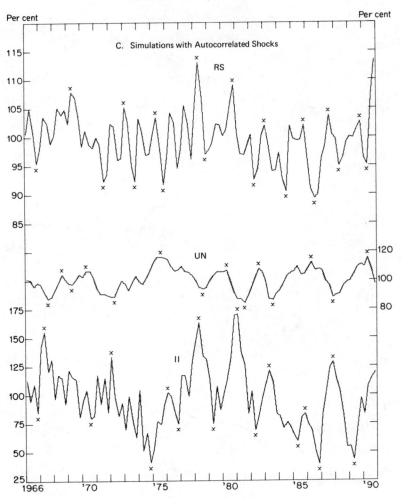

CHART 4.9 (*concluded*)

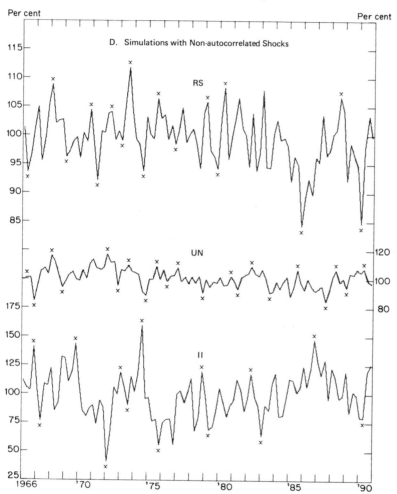

D. Simulations with Non-autocorrelated Shocks

TABLE 4.13

Stochastic 100-Quarter Simulations, OBE Model: Average Duration of Rises and Declines in Relative Deviations from Trend in Quarters, Twenty-One Variables, Actuals and Three Simulation Runs

Line	Variable Symbol[a]	Rise (R) or Decline (D)	Actuals: Ratio to Exponential Trend 1953-II– 1966-IV (1)	Stochastic Simulations: Ratio to Control Solution		
				Uncorrelated Shocks (Run 205) (2)	Serially Correlated Shocks (Run 107) (3)	(Run 110) (4)
1	GNP	R	3.1	2.0	3.4	2.6
2		D	2.3	2.1	2.8	2.8
3	GNP58	R	2.3	2.0	3.3	2.4
4		D	2.2	1.7	2.9	2.8
5	C	R	2.1	1.7	2.0	1.9
6		D	1.9	1.5	2.1	2.0
7	IH	R	3.5	2.1	2.1	2.4
8		D	4.7	2.1	2.6	2.9
9	ISE	R	6.4	2.1	2.5	3.4
10		D	5.5	2.3	2.6	3.0
11	II	R	3.3	1.7	2.2	1.8
12		D	11.0	1.6	1.8	1.9
13	NE	R	2.0	1.6	2.2	2.0
14		D	2.3	1.6	1.8	1.8
15	YP	R	2.5	2.0	2.6	2.8
16		D	2.7	2.0	2.2	2.5

17	P	R	3.2	1.8	2.0	2.3
18		D	3.5	1.8	1.9	1.9
19	LE	R	4.1	1.8	1.8	2.9
20		D	3.6	1.7	2.4	2.8
21	UN	R	2.6	1.5	2.1	2.9
22		D	2.8	1.5	2.2	2.8
23	CPR	R	1.5	1.5	1.7	1.7
24		D	1.6	1.8	1.8	1.7
25	AWW	R	4.3	1.8	1.6	1.4
26		D	4.0	1.9	1.4	1.7
27	OMD	R	1.9	1.7	2.1	1.7
28		D	2.2	1.7	2.0	1.9
29	UMD	R	3.8	2.7	2.7	2.4
30		D	5.2	3.3	2.8	3.1
31	HS	R	3.9	1.5	1.6	1.7
32		D	4.5	1.5	1.7	1.8
33	RS	R	3.0	1.7	2.0	2.0
34		D	3.8	1.5	2.1	2.0
35	RL	R	4.4	1.8	2.1	2.0
36		D	3.3	2.0	2.3	2.3
37	W	R	2.6	1.6	1.8	1.7
38		D	2.5	1.6	1.7	1.7
39	LC/O	R	1.6	1.6	2.1	1.6
40		D	1.5	1.6	2.0	1.7
41	M	R	12.0	2.6	2.8	2.3
42		D	9.0	2.5	3.1	2.2

[a] For meaning of symbols, see Table 1.1.

TABLE 4.14

Stochastic 100-Quarter Simulations, OBE Model: Average Percentage Amplitudes, Per Quarter, of Rises and Declines in Relative Deviations from Trend, Nineteen Variables, Actuals and Three Simulation Runs

Line	Variable Symbol[a]	Rise (R) or Decline (D)	Actuals: Ratio to Exponential Trend 1953-II– 1966-IV (1)	Stochastic Simulations: Ratio to Control Solution		
				Uncor-related Shocks (Run 205) (2)	Serially Cor-related Shocks (Run 107) (3)	(Run 110) (4)
1	GNP	R	0.61	0.40	0.27	0.28
2		D	0.61	0.34	0.31	0.29
3	GNP58	R	0.60	0.30	0.25	0.24
4		D	0.50	0.36	0.22	0.23
5	C	R	0.50	0.33	0.34	0.30
6		D	0.41	0.38	0.31	0.31
7	IH	R	1.74	1.38	1.08	0.93
8		D	1.21	1.39	0.79	0.91
9	ISE	R	0.56	0.82	0.86	0.74
10		D	0.71	0.80	0.63	1.03
11	YP	R	0.44	0.34	0.22	0.25
12		D	0.30	0.35	0.24	0.26
13	P	R	0.16	0.20	0.15	0.13
14		D	0.08	0.19	0.16	0.17
15	LE	R	0.17	0.23	0.21	0.15
16		D	0.21	0.26	0.15	0.21
17	UN	R	3.98	5.75	2.82	3.44
18		D	2.54	5.60	3.00	3.15
19	CPR	R	2.91	2.19	1.83	1.62
20		D	2.16	2.00	1.68	1.49
21	AWW	R	0.06	0.35	0.37	0.44
22		D	0.08	0.36	0.42	0.40
23	OMD	R	4.42	2.88	2.33	2.73
24		D	3.14	3.05	2.43	1.92
25	UMD	R	1.43	1.90	1.48	1.70
26		D	1.62	1.43	1.55	1.35
27	HS	R	1.45	4.60	3.50	2.66
28		D	1.80	4.46	2.50	2.57
29	RS	R	8.65	4.96	4.62	4.41
30		D	4.05	4.70	3.70	3.43
31	RL	R	1.23	1.92	1.34	1.56
32		D	1.80	1.78	1.24	1.20
33	W	R	0.41	0.71	0.53	0.58
34		D	0.28	0.69	0.51	0.51
35	LC/O	R	0.41	0.45	0.28	0.24
36		D	0.31	0.46	0.28	0.23
37	M	R	0.33	0.16	0.16	0.12
38		D	0.43	0.13	0.16	0.13

[a] For meaning of symbols, see Table 1.1.   [b] All figures per quarter.

size of quarterly movements is smaller for the simulated ratio-series than for the corresponding actuals, and 46 instances in which the opposite applies. The sample data suggest that the outcome depends on the type of simulation. The ratio-series with uncorrelated shocks (S_u) show a strong tendency to have larger amplitudes than the ratio-series with autocorrelated shocks (S_c).[53] The average relative amplitudes of S_u are mostly larger — and those of S_c are mostly smaller — than the corresponding measures for the actuals (with majorities of about 60 per cent in either case).

4.2.6 Following the method applied to the Wharton series and described in Section 4.1.6 above, cumulated diffusion indexes based on specific-cycle movements in the ratios of shocked to control series, were constructed for the three randomly chosen simulation runs of the OBE Model. The identification and dating of the specific cycles presented greater difficulties for the ragged series with non-autocorrelated shocks (Run 205) than for the considerably smoother series with autocorrelated shocks (Runs 107 and 110). Accordingly, the results for the former set are probably less dependable than those for the latter sets.

The three cumulated diffusion indexes are displayed in Chart 4.10. Each of them includes twenty-one series; that is, all variables covered in the OBE simulations.

As would be expected, the indexes for the different runs differ greatly in timing and amplitude of fluctuations. As in the Wharton Model, these indexes show distinct movements of cyclical duration. The tabulation on p. 509 indicates that the expansions in the indexes averaged about 6 to 7 quarters, while the expansions in the relative deviations from trends of the postwar GNP and $GNP58$ series averaged 11 to 12 quarters. For contractions, the mean durations are 6 to 11 quarters for the indexes and about 7 quarters for the GNP ratio-series. The differences between these measures are sizable but lie entirely within the range of historically observable variation. For example, without the single extra-long increase in the 1960's, the expansion averages for the GNP ratio-to-trend series would be reduced to 7 to 8 quarters. Mean duration figures for the GNP simulations in current and

---

[53] The figures in column 2 of Table 4.14 exceed the corresponding entries in columns 3 and 4 in nearly 86 per cent of the comparisons.

CHART 4.10

Cumulated Historical Diffusion Indexes for Selected Sets of Stochastic Simulations, Ratios to Control Solutions, OBE Model (1966-I–1990-IV)

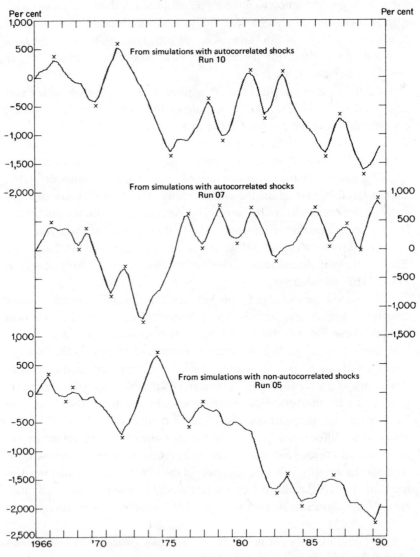

constant dollars are on the whole of the same general order of magnitude.[54]

	Ratios to Control Solution, OBE Model, Indexes of Cumulated Per Cent Expanding			Ratios to Exponential Trend, Actual Data, 1948–68	
	Run 107	Run 110	Run 205	*GNP*	*GNP58*
	(1)	(2)	(3)	(4)	(5)
	Average Duration of Movement, in Quarters				
Expansions	6.1	6.8	5.6	12.5	11.0
Contractions	5.5	9.0	10.8	7.0	6.5
Full cycle	11.6	15.8	16.4	19.5	17.5

4.2.7 Table 4.15 presents the conformity measures (frequencies of unmatched and extra turns) for the simulated ratio-series of the selected OBE runs. The measures result from timing comparisons between these series and the corresponding reference (cumulated diffusion) indexes, CDI. The table also shows the distributions of the leads and lags involved (columns 5 to 12). The average leads and lags are given in Table 4.16.[55]

The series in Run 205 have much higher proportions of extra turning points than the series in either of the other sets (Table 4.15, columns 3 and 4).[56] This is analogous to results shown in Table 4.7 for the Wharton simulations, and the reason is already familiar: the

---

[54] For eight runs (including three with non-autocorrelated shocks, S_u, and five with autocorrelated shocks, S_c), the averages, weighted by the number of cycles per run, are as follows. (The figures refer to ratios of shocked- to control-series and are expressed in quarters.)

> *GNP*: expansions, 9.7; contractions, 9.8; full cycle, 19.5.
> *GNP58*: expansions, 9.5; contractions, 9.5; full cycle, 19.0.

The S_u runs tend to show considerably longer expansions and contractions (averaging 12 to 17 quarters). The S_c runs have somewhat shorter movements (averaging about 8 to 9 quarters in either direction).

[55] The format of these tables is the same as that of the Tables 4.7 and 4.8 for the Wharton Model (in Section 4.1.7 above).

[56] There are 20 series with extra specific-turns in Run 205, 14 in Run 107, and 15 in Run 110. The average percentages of such turns are 31.0, 16.0, and 21.6, respectively.

TABLE 4.15

Cyclical Conformity and Timing of Simulated Ratio-Series, with Reference Chronologies Based on Cumulated Diffusion Indexes, OBE Model, Three Runs

		Reference Turns Not Matched[b]		Extra Specific Turns[c]		Number of Timing Observations							
						At Reference Peaks				At Reference Troughs			
									Long Leads and Lags[d]				Long Leads and Lags[d]
Line	Variable Symbols[a]	Number (1)	Per Cent (2)	Number (3)	Per Cent (4)	Leads (5)	Co-incidences (6)	Lags (7)	(8)	Leads (9)	Co-incidences (10)	Lags (11)	(12)
						Run 205: with non-autocorrelated shocks[e]							
1	GNP	0	0	0	0	0	4	2	2	0	5	1	1
2	GNP58	0	0	4	25.0	1	3	2	3	1	3	2	2
3	C	0	0	6	33.3	1	4	1	2	4	2	0	1
4	IH	0	0	6	33.3	3	1	2	3	3	1	2	3
5	ISE	1	8.3	4	26.7	1	0	4	1	3	1	2	0
6	II	2	16.7	4	28.6	1	2	2	2	2	2	1	2
7	NE[f]	1	8.3	4	26.7	1	0	4	2	2	2	2	3
8	YP	0	0	4	25.0	1	3	2	2	0	5	1	1
9	P	1	8.3	2	15.4	0	0	5	2	2	1	3	4
10	LE	0	0	6	33.3	1	2	3	0	1	4	1	1
11	UN[f]	0	0	9	42.9	1	1	4	1	1	2	3	2
12	CPR	1	8.3	4	26.7	4	0	1	0	4	2	0	1
13	AWW	0	0	8	40.0	2	2	2	1	1	3	2	0
14	OMD	3	25.0	5	35.7	2	2	0	1	3	1	1	2

15	UMD	4	33.3	1	11.1	1	1	2	1	1	1	2	1
16	HS	3	25.0	5	35.7	2	1	2	3	4	0	0	3
17	RS	3	25.0	8	47.1	2	0	2	3	1	2	2	3
18	RL	3	25.0	3	25.0	2	1	2	4	2	1	2	3
19	W	2	16.7	8	44.4	3	1	1	2	3	0	3	3
20	LC/O	1	8.3	6	35.3	0	1	4	2	3	1	2	4
21	M	2	16.7	4	28.6	0	2	3	3	2	1	2	1

Run 107: with autocorrelated shocks[g]

22	GNP	0	0	0	0	1	5	3	0	1	6	1	0
23	GNP58	0	0	0	0	2	6	1	1	2	5	1	1
24	C	0	0	0	0	4	5	0	0	4	2	2	1
25	IH	3	17.6	4	21.1	1	2	4	1	2	2	3	0
26	ISE	5	29.4	0	0	0	4	2	1	2	1	3	2
27	II	0	0	2	11.8	4	3	2	0	3	2	3	2
28	NE[f]	4	23.5	1	7.1	2	3	2	0	2	2	2	2
29	YP	0	0	0	0	2	6	1	1	2	6	0	0
30	P	3	17.6	4	22.2	1	2	4	2	0	3	4	1
31	LE	2	11.8	2	11.8	3	2	3	1	1	1	5	0
32	UN[f]	1	5.9	4	20.0	2	2	4	1	2	2	4	0
33	CPR	0	0	2	10.5	4	2	3	1	1	4	3	1
34	AWW	1	5.9	0	0	4	2	2	3	7	0	1	4
35	OMD	2	11.8	2	11.8	5	2	1	3	4	1	2	2
36	UMD	8	47.1	0	0	1	3	1	1	4	0	0	1
37	HS	2	11.8	3	16.7	4	1	3	2	4	2	1	1
38	RS	2	11.8	3	16.7	4	0	4	3	2	3	2	0
39	RL	2	11.8	3	16.7	0	3	5	0	2	3	2	1
40	W	0	0	4	19.0	3	1	5	0	3	4	1	1
41	LC/O	3	17.6	5	26.3	1	0	6	1	1	3	3	0
42	M	3	17.6	2	12.5	4	2	1	0	4	2	1	0

(continued)

TABLE 4.15 (continued)

Line	Variable Symbols[a]	Reference Turns Not Matched[b]		Extra Specific Turns[c]		Number of Timing Observations							
						At Reference Peaks				At Reference Troughs			
		Number (1)	Per Cent (2)	Number (3)	Per Cent (4)	Leads (5)	Coincidences (6)	Lags (7)	Long Leads and Lags[d] (8)	Leads (9)	Coincidences (10)	Lags (11)	Long Leads and Lags[d] (12)
						Run 110: with autocorrelated shocks[e]							
43	GNP	0	0	0	0	1	3	2	0	0	5	1	1
44	GNP58	0	0	0	0	1	5	0	0	0	4	2	0
45	C	0	0	0	0	1	4	1	0	2	2	2	0
46	IH	0	0	4	25.0	5	0	1	2	3	1	2	0
47	ISE	0	0	0	0	0	2	4	1	1	2	3	0
48	II	0	0	5	29.4	2	2	2	0	1	3	2	1
49	NE[f]	2	16.7	1	9.1	1	0	4	1	2	1	2	1
50	YP	0	0	0	0	1	2	3	0	2	3	1	0
51	P	2	16.7	3	23.1	0	0	5	3	2	0	5	3
52	LE	0	0	0	0	1	1	4	0	0	3	3	1
53	UN[f]	0	0	2	14.3	0	1	5	0	1	2	3	2
54	CPR	0	0	2	14.3	0	5	1	0	1	3	2	0
55	AWW	0	0	4	25.0	2	0	4	0	2	1	3	3
56	OMD	0	0	4	25.0	2	4	0	1	2	3	1	1
57	UMD	1	8.3	1	8.3	0	2	4	1	0	3	2	0
58	HS	1	8.3	6	35.3	5	0	0	3	5	0	1	0

TABLE 4.15 (concluded)

| | | Reference Turns Not Matched[b] | | Extra Specific Turns[c] | | Number of Timing Observations | | | | | | | |
| | | | | | | At Reference Peaks | | | | At Reference Troughs | | | |
Line	Variable Symbols[a]	Number (1)	Per Cent (2)	Number (3)	Per Cent (4)	Leads (5)	Co-incidences (6)	Lags (7)	Long Leads and Lags[d] (8)	Leads (9)	Co-incidences (10)	Lags (11)	Long Leads and Lags[d] (12)
						Run 110: with autocorrelated shocks[e] (continued)							
59	RS	0	0	7	36.8	2	2	2	2	2	2	2	2
60	RL	2	16.7	2	16.7	1	1	3	2	1	2	2	3
61	W	2	16.7	5	33.3	1	2	2	1	2	2	1	2
62	LC/O	0	0	1	7.7	0	0	6	0	2	1	3	3
63	M	0	0	3	20.0	1	3	2	0	3	1	2	2

[a] For meaning of symbols, see Table 1.1.
[b] Turns in the cumulated diffusion indexes (CDI) not matched by turns in the simulated series. For number of the reference turns (in CDI), see footnotes d and e.
[c] Turns in the simulated series that have no matching turns in CDI.
[d] Leads and lags of three or more quarters.
[e] Twelve reference turns (6 peaks and 6 troughs).
[f] Inverted (peaks matched with reference troughs; troughs, with reference peaks).
[g] Seventeen reference turns (9 peaks, 8 troughs).

TABLE 4.16

Average Timing of Simulated Series (Ratios to Control Solutions) at Reference Dates Based on Cumulated Diffusion Indexes, OBE Model, Three Runs

(Mean (M) and Median (Md) Leads (−) or Lags (+) in Months)

Line	Variable Symbol[a]	Run 205[b]					Run 107[c]					Run 110[c]				
		Peaks		Troughs		All Turns	Peaks		Troughs		All Turns	Peaks		Troughs		All Turns
		M	Md	M	Md	M	M	Md	M	Md	M	M	Md	M	Md	M
		(1)	(2)	(3)	(4)	(5)	(6)	(7)	(8)	(9)	(10)	(11)	(12)	(13)	(14)	(15)
1	GNP	+5.5	0	+1.5	0	+3.5	+1.0	0	0	0	+0.5	+1.0	0	+1.5	0	+1.2
2	GNP58	+5.5	0	+0.5	0	+1.5	-1.0	0	+0.7	0	-0.1	-0.5	0	+1.0	0	+0.2
3	C	+1.0	0	-4.0	-3	-1.5	-2.0	0	-0.7	-3	-1.4	0	0	0	0	0
4	IH	-3.0	-3	-3.0	-3	-3.0	+3.4	+3	+0.4	0	+1.9	-7.0	-4.5	-2.5	-1.5	-4.7
5	ISE	+4.2	+6	-1.0	-1.5	+1.4	+2.0	0	+0.5	+1.5	+1.2	+3.5	+3	+1.0	+1.5	+2.2
6	II	+4.8	0	-3.6	0	+0.6	-1.0	0	-0.3	0	-0.7	0	0	-0.5	0	-0.2
7	NE[d]	+13.8	+6	-4.5	0	+3.8	0	0	+1.5	0	+0.7	+3.6	+3	-1.2	0	+1.2
8	YP	+2.0	0	+1.5	0	+1.7	-1.0	0	-1.1	0	-1.1	+2.0	+1.5	-0.5	0	+0.7
9	P	+7.8	+7.5	0	+1.5	+3.6	+3.4	+3	+3.4	+3	+3.4	+10.8	+9	+15.0	+9	+12.9
10	LE	+1.5	+1.5	+0.5	0	+1.0	+1.5	0	+1.7	+3	+1.6	+2.0	+3	+3.5	+1.5	+2.7
11	UN[d]	+3.5	+3	+1.0	+1.5	+2.2	+0.4	+1.5	+0.4	+1.5	+0.4	+3.0	+3	+4.0	+1.5	+3.5
12	CPR	-1.2	-3	-5.0	-4.5	-3.2	-1.0	0	+2.2	0	+0.5	+0.5	0	+0.5	0	+0.5
13	AWW	+1.0	0	0	0	+0.5	-3.7	-1.5	-7.5	-6	-5.6	+0.5	+3	+2.5	+3	+1.5
14	OMD	-3.8	-3	-0.6	-3	-2.0	-4.1	-3	-4.7	-3	-4.4	-2.5	0	-1.5	0	-2.0
15	UMD	+9.7	+4.5	-0.8	+1.5	+4.5	-1.8	0	-6.7	-4.5	-4.0	+6.0	0	+3.6	+3	+4.0

TABLE 4.16 (concluded)

Line	Variable Symbol[a]	Run 205[b] Peaks M (1)	Md (2)	Troughs M (3)	Md (4)	All Turns M (5)	Run 107[c] Peaks M (6)	Md (7)	Troughs M (8)	Md (9)	All Turns M (10)	Run 110[c] Peaks M (11)	Md (12)	Troughs M (13)	Md (14)	All Turns M (15)
16	HS	+3.0	0	−21.0	−15	−7.7	−0.8	−1.5	−1.7	−3	−1.2	−10.8	−9	−3.0	−3	−6.5
17	RS	+3.8	+6	+3.0	0	+3.3	+1.5	0	−0.4	0	+0.6	+4.5	0	0	0	+2.2
18	RL	+1.8	0	+1.8	+3	+1.8	+2.6	+3	+3.9	0	+3.2	+10.2	+3	+1.8	0	+6.0
19	W	−1.2	−3	−1.2	+3	−1.2	+0.3	+3	−1.9	0	−0.7	+5.4	0	−4.8	0	+0.3
20	LC/O	+6.0	+6	−1.0	−1.5	+2.2	+4.3	+3	+0.8	0	+2.4	+5.0	+6	+2.0	+3	+3.5
21	M	+5.4	+9	−3.6	0	+0.9	−1.7	−3	−1.7	−3	−1.7	+1.0	0	−2.0	−1.5	−0.5

NOTE: The average leads and lags listed in this table cover the timing observations that are included in the frequency distributions of columns 5 to 12 of Table 4.15.

[a] For meaning of symbols, see Table 1.1.
[b] With non-autocorrelated shocks.
[c] With autocorrelated shocks.
[d] Inverted (see footnote f in Table 4.15).

S_u series are a good deal more volatile than the S_c series. Again, there is no systematic difference between S_u and S_c in matching the reference turns.[57]

Four of the simulations in Run 107, and six in Run 110, have perfect conformity scores (no unmatched reference or extra specific-turns), but there is only one such series (*GNP*) in Run 205. All of these cases of one-to-one correspondence between the cyclical fluctuations in CDI and the ratio-series relate to comprehensive aggregates that are expected to indicate closely the economy's broad movements. These include *GNP* in current and constant dollars, and total civilian employment; also, the cyclically sensitive, though lagging, business fixed-investment outlays, *ISE*, and *YP* and *C*, which recently have shown rather muted (but recurrent) reactions to cyclical developments.

The worst conformity-scores (highest totals of the percentage in columns 2 and 4 in Table 4.15) belong to the interest rates, price and wage levels, housing starts, and new and unfilled orders. Actual data, especially for the post-World War II period, do show *P* and *W* to conform poorly, and *HS* somewhat indifferently, but the interest rates and orders series should have performed substantially better according to their historical records.

4.2.8   According to the criteria specified in Section 4.1.8, the simulated ratio-series of the OBE Model can be classified by timing, with relatively little doubt for most variables.

(1) *GNP, GNP58, C, II, YP, LE*. These series belong in the *RC* (roughly coincident) group. For *GNP*, exact coincidences are most frequent and lags are somewhat more numerous than leads; the means are predominantly small positive ones (short lags), medians zero (coincidences). For *GNP58* the measures are similar, with somewhat more frequent leads at peaks. For *C*, there are a few more leads in two of the runs, but they are, on the whole, short. For *II*, leads are quite frequent — especially at peaks — in one run (107), and a few are long; but elsewhere, lags and coincidences are as frequent or more, and the medians are zero throughout. The *YP*

---

[57] There are 13 series that fail to match all reference-turns in Run 205, 14 such series in Run 107, and 6 in Run 110. The average percentages of unmatched reference-turns are 17.3, 17.2, and 13.9 for the three runs, respectively (Table 4.15, columns 1 and 2).

series show a few longer lags in two runs, but once more the averages are all in the *RC* range, and all but one of the medians are zero. For *LE*, lags are more numerous than either leads or coincidences, and most of the timing averages are lags of one to three months. The *LE* series, then, could be classified as roughly coincident with some tendency to lag, *RC-Lg*.

(2) *HS, OMD*. Predominantly leaders, *L*. There are long average leads at troughs in Run 205, and at peaks in Run 110, for the housing starts, and short average leads in Run 107. (However, leads and lags balance each other at peaks in Run 205.) For new orders, all means and most medians are leads, but they are short, from two to five months. The leads tend to be somewhat longer at peaks than at troughs. In at least two of the three runs, the *OMD* series can be viewed as roughly coincident with a tendency to lead, *RC-L*.

(3) *ISE, UN, P, RL, LC/O*. Generally, laggers, *Lg*. Most of the individual observations for plant and equipment investment are lags, and so are most of the averages; but they are short, in the *RC* range. The same statements apply to the series for unemployment (inverted). Both *ISE* and *UN*, therefore, qualify as roughly coincident with a tendency to lag, *RC-Lg*. The lags are often much longer for the other variables in this group, particularly for *P* and *LC/O* at peaks in Runs 205 and 110.

The evidence is somewhat more ambiguous for the remaining variables, but it permits some further groupings and observations.

(4) *IH, CPR, AWW*. The timing of these series is mainly leading or roughly coincident, *L, RC*. Investment in housing leads, on the average, by three months in Run 205, and by longer intervals in Run 110 (especially at peaks), but it shows small mean lags elsewhere. For profits, leads prevail in the averages of one run; but for the rest, the medians are zero and the means are small lags. Much the same applies to *AWW*: there are sizable leads here in one run (107), and average coincidences and short lags in the other two runs.

(5) *RS, W, M*. These are all roughly coincident series, according to the over-all timing averages (for "all turns"), but leads and lags — some of them quite long — are here much more numerous than coincidences, and just about offset each other. There are a few

long lags at peaks in two of the short-term interest-rate series. For wages, lags somewhat outweigh leads; while for money, the opposite applies.

(6) *UMD, NE.* Here the timing is particularly mixed. For unfilled orders, lags prevail in two runs, and leads in one — yielding over-all averages of about +4 and −4 (months), respectively. Net exports, when treated on an inverted basis, conform fairly well (on a positive basis, very poorly).[58] Lags dominate the averages for *NE* at peaks in two runs; in one of which, they are rather long. Elsewhere the timing of *NE* is roughly coincident.

For the most part, the timing of the simulated ratio-series for the OBE Model agrees broadly with the timing of the corresponding variables, as established from historical data.[59] The agreement extends beyond the roughly coincident national product, income, and consumption aggregates (*GNP, GNP58, YP, C*) to some sensitive leading indicators (*HS, OMD*) and some laggards (*W, LC/O,* and probably also *P*). To be sure, there are deviations from this over-all correspondence in that the behavior of some of the *S* series is occasionally contrary to expectations (e.g., *HS* at peaks in Run 205), but the similarities do prevail.

In several cases, the differences are more quantitative than qualitative and not very large. Thus *LE* and *UN* are roughly coincident according to over-all timing averages for past data; in the OBE simulations, they also belong in the *RC* group but show distinct lagging tendencies.[60] *ISE* is recognized as a lagging indicator; in the simulations, it often lags but on the average by short intervals, and hence might be labeled *RC-Lg;* however, the average lag of *ISE* has been very short in the past, too. Something similar might be said about the interest rates, where *RS* also is coincident-lagging; here, the runs with

---

[58] As noted in Section 4.1.8 (text and footnote 47), no meaningful timing comparisons could be made for this variable in dealing with the Wharton simulated series (on either basis). The rationale for the inverted treatment is that imports, which should conform positively, enter *NE* with a negative sign (*NE* = exports minus imports).

[59] See Section 4.1.8 above for a discussion of some of these historical timing patterns and related analytical problems.

[60] The unemployment rate (inverted) has often led at business-cycle peaks and lagged at troughs; but here, *UN* shows some average lags at peaks, too.

autocorrelated shocks must also be credited with having RL lag behind RS.

Investment in housing, IH, leads in two runs, and in one case by longer intervals at peaks: this agrees with its timing according to the postwar data. However, in one run (107) IH shows, perversely, some tendency to lag at peaks.

CPR — corporate profits after taxes — was included in the RC group in the 1950 list of NBER indicators, but ten years later it was shifted to the L group, in view of its longer leads in the postwar period. The average lead of CPR in Run 205 agrees approximately with the recent record, but the prevalence of coincidences and lags in Runs 107 and 110 does not.

There is evidence, too, that the timing since World War II has become earlier for another leader, the change in business inventories, II. Here the apparent discrepancies are quite considerable, since the simulations show II as roughly coincident, with leads about as frequent as either exact coincidences or lags.

The average workweek, AWW, belongs to the most dependable leaders; its median lead since 1921 has been 5 months. Only one of the simulated series (in Run 107) has a similar timing pattern, while the two others (in the RC or RC-Lg categories) definitely do not. The simulations for UMD seem rather inconsistent from run to run, and their timing is certainly quite different from that of the actuals (RC, with leads at peaks). For net exports, it is difficult to know what to expect: the series has not conformed well to domestic business cycles.[61]

The record for the money supply, M, is also easy to interpret. Total M has often shown retardations rather than absolute declines during relatively mild recessions; but where timing comparisons can be made, they suggest rough coincidence. The rate of change in M tends to lead by irregular, but frequently long, intervals. The RC patterns of most of the simulated series for this variable are probably not necessarily in conflict with the historical evidence, given the type of measurements here applied, but the long lags at peaks in one run (205) are.

[61] See Ilse Mintz, *Cyclical Fluctuations in the Exports of the United States Since 1879*. New York, Columbia University Press for the National Bureau of Economic Research, 1967, Chapter 5. Also, see footnote 58 above.

In summary, the timing of the simulations for II, AWW, and UMD disagrees with the recorded timing for these variables; and there are also considerable partial discrepancies for a few other variables, notably IH and CPR. The results seem to be better here than for the Wharton Model with respect to the verisimilitude of timing for LE, P, and RS; but the reverse applies to II, UMD, and, perhaps, AWW.

4.3 STOCHASTIC SIMULATIONS: A SUMMARY

The main results of this part of our study are based on two sets of measures: (1) frequency, duration, and relative amplitude of rises and declines, and (2) conformity and timing of cyclical expansions and contractions. They will be summarized in this order for both the stochastic simulations proper (levels) and the relative deviations of these S series from their presumed trends (ratios of shocked- to control-series). The stochastic simulations must be seen against the background of the underlying control solutions and compared with sample-period realizations in some suitable form.

4.3.1 The *control solutions* for both the Wharton and OBE Models produce, for the most part, smooth series with upward trends. There are some mild effects of the start-up shock in the Wharton Model, but no recession develops. There are some fluctuations, downward trends, or trend reversals in one or both of the control series for eight variables (II, NE, UN, CPR, AWW, OMD, RS, and RL). The trendlike control series contrast sharply with the nonstochastic sample-period simulations, which do show recurrent fluctuations, although in markedly damped form. One probable reason for this contrast lies in the fluctuations of the exogenous variables, which are included in the sample-period simulations but not in the ex ante stochastic simulations; another reason (compatible with the first one) would be specification errors of the models.

The *stochastic simulations* proper are strongly trend-dominated for GNP in current and constant dollars, and for several other comprehensive aggregates, viz., personal income and consumption, employment, price and wage levels, and money supply. There are systematic differences between the series with non-autocorrelated shocks (S_u) and those with autocorrelated shocks (S_c): the latter are far smoother than the former, hence tend to have larger average durations (AD) and smaller average percentage amplitudes (APA) of rises and declines. The Wharton S_u series for GNP and $GNP58$ show somewhat shorter and smaller declines than the historical data, while the S_c series show much fewer declines, which are all very short, and much too few rises, which are all very long. In the corresponding OBE simulations of either type, declines are altogether rare, short, and small.

For the other variables listed in the preceding paragraph, the AD of rises in the sample-period actuals are often overestimated by the S_c series and underestimated by the S_u series, particularly in the OBE runs; the AD of declines tend to be underestimated by both S_c and S_u figures. The series that have weaker trends and stronger fluctuations (relating to investment processes, unemployment, average workweek, orders, and interest rates) tend to have shorter movements than the actuals in either direction. The S_c series often underestimate the length of the movements recorded in the historical data less than do the S_u series.

For the Wharton simulations, the APA of quarterly changes tend to be too large in S_u and too small in S_c, when compared with the actuals. The OBE series have, for the most part, too small declines, and here the S_u series have the advantage of understating the APA of the actuals less than the S_c series do.

The criterion of duration is presumably more important than that of amplitude. (See p. 438.) When this is taken into account, the balance of our comparisons favors the S_c over the S_u simulations for most variables in both models. However, the S_u series yield results which are definitely better than those of the S_c series for GNP and $GNP58$ in the Wharton Model. (In the OBE Model, neither type of simulation gives directly acceptable approximations to the historical behavior of these aggregates.)

Our charts and measures leave little doubt that the shocked simulations of both models can produce extremely diversified behavior-patterns in the different variables. Indeed, it appears that they accentuate—and often overstate by historical standards—the persistence of growth in national output, income, and employment aggregates on the one hand; and the frequency of short irregular fluctuations in the more sensitive series for investment and other partial indicators, on the other. It is the intermediate, cyclical movements that seem to become blurred. But this could be due, in large measure, to the inadequate handling or scaling of the shocks — in particular, to the neglect of disturbances in the exogenous variables. Hence the proposal to analyze the *relative deviations of shocked-series from control-series,* as such experimental data might be expected to be more sensitive to, and indicative of, the cyclical effects of relatively weak impulses.

It took some working familiarity with these simulated ratio-series to recognize that the method can, and does, bring out errors of measurement, as well. Short erratic movements, often of relatively large amplitude, are a feature of many of the ratio-series, and the presence of longer cyclical movements that are not mere statistical artifacts is not always clear. Some of the control-series are probably rather arbitrary, and the procedure can, perhaps, reduce errors from this source.

It is particularly the ratios of S_u to the control-series that are highly erratic in many cases; the ratios for S_c are much smoother. The S_c ratio-series have larger AD than the S_u ratio-series in about 80 per cent of all cases, for both models; also, the former series generally have smaller relative movements (APA) than the latter. (These observations for the ratios, it will be noted, parallel those for the levels of the S series.) The simulated ratios tend to understate the AD of the corresponding sample-period actuals (relative deviations from trend), but often by much smaller margins for the S_c than for the S_u runs; indeed, the deviations are very small for the former series in a substantial proportion of the comparisons. The APA of the S_u ratios are often larger, while those of the S_c ratios are generally smaller, than the corresponding amplitude measures for the actuals; and here, the differences are frequently smaller for S_u than for S_c.

The trend-adjusted postwar GNP series in current and constant dollars are, in most cases, better approximated by the S_c than by the S_u ratios, in terms of the frequency and average durations of rises and declines. Again, giving more weight to the duration than to the amplitude criterion, the results for the ratio-series generally favor the S_c over the S_u simulations, and do so rather more strongly than do those findings based on the level comparisons.

4.3.2 In their original form, many of the stochastic simulations show only short declines — isolated or more frequent — but no recurrent fluctuations in the nature of specific cycles. This applies particularly to the comprehensive income, production, and employment aggregates; and still more to the OBE than to the Wharton series (as is evident from the charts). Accordingly, the cyclical conformity and timing analysis could be carried out fully only for the ratios of shocked-series to control-series, not for the shocked-series proper.

Using the ratio-series, cumulative diffusion indexes (CDI) were constructed for three randomly chosen runs of the Wharton Model and for three of the OBE Model. For either model, the selection includes one set of series based on the S_u simulations and two based on the S_c simulations. Each of the CDI shows reasonably well-defined cyclical movements, whose turning point dates can be used as a reference chronology with which to compare the timing of the simulated series in the given set. The average durations of the specific cycles in the CDI are of the same general order of magnitude as the average durations of cycles in the relative deviations from trends of the postwar *GNP* and *GNP58* series.

The lower the proportions of those turns in CDI and the simulated ratio-series that cannot be matched, the higher the *cyclical conformity* of the series. In general, the series involving autocorrelated shocks show fewer "extra" turns and, therefore, have better conformity scores than the more erratic series with serially uncorrelated shocks. Among the best conformers, in the models as in the historical data, are the national product and income aggregates in current and constant dollars, and also some of the largest real-expenditure components (*C*, *ISE*); among the poorest are the price and wage levels, and net exports. The interest rate simulations show relatively poor conformity in both models, and so do the Wharton series for profits, and the OBE series for new and unfilled orders — all contrary to the actual records.

Measures of *relative timing* (based on comparisons at the reference or CDI turns) show *GNP*, *GNP58*, *YP*, *C*, and *UN* all to be roughly coincident, in the simulated as in the actual data. Both models agree broadly with historical records in regard to *IH* and *CPR*, which are predominantly leading, and *ISE*, *RL*, and *W*, which tend to lag. In the Wharton Model, the average timing measures for *II* and *UMD* (leads

TABLE 4.17

Stochastic 100-Quarter Simulations (Ratio-Series) for Two Models,
Absolute and Relative Frequency Distributions of Leads and Lags
at Turns in Cumulated Diffusion Indexes
(number and per cent)

Line	Grouped Variables[a]	Total (1)	Leads (2)	Exact Coincidences (3)	Lags (4)
		Timing Observations at Business Cycle Turns			
		Wharton Model[b]			
	Leading (5)				
1	Number	159	76	42	41
2	Per cent	100.0	47.8	26.4	25.8
	Coincident (6)				
3	Number	192	45	82	65
4	Per cent	100.0	23.4	42.7	33.9
	Lagging (3)				
5	Number	89	25	19	45
6	Per cent	100.0	28.1	21.3	50.6
		OBE Model[c]			
	Leading (7)				
7	Number	256	111	72	73
8	Per cent	100.0	43.4	28.1	28.5
	Coincident (7)				
9	Number	279	62	132	85
10	Per cent	100.0	22.2	47.3	30.5
	Lagging (4)				
11	Number	142	34	36	72
12	Per cent	100.0	23.9	25.4	50.7

[a] Classified according to the timing of actuals (historical series). The variables included in each group are those used in Table 3.14, lines 1 to 6 and 7 to 12 (based on Tables 3.4 and 3.8 for the Wharton and OBE Models, respectively).

[b] Based on Table 4.7. The count includes all observations at reference (CDI) peaks and troughs for the three runs (31, 14, and 26) combined.

[c] Based on Table 4.15. The count includes all observations at reference (CDI) peaks and troughs for the three runs (205, 107, and 110) combined.

and RC) are also correct in terms of past behavior, but this is not so in the OBE Model. On the other hand, the timing patterns of LE, P, and RS are reproduced better in the OBE than in the Wharton simulations. The leading tendency of AWW is largely missed in both models. No major inconsistencies prevail in the relative timing of the OBE simulations for OMD, HS, LC/O, and M (variables not included in the Wharton Model).

Both models score relatively well on timing according to these comparisons, and neither appears clearly superior to the other. From the timing measures alone, it would not be possible to say that the S_u runs are systematically worse (or better) than the S_c runs. However, the quality of these measures seems particularly uncertain for S_u, because these series have greater frequencies of turns (all and extra) and, hence, conform worse than do the S_c series.

Table 4.17 sums up the evidence on cyclical timing of the simulated ratio-series. Like Table 3.14 for the sample-period simulations, it attempts to answer the question: How well do the models differentiate between the groups of historically leading, coinciding, and lagging indicators? These distributions classify the observations by model and timing group only, combining the individual runs and the measures at peaks and at troughs within these categories. The results are reasonably satisfactory in that, in both models, leads are more frequent than either lags or coincidences for the group of leading indicators; and, similarly, coincidences represent the modal class for the roughly coincident group, while lags represent the modal class for the lagging group. Indeed, these distributions appear to be better than those based on the sample-period simulations for Wharton and OBE in discriminating between the timing categories, because of a superior performance with respect to the group of coinciders (compare Table 4.17 with Table 3.14, lines 1 to 12, columns 6 to 9). However, the differences between the leaders and the laggers are still less pronounced here than in the distributions for the sample-period actuals (Table 3.14, columns 2 to 5).

5 CONCLUSION AND SUGGESTIONS FOR FURTHER RESEARCH

TO COMPLETE this report, three inter-related tasks remain to be done. We shall now sum up the main findings of this study, identify its principal limitations, and consider its implications for future work.

5.1 SURVEYING THE RESULTS

(1) The nonstochastic simulations analyzed in Parts 2 and 3 refer to the periods to which the models were fit and use the correct ex post values of the exogenous variables; hence, they do not provide tests of the predictive powers of the models. They do, however, subject the models to rather demanding tests of a different kind, since, in simultaneous estimation, errors are liable to cumulate across a model and over time. There is evidence that the calculated values do tend to drift away, though not necessarily continuously, in simulations that cover more than one or two business cycles. The drift is easy to spot visually on some charts for trend-dominated variables such as GNP, where it takes the form of increasing underestimation of growth. Generally, the discrepancies between the levels of the simulated and actual series are much greater than those between the corresponding quarterly changes. The reason lies in autocorrelated errors, which cumulate, thus throwing off base the long multiperiod predictions that are involved here.

(2) Simulation of turning points presents a particularly difficult test for the models. Missed turns, large discrepancies in timing, and drastically reduced amplitudes of fluctuation are all major sources of error in the simulated series that are associated with directional shifts in the actuals. For more cyclical and volatile variables, such timing and amplitude differences result in especially large errors.

(3) The nonstochastic sample-period simulations indicate that models such as the Wharton and OBE produce a progressively — and heavily — damped time-path of aggregate output (real income). Only the first one or two recessions covered have found some reflection in the declines of the simulated $GNP58$ series for these models. The FMP series, being quite short, allow no examination of whether this

model would have simulated another contraction in *GNP58* beyond the first two rounds.

(4) It is consistent with these results that the six-quarter simulations, which cover only one business-cycle turn each, disclose no dampening or other systematic changes over time. Since each of these short simulations starts from new (correctly measured) initial conditions, any one of the included episodes has an approximately equal chance to be replicated. Small shifts in the base have rather little effect; the simulations are not significantly better when they start one quarter ahead of a reference peak or trough than when they start two or three quarters ahead. About 75 per cent of the specific-cycle turns in the actual series are matched in these short simulations when the differences in timing are disregarded, whereas the corresponding proportion for the long sample-period simulations is close to 65 per cent.[62]

(5) Common to both short and long nonstochastic simulations is a strong tendency to underestimate the amplitudes of the observed cyclical movements. Since these simulations exclude the component of random disturbances which is present in the actuals, the total variance of any of them must be smaller than the variance of the corresponding historical series. However, the six-quarter and reference-cycle amplitudes refer to separate cyclical episodes, as reflected in the complete-model simulations; underestimation could well show up much less consistently in such measures than in the over-all changes in the *S* series, and it does. To the extent that the simulations underpredict the longer cyclical movements and not just the short irregular variations in the actuals, errors of this kind acquire a systematic and undesirable element.[63]

(6) The simulated series are, for the most part, classifiable according to their timing at business-cycle turns; but some of them are not,

---

[62] The gain from reducing the span of the calculations is considerably larger for real *GNP*, where short simulations still reproduce about 70 per cent of the turning points, while long simulations match only 55 per cent. There may be some bias in these comparisons in favor of the long simulations to the extent that *S* and *A* have corresponding turns that either lead or lag at the reference dates by long intervals, for such observations are included in the counts for the sample-period series but may not be included in those for the six-quarter runs. (However, the admission of the "inferred prior turns" in the latter measures—see Table 2.1 and text—should counteract some of this bias.)

[63] Underestimation of changes is not per se undesirable—indeed, it is a property of unbiased and efficient forecasts—but it can also occur in grossly incorrect predictions. See [24, p. 18] and [29, p. 43].

because they have too few turning points. The series in this subset consist mainly of comprehensive aggregates for *GNP,* employment, personal income, and consumption—series that should have shown good cyclical conformity and roughly coincident timing. Although the simulations do differentiate broadly between the groups of leading, coincident, and lagging indicators, these distinctions are much less sharp here than in the actual data. This applies to both the short, and the long, nonstochastic simulations. In particular, for the coincident indicators, the simulations show a preponderance of leads and lags that balance each other, rather than the large percentages of exact coincidences (in quarterly terms) that typify the recorded timing distributions for these series.

(7) The ex ante simulations (control-solutions), by reaching far into the unknown future, confront the models with difficult problems of internal consistency. They include, for both models examined here (Wharton and OBE), some series that are either made to behave in a more-or-less arbitrarily predetermined fashion or are permitted to behave in ways that would seem difficult to rationalize (as illustrated by the simulations for unemployment and interest rates). For the comprehensive indicators of over-all economic activity, the nonstochastic simulations for future periods, unlike those for the sample periods, produce smooth trend-dominated series rather than series with recurrent, if damped, fluctuations. Thus these models do not generate cyclical movement endogenously.[64]

(8) In the stochastic ex ante simulations many fluctuations do occur, but they are in large part too short to qualify as cyclical movements. The series with autocorrelated shocks are much smoother than those with non-autocorrelated shocks; that is, they have longer, but also smaller, declines, which interrupt their upward trends less frequently. The use of autocorrelated shocks is helpful in many—but not in all—cases: it works better for the more volatile series than for the comprehensive aggregates with dominant growth trends and sub-

---

[64] It is important to recall that here the models are unaided by fluctuations in the exogenous variables, which in reality—as reproduced in the sample-period simulations—are often pronounced. The projections for these variables are essentially monotonic growth trends, and the models evidently contain no mechanisms that would cause the simulated system to undergo fluctuations in the absence of any shocks (either in the exogenous quantitites or in the relationship with the endogenous variables).

dued fluctuations. In general, the cyclical aspects of the simulated series are much weaker than those observed in the historical series, in contrast to the long trends and short erratic variations that are often considerably stronger.

(9) Since the shocks used may not be adequately scaled, ratios of the stochastically simulated to the control series were also analyzed, in the expectation that they would show greater cyclical sensitivity. This expectation was confirmed, but the ratio-series are also much more erratic than the shocked-series proper, reflecting not only greater over-all susceptibility to the effects of the shocks but presumably, also, a telescoping of measurement errors. The ratios based on simulations with serially uncorrelated shocks are particularly volatile; those with autocorrelated shocks are substantially smoother and generally more plausible.

(10) Cumulated diffusion indexes constructed from the ratio-series exhibit specific cycles whose average duration is similar to that of cycles in trend-adjusted GNP, as recorded in the postwar period. Series that incorporate autocorrelated shocks conform better to these reference indexes than do those with non-autocorrelated shocks. The comprehensive indicators of national product, income, and expenditures, which historically rank high on conformity, also score relatively well according to these comparisons.

(11) There is considerable correspondence between the relative timing of the ex ante stochastic simulations and of the historical data for the same variables, as indicated by the average leads, coincidences, and lags of the ratio-series at reference-cycle dates — that is, at the major peaks and troughs in the appropriate diffusion indexes. The distributions of the timing observations for these series are at least as good as those for the sample-period simulations in differentiating between the groups of typical leaders and laggers — and appreciably better in identifying the coinciders. However, the total picture is less favorable than these measures alone would imply, for many turns in the more volatile ratio-series cannot be matched with the reference turns; and some that can be, are difficult to date, so that the timing comparisons involved are rather uncertain.

5.2 SOME PROBLEMS AND AGENDA

(1) One of the basic questions raised at the outset of this study has been answered in the negative by our results for the Wharton and OBE simulations: neither of these models endogenously produces movements corresponding to the historical business cycles. To answer this question for the FMP Model, nonstochastic post-sample-period simulations would be needed.

(2) The absence of any "shocks" or fluctuations in the projected exogenous variables is an unrealistic feature that could, to a large extent, be responsible for the weakness of the cyclical elements in the stochastic simulations here examined. Further experiments should test whether this weakness can be remedied, or reduced, by imposing more-or-less sporadic disturbances on the exogenous factors.

(3) More-standardized simulations for the different models are required in dealing with a comparison of the models regarding their ability to approximate the main characteristics of major short-term fluctuations of the economy. The need here is, at least, for a suitable common sample-period for the different models. Such standardization would also help to solve some analytical problems. For example, it should then be possible to learn more about the relative "damping" properties of the models.

(4) Every econometric model embodies a set of tentative hypotheses, and these theoretical frameworks can differ in important respects without any one of them being obviously unreasonable or inferior to the others: economic theory is not so well developed — and anyhow, cannot be as specific — as to preclude this situation. To the extent that this is so, the more differentiated the models are, the greater should be the potential gains from empirical studies of such models. From this point of view, it is of major interest to obtain and examine the ex ante stochastic simulations for the FMP Model, which differs importantly from other models. Comprehensive simulation studies are needed, as well, for the large Brookings system and for some other more modest, but interesting, models.

(5) This leads directly to the contributions that simulation analysis can make to a comparative study of specification errors in different

models. While we believe this to be a promising area that should be explored systematically, the subject is as vast and difficult as it is important and it was largely left outside the scope of the present report.

REFERENCES

[1] Adelman, Irma, "Simulations: Economic Processes," *International Encyclopedia of the Social Sciences*. New York, Macmillan and Free Press, 1968, Vol. 14, 268–274.

[2] ———, and Adelman, Frank L., "The Dynamic Properties of the Klein-Goldberger Model," *Econometrica* (October, 1959), 596–625.

[3] Ando, Albert, and Modigliani, Franco, "Econometric Analysis of Stabilization Policies," *American Economic Review*, Papers and Proceedings (May, 1969), 296–314.

[4] Bry, Gerhard, and Boschan, Charlotte, *Cyclical Analysis of Time Series: Selected Procedures and Computer Programs*. New York, National Bureau of Economic Research, Technical Paper 10, 1971.

[5] Burns, Arthur F., and Mitchell, Wesley C., *Measuring Business Cycles*. New York, National Bureau of Economic Research, 1946.

[6] Chow, Gregory C., and Moore, Geoffrey H., "An Econometric Model of Business Cycles." Paper prepared for the Conference on Econometric Models of Cyclical Behavior and printed in this volume.

[7] Cooper, Ronald, "The Predictive Performance of Quarterly Econometric Models of the U.S." Paper prepared for the Conference on Econometric Models of Cyclical Behavior and printed in this volume.

[8] Duesenberry, James S., Eckstein, Otto, and Fromm, Gary, "A Simulation of the United States Economy in Recession," *Econometrica* (October, 1960), 749–809.

[9] ——, Fromm, Gary, Klein, Lawrence R., and Kuh, Edwin, eds., *The Brookings Quarterly Econometric Model of the United States.* Chicago, Rand McNally, 1965.

[10] ——, Fromm, Gary, Klein, Lawrence R., and Kuh, Edwin, eds., *The Brookings Model: Some Further Results.* Amsterdam, North-Holland; and Chicago, Rand McNally, 1969.

[11] de Leeuw, Frank, and Gramlich, Edward, "The Federal Reserve-MIT Econometric Model," *Federal Reserve Bulletin* (January, 1968), 11–40.

[12] Evans, Michael K., Haitovsky, Yoel, and Treyz, George I., assisted by Vincent Su, "An Analysis of the Forecasting Properties of U.S. Econometric Models." Paper prepared for the Conference on Econometric Models of Cyclical Behavior and printed in this volume.

[13] ——, and Klein, Lawrence R., *The Wharton Econometric Model.* Studies in Quantitative Economics No. 2, Economics Research Unit, University of Pennsylvania, Philadelphia, 1967.

[14] ——, Klein, Lawrence R., and Saito, Mitsuo, "Short-Run Prediction and Long-Run Simulation of the Wharton Model." Paper prepared for the Conference on Econometric Models of Cyclical Behavior and printed in this volume.

[15] Fisher, G. H., "Some Comments on Stochastic Macro-economic Models," *American Economic Review* (September, 1952), 528–539.

[16] Frisch, Ragnar, "Propagation Problems and Impulse Problems in Dynamic Economics," *Essays in Honor of Gustav Cassel.* London, Allen and Unwin, 1933.

[17] Fromm, Gary, and Taubman, Paul, *Policy Simulations with an Econometric Model.* Washington, Brookings Institution, 1968.

[18] Green, George R., in association with Liebenberg, Maurice, and Hirsch, Albert A., "Short- and Long-Term Simulations with the OBE Econometric Model." Paper prepared for the Conference on Econometric Models of Cyclical Behavior and printed in this volume.

[19] Haavelmo, Trygve, "The Inadequacy of Testing Dynamic Theory by Comparing Theoretical Solutions and Observed Cycles," *Econometrica* (October, 1940), 312–321.

[20] Howrey, E. Philip, "Dynamic Properties of a Condensed Version of the Wharton Model." Paper prepared for the Conference on Econometric Models of Cyclical Behavior and printed in this volume.

[21] Klein, Lawrence R., "A Postwar Quarterly Model: Description and Applications," *Models of Income Determination*. Studies in Income and Wealth, Vol. 28. Princeton, Princeton University Press for the National Bureau of Economic Research, 1964.

[22] ———, and Goldberger, Arthur S., *An Econometric Model of the United States 1929-1952*. Amsterdam, North-Holland, 1955.

[23] Liebenberg, Maurice, Hirsch, Albert A., and Popkin, Joel, "A Quarterly Econometric Model of the United States: A Progress Report," *Survey of Current Business* (May, 1966), 13-39.

[24] Mincer, Jacob, and Zarnowitz, Victor, "The Evaluation of Economic Forecasts," *Economic Forecasts and Expectations: Analyses of Forecasting Behavior and Performance*. Jacob Mincer, ed. New York, Columbia University Press for the National Bureau of Economic Research, 1969.

[25] Modigliani, Franco, "Econometric Models of Stabilization Policies." Paper prepared for the Third Far Eastern Meeting of the Econometric Society, June, 1968.

[26] Moore, Geoffrey H., ed., *Business Cycle Indicators*. Volume I. Princeton, Princeton University Press for the National Bureau of Economic Research, 1961.

[27] Rasche, Robert H., and Shapiro, Harold T., "The F.R.B.-M.I.T. Econometric Model: Its Special Features," *American Economic Review* (May, 1968), 123-149.

[28] Slutsky, Eugen, "The Summation of Random Causes as the Source of Cyclic Processes." Vol. III, No. 1, Conjuncture Institute of Moscow, 1927 (in Russian). English translation in *Econometrica* (1937), 105-146.

[29] Zarnowitz, Victor, *An Appraisal of Short-Term Economic Forecasts*. NBER Occasional Paper 104. New York, Columbia University Press for the National Bureau of Economic Research, 1967.

[30] ———, "On the Dating of Business Cycles," *Journal of Business* (April, 1963), 179-199.

DISCUSSION

IRMA ADELMAN

NORTHWESTERN UNIVERSITY

Zarnowitz et al. are to be congratulated on their unusually careful analysis of the dynamic properties of the recent econometric models. On the whole, their tests offer confirmation of the findings of my husband and myself in our earlier paper on the dynamic properties of the Klein-Goldberger model.[1] All the models tested by them were non-cyclical in their behavior in the absence of shocks;[2] the amplitudes and frequencies of oscillation in the presence of shocks were rather similar to those in the U.S. economy. Nevertheless, the basic issue raised by our paper (namely: Are the cycles induced by stochastic forces exogenous to the models, or are the models a poor representation of the actual economy?) remains unsolved. This is so because all of the models tested strongly resemble the Klein-Goldberger Model in their basic structural specification of the economy. The only model whose economic and mathematical structure is somewhat different (the MIT-FRB Model) could not be tested, since the simulation results were not made available to Zarnowitz et al. while their paper was being prepared. If the analysis of the simulation results with the MIT-FRB Model leads to conclusions similar to those derived from the other models, this will, to my mind, tip the scale in favor of the hypothesis that the origin of business cycles in the real economy is truly stochastic.

Naturally, even if the dynamic simulations—whether shocked or nonshocked—indicate that the dynamic properties of a model resemble those of the U.S. economy exactly, this cannot be taken as a sufficient test of the validity of the model. The reason for this is that the dynamic simulations are based on simultaneous solutions of the *reduced forms*

---

[1] I. Adelman and F. L. Adelman, "The Dynamic Properties of the Klein-Goldberger Model," *Econometrica* (Oct., 1959), 596–625.

[2] In this connection, it is only the stochastic simulations for 25 years, using the extrapolated values of the exogenous variables, which are truly free of shocks over the sample period. Both the nonstochastic simulations using actual values of the exogenous variables and the nonstochastic simulations over six quarters—starting from actual values—contain shocks. The first set of simulations includes shocks in exogenous variables, while the second set incorporates shocks in initial conditions.

of the models, with the lagged endogenous variables treated as endogenous; but to any given reduced form there can correspond an infinite number of differently specified structural models, even when the model is identified in the statistical sense. Identification of structural parameters requires equating certain coefficients of the structural model with specific combinations of coefficients of the reduced forms; in the absence of both the structural specification and the reduced form estimates, one cannot infer a particular model structure from a specific set of reduced forms. Therefore, an exploration of the dynamic properties of a model is not a substitute for an equation-by-equation validation of the structural specification of the model, as carried out, for example, in the Griliches review of the Brookings Model,[3] or in the Christ review of the Klein-Goldberger Model.[4] At a minimum, models must pass the analytic-structural tests, the dynamic simulation tests, and the forecasting tests before one can have some confidence in their validity as good approximations to the behavioral relationships of a real economy.

There is some evidence in the Zarnowitz results that a combination of Type I and Type II shocks would perform better than either kind of shock taken in isolation. The tests also offer some ground for the belief that a combination of correlated and uncorrelated shocks would be superior to either purely random (both across variables and across equations), or purely correlated, shocks. In this connection, it would be interesting to create a set of mixed correlated and uncorrelated shocks by using the output of a control-model (in the engineering sense) to generate shocks upon some of the basic input variables. The model would be used to forecast the future levels of some of the target variables (e.g., GNP, price levels, and unemployment) and then the shocks upon specific instrument variables (money supply, interest rates, government expenditures, taxes) could be determined by specifying a set of control functions. The control function for each variable would have the form

$$\delta_i^t = F_i(y_1^{ft} - y_1^{dt}, y_2^{ft} - y_2^{dt}, \ldots)$$

---

[3] Zvi Griliches, "The Brookings Model: A Review Article," *Review of Economics and Statistics*, Vol. L, No. 2 (1968), 215–234.

[4] C. F. Christ, "Aggregate Econometric Models," *American Economic Review*, Vol. XLVI (1956), 385–408.

where δ_i^t is the shock imposed by the control authorities (Federal Reserve, Bureau of the Budget, and Congress) upon instrumental variable i at time t; y_j^{ft} is the level of the jth target variable forecast for time t; and y^{dt} is the desired level of that variable for that point of time. The sign of $\dfrac{\partial fi}{\partial (y_j^f - y_j^d)}$ should be set by Keynesian conventional wisdom, and the order of magnitude of the shocks would be fixed by reference to the variance of such shocks in the past. The function F_i would probably be quadratic. Each variable in the model could then be subjected to a shock: $\mu_i^t = \lambda_i \rho_i^t + (1 - \lambda_i)\, \delta_i^t$; where ρ_i^t is an uncorrelated shock with zero mean and a fixed variance; δ_i^t is the shock calculated from the control function; and λ_i is a weighting factor $1 \geqslant \lambda_i \geqslant 0$. Such an approach to the generation of shocks would appear to be more realistic than either of the two extreme specifications employed by Zarnowitz et al. By varying λ_i towards unity one could also, incidentally, have a test of the Friedman hypothesis.

Tests of the type performed by Zarnowitz et al. are important inputs, aiding insight into both the properties of econometric models and the dynamics of a real economy. Unfortunately, the results of the careful tests performed upon the existing quarterly econometric model in the present paper suggest that we have not progressed substantially along either front during the decade since publication of the original paper by my husband and myself.

SAUL H. HYMANS

UNIVERSITY OF MICHIGAN

1. INTRODUCTION

The main task of this Conference should be to assess the existing econometric evidence as it bears on the causes of business cycles. An alternative view — and one that I tend to reject — is that we are gathered to assess various econometric models. None of the models before us is a bad model; after all, each was built by competent economists who were then willing to publish the model, to use it, and to submit it to the scrutiny of both members of the profession and the *Survey of Current Business*. Each model has had moments of glory — even forecasting real *GNP* correctly for two quarters in succession is enough to warm the heart of a model-builder. And, at times, each model will surely be very wrong. It takes very little to remember 1968.

One of the significant findings of this Conference has been the fact that the record of ex ante forecasting by a particular model has generally been superior to the model's ex post forecasting performance over the same period. The reason for this is immediately obvious to anyone who operates a model. No operator — at least, not one with much success as a forecaster — lets the computer center run his model. Rather, the operator considers the model to be nothing better than the best statement of the internal logic of the economy which he happens to have available. While he rarely tampers with the model's interactive logic, he recognizes that there are relevant factors which he *thinks* he knows, and which he is *sure* the model does not know, about current realities in the economy. In some way, he attempts to communicate this information to the model. The value of an operation like Wharton-EFA is that someone who really understands the interactions in that model will be the one to phase in the removal of the investment tax credit, or to take account of a strike, or to tell the model that it simply does not understand the state of expectations in the business sector. And what is most important, much of the relevant information which has to be communicated to the model is simply not contained in the values of the exogenous variables. That is why an outsider who does no more than feed in the exogenous data is really only testing whether the model possesses the necessary property of a dynamic structure which keeps its endogenous motion *within* the extreme limits of reality.

2. SAMPLE-PERIOD TESTS

What, then, do we make of the performance of these models in the ex post tests run by Zarnowitz, Boschan, and Moore? Specific peculiarities aside, the over-all performance was fairly successful. The major intermodel discrepancy seems to have been that FMP was capable of picking up the cyclical peak — though not the succeeding amplitude —

in 1957. In the section on sample-period simulation, Zarnowitz, Boschan, and Moore speculate that the superior performance of FMP in 1957 may be due to its having been initiated in 1956, a period far closer to the 1957 peak than the initiation period of either Wharton or OBE. However, in the section on six-quarter simulations, the authors point out that FMP's superior ability to pick up turns is maintained even when the comparison is restricted to the 1957–61 period—in which case, all the models would have been identically initiated.

Since full data were not provided, one can only speculate about the reason for this difference in behavior. One obvious possibility is that FMP does have better structural equations—at least in the particular aspects which were, at the margin, critical in reproducing the 1957 peak. A look at the available charts, the actual data, and the FMP structure does, however, suggest a plausible alternative. In real terms, GNP fell by \$7 billion in the final quarter of 1957. Final sales, on the other hand, declined by only \$1½ billion, while inventory investment experienced a sharp drop of \$5½ billion. FMP completely misses the decline in inventory investment, and projects real GNP to rise from third to fourth quarter. The sense in which FMP does pick up the cycle is in the simulation of a drop in real GNP of \$6–7 billion over the two-quarter period, 1957.4 to 1958.2, concurrent with a very small initial drop in inventory investment from fourth to first quarter, and a larger decline in the following quarter. The Wharton Model actually does a much better job than this regarding the direction and timing of simulated inventory investment, but it fails to show any decline in real GNP. Wharton, of course, is simulating all of net exports endogenously—and probably poorly enough to miss the \$3½ billion decline which followed the artificial boost from the Suez Crisis—while FMP is being fed an exogenous \$3.3 billion decline in exports. It is therefore quite possible that the discrepancy between the Wharton and the FMP simulations in late 1957 rests largely on the differences in endogeneity of the two models.

All three models produce distinct biases in their sample-period simulations. This may not be of grave concern in short-term applications of the models, though it can serve to point up weaker elements in the structure. For example, the real expenditure sectors in the three models seem to be superior in performance to the wage-price sectors, by and large. The models in question treat all, or most of, government spending exogenously, and determine endogenous interest rates largely via term-structure equations based on an exogenous short-rate or discount rate. These major inputs to the expenditure sector are, therefore, well determined in ex post simulations. Since the wage-price sector is treated as only a minor input to the expenditure sector, it is hardly surprising that the latter performs creditably. On the other hand, small errors in output-expenditure determination are capable of resulting in serious distortion of the wage-price-productivity configuration. The relative sector performances are thus not difficult to trace down.

3. STOCHASTIC SIMULATIONS

The sample-period tests revealed that under a regime of fixed-parameter simulation, the models would respond to the true values of the exogenous variables by cycling—but well within the limits of reality. Under these circumstances, the noncyclical path in response to twenty-five years of smooth exogenous variables is readily understood. This situation is about as close as we can come in practice to the textbook ideal of investigating the properties of the pure endogenous system. It corresponds to a laboratory experiment free of external shocks, free of differential policy errors, and free of changing expectations. All these results, combined with the subsequent stochastic simulations, lead me to pose the following alternative inferences.

(i) The models contain extreme specification errors. A more nearly correct specification would produce endogenous cycles even with smooth exogenous variables.

or (ii) The business cycle is not endogenous; rather it is the result of a normally stable, or damped, system reacting to external influences.

I suggest that the time has come to admit that the weight of reasoned evidence is on the side of the latter. There is simply no clear evidence to support the view that the business cycle results from the endogenous interaction of consumption and investment spending as they are *normally* determined in an industrialized market economy free of external shocks. Any stock-adjustment model which exhibits endogenous cycles, clearly rests on a gross denial of the ability of the business sector to understand the realities of an aggregative natural growth-rate. This seems particularly inappropriate as the *general* description of a highly industrialized economy with concentrated market structures.

The parameters which we estimate in our models are surely not correct — nor is the structure correct. But within the general structure, it requires only minor changes in particular parameter values to get a model to reproduce closely any cyclical episode which it does not duplicate under a fixed-parameter regime. The altered parameters cannot, however, be expected to work well in the majority of time which lies outside the turning point areas; nor will the parameter alterations adequate for one episode be those required for the next. In an important sense, then, we live with variable parameter sets. Most of the time, one set serves well to represent the system. At other times, the normal set is a poor approximation.

At some junctures, the effective parameter set may change for reasons which are not immediately clear to any observer. Such episodes are more apt to produce data outliers than anything else. They correspond in spirit to the uncorrelated shocks which — in the Type I ratio simulations — generally failed to produce a path with marked similarity to the cycles of experience.

The effective parameter set is almost sure to change when external shocks conspire to push the economy steadily away from the path on which normal expectations are fulfilled, and normal decision criteria are suitably rewarded. Such episodes are quite likely to result in a cyclical response pattern. They correspond in spirit to the correlated shocks which — in the Type II ratio simulations — succeeded in producing a path of alternating activity with duration and timing patterns remarkably close to those in the observed data.

We are as certain as we can be that throughout the past twenty-five years, expectations changed markedly at certain critical times: external factors of monetary policy, fiscal policy, and world-trade circumstances impinged on the economy; and production technology and demographic patterns changed substantially. And this is only an abbreviated list. Given the mildness of the business cycle over the same period, how can we expect the data to reveal anything other than a system which would be stable or damped in the absence of such factors?

In an obvious sense, this returns us to Frisch and his emphasis on external shocks. But more specifically, it suggests that the cycle itself arises *after* the economy has already been displaced from its normal path. The process by which the economy gropes its way back from unfamiliar events to a self-justifying set of decisions constitutes the cycle, as we know it. And that, in fact, returns us to Schumpeter. Maybe that is not such a bad place to be after all.

APPENDIX TO PART ONE: EQUATIONS AND DEFINITIONS OF VARIABLES FOR THE FRB-MIT-PENN ECONOMETRIC MODEL, NOVEMBER, 1969

ALBERT ANDO · University of Pennsylvania
FRANCO MODIGLIANI · Massachusetts Institute of Technology
ROBERT RASCHE · University of Pennsylvania

IN what follows, we define the variables and list the equations for a version of the FRB-MIT-Penn Model that was used to generate the simulation results for the analysis by the National Bureau team headed by Professor Victor Zarnowitz. This is also the version of the model used for the analysis reported by Ando and Modigliani in "Econometric Analysis of Stabilization Policies," *Papers and Proceedings of the American Economic Association,* May, 1969.

A substantial revision and reestimation of the model was recently undertaken, the version of the model given below being replaced in the spring of 1970.

The equations are listed as they appear in the coding for computer simulation of the model. The variable on the left of the equality sign is the one for which the equation was normalized. The variables on the right of the equality sign are separated into two groups. The terms between the equality sign and the line of three dots, under the heading "Solve," are the ones that must be solved simultaneously for the model in the current period. The terms to the right of the dotted line under the heading "Constant" contain only exogenous and lagged endogenous variables and constants, and therefore can be taken as given in solving the model for the current period. It should be noted that the form of coding for simulation is not necessarily the form in which the behavior represented by the equation was originally conceptualized and estimated. Thus, for instance, in equation (4), CON is listed as the dependent variable, although the theory and estimation were carried out with *CON/N* as dependent (the alphabetical list of definitions begins on page 556). The demand equation for money, equation (87), is expressed with *RTB* as the dependent variable, although the original formulation was with *MD$/XOBE$* as dependent. These alterations for simulation coding will become fairly obvious as the reader becomes familiar with the listing, and he is requested to make the necessary readjustment in order to understand the behavioral hypotheses embodied in each of the equations.

The *a*'s with subscripts represent fixed numerical coefficients. Most of these are estimated from the time series data through a variety of methods, but some of them are fixed a priori in accordance with well-defined theories. The subscripts refer to positions in the coefficient matrix in the simulation program; the numerical values of these coefficients are given at the end of each sector.

R refers to the estimation error of *the previous period* for the equation in which it appears; and, therefore, the coefficient *a* attached to *R* is the autocorrelation coefficient of the error for the equation.

The variables are listed first in their numerical order in the system and then in the alphabetical order of their names. Endogenous variables are given plain numbers, and the number given to a variable corresponds to the number given to the equation explaining that variable. Exogenous variables are given a number preceded by either E or AC. The latter are those policy variables which are most commonly used for stabilization, though not all policy variables in the system are given numbers preceded by AC. The special dummy variables are unnumbered. They are mostly associated with strikes that are in the system but not explicitly carried in our data matrix.

Variables that can be measured in monetary units are either in billions of current dollars (denoted by a dollar sign after the name symbol) or in billions of 1958 dollars (without the dollar sign), except for revenues and transfer payments of governments, which are measured in billions of current dollars but have no dollar sign.

All flow variables are expressed at an annual rate. All ratio variables, such as interest rates and the rate of unemployment, are expressed as percentages.

NUMERICAL LISTING OF VARIABLES: FRB-MIT-PENN MODEL

1	X	Gross output
2	$XOBE$	GNP, OBE definition
3	XB	Gross private domestic business product
4	CON	Consumption
5	YH	Household product
6	EC	Consumer expenditures on durable goods
7	WC	Depreciation of consumer durable goods
8	KC	Stock of consumer durables, end of period
9	YC	Net imputed rent on consumer durables
10	$D - I$	Nonfarm inventory investment (1958 dollars)
11		
12		
13	RH	Rent index for residential structures (taken exogenously)
14		
15	$EH\$$	Expenditure on residential construction
16		
17	OPD	New orders for producers' durables
18	KPS	Net stock of producers' structures, end of period
19	EPS	Expenditures on producers' structures
20	EPD	Expenditures on producers' durables
21	SME	Shipment of machinery and equipment
22	OME	Net new orders for machinery and equipment
23	$OUME$	Unfilled orders for machinery and equipment, end of period
24	RPD	Cost of capital for producers' durables
25	$RTPD$	Current dollar rent per unit of new producers' durables
26	XBC	Production capacity of producers' durables
27	RPS	Cost of capital for producers' structures
28	$RTPS$	Current dollar rent per unit of new producers' structures

NOTE: Numbers without definitions or symbols denote vectors in the data matrix which are at present unoccupied.

29	*VWPD*	Present value of depreciation deduction for producers' durables
30	*KPD*	Net stock of producers' durables, end of period
31	*VWPS*	Present value of depreciation, deduction for producers' structures
32	*VPD*	Equilibrium ratio of producers' durables to output, multiplied by a constant
33	*VPS*	Equilibrium ratio of producers' structures to output, multiplied by a constant
34	*WPD$*	Bookkeeping depreciation in producers' durables
35	*WPS$*	Bookkeeping depreciation in producers' structures
36	*EGSC$*	Construction expenditures by state and local government
37	*EGSO$*	Other expenditures on goods and services by state and local government
38	*EGSL$*	Employee compensation by state and local government
39	*I*	Stock of nonfarm business inventory multiplied by 4.0, end of period
40	*XBNF*	Nonfarm business product and product of households
41	*YCR$*	Corporate retained profits
42	*QEIM*	Natural log of imports (*EIM*, 43)
43	*EIM*	Imports
44	*ECO*	Personal consumption expenditures
45	*EGS$*	State and local government expenditure on goods and services
46	*XB$*	Gross private domestic business product
47	*YH$*	Income originating in households
48	*XOBE$*	GNP, OBE definition
49	*EPD$*	Expenditures on producers' durables
50	*EPS$*	Expenditures on producers' structures
51	*ECO$*	Personal consumption expenditures
52	*EC$*	Consumer expenditures on durables
53	*XBNF$*	Nonfarm business product and products of households

54	YL$	Labor income, nonfarm business sector
55	YNI$	National income, OBE definition
56	YPG$	Total profit after depreciation and before income taxes, nonfarm business sector
57	YPC$	Net profits before income taxes of corporations
58	TCIS	Corporate income tax liability, state and local government
59	TCIF	Corporate income tax liability, federal government
60	YPCT$	Net corporate profits after taxes
61	YPCC$	Cash flow of corporations after taxes
62	YDV$	Corporate dividends
63	QTXF	Natural log of federal excise taxes (TXF, 64)
64	TXF	Federal excise taxes
65	TIBF	Federal indirect business taxes
66	TIBS	State and local government indirect business taxes
67	QTO	Natural log of OASI contributions (TO, 68)
68	TO	OASI contributions
69	QTU	Natural log of unemployment insurance contribution (TU, 70)
70	TU	Unemployment insurance contribution
71	QGB	Natural log of unemployment insurance benefits (GB, 72)
72	GB	Unemployment insurance benefits
73	GSP	State and local government transfer payments to persons
74	YP$	Personal income
75	QYTF$	Natural log of taxable income for federal personal income taxes ($1-YTF\$/YP\$$) (76, 74)
76	YTF$	Taxable income for federal personal income taxes
77	TPF	Federal personal income tax liability
78	TPS	State and local government personal income tax and nontax payments
79	YD$	Disposable personal income
80	YS$	Gross national product net of federal taxes and transfers

81	*TSC*	State and local government contributions to social insurance
82	*EGSN$*	Net state and local government expenditures
83	*QMC$*	Natural log of currency outside banks (*MC$*, 84)
84	*MC$*	Currency outside banks
85		
86	*MD$*	Demand deposits adjusted at all commercial banks
87	*RTB*	Treasury bill rate
88	*RCP*	Commercial paper rate
89	*MDS$*	Adjusted net demand deposit at all member banks
90	*MRU$*	Unborrowed reserves at all member banks
91	*RCB*	Corporate bond rate
92	*RCL*	Commercial loan rate
93	*DCL$*	Commercial and industrial loans at all commercial banks
94		
95		
96		
97		
98	*QJMSB*	Natural log of blowup factor to convert net adjusted demand deposits at member banks to those at all commercial banks (*JMSB*, 99)
99	*JMSB*	Blowup factor to convert net adjusted demand deposits at member banks to those at all commercial banks
100	*VG$*	Residual in net worth identity, billions of dollars
101	*YSG$*	State and local government income
102	*KSL*	Stock of capital owned by state and local government
103	*RSLG*	Municipal bond rate
104	*RM*	Mortgage rate
105	*ZINT*	Interpolation variable for the passbook savings equation
106	*RTP*	Effective rate on passbook savings deposits at commercial banks

107	*RSL*	Effective rate on savings and loan association shares
108	*RMS*	Effective rate on deposits at mutual savings banks
109	*RCD*	Rate on certificate of deposits
110	*QMPTA$*	Natural log of passbook savings at member banks, seasonally adjusted (*MTPA$*, 111)
111	*MTPA$*	Passbook savings at member banks, seasonally adjusted
112	*MCDA$*	Nonpassbook savings deposits of public at member banks seasonally adjusted
113	*MCD$*	Nonpassbook savings deposits of public at member banks
114	*MTM$*	Total time deposits at member banks
115	*MFR$*	Free reserves at all member banks
116	*QMSL$*	Natural log of savings and loan association shares (*MSL$*, 117)
117	*MSL$*	Savings and loan association shares
118	*QMMS$*	Natural log of mutual savings bank deposits (*MMS$*, 119)
119	*MMS$*	Mutual savings bank deposits
120	*QMIS$*	Natural log of life insurance reserves (*MIS$*, 121)
121	*MIS$*	Life insurance reserves
122	*MT$*	Time deposits at all commercial banks
123	*YD*	Disposable personal income
124	*LU*	Unemployment
125	*LE+LA*	Total employment including armed forces
126	*RDP*	Dividend-price ratio
127	*RCH1*	Cost of capital for single family dwellings
128	*RCH3*	Cost of capital for multifamily dwellings
129	*PXB*	Implicit price deflator for *XB* (3)
130	*POBE*	Implicit deflator of *XOBE* (2)
131	*PC*	Implicit price deflator for *EC* (6)
132	*PCON*	Implicit price deflator for *CON* (4)
133	*PPD*	Implicit price deflator for *EPD* (20)
134	*PRS*	Implicit price deflator for *EH$* (15)
135	*PS*	Implicit price deflator for *EGS* (45)

136	*PHC*	Construction cost index
137		
138	*VCN$*	Net worth of households
139	*LMHT*	Man-hours private domestic nonfarm business sector, including proprietors
140	*D − I$*	Nonfarm inventory investment
141	*PPS*	Implicit price deflator for *EPS* (19)
142	*LH*	Total hours per man in nonfarm private domestic business and household sectors
143	*LF+LA*	Labor force, including armed forces
144		
145	*QLMHT*	Natural log of man-hours private domestic nonfarm business sector, including proprietors (*LMHT*, 139)
146	*QLH*	Natural log of total hours per man in nonfarm private domestic business and household sectors (*LH*, 142)
147	*LEBT*	Employment, private domestic nonfarm business sector, including proprietors
148	*LE*	Total civilian employment
149		
150	*ULU*	Unemployment rate
151		
152	*PL*	Employee compensation rate in nonfarm private domestic business
153	*QYPC$*	Natural log of net profits before income taxes of corporations (*YPC$*, 57)
154	*QPXB∗*	Natural log of price deflator for nonfarm business product (*PXB∗*, 189)
155	*TSS*	Current surplus of state and local government enterprises
156	*PXBNF*	Implicit deflator for *XBNF* (40)
157	*MTP$*	Passbook savings at member banks
158	*PCO*	Implicit price deflator for *ECO* (44)
159	*IVA$*	Inventory valuation adjustment
160		
161	*GDSF*	Net deficit of federal goverment

162	*GDSS*	Net deficit of state and local government
163	*WCCA$*	Capital consumption allowance, total
164		
165	*YNNP$*	Net national product
166	*YRT$*	Rental income of persons
167	*YII$*	Interest income
168	*PI*	Price deflator for stock of inventories
169	*WCO$*	Corporate capital consumption allowances
170		
171	*UPC*	Exogenous
172	*UPCON*	Exogenous
173	*UPPD*	Exogenous
174	*UPPS*	Exogenous
175	*UPS*	Exogenous
176	*UPHC*	Exogenous
177	*UPRS*	Exogenous
178	*UPI*	Exogenous
179		
180		
181	*QHS1$*	Ln $(HS1\$/((N - N20)*(NS/NA)*PHCA))$, ln $(182/(E5 - E17)*(E88)*(188))$
182	*HS1$*	Housing starts, single dwelling units
183	*QHS3$*	Ln $(HS3\$/((N - N20)*(1 - NS/NA)*PHCA))$ $= \ln (184/(E5 - E17)*(1 - E88)*(188))$
184	*HS3$*	Housing starts, multifamily dwelling units
185	*D − DSL*	Flow of funds into savings and loan associations and mutual savings banks
186	*KH1*	Stock of single family houses
187	*KH3*	Stock of multifamily houses
188	*PHCA*	Construction cost adjusted
189	*PXB**	Price deflator for nonfarm business product
E1	*EEX*	Exports
E2	*EGF*	Federal government expenditures on goods and services
E3	*YRW*	Income originating in the rest of the world
E4	*EGFL$*	Compensation of federal government employees
E5	*N*	Population

E6		
E7		
E8		
E9	*UWPS*	Rate of depreciation of producers' structures
E10	*TIME*	Time, 1 in 1947-1
E11	*UDC*	Desired proportion of debt in corporate capital
E12	*UWPD*	Depreciation rate for producers' durable equipment
E13	*ZLNG*	Dummy variable for long amendment on depreciation basis
E14	*D − IF*	Farm inventory investment
E15	*WAPD*	Proportion of new equipment depreciated using accelerated depreciation method
E16	*WAPS*	Proportion of new structures depreciated using accelerated depreciation method
E17	*N20/N*	Ratio of population under 20 to total population
E18	*GFS*	Federal grants-in-aid to state and local governments
E19	*EGPD+*	Federal government defense procurement expenditures, led one period
E20	*NDI*	Number of man-hours idle (>10 million) due to major strikes
E21	*WPIF*	Wholesale price index for rest of world
E22	*JCAA*	Dummy variable for Canadian auto agreement
E23	*YRW$*	Income originating in rest of the world
E24	*TCDF*	Federal customs duties
E25	*JOA*	Dummy variable for OASI coverage change
E26	*JOB*	Dummy variable for OASI coverage change
E27	*JOC*	Dummy variable for OASI coverage change
E28	*JOD*	Dummy variable for OASI coverage change
E29	*TUIC*	Ratio of covered to total labor force
E30	*L26U*	Percentage of unemployed who are unemployed twenty-six weeks or less
E31		
E32	*TEGF*	Federal estate and gift taxes
E33	*GBFC*	Unemployment benefits beyond twenty-six weeks paid by federal government 1958–1961

E34	GFL	Federal government interest payments
E35	GFP	Federal government transfer payment to persons other than unemployment insurance benefits
E36	GFG	Federal government subsidies less surpluses of government enterprises
E37	$TUIB$	Maximum weekly benefits payable under unemployment insurance system
E38	GSI	State and local government interest payments
E39	$JS2$	Seasonal dummy variable for the second quarter
E40	$JS3$	Seasonal dummy variable for the third quarter
E41	$JS4$	Seasonal dummy variable for the fourth quarter
E42	JCD	Dummy variable for the development of CD's
E43	$JMSA$	Seasonal adjustment factor for $MD\$$
E44	$MGF\$$	U.S. government deposits at all commercial banks
E45		
E46	$JCLS$	Seasonal adjustment factor for commercial loans
E47		
E48		
E49		
E50	$JCDS$	Seasonal adjustment factor for nonpassbook time deposits at all member banks
E51		
E52		
E53		
E54	JMT	Blowup factor to convert time deposits at all member banks to those at all commercial banks
E55	PGE	Implicit deflator for compensation of government employees
E56	PYH	Implicit deflator for YH
E57	LA	Armed forces
E58	$N16$	Total noninstitutional population over 16
E59	$JR1$	Productivity time trend for man-hours equation
E60	$JR2$	Productivity time trend for man-hours equation
E61	$JR3$	Productivity time trend for man-hours equation

E62		
E63	*TT60*	Decreasing time trend, 59 in 1947-I, 1 in 1961-II, 0 thereafter
E64	*LEO*	Employment not otherwise classified
E65	*XBF$*	Farm business output
E66	*XBF*	Farm business output
E67	*JTPS*	Seasonal adjustment factor for passbook savings deposits at member banks
E68	*LPRI*	Number of males employed ages 25–65, millions
E69	*JIC*	Dummy variable for 1964 automobile strike
E70	*JSTK*	Dummy variable for 1962 stock market crash
E71	*YRC$*	Interest paid by consumers
E72	*YFT$*	Personal transfer payment to foreigners
E73	*YCRW$*	Corporate profits originating in the rest of the world
E74		
E75	*PEGF*	Price deflator for federal purchases of goods and services
E76	*TOSI*	Contribution to social insurance other than OASI and unemployment insurance
E77	*YSD$*	Statistical discrepancy
E78	*GFR*	Government transfers to rest of world
E79	*YBT$*	Business transfer payments
E80	*YPF$*	Proprietors' income in agriculture
E81		
E82	*YLAG$*	Compensation of employees, agriculture
E83	*JT1*	Strike dummy, man-hours equation
E84	*JT2*	Strike dummy, man-hours equation
E85	*JT3*	Strike dummy, man-hours equation
E86	*JT4*	Strike dummy, man-hours equation
E87	*UTP*	Property tax rate used in housing equation
E88	*NS/NA*	Proportion of persons expected to live in single-family houses
E89	*RFVA*	Average FHA-VA ceilings on mortgage rate
E90	*EHF$*	Expenditure on residential houses, farm
E91		
E92	*PWM*	Raw materials price, imports

E93	*PFM*	Raw materials price, farm
E94		
AC1	*UTC*	Marginal rate of corporate income tax
AC2	*TCPD*	Effective rate of tax credit on investment in producers' durables
AC3	*UTXF*	Index of federal excise-tax rate
AC4	*UTO*	OASI contribution rate, total
AC5	*UTU*	Unemployment insurance contribution rate
AC6	*UTPF*	Effective rate of federal personal income tax
AC7	*ZRD*	Implicit reserve requirement against net demand deposits at all member banks on call date
AC8	*ZRT*	Implicit reserve requirement against time deposits at member banks
AC9	*ZDRA*	Federal Reserve discount rate
AC10	*ZMS*	Unborrowed reserves at member banks plus currency outside of banks
AC11	*ZDR*	Federal Reserve discount rate for the first fifteen days of the quarter
AC12	*JL*	Legal reserve change dummy variable
AC13	*TEX*	Per capita exemption for federal personal income tax
AC14	*ZCT*	Ceiling rate on passbook saving deposits
AC15	*RCDC*	Ceiling rate on single maturity time deposits of one hundred thousand dollars or more
AC16		
AC17		
AC18	*SLPD*	Service life of producers' durable equipment for tax purposes
AC19	*SLPS*	Service life of producers' structures for tax purposes
AC20		

The following variables appear in the coding sheets but have not yet been assigned a position in the data matrix:

C(I)	Denotes a residual used to satisfy an identity
JIA	Dummy variable for 1959 steel strike

| | *JIB* | Dummy variable for dock strike |
| | *JID* | Time trend variable |

ALPHABETICAL LISTING OF VARIABLES: FRB-MIT-PENN MODEL

	C(I)	Denotes a residual used to satisfy an identity
4	*CON*	Consumption
93	*DCL$*	Commercial and industrial loans at all commercial banks
185	*D − DSL*	Flow of funds into savings and loan associations and MSB
E14	*D − IF*	Farm inventory investment
140	*D − I$*	Nonfarm inventory investment
10	*D − I*	Nonfarm inventory investment (1958 dollars)
51	*ECO$*	Personal consumption expenditures
44	*ECO*	Personal consumption expenditures
52	*EC$*	Consumer expenditures on durables
6	*EC*	Consumer expenditures on durables
E1	*EEX*	Exports
E4	*EGFL$*	Compensation of federal government employees
E2	*EGF*	Federal government expenditures on goods and services
E19	*EGPD+*	Federal government defense procurement expenditures, led one period
36	*EGSC$*	Construction expenditures by state and local government
38	*EGSL$*	Employee compensation by state and local government
82	*EGSN$*	Net state and local government expenditures
37	*EGSO$*	Other expenditures on goods and services by state and local government
45	*EGS$*	State and local government expenditure on goods and services
E90	*EHF$*	Expenditure on residential houses. farm
15	*EH$*	Expenditure on residential construction
43	*EIM*	Imports
49	*EPD$*	Expenditures on producers' durables

20	*EPD*	Expenditures on producers' durables
50	*EPS$*	Expenditures on producers' structures
19	*EPS*	Expenditures on producers' structures
E33	*GBFC*	Unemployment benefits beyond twenty-six weeks paid by federal government 1958–61
72	*GB*	Unemployment insurance benefits
161	*GDSF*	Net deficit of federal government
162	*GDSS*	Net deficit of state and local government
E36	*GFG*	Federal government subsidies less surpluses of government enterprises
E34	*GFI*	Federal government interest payments
E35	*GFP*	Federal government transfer payment to persons other than unemployment insurance benefits
E78	*GFR*	Government transfers to rest of world
E18	*GFS*	Federal grants-in-aid to state and local government
E38	*GSI*	State and local government interest payments
73	*GSP*	State and local government transfer payments to persons
182	*HS1$*	Housing starts, single dwelling units
184	*HS3$*	Housing starts, multifamily dwelling units
159	*IVA$*	Inventory valuation adjustment
39	*I*	Stock of nonfarm business inventory multiplied by 4.0, end of period
E22	*JCAA*	Dummy variable for Canadian auto agreement
E50	*JCDS*	Seasonal adjustment factor for nonpassbook time deposits at all member banks
E42	*JCD*	Dummy variable for the development of CD's
E46	*JCLS*	Seasonal adjustment factor for commercial loans
E69	*JIC*	Dummy variable for 1964 automobile strike
AC12	*JL*	Legal reserve change dummy variable
E43	*JMSA*	Seasonal adjustment factor for *MD$*
99	*JMSB*	Blowup factor to convert net adjusted demand deposits at member banks to those at all commercial banks
E54	*JMT*	Blowup factor to convert time deposits at all

		member banks to those at all commercial banks
E25	JOA	Dummy variable for OASI coverage change
E26	JOB	Dummy variable for OASI coverage change
E27	JOC	Dummy variable for OASI coverage change
E28	JOD	Dummy variable for OASI coverage change
E59	JR1	Productivity time trend for man-hours equation
E60	JR2	Productivity time trend for man-hours equation
E61	JR3	Productivity time trend for man-hours equation
E70	JSTK	Dummy variable for 1962 stock market crash
E39	JS2	Seasonal dummy variable for the second quarter
E40	JS3	Seasonal dummy variable for the third quarter
E41	JS4	Seasonal dummy variable for the fourth quarter
E67	JTPS	Seasonal adjustment factor for passbook savings deposits at member banks
E83	JT1	Strike dummy, man-hours equation
E84	JT2	Strike dummy, man-hours equation
E85	JT3	Strike dummy, man-hours equation
E86	JT4	Strike dummy, man-hours equation
8	KC	Stock of consumer durables, end of period
186	KH1	Stock of single-family houses
187	KH3	Stock of multifamily houses
30	KPD	Net stock of producers' durables, end of period
18	KPS	Net stock of producers' structures, end of period
102	KSL	Stock of capital owned by state and local government
E57	LA	Armed forces
147	LEBT	Employment, private domestic nonfarm business sector, including proprietors
125	LE+LA	Total employment including armed forces
E64	LEO	Employment not otherwise classified
148	LE	Total civilian employment
143	LF+LA	Labor force, including armed forces
142	LH	Total hours per man in nonfarm private domestic business and household sectors
139	LMHT	Man-hours private domestic nonfarm business sector, including proprietors

E68	*LPRI*	Number of males employed ages 25–65, millions
124	*LU*	Unemployment
E30	*L26U*	Percentage of unemployed who are unemployed twenty-six weeks or less
112	*MCDA$*	Nonpassbook savings deposits of public at member banks, seasonally adjusted
113	*MCD$*	Nonpassbook savings deposits of public at member banks
84	*MC$*	Currency outside banks
86	*MD$*	Demand deposits adjusted at all commercial banks
89	*MDS$*	Adjusted net demand deposit at all member banks
115	*MFR$*	Free reserves at all member banks
E44	*MGF$*	U.S. government deposits at all commercial banks
121	*MIS$*	Life insurance reserves
119	*MMS$*	Mutual savings bank deposits
90	*MRU$*	Unborrowed reserves at all member banks
117	*MSL$*	Savings and loan association shares
114	*MTM$*	Total time deposits at member banks
111	*MTPA$*	Passbook savings at member banks, seasonally adjusted
157	*MTP$*	Passbook savings at member banks
122	*MT$*	Time deposits at all commercial banks
E20	*NDI*	Number of man-hours idle (>10 million) due to major strikes
E88	*NS/NA*	Proportion of persons expected to live in single-family houses
E5	*N*	Population
E58	*N16*	Total noninstitutional population over 16
E17	*N20/N*	Ratio of population under 20 to total population
22	*OME*	Net new orders for machinery and equipment
17	*OPD*	New orders for producers' durables
23	*OUME*	Unfilled orders for machinery and equipment, end of period
131	*PC*	Implicit price deflator for *EC* (16)

158	*PCO*	Implicit price deflator for *ECO* (44)
132	*PCON*	Implicit price deflator for *CON* (4)
E75	*PEGF*	Price deflator for federal purchases of goods and services
E93	*PFM*	Raw materials price, farm
E55	*PGE*	Implicit deflator for compensation of government employees
188	*PHCA*	Construction cost adjusted
136	*PHC*	Construction cost index
168	*PI*	Price deflator for stock of inventories
152	*PL*	Employee compensation rate in nonfarm private domestic business
130	*POBE*	Implicit deflator of *XOBE* (2)
133	*PPD*	Implicit price deflator for *EPD* (20)
141	*PPS*	Implicit price deflator for *EPS* (19)
134	*PRS*	Implicit price deflator for *EH$* (15)
135	*PS*	Implicit price deflator for *EGS* (45)
E92	*PWM*	Raw materials price, imports
156	*PXBNF*	Implicit deflator for *XBNF* (40)
189	*PXB∗*	Price deflator for nonfarm business product
129	*PXB*	Implicit price deflator for *XB* (3)
E56	*PYH*	Implicit deflator for *YH* (5)
42	*QEIM*	Natural log of imports (*EIM*, 43)
71	*QGB*	Natural log of unemployment insurance benefits (*GB*, 72)
181	*QHS1$*	Ln $(HS1\$/((N - N20)*(NS/NA)*PHCA))$, ln $(182/(E5 - E17)*(E88)*(188))$
183	*QHS3$*	Ln $(HS3\$/((N - N20)*(1 - NS/NA)*PHCA))$ $= \ln (184/(E5 - E17)*(1 - E88)*(188))$
98	*QJMSB*	Natural log of blowup factor to convert net adjusted demand deposits at member banks to those at all commercial banks (*JMSB*, 99)
146	*QLH*	Natural log of total hours per man in nonfarm private domestic business and household sectors (*LH*, 142)
145	*QLMHT*	Natural log of man-hours private domestic nonfarm business sector, including proprietors (*LMHT*, 139)

83	QMC$	Natural log of currency outside banks (MC$, 84)
120	QMIS$	Natural log of life insurance reserves (MIS$, 121)
118	QMMS$	Natural log of mutual savings bank deposits (MMS$, 119)
110	QMPTA$	Ln (MPTA$)
116	QMSL$	Natural log of savings and loan association shares (MSL$, 117)
154	QPXB*	Natural log of price deflator for nonfarm business product (PXB*, 189)
67	QTO	Natural log of OASI contributions (TO, 68)
69	QTU	Natural log of unemployment insurance contribution (TU, 70)
63	QTXF	Natural log of federal excise taxes (TXF, 64)
153	QYPC$	Natural log of net profits before income taxes of corporations (YPC$, 57)
75	QYTF$	Ln (1-YTF$/YP$) (76, 74)
91	RCB	Corporate bond rate
AC15	RCDC	Ceiling rate on single maturity time deposits of one hundred thousand dollars or more
109	RCD	Rate on certificate of deposits
127	RCH1	Cost of capital for single family dwellings
128	RCH3	Cost of capital for multifamily dwellings
92	RCL	Commercial loan rate
88	RCP	Commercial paper rate
126	RDP	Dividend-price ratio
E89	RFVA	Average FHA-VA ceilings on mortgage rate
13	RH	Rent index for residential structures
108	RMS	Effective rate on deposits at mutual savings banks
104	RM	Mortgage rate
24	RPD	Cost of capital for producers' durables
27	RPS	Cost of capital for producers' structures
103	RSLG	Municipal bond rate
107	RSL	Effective rate on savings and loan association shares
87	RTB	Treasury bill rate

25	RTPD	Current dollar rent per unit of new producers' durables
28	RTPS	Current dollar rent per unit of new producers' structures
106	RTP	Effective rate on passbook savings deposits at commercial banks
AC18	SLPD	Service life of producers' durable equipment for tax purposes
AC19	SLPS	Service life of producers' structures for tax purposes
21	SME	Shipment of machinery and equipment
E24	TCDF	Federal customs duties
59	TCIF	Corporate income tax liability, federal government
58	TCIS	Corporate income tax liability, state and local government
AC2	TCPD	Effective rate of tax credit on investment in producers' durables
E32	TEGF	Federal estate and gift taxes
AC13	TEX	Per capita exemption for federal personal income tax
65	TIBF	Federal indirect business taxes
66	TIBS	State and local indirect business taxes
E10	TIME	Time, 1 in 1947-1
E76	TOSI	Contribution to social insurance other than OASI and unemployment insurance
68	TO	OASI contributions
77	TPF	Federal personal income tax liability
78	TPS	State and local government personal income tax and nontax payments
81	TSC	State and local government contributions to social insurance
155	TSS	Current surplus of state and local government enterprises
E63	TT60	Decreasing time trend, 59 in 1947-I, 1 in 1961-II, 0 thereafter
E37	TUIB	Maximum weekly benefits payable under unemployment insurance system

E29	*TUIC*	Ratio of covered to total labor force
70	*TU*	Unemployment insurance contribution
64	*TXF*	Federal excise taxes
E11	*UDC*	Desired proportion of debt in corporate capital
150	*ULU*	Unemployment rate
172	*UPCON*	Exogenous
171	*UPC*	Exogenous
176	*UPHC*	Exogenous
178	*UPI*	Exogenous
173	*UPPD*	Exogenous
174	*UPPS*	Exogenous
177	*UPRS*	Exogenous
175	*UPS*	Exogenous
AC1	*UTC*	Marginal rate of corporate income tax
AC4	*UTO*	OASI contribution rate, total
AC6	*UTPF*	Effective rate of federal personal income tax
E87	*UTP*	Property tax rate used in housing equation
AC5	*UTU*	Unemployment insurance contribution rate
AC3	*UTXF*	Index of federal excise-tax rate
E12	*UWPD*	Depreciation rate for producers' durable equipment
E9	*UWPS*	The rate of depreciation of producers' structures
138	*VCN$*	Net worth of households, trillions of dollars
100	*VG$*	Residual in net worth identity, billions of dollars
32	*VPD*	Equilibrium ratio of producers' durables to output, multiplied by a constant
33	*VPS*	Equilibrium ratio of producers' structures to output, multiplied by a constant
29	*VWPD*	Present value of depreciation deduction for producers' durables
31	*VWPS*	Present value of depreciation deduction for producers' structures
E15	*WAPD*	Proportion of new equipment depreciated using accelerated depreciation method
E16	*WAPS*	Proportion of new structures depreciated using accelerated depreciation method
163	*WCCA$*	Capital consumption allowance, total
169	*WCO$*	Corporate capital consumption allowances

7	*WC*	Depreciation of consumer durable goods
34	*WPD$*	Bookkeeping depreciation in producers' durables
E21	*WPIF*	Wholesale price index for rest of world
35	*WPS$*	Bookkeeping depreciation in producers' structures
26	*XBC*	Production capacity of producers' durables
E65	*XBF$*	Farm business output
E66	*XBF*	Farm business output
53	*XBNF$*	Nonfarm business product and households' output
40	*XBNF*	Nonfarm business product and product of households
46	*XB$*	Gross private domestic business product
3	*XB*	Gross private domestic business product
48	*XOBE$*	GNP, OBE definition
2	*XOBE*	GNP, OBE definition
1	*X*	Gross output
E79	*YBT$*	Business transfer payments
41	*YCR$*	Corporate retained profits
E73	*YCRW$*	Corporate profits originating in the rest of the world
9	*YC*	Net imputed rent on consumer durables
79	*YD$*	Disposable personal income
62	*YDV$*	Corporate dividends
123	*YD*	Disposable personal income
E72	*YFT$*	Personal transfer payment to foreigners
47	*YH$*	Income originating in households
5	*YH*	Household product
167	*YII$*	Interest income
E82	*YLAG$*	Compensation of employees, agriculture
54	*YL$*	Labor income, nonfarm business sector
55	*YNI$*	National income, OBE definition
165	*YNNP$*	Net national product
61	*YPCC$*	Cash flow of corporations after taxes
57	*YPC$*	Net profits before income taxes of corporations
60	*YPCT$*	Net corporate profits after taxes

E80	*YPF$*	Proprietors' income in agriculture
56	*YPG$*	Total profit after depreciation and before income taxes, nonfarm business sector
74	*YP$*	Personal income
E71	*YRC$*	Interest paid by consumers
166	*YRT$*	Rental income of persons
E23	*YRW$*	Income originating in rest of the world
E3	*YRW*	Income originating in the rest of the world
E77	*YSD$*	Statistical discrepancy
101	*YSG$*	State and local government income
80	*YS$*	Gross national product net of federal taxes and transfers
76	*YTF$*	Taxable income for federal personal income taxes
AC14	*ZCT*	Ceiling rate on passbook saving deposits
AC9	*ZDRA*	Federal reserve discount rate
AC11	*ZDR*	Federal reserve discount rate for the first fifteen days of the quarter
105	*ZINT*	Interpolation variable for the passbook savings equation
E13	*ZLNG*	Dummy variable for long amendment on depreciation basis
AC10	*ZMS*	Unborrowed reserves at member banks plus currency outside of banks
AC7	*ZRD*	Implicit reserve requirement against net demand deposits at all members banks on call date
AC8	*ZRT*	Implicit reserve requirement against time deposits at member banks

The following variables appear in the coding sheets but have not yet been assigned a position in the data matrix:

C(I)	Denotes a residual used to satisfy an identity
JIA	Dummy variable for 1959 steel strike
JIB	Dummy variable for dock strike
JID	Time trend variable

I. FINAL DEMAND EQUATIONS

A. CONSUMPTION SECTOR

	Normalization — Solve	Constant
(4)	$CON = a_1*YD + a_{476}*(VCN/(.01*PCON))$	$+ N(a_2*YD_{-1}/N_{-1} + \cdots + a_{12}*YD_{-11}/N_{-11} + a_{477}*(VCN_{-1}/.01*PCON_{-1}*N_{-1}) + \cdots + a_{479}*(VCN_{-3}/.01*PCON_{-3}) + a_{480}R_4)$
(6)	$EC = a_{491}*YD + CON(a_{495}(PC/PCON)*(.225 + .01RCB) + a_{493} + a_{494}*JIC + a_{496}(PC_{-1}/PCON_{-1})*(.225 + .01RCB_{-1}) + \cdots + a_{500}(PC_{-5}/PCON_{-5})*(.225 + .01RCB_{-5}))$	$+ a_{492}*KC_{-1} + a_{17}*N + a_{18}R_6*CON$
(7)	$WC = .05625*EC$	$+ .225KC_{-1}$
(8)	$KC = .25*(EC - WC)$	$+ KC_{-1}$
(9)	$YC = .0379*(EC/8.0)$	$+ .0379*KC_{-1}$
(5)	$YH = (a_{14}CON + a_{15}YD + a_{16} + a_{405}R_5)*(PCON/PYH)$	

B. INVESTMENT IN EQUIPMENT AND PLANTS

1. Equipment

	Normalization — Solve	Constant
(17)	$OPD = .01*(a_{43}VPD_{-2}*XB)$	$+ .01((a_{44}*VPD_{-2}*XB_{-1}) + (a_{45}*VPD_{-3}*XB_{-2}) + \cdots + (a_{53}*VPD_{-11}*XB_{-10}) + a_{60}*VPD_{-1}*XB_{-1} + a_{61}*VPD_{-2}*XB_{-2} + \cdots + a_{70}*VPD_{-11}*XB_{-11})$
(20)	$EPD = (a_{94} + a_{100}(OUME_{-1}/SME_{-1}))*OPD$	$+ (a_{95} + a_{101}(OUME_{-2}/SME_{-2}))*OPD_{-1} + \cdots + (a_{99} + a_{105}(OUME_{-6}/SME_{-6}))*OPD_{-5}$

566

			Constant
(24)	RPD	$= (1.0 - UDC*AC_1)*(a_{112}*RCB + a_{113}*RDP)$	$+ a_{114}(1.0 - UDC*AC_1)$

$$AC_1 = UTC$$
$$AC_2 = TCPD$$
$$AC_{18} = SLPD$$

(25) $RTPD$ $= 0.1*PPD(.01*RPD + UWPD)*(1.0 - AC_1*VWPD - ZLNG*AC_2)*(1.0 - AC_2*(1.0 - ZLNG))/(1.0 - AC_1)$

(29) $VWPD$ $= (1.0 - WAPD)(1.0 - EXP(-.01*RPD*AC_{18}))/(.01*RPD*AC_{18}) + 2.0*WAPD*(1.0 - (1.0 - EXP(-.01*RPD*AC_{18}))/(.01*RPD*AC_{18}))/(.01*RPD*AC_{18})$

(30) KPD $= .25EPD$ $+ KPD_{-1}*(1.0 - UWPD)/4.0$

(32) VPD $= ((.01*PXB/(0.1*RTPD))**a_{128})*EXP(a_{129}*(TIME - 46.5))$

(34) $WPD\$$ $= (.01*PPD*UWPD*KPD_{-1})/4.0$

2. Plants

		Normalization	Solve	Constant
(19)	EPS	$=$		$= .01(a_{77}VPS_{-1}*XB_{-1} + \cdots + a_{87}VPS_{-11}*XB_{-11})$ $+ a_{93}*KPS_{-1} + a_{92}R_{19}$ $+ KPS_{-1}*(1.0 - .25UWPS)$ $+ (1.0 - UDC*AC_1)*a_{411}$
(18)	KPS	$= .25EPS$		
(27)	RPS		$= (1.0 - UDC*AC_1)*(a_{126}RCB + a_{127}*RDP)$	
(28)	$RTPS$		$= 0.1*PPS(.01*RPS + UWPS)*(1.0 - AC_1*VWPS - ZLNG*AC_{17})*(1.0 - AC_{17}*(1.0 - ZLNG))/(1.0 - AC_1)$	$AC_{17} = TCPS$

NOTE: Numerical values for coefficients begin p. 588. (continued)

I. FINAL DEMAND EQUATIONS (continued)

B. INVESTMENT IN EQUIPMENT AND PLANTS (continued)

2. Plants (continued)

Normalization	Solve	Constant
(31) $VWPS$	$= (1.0 - WAPS)*(1.0 - EXP(-.01*RPS*AC_{19}))/(.01RPS*AC_{19})$ $+ 2.0*WAPS*(1.0 - (1.0 - EXP(-.01*RPS*AC_{19}))/(.01*RPS*AC_{19}))/(.01*RPS*AC_{19})$	$AC_{19} = SLPS$
(33) VPS	$= ((.01*PXB/(0.1*RTPS))**a_{130})*EXP(a_{131}*(TIME - 46.5))$	
(35) $WPS\$$	$= (.01*PPS*UWPS*KPS_{-1})/4.0$	

3. Supplementary Equations

Normalization	Solve	Constant
(21) SME	$= a_{106}EPD*(PPD*.01)$	$+ a_{107} + a_{108}*R_{21}$
(22) OME	$= a_{109}*OPD*(PPD*.01)$	$+ a_{110} + a_{111}*R_{22}$
(23) $OUME$	$= .25OME - .25SME$	$+ OUME_{-1}$
(26) XBC	$=$	$+ a_{115}XB_{-1} + \cdots + a_{125}XB_{-11} + (1.0 - a_{21})*XBC_{-1}$

C. HOUSING

Normalization	Solve	Constant

(181) $\ln(HS1\$/)$
$= a_{571} \ln(CON/.001*N) + a_{572} \ln RCH1$
$+ a_{582} \ln RCH1_{-1} + \cdots + a_{584} \ln RCH1_{-3}$
$+ a_{585} \ln(D - DSL)_{-1} + \cdots + a_{587} \ln(D - DSL)_{-3}$
$+ a_{575} \ln(PCON/PHCA)_{-1} + \cdots$
$+ a_{581} \ln(PCON/PHCA)_{-7} + a_{588}(TIME - 4.0)$
$+ a_{589} + a_{590} \ln((KH1/(1 - N20/N)*NS/NA*N*.001)_{-1}) + a_{591}R_{181}$

(183) $\ln(HS3\$/)$
$= a_{592} \ln(100.0RH/PHCA) + a_{593} \ln(RCH3)$
$+ a_{594} \ln(D-DSL)$
$+ a_{595} \ln(RCH3)_{-1} + \cdots + a_{601} \ln(RCH3)_{-7}$
$+ a_{602} \ln(100.0RH/PHCA)_{-1} + \cdots$
$+ a_{604} \ln(100.0RH/PHCA)_{-3} + a_{605} \ln(D-DSL)_{-1}$
$+ \cdots + a_{609} \ln(D-DSL)_{-5} + a_{610}(TIME - 4.0)$
$+ a_{611} + a_{612}(1.0/KH3_{-1} - 60.0) + a_{613}R_{183}$

(182) $HS1\$$
$= EXP(\ln(HS1\$/))*(1.0 - N20/N)*NS/NA*N*PHCA*.001$

(184) $HS3\$$
$= EXP(\ln(HS3\$/))*(1.0 - N20/N)*(1.0 - NS/NA)*N*.001*PHCA$

(15) $EH\$$
$= a_{614}(HS1\$ + HS3\$)$
$+ a_{615}*(TIME - 4.0) + a_{616}*(HS1\$ + HS3\$)_{-1}$
$+ a_{617}*(HS1\$ + HS3\$)_{-2} + a_{618} + EHF\$ + a_{619}R_{15}$

(127) $RCH1$
$= (1.0 - UTPF*.01)*(a_{557}RM + a_{558}RCB)$
$+ (1.0 - UTPF*.01)*a_{559}UTP + a_{560}$

(128) $RCH3$
$= a_{561}RM + a_{562}RCB$
$+ a_{563} + a_{564}UTP$

(186) $KH1$
$= a_{547}*(a_{548} + a_{549}*(TIME - 4.0))/(4.0*PRS*.01)$
$+ a_{546}*KH1_{-1} + (HS1\$/(.01*PRS))_{-1}$

(187) $KH3$
$= a_{565}*(a_{566} + a_{567}*(TIME - 4.0))/(4.0*PRS*.01)$
$+ a_{568}*KH3_{-1} + a_{569}*(HS3\$/(PRS*.01))_{-2}$
$+ a_{570}*(HS3\$/(PRS*.01))_{-3}$

(188) $PHCA$
$= \dfrac{PHC*PHCA_{-1}}{PHC_{-1}}$
$+ PHCA_{-1}*(-.0025)$

(continued)

569

I. FINAL DEMAND EQUATIONS (*concluded*)

D. STATE AND LOCAL GOVERNMENT EXPENDITURE

Normalization	Solve	Constant

$$(36) \quad EGSC\$ = \left[a_{700} + a_{701}* \left[\frac{YS\$}{N*POBE*.00001} \right] + \cdots \right.$$

$$+ a_{712}* \left[\frac{YS\$}{N*POBE*.00001} \right]_{-12}$$

$$+ a_{713}* \left[\frac{YS\$}{N*POBE*.00001} \right] (RSLG) + \cdots$$

$$+ a_{715}* \left[\frac{YS\$}{N*POBE*.00001} \right]_{-3} * (RSLG_{-3})$$

$$+ a_{716}* \left[\frac{YS\$}{N*POBE*.00001} \right] \left[\left[\frac{100(PS - PS_{-4})}{PS_{-4}} \right] + \cdots \right.$$

$$+ a_{725}* \left[\frac{YS\$}{N*POBE*.00001} \right]_{-9} \left[\frac{100(PS_{-9} - PS_{-13})}{PS_{-13}} \right]$$

$$* + a_{727}* \left[\frac{YS\$}{N*POBE*.00001} \right] * \left[\frac{PS}{POBE} \right]$$

$$+ a_{728}* \left[\frac{YS\$}{N*POBE*.00001} \right] (N20/N)$$

$$\left. + a_{729}* \left[\frac{KSL_{-1}}{N} \right] * PS*.0001*N \right. \qquad + a_{726}*GFS$$

(102) KSL $= .25*EGSC\$/(.01*PS)$ $+ .9956KSL_{-1}$

(37) $EGSO\$$ $= (a_{161}*YS\$/(.01*POBE) + a_{162}*(YS\$/(.01*POBE))*$ $+ a_{165}*GFS$
$(PS/POBE) + a_{163}*(YS\$/(.01*POBE))*N20/N$
$+ a_{164}*(.001*N) + a_{166}*(.001*N)*R_{37})*(.01*PS)$

(38) $EGSL\$$ $= (a_{168}*YS\$/(.01*POBE) + a_{169}*(YS\$/(.01*POBE))*$ $+ a_{173}*GFS$
$(PS/POBE) + a_{170}*(YS\$/(.01*POBE))*N20/N$
$+ a_{171}*(.001*N) + a_{172}*(.001*N)*R_{38})*(.01*PS)$

(45) $EGS\$$ $= EGSC\$ + EGSL\$ + EGSO\$$

(82) $EGSN\$$ $= EGSL\$ + EGSO\$ + GSP\$ - TSC$ $+ GSI - .70*GFS$

E. INVENTORY INVESTMENT

	Normalization	Solve	Constant
(39)	I	$= a_{177}ECO + a_{186}OPD$	$+ a_{178}ECO_{-1} + a_{179}ECO_{-2} + a_{180}I_{-1} + a_{181}I_{-2}$ $+ a_{182}EGDP + a_{183}EGDP_{-1} + a_{184}NDI + a_{185}NDI_{-1}$ $+ a_{187}OPD_{-1} + \cdots + a_{191}OPD_{-5}$
(10)	$D-I$	$= I$	$-I_{-1}$

F. IMPORTS

	Normalization	Solve	Constant
(42)	$\ln (EIM)$	$= a_{192} \ln (XOBE) + a_{193} \ln (1.0/(1 - XB/XBC))$	$+ a_{194} + a_{195}JCAA + a_{196} \ln (JID) + a_{488}JIA + a_{489}JIB$
(43)	EIM	$= EXP(.01*\ln (EIM))$	

II. DISTRIBUTION OF INCOME

A. DEFINITION OF OUTPUTS

	Normalization	Solve	Constant
(1)	X	$= CON + EC + EH\$/(.01*PRS) + EPD + I + EPS$ $+ EGS\$/(.01*PS) - EIM$	$+ EEX + EGF - I_{-1} + D\text{-}IF$
(2)	$XOBE$	$= X - YC - WC$	
(3)	XB	$= XOBE - EGSL\$/(.01*PGE) - YH$	$- YRW - EGFL\$/(.01*PGE)$
(40)	$XBNF$	$= XB + YH$	$- XBF$
(44)	ECO	$= CON + EC - YC - WC$	

B. NET NATIONAL PRODUCT AND NATIONAL INCOME

	Normalization	Solve	Constant
(165)	$YNNP\$$	$= XOBE\$ - WCCA\$$	
(55)	$YNI\$$	$= YNNP\$ - TIBS - TIBF - TSS$	$- YBT\$ - YSD\$ + GFG$

C. LABOR INCOME

	Normalization	Solve	Constant
(54)	$YL\$$	$= (.01*PL)*LMHT$	

D. NONLABOR INCOME

	Normalization	Solve	Constant
(56)	$YPG\$$	$= YNI\$ - YL\$ - EGSL\$ - YRT\$ - YII\$$	$- YLAG\$ - EGFL\$ - YPF\$$

E. CORPORATE PROFITS, CASH FLOWS AND DIVIDENDS

	Normalization	Solve	Constant
(153)	$\ln (YPC\$)$	$= a_{482} \ln (YPG\$) + a_{443} \ln (XB/XBC)$	$+ a_{444} \ln (XB/XBC)_{-1} + a_{445}TIME + a_{446} + a_{481}R_{153}$
(57)	$YPC\$$	$= EXP(.01*\ln YPC\$)$	
(60)	$YPCT\$$	$= YPC\$ - TCIF - TCIS$	
(61)	$YPCC\$$	$= YPCT\$ + WCO\$$	
(169)	$WCO\$$	$= WCCA\$ - .04*PRS(a_{546}*KH1_{-1} + a_{568}KH3_{-1})$	$+ C(169)$
(62)	$YDV\$$	$= a_{205}YPCC\$$	$+ a_{206} + a_{208}YPCC\$_{-1} + \cdots + a_{215}YPCC\$_{-8}$ $+ a_{408}R_{62}$
(41)	$YCR\$$	$= YPC\$ - YDV\$ - TCIF - TCIS - IVA\$$	

F. PERSONAL INCOME AND DISPOSABLE INCOME

	Normalization	Solve	Constant
(74)	$YP\$$	$= YNI\$ - YPC\$ - TO - TU + YDV\$ + GB + GSP$ $- TSC$	$- TOSI + GSI + GFI + GFP + YRC\$ + YBT\$$
(79)	$YD\$$	$= YP\$ - TPF - TPS + .01*RCB*(KC_{-1}*PC + EC\$/8.0)$	$- TEGF - YRC\$$

(continued)

II. DISTRIBUTION OF INCOME *(concluded)*

G. INVENTORY VALUATION ADJUSTMENT

	Normalization	Solve	Constant
(159)	$IVA\$$	$= a_{507}*PI + a_{508}*PI*I_{-1}$	$- a_{508}PI_{-1}*I_{-1} - a_{507}PI_{-1} + a_{509}$
(140)	$D\text{-}I\$$	$= .01*I*PI + IVA\$$	$- I_{-1}*.01*PI_{-1}$

H. SAVING AND NET-WORTH IDENTITY

	Normalization	Solve	Constant
(138)	$VCN\$$	$= .05*(YDV\$/RDP)$	$+ VCN\$_{-1} + (.25*(YD\$_{-1} - CON_{-1}*.01*PCON_{-1}) + .01*(PRS_{-1} - PRS_{-2})*(KH1_{-2} + KH3_{-2}) + .01*(PC_{-1} - PC_{-2})*KC_{-2} - 50.0*YDV\$_{-2}/RDP_{-2} + VG\$_{-1})*.001$

I. MISCELLANEOUS ITEMS

	Normalization	Solve	Constant
(80)	$YS\$$	$= XOBE\$ - TCIF - TIBF - TO - TPF - TU + GB$	$+ GFI + GFP + GFG + TEGF - TOSI$
(166)	$YRT\$$	$= .0414*RH*KH1_{-1}*C(166)$	
(167)	$YII\$$	$= EXOGENOUS$	
(163)	$WCCA\$$	$= (WPD\$ + WPS\$)*4.0 + .04*PRS*(a_{546}KH1_{-1} + a_{568}KH3_{-1})$	$+ C(163)$

III. TAXES AND TRANSFERS

A. CORPORATE INCOME TAXES

Normalization	Solve	Constant	
(58) $TCIS$	$= a_{197}(YPC\$ - IVA\$) + a_{198}EGSN\$$	$+ a_{199} + a_{200}R_{58}$	
(59) $TCIF$	$= a_{202}*AC_1*YPC\$ + a_{203}*AC_2*EPD\$$	$+ a_{204} + a_{207}R_{59}$	$AC_1 = UTC$

B. INDIRECT BUSINESS TAXES

Normalization	Solve	Constant	
(63) $\ln TXF$	$= a_{216} \ln ECO\$$	$+ a_{217} \ln (AC_3) + a_{218} + a_{167}R_{63}$	$AC_3 = UTXF$
(64) TXF	$= EXP(.01 \ln TXF)$		
(65) $TIBF$	$= TXF$		
(66) $TIBS$	$= a_{219}YS\$ + a_{220}EGSN\$$	$+ TCDF$ $+ (a_{223} + a_{224}(YS\$_{-1}/(.001*N_{-1})) + a_{225}(EGSN\$_{-1}/(.001*N_{-1}) + a_{221}*R_{66})*(.001*N)$	

C. PERSONAL INCOME TAXES

Normalization	Solve	Constant	
(75) $\ln\left(1 - \dfrac{YTF\$}{YP\$}\right) = a_{249} \ln YP\$$		$- a_{249} \ln N + a_{250} \ln (AC_{13}) + a_{251}$	$AC_{13} = TEX$

(continued)

III. TAXES AND TRANSFERS (concluded)

C. PERSONAL INCOME TAXES (continued)

	Normalization	Solve	Constant
(76)	$YTF\$$	$= (-EXP(\ln(1 - \frac{YTF\$}{YP\$})) + 1)*YP\$$	
(77)	TPF	$= AC_6*YTF\$/100.0$	$AC_6 = UPTF$
(78)	TPS	$= a_{252}YP\$ + a_{253}EGSN\$$ $+ a_{255}*N*.001$	

D. CONTRIBUTIONS TO SOCIAL INSURANCE

	Normalization	Solve	Constant
(67)	$\ln(TO)$	$= a_{226}\ln YP\$$ $+ a_{227}JOA + a_{228}JOB + a_{229}JOC + a_{230}JOD + a_{231}$ $+ a_{232}\ln(AC_4)$	$AC_4 = UTO$
(68)	TO	$= EXP(\ln TO)$	
(69)	$\ln TU$	$= a_{233}\ln YP\$$ $+ a_{234}\ln(TUIC) + a_{235} + a_{236}\ln(AC_5)$	$AC_5 = UTU$
(70)	TU	$= EXP(\ln TU)$	
(81)	TSC	$= a_{257}*EGSL\$$ $+ a_{417} + a_{256}R_{81}$	

E. TRANSFER PAYMENTS

	Normalization	Solve	Constant
(71)	$\ln GB$	$= a_{237}\ln(LU)$	$+\, a_{238}\ln(TUIC) + a_{239}\ln TUIB + a_{240}\ln(L26U)$ $+\, a_{241} + a_{409}R_{71}$
(72)	GB	$= EXP(.01*\ln GB)$	
(73)	GSP	$= (a_{242}YS\$/(.01*POBE)$ $+\, a_{243}(LE+LA/N)YS\$/(.01*POBE) + a_{246}$ $+\, a_{247}R_{73})*(.00001*N*PS)$	$+\, a_{245}GFS$
(155)	TSS	$= a_{501}*YS\$ + a_{502}*EGSN\$$	$+\, a_{505} + a_{506}*YS\$_{-1} + a_{503}R_{155}$

F. NET DEFICIT OF GOVERNMENT

	Normalization	Solve	Constant
(161)	$GDSF$	$= TPF + TCIF + T + TO + TU - GB$	$+\, TEGF + TOSI - EGF\$ - GFP - GFS - GFI$ $-\, GFG - GFR$
(162)	$GDSS$	$= TPS + TCIS + TIBS + TSC - EGS\$ - GSP + TSS$	$+\, GFS - GSI$

IV. LABOR MARKET

A. DEMAND FOR MAN-HOURS AND HOURS/MAN AND EMPLOYMENT

	Normalization	Solve	Constant
(139)	$LMHT$	$= EXP(.01*\ln LMHT)$	
(145)	$\ln (LMHT)$	$= \ln (XBNF) + a_{458} \ln (XB/XBC) + a_{459} \ln (ULU)$ $+ a_{460} \ln (XBNF)$	$-a_{460} \ln (XBNF_{-1}) + a_{461}JR1 + a_{462}JR2 + a_{463}JR3$ $+ a_{468}JT1 + a_{469}JT2 + a_{470}JT3 + a_{471}JT4 + a_{486}$ $+ a_{465}R_{145}$
(142)	LH	$= EXP(.01*\ln (LH))$	
(146)	$\ln (LH)$	$= a_{466} \ln (LMHT)$	$-a_{466} \ln (LMHT)_{-1} + a_{467} \ln (LH_{-1}) + a_{473}TT60$ $+ a_{474} + a_{475}R_{146}$
(147)	$LEBT$	$= LMHT/LH$	
(148)	LE	$= LEBT$	$+ LEO$
(125)	$(LE+LA)$	$= LE$	$+ LA$

B. SUPPLY OF LABOR AND UNEMPLOYMENT

	Normalization	Solve	Constant
(143)	$LF+LA$	$= a_{447}*(LE+LA)*\left(1.0 - \dfrac{LPRI}{N16}\right)$	$N16*\Big(a_{448}*\dfrac{(LE+LA)_{-1}}{N16_{-1}}*\left(1.0 - \dfrac{LPRI}{N16_{-1}}\right)$ $+ \cdots + a_{455}*\dfrac{(LE+LA)_{-8}}{N16_{-8}}*\left(1.0 - \dfrac{LPRI}{N16_{-8}}\right) + a_{456}$ $+ a_{457}* \ln (TIME + 88.0) + a_{487}*\left(1.0 - \dfrac{LPRI}{N16}\right)$ $+ a_{485}R_{143}\Big)$
(124)	LU	$= (LF+LA) - (LE+LA)$	
(150)	ULU	$= (LU/(LF+LA))*100.0$	

A. THE WAGE RATE

Normalization	Solve	Constant
(152) PL	$= (a_{635}/(ULU + ULU_{-1}) + a_{636}*YPCC\$/(YPCC\$_{-1}$ $+ YPCC\$_{-2}))*PL_{-2}$	$(1.0 + a_{637}*(PCON_{-2} - PCON_{-4})/PCON_{-4} + a_{638}$ $+ a_{639}R_{152})*PL_{-2} + a_{640}(UTO - UTO_{-2})*PL_{-2}$

B. THE GENERAL PRICE LEVEL

Normalization	Solve	Constant
(154) $QPXB$	$= \ln(PL) - a_{621}\ln(PL)$ $+ a_{622}(OUME/SME)*EXP(.002698(TIME - 80.0))$ $+ a_{624}(\ln XBNF - \ln LMHT)$	$+ a_{625} + a_{621}QPXB_{-1} + a_{627}\Delta \ln(31.91*PWM$ $+ 68.09*PFM)$ $+ a_{628}[(OUME/SME)*EXP(.002698(TIME - 80))]_{-1}$ $+ a_{629}JS1 + a_{630}JS2 + a_{631}JS3 + a_{632}TIME$
(189) $PXB*$	$= EXP(QPXB)/(1.0 - (TIBF/XB\$))$	

C. ALL OTHER PRICES ARE DEFINED IN TERMS OF PROPORTIONALITY TO THE GENERAL PRICE AND THESE PROPORTIONALITIES ARE TAKEN AS EXOGENOUS IN THE CURRENT VERSION OF THE MODEL, AS FOLLOWS:

Normalization	Solve	Constant
(156) $PXBNF$	$= 100.0*(.01*PXB*(XBNF - YH) + YH\$)/XBNF$	
(129) PXB	$= 100.0*(XBNF\$ - YH\$ + XBF\$)/(XBNF - YH$ $+ XBF)$	

(continued)

579

V. PRICES (concluded)

C. ALL OTHER PRICES ARE DEFINED IN TERMS OF PROPORTIONALITY TO THE GENERAL PRICE AND THESE PROPORTIONALITIES ARE TAKEN AS EXOGENOUS IN THE CURRENT VERSION OF THE MODEL, AS FOLLOWS: (continued)

	Normalization	Solve	Constant
(130)	POBE	$= \dfrac{100.0*(XB\$ + EGSL\$ + YH\$ + YRW\$ + EGFL\$)}{(XB + (EGSL\$/PGE) + YH + (EGFL\$/PGE) + YRW)}$	
(131)	PC	$= UPC*PXBNF$	
(171)	UPC	$= EXOGENOUS$	
(132)	PCON	$= UPCON*PXBNF$	
(172)	UPCON	$= EXOGENOUS$	
(158)	PCO	$= PCON*(ECO - EC + WC + .0379*(KC_{-1}$ $+ EC/8.0))/ECO - PC*(-EC + WC$ $+ .01*RCB*(KC_{-1} + EC/8.0))/ECO$	
(133)	PPD	$= UPPD*PXBNF$	
(173)	UPPD	$= EXOGENOUS$	
(134)	PRS	$= UPRS*PXBNF$	
(177)	UPRS	$= EXOGENOUS$	
(135)	PS	$= UPS*PXBNF$	
(175)	UPS	$= EXOGENOUS$	

(136) PHC   = UPHC*PXBNF

(176) UPHC   = EXOGENOUS

(141) PPS   = UPPS*PXBNF

(174) UPPS   = EXOGENOUS

(168) PI   = UPI*PXBNF

(178) UPI   = EXOGENOUS

D. TRANSFORMATION BETWEEN THE CURRENT DOLLAR VARIABLES AND REAL VARIABLES

	Normalization	Solve	Constant
(46) XB$	= XB*(PXB*.01)		
(47) YH$	= YH*(PYH*.01)		
(48) XOBE$	= XOBE*(POBE*.01)		
(49) EPD$	= EPD*(PPD*.01)		
(50) EPS$	= EPS*(PPS*.01)		
(51) ECO$	= ECO*(PCO*.01)		
(52) EC$	= EC*(PC*.01)		
(53) XBNF$	= XBNF*(PXBNF*.01)		
(123) YD	= YD$/(.01*PCON)		

VI. FINANCIAL SECTOR

A. MONEY MARKET
1. Demand for Currency

	Normalization	Solve	Constant
(83)	$\ln MC\$$	$= (1.0 - a_{258}) \ln ECO\$ + a_{259} \ln RTP$	$+ a_{260} + a_{258}(\ln MC\$)_{-1} + a_{261}R_{83}$
(84)	$MC\$$	$= EXP(.01*\ln MC\$)$	

2. Demand for Demand Deposits

	Normalization	Solve	Constant
(87)	RTB	$a_{262}*MD\$/XOBE\$ + a_{263}*RTD$ $+ a_{264}(.01*POBE*N)/XOBE\$ + a_{265}*MD\$_{-1}/XOBE\$$	$+ a_{266} + a_{267}R_{87}$
(86)	$MD\$$	$(MDS\$*JMSB*JMSA)$	$- MGF\$*JMSA$

3. Demand for Free Reserves

	Normalization	Solve	Constant
(115)	$\underline{MFR\$}$	$= a_{268}*(1.0 - AC_7)*MRU\$ + a_{274}*\left(\sum_{i=1}^{4} .25MDS\$_{-i}\right)*RTB$ $+ a_{277}*AC_7*DCL\$*JCLS$	$- a_{268}*(1.0 - AC_7)*MRU\$_{-1} + a_{269}*((AC_8$ $- AC_{8,-1})*MTM\$_{-1} + (AC_7 - AC_{7,-1})*MDS\$_{-1})$ $+ (a_{270} + a_{271}*JS1 + a_{272}*JS2 + a_{273}*JS3$ $+ a_{275}*ZDRA)*\left(\sum_{i=1}^{4} .25MDS\$_{-i}\right) + a_{276}MFR\$_{-1}$

4. Relation Between the Treasury Bill Rate and Commercial Paper Rate

	Normalization	Solve	Constant
			$- a_{277}*AC_7*DCL\$_{-1}*JCLS_{-1}$
			$+ a_{278}R_{115}\left(\sum_{i=1}^{4}.25MDS\$_{-i}\right)$
(88)	RCP	$= (a_{279} - a_{280})RTB$	$+ a_{280}RTB_{-1} + a_{281}JCD + a_{410}$

5. Reserve and Commercial Bank Balance Sheet Identities

	Normalization	Solve	Constant
(89)	$MDS\$$	$= (MRU\$ - MFR\$ - AC_8*MTM\$)/AC_7$	
(90)	$MRU\$$	$= -MC\$$	$+ AC_{10}$
			$AC_{10} = ZMS$

6. Supplementary Equations

	Normalization	Solve	Constant
(98)	$\ln(JMSB)$	$= a_{323}*\ln(MDS\$)$	$+ a_{324} + a_{325}JS2 + a_{326}JS3 + a_{327}JS4$
			$+ a_{328}\ln(MDS\$)_{-1} + a_{329}\ln(JMSB)_{-1}$
(99)	$JMSB$	$= EXP(.01*\ln JMSB)$	

(continued)

VI. FINANCIAL SECTOR (continued)

B. TERM STRUCTURE EQUATION FOR CORPORATE BOND RATE

	Normalization	Solve	Constant
(91)	RCB	$= a_{282}RCP$	$+ a_{283}RCP_{-1} + \cdots + a_{300}RCP_{-18} + a_{400} + a_{401}R_{91}$

C. COMMERCIAL LOAN MARKET

	Normalization	Solve	Constant
(92)	RCL	$= a_{302}*DCL\$/(MD\$ + MT\$ - DCL\$) + a_{303}RCB$ $+ a_{304}(MCDA\$/(MD\$ + MT\$))$	$+ a_{305}AC_{11} + (a_{306} - a_{305})AC_{11,-1} - a_{306}AC_{11,-2}$ $+ a_{307}RCL_{-1} + a_{308}JS2 + a_{309}JS3 + a_{310}JS4 + a_{311}$ $AC_{11} = ZDR$
(93)	$DCL\$$	$= a_{312}(D - I\$) + a_{313}EPD\$ - .25*a_{315}*EPS\$ + a_{316}(XBNF\$$ $- YH\$ - (D-I\$)) + (a_{318}*(RTB - RCL) + a_{416}*(RCB$ $- RCL))*(XBNF\$ - YH\$ - XBNF\$_{-1} + YH\$_{-1})$ $+ a_{314}WCO\$$	$+ a_{315}.25*(D - I\$_{-1} + EPD\$_{-1} + EPS\$_{-1} - WCO\$_{-1})$ $+ (1 - a_{315})DCL\$_{-1} + a_{315}DCL\$_{-2}$ $+ (a_{317} - a_{316})*(XBNF\$_{-1} - YH\$_{-1} - (D-I\$)_{-1})$ $- a_{317}*(XBNF\$_{-2} - YH\$_{-2} - (D-I\$)_{-2})$

D. MUNICIPAL BOND RATE

	Normalization	Solve	Constant
(103)	$RSLG$	$= a_{770}*RCB + a_{771}*RCB_{-1} + a_{772}DCL\$/MT\$$	$+ a_{769} + a_{771}*RCB_{-1} + a_{773}R_{103}$

E. DETERMINATION OF MORTGAGE RATE

Normalization	Solve	Constant
(104) RM	$= a_{550}RCB$	$+ a_{551}RCB_{-1} + a_{552}RCB_{-2} + a_{553}RCB_{-3} + a_{554}JCD_{-3}$ $+ a_{555} + a_{556}R_{104}$

F. TIME DEPOSITS AT COMMERCIAL BANKS
1. Passbook Savings Accounts

Normalization	Solve	Constant
(106) RTP	$= a_{350}RM + a_{351}ZINT$	$+ a_{352}RTP_{-1} + a_{415}$
(157) $MTP\$$	$= MTPA\$ * JTPS$	
(105) $ZINT$	$=$	$= .5333(AC_{14} - AC_{14,-1} + ZINT_{-1})$ $AC_{14} = ZCT$
(110) $\ln(MTPA\$)$	$= a_{363}\ln RTP + a_{364}\ln RSL + a_{365}\ln RCB$ $+ a_{366}\ln(.01*PCON) + (1.0 - a_{367})\ln(VCN\$*1000)$	$+ a_{368}\ln MTP\$_{-1} + a_{369}\ln(.01*PCON_{-1}) + a_{370}$
(111) $MTPA\$$	$= EXP(.01*\ln MTPA\$)$	

2. Nonpassbook Time Deposits

Normalization	Solve	Constant
(109) RCD	$= a_{360}RTB$	$+ a_{361}RCD_{-1} + a_{362}$
(112) $MCDA\$$	$= EXOGENOUS$	
(113) $MCD\$$	$= JCDS*MCDA\$$	

(continued)

VI. FINANCIAL SECTOR (concluded)

F. TIME DEPOSITS AT COMMERCIAL BANKS (continued)

3. Accounting Identity

Normalization	Solve	Constant
(114) $MTM\$$	$= MCD\$ + MTP\$$	
(122) $MT\$$	$= JMT*MTM\$$	

G. SAVINGS AND LOAN ASSOCIATIONS

Normalization	Solve	Constant
(107) RSL	$= a_{353}RTP + a_{354}RM + a_{355}RSL_{-1} + a_{356}$	
(116) $\ln MSL\$$	$= a_{374} \ln RTP + a_{375} \ln RSL + a_{376} \ln RCB$ $+ a_{377} \ln (.01*PCON) + (1.0 - a_{378}) \ln (VCN\$*1000)$	$+ a_{379} \ln MSL\$_{-1} + a_{380} \ln (.01*PCON_{-1}) + a_{381}$
(117) $MSL\$$	$= EXP(.01*\ln MSL\$)$	

H. MUTUAL SAVINGS BANKS

Normalization	Solve	Constant
(108) RMS	$= a_{357}RSL$	$+ a_{358}RMS_{-1} + a_{359}$
(118) $\ln MMS\$$	$= a_{382} \ln RSL + a_{383} \ln RMS + a_{384} \ln RCB + (a_{385}$ $+ a_{386} + a_{387}) \ln (VCN\$*1000) + (a_{388}$ $+ a_{389}) \ln (.01*PCON)$	$+ a_{390} \ln MMS\$_{-1} + a_{391} \ln N + a_{392} \ln (.01*PCON)$ $+ a_{393}$
(119) $MMS\$$	$= EXP(.01*\ln MMS\$)$	

I. LIFE INSURANCE RESERVES

Normalization	Solve	Constant
(120) $\ln MIS\$$	$= a_{394} \ln RCP + (1.0 - a_{395}) \ln (VCN\$*1000)$ $+ a_{396} \ln (.01*PCON')$	$+ a_{397} \ln MIS\$_{-1} + a_{398} \ln (.01*PCON_{-1}) + a_{399}$
(121) $MIS\$$	$= EXP(.01*\ln MIS\$)$	

J. DIVIDEND PRICE RATIO

Normalization	Solve	Constant
(126) RDP	$= a_{425}*RCB$	$+ a_{426}*RCB_{-1} + a_{427}*RCB_{-2} + a_{428}*RCB_{-3} + a_{429}RCB_{-4}$ $+ a_{430}*RCB_{-5} + a_{431}*RCB_{-6} + (-a_{432} - a_{433} - a_{434}$ $- a_{435} - a_{436} - a_{437} - \cdots - a_{441}) + a_{432}(PCO_{-4}/PCO_{-5})$ $+ \cdots + a_{441}(PCO_{-13}/PCO_{-14}) + a_{421}JSTK$ $+ a_{422}\dfrac{1.0}{(TIME - 3.0)} + a_{423} + a_{484}R_{126}$

K. SAVINGS FLOWS FOR HOUSING STARTS

Normalization	Solve	Constant
(185) $D\text{-}DSL$	$= \dfrac{11.0*(MSL\$ + MMS\$)}{1.12(MSL\$_{-1} + MMS\$_{-1} - MSL\$_{-12} - MMS\$_{-12})}$	$\dfrac{-11.0*(MSL\$_{-1} + MMS\$_{-1})}{1.12(MSL\$_{-1} + MMS\$_{-1} - MSL\$_{-12} - MMS\$_{-12})}$

587

NUMERICAL VALUES FOR COEFFICIENTS
(TABLE I)

I. A.

(4) $a_1 =$ .0794 $a_8 =$ .0448

$a_{476} =$ 37.9982 $a_9 =$ .0372

$a_{404} =$ .0954 $a_{10} =$ .0289

$a_2 =$ .0764 $a_{11} =$ .0199

$a_3 =$ .0728 $a_{12} =$ .0103

$a_4 =$ .0686 $a_{477} =$ 17.1962

$a_5 =$ .0636 $a_{478} =$ 2.1265

$a_6 =$ .0580 $a_{479} =$ .000

$a_7 =$ .0517 $a_{480} =$ .6055

(6) $a_{491} =$ .3588 $a_{498} =$ −.0011

$a_{495} =$ −.0008 $a_{499} =$ −.0009

$a_{493} =$ .2119 $a_{500} =$ −.0005

$a_{494} =$ −.0030 $a_{492} =$ −.3312

$a_{496} =$ −.0010 $a_{17} =$ −.2612

$a_{497} =$ −.0011 $a_{18} =$ .6342

(5) $a_{14} =$ .0791 $a_{16} =$ −6.4838

$a_{15} =$ −.0168 $a_{405} =$ .4435

B. 1.

(17) $a_{43} =$ 11.3460 $a_{61} =$ −10.1810

$a_{44} =$ 10.4400 $a_{62} =$ −8.9030

$a_{45} =$ 9.4480 $a_{63} =$ −7.7250

$a_{46} =$ 8.3890 $a_{64} =$ −6.6330

$a_{47} =$ 7.2780 $a_{65} =$ −5.6080

$a_{48} =$ 6.1580 $a_{66} =$ −4.6350

$a_{49} =$ 5.0250 $a_{67} =$ −3.7000

$a_{50} =$ 3.9080 $a_{68} =$ −2.7830

$a_{51} =$ 2.8250 $a_{69} =$ −1.8720

$a_{52} =$ 1.8000 $a_{70} =$ −.9500

$a_{53} =$ .8510

$a_{60} =$ −11.5750

(20)	$a_{94} =$	.6475	$a_{98} =$	.0090
	$a_{100} =$	−.7150	$a_{102} =$	.2122
	$a_{95} =$	.2555	$a_{103} =$	.3562
	$a_{101} =$	−.1448	$a_{104} =$	.2862
	$a_{96} =$	.0598	$a_{99} =$	.0302
	$a_{97} =$	−.0018	$a_{105} =$	.0044

(24)	$a_{112} =$	2.1010
	$a_{113} =$	1.3775
	$a_{114} =$	3.5539

(32)	$a_{128} =$	1.0000
	$a_{129} =$	0.0

2.

(19)	$a_{77} =$	.3512	$a_{84} =$	.3183
	$a_{78} =$	.5328	$a_{85} =$	.2865
	$a_{79} =$	.5822	$a_{86} =$	.2457
	$a_{80} =$	.5537	$a_{87} =$	.1647
	$a_{81} =$	.4894	$a_{93} =$	−.2067
	$a_{82} =$	.4190	$a_{92} =$	.5792
	$a_{83} =$	.3602		

(27)	$a_{126} =$	.0263
	$a_{127} =$	.7258
	$a_{411} =$	−1.8330

(33)	$a_{130} =$	.4500
	$a_{131} =$	−.0029

3.

(21)	$a_{106} =$	.8941
	$a_{107} =$	7.2440
	$a_{108} =$	.7693

(22)	$a_{109} =$	.8941
	$a_{110} =$	7.2440
	$a_{111} =$	.7693

(26) $a_{115} =$ 0.0 $a_{121} =$ .0025

$a_{116} =$ −.0004 $a_{122} =$ .0020

$a_{117} =$ .0013 $a_{123} =$ .0022

$a_{118} =$ .0023 $a_{124} =$ .0008

$a_{119} =$ .0028 $a_{125} =$ .0002

$a_{120} =$ .0028 $a_{21} =$ .0400

C.

(181) $a_{571} =$ 2.1213 $a_{576} =$ .1541

$a_{572} =$ −.8447 $a_{577} =$ .7927

$a_{573} =$ .0600 $a_{578} =$ 1.1656

$a_{574} =$ −1.9201 $a_{579} =$ 1.2728

$a_{582} =$ −0.9502 $a_{580} =$ 1.1142

$a_{583} =$ −0.8445 $a_{581} =$ .6900

$a_{584} =$ −0.5278 $a_{588} =$ .0050

$a_{585} =$ .0590 $a_{589} =$ 10.7379

$a_{586} =$ .0486 $a_{590} =$ −2.1213

$a_{587} =$ .0290 $a_{591} =$ .6465

$a_{575} =$ −.7501

(183) $a_{592} =$ −1.8011 $a_{603} =$ 2.8911

$a_{593} =$ −.7765 $a_{604} =$ 2.3934

$a_{594} =$ .0622 $a_{605} =$ .1157

$a_{595} =$ −.4423 $a_{606} =$ .1436

$a_{596} =$ −.1759 $a_{607} =$ .1460

$a_{597} =$ .0228 $a_{608} =$ .1229

$a_{598} =$ .1538 $a_{609} =$ .0742

$a_{599} =$ .2170 $a_{610} =$ .0050

$a_{600} =$ .2124 $a_{611} =$ 4.4551

$a_{601} =$ .1401 $a_{612} =$ −3.5173

$a_{602} =$ 1.4929 $a_{613} =$ .6114

(15) $a_{614} =$ 2.0771 $a_{617} =$ .7631

$a_{615} =$ .0184 $a_{618} =$ 2.9980

$a_{616} =$ 1.6145 $a_{619} =$ .3247

(127) $a_{557} =$ .7000 $a_{559} =$ 80.000

$a_{558} =$ .3000 $a_{560} =$ −1.1400

(128) $a_{561} =$ .9500 $a_{563} =$ −2.4400
       $a_{562} =$ .0500 $a_{564} =$ 80.000

(186) $a_{547} =$ .8500 $a_{549} =$ .0408
       $a_{548} =$ 2.9658 $a_{546} =$ .9933

(187) $a_{565} =$ .1500 $a_{568} =$ .9950
       $a_{566} =$ 2.9658 $a_{569} =$ .6667
       $a_{567} =$ .0408 $a_{570} =$ .3333

D.

(36) $a_{700} =$ −61.9952 $a_{716} =$ .0001
       $a_{701} =$ −.0085 $a_{117} =$ .0001
       $a_{702} =$ −.0043 $a_{718} =$ .0001
       $a_{703} =$ −.0007 $a_{719} =$ .0001
       $a_{704} =$ .0023 $a_{720} =$ .0001
       $a_{705} =$ .0046 $a_{721} =$ .0001
       $a_{706} =$ .0063 $a_{722} =$ .0001
       $a_{707} =$ .0073 $a_{723} =$ .0001
       $a_{708} =$ .0077 $a_{724} =$ .0001
       $a_{709} =$ .0075 $a_{725} =$ .0001
       $a_{710} =$ .0066 $a_{726} =$ .3763
       $a_{711} =$ .0050 $a_{727} =$ −.0537
       $a_{712} =$ .0028 $a_{728} =$ .2341
       $a_{713} =$ −.0011 $a_{729} =$ −.0482
       $a_{714} =$ −.0006
       $a_{715} =$ −.0002

(37) $a_{161} =$ .0250 $a_{164} =$ −25.0807
       $a_{162} =$ −.0098 $a_{166} =$ .6000
       $a_{163} =$ .0231 $a_{165} =$ .2815

(38) $a_{168} =$ −.0705 $a_{171} =$ 51.4739
       $a_{169} =$ .0607 $a_{172} =$ .5000
       $a_{170} =$ .0926 $a_{173} =$ .4310

E.

$$
\begin{array}{llll}
(39) & a_{177} = & -.1380 & a_{184} = -27.6000 \\
& a_{186} = & -.0200 & a_{185} = 27.6000 \\
& a_{178} = & .7110 & a_{187} = .2340 \\
& a_{179} = & -.5730 & a_{188} = .1170 \\
& a_{180} = & 1.4240 & a_{189} = .0040 \\
& a_{181} = & -.4240 & a_{190} = -.1110 \\
& a_{182} = & .3870 & a_{191} = -.2240 \\
& a_{183} = & -.3870 &
\end{array}
$$

F.

$$
\begin{array}{llll}
(42) & a_{192} = & 1.0148 & a_{196} = .0817 \\
& a_{193} = & .1349 & a_{488} = .0751 \\
& a_{194} = & -3.3794 & a_{489} = .0518 \\
& a_{195} = & -.0170 &
\end{array}
$$

$$
\begin{array}{lll}
(169) & a_{546} = & .0050 \\
& a_{568} = & .0067
\end{array}
$$

NUMERICAL VALUES FOR COEFFICIENTS
(TABLE II)

II. E.

$$
\begin{array}{llll}
(153) & a_{482} = & .9638 & a_{445} = .0019 \\
& a_{443} = & .3867 & a_{446} = -.0316 \\
& a_{444} = & -.1059 & a_{481} = .9090
\end{array}
$$

$$
\begin{array}{llll}
(62) & a_{205} = & .0623 & a_{212} = .0203 \\
& a_{206} = & .2151 & a_{213} = .0137 \\
& a_{208} = & .0518 & a_{214} = .0070 \\
& a_{209} = & .0426 & a_{215} = 0.0 \\
& a_{210} = & .0345 & a_{408} = .2570 \\
& a_{211} = & .0272 &
\end{array}
$$

$$
\begin{array}{lll}
(169) & a_{546} = & .0067 \\
& a_{568} = & .0050
\end{array}
$$

G.

(159) $a_{507} =$ 0.0

        $a_{508} =$ $-.0103$

        $a_{509} =$ $-.0513$

I.

(163) $a_{546} =$ .0067

        $a_{568} =$ .0050

NUMERICAL VALUES FOR COEFFICIENTS
(TABLE III)

III.   A.

(58) $a_{197} =$ .0150 $a_{199} =$ $-.3599$

       $a_{198} =$ .0277 $a_{200} =$ .4792

(59) $a_{202} =$ .8908 $a_{204} =$ -1.6475

       $a_{203} =$ $-.1786$ $a_{207} =$ .8971

B.

(63) $a_{216} =$ .5995

       $a_{217} =$ 1.0000

       $a_{218} =$ .7653

       $a_{167} =$ .6300

(66) $a_{219} =$ .0322 $a_{223} =$ 13.6903

       $a_{220} =$ .1314 $a_{224} =$ .0167

       $a_{221} =$ .95 $a_{225} =$ .1573

C.

(75) $a_{249} =$ $-.3225$

       $a_{250} =$ .2751

       $a_{251} =$ -2.1074

(78) $a_{252} =$ .0187

       $a_{253} =$ .1629

       $a_{255} =$ -30.8473

D.

(67)	$a_{226} =$	.8611	$a_{230} =$	$-.1169$
	$a_{227} =$	$-.2642$	$a_{231} =$	-4.5190
	$a_{228} =$	$-.2751$	$a_{232} =$	1.0000
	$a_{229} =$	$-.1045$		
(69)	$a_{233} =$	.5412	$a_{235} =$	-6.9292
	$a_{234} =$	.9974	$a_{236} =$	1.0000
(81)	$a_{257} =$	.0780		
	$a_{417} =$	1.1956		
	$a_{256} =$	.9500		

E.

(71)	$a_{237} =$	1.3956	$a_{240} =$	.8480
	$a_{238} =$	1.0000	$a_{241} =$	-9.7437
	$a_{239} =$	.2443	$a_{409} =$	.6341
(73)	$a_{242} =$	.0207	$a_{246} =$	4.6314
	$a_{243} =$	$-.0315$	$a_{247} =$	.9022
	$a_{245} =$	.0257		
(155)	$a_{501} =$	$-.0010$	$a_{505} =$	1.2159
	$a_{502} =$	.0133	$a_{506} =$	.0029
	$a_{503} =$	.9500		

NUMERICAL VALUES FOR COEFFICIENTS
(TABLE IV)

IV. A.

(145)	$a_{458} =$	$-.4360$	$a_{468} =$	$-.0044$
	$a_{459} =$	$-.0293$	$a_{469} =$	$-.0058$
	$a_{460} =$	$-.2750$	$a_{470} =$	$-.0033$
	$a_{461} =$	$-.0079$	$a_{471} =$	$-.0025$
	$a_{462} =$	$-.0059$	$a_{486} =$	$-.9629$
	$a_{463} =$	$-.0066$	$a_{465} =$	.6022

(146)	$a_{466} =$	.2986	$a_{474} =$	.2525
	$a_{467} =$	.6362	$a_{475} =$	0.0
	$a_{473} =$	.0003		

(143)	$a_{447} =$	.2695	$a_{454} =$	−.0116
	$a_{448} =$	.1905	$a_{455} =$	0.0
	$a_{449} =$	.1244	$a_{456} =$	.8369
	$a_{450} =$	.0714	$a_{457} =$	.0510
	$a_{451} =$	.0312	$a_{485} =$	.5868
	$a_{452} =$	.0040	$a_{487} =$	−1.0526
	$a_{453} =$	−.0103		

NUMERICAL VALUES FOR COEFFICIENTS
(TABLE V)

V. A.

(152)	$a_{635} =$	.2185	$a_{638} =$	−.0324
	$a_{636} =$	.0542	$a_{639} =$	.5288
	$a_{637} =$	.4238	$a_{640} =$	.3261

B.

(154)	$a_{621} =$	.7472	$a_{627} =$	−.0512
	$a_{622} =$	.0806	$a_{628} =$	−.0390
	$a_{624} =$	−.1090	$a_{629} =$	0.0
	$a_{625} =$	−.0409	$a_{630} =$	−.0013
	$a_{621} =$	.7472	$a_{631} =$	−.0012
			$a_{632} =$	−.0016

NUMERICAL VALUES FOR COEFFICIENTS
(TABLE VI)

VI. A. 1.

(83)	$a_{258} =$	.8117	$a_{260} =$	−.4013
	$a_{259} =$	−.0467	$a_{261} =$	.7518

2.

(87) $a_{262} = -212.5539$ $a_{265} = 139.9768$
      $a_{263} = -2.0931$ $a_{266} = 27.1245$
      $a_{264} = -6.1365$ $a_{267} = .6821$

(115) $a_{268} = .6573$ $a_{274} = -.0016$
       $a_{269} = -.3464$ $a_{275} = .0013$
       $a_{270} = .0027$ $a_{276} = .6484$
       $a_{271} = -.0020$ $a_{277} = -.5124$
       $a_{272} = -.0023$ $a_{278} = .2271$
       $a_{273} = -.0022$

4.

(88) $a_{279} = 1.0486$ $a_{281} = -.2346$
      $a_{280} = .3331$ $a_{410} = .5463$

6.

(98) $a_{323} = -.0946$ $a_{327} = -.0008$
      $a_{324} = -.3326$ $a_{328} = .1765$
      $a_{325} = -.0028$ $a_{329} = .6514$
      $a_{326} = -.0010$

B.

(91) $a_{282} = .3082$ $a_{293} = .0371$
      $a_{283} = -.0328$ $a_{294} = .0323$
      $a_{284} = .0121$ $a_{295} = .0286$
      $a_{285} = .0413$ $a_{296} = .0257$
      $a_{286} = .0581$ $a_{297} = .0228$
      $a_{287} = .0657$ $a_{298} = .0186$
      $a_{288} = .0665$ $a_{299} = .0117$
      $a_{289} = .0630$ $a_{300} = 0.0$
      $a_{290} = .0571$ $a_{400} = 1.1709$
      $a_{291} = .0500$ $a_{401} = .7364$
      $a_{292} = .0432$

C.

(92) $a_{302} =$ 1.9060 $a_{307} =$ .7274
$a_{303} =$ .1884 $a_{308} =$ .0582
$a_{304} =$ −2.1317 $a_{309} =$ .0527
$a_{305} =$ .2636 $a_{310} =$ .0457
$a_{306} =$ .1304 $a_{311} =$ .0063

(93) $a_{312} =$ .2018 $a_{318} =$ .0175
$a_{313} =$ .0861 $a_{416} =$ .0583
$a_{315} =$ −.3187 $a_{314} =$ −.3057
$a_{316} =$ .0495 $a_{317} =$ −.0246

D.

(103) $a_{769} =$ −.8332 $a_{772} =$ 1.7044
$a_{770} =$ .8661 $a_{773} =$ .5000
$a_{771} =$ −.1624

E.

(104) $a_{551} =$ .2204 $a_{554} =$ −.2273
$a_{552} =$ .1728 $a_{555} =$ 2.9001
$a_{553} =$ .0993 $a_{556} =$ .7000

F.   1.

(106) $a_{350} =$ .0486 $a_{352} =$ .9650
$a_{351} =$ .4243 $a_{415} =$ .1590

(110) $a_{363} =$ .1230 $a_{367} =$ .9125
$a_{364} =$ .000 $a_{368} =$ .9125
$a_{365} =$ −.1334 $a_{369} =$ −.9125
$a_{366} =$ .9125 $a_{370} =$ −.1986

2.

(109) $a_{360} =$ .9485
$a_{361} =$ .2143
$a_{362} =$ −.3110

G.

(107) $a_{353} =$ .0742 $\qquad$ $a_{355} =$ .8581

$a_{354} =$ .0815 $\qquad$ $a_{356} =$ −.1195

(116) $a_{374} =$ −.0040 $\qquad$ $a_{378} =$ .9529

$a_{375} =$ .1002 $\qquad$ $a_{379} =$ .9529

$a_{376} =$ −.0400 $\qquad$ $a_{380} =$ −.9529

$a_{377} =$ .9529 $\qquad$ $a_{381} =$ −.2018

H.

(108) $a_{357} =$ .1568

$a_{358} =$ .8581

$a_{359} =$ −.0673

(118) $a_{382} =$ −.0230 $\qquad$ $a_{388} =$ .9982

$a_{383} =$ .0937 $\qquad$ $a_{389} =$ .0653

$a_{384} =$ −.0497 $\qquad$ $a_{390} =$ .9982

$a_{385} =$ 1.0000 $\qquad$ $a_{391} =$ .0653

$a_{386} =$ −.9982 $\qquad$ $a_{392} =$ −.9982

$a_{387} =$ −.0653 $\qquad$ $a_{393} =$ −.1669

I.

(120) $a_{394} =$ −.0117 $\qquad$ $a_{397} =$ .9297

$a_{395} =$ .9297 $\qquad$ $a_{398} =$ −.9297

$a_{396} =$ .9297 $\qquad$ $a_{399} =$ −.1798

J.

(126) $a_{425} =$ .2291 $\qquad$ $a_{436} =$ −5.6400

$a_{426} =$ .2192 $\qquad$ $a_{437} =$ −4.6700

$a_{427} =$ .1980 $\qquad$ $a_{438} =$ −3.4500

$a_{428} =$ .1655 $\qquad$ $a_{439} =$ −2.1600

$a_{429} =$ .1217 $\qquad$ $a_{440} =$ −.9800

$a_{430} =$ .0666 $\qquad$ $a_{441} =$ .0900

$a_{431} =$ 0.0 $\qquad$ $a_{421} =$ .4991

$a_{432} =$ −3.1400 $\qquad$ $a_{422} =$ 169.0089

$a_{433} =$ −5.1000 $\qquad$ $a_{423} =$ −3.9299

$a_{434} =$ −6.0300 $\qquad$ $a_{484} =$ .7883

$a_{435} =$ −6.1500